RIVERSIDE COMMUNITY COLLEGE
1916

LAND AND POWER : THE ZIONIST R
DS 149 S497158 1992

D0744133

JA 1			

DEMCO 38-296

Land and Power

STUDIES IN JEWISH HISTORY
Jehuda Reinharz, General Editor

Other Volumes Are in Preparation

LAND

AND

POWER

The Zionist Resort to Force,

1881–1948

ANITA SHAPIRA

Translated by William Templer

New York   Oxford
OXFORD UNIVERSITY PRESS
1992

Riverside Community College
Library
4800 Magnolia Avenue
Riverside, California 92506

APR   '93

Oxford University Press

Oxford   New York   Toronto
Delhi   Bombay   Calcutta   Madras   Karachi
Petaling Jaya   Singapore   Hong Kong   Tokyo
Nairobi   Dar es Salaam   Cape Town
Melbourne   Auckland

and associated companies in
Berlin   Ibadan

Copyright © 1992 by Oxford University Press, Inc.

Published by Oxford University Press, Inc.
200 Madison Avenue, New York, New York 10016

Oxford is a registered trademark of Oxford University Press

All rights reserved. No part of this publication may be reproduced,
stored in a retrieval system, or transmitted in any form or by any means,
electronic, mechanical, photocopying, recording, or otherwise,
without the prior permission of Oxford University Press.

Library of Congress Cataloging-in-Publication Data
Shapira, Anita.
Land and power : the Zionist resort to force, 1881–1948/
Anita Shapira : translated by William Templer.
p.   cm. — (Studies in Jewish history)
Includes bibliographical references and index.
ISBN 0-19-506104-7
1. Zionism—Philosophy.   2. National characteristics, Israeli.
3. Jewish-Arab relations—To 1917—Public opinion.
4. Jewish-Arab relations—1917–1949—Public opinion.
5. Jews—Palestine—Attitudes.
6. Public Opinion—Palestine.   I. Title. II. Series.
DS149.S497158   1992   320.5′4′095694—dc20   91-28984

2 4 6 8 9 7 5 3 1

Printed in the United States of America
on acid-free paper

One Jew said to another: "I was too weak." This saying could serve as a motto for a history of Judaism

HEINRICH HEINE

Preface

The idea for this book came to me in 1982, after reading an article by Menahem Begin, then prime minister of Israel, entitled "On Behalf of a War of Choice." That was at the time of the ill-fated Israeli invasion of Lebanon, and a fierce debate was being waged in Israel between supporters and opponents of the war. While reading Begin's article, it occurred to me that this was the first time in Zionist history that a leading public figure had openly advocated war. Previous Zionist and Israeli leaders were careful to avoid being viewed as trigger-happy politicians. Whenever they deemed it necessary to engage in hostilities, they justified their decision by pointing to the deeds of the adversary, claiming that it was a question of survival. War was always viewed as unavoidable, a matter of necessity and not of choice. Thus, Begin's position constituted a significant departure from a long and highly respected Zionist tradition, heralding a new era with respect to the use of force.

The Zionist reticence toward armed conflict did not derive solely from the common wisdom that war was evil and should be avoided if possible. Its motivating causes ran deeper. For nearly two thousand years Jews had been a noncombative people. From the time of the Christianization of Rome, and especially after the rise of a feudal social order in Europe and the spread of Islam, Jews in the Mediterranean had been confined to the noncombatant classes. Even when other town dwellers began to carry weapons, Jews continued to be excluded from bearing arms. They accepted their weakness and dependence on others for protection as God's will, not to be challenged or questioned.

Over the course of generations, the aversion to force among Jews took on the proportions of a Jewish trait, distinguishing them as a distinct community from their neighbors. Apparently, many Jews were aware of the humiliation this state of affairs engendered, and did not always meekly accept it. Burning rage erupted on occasion, shattering the seemingly tranquil surface—as manifested by the messianic movements, which gave vent to deep-seated yearnings for redemption. But these were exceptional occurrences. On the whole Jews tended to conform and unquestioningly to accept their fate.

During the nineteenth century, Jews in Europe began to enlist in the evolving national armies, thereby demonstrating their eagerness to become active citizens in the emerging nation–states. Emancipation, integration, and secularization were the principal processes to achieve this. Their readiness to enlist and fight was intended to underscore Jewish loyalty to, and identification with, their state. Yet this new trend involved only a small segment of the Jewish population, with the majority continuing to pursue their traditional lifestyles and manifesting little zeal for conscription—especially in the czarist empire, where emancipation and integration were still unrealizable goals.

The willingness to fight exhibited by emancipated Jews was not associated with a change in Jewish self-identity. Rather, it was linked to a readiness to immerse that identity in a broader and more appealing one. This new attitude toward conscription was perceived not as an indication that Jews were adopting new characteristics, but as part of a process by which Jews were losing their own specificity. Consequently, it did not give rise to the emergence of a new ethos regarding Jewish attitudes toward power; nor did it lead to a change in the traditional acquiescence on the part of Jews in their helplessness in the face of belligerent neighbors.

This mindset did not disappear with the appearance of a Jewish national movement. The Jewish self-image as a people abhorring violence in any form was too deeply rooted in the national psyche to be easily dismissed. Nevertheless, a century later an Israeli prime minister considered it legitimate to express views diametrically opposed to the most basic tenets of this self-image. The Jewish state came to be identified with military might, distinguished by the spirit and valor of its soldiers. The self-image of the Israelis, as well as their prevalent stereotype, is that of a people who do not hesitate to resort to force when deemed necessary. This defiant mood is also reflected in the consciousness of Jews living outside Israel. The past century witnessed a fundamental transformation in what were assumed to be abiding and genuine Jewish characteristics. A new national ethos emerged, accompanied by a newly forged identity and set of values.

This transformation is the subject of the present study, which explores the changes in mores, behavioral codes, and priorities, as well as the evolving worldview and stereotypes built into the Zionist ideology and practice during the formative decades preceding the establishment of the Jewish state (1881–1948). Whatever subsequent changes took place should be viewed as a consequence of the major psychological shift that occurred during this relatively short span of time.

This study deals less with facts and more with their interpretation. Indeed, the principal facts are generally known: the Jewish colonization of Palestine; Zionist confrontation with Arab nationalism; and the political triangle consisting of the British, Arabs, and Jews. An attempt is made to explore how people understood that reality and to trace the events they were confronted with and how they coped with them politically, ideologically, and emotionally. What were the conceptual frameworks they constructed for this purpose? How were those concepts reflected in the myth making, literature, and norms of the era? What was the fate of the imagery and ideas transposed from one environment to another? This study explores how concepts derived from Jewish antiquity gained new vitality and were translated from the lofty plane of abstraction to the sphere of practical action. It also examines how concepts, imported from a European ambience, were internalized by a new generation confronting the reality of Palestine.

I have also attempted to examine how and when the Zionists realized that the acquisition of Palestine would entail the use of force. This is quite a complicated question that can only be answered after a careful investigation of several issues: How did the founding fathers perceive Jewish colonization in the Holy Land? Were they aware of Arab opposition from the outset? What was their vision of Jewish–Arab relations? How, when, and why did this concept change—or did it remain basically the same? The realization that the use of force was inevitable did not occur simultaneously among all parties concerned. What were the different stages? How did it affect different social circles and political groups?

Given the rich diversity of thought among Zionists, it proved impossible to deal adequately with each strand within the scope of this study. I have chosen to concentrate principally on the so-called mainstream group, namely, socialist Zionism. This had been the most dynamic force in Zionism since the early 1920s and was to a large degree representative of the widest body of opinion in the Zionist camp. For some fifty years Mapai remained the predominant political party within the Jewish community in Palestine, within the Zionist movement in general and later within the newly created State of Israel. More than any other factor, it molded the Israeli ethos, defining its basic tenets and shaping the minds of young people associated with it. I have not dwelt in detail on some of the smaller parties of the Zionist Left except where their approach differed significantly from that of the mainstream. This study does explore at some length both ends of the political spectrum, namely, the militant nationalists, who represented an extreme position on the question of the Jewish attitude toward the Arabs, and the doves, who represented the opposite position. Yet these two groups, though by no means negligible, only had a limited impact. Moreover, once they had formulated their basic approach, it underwent only minor changes during the course of events. It was the predominant party, motivated by the constraints and responsibilities of the power invested in it, that found it necessary to test its concepts and beliefs against changing circumstances. This involved flexibility, much soul searching, and a gift for adaptation. Consequently, the ruling party and its evolving positions reflected the ongoing shifts in ethos, worldview, and educational and political conceptions far better than its militant adversaries.

A point of terminology: The State of Israel was created in 1948. According to Jewish tradition, the name of the land was always Eretz Israel (the Land of Israel)—a holy term, vague as far as the exact boundaries of the territory are concerned but clearly defining ownership. For many centuries non-Jews used the name Palestina, which the Romans gave the land in the year 135, after quashing a Jewish rebellion against them. This name attributed the country to the Philistines, eradicating the centuries-old Jewish bond of attachment and ownership. In the modern era the name Palestine was commonly used to refer to the country. During the British Mandate, that was the official name in English and (with a slight phonetic difference) in Arabic, while Eretz Israel predominated in Hebrew. Palestine designated the country, and Palestinian its people, both Jews and Arabs. The same holds true for terms derived from it, such as Palestinocentrism, an expression often used among Jews to denote the Zionist trend that perceived Palestine as the focus of Jewish interests. One should bear in mind that the association of Palestine and Palestinian with the Arab population of that country now living outside Israel did not develop until after the establishment of the state. During the mandate period local Arabs were referred to as Arabs (as contrasted with Jews), and both were considered Palestinians. Since this book is being published in English, I have tended to follow the usage of the terms common in English—and, to a certain extent, in Hebrew as well—at the time.

Most of the work on this book was done while I was a fellow at the Annenberg Research Institute in Philadelphia during 1989–1990. The intellectual give-and-take in the weekly seminar there, conducted by Bernard Lewis, gave birth to a number of the ideas developed here. Daily discussions with my colleagues, especially Gavriel Warburg at Haifa University and David Berger at Brooklyn College of the City University of New York, were extremely stimulating. The assistance of the devoted staff members, librarians, and secretaries at the Annenberg Research Institute contributed significantly to my having been able to accomplish so much there.

   I am grateful to the Rockefeller Foundation, whose support allowed me the needed respite to put the final touches on this manuscript as a fellow at the Bellagio Study and Conference Center, Bellagio, Italy. This volume would not have been completed without the assistance of the Memorial Foundation for Jewish Culture, New York City.

   Shaike Weinberg read the entire manuscript and made important and helpful comments, as did Ahuvia Malkin. Aviva Halamish went over the English translation, editing the text and checking all notes, thereby saving me from many a pitfall; I am indebted to her for her thoroughness and accuracy. Ahuva Dotan and Asnat Shiran were of great assistance to me in researching the contents of archives and collecting material for me, and I am grateful for their help. I owe a special debt of gratitude to William Templer, who translated the manuscript from the Hebrew. Considering the complexity of the material, which includes references to poetic, religious, and archaic terms, this was not an easy assignment; and he accomplished the task with great devotion and much flair.

   I would also like to take this opportunity to express my heartfelt thanks to the many persons who provided assistance at different stages: Shulamit Laskov supplied source material on Ahad Ha-Am and Berdichevsky. Eliyahu Ha-Cohen allowed me to consult his extensive collection of early Israeli folk songs and was extremely generous with his time. Dr. Chanita Goodblatt assisted me in translating some of the poems and in locating English translations already in print. Ilan Gal-Pe'er, the librarian at the Labor Archives in Tel Aviv, aided me in locating lost documents. Baruch Tor Raz, at the Labor Party Archives in Bet Berl, was helpful and very patiently processed my requests.

   Last, but not least, I would like to express my thanks to my friend and colleague Jehuda Reinharz, at Brandeis University. Without his encouragement this book could not have been written.

Tel Aviv   A.S.
February 1991

Contents

I

THE CRYSTALLIZATION
OF A
DEFENSIVE ETHOS,
1881–1921

1

The Birth of a National Ethos

The Zionist movement was born out of deep disappointment: the dream of the nineteenth century that progress was destined to carry the world forward toward an enlightened future in which the distortions, legal perversions, and discrimination of past eras would appear like a passing nightmare, revealed itself to be nothing but a figment of the imagination by the close of that century. Modern antisemitism erupted onto the scene during the 1880s in Central Europe. The vision of Jewish integration within German society, the fervent wish of the three previous generations, seemed more beyond reach than ever in the face of virulent racist antisemitism that now overnight transformed well-established German citizens into loathsome aliens contaminating the land.

The truly alarming manifestations were associated with a salient shift in the role of antisemitism as it became a political force. Mass participation in politics, beginning with the introduction of universal adult suffrage, did not set free the naturally benevolent inclinations of man (as had been envisaged by well-wishing humanist thinkers) but, rather, gave license to passions and prejudices that up to then had been restrained, held in check by the strict hand of authoritarian regimes. Left and Right found common ground in their shared hatred of the Jew. This was not hatred of the stranger and his alien tongue; rather, it was animosity directed specifically toward persons who were similar to themselves, who aspired to be part of the nation, to enjoy the same rights, compete in the same market of professions and positions, and participate in the national culture.

Newspapers and popular literature cultivated the stereotype of the sly and cunning Jew, devious, cowardly, overly ambitious, ugly—stereotypes that expressed the latent fears of a society in the throes of crisis as it evolved from a conservative, stable agrarian social order to urban industrialism, with its associated weakening of family structures, mores, and established outlooks on life and the world.[1]

There were numerous Jews who discounted the gathering storm on the horizon, viewing the antisemitic excesses as a kind of childhood malady of German society,

3

destined to disappear quickly; indeed, such Jews were in fact the majority. In his memoirs, Gershom Scholem has described his father, a man who saw himself first and foremost as a German nationalist and kept his distance from anything that smacked of Jews and Judaism. He contended that the only place it was good to go with Jews was to the synagogue—nowhere else. The elder Scholem refused to acknowledge that non-Jews never visited their home and also failed to face up to the fact that he had been obliged to withdraw from the German associations he was a member of because of mounting antisemitism.[2]

What distressed the Jews most deeply were not events in the political sphere (although, from a long-term perspective, these were the most dangerous) but, rather, the trivial, direct incidents of everyday life, like the accidental encounter with abusive language, drunken derisive laughter, and discriminatory behavior on the street. When Herzl tried to explain antisemitism, he characterized it by centering on quotidian encounters such as these, even if his understanding of the phenomenon was far more profound.[3]

In Eastern Europe, there was a parallel disappointment: In the vast expanses of czarist Russia, hopes were dashed that the reforms introduced by Alexander II in respect to Jewish life (which, among other things, had opened up the path for the Jewish elite to enter institutions of higher learning) would serve as a basis and reference for additional reforms in the future. In their stead, in 1881, came a series of vicious pogroms that raged through scores of cities and towns in Southern Russia. These were the most extensive anti-Jewish disturbances since the slaughter of Jews in Poland in 1648–1649. The authorities, suspected by the Jews of collusion with the rioters, subsequently carried out what was dubbed the "cold pogrom": they alleged that the riots were the product of the exploitation of the Russian masses by the Jews and enacted a series of decrees in 1882 (the May Laws) further circumscribing the Pale of Settlement (the Pale) of the Jews in Russia and reducing to a minimum the opportunities for Jewish students to study at institutions of higher education.

In Russia popular antisemitism of the street and gutter was an integral part of daily life and came as no surprise to Jews accustomed to its vulgar ubiquity. But the phenomenon of reaction from above—a retreat from the path of progress and reform—was a painful blow. Multitudes of Jews now decided to flee the blood-soaked czarist empire, emigrating in massive numbers to the West, in particular to the United States, the golden Medina beyond the sea. They expected nothing from the authorities and thus were not disappointed: The steps they took were aimed primarily at ensuring the safety of their families.

Yet the hopes of the Jewish intelligentsia that had been nurtured during the period of Alexander II lay shattered: the great dream of acculturization and integration with the Russian people, in particular its educated classes, dissipated and dissolved in the acrid smoke billowing up from the Jewish hamlets set aflame. The Russian-educated classes did not raise their voices in defense of the Jews; and there were those among the revolutionaries who viewed the outbreak of the riots as a propitious sign, portending the awakening of the Russian people, and even published a leaflet in praise of the pogroms.[4]

The theme of the rejected suitor was repeated in both Eastern and Central

Europe, under dissimilar historical circumstances and even differing stages in the process, as Jews attempted to forge closer links with the peoples among whom they dwelt. The awakening of *active* national feelings among Jews (an instinctive national identification without need of any definition or proofs had existed among Jews in Eastern Europe and, to a limited extent, among German Jews, as well) was accompanied by a sense of deep humiliation—the mortification felt by someone who wished to be an accepted member of the nation and had been spurned. Anyone who reads Leo Pinsker's "Auto-Emancipation" of 1882 or Herzl's diaries cannot help but feel the profound sense of shame, mingled at times with a feeling of outrage and anguish (Pinsker), or a more covert sense of hurt, expressing itself as profoundly felt insult and indignity (Herzl).[5]

It was no glorious path that had led the Jews to the Zionist idea. On the contrary, the disappointment and humiliation, the rage and rejection, and the sense of shame that frequently went hand-in-hand with such mortification and nonacceptance—this was the gossamer web from which the idea was spun, "If they don't want us, we don't need them." Indeed, in the middle of the nineteenth century thinkers such as Yehuda Alkalay, Zvi Hirsch Kalischer, and, in particular, Moses Hess wove their dreams about the renewal of Jewish national life in the ancient Land of Israel around the great guiding aspirations for the advancement of mankind, conceived as part of the forward march by the entire world toward a better future. Hess viewed his pre-Zionist solution as the final step on the path of the salvation of humankind. In the eyes of the precursors of Zionism, the present appeared to promise positive tidings for the world and the Jewish people. Consequently, their Zionist idea was imbued with great optimism about the natural inborn goodness of the human heart, the readiness of the nations of the world to assist the children of Israel in rebuilding its ruins, and the understanding among the enlightened world of the need felt by the Jewish people for a national expression of its own. In an age when national movements sought to integrate the particularistic and the general, nationalism and a global order, national and universal missions, the conceptions of the three main proto-Zionists, especially Hess, seemed to express the spirit of the era.[6]

The fact is that Zionism was late in coming: when Hess's book *Rome and Jerusalem* appeared in 1862, the national wave that had forged a fraternal pact with the democratic movements against autocratic regimes was already in retreat, receding in the wake of its searing defeat in the abortive 1848 revolutions. Europe was drawing its conclusions: The unification of Italy, which had been the source of Hess's inspiration, was already stamped with the mark of the new style of national movement, which seized power from above by armed force, a style that the unification of Germany under Bismarck turned into a paradigm. By the time the Zionist movement emerged onto the scene, even in its modest early beginnings in the 1880s, all the previous hopes and illusions had faded. Nationalist doctrines and teachings that aspired to link up with universalistic worldviews, seeking justification and a meta-historical mission, had lost their original appeal. They were supplanted by the doctrine of "blood and iron," whose justification was based on egoistic national interest.

This conception was accompanied by a complex of notions in tune with its basic thrust, and a spirit of pessimism descended on Europe at the end of the century.

The great hopes that were animated by the French Revolution at the beginning of the century seemed, by its closing decade, to have been proven hollow. Faith in the goodness of human nature and the virtue of the nations of the world had been significantly eroded. Applications were found for Darwinian theory in social and national relations, and the concept of racial superiority gained impetus and strength in its wake.[7] The thinking of Artur Schopenhauer, Friedrich Nietzsche, Oswald Spengler, and Max Nordau, marked by a profound lack of faith in the future of European civilization, and anticipating the waning of Judeo–Christian morality, gave apt expression to the darkened spirit of the age.

Zionism was a product of its times. That assertion, which would appear self-evident, can nonetheless generate much wearying dispute about the question of the nature of Zionism and its sources. For purposes of the present study, it should suffice to point out that the concept Zionism, as used here, refers to a movement that wished, by its actions and activities, to renew the national life of the Jewish people in Palestine, the historical Land of Israel, and to eventually establish an independent Jewish entity there. Zionism was a child of its era in a double sense. First, it was able to transform itself from a vision that had been the cherished idea of a few marginal fantasts—a small circle of obsessed enthusiasts—into a genuine movement and succeeded in doing so precisely at that pivotal point in European history. Second, it absorbed ideas and intellectual stances, tendencies and patterns of action, characteristic of its age. There is a very evident and essential link between the failure of progress to solve the Jewish problem in the foreseeable future, the emergence of modern antisemitism, and the birth of the Zionist idea. This does not mean to imply that there were no other motives behind the emergence of Zionism, whose sources should also be sought in the processes of internal cultural development among Jews in Eastern Europe (processes, of course, influenced by the spirit of the times). Yet when Herzl described the Jewish predicament, whose root cause was antisemitism, as the "steam power" that would propel the Jews forward to the establishment of a Jewish state, he was outlining the dynamics of Zionism: By dint of that "engine," a marginal idea, hitherto lacking any social anchor, would be transformed into a viable political force.[8]

Varieties of Jewish Nationalism and Their Approach to Power

Historians tend to classify nationalism into two basic categories. The first has its origin in the French Revolution, is based on the secular and rationalistic traditions of the Age of Enlightenment, and views the state as an entity founded on the notion of a social contract, expressing the will of its citizenry. This concept of nationalism and nationality contains a subjective dimension: A person can feel that he or she belongs to a specific nation and can affiliate by desire and choice with that people; as long as that individual does not violate the agreement between them, he or she is a part of that nation. The second category originated in the period of revolt against rationalism in the Romantic era. That concept of nationhood and nationalism is based on an organic notion of society deriving from blood ties and common ethnic origin, culture, and history. Usually, it is linked geographically to a specific territory where the nation arose and evolved its system of values. The nation constitutes a mystic bond whose origin lies in a common past. It demands a "unity of hearts" far beyond the normal allegiance to the state expected from its citizens: A person has value only insofar as he or she is a part of the nation. This conception seeks the key to the national spirit in a past era, viewing this as the Golden Age, the lost paradise of the nation's youth. It often rejects forms and patterns of modern life that crystallized after the industrial revolution. The collapse of traditional frameworks, the loss of time-honored values, the processes of urbanization and the concomitant sense of alienation they generate—all these are conceived as destructive of the true spirit of the nation. This conception of nation and nationalism leads to an "objective" definition of the composition of the people: Those who did not participate in that process of growth and genesis of the national spirit can never be a part of it.

The concept of nation that originated in the French Revolution was not serviceable as a basis for a Jewish conception of nationhood. A stateless people, the Jews could not embrace the idea of citizenship based on the notion of a state. Ironically, it was the Romantic–exclusivistic brand of nationalism (whose prescriptions meant that the Jews could never be an integral part of the organic nation) that contained certain ideas able to function as a basis for an elaborated notion of a Jewish nation and national movement.[9]

Ostensibly, Jews continued the dispute that emerged at the beginning of the nineteenth century at the time of the struggle for emancipation and was still a matter of vehement debate among them at the century's close. The issue was "To be or not to be?"—assimilation to Gentile society or preservation of a separate Jewish existence and identity. For at least a segment of Jewish society, that dispute lost much of its relevance as soon as a key fact became clear: In the context of Central and Eastern Europe, the "host peoples" were not, in fact, prepared to accept Jewish assimilation hospitably. But the controversy raged on, offering proof that consciousness always lags behind reality.

However, a kind of hidden stratum formed among Jews, a set of silent understandings requiring no proof, namely, that (1) there was a Jewish people that had existed for centuries, (2) Jews wished to continue to exist as a people, and (3) the nucleus that can account for the continued existence of the people since its inception was not religious tradition but, rather, Jewish national feeling. The "instinct for national survival," as Ahad Ha-Am[10] called it, had been wrapped in the sheath of religion for generations. Now, after religion had declined in importance and its hold had weakened, the previously covert impulse for survival had emerged from hiding and was searching for a proper mode and means of expression. The shared fabric of ethnic–cultural bonds uniting all Jews (its existence had never been doubted by Jews in Eastern Europe, and it had preserved its vitality also in the period under discussion) provided a natural and convenient soil for adopting and transplanting concepts deriving from German or Pan-Slavic sources of *völkisch* nationalism.

The notion of the nation as an organic unity was espoused by the two key protagonists in the great central debate of the age, namely, Micha Joseph Berdichevsky and Ahad Ha-Am. Ahad Ha-Am's thinking was rationalistic in orientation, paying respects to such British philosophers as John Stuart Mill, Jeremy Bentham, and Herbert Spencer. In contrast, Berdichevsky espoused the idea that primeval instinctive urges should be given free rein and admired the thought of Friedrich Nietzsche. Yet when it pertained to the concept of Jewish nationhood, there was no essential difference in their views: whoever wished to believe in the continued existence of the Jewish people, without relying on the props of religion or an existing state framework, had no choice but to turn to more deeply rooted dispositions to provide an explanation for the nation's past and serve as a source of faith in its future.

The mythohistorical spirit also affected radical national Zionist groups within the sphere of German culture. The Bar Kokhba Association in Prague (especially Martin Buber) adhered to a Jewish nationalism organically linked to Palestine. In their view, it was only there that the creativity of the Jewish people could find adequate expression, and regain its special and unalloyed connection with divinity. That conception was replete with motifs drawn from Romanticism and German *völkisch* thought. Deep disdain for the materialism of modern society; a rejection of Marxist determinism; the aspiration to return to more simple and pristine patterns and forms of living, and especially a return to the soil; the desire for human relations more whole and honest; and a preference for organic community *(Gemeinschaft)* over society *(Gesellschaft)*—these were all notions drawn from the reservoir of German *völkisch* thought. They were adopted, after undergoing a certain metamorphosis, as part of the Zionist arsenal of this idealistic group.[11]

Perhaps the thinker whose approach came closest to the definition of citizenship in the sense of the French Revolution was Theodor Herzl. His concept of *peoplehood* (born out of the experience of rejection, humiliation, and shame) was essentially based on a rationalistic form of reasoning: a logical solution for a well-defined problem. The state he envisaged was basically an artificial construction, to be built according to a blueprint. He was not attracted by mysticism's harking back to a primordial era and had little passion for ancient, millennia-old Jewish traditions. Herzl lacked both the requisite knowledge and emotional disposition for such enthusiasms. The state he dreamed of was meant to be a European, liberal polity of the kind aspired to by Jews who had undergone a process of acculturation and that had eluded them with the advent of modern antisemitism. The culture he wished to see in the state he envisioned was European in origin. This was the culture he understood, had loved, and thought was his own—until, alas, events taught him otherwise.

Herzl's utopian novel *Altneuland,* written as a description of the Jewish state after its establishment, was based on the principles of tolerance between the three great monotheistic faiths, mutual respect, and brotherhood—and on a total abrogation of any advantages deriving from religion or race. The culture of his Jewish state was devoid of any distinctively Jewish qualities. It was completely immersed in a fluid of enlightened German *Gemütlichkeit,* in accordance with the idealized way Herzl wished to picture German culture to himself: an amalgam of civility, cleanliness and charming manners, and theater and opera. The Jewish state would implement what was regarded in Europe as enlightened but that had not been fully realized there.[12]

The revolutionary element in Herzl's rather bourgeois Jewish state was that it was designed to provide a total and immediate answer to the Jewish Problem. Apart from that, Herzl kept his distance from revolutionary notions. He was never carried away by ideas postulating an organic basis for society and the state. Herzl was a man of the modern world, a great admirer of technology and machines; he envisaged Zionism as a massive emigration movement, whose ultimate success would derive from its being a part of that innovative new world. Herzl was a resident of the Viennese metropolis, loved opera and the theater, and frequented coffee houses. He had received his political education in Paris, where he served as a correspondent of the *Neue Freie Presse.* Indeed, Herzl was passionately at home in the urban environment. He had no patience with romantic ideas about a return to preindustrial ways of life, rejection of city life and longing for the rustic pleasures of rural living.[13] Thus, he initially had no preference when it came to the specific geographical territory to which the stream of emigration should be directed. In his view, the utilitarian factor was the primary consideration in choosing a country, not memories of past glory or ancient myths.

After the Zionist Organization was established in 1897 and Herzl had come into contact with Zionists from Eastern Europe, who, indeed, provided the major source of strength of the movement, he grasped the importance Palestine had for them. Nevertheless, this was a kind of external comprehension, the understanding of someone who is enlightened as to a certain matter and then can comprehend it intellectually but is unable to internalize the insight and make it his own. Hence, in 1903, when British colonial secretary Joseph Chamberlain suggested to him as a possible alternative to Palestine (which seemed as beyond reach as ever in view of Ottoman opposition to Jewish settlement there) East Africa, he did not appreciate the explosive controversiality of that alternative for the Zionist Congress when he placed this seemingly innocent proposal on the agenda.

The depth of emotions and impulses aroused by the Uganda Controversy (the term under which the East Africa proposal is known in Zionist historiography) was alien to Herzl. When he swore the oath "If I ever forget thee, Jerusalem" in front of the agitated opponents, who were threatening to split the Zionist movement over this issue, he did so because he understood that this was the right way to preserve the movement's unity, not because the frame of mind that had unleashed this storm of emotions had become any more comprehensible to him.[14]

Herzl's projected state was to be set up as the result of an international agreement. Jews would then emigrate from their countries of residence—gradually, in order to avoid inflicting any damage on the local economies of these European countries.[15] The country to which they were to emigrate would be granted them by the local authorities and be paid for in full, under the auspices of the European Great Powers.[16]

It is evident that the question of force—or its possible use in occupying Palestine—was never a relevant issue for Herzl. When youthful enthusiasts expressed such ideas to him, he ignored them, choosing not to respond.[17] In his book *The Jewish State,* he devoted a short and rather perfunctory paragraph to the topic of defense of the proposed polity: "The Jewish state is conceived as a neutral one. It will therefore require only a professional army, equipped, of course, with every requisite of modern warfare, to preserve order internally and externally."[18]

Significantly, Herzl allotted far more space to describing how steam engines were changing the face of the earth than to the topic of the defense of the proposed state. In his diaries, he dropped an occasional thought on the subject of the army. For example, in the entry for June 6, 1895, one can read: "Keep the army well in hand."[19] And a day later, he wrote, "After a hundred years, universal military service should be introduced," yet felt it necessary to qualify this by adding, "but who knows how far civilization will have progressed by then."[20] His remarks in *Altneuland* presume that a basis would be created for amicable relations and peace between Jews and Arabs, who would be citizens with equal rights in the proposed state.

In a touching and revealing passage, Herzl elaborated on what he understood by the phrase Promised Land:

> The Promised Land, where it is all right for us to have hooked noses, black or red beards, and bandy legs without being despised for these things alone. Where at last we can live as free people on our own and die in peace in our own homeland. Where we, too, can expect honor as a reward for great deeds; where we shall live at peace with all the world, which we shall have freed through our own freedom, enriched by our wealth and made greater by our greatness.[21]

The passage does not contain a single word referring to the past. The present is depicted here as the latent opposite of the future. The need for a Jewish state is existential, concrete, and psychological. He demanded the same rights for Jews that any other nation and language had, the right to be themselves. The Promised Land he called for was destined to bring peace to the Jews and to the world as a whole.

Among Zionism's founding fathers, Herzl was the most characteristic representative of the liberal, German–Jewish school, an approach deemed already obsolete by the youthful enthusiasts during the final decade of the nineteenth century and even more so by the beginning of the twentieth. This school of Zionist thought did not delve deeply into the historical and conceptual roots of the Zionist idea but, rather, sought an immediate, practicable answer to the existential plight and hardship of the Jews. It was no accident that its ideology was espoused specifically by the Zionists who had first traveled down the path of assimilation and, after having despaired of this direction, had returned to their people, albeit by another road. Their Zionism was secular, political, lacking in depth, oriented toward the future rather than the past, and devoid of cultural roots.

To an appreciable extent, Herzl's predecessor, Leo Pinsker, the author of "Auto-Emancipation," could also be classified in these terms. His stirring pamphlet, published after the 1881 pogroms in Russia, initiated the process of the formation of the Hibbat Zion (Love of Zion) movement, a predecessor of the Zionist movement. Pinsker, too, had initially wished to assimilate to the Russian people, and after his disappointment, proposed the idea of a Jewish territory where Jews might free themselves from the age-old burden of having to live as a minority dispersed among other peoples. He was also prepared to consider countries other than Palestine.[22]

This was likewise the path traversed by Max Nordau, a German writer and thinker, the most important personality Herzl succeeded in recruiting to the Zionist cause. A similar personage active in the movement was Dr. Max Emmanuel Mandelstamm, a renowned ophthalmologist from Odessa and a man deeply immersed in Russian culture, who was one of Herzl's most ardent supporters. A kindred perspective was also espoused by Bernard Lazare, the French socialist, who was attracted for a time to Zionist activity by the power of the Herzlian vision.

These men were all relatively sophisticated and experienced in the affairs of the world; their thinking, especially in the case of Herzl, was in terms of concepts culled from the European political arsenal: "The matter of who is a foreigner in the country can be determined by the majority; this is a question of power, like all things in relations between peoples." Thinking along these lines was alien to Jews in the Pale of Settlement but came quite naturally to a person who had frequented the Palais de Bourbon.[23] Reception of European concepts was bound up with tacit acceptance of certain elements prevalent in anti-Jewish stereotypes. Jewish vulnerability to antisemitism varied in direct proportion to the involvement of Jews in Gentile society. The Orthodox Jew, shut up in his circumscribed Jewish world, had little interest in what non-Jews thought about him and most certainly did not consider their opinion of him to be a criterion for his own self-esteem and appraisal. Yet that was not the case when it came to the Jews who had undergone a process of acculturation and had internalized the criteria for evaluation, and the accepted norms, of European society.

It is no surprise, then, that the question of how the Jew appeared in the eyes of the non-Jew and how he was evaluated played a central role in fashioning the worldview of the Zionists who came from "outside." Antisemitic images penetrated into their world of symbols and imagery. Thus, Pinsker accepted as essentially correct the view that Jews were lacking in genius. To be sure, he attributed this wretched situation to the oppressive treatment of the Jews at the hands of Gentile society, but he had no doubts about its truth. "What a pitiful figure we cut!" he wrote in anguish.[24] Herzl felt Jews possessed certain odious traits, such as snobbishness and crudely excessive ambitiousness.[25] Nathan Birnbaum, who coined the expression Zionism, treated widespread antisemitic stereotypes as objective facts.[26] In a somewhat perverse vein, it is possible to imagine that even Herzl's mystical faith in the unlimited abilities of the Jewish people ("If you will, it is no fairy tale") was itself an expression of the well-known antisemitic stereotype regarding the alleged "omnipotent capabilities" of the Jews.

Of all the failings that antisemites accused Jews of, the one that stung most was the assertion that Jews lacked self-dignity. Pinsker, Herzl, and the rest of their contemporaries were virtually obsessed with the topic of the lost dignity of the Jewish people. The educated Jew was conscious of the contempt, mockery, and scorn of the Gentiles. The wandering Jew—homeless, weak, and vulnerable, responding with fear to brutality and injury—incited the disdain of the non-Jewish environment. Pinsker viewed Jewish willingness to accept insult and injury as an expression of their loss of "self-respect and the consciousness of human dignity."[27] Birnbaum ranked cowardice among the shameful Jewish traits, indicative of a lack of self-pride.[28]

The topic of Jewish honor and respect was constantly on Herzl's mind while he was writing *The Jewish State*. All manner of details when Jews were about to leave

Europe and enter Palestine were sketched out with one purpose in mind: the need to assure that Jews would appear respectable and be respected. Thus, for example, Herzl wanted the matter of the liquidation and sale of Jewish businesses in Europe to be handled by distinguished and respected antisemites. He also made it a point to stress that the acquisition of land from residents in Palestine should be carried out without "swindling"; and he added with satisfaction, "After all, through us the world shall be acquainted with something that has not been considered possible for 2,000 years: Jewish honor."[29] Herzl was so troubled about derision for the Jew that he noted in his diary that he would wage a powerful struggle against Jewish humor, which had a tendency toward self-mockery.[30] To effect a change in the image of the Jew from a people scorned to that of a respected and honored nation was one of the chief objectives of the young Zionist movement.

The concept of dignity had been associated since time immemorial with the status of the fighter, able to defend his honor and likewise ready to risk his life for that end. Hence, from the very inception of emancipation, Jews sought out opportunities to prove their dignity by deeds of valor and self-sacrifice. It was no accident that Ferdinand Lassalle, the assimilated Jew, did not permit himself to withdraw from the duel he had become embroiled in and that eventually brought his life to an abrupt end. The dueling scars on the faces of German students were an entrance ticket to respected student fraternities, the doors of which had already been slammed shut for Jews in the period under discussion. For that reason, young Jews used to pick an argument with young antisemites in order to demonstrate their readiness to defend Jewish honor with their blood. That tendency was popular at German universities, and was one of the manifestations of increasing militancy among Jewish students. The Zionist journal *Die Welt* reported with satisfaction that young Zionists in Vienna had come out to fight their humiliators with fists and clubs.[31] Herzl considered independent dueling to be a mode of fighting suitable for "honorable gentlemen," an expression of cultural refinement, and a means for educating "true officers." He therefore wrote that dueling would be legal in the Jewish state he envisaged.[32]

Assimilated Jews sought to redeem lost Jewish honor by adoption of the traits of courage and fortitude held up as ideals in the Gentile world. The Jewish state would nurture a new type of Jew, liberated from the complexes spawned by the abnormal situation of living as a despised minority. Herzl wanted to educate a new generation of free and strong individuals, prepared to take on any mission or task. The means he hoped to utilize in order to achieve this end were those familiar to him from the German nationalist movement: patriotic songs, glorification of the heroes of the nation's past, such as the Maccabees, emphasis on Jewish "dignity," and even military education.[33] It appears that what Herzl had in mind were the dashing uniforms of the Hapsburg Empire rather than the less savory functions of a real army. In his proposed state, he assigned the armed forces the task of police duties. This is not surprising when one considers that in the twenty-five years preceding the writing of *The Jewish State,* Europe had not experienced a single war. The educational example he wished to adopt as a paradigm for the Jewish state was the British model of education, due to the emphasis it placed on group games.[34] These thoughts, albeit fragmentary, are useful in order to understand Herzl's orientation and cast of mind: though his perspective had little in common with meta-historical, nonrational modes of thought, Herzl aspired to mold a new and different Jewish youth. This led him to embrace educational methods popular in the German youth movement at the time. Although Herzl was not militaristic in outlook, he viewed the army and the symbols of sovereignty as an essential component of the national pattern he wished to forge. His desire to prove that Jews were capable of creating a state endowed with all the attributes of a modern polity also led him to embrace the full panoply of symbols of national sovereignty: ceremonies, uniforms, and emblems. He opted for such symbols despite the fact that the model state he proposed not only embodied the concepts of brotherhood and liberalism, but had no practical need for a standing army.

This same line of thought also gave rise to the plan put forward by Max Nordau and labeled *Muskeljudentum* (Judaism of the muscles). Nordau asserted that the intellectual abilities of the Jew—incisive intellect, quick grasp and flexibility of thought—were regarded by antisemites as "Jewish traits" and accordingly stigmatized. In contrast, Jews were pictured as physically inferior: short in stature, bow-legged, lacking in agility, and endowed with a posture and carriage hardly inclined to evoke respect. These traits, seized upon by the antisemites to mock and deride the Jew, could be overcome by physical exercise and strength of willpower. In his view, developing of the athletic abilities of the Jew would heighten his esteem in the eyes of the non-Jew and, consequently, in his own eyes as well.[35] The German athletic associations that apparently served Nordau as a model were already tainted at that time by a virulent antisemitism and had expelled their Jewish members. In 1898 Nordau gave a speech in one of the committees of the Zionist Congress in which he proposed development of the physical abilities of Jewish youth. Two years later, the Jewish athletic association made its appearance in Berlin. Not by accident, the organization bore the name Bar Kokhba: "Whoever embraces the slogan of 'Bar Kokhba'," Nordau proclaimed with satisfaction, "signifies that there is a latent aspiration for honor in his heart."[36]

Inadequate physical ability was but one item in a far-too-lengthy list of failings that antisemites imputed to Jews. Nordau and his ideological associates wished to prove that Jewish weaknesses and deficiencies were rooted in historical causes and would consequently be remedied by changing these circumstances. In their case, acceptance of the antisemitic diagnosis did not entail concomitant acceptance of the racist deterministic prognosis preached by antisemitic ideologues. Thus, they were able to agree on the present situation of the Jews. Yet that analysis did not contain any self-hatred, along the lines of Otto Weininger and others; rather, it harbored a wish for self-improvement. Enhancement of the sense of Jewish solidarity, awareness of Jewish ethnicity, bolstering of self-pride—all these were to be the necessary preliminary stages preceding the truly momentous task that lay before the Jews as a people, namely, "to prove that the [Jewish] people—no less so than other nations, which are justifiably proud of the fact—is endowed with those same qualities that serve to establish and maintain political organisms."[37]

German historiography tended to present the Germans as a people who had built cities and states, the Slavs and other inferior peoples having later borrowed this advanced culture from them. The popular antisemitic argument held that the

Jews were similar to parasitic plants that could exist only by preying on a larger host and that this was why the Jews lived in the midst of other peoples. Richard Wagner's claim that the Jews were lacking in genuine creativity enjoyed particular support when it came to a key political question, namely, whether the Jews were truly capable of setting up a state and maintaining a national existence. That criticism was echoed in Jewish self-doubts in this regard. Physical strength and nation building were thought to be two closely linked qualities that Jews were sorely deficient in. It is therefore little wonder that ideas about building a Jewish state based on a European model were bound up with the concept of creating a new type of Jew, similar physically and mentally to his tall and powerful neighbors.

Quite naturally, one also recalled a primary paradigm from the Jewish past, the Maccabees. The story of the Hasmoneans had been one of the most popular ancient tales of valor among Christians and had served as a subject for numerous artistic creations. In particular, those with a spotty knowledge of their people's past were often the ones who cited the Maccabees as an example of Jewish bravery and prowess. Summing up the sorry state of the Jewish people among the nations, Pinsker, troubled by anguish, had written, "What a contemptible role for a people which once had its Maccabees!"[38] And when Herzl chose to conclude *The Jewish State* on a note of confidence in a bright future, he wrote, "Therefore I believe that a wondrous generation of Jews will spring into existence. The Maccabeans will rise again!"[39] Maccabee was widespread as a name for Jewish student organizations, stemming from the same motivation of enhancing Jewish pride and focusing the spotlight on past grandeur that nullified racist derision of the day.

The name Bar Kokhba, belonging to a second-century insurgent who had led an uprising against Rome, also appeared in this context. As in the case of the Maccabees, the historical knowledge required for recognition of the name was minimal; but the connotation it bore associated with Jewish valor was clear. This is the origin of the name of the Jewish athletic association that had so pleased Nordau when it was founded, as well as the source for the association Bar Kokhba in Prague. The purpose of that organization was a renewal of Jewish intellectual life and was far removed from any notion of the use of physical force. The Prague group probably viewed the legendary hero as a symbol of past genius, calling for a future renewal of Jewish life yet without touching upon the specific historical content of the Bar Kokhba tale. In contrast, Nordau used the name of Bar Kokhba as a symbol of a politician who grasped the importance of fighting for the land to achieve a "national existence on the soil of the forefathers" and as an example of a heroic figure who knew how to die with dignity.[40]

The emphasis on the motifs of national honor and past glories did not contradict the basic assumption that the state envisioned by Pinsker, Herzl, and associates would be established by peaceful means, exploiting in a positive way the desire among antisemites to be finally rid of the Jews. In a passage in his diary that seems ghastly prophetic today, Herzl summed up the future prospects of the Jewish people, likening them to a stone hurtling down a slope. He analyzed the phenomenon of the growing power of the masses and concluded, "So they will chase us out of these countries, and in the countries where we take refuge they will kill us."[41] Yet that vision, a seeming premonition of the Holocaust, appeared valid to Herzl only if the modern exodus he called for did not materialize. The fundamental assumption underlying his entire program was that "the world" (i.e., Europe) indeed hated the Jews and wished to get rid of them but that it was an enlightened world, ashamed of its biases, and would therefore be prepared to assist in the establishment of the Jewish state as a means to free itself from internal tensions and from the contradictions between progress and prejudice, humanism and antisemitism. Zionism would only be realized in a world at peace and would further enhance the stability of Europe.

As mentioned, Herzl showed little interest in questions pertaining to the defense of the future Jewish state. Pinsker did not deal at all with what would happen after the establishment of the state. His "Auto-Emancipation," though a brilliant analysis of antisemitism, lacks substance as a political program. Yet it is unlikely that these two thinkers were unaware of the problem. The publication of Pinsker's work aroused considerable debate in the press, a controversy in which all the questions were raised that the young Hibbat Zion movement preferred not to deal with. *Voskhod,* a Jewish Russian-language paper appearing in Petersburg and considered to be the mouthpiece of the liberal–assimilationist forces in Russian Jewry, published an article in 1882 written most probably by its editor Adolph Landau. The piece attacked both the basic hypothesis of Pinsker that progress had failed and the solution he had proposed, namely, the acquisition of a piece of land where Jews could settle in security and engage in self-rule:

> One can assume that even in the most secret corner of the Jewish soul, we have no dream that Jews will become a kind of omnipotent new Roman empire. Rather, at the most, we shall aspire to some sort of status as semisubjugated "protected" Jews. And in that case, who can guarantee that some dark day, following some excuse of war, so easy to invent, that powerful ruler, our protector, will not rise up against us to grind us into dust? Or that a new "world leader" in the guise of a 22d-century Titus—on the basis of those same international covenants for whose achievement we so vehemently struggle and whose "sacred stability" is manifested over and over again by every new war—will not scatter us once again to the four corners of the globe? And finally, who can guarantee that some neighbor, agitated by internal turbulence, will not decide, like Napoleon III, to deflect public attention from internal events by the cheap laurels of victory at our expense?[42]

The diagnosis by this writer in *Voskhod* of the risks and responsibilities inherent in self-government did not make him into a greater realist than Pinsker or Herzl. In that same article, he expressed the view that the recent antisemitic outbursts in Germany were only a temporary setback in the march of progress.

It would appear that the absence of any reference by the Zionist leadership to the security problems of the envisioned Jewish state emanated from their lack of governmental experience: after all, Jews had never borne any responsibility for the security of the state they were living in. In any event, neither Pinsker, nor Herzl, nor their predecessor Moses Hess voiced any opinion about this basic question. It is likely that Hess and Pinsker were both contemplating the possibility of a special status under the protective wing of one of the enlightened European powers. As mentioned, Herzl thought that the establishment of a Jewish state should be an enterprise the safety of which would be guaranteed by the European powers. He broached the idea of a charter (i.e., a document of authorization certified in terms of international law) that would permit Jews to develop Palestine and settle there protected by one of the Great Powers. Under those circumstances, the question of the defense of the Jewish state was not a pressing issue. Moreover, Herzl and Pinsker provided an excellent description and analysis of the situation in Europe and the various countries that Jews would emigrate from. However, they did not elaborate on the specifics of the land they were supposed to immigrate *to*. Pinsker sufficed with a few general remarks, while Herzl was still vacillating between Palestine and Argentina when he wrote *The Jewish State*. In *Altneuland,* he let his imagination roam, avoiding any reference to present conditions in Palestine. For these thinkers, the Promised Land was a country where Jews would be able to dwell among themselves and develop their national life as a people. They did not have a concrete country in mind but created an abstract conception. For that reason, they were unperturbed by the more mundane questions stemming from the maintenance of sovereignty over territory.

It is surprising that the man who did, in fact, treat the concrete situation prevailing in Palestine was Zvi Hirsch Kalischer, rabbi of the city of Torun in Poznan. In his book *Derishat Tziyon* (Seeking Zion), which appeared in 1862, he detailed a plan for Jewish settlement in Palestine. Among other things, Kalischer commented on the need to train Jews for a home guard to protect the settlers against bedouin marauders and to preserve law and order.[43] It is impossible to determine whether this proposal derived from a knowledge of realities in Palestine, or was based on abstract assumptions about what might be expected there. It remains a curious fact, nonetheless, that among the early proponents of the Zionist idea, the thinker who was seemingly furthest from concrete experience in the mundane world was the only one to remark in any way on the security situation in Palestine.

In *The Jewish State,* Herzl dealt very little with the population of Palestine. As mentioned, he had not yet decided whether the land for future Jewish settlement should be Palestine or Argentina. Hence, it is not surprising that he did not mention the Arabs by name. Herzl reminded readers that the land eventually promised to Jews under international law would also have to be acquired by legal means in terms of private law. He was concerned about speculation and an uncontrolled rise in the price of real estate in the wake of Jewish immigration. Yet he did not imagine the possibility that the local inhabitants might refuse to sell their land.[44] In his diary, he spoke about "voluntary expropriation," to be implemented by secret agents who would pay the inhabitants uncommonly high prices for their land. Needy segments of the native population would be persuaded to leave the country by assuring them jobs in neighboring countries and by causing temporary unemployment in Palestine.[45]

The orientation of the world prior to 1914 was Eurocentric: in the age of imperialism, the accepted norm was to give preference to European interests over those of native populations. Herzl's plan was more generous toward the local population than had been the prevailing norm. That generosity and caution stemmed from Herzl's personal ethical stance, on the one hand, and his awareness that every step toward construction of the Jewish state would be put to severe scrutiny by the entire enlightened world, on the other.

He was not troubled by the possibility that purchase of land and eviction of the impoverished natives might result in negative international publicity. In terms of public opinion in the wealthy European countries, such acts of acquisition and dispossession of the local population were not considered unusual. What did disturb Herzl was the shadow of possible financial scandal: It might once again associate Jews with swindling and fraud. Herzl was aware of two models of international enterprises in developing countries: the notorious Panama Canal affair, a symbol of public corruption, and the famous Suez Canal Company, praised as a positive example of international cooperation. He wanted desperately to avoid the pitfalls of the first model and emulate the second.

Historical Nationalism and Power: Two Conceptions

Nationalism of Herzl's type was based on the inevitability of the continued existence of the Jewish people—a necessity that unfortunately could not be avoided and should therefore serve as the springboard for a fresh start. Yet that perspective was unacceptable to Jews for whom the possibility of total assimilation had never been a viable alternative in any case. Jews in Eastern Europe had no need for any proof to corroborate their being a people. Multitudes were living there in densely populated urban neighborhoods, villages, and hamlets under distressing conditions and constant pressure from both the authorities and their non-Jewish neighbors. Manners and mores, customs, festivals and holidays, education, the private and public spheres—all emphasized the distinctiveness of the Jewish experience, the special character of Jewish existence. Religious culture still reigned supreme; but a powerful intellectual ferment had also emerged, generating a secular Jewish culture. The sense of a shared fate and common solidarity remained predominant, even in the instances where the power of religion had weakened. Herzl's discovery, "We are a people, one people"[46] was not considered in the Pale of Settlement to be a discovery.

Consequently, it is not surprising that one of the few topics on which there was general agreement (albeit in differing styles) between Ahad Ha-Am and Micha Joseph Berdichevsky was their basic opposition to Herzl's idea that Jewish nationalism was the result of external pressures. "Antisemitism begat Herzl, Herzl begat the 'Jewish State', the Jewish state—'Zionism', Zionism—the Congress," wrote Ahad Ha-Am, mocking the naive doctor from Vienna who was brazen enough to presume to teach Zionist traditions to the Jews of Eastern Europe.[47] Herzl limited the application of Zionism to Jews "who do not wish or are unable to assimilate."[48] His underlying assumption was that there were Jews who had retained their Jewishness solely because the non-Jewish environment was opposed to their integration. That hypothesis disqualified Herzl in Ahad Ha-Am's eyes. It was not antisemitism but rather the innate "instinct for national survival" that had maintained the nation, Ahad Ha-Am proudly proclaimed. Antisemitism was only the catalyst that aroused the innate instinct. Berdichevsky was also offended by the idea that the national feeling of Jews had been stirred as a result of Gentile hatred: "In my view, there is no greater act of submissiveness than for an entire people to render its very being dependent on the inclinations of others toward it!" In his perspective, no nation could exist solely by dint of external pressure. "Every people is a people because it is a people, regardless of whether others wish that to be so or not."[49] Anti-semitism, he reasoned, could not lead to the resurgence and revival of the people. Such revival has its source in the psychological need deriving from the *will,* a concept frequently used by Berdichevsky, connoting the vitality of the nation.

Ahad Ha-Am and Berdichevsky employed different phrases—"instinct for national survival" and "will of the people"—but their message was similar. The nation is not the product of free convention but the outgrowth of mythical forces, uncontrollable and beyond the realm of individuals and their desires, forces that compel them to act in a certain way, unconsciously and without knowing it. The people and its destiny—its past and future—are the dominant values, rather than the fate of individuals making up the people. Ahad Ha-Am blurred this fact by utilizing the concept *Judaism* instead of *people.* He accorded national culture an autonomous standing, separate from the individuals that bear that culture. National culture and its fate—rather than individuals and their fate—were, in his conception, the central topic shaping the activity of the Zionist movement. The national Jewish symbols were principally associated with Jewish cultural distinctiveness. However, if we strip Ahad Ha-Am's conception of its festive cultural attire, it becomes evident that there is no difference between the instinct for national survival and the "spirit of the nation" or any other romantic national abstraction drawn from the European arsenal. Berdichevsky, in that respect, was much more open and unburdened by complexes. He sought the path for the revival of the nation in a secular context, without any reference to traditional Jewish concepts.

On the face of it, the dispute between Ahad Ha-Am and Berdichevsky, which soon became a dispute between the Veterans (the school of Ahad Ha-Am) and the Youngsters (the school of Berdichevsky), was an argument between two schools of literary thought. In actual fact, at a certain stage of the controversy, it did, indeed, center on an essentially literary topic, namely, the proper content of Hebrew literature. Should it deal with scholarly issues, based on specifically Jewish sources, a kind of *Wissenschaft des Judentums* in a new guise (Ahad Ha-Am), or did it need to be a literature similar to that of all other peoples, treating the gamut of topics that abound in the imaginative literatures of the world's peoples (Berdichevsky)?[50] Yet even this apparently literary issue reflected the presence of basic differences in approach between the two thinkers, differences affecting the entire breadth of their respective national conceptions.

Ahad Ha-Am's point of departure was the special national character of the Jewish people. In his view, this distinctiveness had been expressed from time immemorial in the ethical conceptions of the people: "Almost everybody acknowledges the ethical 'genius' of the people of Israel and recognizes that in this field, it is 'superior' to all other nations." Ahad Ha-Am did not offer an explanation for the origin of this special "mutation" among the Jewish people. Yet he noted that the people had been cognizant of this singular quality since ancient times. It had been the source for the concept of election of the people: The Jews were the Chosen People, singled out not to exercise worldly power but to be a model unto the nations, a nation guided by ethical principles.[51]

This conception led Ahad Ha-Am to develop his own special interpretation of Jewish History: "The secret of the survival of our people is . . . that already in ancient times, the prophets taught it to respect spiritual power alone, and not to be impressed by physical strength."[52] By dint of this special characteristic, it did not humble itself to those who were stronger and had thus managed to survive, while other peoples greater than it had vanished into oblivion. From the time of its advent on the stage of history, its essence was a "kind of constant and powerful protest on the part of spiritual strength against physical force and the saber."[53] This philosophy of history led Ahad Ha-Am to grant a special importance to certain chapters in Jewish history. In his conception, *prophecy* embodied the spirit of Judaism by virtue of its ethical and social protest. During the period of the Second Temple, the bearers of the spirit of Judaism were the Pharisees, who had opposed the materialism of the Sadducees. The Sadducees, in contrast, wished to assimilate to Greek culture: They wanted the Jewish state to be just like all the other states and to act in accordance with its interests, without any special unique spiritual quality. After the destruction of the Temple, the vessel of Jewish political existence, the Pharisees understood the need to take action to assure the continued survival of the people: "The political Zealots remained sword in hand on the walls of Jerusalem, and the Pharisees, Torah in hand, went to Yavneh."[54]

Ahad Ha-Am praised Rabbi Yohanan ben Zakkai, who, according to legend, had fled from Jerusalem hidden in a coffin when the city was under siege and its fate had been sealed, and established "Yavneh and its suburbs," the rabbinical center of learning that eventually served as a substitute for the Temple that had been destroyed. On the other hand, Ahad Ha-Am was quite reserved when it came to the Zealots, who were fighting at that same time on the walls of Jerusalem: Blessed be their memory, he commented, but those who had truly saved the people of Israel from annihilation were the men who sat and studied in Yavneh, not those who had spilled their blood in a hopeless battle against the Romans.[55]

Ahad Ha-Am rejected the widespread tendency among Zionists to view the Diaspora as a period of stagnation in which Jewish creativity had ceased. He pointed to the Talmud and the Shulhan Arukh, two codificatory works that had been composed in the Diaspora and served as the basis for the life of the people, as proof that creativity had continued unabated.[56]

Ahad Ha-Am utilized his interpretation of the past in current controversies. The First Zionist Congress in Basel, where Herzl, a veritable upstart, stole the show and captured the hearts of the Jewish masses, engendered for a moment the hope that perhaps, against all odds, he might achieve the impossible, a Jewish state. Faced with that "apprehension," Ahad Ha-Am wrote that the establishment of a Jewish state at that juncture in world history could only lead to the creation of something small and pitiable, a polity that would be a plaything in the hands of its more powerful neighbors. It was inconceivable that a people that had sacrificed so much over the course of thousands of years should finally acquiesce in accepting the very same recompense that other nations, of lesser claim to fame, had achieved quickly and with comparatively little effort. Only when the vision of the prophets became reality and the "wolf lay down with lamb"—only then would Israel dwell in safety in its land and the Jewish state be established, Ahad Ha-Am contended.[57] He ended his words with a ringing line that has often been quoted since: "Israel's salvation will be brought about by 'prophets', not 'diplomats'."[58]

Ahad Ha-Am's basic Zionist perspective is reflected in this passage: He was not alarmed by the "plight of the Jews"—the existential hardship that characterized Jewish life in Eastern Europe and the fear and sense of estrangement engendered by antisemitism in the West. He proposed to solve the material problems of the existence of the Jewish people by mass emigration overseas, to Argentina or the United States. In his view, Palestine was meant to bring forth a spiritual revival of the people, to fashion its image anew based on the vision of the prophets. The Jewish community in Palestine should be built up slowly, in an evolutionary manner, step by step, since Ahad Ha-Am was wary of any revolutionary, sudden moves, cutting the Gordian knot as Herzl would have done. Ahad Ha-Am's greatest fear was not so much that Herzl would fail and lead the movement to disappointment (a point he often stressed) but, rather, that Herzl would succeed. The slow pace of development was a part of the system of educational control, meant to prevent the possibility that the proposed Jewish state would be a state like any other. From Ahad Ha-Am's perspective, that would not be a genuinely *Jewish* state. In his view, a Jewish state was not simply a state of and for Jews along the lines proposed by Herzl but, rather, an abstraction representing and exemplifying the "spirit of the nation" as Ahad Ha-Am conceived it.

He presented the attitudes of Herzl and Nordau toward dueling as an illustration of the misconception by these "Westerners" of the true "spirit of the nation" (or, as Ahad Ha-Am termed it, "Jewish culture"). Central characters from Herzl's play *The New Ghetto* and Nordau's *Dr. Cohen* end their lives in a duel against a Gentile who has insulted them. Dr. Cohen even explains that he cannot desist, since it is a fight to defend Jewish dignity. Ahad Ha-Am viewed these fictive representations as proof that neither of the authors had understood the spirit of Judaism: The dignity of the "genuine Jew" would not be offended because some numbskull chose to insult him. Instead of fighting him, such a Jew would turn aside in contempt, without sensing any need to sacrifice his life on this account.[59]

In Ahad Ha-Am's view, the Jewish people was morally superior to all other peoples. As a consequence, it had a natural disgust for physical power and its use. Accordingly, the "true Jew" was not ashamed of his physical weakness. While the Gentiles are busy shedding blood in power struggles, the Jew looks on in dismay at their backwardness and lack of moral virtues. Thus, the Jewish state must, first of all, be a "light unto the Jews," acting as a focus of creativity and national renewal for the entire people. But it must also be a "beacon unto the nations," because the Jewish people did not suffer so much affliction for thousands of years just to achieve the mundane goal of bringing into being still another tiny polity like Serbia or Montenegro. For Ahad Ha-Am, it was inconceivable that the Jewish state should be nothing more than a state like any other, aggrandizing its material might and venerating symbols of power and physical valor.

Ahad Ha-Am remained enclosed within the ambit of a Jewish ethnic and cultural world. He did not wish to fling open the portals to the broader world outside and was uninterested in what non-Jews thought of him. Paradoxically, he apparently adhered to the traditional Jewish postulate that non-Jews could offer no understanding or empathy. For him, the integration of the new Jew into the non-Jewish world was not an advantage but a fault. He sought means to defend Jews against the danger of assimilation. Consequently, Ahad Ha-Am regarded any sign of Jewish acceptance of the behavioral and value norms of non-Jewish society as an existential threat. It was no accident that he criticized Nordau for the fact that the main protagonist in his play *Dr. Cohen* pursues a German Christian woman and expresses his willingness to enter into a mixed marriage. In Ahad Ha-Am's Judeo-centric world, Nordau's position was interpreted as a blow to the physical survival of the people and to Jewish morality. Although he preferred to avoid explaining in specific terms why he thought this was injurious to Jewish morality, there is no doubt that this is how he saw the situation. On the other hand, he felt it was a "moral obligation" for a person endowed with a sense of national consciousness "to defend the existence of his people" by avoidance of mixed marriage.[60] He often used the concept *morals* when referring to values rooted in national Jewish interests. For Ahad Ha-Am, morality was conceptualized as "national," that is, an expression of the "instinct for national survival." In his thinking, it is not a universal human attribute. Thus, he also hypothesized that there was one morality for Jews and another for non-Jews. Although he placed morality at the very top of the scale of values characterizing the Jewish spirit, Ahad Ha-Am's Judeocentrism left latitude for far-reaching interpretations.

Micha Joseph Berdichevsky felt obligated toward a totally different spiritual world. He was well versed in Jewish sources, as befitting a former Yeshiva student and simultaneously viewed himself as a follower of Friedrich Nietzsche. Berdichevsky was attuned to a highly characteristic spiritual–intellectual current of the late nineteenth and early twentieth century, namely *vitalism.* He never considered assimilation; and even when he drew sustenance from foreign sources, he internalized their content and applied them to Jewish topics and concerns. In contrast with Ahad Ha-Am, who desired a secular Judaism that would preserve the system of values adhered to by Jews at the time by dint of religion, Berdichevsky recognized the existence of a complete severance between the old world of Jewish values and the new nationalism. Moreover, he actually welcomed this schism. In his perspective, everything the Jewish people had created since it had gone into exile was a product of weakness, degeneration, and defilement, not a genuine expression of the national spirit. Only when the people would be liberated from the fetters and restrictions of exile and would return to its vital ancient roots, a wellspring prior to the time when it had taken on the image of the People of the Book—only then would the Jewish people be capable once again of true creativity.

Berdichevsky wanted the Jewish people to be accepted as a peer, a nation among the nations. In contrast to Ahad Ha-Am, he was attentive to what was said about Jews by the antisemites and even accepted a portion of that criticism. He did not consider Heinrich von Treitschke, the renowned German historian who had written in an extremely negative vein on the Jews, to be an enemy. Treitschke asserted that the Jews were a people in their own right and that for that reason it was impossible for them to assimilate to the German people. While many Jews viewed this approach as antisemitic, Berdichevsky felt he was simply stating the truth. Berdichevsky claimed that Treitschke's critique of Heinrich Heine and Ludwig Börne, although excessive, contained a kernel of truth: The same elements in the works of these two authors that Jews praised as being fundamentally Jewish, Treitschke criticized as "non-German." On the whole, Berdichevsky argued, what Treitschke had underscored was the "national obduracy" of the Jews; and this was no reason to fault him.[61]

The fundamental dispute between Berdichevsky and Ahad Ha-Am revolved around the national essence of the Jewish people. Ahad Ha-Am selected certain elements from Jewish history and fashioned them into a vision of a monolithic Judaism, any deviations from which were mere aberrations unrepresentative of the general and homogeneous course of Jewish character. Berdichevsky disputed the existence of such an essential character. Judaism had, he contended, never been a single and unified system of values, beliefs, and opinions. Rather, it was a constantly altering complex of values whose source lay in changing external conditions.

Ahad Ha-Am postulated the existence of a national morality that derived from the essence of the national spirit. He had a certain difficulty in adequately explaining, without reference to religious imperatives, just how that special morality had come into being and maintained its existence. Berdichevsky did not need to resort to such intellectual exercises. As a relativist, it was clear to him that it was impossible to speak about absolute morality. Rather, morality, like all other values, was relative and the product of circumstances.

"The core of the national morality," Berdichevsky noted, "is simple: *the people's love for itself,* for *that same* people and its advantage, even if such love speaks in the name of the Lord who chose the people, bequeathing it everything as an inheritance."[62] Even if the "national morality" aims to establish a "spiritual center" along the lines suggested by Ahad Ha-Am, it is "founded on the nonmorality of conquest, expansion of borders, destruction of the weak, and resettlement in their stead."[63] This is how it had always been: Whoever wrote the command "Not a soul shall survive" was not inspired by moral considerations but, rather, by national interests.[64] Jewish history, portrayed by Ahad Ha-Am as a kind of moral tale of our noble forefathers supposedly endowed with fine virtues looked different in actual reality, Berdichevsky contended: It was steeped in bloodshed, violent struggle, and mutual slaughter.

Berdichevsky suggested looking carefully at representative examples drawn from biblical literature: Sarah asks Abraham to send away Hagar and Ishmael, and the Lord gives his blessing to that perverse deed. Jacob steals the birthright of Esau, and it is written, "Jacob I loved, and Esau did I hate." There were the fraternal wars between the sister kingdoms of Judea and Israel. Abimelech murders seventy of his brothers on one stone. Cunningly, David has the entire house of Saul done away with. Covenants with neighboring peoples are repeatedly broken. Ezra enforces the rule of the Torah over the people of Zion by the coercive power of the kings of Persia. The Hasmoneans conquer the land in bloody battle and then fight among themselves. Ultimately, Herod comes and annihilates them. The dispute between the Pharisees and Sadducees was not about the intricacies of the Law but about who should have power. Moreover, one should recall the strife and contention in Yavneh, Babylon, and elsewhere. It is enough to read the records of the Jewish communities and the rabbinical *responsa,* Berdichevsky noted, to discover that the most powerful in the community always abused the weak. Not only did Berdichevsky point to the stories of injustice cited in the Bible, rulings laid down by man and God and not understandable in terms of a simple human decency. He also drew attention to the moral contradictions in the Bible. Is Jewish morality that of "visiting the sins of the fathers unto the sons" or that of "sons shall not die because of their fathers"? Is it the morality of Saul, who, according to legend, compassionately refused to carry out Samuel's order to slaughter Amalek and his kin by the sword or that of the divine voice that was angered and commanded him not to be self-righteous? Is it the morality that commands you to love your enemy or the one that states that vengeance against Edom was also one of the gifts granted the world in the six days of creation? For Ahad Ha-Am, one of Judaism's key virtues was that it did not seek revenge and was generous and forgiving. But those same Scriptures wrote that the "righteous shall rejoice when he beholds vengeance"; and the Talmud states, "Greater is the vengeance given between two letters [two names of God], as is written: A God of vengeance is the Lord."[65]

Berdichevsky was especially enraged about Ahad Ha-Am's claim that the typical trait of Jewish national character was the disdain of physical force and veneration of spiritual superiority. In contrast with the symbols of the nation praised by his intellectual adversary, Berdichevsky resurrected other national symbols till then persistently neglected by the Jewish educational system and nearly forgotten: Abimelech, who demanded from his armorbearer that he kill him after he had been injured by a woman; Saul, who, facing defeat and disgrace, fell upon his own sword, his servant with him; Samson, who chose to die with the Philistines. To these biblical examples of valor, Berdichevsky added the episode of the collective suicide of the defenders of the Massada, headed by their leader Elazar ben Yair. Indeed, this appears to be one of the first references by a Jewish writer to the Massada saga as a tale of Jewish heroism.[66]

The Maccabees held a prime place in the national pantheon created by Berdichevsky, but the Zealot *biryonim* (hooligans), upon whom Jewish tradition had placed a crown of thorns, were even more important in his eyes. Berdichevsky noted that in his youth, when he read the tale of the destruction of the Temple, particularly the legend of the burning of the food reserves in Jerusalem by those Zealot extremists, he was bitterly moved by their act of destruction. But "years have passed, I've grown distant from the *heder* and its atmosphere, and my views have also changed. Had I been living then, I would have assisted them, and would also have shared their conviction."[67] The siege of Jerusalem, on the one hand, and the departure of Rabbi Yohanan ben Zakkai to Yavneh on the other, are depicted by him as two poles in Jewish history. Representative of the true Jewish national spirit is not the man who went to Yavneh but, rather, those who remained in the city to die on its walls. "Greater than those who fled out of the walls and hid in coffins were those who died by the sword," Berdichevsky asserted.[68] The fall of Jerusalem did not spell the end of the fighting tradition among Jews. Rabbi Akiva and thousands of his pupils rallied to the cause of war when animated by political hope in the guise of Bar Kokhba.[69] Only over the course of many generations, after the people had been separated from its land and had ceased to live a normal life, did a new interpretation appear, exalting the action of Yohanan ben Zakkai: "The leaders of the people deflected its natural inclination by a false spirituality and taught the people to prefer Yavneh to the fortress of Jerusalem, that is, to the fortress of the people and its survival."[70]

Berdichevsky did not deny that Ahad Ha-Am's perspective expressed the accepted conception of Jewish history. Yet he wished to emphasize an alternative historical perspective with different heroes, alternative critical crossroads and moral lessons. The traditional Jewish conception gave little weight to physical prowess and exalted the notion "Not by power and might, but by my spirit" (or in the secular version of Ahad Ha-Am, by spirit[71]). Berdichevsky contended that this conception had developed as a result of Jewish weakness and expressed that weakness. When the people was a people like all others, vital, creative, full of strength and courage, its veneration was not for righteous men but for heroes in war. The period of strength of the people and its conquest of the land coincided with the time when the children of Israel did *evil* in the eyes of the Lord.[72] In its youth, the people placed greater emphasis on the love of nature than the love of God, admired power rather than love, instinct and impulse over moral values. This was a people that had conquered its land by military force, and did not care about what other nations might say.[73] This was a people that was unashamed to dream the dream of the psalmist, "O daughter of Babylon, who art to be destroyed, . . . happy shall he be that taketh and dasheth thy little ones against the stones" (Psalms 137:8–9). Only during the talmudic period did the metaphor arise of Israel as a lamb among wolves. "I cannot comprehend," wrote Berdichevsky in wrath, "how a whole people can perceive itself to be a lamb and be content with that."[74]

Berdichevsky set out his view of Jewish history as being divided into two periods: (1) the epoch before the Torah took control of life, a period of strength, courage, and vitality, and (2) the subsequent era of failure and disgrace. He dubbed the first period the Age of Shammai, the "generation of strength and life," and the second the Age of Hillel, an era when "spirituality crushed vitality."[75] The humiliation of such a life was, he argued, manifested not only in the despicable weakness of the Jewish people among the other nations but also in the alienation of the people from nature, real life, knowledge of the world, and creative thought. Over the course of generations, the Jewish people pursued erudition but did not bring forth new creations. Though Jews wrote many books, these were devoid of originality. Religious learning had transformed the Jew into a "person endowed with brains, yet lacking a heart."[76] According to Berdichevsky, a chasm existed between the period of youth and simple purity of the people, marked by its struggle for the land, and the two thousand years of exile, distinguished by its divorce from genuine life as a people.[77] Berdichevsky's call for liberation from the fetters of Jewish morality and a return to the ancient instincts of the natural people—to that state of affairs before their desires, wishes, and behavior had been stifled, bridled by counterfeit norms—was the Hebrew version of the Nietzschean critique of Judeo–Christian morality and its chains.

One might expect that Berdichevsky's verbal aggressiveness would have led him to the path of radical, egoistic, reclusive nationalism. Yet in contrast with Ahad Ha-Am, who viewed the non-Jewish world with suspicion and even enmity, Berdichevsky wanted to raze the walls between him and that world. The biblical injunction "not to follow after their laws" was viewed by Berdichevsky as the "greatest repression of the spirit of Israel." It had resulted in the seclusion of the Jews from the larger world and its manifestations. He totally rejected the Jewish self-complacency ingrained in the doctrine of the Chosen People and wrote that "any *distinction or limitation* between peoples or individuals is a curse on life."[78]

We are thus presented with a genuine paradox: The proponent of raging, militant nationalism advanced the concept of "open windows" to the non-Jewish world, while the thinker who espoused ethical and humanistic concepts of nationalism carried aloft the banner of Jewish seclusion, stressing Jewish specificity as an ideal. Berdichevsky's militancy, his cultivation of a pantheon of heroes of yore, his abundant use of aggressive terminology—all this was meant to make up for what had been lacking in Jewish life. If the aspiration was to establish the Jews as a normal people, settled on their own soil, prepared to fight for and defend it, then it was necessary to foster an admiration within the people for a new set of values, hitherto alien to it or long suppressed.

The major difference between the national conceptions of Ahad Ha-Am and Berdichevsky lay in their attitude toward Jewish life in the Diaspora. Ahad Ha-Am viewed it positively. He did not conceal his affinity with, and fondness for, Simeon Dubnow and his concept of Jewish autonomy in the Diaspora and had greater sympathy for the diasporic "nationalists" of the Dubnowian school of thought than for the "statist" Zionists of Herzlian persuasion.[79] He expected Jewish life in the Diaspora to continue to exist even if the Zionist experiment succeeded. Indeed, Ahad Ha-Am considered diasporic existence to be an essential and integral component of Jewish national life.

In contrast, Berdichevsky saw life in the Diaspora as a process of constant and ongoing degeneration, from both the spiritual–intellectual and physical point of view. Ahad Ha-Am's theory of nationalism posited a continuity between Jewish existence in the Diaspora in the past, present, and future. In contrast, Berdichevsky created a theory of secular Jewish nationhood, drawing its sustenance from the ancient Jewish nation before it had accepted the yoke of the Law and the commandments. Berdichevsky's conception centered on a renewal of that nation. It would not necessarily be a people that relished the shedding of blood. But if the quality that characterized the Jews according to Ahad Ha-Am was the rejection of the sword (in practical terms denying any possibility of independent Jewish political life), then, quite naturally, those who desired national rejuvenation along the lines of the German or Italian example (Bismarck and Garibaldi being considered model leaders in this respect) emphasized this element as an antithesis.

Berdichevsky was not the only thinker who engaged in a revision of the interpretation of Jewish history. In the public debate among Zionists in Eastern Europe at the end of the nineteenth and beginning of the twentieth century, a strong tendency emerged for a revaluation of the Jewish past. Concretely, what that meant was a distancing from the traditional Jewish view of Israel as a lamb among the nations, a people guided by moral values, a nation of the righteous. This traditional conception had various roots. First of all, there was the Jewish self-image, the product of generations of persecution and weakness. Second, Jewish apologetic literature, from the time of the disputations between Jews and Christians, Jews and apostates, had placed emphasis on the qualities of love for one's fellow man, a sense of humanity, and other elevated virtues apparently possessed by the people of Israel. This was supplemented by the apologetic literature of the nineteenth century, which brought to new heights the self-image of Israel as a people (or, more correctly, a *religion*) entrusted with an exalted spiritual mission. The antisemites portrayed the Jews as wretched and weak. Concurrently, they accused them of lacking integrity and being rapaciously hungry for profit and distinguished by an absence of moral inhibitions. Jews reacted by emphasizing their devotion to the homeland, and their readiness to fight for it. In the main, however, the Jewish argument was based on emphasizing the qualities that were the very opposite of the traits imputed to them by the antisemites; and they cited Jewish Scripture, the Talmud, and the rabbinical literature as evidence. The claim of Jewish moral superiority derived from two sources: the generations-old tradition of the Chosen People, employed by the weak to defend themselves against self-denigration and the nineteenth-century tendency to respond to antisemitic charges with rational arguments drawn from the Bible. The emergence of a new national ethos, whose central significance was the return of the Jews to history as a normal people, led to the flowering of a new self-image. No longer were Jews conceived as a just, but weak and hence contemptible, people. Rather, the new image was that of a people endowed with virtues and defects similar to those of all other nations, not distinguished by any special sanctity, whose supposedly moral traits and disposition had been the product of historical factors and circumstances.

This revision of Jewish history entailed a fair portion of self-criticism, a refreshing openness, unencumbered by the complexes and self-righteousness that had characterized such deliberations in the past. In contrast with the tendency to associate altruistic motives, for the good of all mankind, with the Jews and their continued existence, it was asserted that "nationalist ends . . . are always *egotistic and materialistic* in the broader sense." It is obvious that peoples attempt to blur and conceal these aims, and tend to bestow epithets such as "war for freedom" or "cultural war" on their egoistical aspirations. That is the way of the world. The Jews are no exception in this regard: Indeed, they pray that the "rule of wickedness shall pass from the earth" but do not see it as their task to accelerate the coming of that day. It is conventionally assumed that Jews joined the vanguard of all wars for justice around the globe, struggling for freedom and socialism. However, in actuality, Jews only made common cause with the revolutionaries in those states where their own rights had not been guaranteed. In contrast, in countries where their position was strong, Jews tended to defend the existing order and support parties at the political center.[80]

As to any Jewish proclivity to turn the other cheek, it was argued that such a characteristic did not stem from some special Jewish moral trait but had its origin in historical circumstances: "Such views always arise at times when spiritual strength outweighs physical power, in periods of political weakness."[81] The same held true for other fine traits attributed to the Jews, such as purity of family life and charity and mercy toward the needy in the Jewish community: These virtues had not stood the test of emancipation and were disappearing. Moreover, even in the past, when their material well-being was affected, Jews had not hesitated to find a way to get around the moral laws of the Torah: The Law forbade receiving usury from fellow Jews, but in practice a legal way was found to circumvent it.[82] Highly uncomplimentary criticism was also voiced regarding Jewish creativity in the past: "Aside from the hair-splitting pedantry of ritualistic religion and literature deriving from a narrowness of spirit and poverty of thought (e.g., the *poskim*, rabbinical *responsa* literature, and the like), the culture of our people was not distinguished in any way during the Middle Ages."

The argument advanced by Richard Wagner and like-minded critics postulating a lack of Jewish creativity was now reiterated by Jews themselves: Even in the modern period, the Jewish people had not innovated anything but, rather, had drawn their sustenance from the other nations.[83] The relation of the Jew to the non-Jew—in the past subject to severe self-imposed censorship—was now ventilated, at least partially: Indeed, the prophet Isaiah (49:6) had stated, "It is too light a thing that thou shouldest be my servant, . . . I will also give thee for a light to the Gentiles." Yet when the Jews, in their own land, were required to put that fraternal friendship for other nations into practice, they answered, "Ye have nothing to do with us to build a house unto our God" (Ezra 4:3). Even among the Jews of Hellenistic Alexandria, whose literature had universal characteristics, carrying a message of peace and truth to all peoples, there were some who taught "the doctrine of self-defense to all Jews in the Diaspora, in the days of Vespasian and Trajan."[84]

One of the new trends was a sense of weariness regarding claim to a special national mission. This missionary concept contained appealing components; its roots lay in the idea of the mission in the early nineteenth century and continued, in another guise, in the notion of Ahad Ha-Am that the Jewish state would have to be a "light unto the nations." The universalism it harbored liberated the Jewish national concept from the provincialism of a small and narrow national movement involved in matters that were marginal to the great world events of the time. It also endowed the propagation of the national idea with a character and meaning beyond its immediate objectives. Yet such a view could also lead to anti-Zionist interpretations: Should it turn out that the Jewish state was nothing more than a Serbia or Montenegro, why, then, should such great efforts be undertaken in the first place?[85] It is thus not surprising that within the framework of the general revision of past values and the process of merciless self-exposure, doubts also arose regarding the concept of a national mission or destiny. The pretension this idea was imbued with was out of all proportion to the actual capabilities of the Zionist movement. It also served as a source for a substantial degree of self-complacency. This, in turn, provoked disgust among youth thirsty for action, who clearly discerned the gap between the humble facts of mundane existence and the overblown rhetoric.

"We are a purpose unto ourselves, and there is no need to search for missions beyond that of our own survival." That, in essence, was the rebuke in reply to those who continued to look for world-embracing missions: "As though we have only been created to serve as a tool for others and are unable, unlike all other peoples, to be a purpose unto ourselves! As though we did not have a right to demand the freedom that has been stolen from us and our independence without promising a world to come for others!"[86] This meant that it was enough for the Jews to have a state like other states: "And for that reason, it is no misfortune 'if we have an insignificant state like that of Serbia or Montenegro'." Again, "For the sick man, it is enough that he regain his health; and there is no need for him to aspire to the strength of Samson." Not that it is forbidden to dream "that out of Zion shall go forth the Law": "After all, there is no tariff on aspirations, and it is our right to aspire without end."[87] However, this hope should not come instead of action or foster the notion that the existence of a Jewish national entity is justified only if it serves universal aims.[88]

The crystallizing national ethos was marked by a growing realism and departure from the generations-old Jewish tendency to regard an intellectual dispute on philosophical questions as a political act. The distinction between the world of ideas and the world of action was not yet sharp enough. However, efforts were made to neutralize the discussion, avoiding value judgments and shifting its focus to the plane of reality. The inclination to place excessive emphasis on Machiavellian elements in Jewish history, manifested by the heralds of the new ethos, was rooted in a need to delineate the departure from the accepted practice. The transition from a people *in potentia* to one in actuality entailed a psychological willingness to change one's self-image, and recognize the fact that normalization also meant embracing the less appealing aspects of political life. This was not a straightforward, steady process; rather, it experienced periods of progress and retreat.

Two contradictory messages were broadcast simultaneously by the evolving national ethos. One, characteristic of Ahad Ha-Am and his followers, viewed Judaism in terms of a special moral quality, conceiving of national revival as the means to strengthen and promote this quality. The second denied the existence of Judaism as a secular abstract value separate from Jewish religion and demanded a revival and resurgence of the Jews as a normal people. The key phrases were "spiritual" versus "material," "light unto the nations" versus "like all other peoples," and "Yavneh" versus "Betar." Both messages rested to a large extent on the Bible as the proof of Jewish exploits in the past and as a fountainhead of hope for the future.

It is not farfetched to contend that the Bible was the battlefield on which the struggle over the nature of the new national ethos was waged. Both camps were able to claim that they represented true Judaism as manifested in the most important work given the world by the Jewish people. The Hebrew Bible recounts the blood-drenched history of the conquest and settlement of the land by the Hebrew tribes and chronicles the later kingdoms of Saul, David, and their successors. It also contains some of the most exalted chapters ever written in moral literature. One of the most cherished and cultivated components of the new Jewish self-esteem was pride in the fact that it was the Jewish people that had created the Bible. Simultaneously, the Bible was also viewed as a source of written proof—evidence in support of the right of Jews to their land. Neither camp was able to delegitimize the aspects of the Bible unacceptable to them. The upshot was that the national message in regard to these basic questions was not straightforward but marked by contradictory components. There was constant dispute about these elements, and they ultimately served as the basis for the emergence of competing groups expressive of conflicting political cultures. Yet both these trends were considered a legitimate and integral part of the national ethos.

It is doubtful whether ideas dictated the course of actual events. However, it is important to note the formation of potential ideas—seeds of concepts and attitudes that would, indeed, become essential components in ideology, a stimulus for action, and a moral justification in another place and time.

The National Ethos in the Poetry of the Period

In its early period (down to World War I), the Zionist movement was more distinguished by the presence of intellectuals, incisive polemicists, brilliant lecturers, and, of course, sharp-penned journalists than by the men who took bold concrete action. Such a feature is quite natural for a movement whose cultural structure predated its social constitution and long predated its political makeup. That cultural fabric, woven from soul-searching deliberations on the essence of the people in the past, present, and future, had given sustenance to rabbinical students and graduates, accustomed to the hair-splitting argumentation characteristic of talmudic study. But it was no nourishment for a people's movement that needed to be galvanized into action and inspired. As one of the zealous young men of the Second Aliyah proclaimed, a single poem by Bialik contributed more to the spirit of the national movement than all the tomes of research written on the essence of Judaism.[89] It is thus instructive to pursue the character of the emerging national ethos as it was manifested in the Hebrew poetry of the day.

The 1890s saw the emergence of two giants of Hebrew poetry: Chaim Nahman Bialik and Shaul Tchernichovsky. Bialik's first poem, "El ha-zippor" (To the bird) of 1891, describes the longing of a Jewish boy in cold Russia for Palestine, the warm land. The contrast between *here,* where things are bad, and *there,* where all is good, constitutes the axis of the poem. Palestine is described in its full mythic splendor. The young man is well versed in the Bible and depicts the country as he has learned about it from that source. He mentions places he knows from the Bible, without their necessarily having any connection with the landscape of the present: Sharon, Lebanon, Jordan, Zion. The plants of Palestine are familiar to him from the so-called seven varieties and other biblical references: almonds, date trees, cereals. This is "the land where spring forever dwells" and where those who sow in tears will reap in joy.

In the past, Jews had lived in this land. What occurred from the time the Jews were banished from their land down to the present is of no interest to the poet. There is a kind of hidden assumption in the poem that the land has, in fact, been desolate since that time: "Did the Lord have compassion on Zion, did he comfort it, / Or is it still deserted, desolate in ruins?" The physical description of the land does not include any mention of a living soul.[90] Eretz Israel of the young Bialik is a land of the Bible and of legend and has no connection with the actual Palestine of the present. In that respect, it is reminiscent of the biblical novels of Abraham Mapu—*Ahavat Tziyon* (Love of Zion) and *Ashmat Shomron* (Guilt of Samaria)—that excited the hearts of many young people in the period of the Hebrew Haskalah

(Enlightenment) in the 1850s and 1860s. They played an important role in awakening consciousness about Palestine but were completely divorced from the prosaic facts of the actual country.

Several years later, Tchernichovsky composed what eventually became one of the most popular of Zionist songs. It was a lullaby that is known to many by its first two words, Nitshu tzlalim (Shadows are Spreading). In a few lines Tchernichovsky captured the essence of sentiments underlying the Zionist idea: a mixture of national pride and deep-seated shame: "You are a Hebrew, my son; yet this is / Your happiness, this your disaster." A splendid past, shameful present, and bright future intermingle here. Once this was a people that ruled over nations and performed great deeds. Now it is to renew its days as of old in that same land in the East. The poem is written from the depths of a tragic feeling of great weakness of the Jews, fighting against insurmountable forces. The hope for a glorious future has no actual basis and stems from the mystical faith in the future of the people. The poet believes that the "day of salvation" will come, but he also prepares for possible disappointment: "Despair not, prisoner of hope, / Our sun will still rise." The focus of the poem is not the faraway country where the sun rises but the bitter reality of the Diaspora. Yet the lullaby's last stanza, which was generally forgotten, reads:

> On the Jordan and in Sharon,
> Where the Arabs camp,
> This will be our land!
> You, too, are among the builders!
> And some day the standard-bearers will arise,
> Do not betray them!
> To your weapons among the heroes,
> Our sun shall rise.[91]

On the face of it, there are elements here that can be interpreted as hinting at the beginning of an aggressive ethos. But a more sophisticated approach to this poem appears necessary. The description of the Jordan and Sharon, as well as of the Arabs, is not based on real acquaintance any more than is the description in the poem by Bialik. It is still a mythical Palestine; and the Arabs are one of the natural components that are part of that landscape, like the Jordan River and the plain of Sharon. Even the proud proclamation that the land someday will be owned by the Jews is not meant to stand in contrast to the Arab inhabitants. The passage contains hints of two actions: construction and warfare. Construction precedes the waging of war. The call to arms is not presented in realistic dimensions but, rather, as a symbol of the revival of the people. Bravery and heroism will characterize the Jew returning to his homeland, contrasted with the fears and apprehensions plaguing him at present. Nonetheless, the mention of the Arab inhabitants, the claim of ownership over the land, and the mention of weapons—all uttered almost in a single breath—is a combination with a certain significance even though at the time of composition it had only a mythical value. Words carry weight in the crystallization of a national ethos.

Tchernichovsky belonged to the vitalist school of thought. His poems reflect a longing for a rejuvenation of the people and its liberation from the chains of religion. He linked national renewal with the hope for universal salvation: The improvement of the world in the spirit of socialism and world peace were, in his outlook, the preconditions for the Jewish national renaissance. Then the Jewish people would also be liberated from its religious fetters:

> They will live, love, act, do,
> A [native] generation indeed living in the land,
> Not in the future, in the heavens—
> For them, the spiritual life will not suffice.[92]

This is the first appearance of the myth of a generation raised in Eretz Israel. The link with the land will, it is imagined, lead to the creation of a new type of Jew: passionate, down-to-earth, at one with nature, a builder of the land. And indeed, this people once possessed those qualities—in its pristine youth, when it came storming out of Egypt and conquered the land of Canaan by force. The youth of the people was stamped by the primacy of the experience of the conquest:

> The God of wonders of the wilderness,
> The God of conquerers, who took Canaan by storm
> Before they bound him in phylacteries.[93]

For Tchernichovsky, paganism and Hellenism symbolized life, youth, and beauty. In contrast, Judaism symbolized mutiny against the light, the agony of prolonged death, old age, the loss of vitality. The masculine virtues of physical strength and valor were expressed in the conquest of the land for the purpose of settling the people. Tchernichovsky imputed a mythical significance to the act of conquest, a manifestation of past vigor and a condition for future vitality. He sensed no contrast between the universal ideals he espoused and the act of conquest he so admired. Thus, it appears that he attached greater importance to the virtue of valor and the readiness to take risks than to the actual act of conquest. It is possible that what underlay his words was the perception that a right to a country must be earned, won by armed struggle. However, his words still remained on a symbolic, mythical plane, without concrete practical implications.

Another poem by Tchernichovsky, the ballad "Be–En–Dor" (In En-Dor) was to play an important role in the crystallization of the national ethos. The ballad describes the last night in the life of Saul, the first king of Israel. He travels to a woman possessed with a familiar spirit; is confronted with Samuel the prophet; and at the end, devoid of hope, returns to his encampment to fight his last battle. From the first lines, the sympathy of the reader is directed to the tragic figure of Saul, taken from the shepherd's flock to rule as a king over Israel. Samuel, the preferred hero of the tale according to Jewish tradition, appears in this poem as merciless and almost inhuman. Although the landscapes described are the fruit of the poet's imagination, they lend the work a concrete background, almost sensual, of the Land of Israel.[94] The situation on the eve of battle and the unhappy end—not elaborated upon but known to every youngster (Saul falling on his own sword)—all this generated strong emotions among the poem's readers. More than the essays by Berdichevsky, Tchernichovsky's poems played an important role in the education of youth, evoking dreams of heroism, national glory, and the land of their forefathers, a past to be appropriated and reacquired.

Although Bialik was never attracted by pagan myths, he also made use of the imagery of courage drawn from the biblical past and the era of the Second Temple. The evocation of past exploits, such as those of the Maccabees, was meant to spark the enthusiasm of the people and galvanize them into taking more decisive action for their own salvation.[95] The poem "Metei midbar" (The Dead of the Desert) was more ambivalent. The image of the desert generation, destined to perish before reaching the Promised Land, can be interpreted as an expression of doubt in the ability of humankind to disobey divine will. Yet it was not the image of the dead in the desert that caught the imagination of the readers but, rather, the scene in which the dead were awakened and began to cry out, "We are the brave! / Last of the enslaved! First to be free!" God commanded them to remain in the desert, but they defy the heavens and strive to conquer the mountain.[96] In the consciousness of the reader, they were depicted as the new Jews who rebel against a bitter Jewish fate, taking their destiny in their own hands.

The image of ascent to the summit of the mountain was a very natural motif to choose: It had already served several national movements in their early period. In the Zionist context, it acquired a special justification in view of the concept of *aliyah* (ascent) to Palestine. The term *aliyah* is laden with deep emotions and bestows upon the act of immigration to Eretz Israel a supernatural meaning, far beyond the limits of the prosaic equivalent *immigration.* The motif of ascent can be found in the poem of another young poet at the time, Yaakov Cahan. The figure of the Jewish pioneer is symbolized by a climber heading to the top of the mountain, who is not deterred by the corpses he passes by during his ascent. Cahan apparently drew his inspiration from the mountains of Switzerland, where he was studying when he composed these poems.[97] But the image of the conquest of a mountain as a metaphor for the implementation of the national mission would be used in future Hebrew poetry and belles lettres.

Cahan won himself a place in the evolving national ethos by virtue of a single poem, Ha-biryonim (The Hooligans). He avoided using the more neutral term *Kana'im* (Zealots), standard in historiographical literature, preferring the pejorative epithet from talmudic tradition *biryonim* (hooligans, roughnecks). The very use of this expression signified a Berdichevsky-like denial of the entire approach to the Jewish war against the Romans prevalent in Jewish tradition and also a rejection of the concept of Yavneh and its sages. The tendency toward a revision of the dominant traditional interpretation of the heroic disasters of the Second Temple had begun. No longer was it the outcome of the struggle that counted; rather, the struggle itself was considered an expression of spiritual strength, vitality, and the superiority of those who fight over those who surrender.[98]

The essence of "The Hooligans" is a description of the awakening of the new generation of *biryonim:*

> We arose, returned, we, the *biryonim!*
> We came to redeem our oppressed land—
> With a strong hand, we demand our right!

In blood and fire did Judea fall.
In blood and fire shall Judea rise.[99]

The awakening is associated with a mighty war, in which the "camp of Judea" stands opposed to an adversary whose identity is not specified. The clash between these two rival camps takes place "on the open steppe" (recalling more the steppes of Russia than the landscape of Palestine). The war has mythical dimensions, and all the universe participates in it. This is not a modern war; it possesses features reminiscent of ancient warfare: trumpets, horsemen, and lances join in battle. It seems that what the poem portrays is not the depiction of the conquest of Palestine but, rather, a vision of an apocalyptic struggle between the people of Israel and its enemies from time immemorial. Like his great predecessors, Cahan also wrote his poems in the Diaspora: For him, as well, Palestine was still an abstraction.

He also anticipated the emergence of a new generation: "Proud and courageous, generation of masters / Generation of fire and desire, fanatic and vengeful, generation of freedom and victory."[100] This envisioned generation is devoid of spiritual qualities and is characterized by its instinctuality, valor, and belligerency.

Self-Defense

One of the most central—and perhaps most important—phenomena marking Jewish life in the twentieth century was the increasing feeling of insecurity and mounting threat to Jewish physical survival. Popular Jewish historiography tended to present the history of the Jews since the destruction of the Second Temple as a running tale of suffering, woe, and pogroms. The lacrimonious history of the Jewish people mirrored the relation of the Jew to himself and his environment, a lamb among wolves, the eternal victim of his neighbors' violence. Yet when analyzing the collective historical experience of Jewish existence in the Diaspora, breaking it down into its actual forms and patterns, the actual experience appears to have been different. There were centuries of coexistence, sometimes more harmonious, sometimes less, interspersed between waves of pogroms and physical violence. Jewish collective memory preserved the recollection of the bitter times, but this did not necessarily lead the Jews to attribute any contemporary meaning to them. Some 230 years lay between the slaughter of the Jews in Poland by Bogdan Chmielnicki (1648–1649) and the next great wave of pogroms in the 1880s. It is true that there were sporadic outbreaks here and there, which were considered to be an integral component of the life of the Jews as a vulnerable minority among a backward, easily incited non-Jewish population. Despite this fact, there was a substantial degree of cooperation between Jews and non-Jews. With the emergence of the modern European states based on the principles of law and order, violent outbreaks seemed to belong to a past era, far removed from prevailing realities. The Jews harbored the expectation that with the advent of progress, they would ultimately become a historical relic.

But events took a different turn. From the beginning of the twentieth century on, Jewish life was darkened by a constant shadow, growing ever denser and more oppressive, namely, the sense of a threat to their very existence. This shadow, which extended across the borders of states and regimes, became more ominous the further east one moved from the Vistula. The fear of death became one of the characteristic features of daily life. More than any other factor, that existential anxiety shaped the attitude of the Jew to his environment and ultimately to himself, as well.

When the Southern Maelstorms erupted, the wave of pogroms in Southern Russia in 1881, Jews were shocked and dismayed: How were such events possible in a civilized and well-organized state like czarist Russia? After Moses Leib Lilienblum received information that mobs were planning to attack Jews on the coming Easter, his immediate response was, Why are the enemies of the Jews trying to bring back the Middle Ages, whose time has long passed? But reports soon arrived of pogroms in Elisavetgrad and elsewhere. The anxious suspense preceding the riots was an experience that left its imprint on all those who lived through the ordeal: the rush to hide the silver and bedding, sleeping in one's clothes, checking fearfully through the closed gate of the courtyard to see whether rioters might be approaching. The terror, the sense of helplessness: What will happen to the children? and the anguished question, "Will they take pity on the small babies, who do not even know yet that they are Jews?" Then the actual pogrom: the wailing of the women, the children in their arms; the men, weak and humiliated in front of the mob. Lilienblum's family was rescued thanks only to the intervention of the army. When he summed up what he had experienced, Lilienblum found solace in Jewish solidarity: "It is good that I suffered, that at least once in my life I was able to experience what my forefathers went through all their life. Their existence was fraught with fear and alarm." But the painful shock was too severe for him to take solace in the fact that Jews had already endured similar experience in the past. And he added sarcastically, "How great now is my satisfaction, since I was given the opportunity to learn and feel the life of my people in its exile!"[101] Lilienblum and his contemporaries saw the riots as a setback, a retreat from the cherished hopes for progress. First and foremost, however, the violence undermined their confidence that the authorities were determined to ensure the safety and well-being of the Jewish citizenry. Although no one had any proof that the central authorities in Russia were directly implicated in the riots, the very fact that these disturbances had been able to take place at all served after the fact as proof that those in power did not oppose them. This was the onset of the feeling that security for the Jew, personally and for his family, was quickly eroding.

Nonetheless, more than twenty years were to pass between the 1881 riots and the subsequent traumatic event, the 1903 pogrom in Kishinev. In the meantime, a new generation had matured that had never experienced a pogrom. Hence, the events in Kishinev had the impact of an earthquake on the younger generation. The pogrom there was also traumatic due to the sheer degree of its violence. In the 1881 pogroms, there had been numerous acts of rape, robbery, the burning of property, and injuries; but acts of murder had been relatively rare. In Kishinev, many were massacred—men, women, and children. The cruelty that marked these killings added a special dimension to the feeling of terror and shock that spread in their wake.

People had not yet recovered from the trauma of the Kishinev atrocities when political events of great import occurred in Russia with the outbreak of the 1905 revolution. Hopes soared among Jews that the Pale of Settlement would be abolished. Another expectation appeared to be crystallizing, namely, that with the advent of a revolution for the Russian people, the liberation of the Jewish people dwelling in its midst would also be placed on the agenda for action. Indeed, there were already developments during Easter 1905 that hinted at the presence of a smoldering volcano; but no one was prepared for what later, in fact, took place. In October 1905, the czar published a manifesto proclaiming a new constitution for the Russian people. The morning after the proclamation, a series of pogroms broke out. They raged for twelve days, sweeping through a total of some six hundred cities, towns, and villages. There had been scores of victims in Kishinev; but the number of dead now reached almost one thousand, not to mention the many thousands who were raped, injured, and lost all their possessions. This time, there was no doubt about the role played by the government in the unrest: Both the army and the police took active part on repeated occasion in the riots.[102]

The pogrom became an integral component of the routine of life for Jews in the Pale. It played an important role in shaping the personality of the generation then reaching maturity, equivalent to the influence of other salient factors, such as the abandonment of religious tradition, studying at government schools, or contact with the Socialist movement. Zalman Aranne (Aharonowitz, subsequently a minister in the Israeli government), a boy at the time, described the atmosphere of dread preceding an imminent pogrom that hung in the air in his hometown for weeks on end. One morning, his older brother rushed in, and shouted in Yiddish in a voice no longer his own, "My dearest ones, it's a pogrom, save yourselves!" A panic broke out in the house. His father, the circumciser, took his knives in one hand, a towel, bread, and a bottle of valerian in the other; and the family hurried to a place of hiding, where other Jewish families were already concealed. In the suddenly abandoned street, a Jew could be seen walking, carrying the short, elderly rabbi aloft on his shoulders. In the nearby courtyards, the feathers from pillows and quilts, ripped open by the rioters, began flying through the air: "During the years 1906–1907, the Jewish milieu was saturated with fear of the goy—direct and immediate physical fear."[103]

The pogrom riots had a dynamics of their own. Each series of new riots was worse than the one preceding, as if every bloodbath provided a permit for an even worse massacre. Each time, it seemed that things could get no worse: The atrocities of the civil war in Russia dwarfed those of 1905, while the later atrocities of the Nazi Holocaust caused people to forget Petlyura and his associates, who had perpetrated massacres of Jews in the Ukraine in 1919–1920. The Jew's sense of security and survival continued to be undermined, and these anxieties were to remain persistent throughout the first half of the twentieth century.[104] The feeling "All the world is my gallows"[105] was not a rhetorical flourish but rather a description of the psychological truth and state of mind of the contemporaries who experienced the violence firsthand, and whose psyches bore its scars.

This fundamental fact is important for understanding the mentality of the generation that reached maturity at the turn of the century. People realized that pogroms were a permanent, recurring phenomenon and that Jewish blood could be spilled at will. They concluded that Jews would continue to be under ever-increasing threat. This became the dominant mood and somehow had to be dealt with, an answer had to be found.[106]

The fin-de-siècle generation differed significantly from that of its fathers. The process of secularization was accelerating throughout Jewish society, accompanied by the growing influence of socialism. The Bund (the Jewish Social–Democratic party established in 1897) educated its members to greater self-consciousness, rejection of fatalistic acceptance of persecution, and an active response to acts of discrimination and injustice. The quickening pace of industrialization led to the formation of large concentrations of Jews in the urban centers of the Pale, giving them an enhanced sense of self-esteem and a feeling of greater security in the street. The impact of the martyrology of Russian revolutionary youth was electrifying: young people, Jews among them, who were unwilling to accept present oppressive realities and stood prepared to sacrifice their very lives for the sake of correcting the injustice that permeated Russian society. A philosophy of *activism* (the principle of action aimed at changing reality) was shared by the Jews who took their destiny into their own hands and emigrated to the United States, as well as by those who joined the Russian revolutionary movement, became active in the Bund, or chose to struggle for the establishment of a Jewish state in Palestine. All of them found it impossible to accept quiet submission to the pogroms.

Kishinev was the watershed event: There was a salient difference in the relation of Jewish youth to attacks against them before Kishinev and after. People were no longer ready to acquiesce in acceptance either of the physical injury or of the insults to human dignity and the loss of humanity that such affronts entailed. The impotent rage was a kind of revolutionary explosive charge that demolished traditional Jewish responses, insisting on a new demonstration that the Jew was also a human being, whose blood would not be shed with impunity. Ahad Ha-Am, together with Simeon Dubnow and several other Jewish writers, called, this time, for the organization of Jewish self-defense. "It is a disgrace for five million human beings to place themselves at the mercy of others, to hold out their throats to be cut and to cry for help, without any attempt to defend their property, honor, and lives by their own efforts," they wrote in a leaflet they published; "and who knows if this disgrace is not the initial reason for our being despised in the eyes of the population. . . . Only a person who is able to protect and defend his dignity is respected by others." For that reason, they wrote, "Stop crying and pleading, cease lifting your hands in supplication to your enemies and ostracizers, asking for their succor. Let your own arms save you!"[107] Keeping in mind Ahad Ha-Am's profound reservations regarding any use of force by Jews, this call heralded a revolutionary change in his way of thinking and response. It underscored the deep sense of despair that weighed down upon the nationalist segment of Jewish leadership regarding the prospect that the government would eventually act to guarantee the most elementary thing a government is supposed to ensure, namely, the peace and safety of its citizens.

The individual who jolted the Jewish public and brought about a genuine shift in its ways of responding was Bialik. Bialik was sent to Kishinev in order to write a report on the events that had taken place there. The report turned out to be of little importance, since the world press, in the meantime, had published all the gory details. However, Bialik soon published his poem "Massa Nemirov." Because of the Russian censorship, he was unable to make direct reference to Kishinev and therefore made use of the name of a town where Jews had been massacred during the time of the 1648–1649 pogroms. The real title of the poem was "Be-ir ha-har-ega" (In the City of Slaughter). This poem belongs to a special category of literary works that had a major impact in their own time on contemporary consciousness. Bialik's depiction of the cowardly behavior of the Jews had a greater effect than the description of the acts of the rioters. The Jews hid in hovels and holes, praying that evil would not befall them while their mothers, wives, and daughters were raped and murdered before their very eyes. Commenting in bitter sarcasm on the "children of the children of the Maccabees," who demonstrated their courage by finding filthy places to hide, Bialik utilized the traditional image of Jewish bravery as a whip for self-flagellation. Feelings of pain and deep shame predominate in the poem. Together they were molded into a fiery fist raised in protest against Jewish passivity. That passive attitude sufficed in the sanctimonious expectation of ultimate divine deliverance. Defying God, Bialik claimed that in the hour of Jewish distress, the heavens had been silent. Now the Jews rush to beg forgiveness for their sins, as though they themselves were to blame for the slaughter:

> Wherefore their cries imploring, their supplicating din?
> Speak to them, bid them rage!
> Let them against me raise the outraged hand,
> Let them demand!
> Demand retribution for the shamed
> Of all the centuries and every age! Let fists be flung like stone
> Against the heavens and the heavenly throne![108]

Bialik's words were like a searing flame for contemporaries. The sense of shame, desire for revenge, and particularly the urge to take action and no longer wait like cowards in hiding for the murderers to come, became the predominant sentiments of the generation. A Jew is obliged to defend himself; otherwise, he will perish. This was the conclusion.

A few years prior to that, in 1901, Tchernichovsky's poem "Barukh mi-Magentza" (Baruch from Meinz) had been published. It tells the story of a father who kills his two daughters to sanctify the name of God; and after his wife has been murdered, and he is forced to convert to Christianity, he sets fire in rage to his town. The burning of the entire town as an act of vengeance was a kind of intermediate response somewhere between the traditional Jewish reaction, martyrdom, and the new response, manifested in the organization of self-defense.[109] Separating the poems "Baruch from Meinz" and "In the City of Slaughter" were the events in Kishinev, which became a symbol of Jewish helplessness and in retrospect were seen as a turning point in the relation of the Jews toward self-defense.

If Bialik gave expression to the feeling of rage and the need for a different Jewish response, Y. H. Brenner wrote the manifesto of the young generation. His prose piece "Hu amar la" (He Told Her) is the monologue of a young Jewish boy addressed to his mother on the eve of a pogrom. She tries to dissuade him from joining a "self-defense" group; and in response, he explains to her why it is impossible for him not to go. Brenner sketches Jewish history in Russia as a chronicle perenially drenched in blood, especially in the two previous generations. He juxtaposes the generation of the fathers, symbolized by the figure of the father, and the generation of the sons, symbolized in the monologue by the young man who goes to join the "self-defense" group. The father is beaten to death in one of the neighboring villages, where he had gone to try to convince a converted woman to return to her people: "And when the good, simple villagers fell upon him, he gave no signs of valor. My father was a coward, as I said. He tried to escape. . . . He was not a pretty sight while fleeing. . . . They caught up with him." Trusting in divine help, the fathers did not try to defend themselves. However, the sons, who abandoned the tradition of their fathers, were no longer prepared to accept a despicable death as though it were a kind of divine decree. Defense of the "dignity of Israel" was no less important to them than the defense of life itself: "Hear, O Israel! Not an eye for an eye. Two eyes for one, and all their teeth for any kind of humiliation!" Those who assimilate, Brenner said, will go to the authorities to implore them to grant protection. But Jews who are true and loyal to their people will not degrade themselves by asking the authorities, the instigators of the pogrom, for protection. The mother in the monologue articulates the traditional Jewish arguments against self-defense. Jews are few in number, she says; the Ukrainians (the scene is Kiev) are many; and they are backed by the government and the army. Self-defense is a kind of "cold therapy," it cannot save anybody. But the young man shakes off that time-worn logic of generations: "Let me go. Know that *from very the first hour of my existence, I have been waiting in anticipation for this time.* What, this is not a remedy? Yet the people's world is also founded on consoling the bereaved, on vengeance and honor!" The symbolic value of self-defense is more pertinent than its practical value. Its importance lies in the very willingness of the Jew not to flee, not to run and hide, but rather to stand face to face with the rioters, a "war of the poor sons of Jankel against the powerful descendants of Chmielnicki, from generation to generation." And Brenner adds, as a kind of final lesson from Kishinev, "Cursed be he who says, 'A place to hide!'"[110]

The assimilating Jewish intelligentsia rejected the concept of Jewish history as a continuing battle between weak and strong, between victims and murderers, as conceived in the Brennerian perspective. That intelligentsia regarded the regime in Russia as the source for all the evils that had befallen the Jews and placed its trust in the imminent revolution to bring about a change in the situation. Latent in this conception was an idealization of the simple Russian masses, which the Jewish intelligentsia had adopted from the populist currents in the revolutonary movement sweeping over Russia. The Russian people was portrayed as a paragon of all virtues, ignoring the cruelty, crudeness, ignorance, and religious fanaticism that were also integral components of the life of the masses. The revolutionaries themselves had an ambivalent attitude toward anti-Jewish riots. Although they had a fundamental abhorrence for antisemitism, many among them, including Jews, viewed the pogroms instrumentally—as a means to rouse the masses against the regime. Theory suggested that if the people were to rise up against the Jews, the dynamic process of violating law and order and casting off the yoke of oppression would continue, leading to a popular uprising against the authorities. "Oil for the wheels of the revolution" was a popular expression among many active in "progressive circles" to characterize the riots. This was an indirect justification of the pogroms as part of a "progressive" process.[111] Young Jews rebelled against this tendency to view the life of Jews as a kind of pawn on the revolutionary chessboard. Bialik wrote,

> If there is justice,
> Let it appear now,
> But if after my annihilation from the face of the earth,
>   justice should appear,
> Let his throne be razed forever![112]

Among other things, the position of the assimilationists reflected the difficulty the Jews had in accepting the fact that they had to defend themselves. It was bound up with a total loss of faith not only in the authorities and the simple masses (and this matter in itself was quite complex) but also in the enlightened strata and groups within Russian society that symbolized the hope for a brighter future. The principal significance of self-defense was that Jews had no one to rely on except themselves. This concept, one that every American settler in the Wild West adopted as his or her own right from the very first day there, was difficult for the Jew to absorb and digest. It stood in total contrast with the customary system of relations that had prevailed over countless generations between the Jews, as a small and despised minority, and their non-Jewish neighbors. Jews were always in need of protection. The recognition that there was no one who could give Jews that protection was extremely bitter and required the adoption of new traits, another mode of self-awareness, and a different relation to the surrounding world. It was a difficult task, both physically and mentally, for Jews—and particularly for the Jewish intelligentsia—to take up arms to defend themselves. Even though Berdichevsky's words and Tchernichovsky's poems stirred their hearts and excited their blood, most Jews felt great inhibitions when it came to physical violence. It was precisely the attitude of Ahad Ha-Am—otherwise generally unacceptable to them—that gave incisive expression to such reservations. It was no simple matter to inculcate the notion that Jews had need of weapons and should risk their lives in defending themselves in the event of a pogrom.

Groups for self-defense, from the ranks of the Bund and the Zionists, were organized, especially in the period 1903–1905; but the great majority of the Jewish community did not join their ranks. The Jewish tradition of noncombativeness was still very powerful. For that reason, its proponents endowed self-defense with a special ethical value right from the start. From the moral standpoint, it was argued, a Jew who defends himself is superior to one who does not. The Jews who ran and hid in Bialik's "In the City of Slaughter" were not only wretched and pitiable but also marred by a moral deficiency. The young man in "He Told Her" who goes forth to take part in a defensive war is morally preferable to his father who sacrificed his life without responding to his assailants. The Jews still lacked what was an integral component of national ethos among other peoples; it was a characteristic that would have to be acquired.

In terms of its internal logic, the act of self-defense was no different from rebellion against other sorts of degradation and affronts to human dignity. The Socialist movement, striving to foster the sense of self-esteem among the masses, welcomed acts of rebellion against the authorites. It was thus quite natural that groups for self-defense proliferated specifically in the areas where there was a pronounced socialist presence, mainly in White Russia. The socialists, particularly from the groups of the Social Revolutionary party, justified violence not only in the defense of human life but likewise in the name of human dignity. Hirsch Lekert, who attacked and injured the governor of Vilna District in 1902 because he had ordered Jewish political prisoners to be flogged, was a member of the Bund. That defiant act by Lekert, the first Jew to take vengeance, became a popular theme for balladry. A year later, Pinhas Dashewski, a student active in Zionist–socialist circles, attempted to assassinate the person who was the alleged instigator of the Kishinev pogrom.[113] The moral pathos that characterized the Socialist movement was also applied to the field of self-defense. In this way, recruitment of Jews for self-defense was endowed with the same value as their mobilization to the struggle for a just society.

The European national movements did not lose sleep over the question of whether the use of armed force for furthering national interests was morally justified or not. For them, the principle was obvious that the realization of national aspirations had priority over considerations of morality or justice; the latter had validity in interhuman relations but not in those between nations. The omnipotence of the nation is superior to all other systems. The reservations about this question in the early stages of the Zionist movement, manifested in the dispute between Ahad Ha-Am and Berdichevsky, expressed the traditional misgivings of the Jew about the use of force. Ultimately, the main factor that convinced the Jews it was absolutely necessary for them to employ force was the mounting violence against them in the Pale of Settlement. Few, if any, national movements can point to so tragic and bloody a beginning on their path to power.

The "Arab Problem": A View from the Diaspora

One of the covert assumptions present among all the poets and the majority of Zionist thinkers and leaders was that Jews had a special right to the Land of Israel, that is, Palestine. In a short passage where Lilienblum described in his memoirs how he came to the Zionist idea, he explained that in order to be liberated from the sense of alienness, Jews must return to the ancient homeland of their forefathers and slowly settle the land: "Why should we be strangers in Gentile countries while the land of our fathers has not yet disappeared from the face of the earth, is still desolate, and can, along with its neighboring environs, incorporate our people?"[114] The concept "land of our fathers," mentioned nine times in a passage consisting of some thirty lines, expresses both the historical link and the hereditary title to the land. In the essays, poems, and thought of the period the right of the Jews to their ancestral land was considered to be an obvious proposition. Eretz Israel had belonged to the Jews in the past, they had lived there as a people, bringing forth immortal creations for all of humankind; and there the life of the Jewish people would be renewed. The continuity of rights in the past and the future was not subject to questioning.

The belief in the proprietary right to Palestine included the assumption that

Jews would be able to settle there peacefully. If ideas of conquest were aired during this period, they derived more from the needs of national romanticism for exploits of great valor than from any feeling that it would really be necessary to conquer the land by force due to resistance to Jewish immigration. The concept *kibbush* (conquest) is frequent in the literature of the period; but it has a connotation of settlement, not militant action. In the terms employed before World War I, "conquering the land" generally meant one thing: settling in Palestine: "The war for which we are being prepared is very simple, not dangerous in the least. What we desire is to engage in patient labor, work devoid of any bloodshed, work that is only civilized colonization. Diligent labor is our sword and bow. In the end, no one will oppose us in enmity."[115] This description of Zionism's objectives and the path of their realization, penned by Dr. Max Emmanuel Mandelstamm, one of Herzl's ardent followers, makes use of concepts associated with militant combat to describe tasks that are all quite peaceful in nature. Likewise, Ahad Ha-Am utilized the phrase "heavy warfare" in order to emphasize the need for scrupulous planning prior to settlement in Palestine.[116] This ambivalence was characteristic of the Zionist style of expression in that period: It expressed a longing for manifestations of force, but these were not translated into a plan of action.

The basic assumption regarding the right of Jews to Palestine—a right that required no proof—was a fundamental component of all Zionist programs. In contrast with other prospective areas for Jewish settlement, such as Argentina or East Africa, it was generally believed that no one could deny the right of the Jews to their ancestral land. Even Ahad Ha-Am, the eternal skeptic, commented that this was "a land to which our historical right is beyond doubt and has no need for farfetched proofs."[117] Others, such as Lilienblum, did not even think it necessary to dwell on this matter.

It is possible that this attitude resulted from the growing influence of the Bible in conjunction with the expansion of secularization among educated Jews. Through the study of the Bible by non-Jews, Jews rediscovered it as a great work of literature, a historical source, and a basis for envisioning the future of the people. The dream of Jews returning to their homeland was quite common among Christian Protestant sects, and contained a recognition of the right of Jews to that homeland. Christians who envisaged Jews returning to their ancient land, such as Sir Lawrence Oliphant,[118] played an important role in the Hibbat Zion movement and in the history of the Zionist movement (e.g., the Grand Duke of Baden, who had been influenced by the preacher William Henry Hechler).[119] There was a link between the rise in Christian missionary activity in Palestine in the nineteenth century and this idea of Jewish return. That upsurge in activity was also associated, of course, with the growing interest of the Great Powers in the Levant. Distinguished non-Jewish personalities demonstrated enthusiasm and a cultural affinity for this concept. No wonder, then, that Jews also viewed it in that light.

This conception of return was closely related to another, namely, that the land was desolate, pining away in expectation for Jews to come and settle there. That was the fundamental assumption of Bialik, Lilienblum, Mandelstamm, and many others. In *The Jewish State,* Herzl did not mention the inhabitants of Palestine. When he described the land of the future in the novel *Altneuland,* he depicted

"European" Arabs, who wanted only good for the Jews. The slogan "A land without a people for a people without a land" was common among Zionists at the end of the nineteenth, and the beginning of the twentieth, century. It contained a legitimation of the Jewish claim to the land and did away with any sense of uneasiness that a competitor to this claim might appear.

Ahad Ha-Am was the first to depict the real and genuine Palestine to the lovers of Zion in the Diaspora. His first trip to Palestine took place in 1891, lasted three months, and was in the spirit of "A fleeting guest sees all faults." With a critical mind and discerning eye, Ahad Ha-Am traveled the length and breadth of Palestine and was the first to give a realistic picture of the actual situation there, differing from portrayals of the land in Zionist propaganda. That propaganda (and in this regard there was no difference between Hibbat Zion and the Zionist movement) presented Palestine as a land blessed with all positive qualities. Biblical phrases such as "every man under his vine and under his fig-tree" (1 Kings 5:5) served as a seemingly authentic description of the actual situation. Already in the poems of the First Aliyah (1882–1903) one could read, "In the beloved land of our fathers, all hopes will soon be realized." Literary models, such as those embodied in the novels of Mapu, were presented as an authentic description of prevailing realities. Such descriptions were partially the result of simple error and ignorance: Not every person who wrote about Palestine knew what he was talking about. Yet some of these idealizing, flowery depictions were intentional, designed to galvanize national feeling among the Jews and to play down the difficulties, so as not to malign Palestine. Zionist propaganda had a dubious reputation as far as truth was concerned.[120] The idealization of Palestine tended to obscure all the aspects of the country that were less pleasant: the hot climate, difficulties of adjustment, the hardship involved in earning a living there, the hostile attitude of Ottoman authorities; and, of course, it blurred the fact that there were inhabitants living there who might claim the country as their own.[121]

In his essay "Emet me-Eretz Israel" (Truth from Palestine) Ahad Ha-Am did not hesitate to demolish all the accepted truths about the land: He was unconcerned about any jubilation his report might cause in non-Zionist circles. He described all the weaknesses of Jewish settlement in Palestine, unsparingly, mercilessly, using the whetted knife of sarcasm. The gulf between the description of Zionist propaganda and the realities in the field served as a central motif in his attack. He opened his essay with the words "We are accustomed abroad to believe" and then went on to present three key areas in which there was no connection between what was believed and actual facts. Jews in the Diaspora believe that Palestine is desolate and waiting for them to come and acquire land to settle there. But the truth is that given the accepted level of cultivation in Palestine, there are no unoccupied fields waiting to be bought and cultivated. Jews in the Diaspora believe that "all Arabs are savages of the desert, a people similar to a donkey." Thus, Jews can come, buy up land and settle there, while the Arabs fail to grasp what is actually going on. But the truth is that Arabs do understand Jewish intentions quite well. At present, the realization of Jewish objectives does not appear to them to pose a genuine threat. For that reason, they prefer for the time being to exploit the Jews and enjoy the economic benefit gained from selling land at high prices. "However," Ahad Ha-Am warns, "should the time come when the life of our people in Palestine begins to develop to such an extent that they will supplant the natives to a smaller or greater degree, then that people will not easily surrender its place."[122] People believe that the Ottoman authorities are corrupt—open both to taking bribes and to pressure from European consulates. The truth is that the Turkish officials are patriots, zealous adherents of their religion and government, and likely to resist foreign intervention in their affairs, Ahad Ha-Am argued.

One of the factors rendering it difficult for the scholar today to reconstruct attitudes at that time toward the Arab problem, especially in the Diaspora, is the element of internal censorship. It is possible to assume with a high degree of certainty that in private conversation comments were made about Arabs. The manner in which Ahad Ha-Am presented his criticism suggests the existence of a secret, more covert level of discourse, based on certain presuppositions regarding the situation in Palestine.

The image of the Arab as naive and lacking in reason and intelligence—presented by Ahad Ha-Am as a widespread belief among the Jewish public—was vital for the assumption that it was indeed possible to settle the land without those native savages' placing any obstacles in the path. Paradoxically, Arab backwardness was utilized as evidence to support the notion of the feasibility of peaceful Jewish settlement. Ahad Ha-Am warned about underestimating potential Arab resistance in the future, hinting at the future link between its development and the progress of the Zionist enterprise. Yet even he did not regard the Arabs at the time as constituting any kind of a genuine threat to the Zionist program. The "spiritual center" that he visualized as the ideal Jewish settlement in Palestine was understood by his contemporaries as a spiritual hub, rather than a center of population. He did speak explicitly about the need to create a Jewish majority in the land; yet in that context, he never alluded to the Arabs.[123]

The impression Arabs made at that time on anyone who chose to investigate them (and precious few had any such interest) was, on the whole, rather negative. The urban Arabs were depicted as being sly, underhanded, and cruel, prepared to exploit their brothers. The fellahin left a more positive impression, although "most are cunning and lack that naive simplicity thought in other countries to be a characteristic of farmers." The bedouin, like their brethren, the fellahin, do not consider it sinful to steal, commit violent acts, or lie. On the other hand, they are hospitable and show great respect for those who are courageous and for deeds of valor. Moreover, "the bedouin are always prepared to lay down their lives to save persons requesting their help or protection; and it won't be difficult at all to live with them peacefully, and then they will act as a protective wall for their allies."[124]

This description was published in the influential journal *Ha-Shilo'ah* as part of a series of three articles on Palestine. The first part dealt with the prevailing physical conditions, the second with the "natives of the land," and the third with the new Jewish colonies that had been established there. The writer apparently was not directly familiar with the situation among the Arab population and based his remarks on secondhand sources.[125]

The comment about the bedouin, hinting at the concealed level of discussion just alluded to, is quite instructive: It was reassuring to read that the bedouin, as the fighting element among the "natives," were not plotting any evil against the Jews.

Even more interesting is the fact that the Arabs of Palestine are not specifically referred to in the article. They are designated by the general phrase "natives of the land" or by sectorial terms, such as "urbanites," "fellahin," "bedouin," or "Christians." They are presented as lacking a collective entity, devoid of common interests, that is, of national qualities. Was this intentional or due, rather, to the oversight of the author? Since the number of articles focusing on a description of the Arab population in Palestine was extremely limited at that time, it is difficult to ascertain what may be hidden behind this fact.

The assumption that the Arabs would not oppose Jewish colonization in Palestine was associated quite naturally with the concept of brotherhood among all the sons of Shem. It was contended that the Arabs had never hated the Jews, since they were of the same Semitic race and, like their Jewish brethren, were distinguished by a sharp sense of justice and fairness. Unfortunately, due to historical reasons in recent generations, those sentiments had been suppressed; and Arabs had begun to demonstrate feelings of hatred toward Jews. Yet that hatred was quite unnatural for the Arabs, it was argued, and had been precipitated principally by the missionary activities of Christians in the Middle East. The philosemitic tendencies that appeared already at the end of the nineteenth century were also mobilized to allay anxieties about Arab enmity in Palestine: The resentment Arabs had regarding Jews coming to settle in their land stemmed, it was reasoned, from their suspicious attitude toward foreigners in general. It was due to hate propaganda from non-Arab sources to which they were exposed; and it was inflamed by the indifference shown them by the Jewish settlers. There was a necessity for Jews to take action against the hate literature that had begun to surface among the Arabs. More generally, Jews should attempt to become familiar with the culture of the region—"as important 'houseowners', and not as guests."[126]

The Herzlian period in the Zionist movement (1897–1904) was characterized by the search for a path to the Sublime Porte in Constantinople in order that Jews might be given some sort of permission to settle in Palestine as a national entity. Herzl's idea of obtaining a charter for Jews in Palestine (i.e., a permit for colonization protected under the law) was the brainchild of his era. Colonization projects in which entrepreneurs or private bodies acquired settlement rights from the ruling power in return for payment had been an accepted practice in the British Empire since the establishment of the East India Company. The later example of Cecil Rhodes was also considered in a positive light at that time. Economic concessions were a regular practice in the United States, Russia, and, of course, the Ottoman Empire, where there was a great need for economic development. The prevailing concept was not tainted by any element of discredit. The Ottomans were the ruling power in Palestine. Naturally, they were a prime target for activity by the Zionist movement. It was ultimately in their power to permit or prohibit in Palestine not only Jewish political activity but activity of any sort.

In 1905, in the wake of Sixth Zionist Congress (known by the epithet Uganda Congress), a certain discussion arose regarding the Arabs in Palestine and the implications of their presence for the possibility of the realization of the Zionist dream. In the history of the Zionist movement, there were a number of watersheds that can rightfully be termed "moments of truth." The first of these was the Uganda Congress, which revealed for the first time the potential tension present in the Zionist movement between the aspiration to renew the existence of an ancient people in the land of its forefathers and the desire to effect immediate relief to ease the plight of Jews in Eastern Europe.

The bitter dispute in the wake of the congress revealed layers of fear and anxiety whose exposure had previously been prevented by self-censorship. The question whether Palestine was attainable, whether the dream of the renewal of Jewish sovereignty there was feasible or nothing but a delusion, became a topic of public debate between the territorialists and the "Zionists of Zion." As usual, all of the problems that Zionists preferred to sweep under the rug and not think about at that stage were raised by those who no longer felt any commitment to the Zionist idea. This phenomenon of uncovering the hidden layers of the national psyche precisely by persons already outside the camp would be repeated on various occasions in the history of the movement.

An incident occurred in the course of this dispute that provided food for thought and served as a topic for a parallel dispute. In a meeting of the cultural association Ivriya that was held simultaneously with the Seventh Zionist Congress in Basel in 1905, in which the Zionists of Zion proved stronger than the territorialists, Yitzhak Epstein, a well-known and enlightening teacher from Palestine, gave a lecture entitled "A Hidden Question." Its topic was the Arabs of Palestine and Jewish attitudes toward them: "Among the difficult problems associated with the idea of the renewal of life of our people in its land, there is one question that outweighs all the others, namely, the question of our attitude to the Arabs." After he had emphasized the importance of the problem as he viewed it, he added, "We have overlooked a rather 'marginal' fact—that in our beloved land there lives an entire people that has been dwelling there for many centuries and has never considered leaving it."[127]

Epstein's words sparked a heated debate; and subsequent to their publication in the periodical *Ha-Shilo'ah* some two years after the speech (with a note by the editor indicating his reservations about the content of the article), they triggered a further wave of controversy, this time in Palestine. We will focus here on the first wave of reactions. At about the same time, Menahem Ussishkin, the Russian Zionist leader and among Herzl's most important opponents, published an essay entitled "Our Program." This was the manifesto of practical Zionism against the "statists" and territorialists. In this essay Ussishkin declared: "The Arabs live on the most friendly and peaceful terms with the Jews. They recognize unconditionally the historical title of Jews to the land."[128] These remarks were in the context of Ussishkin's demand to hasten the purchase of land in Palestine. He argued that after Jews were given the charter according to Herzl's plan, the Arabs, noted for their greed, would be sure to raise the prices of land. Ussishkin's comments, stated very authoritatively after his visit to Palestine, provoked ironic responses. For example, Berdichevsky presented the difficulties bound up with the matter of the right to the land: It is a fact that that right had been acquired by the Jews in ancient times by dint of force and occupation, just like the right of those who had conquered it after them: "The country is not ours, inasmuch as for a thousand years it was forsaken by us, and other peoples conquered it in blood, saturating its soil. Thus, doubt speaks in our hearts, on occasion, adding another burden for us to carry."[129] He quoted Epstein at length to counter Ussishkin's statement but left it to the reader to draw his own conclusions. Since Berdichevsky rejected any notion of another country to replace Palestine as the goal of Jewish settlement, he had no option but to continue to agonize on this question.

In contrast, Hillel Zeitlin, a Zionist who went over to the camp of the territorialists, did not hesitate to touch on all the painful issues. Zeitlin claimed the Zionist enterprise had no chance for success because of the fact that there were half a million Arabs in the country: "What all the Palestinians [i.e., the Zionists of Zion] forget, mistakenly or maliciously, is that Palestine belongs to others, *and it is totally settled.*" In Zeitlin's view, it was impossible to bring Jews into the land without removing Arabs, something no one could do. For that reason, Jews would have to look for another country that could provide an answer to the problem of Jewish existential distress. Zeitlin rejected Ussishkin's optimistic evaluation as unrealistic and embraced the facts as presented by Epstein. Among each and every people, Zeitlin challenged, writers and philosophers were allowed to amuse themselves with romanticism, with longing for bygone eras. However, a people should not forfeit its life because of such a mirage.

During the Congress and in the disputes that raged around it, there were whisperings about two possible solutions to the Arab problem. The first was attributed to Nordau, the veteran among the advocates of a Jewish state; and the second was associated with the Young Guard—apparently, followers of the grouping "democratic fraction." Nordau's conception was a direct continuation of the thinking of Herzl, but more outspoken. The Arabs, he said, are in the process of revolt against the Turks. They endanger the Ottoman Empire. It is in line with the interests of the European powers that would like to prevent the breakup of the Ottoman Empire to settle a neutral element in Palestine, namely, the Jews, who would be loyal to the Turks and not rebel against them. Zeitlin argued that this idea was based on a fundamental contradiction. From the floor of the Congress, the Jews had urged that the despotic regime in Russia should be resisted and assistance given to the struggle of the revolutionary forces there. Should they now be the ones to serve as adjuncts to Turkish tyranny? The Jews in Europe are regarded as a dangerous revolutionary element. Would the Turks then choose precisely that element to try to pacify the situation in the Ottoman Empire? Moreover, the European powers (and this basically meant Great Britain) usually deal with rebellious peoples according to local circumstances: They try to suppress them if possible; and if not, they try to arrive at some compromise. "Yet we have never heard," Zeitlin remarked, "that the peoples of Europe might drive out the peoples in those countries and settle their own element instead."

The Young Guard was disgusted by the idea of being on the same side of the barricades together with the Ottoman authorities. In the corridors, they talked about the possibility of creating a Jewish–Arab alliance. In return for assisting the Arabs in realizing their national aspirations, the Jews would be given Palestine as a gift. Zeitlin also rejected this idea. In his view, the Jews had nothing to offer the Arabs: "What will you give to the Arabs? Do they need your strength? Do they require your wisdom?" But the fundamental point was that there was no political logic behind this approach: "For what reason and why would they give you Palestine . . . at the same time that they themselves want to be the lords of the land, they who are the ones who are settled there and till the land and who wish to rule over it?"

The Zionists of Zion, particularly the younger members among their ranks, answered these pointed questions by the reply that if Palestine were not given to them, they would take it by force. This challenge provoked Zeitlin to the response, "They are forgetting one small thing, namely, that in order to take something by force, that force has to exist." A people that is not on its own territory is unable to fight for freedom the way other oppressed peoples can that are settled on their own land. The Zionists of Zion argued that a Jewish infrastructure would be built in the land by means of education and culture. A new generation would mature, and it would fight the battle for the land of Palestine. Zeitlin replied it would take many years until anything substantial was built in Palestine and a generation of Jewish fighters arose. In the meantime, the Jews would assimilate or perish. Moreover, until then, "there would already be a strong Arab government in Palestine, so that no person anywhere would be insane enough to still be able to contemplate its conquest."[130]

Such thoughts about obtaining Palestine as the result of a Jewish–Arab alliance or because of common interests in the region between Jews and the European powers were to have a long vitality within the Zionist movement. What was special about Zeitlin's remarks was the blunt discussion of the fact that there were half a million Arabs living in Palestine. It would appear that as a result of the debate between the territorialists and the Zionists of Zion, Epstein's lecture "A Hidden Question" had a decided impact.[131] The moral consideration—that is, that it was inconceivable to dispossess the Arabs who toil on the land—appears repeatedly in Zeitlin's exposition. He—and apparently others, as well—rejected the attempt to circumvent the problem of Arab inhabitants by means of the two aforementioned political solutions, not just because he considered it unrealistic but also because he viewed it as immoral.

Arguments drawn from the romantic arsenal gained renewed strength in the debate with the territorialists. One of the impressive figures in this area was a young man from Odessa who had earned himself a name as an experienced journalist there. He later became an active Zionist and soon demonstrated remarkable abilities, especially as a gifted orator. In his address to the Zionist Congress, Vladimir Jabotinsky developed the idea of the "Palestinian personality" of the Jewish people: The original national essence of the Jewish people had arisen in the Land of Israel; had been influenced during its formative period by the landscape, climate, and nature of the land; and could not rejuvenate anywhere except within the borders of that land.[132] Zeitlin wrote sarcastically on Jabotinsky's presentation: "We still do not have a single decent colony in Palestine and still have not yet started to do a thing there after 25 years of noise and commotion; and in comes Jabotinsky, stands at the rostrum of the Congress, and proclaims that we shall take Palestine by force."[133] In the version of the speech subsequently published in Jabotinsky's writings, there is no reference to such an assertion regarding force, though this is no proof that it was not said. Statements uttered in the heat of argument, whose value was strictly declarative, were not uncommon during debates among Zionists. It is certainly possible to imagine a response of this kind by Jabotinsky to some provocation by the territorialists. This incident remains significant in that it may shed a certain light on hidden aspirations at the time. It was also the first exposure of the public to Jabotinsky and his approach.

There are two references in this debate particularly worth noting. One was the question of eviction of Arabs from Palestine. Zeitlin broached the idea and rejected it as impossible to implement. As far as is known, it was not mentioned by the Zionists themselves. Even if we assume there were some who toyed with that notion, it was so far removed from reality that it was not commented on anywhere in writing.

The second reference alludes to the character of the generation growing up in the land. What stands out is that expectation that the generation educated in Palestine would, unlike their parents, be capable of fighting for the country. The hope for a new type of Jew contained an element of healthy aggressiveness, as in Nordau's "Judaism of the muscles" or the ancient heroes of Berdichevsky. That aggressiveness was necessary more for internal than external purposes, as a component in national education to counteract the old image of the Jew. However, there was also a potential of aggression here that was capable of being directed outward.

The dispute with the territorialists led Ber Borochov, one of Ussishkin's faithful supporters at that time, to formulate his prognosis regarding the question of the Arabs in Palestine. Borochov, one of the more prominent leaders and theorists of the Poalei Zion movement—the Zionist Socialist movement then in the process of formation—made use of Marxist methodology to substantiate the claims of Zionism. Borochov's analysis was characterized by great skill and an unusual degree of penetration. Yet his approach to the Arab problem revealed how far removed the actual land of Palestine was from the thoughts of its lovers in exile. Ussishkin used to speak very authoritatively on any subject, including the Arabs, though he was innocent of any firsthand knowledge about them. Borochov did likewise. He embraced the concept of the brotherhood between all descendants of Shem and made that the basis of his outlook. In his perspective, the Arabs of Palestine were the descendants of Jewish and Canaanite fellahin who had lived in the land for generations and had accepted Islam after the Muslim Conquest—"people akin to us in blood and spirit."[134]

The question Borochov addressed (though without further explication) was, Are the Arabs hostile to the Jews, and will they interfere with their settlement in Palestine, as the territorialists argue and quite a few Zionists of Zion suspect? He replied that the population in Palestine would assimilate among the Jewish immigrants, who were superior to the Arabs culturally and economically. Assimilation would be the result of a process of development of the land by the Jews: "And for that reason, we have no fears about a possible national rivalry on their part."[135]

Borochov had two versions regarding the pace of Jewish colonization and the anticipated Arab assimilation. The first, developed in his article "On the Question of Zion and Territory" (1905) anticipated a relatively slow pace—"smooth." The second, spelled out in his essay "Our Platform" (1906) expected a rapid process of change that would lead to tensions and conflict between the Jews and certain segments of the local population that chose to resist Jewish predominance. Here, Borochov described a less ideal process than he had depicted a year earlier: "Such a profound and fundamental upheaval in Jewish life as is entailed by colonization cannot be imagined without a harsh struggle, acts of cruelty and injustice, suffering by the innocent and the guilty. Such upheavals are not written in ink or in words pleasing to the ear. They are written in sweat, tears, and blood."[136] According to both these versions, the Arab problem would be solved by their assimilation within the Jewish population by dint of the racial similarity between the two peoples. The difference between these approaches did not derive from a new insight that Borochov had had regarding the problems in Palestine but, rather, was a consequence of his general views on society: Processes of social change necessarily entailed cruel and bloody struggle.

The perspective advanced by Ussishkin and Borochov was one of peace. Both thought that the progress brought by Jews to Palestine was a factor that would encourage Jewish–Arab cooperation at one level or another. This approach was part of a campaign of self-persuasion that the fact of the presence of Arabs in Palestine did not contain any element that threatened the prospects for realization of Zionist aims or endangered the hope that this could be accomplished by peaceful means.

All in all, there was basically, as yet, no real dispute in the Zionist camp regarding the Arab question. Comments on the topic in writing were rare and scattered. If the territorialists had not raised the matter as part of their propaganda campaign against the "Palestinians," it is doubtful whether the subject would have been given the degree of attention it received. Epstein was lucky to have delivered his speech precisely at the high point of that dispute; accordingly, his words were accorded considerable attention. There was a certain unease stemming from the realization that an Arab population was living in the land of the forefathers. That disquietude manifested itself principally in the question as to whether the Arabs were opposed to the Jews. But the prime focus of Zionist attention that year was not on what was happening in Palestine. Interest centered on the momentous events in Russia in the aftermath of the First Russian Revolution (1905). Moreover, the Zionists were busy with the implementation of the Helsingfors (Helsinki) Program, which required much grass-roots work among the Jewish communities. Soon after, the reaction set in in Russia; and for some years, there was a decline in public Zionist activity.

A renewed interest in what was occurring in Palestine was generated in the wake of the Young Turk Revolution (1908). One can see from an enthusiastic essay by Ahad Ha-Am about the Young Turks just how far the Zionists still were from any serious understanding of the political events. He viewed their victory as an example of the primacy of spiritual over physical power—a trait that he attributed to all Asians.[137] Palestine returned to the headlines at that time, since hopes mounted for a positive development in the prospects for activity there, thwarted until then by the Ottoman authorities. Parallel with this, there was a small incident that was given major coverage by the press and once again exposed the raw nerve of the Zionists as far as the Arab problem was concerned.

On the eve of Purim 1908, a brawl broke out among Jews and Arabs in Jaffa. At a certain point in the course of the squabble, the Turkish authorities intervened; and a group of soldiers forced its way into the hotel where the Jews were staying, arrested several of them, and injured thirteen Jews—all of them Russian citizens. The event was widely reported in the Jewish press in Russia and stirred considerable emotions, to the point that it was thought "to have discouraged the fearful and faint-hearted among the Zionists." It was not the brawl itself that was frightening; after all, much worse things had happened to Jews in Russia just three years earlier. Rather, the question was raised, Are Jews, even in the land of their forefathers, going to be subjected to persecution because they are Jews? The anti-Zionist press reacted with a touch of satisfaction to the news of the incident and was quick to dub it with a notorious epithet—*pogrom*.[138] This was not the first time that the Jewish Diaspora had overreacted to a brawl between Jews and Arabs. There had been an incident of this type in Petah Tikvah in 1886.[139] The Jewish press responded nervously. The term *ra'am* (thunder), used to designate the 1881 wave of pogroms in Russia, was now also applied to describe the modest incident in Petah Tikvah. And the question arose immediately as to whether those events were an indication of the existence in Palestine of antisemitism or religious hatred of the Jews along European lines.[140]

Simultaneously, a far more important question was asked (or, rather, only hinted at), namely, whether there were signs here of any Arab resistance to Jewish settlement for nationalist reasons. Was this incident proof of the existence of Arab nationalist fanaticism?[141] Fears about the emergence of a national Arab movement in Palestine were bound up with apprehensions about resistance to the Zionist project. Like the entire Arab question, this specific issue was not dealt with except in a haphazard and reluctant manner. In his article "A Hidden Question," Epstein had noted that no Arab national movement existed at present. Yet at the same time, he qualified himself by adding that in actuality, the Arab people had never died and therefore had no need for a movement of national revival.[142] This statement lent itself to the interpretation that a national movement did in fact exist—at least potentially, if not in practice.

When reporting on disturbing incidents, the Zionist press tried to lessen tensions and allay apprehensions. Their general argument ran as follows: There was no reason for worry; the Arabs harbored no hatred for Jews like the peoples in Europe; and there were no signs of a national Arab movement on the horizon. The incidents that had occurred were presented as being of marginal importance. In the case of Petah Tikvah, it was alleged that the source of the trouble had been a quarrel between neighbors; in the case of Jaffa, a squabble between Jewish workers and young Arabs. In connection with both incidents, journalists made an effort to stress the negative role played by the Jews in the disturbances: It was their provocative behavior that had caused the complications. If the Jews had acted properly, it would have been possible to prevent—or at least postpone—the clashes with their neighbors.[143]

The nervousness among Zionists in the Diaspora that broke to the surface every time the press carried a report on a Jewish–Arab clash and the nature of the questions asked (and answers given) are instructive in providing a key for understanding the phenomenon of sidestepping the Arab problem. That tendency to avoid the issue was criticized by Epstein, Zeitlin, and (to a certain degree) Ahad Ha-Am. "In all of 'Palestinian' [i.e., *about* Palestine] literature and in all the speeches and dis-

putes of the Palestinians [Zionists of Zion], the Arabs, their presence, and their settlement in Palestine are belittled and nullified, as if they did not exist," wrote Zeitlin.[144] Not that there was no clarity about the nature of the problem at issue
(settlement in a country where another people was already living), at least in the
minds of the intellectual–political elite of the Zionist movement. Even if they had
so desired, the opponents of Zionism would not have allowed them to ignore the
issue. Nonetheless, what were Zionists in the Diaspora supposed to do, given
the state of weakness and inertia that characterized the Zionist movement after the
shining days of Herzl, the hostile Ottoman rule in Palestine, and the embryonic
stage of Jewish colonization there? As stated, the Arabs in Palestine were viewed as
one more of the many misfortunes present in Palestine, like the Ottoman authorities, the climate, difficulties of adjustment—no greater or smaller than other troubles the settlers had to grapple with. It is doubtful whether the Zionists in Eastern
Europe were able to do much more when it came to this question than carefully
follow what was happening. It is true that the Zionist Organization did not discuss
this issue during that period and did not formulate a political line on it. Yet at that
particular juncture in the movement, such deliberations had no more practical significance than the question of what type of government would be established in
Palestine after obtaining the charter. When it came to their concrete relevance, such
deliberations about Arabs in Palestine had about the same importance as the
learned disputations customarily held in the courtyards of Hassidic rabbis regarding what would happen after the coming of the messiah.

Up until World War I, there were basically two approaches to the Arab question
in Palestine among Zionists in the Diaspora. The first, expressed in the slogan "A
land without a people for a people without a land," tended to avoid the existence
of the problem entirely or at most to accord it a miniscule importance. The second,
that generally emerged in the wake of incidents in Palestine, kept nervous track of
developments in the relationship of the Arab population to Jewish settlers there.
The greater the level of individual Zionist fanaticism, the more powerful was the
tendency for a person to close his eyes to the existence of the problem. Ussishkin's
attitude toward the issue is characteristic.

So far as one can determine, based on various publications, there was a widespread belief that the Arabs would not interfere with Jewish settlement, that is, that
the process of settlement and colonization could be carried out peacefully: "All our
hope that someday we will be the masters of the land of our forefathers is not
founded on the sword or the fist but, rather, on the cultural advantage we enjoy over
the Arabs and the Turks, an advantage due to which our influence in the land will
slowly increase. Ultimately the inhabitants there will subject themselves to this cultural influence, since they will find it brings benefit and blessing even for them."[145]
This conception, quite similar to that of Borochov, though without his Marxist
embellishments, appears to express the accepted view. There is no note of enmity
toward Arabs or any fear of them. Any apprehension, to the extent it did exist, was
of the *potential* for a possible dispute and did not relate to any real phenomenon at
the time.

The stereotype of the Arab as it had crystallized in the Diaspora was of a primitive person, backward, a bit childish, with a tendency toward violence, yet also

endowed with the positive virtues of hospitality, the readiness to respond positively to a positive approach, and a laudatory respect for the attributes of courage and heroism. That stereotype served to underpin the fundamental assumption that Jewish settlement in Palestine was indeed feasible and could be implemented without a bloody struggle against the local population. Moreover, the local Arab population would, it was believed, ultimately advance and reap material benefits from such colonization. In this context, considerations as to whether a national movement already existed among the Arabs of Palestine were of utmost significance, since, if it did, that was likely to confound the entire conception. Well versed in the history of national movements in Europe, the Jews anticipated that nationalism would also come to the Middle East. Similar to their approach to Palestine more generally, they did not base their projections in this matter on a knowledge of the actual situation in the field. Rather, what they projected was founded on an analysis in terms of European conceptions, attuned to the situations they were familiar with there.

That analysis introduced a key new dimension into the discussion at this early stage in the development of the Zionist movement, namely, that of time. How much time did the movement have at its disposal in order to realize its vision? That question would later become the most crucial in the history of the Zionist enterprise and have major implications for the issue of the use of force. In the meantime, however, the problem was more latent than actual, especially for those who did not live in Palestine.

2

The First and Second Aliyah

"Usually, those preparing to travel to Palestine tend to keep in mind the romantic, beautiful Palestine and think about its future, the memories of its exalted past and enchanting antiquity, disregarding the real Palestine, with its simple, crude every-day life."[1] This is how the young David Ben Gurion, in one of his first letters to his father from Palestine, depicted the gap between the expectations of the Zionist immigrant and the reality he encountered in the country. Zionist propaganda did not prepare immigrants for an encounter with an Oriental country: a wild land-scape devoid of trees and shade, where a merciless sun beat down, sapping human strength, where the swamps swarmed with malarial mosquitos and the inhabitants were strange and alien, wild like the land itself. The chasm between the image of the country inscribed in the hearts of those dreaming of the "beloved land of our fathers" and the actual land of Palestine was the source of many a trauma.

The Jewish immigrant who came on the First Aliyah (1881–1904)—and even he who came on the Second Aliyah (1904–1914)—harbored great expectations: He thought he was coming to the biblical Eretz Israel, a pleasant land in which Jews could live in peace and comfort, every man under his vine and fig tree. The conception of a "land of wonders" is common in the literature of memoirs and expresses the exalted vision the immigrants had about the country they were about to immigrate to.[2] Many at the time of the First Aliyah also believed that they would find abundance in Palestine and a suitable livelihood; indeed, the First Aliyah was remarkable for its heady degree of optimism. Yet beyond all utopian images of the land that stirred their imagination was the vision that this would be a country of and for Jews: Jews would be able to dwell there in safety and have no need to worry about what Gentiles might think of them: "Before I came here, for some reason, I beheld Palestine in my mind's eye as a single city, inhabited by Jews who were free and surrounded by many empty fields—empty, empty, waiting for more people to come and toil upon them."[3]

For most immigrants, the first encounter with the land and its inhabitants took

53

place in the principal port of entry to the country, the harbor town of Jaffa. In the variegated and colorful din of an Oriental port, one heard the penetrating shouts of the strapping Arab sailors, who would assist the passengers and their baggage down from the ships, tossing them, without much ado, into waiting rowboats and then ferrying them to the shore. Thus, the initial encounter with the land also was the immigrant's first experience with its Arab inhabitants.[4] Naturally, the impression left by that experience differed from individual to individual. Reuven Yosef Paicovitch (the father of Yigal Allon, Palmach commander and a deputy prime minister in the Israeli government) felt that the young Arabs of Jaffa were hostile toward Jews and insolent. As a precaution, he made some wooden clubs for himself and his brothers very soon after arrival. When they walked through the narrow streets of the densely populated Arab town, they beat their clubs on the ground and felt that this gesture of defiance earned them the respect of the population.[5] Others, like Berl Katznelson or Ben Gurion, were not particularly impressed by their first encounter with the inhabitants of Palestine. Ben Gurion, for example, was impressed by the twisting, narrow lanes of Jaffa, the sight of a young Jew riding on a horse or a young Jewish girl on a donkey. Yet he found no need to make mention of the Arab inhabitants thronging the streets of Jaffa.[6] The excitement about their arrival in Palestine, the new tastes of the land and meeting with all sorts of Jews eclipsed their encounter with the local Arab inhabitants. The latter were possibly regarded as a fixture in the strange, exotic scene, not worthy of any particular attention.

Yet in the eyes of others, such as the writer Brenner, that encounter was indeed traumatic. The first night he arrived in Palestine, while walking the streets of Haifa, a group of young Arabs emerged and moved toward him from one of the filthy alleyways, shouting, "Yahud!" Reacting in keeping with what he deemed appropriate for a native son back in his own land, he wanted to start a fight. But those accompanying him reminded him that Haifa was a completely non-Jewish city: "So . . . once again . . . there's *another* sort of alien in the world that one must suffer from. . . . Even from that filthy, contaminated lot, you have to suffer!"[7]

If the meaning of Zionism was to liberate the Jew from the ambivalence of living as a minority among a non-Jewish majority, and to give them a place in the sun where he would be free of the need to have constantly to take a foreign people into account, that first meeting with the reality of Palestine undermined such hopes. The feeling of belonging, of being a part of the land (or, more precisely, the feeling that the land belonged to him) was marred by a salient flaw: the ubiquitous presence of non-Jews that had to be taken into consideration. Brenner referred to Palestine as "my land" in quotation marks, thus symbolizing the dubiousness of his sense of belonging, in the wake of the encounter with the local Arab population.[8]

Brenner's awareness that there was another people in the land claiming to be its masters was a traumatic realization that haunted him all the years of his life in Palestine. Along with the crisis of adjusting to the rigors of physical labor, a physical challenge that taxed the men and women of the Second Aliyah, that recognition was the most difficult: "Who can imagine the pain of the unfortunate *intelligent* Jew who comes here, desirous of a different life, more wholesome, filled with physical labor, the fragrance of the fields—and who, after a few days, realizes that his dream was false, that the land already belongs to Arab Christians, that our farmers are but farmers in the abstract, and that there is no hope here for our people?"[9]

Surprisingly, that awareness had not been part of the consciousness of the men and women of the First Aliyah who began arriving in Palestine at the beginning of the 1880s. Their relationship with Palestine was characterized by two elements. First, there was the total conviction that Palestine was the land of the Jews. From the minute the foot of the first Jew touched the land in this modern return to Zion, he acted as though he were lord and master of the land. These men and women had no doubt that it was they who were the decisive component and factor in the country. That fact was also reflected in their behavior. The contrast between the actual situation in Palestine and their image of it can serve as a sort of proof of the power of ideology to shape a consciousness that would *eventually* change reality—yet with total disregard for the actual facts of life at the time. After all, Palestine in those years had a population numbering some seven hundred thousand, less than 10 percent of which was Jewish; and of these, only a miniscule percentage were imbued with a Zionist historical consciousness. Second, related to this image was a sense of power; but this feeling, too, bore no relationship to the empirical facts of the situation.

A letter written by Vladimir (Zeev) Dubnow, a member of Bilu (the first organized group of young Russian Jews to come to Palestine motivated by Zionist ideology), to his brother Simeon Dubnow, the famous historian and advocate of the national rights of Jews in the Diaspora, can serve as an illustrative example. On October 20, 1882, only a few short weeks after landing in Jaffa, this Russian student wrote: "The ultimate aim or *pia desideria* is to take control of Palestine in due time and to return to Jews the political independence they have been deprived of for two thousand years. Don't laugh, this is not a delusion." He explained that the way to achieve this was by creating a strong and solid Jewish economic foundation in Palestine. "In brief: to try to make sure that all land and all production is in Jewish hands." Dubnow went on: "In addition, it is necessary to teach the young people today and the coming generation the use of arms (in free and wild Turkey, anything is possible). Then . . . and here I can only guess . . . that grand day will arrive, the day whose coming was prophesized by Isaiah in his empassioned vision in the song of consolation. The Jews will yet arise, weapons in hand (if need be); and, in a loud voice, they shall proclaim themselves the lords and masters of their ancient homeland."[10]

It is beside the point that shortly thereafter, Vladimir Dubnow despaired of the prospect of Jewish settlement in Palestine and returned to Russia. A letter such as this could not have been written by a Jew in the Pale of Settlement, even though many towns and cities in the Pale had a larger Jewish population than the total Jewish population in Palestine at the time. Simeon Dubnow believed that Jews were entitled to national rights in the countries they were living in. Yet instinctive feelings among Jews and non-Jews expressed a different perspective, namely, that a land belongs to its people. Thus, Russia belonged to the Russians; and, by the same token, Palestine belonged to the Jews.[11] For that reason, from the moment Jews landed in Jaffa harbor, they did not behave like a small minority dependent on the good grace of the majority. Rather, their comportment was befitting of persons who were the rightful lords and masters of the land and would, at best, have to take the existence of violent neighbors into proper account.

One of the characteristics of the First Aliyah was the absence of a complex ideology. Their outlook, in so far as they were Zionists, did not go much beyond the desire to live in Palestine in a rural setting—leading a life close to nature. Preference was given to working the soil. They came from Russia and Romania, were orthodox in their religious practices, and preserved the customs of their fathers. They rejected the criticism by the Haskalah of Jewish life-styles in the Diaspora. Hence, their Zionism did not include the modernizing component—namely, changing the image of the Jew and promoting Jewish integration into the modern world—as advocated by secular streams of Zionism.

Not all the groups making up the First Aliyah were cut from the same cloth: The Bilu group, for example, had been influenced by the idealism of Russian revolutionaries. Its members saw themselves as pioneers, blazing the path for the Jewish masses that would follow in their footsteps. They were secular in outlook and aspired to create a model society in Palestine. Some of the settlers in Rehovot were influenced by the ideas of Ahad Ha-Am and tried to implement them in their colony. Yet these were relatively small groups, despite the certain degree of importance they had. Most of the men and women of the First Aliyah were unable to boast of a particularly good education. Abstract questions and issues were not what they enjoyed discussing. The revolution entailed by their coming to Palestine and embracing village life was not accompanied by a revolutionary shift in their consciousness or a change in their way of life at home and on the street. Petah Tikvah, the largest of their colonies, resembled a small town in Lithuania. Zikhron Yaakov and various colonies in Galilee were similar in style. Rishon le-Zion had a somewhat peculiar character, a mixture of a Jewish hamlet and quasi-French manners, due to the influence of the officials of Baron Rothschild who lived there. Most of these colonies remained dependent on the baron's assistance over a period of more than fifteen years, down till the turn of the century.

The Jewish colonies lived by agriculture. No one knew exactly what branches were suitable for the Palestinian soil and climate. The economy of the Arab villages they encountered did not provide a good example for emulation. Its meager output was insufficient for meeting the needs of the Jewish settlers—even those with modest expectations, like the settlers who had come from backward areas in Eastern Europe. The poverty of the Arab village was manifest in their extremely low standard of living, the unacceptable conditions of sanitation and hygiene (even when compared with the situation in Jewish hamlets in Eastern Europe), the scourge of skin and eye diseases, and the lack of any public services (not to mention illiteracy). All this was far worse than what they had known in Russia and Romania. That, then, was the settlers' first impression of their fellahin neighbors.

After Baron Rothschild became involved in the enterprise and decided to support the colonies, which were threatened by extinction due to a lack of capital, he decided to implement monocultural cultivation in Palestine, that is, a farm economy based on a single crop meant for marketing. The first crop that the colonies in Judea and Samaria (areas situated in the southern and northern coastal plain) specialized in was viticulture. Only at a later stage did they begin to develop the citrus branch, a field of agriculture in which the Jaffa Arabs had already succeeded, having made a brand name of their oranges. Both these branches required concentrated labor in short seasons, based on cheap hired hands, especially in connection with fruit harvesting and marketing of produce.

These facts determined the relationship between the Jewish colonists and the nearby Arab villagers. The small number of Jews needed Arab workers to tend to their vineyards and orchards. They also required milk products and vegetables from the Arab villages. A system of relations arose that was based on mutual dependence: The Arabs were in need of income from the Jewish economy to supplement the meager income from their own farms. Arab villages near to Jewish colonies, abandoned earlier in the nineteenth century, were reinhabited as a result of Jewish settlement in the area. The price of land near the colonies rose accordingly; and the villagers refused to sell, since they feared they might lose their jobs in the nearby colonies. Although the Jewish employers paid scanty wages, a supplementary income, especially in cash, was a blessing for the Arab fellahin. On the other hand, the Jews would have been unable to maintain their farms without Arab labor. The Arab workers became an inseparable part of the scene in the Jewish colonies.[12]

In Lower Galilee, where colonies based on field crop cultivation had been established, the colonists required Arab tenants, sharecroppers who hired themselves out for the season in return for a certain percentage of the harvest. The sharecropper and his family lived in a miserable hut in the farmyard of the Jewish farmer (though the houses of Jewish farmers in Galilee were themselves anything but palaces). The father and his children then worked at odd jobs in the fields, while the tenant's wife assisted the farmer's wife with household chores. In contrast with the accepted practice in Judea, where farmers behaved like landowners and would not demean themselves by working, preferring to appoint "overseers," in Galilee the farmer and members of his family toiled side by side with the Arab sharecropper from dawn to dusk.

The pattern of relations that developed in several of the colonies—especially Petah Tikvah, Rishon le-Zion, Nes Ziona in Judea, and Zikhron Yaakov in Samaria—was similar to what was customary in colonial societies elsewhere: a minority of settlers, exploiting local native labor in order to develop the economy. The native population, constituting the great majority, remained in an inferior position, economically, socially, and culturally. The network of interpersonal relations that developed likewise did not differ from the accepted norms in such societies. Its fabric was an interweaving of strands of domination and dependency, alienness and intimacy, contempt and fear.

The Jewish colonists had no particular sympathy for the Arab. In their eyes, he was a foreigner, with strange customs and a religion and system of values different from what they had been accustomed to among their Gentile neighbors in Europe. Their first impression was that this stranger respected strength and that the language of physical force was the only idiom he understood.[13] The tendency of colonists to reach quickly for the whip and beat the offender for every transgression, large and small, committed by the fellahin, is recalled in testimonies describing events in the colonies beginning with the early years of settlement. Thus, for example, the violent riot by fellahin in Petah Tikvah in late March 1886, labeled immediately by the

Zionist press as a "pogrom," was in actual fact the outcome of overbearing behavior on the part of the farmers in the colony. The latter had "confiscated" the donkeys of their neighbors, claiming they had trespassed on the fields of the colony, even though the fellahin were apparently innocent.[14] Already on his first visit to Palestine in 1891, Ahad Ha-Am gained a highly unfavorable impression of the attitude of the colonists toward their Arab neighbors: "They behave hostilely and cruelly toward the Arabs, encroaching upon them unjustly, beating them disgracefully for no good reason, and then they do not hesitate to boast about their deeds."[15]

That phenomenon was also in evidence in the years to come. The colony Rehovot, a notable positive exception among Jewish colonies in Judea in respect to its public administration and adherence to appropriate behavioral norms, was laudable for its prohibition on striking any person; and it was "even forbidden to beat an Arab worker."[16] Yet even the council of Rehovot had to investigate incidents in which an Arab worker had been beaten by his employer, though he had done no wrong.[17] Beating was not limited to one side only: On more than one occasion, Arabs also beat up Jews, both outside and within the colony. In Rehovot, there were a number of incidents where Arab workers attacked and battered their employers or Jewish workers.[18] Likewise, in Kefar Tavor in Lower Galilee, there were numerous incidents in which local tenant farmers did not hesitate to enter the house of their employer and attack him, because he had been late in paying their wages (or similar complaints).[19] There were also cases in which Jewish farmers utilized Arab strongmen against other Jews, especially during disputes with socialist workers from the Second Aliyah.[20] On Ahad Ha-Am's second visit to Palestine in 1903, he was shocked by the attitude of the colonists in Galilee toward the share-cropping tenant Arabs living in their farmyards. "The attitude of the colonists toward their land tenants and families is really very much like their attitude toward their animals," he wrote.[21] Even if we assume that Ahad Ha-Am was exaggerating and that there were other kinds of relations between colonists and their land tenants, there can be no doubt that his description contained a kernel of truth.[22] The expression "a people similar to a donkey" was apparently quite common among Jewish farmers as a description of Arab workers. It derives from the Talmud, used there on several occasions in connection with Canaanite slaves,[23] and was widespread in the Diaspora in referring to Gentiles (to the extent that Jewish internal censorship permitted). In Palestine, there were no restrictions of self-censorship; Jews therefore thought they had a license to use that talmudic expression at will.

The writer Moshe Smilansky, a founder of Rehovot, explained the contemptuous attitude on the part of Jewish settlers toward their Arab neighbors by referring to the preconceived notion that Jews had of Palestine: "From the first moment of the Zionist idea, Zionist propaganda described the land to which we were headed as desolate and forsaken, impatiently waiting for its redeemers." In the minds of the settlers, this attitude created a "feeling of certainty that Palestine was a virgin country." It was that same feeling of certainty (or, as I prefer to describe it, of ownership) that, according to Smilansky, led to an "attitude of contempt" on the part of the first colonists toward the local Arab inhabitants.[24]

The crystallization of stereotypes was not long in coming. Arabs were considered to be lazy loafers. If they had no "supervisor," they would not work at all.[25] On the other hand, they were ready to work to the point of exhaustion for a pittance.[26] Stereotypical wisdom held that the Arab respected strength and valor but was a coward, and gave in at the slightest show of force.[27] The lack of respect with which the fellahin or bedouin treated the property of others—manifested in stealing from the fields, houses, or farmyards—infuriated the Jewish settlers. "The Arabs are all thieves"[28] was a complaint voiced in a number of variations by the settlers.[29] The filth in the Arab villages, their state of neglect, the lack of trees and gardens, the stench of manure that served as fuel for their ovens—these components provided material for criticism, and were used in creating a distinction between the Jewish village, depicted as a positive model, and the local Arab village, abject and backward.

Eye diseases were extremely common among the Arab population, and it was obvious that Jewish children would also come down with them. That fact was mentioned as one of the reasons why it was imperative to keep a distance from the Arabs.[30] Ahad Ha-Am complained about the negative habits that Jewish children were learning from the children of the tenants in the farmyard.[31] Zeev Smilansky detailed the bad characteristics that the young picked up by associating with Arabs: obscenity, ugly habits, and indecent facial expressions and gestures: "This is how the young become accustomed to lying, false oaths, swindling and trickery, stubbornness and unbridled egoism." There was also a certain sexual tension in the air, manifested in the uncomfortable feeling visitors had in Zikhron Yaakov, seeing young girls from the colony out for a stroll in the evening, walking among scores of Arab males.[32]

Contemporaries interpreted the high-handed attitude shown by Jewish farmers toward the Arab population as a product of the revolutionary upheaval that had taken place in their own situation: Coming from oppressive and highly autocratic regimes in their countries of origin, they found themselves in a new environment, the wild freedom of Ottomanic Turkey. Only yesterday they had been members of a small and persecuted minority taking pains to avoid incurring the wrath of its neighbors. Today they were in control of the situation, lord and master in their own house. The Turkish authorities were open to being swayed by baksheesh and by the influence of persons who enjoyed standing with the foreign consulates, like the officials of Baron Rothschild or Jews of Austrian origin in Palestine. Hence, the authorities tended to lean toward the benefit of the settlers in disputes between Jewish colonists and the local population. There was total freedom in everyday life, bordering on license.[33] The complex psychology of "when a slave reigns" (an expression used by Ahad Ha-Am in reference to the arrogance of the upstart colonists)[34] was manifested in the colonial system of relations that developed in the colonies. Those who were born and raised in that atmosphere had a certain "arrogance of the 'lord and master' toward his slaves."[35]

This system of relations engendered a certain intimacy between Jews and Arabs. There were occasions when that closeness of contact resulted in excellent interpersonal relations on a human basis, as Moshe Smilansky portrayed in some of his stories in *Hawaja Musa* (Mister Moses) or in stories of the veteran colonists in Galilee. More frequently, though, it simply reduced the obligatory distance between the status of lords and that of the natives, without creating any sense of mutual fondness. There was little mystique: The Arabs knew their employers intimately, with all their weaknesses. In the course of time, they learned to understand the Yiddish commonly used by the settlers; and there was no secret in the colony that they did not know about, from problems of its defense to common Jewish habits and customs. Just as the colonists had a negative opinion about their Arab workers, the latter had little praise for their employers. Among themselves, they generally ridiculed them and spoke contemptuously about their habits.[36]

At times, there were substantially more Arabs than Jews living in the colonies. The shadow of threat hovered constantly over the colony. The dependence on, and the fear of, Arab workers was the other face of the colonial society. Although those workers were regarded as a vital component in the economic structure of the colony, the founders of the colony and their children never lost sight of the possibility that these half-wild natives might one day rise up against them. On various occasions, employers avoided firing a corrupt worker or guard who had not carried out his assigned duties to the letter, for fear he might someday return and take vengeance. The methods of revenge varied from uprooting seedlings, smashing windows, and stealing cattle all the way to physical assault.[37]

Contact between Jewish settlers and Arabs was limited in functional and social terms. The spheres in which contact took place were circumscribed, and centered on work relations. The veteran Jews in Palestine (part of the "old Yishuv," the orthodox community that had lived in Palestine prior to the Zionist settlements—in particular the Sephardim) had various types of social contact with Arabs. This was not the case with the new settlers: Quite naturally, people have a tendency to avoid social relations with persons they consider inferior. After the dispute in Petah Tikvah in 1886, El'azar Rokeach insisted on inviting Arabs there to a cup of coffee in one of the homes of the settlers: "Everyone familiar with the character of the natives of our land knows the power that rests in a flagon of coffee with which we shall honor the Arab who comes to our home, the power to win his affection for us."[38] In vain. Even if Rokeach's expectations regarding the persuasive powers of a cup of coffee seemed exaggerated, the fact that his proposal and others like it were rejected was indicative of the real situation when it came to relations between the settlers and the native population.

That state of affairs was also reflected on another plane: complaints and criticism voiced even before World War I regarding just how little Jews knew about the Arab population and its customs, especially their lack of knowledge of Arabic.[39] This ignorance derived in part from the fact that Jews tended to have contacts only with certain strata of the Arab population, namely fellahin and bedouin. Occasionally they met the representative of the local authorities, but little beyond that. The urban Arab intelligentsia in Palestine and, of course, the old Arab aristocratic families were considered "out of bounds" when it came to the Jews. It is quite possible that one of the reasons for this low level of contact with higher-placed and more-educated strata in Arab society was the background of the settlers themselves: most of them did not belong to the Jewish intelligentsia, and none were from the ranks of the Jewish aristocracy. It is difficult to imagine them engaged in serious discussion with educated Arabs even if they had sought their company and knew their language. This limitation on the nature and scope of Jewish–Arab relations served to strengthen the stereotype among Jews of the boorish Arab, backward and uncivilized. By the same token, urban Arabs were depicted as scheming and cunning, prone to machinations and evil designs, men that could not be trusted.[40] That stereotype fostered the sense of mastership and was, in turn, nurtured by it.

Nonetheless, simultaneous with this, there was also a tendency among the colonists to adapt and appropriate certain attributes of the local culture. Young people in the colonies, for example, were fond of adopting and imitating the symbols of power in bedouin culture: horseback riding, carrying weapons, and wearing a *kaffia* headdress.[41] In contrast, the meek and humble fellah, who was like a virtual doormat in the colony, awakened feelings of contempt and disrespect. But the bedouin, who often guarded (or robbed) the colony, knew how to impose his will, especially in the smaller and isolated settlements; and it was he who stirred the imagination of the second generation in the colonies. Of course, that romanticizing of the bold noble savage is familiar from the literature of other countries with a history of colonial settlement, and is characteristic of the ambivalent network of relations that can develop between settlers and certain elements in the indigenous population in a colonial context. Yet such romanticism does not necessarily entail active adoption of the native symbols of power by the colonists. In the case of Palestine, imitation of bedouin symbols of power apparently derived from the fact that the Jews as yet had no power symbology of their own and appropriated the symbolism current in the area. This was an external expression of the shift in values that had taken place in coming to Palestine.

There were some who voiced criticism of this adoption of native customs by the Jews, viewing it as a process that might undermine the qualitative advantage Jews enjoyed over Arabs and lead to their assimilation among the Arab population, instead of the reverse.[42] Others thought differently: The eyes of Herzl and other leaders of the Zionist movement, such as Max Bodenheimer and David Wolffsohn, were reportedly filled with tears when they attended a demonstration of riding ability by equestrians from Rehovot during their visit to Palestine in October 1898. The metamorphosis from clothing salesmen to cowboys from the Wild West (such were the comparisons used by Herzl to describe the encounter) appeared to be living proof of the revolution in the image of the Jew that the life in freedom on the soil of his homeland was meant to bring about.[43]

Up to 1908, that is, until the Young Turk revolution, it was difficult to discern any genuine confrontation between Jews and Arabs. The Arab national movement in Palestine was still in its infancy. To the extent that there were Arab intellectuals animated by a nationalist spirit, their impact was not felt in public life in Palestine.[44] On the other hand, an Arab then would have had to have a rich imagination to believe that the few thousand Jewish settlers scattered across the land could someday pose a serious threat to the status of the Arab population in Palestine. During this period, clashes between Jews and Arabs were on the order of a quarrel between neighbors and were quite similar to the kind of disputes that erupted between Arab villages. The cause for the quarrel generally involved differences over water and grazing rights and rights to land. The purchase of land did not always ensure the rights of Jews to have access to the water sources in the area. The war over water was a topic that repeatedly surfaced in relations between Kefar Tavor and its Arab neighbors.[45] Grazing pasture was considered the public domain in Arab society. Arab herds grazed on the field of stubble belonging to Jews, in accordance with local custom. But the Jewish farmers followed another code and wished to preserve the pasture in their fields for their own animals, a decision that brought about disagreements and fights.[46]

The worst problems were associated with the purchase of land. The history of Jewish colonization is replete with stories of acts of fraud by sellers, where the naive Jewish buyers bought land without knowing exactly what they had purchased. The result was a chain of claims and counterclaims, violence and counterviolence. There were also incidents where Jews became embroiled knowingly, as in the case of land purchase in Metulla. Jewish buyers there took advantage of a combination of political circumstances to acquire the land at the expense of the local Druze inhabitants. The upshot was a series of bloody disputes that cost Baron Rothschild's officials a fortune in bribes to resolve. There were instances, for example, the case of Rosh Pinna, where the purchase of land entailed eviction of the Arab tenants.[47] Until the arrival of Jews, a change in land ownership did not involve a concomitant change in the person cultivating the land. The fellahin continued to work their land even after they lost its possession, whether due to chicanery and strong-arm tactics or because of debts owed to shrewd Arab moneylenders. Jewish purchase of land was arranged over the heads of those tenants, by means of agreements with the effendi, the legal owner of the land. In general, compensation was paid to the evicted tenants forced to vacate their land both for the loss of their squalid huts and for the crop (if any) in the fields. Yet all this did not change the fact that the fellahin were transformed overnight from farmers who possessed land in some form (even if as land tenants) into hired hands. That problem of dispossession had troubled people like Yitzhak Epstein or Moshe Smilansky even during this period. Suggestions were made to try to avoid purchasing land where there were tenant farmers and to concentrate on acquiring land in less fertile (hence, less settled) regions of Palestine.[48] These proposals were a part of a broader framework, namely, the entire question of relations between Jews and Arabs.

Members of the Second Aliyah began to arrive in Palestine in 1904. That wave continued, with short interruptions, down to 1914. During that decade, it is generally estimated that some thirty-five thousand Jews arrived as immigrants. Many were advanced in years and wished to spend the remainder of their lives in Palestine and be buried in the Holy Land. A minority, estimated at several thousand, were young people who had migrated to Palestine motivated by Zionist ideology of one or another socialist brand. Over the quarter of a century that had passed since the immigrants of the First Aliyah had left for Palestine, the situation in the Pale of Settlement had undergone a transformation. Now a ferment of revolution was in the air. The Russian revolutionaries served as a model to be emulated by young Jews animated by a desire to change society. Many of them joined the Russian revolutionary movement. Others participated in the activity of the Jewish Socialist party, the Bund. Some, however, created a link between universal and national redemption and arrived at the Zionist conclusion that the Jewish problem would not be solved by a general revolution but that it required its own specific solution. The Zionist outlook of those young people was shaped by a socialist conception of reforming the universe and of recasting the image of the Jewish people into a people of workers.

Physical labor played a central role in the ideology of the Second Aliyah. There were some who were influenced by Narodnik ideology, and regarded the peasant as the cornerstone of a healthy society. Others were affected by "enlightened" conceptions, such as the notion of the productivization of the Jewish people, namely, its transformation from a nation of middlemen into a people living by its own productive labor. In their eyes, only physical labor was worthy of the appellation "work." The Marxists among them felt it was especially important to create a Jewish working class in Palestine: Only when there was a Jewish proletariat would Jews be able to struggle on the right side of the barricades in the coming revolution. Whether influenced by ideas of productivization, the romanticism of agricultural labor or proletarian romanticism, those young people knew that they wished to be agricultural workers in Palestine. In contrast with their predecessors from the First Aliyah, whose gifts were not verbal or literary and who preferred to deal with material problems, viewing intellectual questions with contempt, many members of the Second Aliyah had a veritable passion for lofty questions and issues. Ideology and ideological disputes were the source of their spiritual sustenance. They lived under great intellectual tension and self-scrutiny, constantly examining themselves to discover whether they were indeed living up to their self-imposed commandments and ideals.

A significant number of those young people had concrete experience of pogroms in Russia. From 1905 on, programs there had become more frequent, arousing a growing sense of fury and outrage among young Jews; and such experiences became an integral component of the psychological makeup of the Second Aliyah, in contrast with the First Aliyah. The topic of "self-defense" was one of the key questions on the agenda of that wave of immigrants. Some, in fact, had already participated in self-defense units while still in Russia.

Most of the members of the Second Aliyah were preoccupied with themselves, their individual experience of grappling with Palestinian realities, the hardships faced by a young person in the strange new environment, the burden of loneliness and unhappiness. To all this was added the problem of coping with the challenge of physical labor. It appears that this was indeed the chief problem that occupied the young immigrants. They loved psychological probing and engaged in much mental mortification of themselves and others—as befitted those who emulated a model of life drawn from Russian literature.

To judge from the small quantity of ink expended in its discussion, the men and women of the Second Aliyah had little interest in the Arab problem. They came burdened by a sense of profound pessimism and soon developed the fashion of "despair" about the future of the Zionist enterprise in Palestine. None wrote enthusiastic letters along the lines of Vladimir Dubnow. If they harbored hopes about setting up a Jewish state, they preferred to keep those dreams to themselves, deterred by the enormous gap between the ideal and reality. On their agenda, political issues were not problems that demanded immediate attention. Their lives revolved around social, economic, and cultural issues. The Arabs were marginal to them and remained at the periphery of the drama of their personal lives. They interpreted that drama as a struggle for the rejuvenation of the Jewish people, endowing it with national importance.

The encounter of these young immigrants with life in the colonies was traumatic. Some ten years later, Ben Gurion described that encounter in terms that suggest a sense of profound shock. He spoke about the "honeymoon" in the homeland, when everything seemed so enchanting and magnificent. But despite the flush of early enthusiasm, he soon detected an old, familiar picture: "The first settlers became middlemen and shopkeepers, who traffic in the hopes of their people, selling the aspirations of their youth for a pittance. They introduced the idol of exile to the temple of national rebirth, and the creation of the homeland was desecrated by *avodah zara* [employment of Arab workers, lit. 'alien work']."[49] *Avodah zara* (in its religious sense "idol worship") is a notion pregnant with meaning in Judaism. It was one of the three sins—along with bloodshed and incest—rather than commit which, a Jew preferred to be killed. Application of this concept to describe the work of Arabs in Jewish colonies depicted it as being equivalent to breaking a taboo. In the eyes of these young immigrants, for whom physical labor had the status of a supreme value, the employment of Arabs appeared like a desecration of the sanctity of the land. The semicolonial system that they encountered in the colonies was in total contradiction with the set of values they had brought with them to Palestine. Instead of the new Jew and a normal people, what they found were life patterns and human relations well known to them from the Diaspora. Once again, the Jew was not working but, rather, supervising the work of others. The image of the Jew as leaser of great estates, familiar from the history of Poland, reemerged in the new reality of Palestine.

The servile system that appeared in the colonies could not but repel anyone endowed with a sense of social sensitivity. The confrontation between the young men and women of the Second Aliyah and the colonists became inevitable when the newcomers rejected the colonial ideal and refused to become farmers; in their role as workers, they viewed themselves as bearers of social, national, and human values far superior to those of their predecessors in Palestine.

Thus, the paradox arose that the socialists, who carried aloft the banner of changing the world, fraternity among peoples, and other virtues of peace and nonaggression, found themselves in actual fact on a national collision course with the Arabs. In order to escape from the colonial structure of settlement, they called for the building of a Jewish society by Jews alone, from foundation stone to rafter. More sensitive than their predecessors regarding problems deriving from the relations between a minority and majority, they wanted to break free from all the complications bound up with living as a people in the midst of another people. This was to be brought about by a total separation of the evolving Jewish society in Palestine from Arab society. Concretely, they called for a preferential labor policy: all jobs created by Jewish capital should be reserved for Jewish workers. The importance of this step, were it to be realized, would be the creation of two separate economies, Jewish and Arab. Eventually, this meant the creation of two societies as well. During the Second Aliyah, that remained only an aspiration. Jewish workers were few in number, and soon found themselves in serious conflict with the farmers in the colonies. Here was a confrontation between the representatives of two contrasting systems of value and culture: young versus old, secular versus religious, idealist versus materialist, venerating of physical labor versus despising of it, revolutionary and out to change reality versus reactionary and determined to preserve the past and present.

Kibbush ha-avoda (conquest of labor)—the slogan used by the young pioneers to denote their desire to supplant the Arabs working in the Jewish fields—proved a failure: Arab workers stayed on to work in the Jewish-owned fields. Consequently, the expression gradually took on a new meaning, namely, accustoming the Jewish worker to the rigors of arduous physical labor. But the contours of the public debate on the question of the relations between Jews and Arabs in Palestine were already visible. There was a trend that aspired to integration between Jewish and Arab society (whatever the nature of that integration may have been) contrasted with a current aiming at separation (whatever its objective). These two fundamental approaches in the relations between the two peoples had already been outlined during the Second Aliyah. Precisely because there was no place at that time for serious discussion of basic political questions, due to the nature of the Ottoman regime and the relatively small scope of Jewish settlement, an opportunity presented itself to discuss a broader issue: the nature of the future Jewish society, then in the process of formation.[50]

The workers bestowed the status of a supreme national value on the question of Jewish labor. Anyone who failed to understand its importance was regarded as, at best, dim-witted, at worst, a traitor. Most of the Zionist leaders shared the view of the workers who stressed that it was imperative to ensure the Jewish character of the colonies by employment of Jewish workers—but not all. Ahad Ha-Am, for example, had doubts about the wisdom of "a total conquest of that kind" and feared that such a policy would earn the enmity of the Arabs.[51]

During the First Aliyah, Jews regarded their right to Palestine as self-evident and requiring no proof. That attitude was based, consciously or not, on the historical right of the Jews. Jews even claimed that among the older fellahin, an ancient tradition survived that the Jews would one day return to Palestine and be its masters again, as they were in the distant past.[52] Members of the Second Aliyah found it difficult to accept that approach. In the last resort, they were hard put to advance an alternative justification, so they too, fell back on the argument of the historical Jewish claim to Palestine as an explanation for the right of Jews to settle there. However, as adherents of the Narodnik view that the land belongs to whoever works it, that justification was insufficient. They argued that the historical right provides nothing but the primary right to settle there and that the ultimate right to the land would be determined by actual labor on the land. That approach now became a central strand in the line of Zionist argumentation in general and a crucial component in the justifications advanced by the Zionist Labor movement in particular.

In 1907, as a result of the publication of Epstein's "A Hidden Question" in the journal *Ha-Shilo'ah,* a dispute erupted in the Jewish community in Palestine. Epstein contended that Jews should help in any way possible to promote Arab progress; others disagreed. This issue laid bare the covert submerged layer of competition for Palestine and the feeling among Jews that Arab backwardness was a trump card in Jewish hands in the future struggle for the land. From what was said in that dispute, it is evident that the dominant approach in the Yishuv was that the struggle between Jews and Arabs for Palestine would be resolved at a future date after the arrival of mass Jewish immigration that would transform the Arabs into a small and negligible minority. Until then, Jews would have to behave wisely and abstain from provocative behavior, such as purchasing land that entailed eviction of fellahin. Concurrently, they should not make any special effort to advance the condition of the Arab population.[53]

In this dispute, manifestations of Arab enmity toward Jews were interpreted by applying concepts borrowed from European models of Jewish–Gentile relations: If Arabs hate us, this is not the result of our own actions, it is a decree of fate, the product of the eternal hatred of the world for the eternal people; there is no sense in trying to befriend them. The more Jews ingratiate and demean themselves before the Gentiles, the more they are hated. This perspective had been corroborated by a salient fact of experience in Eastern Europe: All Jewish efforts to endear themselves to the Russian people and the sacrifices of Jewish revolutionaries for the sake of that people had brought nothing but the scourge of riots.[54]

The dominant feeling was optimistic: In 1907, the anxious search for signs heralding the emergence of an Arab national movement (an anxiety that, as will be recalled, had accompanied every manifestation of Arab animosity toward the settlers) had not yet discovered any cause for concern. The commonly accepted view was cautious but sanguine: *For the moment,* there was no sign of any such movement. That assessment of the situation was also associated with the question of the likelihood of an Arab attack on the Jewish settlement. Along with the humanistic arguments he mustered in support of a nonprovocative attitude toward the Arabs, Epstein alluded in his essay to the imminent physical danger that could arise should the Arabs rise up against Jews.[55] It was disputed whether there were concrete prospects for such a violent outburst. Opponents of Epstein's views argued that for the present, this was not a relevant issue. "At the moment, fear of his fist is far from our minds," wrote Nehama Pukhachewsky, a resident of Rishon le-Zion, demanding that the national interest be given priority over any other.[56] Moshe Smilansky, in contrast, was more sensitive when it came to the future danger from the Arabs and called for preparations to meet it, though he, too, did not believe there was any immediate danger in the offing.[57] This question was debated primarily in the ranks of the First Aliyah. The main issue was what was the best way to ensure a peaceful process of colonization. Most of the settlers in the colonies tended to view Arab–Jewish relations optimistically: The Arabs were backward, lacking in political awareness, and (except for the bedouin) cowardly. There was no reason to fear that they might become an obstacle on the road to Zionist settlement. Moreover, the contention was that Jewish settlement brought great economic advantages for the fellahin. In Arab villages located near Jewish villages, there were signs of relative prosperity. Consequently, it was unreasonable to think that the Arabs would oppose such settlement. Fellahin were viewed as persons who were not motivated by "lofty" sentiments (such as national identity), and it was thought they were guided first and foremost by considerations of material advantage. If there was animosity, many believed, it had probably been stirred up by the urban Arabs, especially the Christians—the agitators and troublemakers.

This optimistic perspective was an integral component of the quasi-colonial network of relations. The European settler generally saw the local population as being unable to oppose him, and uninterested in any such opposition. That assumption served as a kind of precondition for settlement, as well as a justification. Thus, it is not surprising that most Jews who employed Arab workers were not afraid of them and voiced contempt in varying degree for the ability of the Arabs to inflict any harm on Jewish settlement in Palestine.[58] The attitude of the colonist elite (whose typical representatives were men like Avshalom Feinberg or Aaron Aaronsohn) toward Arabs was based on the notion of the superiority of the Jewish settler and on the desirability of a certain amount of cooperation between the two populations to the mutual benefit of both, though at different levels.

Members of the Second Aliyah rejected that conception. The ideology of "Jewish labor" advocated national solidarity at the expense of economic or class interests. For the same reasons that the farmers tended to minimize the danger of a future Jewish–Arab conflict, the workers emphasized its potential threat. In order to induce the farmers to oppose their natural inclination to employ cheap workers, it was necessary to stress the immanent contrast in interests between Jews and Arabs by giving decisive weight to national identity and identification. The pessimistic approach regarding the future of Jewish–Arab relations was a built-in component of the opposition to the quasi-colonialist method—an argument for its negation and for a nationalist alternative. This was one of the main reasons why the workers stressed the *national* character of the Jewish–Arab conflict, a tendency that made its appearance in 1907. Ironically, individuals who immigrated to Palestine with a well-defined class consciousness, such as the Poalei Zion party, were the ones who emphasized the national character of the Arab–Jewish contrast. Poalei Zion was an orthodox Marxist party that had embraced the teachings of Ber Borochov in regard to the need for the creation of a Jewish proletariat in Palestine, so that a proper class struggle could develop within the Jewish people.

As mentioned, the revolution of the Young Turks in 1908 led to a growing ferment in the Arab world. Arabs now began to give expression to suppressed national feelings. That ferment was not centered in Palestine but, rather, in Syria; and what was taking place in Palestine was a kind of supplement to the central events there. Scholars agree that it is difficult to find signs at that time of the existence of a specific *Palestinian*–Arab nationalism, separate from Pan-Arab nationalism.[59] Yet this new upsurge in national sentiment found expression in Palestine in the form of demonstrations of animosity toward foreigners, Jews in general, and the Zionist settlers in particular. The activists spearheading these demonstrations were indeed urban Arabs, especially Christians—apparently because they had a better level of education. The paper *El-Carmel* was first published in Haifa in 1908. Anti-Jewish agitation had an important place on its agenda. Arab officials in Nazareth and Tiberias revealed a tendency to prefer Arabs to Jews in their decisions. Moreover, as a result of the Turkish revolution and its aftermath, there was a prevailing consciousness in Palestine that the heavy hand of the authorities had been weakened. In regions far from the center of power, such as Galilee, an atmosphere of license was generated, bordering on anarchy. This reduced the state of security regarding life and property.[60]

Some scholars are inclined to link these events to the tendency that emerged among certain groups in the Second Aliyah to stress the nationalist nature of the Jewish–Arab contrast.[61] Yet one should be cautious about overemphasizing the importance of those events in shaping the attitude of the Second Aliyah people toward the Arabs, their awareness of the national character of the potential confrontation, and their attitude toward the use of force. As was already mentioned, significant segments of the Second Aliyah were hardly troubled by the Arab question. Even when it made the headlines (in the last years before World War I), it was not a topic for deliberation in any political party or in any of the social bodies that had formed in the meantime. It is true that the subject was discussed in the press, but it remains doubtful whether those articles can be considered proof that the Arab problem had been placed at the top of the agenda of the Jewish community in Palestine. Moreover, there were apparently unmistakable indications of a growing militancy toward Arabs among certain circles in the Second Aliyah even before the Young Turk Revolution. Thus, for example, the clash in Jaffa (Purim 1908) preceded the revolutionary events in Turkey in June of that year. The organization Bar Giora, a secret quasi-military order that had far-reaching plans for the future in Palestine along the lines suggested by Vladimir Dubnow, was established in 1907.

The 1908 clash in Jaffa can serve as a model example for elucidating the attitude of Second Aliyah immigrants toward Arabs. In Jaffa, the main port of entry to Palestine, there was a growing concentration of Jewish workers, newcomers from Russia. In 1908, the second wave of the Second Aliyah immigrated to Palestine in the wake of the failure of the 1905 revolution in Russia and the ensuing disappointment and resurgence of reactionary politics. The city of Jaffa did not welcome the Jews; local Arab youth had grown accustomed to harassing Jews out walking the streets of the town. Yet in contrast with earlier incidents, this time, the Jews reacted. A group of young people organized and laid an ambush for the attackers. When they again assaulted a Jewish youngster, his friends rushed to his assistance, returning the blows many times over. After empty bottles were hurled at them from a nearby store, they did not hesitate to enter the premises and give the Arab there a severe beating. This triggered a series of incidents. The Arabs took revenge, and the "Muscovites" (as the new immigrants from Russia were nicknamed by the Arabs) responded in kind; Turkish soldiers intervened, firing on the workers, beating them, and arresting a certain number. Following the intervention by Jewish notables, the case was finally resolved.[62]

In itself, such an incident, featured in headlines in the Diaspora as the "Pogrom Against Us," was without much importance. But it can function to shed light on the differences in style, conduct, and guiding ideas between Second Aliyah immigrants and their predecessors. The psychological bent of mind and methods of action that these immigrants brought with them had been conceived and nurtured in the revolutionary climate of Russia. Their thinking and sentiment had been tempered by the riots that came on the heels of the 1905 revolution. They had directly experienced the abortive attempts at self-defense, the helpless and futile effort to protect and defend Jewish life and dignity. Their extreme sensitivity regarding Jewish dignity was quite understandable. "The workers envisioned a simple, but exalted and great, mission: to raise the desecrated honor of the Jewish name in the eyes of the neighbors."[63] Attitudes acquired in the Diaspora were transferred to the realities in Palestine. They were certain that the non-Jews whom they encountered in Palestine harbored the same feelings toward Jews as the Gentiles they had known in the Diaspora and that the enmity demonstrated by Arabs toward Jews flowed from the same irrational sources that had given rise to antisemitism. They concluded that just as it had been impossible to persuade the peoples of the world of the untruth that lay at the heart of antisemitism, convincing Arabs that Jews had not come to drive them out of Palestine was likewise an impossibility. And just as the hatred of Jews had been utilized in Russia as a means to awaken the people from the slumber of indifference and catalyze an uprising against the authorities, in Palestine the Arab intelligentsia was using the animosity toward Jews it had fostered in order to spur Arab nationalist sentiment.[64] Thus, it was reasoned, there was no sense in wasting words: The Gentile understood but one language, that of force. Only aggressive and courageous acts would liberate the Jews from attacks by their neighbors. Hence, when young people in Jaffa were injured by Arabs, in contrast with their predecessors, they were not willing to exercise restraint or to request compensation by the authorities. Rather, they preferred to take the law into their own hands. This was an additional pattern that characterized the Second Aliyah: One should not rely on assistance from the authorities or request compensation from any oppressor. The only true shield was genuine power.

The Russian revolutionary tradition was supplemented in Palestine by the feeling of being "lord and master." (It should be noted, however, that revolutionary impulses were not implemented exclusively against Arabs: The Petah Tikvah farmers were also alarmed to hear young people of the Second Aliyah speaking about "revolution" and "expropriation.") What Jews and even revolutionaries had been prepared to put up with in the Diaspora was regarded in Palestine as insufferable. They felt they were the initiators of a Jewish revolution; and as such, it was their duty to free themselves from the traditional responses of Jews to Gentiles. The transition from Europe to Palestine was associated with a profound sense of liberation. The concepts embodied in such phrases as "conquest of Palestine" or "freedom" were popular in the flamboyant speeches delivered at the time in the streets of Jaffa. Remarks along the lines of "One must not bow his head" or "It is forbidden to be meek" (a reference to Jewish behavior in the Diaspora) expressed the psychological need of those young people to underscore the difference between themselves in Palestine and their former identity in the Diaspora and to do so aggressively.[65]

The establishment of the organization Bar Giora can serve as an example of the influence of Russian revolutionary tradition. This secret order founded (as I mentioned earlier) independently of current events in Palestine, was meant to serve as a conspiratorial cell (along the lines of Social Revolutionary party tradition in Russia) for a variety of purposes, from advancement of the cause of Jewish labor to defence of Jewish affairs and interests. Two years later, the organization Ha-Shomer was set up as the legal and open arm of Bar Giora. This took place in conjunction with mounting unrest in the colonies in Galilee. However, the decision was not due to the increasing tension there but was rather the outcome of internal developments within the secret organization, which continued to be the internal nucleus of the larger organization.[66]

The new activism found its expression in lively political activity, in violent responses to Arab provocations, and in the establishment of semimilitary organizations. In the final analysis, these expressed a tendency to respond with force to clashes with Arabs. That activism was not the product of Palestinian realities, but had been imported from the Diaspora. The young had not learned national pride in Palestine but had come there as an expression of revolt against the humiliation of the Jew. That activism derived its basic values from Russian revolutionary ideology and practice. Those values included a refusal to acquiesce in accepting the established order of things, a faith in the ability of a small avant-garde to change the course of history, a conviction that a historical mission liberates its bearers from the restrictions of simple morality in the name of higher justice, and a legitimation of the use of force for the sake of generating the desired revolutionary change. They believed that every revolutionary ideology harbors within it the legitimation of the use of violence, since the end justifies the means. Moreover, in every revolution, the active core constitutes a minority within a majority. This scheme represented an acknowledgement of the inevitability of violence. That was the worldview of the Bar Giora members.

Such a transfer of behavioral norms from the socialist to the nationalist sphere was not peculiar to the Zionist movement. An examination of the paths taken by national liberation movements in Eastern Europe reveals an amalgam of methods of action and arguments drawn from the nationalist and social arsenal without careful distinction as to what belongs where. The idea of the vanguard, as well as the right to use force, were equally popular among both the national liberation movements and revolutionary movements. It would not be far-fetched to assert that mutual inspiration between these two types of movement and the transfer of ideas, images, and ways of action were common and frequent. The Russian populists made use of the term *narod* (people) in the sense of workers of the soil. In populist ideology, the people was the true object of revolutionary liberatory activity. The blurring of definitional contours between national and class concepts in the thinking of this movement facilitated their alternate use. Therefore, it should not be surprising that Jewish *nationalist* activism in Palestine drew sustenance from Russian *revolutionary* activism.

The veteran settlers in Palestine wished to postpone the eruption of the Jewish–Arab conflict as long as possible, even if they assumed that it was ultimately unavoidable. Thus, they exercised caution and restraint in relations with their Arab neighbors.[67] However, the conclusion to be drawn from the activist concept was not only that a clash was inevitable but that it was already a reality, and that there was an intrinsic educational value in relishing the coming confrontation. The cautious method was classified by Y. Zerubavel, one of the leaders of Poalei Zion, as an indication of "Diaspora psychology", unsuited for a free and independent Jewish life. In contrast, he praised the method of national confrontation as a natural stage in the process of ultimate Arab acquiescence to Jewish settlement. He viewed that confrontation as a necessary consequence of applying the concept of "Jewish labor" and "Jewish guardsmanship," which pointed to the genesis of an independent Jewish entity in Palestine. Zerubavel argued that individual preference for adaptation or confrontation was a function of the socioeconomic status of the individual: The thinking of the farmer (or, as he put it, of the "Jewish landlord") tended to be based on calculations of utility, while the workers, "whose only capital and property is their healthy sentiment, strong muscles, and aspirations for salvation," were motivated by a healthy national instinct. For that reason, they did not shrink from confrontation.[68]

Rhetoric on the question of confrontation ranged across a broad gamut: Jews might be depicted as innocent victims of irrational hatred, as being "somewhat guilty themselves," or even as a revolutionary factor challenging the forces of the existing order. In any case, it is doubtful whether the Hebrew press was warranted in according hostile articles in the Arab papers such importance. No one was able to establish conclusively the existence of a direct link between these newspaper articles and the decline in the general level of security that occurred during that period in Galilee. The animosity of the *qaimaqam* (regional governor) in Nazareth and Tiberias may have expressed a national enmity, but may perhaps have been only a manifestation of traditional religious hostility toward Jews as infidels. As far as the conflicts between Sejera and its neighbors or Mesha (Kefar Tavor) and its neighbors were concerned, it is doubtful whether one can pinpoint any trace of nationalist motives. The readiness to interpret such incidents in that spirit, characteristic of Poalei Zion, was rooted in the transference of patterns of thought from "there" to "here," as was typical more generally of their approach to relations with non-Jews.[69] The Poalei Zion proclivity to think in terms of Marxist, deterministic concepts also contributed to presenting a potential confrontation as though it were already actually taking place.

Two contradictory tendencies were evident among the Second Aliyah immigrants. Many were inclined to indulge in excessive rhetoric, a lofty tone, and the use of heroic concepts. On the other hand, there was a diametrically opposed tendency among them toward low-keyed expression, modesty, an avoidance of high-sounding phrases. These two currents were clearly evident when it came to the topic of power and the romanticism of violence.

The romanticism of the fighter struck a chord among the members of, Ha-Shomer and the ranks of workers in sympathy with them. The activists of Ha-Shomer adopted bedouin dress, horse riding, rifles, and bullet belts, as had the adolescents in colonies. The bedouin male also served as a model for emulation in respect to their psychological attitudes toward reality (in so far as the young people understood and interpreted it). He symbolized the free soul who did not need to give account to anyone for his actions—the courageous nomad, a kind of Palestinian cowboy.[70] There was an incredible magic about carrying weapons: After all, what was a more eloquent expression of the change that had taken place in the position of the Jew than such an instrument, symbolizing the independence of its owner.[71] The symbols of a secret organization—with an oath of allegiance, binding unto death, a hierarchy, and initiation ceremonies in which weapons played a central role—added a touch of importance and aura of romanticism to the prosaic, dangerous job of the guardsman. His task entailed a nomadic existence, material poverty and suffering on the part of his loved ones and family. An intentional coarseness of manner developed among these guardsmen, a sort of bravado expressed in rough speech and domineering behavior toward the fairer sex. "Masculinity," whose symbols were borrowed in part from practices and attitudes familiar to them from the surrounding Arab environment and appropriated in part from what they imagined as Cossack behavior (an additional paradigm they emulated) was manifested by a refusal to grant women equal rights. There was at least one of them who dreamed about Jewish women modeled after the bedouin female: Such women (unlike the Jewish girls) knew how to accept male authority and did not inconvenience the men with notions of egalitarian ideology.[72]

Ha-Shomer was singled out for criticism by circles in the Second Aliyah opposed to the parent party, Poalei Zion, as well as by people in the party itself. The choice of guard duty as a livelihood was interpreted by many as an attempt to shirk strenuous physical labor for an easier job.[73] In that perspective, the image of the fighter was seen as competing with the dominant image of the worker. In the scale of values predominant in the Second Aliyah, there was a clear preference for the latter. This is apparently the reason behind the open criticism voiced by Yosef Aharonovitz, one of the leaders of the party Ha-Poel ha-Tzair, and editor of the important periodical by the same name. His critique condemned Ha-Shomer for adopting Arab ways of dress, language, and mannerisms. The attempts by Ha-Shomer to create a special way of life of warriors, distinguished in speech by a distinctive argot (a mixture of Yiddish and Arabic) and more generally by a "non-bourgeois" life-style, were severely castigated for reflecting an undesirable mentality.[74] In general, symbols of an exclusive order of fighters were not granted legitimacy by the society of workers; yet the assigned task of Ha-Shomer as the defender of the Jewish colonies was given due praise.

The cultivation of symbols and myths of heroism was part of the trend to cultivate a "lofty tone" in the ranks of Poalei Zion. In 1911 the book *Yizkor* was published in remembrance of several guardsmen and workers. What they shared were the circumstances of their death: they had not died due to natural causes but had been killed by Arabs.[75] The material was hardly the stuff of which tales of valor are made: These men had been killed by Arabs waiting in ambush, and often there was no witness to the shooting. Aside from the fact that Jews went on guard duty willingly despite the risk of possible injury and the fact of their violent death, it is difficult to find sufficient mythopoeic motifs in the basic story of what occurred. Whether the book *Yizkor* in its Palestinian edition (it later appeared in various editions in Europe and the United States) had any significant influence remains doubtful. Echoes of it in the literature produced by the Second Aliyah are rare. But the volume is important as a signpost with respect to the use of imagery (as a first attempt at glorification of those who fell "in battle," in contrast to those who died in the struggle for survival in Palestine) and as the first example of a transference of patterns of remembrance from religious to secular tradition.

The prayer "Yizkor" is the memorial prayer said on the last day of Passover, Shavuot, Shemini Atzereth, and Yom Kippur, usually in remembrance of family members. Yet from the medieval period on, there has been an additional prayer in remembrance of martyrs. The prayer requests God to remember the souls of all those put to death, "whose lives were terminated by being murdered, slaughtered, burned, drowned and strangled for the sake of glorifying the name of God." It justifies the judgment and accepts the acts of God as something that does not require any explanation. There is no protest against the heavens. God remains the source of all authority, and supplication is addressed to him to preserve the memory of those put to death. The mirror image of acceptance of judgment is the passivity of those killed. There is no reference whatsoever to objections or resistance. The prayer has no national connotations. The supplicant usually utters the prayer for the sake of remembrance of his own relatives.

The book *Yizkor* took over the basic pattern of the prayer but challenged its components, giving a different content and meaning to the attempt to preserve the memory of those who were killed. One can already note that difference in the opening passage of the book: "Let the people of Israel remember." Significantly, the prayer is no longer directed to God but to the people. This is a collective memorial service of the people, and the people is supposed to derive conclusions from the death of its heroes and apply them to its new life. Even if several of the editors of the volume did not intend to stress the contrast between the traditional "Yizkor" and this new version, Y. Zerubavel underscored the evident differences. Presenting a historical conception clearly based on Berdichevsky and his school, Zerubavel juxtaposed the ancient Hebrew people, situated on its land (and its active heroes, such as the brave Jews of Modi'in, Gush Halav, Massada, and the Bar Kokhba revolt) to the Jewish people in the Diaspora. The latter had held out its neck for slaughter and was distinguished by passive saints who died as martyrs. History in his conception was marked by a series of contrasts: valor versus holiness, homeland versus exile, activism versus passivism. Mount Meron, the place of burial of Simeon Bar Yohai (one of the Ten Martyrs) and Modi'in, the village of the Hasmoneans, symbolize the people's past and future, respectively. Paraphrasing a verse by Bialik from "In the City of Slaughter" referring to the dead of Kishinev ("We did not know why, for whom and for what you died, / And there is no meaning in your death, as there was none in your life"),[76] Zerubavel wrote, "They lived well, and well they died—there was meaning in their life, meaning to their death."[77] In his eyes, the fact that those martyred had lived as workers and free men gave their death a special value.[78] Since their death was not associated with any outstanding heroic deeds, it had to derive its uniqueness from the new life in Palestine. Just as there was an essential difference between life in Palestine and the Diaspora, death there was also fundamentally different.

One of the recurrent motifs in the collection *Yizkor* is the element of blood. At the end of the article dealing with immortality of the soul, a moderate Jew, Yehoshua Thon, declared the following: "National aspirations are not realized unless a person sacrifices himself for them. Without the seal of blood, not a single national hope has yet been realized in history."[79] This motif returned in an article by K. L. Silman, a teacher at the Herzliya Hebrew Gymnasia: "A people does not build its life except on the foundations of its past, and blood joins with blood."[80] The need of a national movement for saints and heroes fused with the mysticism that links blood and soil. Passages from biblical scripture—such as "Blood crieth from the ground" (Genesis 4:10), "Behold the blood of the covenant" (Exodus

24:8), "For the blood is the life" (Deuteronomy 12:23)—forged the psychological background for absorbing two conceptions in which blood constitutes a central element. In one, blood is what establishes the covenant between man and his land. The graves are the source of the vital link with the land, and they generate the loyalty of man to that soil. In the second, blood fructifies the soil (in an almost literal sense) and heralds the creation of new life.[81] The close etymological connection in Hebrew between *dam* (blood) and *adamah* (soil) was instrumental in assisting this play on symbols.

It is likely this linkage of concepts has a German source. Yet it is possible that there is also some influence present from other liberation movements in Eastern Europe. More important in this case than the sources of influence is the mood reflected here. The longing for courageous deeds, the intuitive recognition of the importance of myths of bravery and of the symbolization of valor, exemplified in the case mentioned in the almost ritualistic utilization of concepts such as blood and soil, reflect a transfer for the first time of Berdichevskian vitalism to Palestinian soil. What is conspicuous here, however, is that it goes beyond what Berdichevsky wrote: The cult of heroes, death, and graves, the first traces of which can be seen in the volume *Yizkor,* are not found in Berdichevsky. The Palestinian reality endowed the historical heroes Berdichevsky had rescued from limbo with a new and far greater importance. The blood of modern heroes constituted the vital link connecting the glorious past with the rising future: "New graves are a sign that new life is forming in Palestine. . . . And who knows, there may be a mysterious thread being spun to connect Modi'in with Sejera, the ancient Zealots with the workers of today."[82] It was thus only natural that the leaflet put out by Poalei Zion to mark the death of three guardsmen who had been killed in Galilee eulogized them in these words: "Offspring of the Maccabees, descendants of Bar Giora and Bar Kokhba, come to replace the fallen heroes, who died in a fight for their freedom and their people."[83]

In this context, it is useful to recall the transformation undergone by poems. "Neither the fire nor the sun, but our blood / Will turn red your mountains, O Zion!" is a line from a poem by Sarah Shapira, a Hebrew poet in Russia (a contemporary of Yehuda Leib Gordon, who had a high opinion of her work and even dedicated a poem to her). She published her poems in the 1880s and 1890s, including "Zion, Let There Be Neither Dew, Nor Rain," set to music and sung during the First Aliyah. It does not contain a hint of militant romanticism. It is all tears and longing, nothing more, and contains the original of the line I have quoted: "Neither the fire nor the sun, but our blood / Will turn your skies red, O Zion!" It appears that this change was not accidental. The blood on the mountains contains an element of concreteness that is lacking in the distant symbolism of red skies. Removed from its naive context and in its "corrected" form, the line is quoted in the volume *Yizkor* by K. L. Silman.[84] The desire to fall as a victim in the Judean mountains is, he maintains, what brought him and his comrades to Palestine. This line, in Silman's version, is repeated and quoted by Y. Zerubavel as an example of the correct spirit with which the young should be inculcated.[85] To what extent this phrase made an impression on contemporaries can be seen from the fact that many years later, Ben Gurion used it as a motto in his memoirs about the period of the Second Aliyah, when he was a worker and guardsman in Judea and Galilee.[86] The transformation of this verse from a sentimental poem lacking any "new Jew" militant content is instructive: It indicates just how much contemporaries were searching for romantic symbols and slogans to hold on to and how they adapted what they found to their specific needs.

Another poem composed in the Diaspora also took on a new vitality in Palestine, namely Tchernichovsky's "Shadows Are Spreading." The poem, set to music, was often sung, but was not viewed as a popular song; rather, it was seen as a hymn expressing the profound hopes harbored by the immigrants of the Second Aliyah. Berl Katznelson, for example, customarily used the pen name Asir Tikvah (Prisoner of Hope), an expression taken directly from that same poem. Ben Gurion, who had little active interest in poetry, cited lines from this poem in a letter he wrote to his father shortly after he arrived in Palestine. The passage he quoted registered the great hope that a new beginning would emerge in the East.[87] An article published in *Ha-Shilo'ah* described the experiences of a young teacher in one of the colonies in Judea. The teacher stressed the importance of creating a bond of emotional identification between the young children and Palestine. This was done by the reading of legends on the destruction of the Second Temple that took on a meaning both historical and contemporary in the context of Palestine; work in the vineyards created the attachment to the landscape. He described how children broke forth in spontaneous song; and of all the stanzas of Tchernichovsky's poem, they specifically sang the one that went

> On the Jordan and in Sharon,
> The Arabs camp.
> This will be our land.
> And you will be among the builders.

The context is totally innocent, and the passage does not contain any militant references. Yet it would seem that the fact this was sung in Judea by children who applied the poem to their own circumstances by changing the last line to "We are among the builders" is quite instructive and indicates the presence of a significant change: When Tchernichovsky described the Arabs as a part of the Palestinian scene, his words were devoid of concrete substance. That is not the case when children who meet Arabs on a daily basis sing them.[88]

The use of passages from poems written in the Diaspora as a part of the new mythology found its best-known expressive manifestation in the slogan adopted by Ha-Shomer, "In blood and fire Judea fell, in blood and fire shall Judea rise again". That line, from a poem by Yaakov Cahan mentioned earlier, "The Hooligans," also underwent concretization in the transition from the Diaspora to Palestine. When Cahan wrote about the mythical uprising of the ancient Zealots, he was describing an apocalyptic vision. But when the members of Ha-Shomer adopted the myth of "blood and fire," there was another significance. It would appear there was some basis in fact to complaints by farmers that members of Ha-Shomer had contributed to an unnecessary heightening of tension in relations with Arabs on a number of occasions.[89]

Despite all the aggressiveness, both in word and deed, within groups of the

Poalei Zion, and especially in the ranks of Ha-Shomer, it is impossible to overlook the restraining influence that their socialist ideology had on their relations with Arabs in Palestine. Their aggressiveness was directed more at rivals in the Jewish camp (particularly farmers) than at Arabs. From its very beginning, the dispute about the Arab question was an internal Jewish affair, influenced by ideological, economic, and political positions within the Jewish community. The thinking of the Poalei Zion did not include any sense of superiority to the local Arab population. The stereotypes of Arabs that were common among the farmers are rare in the literature of Poalei Zion. The Jews are called to sacrifice and heroism; but their potential rivals lack identity, character, and substance. This was not accidental: As stated, although Poalei Zion drew their views in part from the realities in Palestine, they derived them to a greater degree from the European models they had transferred to the new situation. The socialist workers had feelings neither of love nor of hatred for the Arabs. The more acute the matter of Arab labor became, the wider the gulf became and the less amity there was in relations between Jews and Arabs. The workers kept to themselves and avoided becoming better acquainted with the Arab laborers. For that reason, no stereotypes surfaced. The self-image of Poalei Zion as universalists prevented them from consciously cultivating hostile feelings toward Arabs. Showing animosity toward members of other peoples was delegitimized in their ideology. Consequently, the "emphasis on blood" along the lines of Zerubavel and associates should be interpreted more as a call for bravery and sacrifice that was directed toward Jews and less as an expression of fear or enmity toward Arabs.[90]

The trend toward an "elevated tone" was characterized by a kind of hidden optimism that existed parallel to the pessimistic prophecy regarding inevitable confrontation. That conflict was conceived as a vital phenomenon that could strengthen the healthy instincts of the people in its process of renewal. The belief was that ultimately it would also lead, after much suffering, to Jewish victory. Missing from the exploits of bravery and presentation of the victims in the *Yizkor* book was the element of tragedy. Its absence stemmed from the fact that Zerubavel and his comrades were guided by a deep inner conviction, namely, that the death of those victims would serve instrumentally to lubricate the wheels of the Zionist revolution and was therefore a welcome sacrifice for the sake of the advancement of humankind.

The histrionics of Poalei Zion were symptomatic of a tendency for them to take themselves far too seriously—apparently a common failing of every extreme ideological movement. Such a theatrical stance also stemmed from their inclination to picture themselves as the masters of the situation in Palestine—that at a time when they were nothing more than a negligible minority. That tendency, not confined to socialist circles but also prevalent throughout the rest of the Jewish community, prompted sarcastic responses. "The 'Arab question'—how ridiculous that formulation is! Americans have the Chinese question, and we have the Arab one," Brenner commented derisively.[91] The writer A. Reuveni related a story about an old Jewish woman who came to Moscow. After a drunken Russian had given her a shove, she turned toward the heavens, commenting, "Lord of the Universe! When will we finally be rid here of the Gentiles?"[92]

The most pointed expression to that "special Palestinian brand of 'Thou hast chosen us'"[93] and its mockery was given by Brenner in two of his most important literary creations dealing with the Second Aliyah, the story "Bein mayim le-mayim" (Between the Waters) and his novel *Mi-kan u-mi-kan* (From Here and There). If the mood of colonial optimism created a certain perspective on reality in the consciousness of farmers, causing them to disregard the risks and dangers, and if, in the consciousness of a particular circle of socialists, historical determinism created a kind of barrier to reality, Brenner was unblinking in his acute analysis: A writer whose nature it was to peer into the abyss without recoiling, and to force others to do the same. The attempts to repress, disregard, and embellish reality served as grist from which to construct his cruel exposure of the factual and psychological truths hidden behind the optimistic facades.

Like most of the immigrants of the Second Aliyah, Brenner had been brought up in the Pale of Settlement; and the models of Jewish–Gentile relations they imported with them to Palestine were also a part of his consciousness. But while fellow Second Aliyah immigrants tried in consciousness to reshape a seemingly new set of values, Brenner, with characteristic intensity, offered virtual proof that there was no difference between "here" and "there," that it was all the same. Both in Palestine and back in Russia, the Jew was the alien, and the Gentile was lord of the land. Here and back there, Jews lived a life divorced from nature and from working the soil and were dependent on the work performed by Gentiles. Here and back there, Jews considered themselves superior to the Gentile but in actuality were inferior. Here and there, the Jew was weak and cowardly, the Gentile courageous and powerful. Here in Palestine and back in Europe, the fear of violence at the hands of the majority hung like a knife in the air.

As a writer, Brenner loathed idealization. His descriptions of Jews prompted many to think that he was afflicted by Jewish self-hate (which was far from the truth). He applied that same acute, penetrating, merciless criterion when dealing with Arabs. In contrast with his associates, such as Rabbi Binyamin, or Yitzhak Epstein, or well-wishing Jewish journalists, he was not enchanted by the romantic magic of the Orient.[94] Brenner was fully capable of sketching a pastoral picture of the Palestinian countryside, with a young Arab as part of the landscape.[95] With a sympathetic pen, he delineated the beautiful figure of an Arab woman, a pot on her head, and accentuated her vitality, in contrast with a "young man from Galicia, without a drop of blood."[96] This vignette was meant to symbolize the rootedness and earthiness of the Arab as contrasted with the rootlessness and contemptibility of the Jew.

However, that same skillful hand depicted the filth and abomination of Arab society as his eyes saw it. His approach to Arabs was totally external. Acquaintance with them was based primarily on visual impressions. For Brenner, the dirt and filth symbolized the characteristic feature of that society. The narrow lanes, the pus in the children's eyes, the bloated stomachs, the men sitting idle in coffeehouses—these were the features marking Arab social reality as he encountered it. The degeneracy of that society was also expressed in the image of perverted eros: intimations of pederasty and sodomy.[97]

Brenner's disgust was accompanied by envy. Despite all their misery, the Arabs were the true native sons of Palestine, while the Jews simply lived there, and nothing more:[98] "The murderer is a native of the land, . . . of the land . . . his language is the language of the land, . . . he stands in his land . . . kills in his land. . . . While he . . . he . . . the victim, . . . he and his brother—are strangers here, strangers."[99] Brenner underscored the weakness of the Jews, their inability to stand their ground in an encounter with Arabs. There were those capable of the "herosim" of whipping some wretched Arab workers in a Jewish colony. However, when the confrontation takes place outside the colony, on the highway, man against man, the Jew is unable to stand up to his adversary. In the two meetings described by Brenner, he gives the Jews the numerical advantage. Nonetheless, the Jews flee for their lives, abandoning to their fate anyone unable to escape.[100] The strength of the Jews is in brave talk; but when action has to be taken, then the sons of Hagar, seemingly wretched, overpower the man who "thinks he's a hero."[101] The distance between lofty talk about a courageous stand and heroic deeds on the one hand and stark reality on the other is accentuated by Brenner in his description of the reaction by people from the colony to information regarding an attack. Once it was learned that only a Jew had been injured, "the predominant thought, not expressed in words, was that it was good he had not fired his pistol and that no Arab had been killed, since if that had been the case, the Arabs would have been 'taking his blood' in revenge from every Jew in the colony."[102]

"Did you ever see people scrambling over the cliffs of mountains, climbing, getting stuck, falling—and yet talking away incessantly all the while?"[103] That sentence expressed Brenner's basic criticism of the leaders of the small and weak Yishuv. The leadership, including a significant segment of the Labor movement, had as yet failed to prove their constructive abilities. But they had already demonstrated ample aptitude for self-praise and self-embellishment. These were perhaps sufferable behavior on the part of someone in the Diaspora unfamiliar with the facts of life in Palestine, but it was completely unacceptable coming from anyone who lived there. Brenner settled accounts with the "lofty tone" school in his description of the memorial service for a guardsman[104] by paraphrasing a verse from David's lamentation over King Saul, "the national hero who was slain upon high places."[105] Like a sarcastic echo to the remarks by Zerubavel quoted earlier, Brenner stated:

> The chairman of the meeting . . . integrated the event in the idea of national rebirth, told about all the victims who had fallen on the fields of our revival, and consoled both himself and the world by high rhetoric to the effect that the young hero had not died in the land of slaughter from which we had gone forth. Rather, he had fallen on the fields of Israel, where our prophets and heroes have tread from time immemorial. . . . Someone who had been a worker [i.e., he no longer worked] jumped up once again and swore that every movement demands its sacrifices and that all of us, we are all prepared to fill the ranks, to replace the one who was slain. . . . Another person, with a liberal profession, spoke about what lesson we had to learn from this and in which direction we should accordingly aim our actions. That is to say, militia, . . . arms, . . . ah.[106]

In several barbed lines, Brenner debunked all the pomposity and heroic rhetoric of the Poale Zion. The contrast between the lofty words and the empty deeds underscored the baseless pretentiousness of the national myth that preceded the formation of the nation.

Brenner presented the relations between Jews and Arabs as though it were a Palestinian version of the generations-old conflict between the Gentile as aggressor and the Jew as victim. The encounter at a crossroads between the sons of Aryeh Lapidot (modeled on A. D. Gordon, one of the key figures of the Second Aliyah, unique in his moral attributes) and an Arab expressed all the traditional motifs of Jewish weakness: The Arab is riding on horseback, while the Jews are walking. One of the two Jews is a hunchback. The encounter takes place in a situation marked by a total lack of communication. The Arab addresses them, but they are unable to understand him. One of them reacts like a "new Jew"—he pulls out his pistol. Yet drawing that pistol indicates nothing but a semblance of any genuine readiness to fight, because the Arab, effortlessly, proceeds to disarm the Jew, striking him with a club and kicking him several times for good measure. The other Jew, the hunchback, reacts in typically Jewish fashion: He attempts to flee. Yet suddenly, he remembers that it would be good to sit down, since that is exactly what they used to do when they encountered dogs back in Europe—the animal that was the terror of Jews in the Diaspora. The Arab, after stabbing him with elegant nonchalance, empties the pockets of the two brothers. And then he "galloped off on his horse straight for his nearby tranquil village."[107]

The encounter on the open highway with an Arab on horseback armed from head to toe was a traumatic experience for the Jews of the Yishuv. Moshe Smilansky from Rehovot also described such a meeting, with similar motifs. The helpless Jew is attacked by a bedouin tribesman on horseback and is ordered to hand over his money. The Arab calls him by the contemptuous term Yahud; and when he refuses to hand over his money, the attacker beats him with a whip. The author exclaims, "My God! . . . To beat him here, *in his own land,* a few steps *from his colony.*"[108] The humiliation hurt no less than the actual blows. The basic feeling of belonging and, even more, of being the master of the house had suffered a mortal blow. The self-image of the new Jew was undermined as a result of his inferiority when faced with the Arab attacker. No talk about bravery and heroism could replace the instinctive feeling of security that a Jew expected to sense upon arriving in Palestine.

The quasi-colonial reality and the socialist militancy combined to divert attention from the central problem: By coming to Palestine, the Jew had not succeeded in exchanging a life on the verge of extinction for a secure existence; rather, he had exchanged one situation of existential threat for another. The Zionist press in the Diaspora appears to have cooperated in concealing that feeling of a basic lack of security. Only infrequently, in remarks made by those who had left Palestine, could one find an open and candid admission that fear of the Arab had indeed been one of the reasons for leaving.[109] Yet although little was said about this, there was an operative element that can be termed the concept of the *volcano,* that is, the feeling that they were living in the shadow of a live volcano. This feeling was an important component of the psychological infrastructure of the Jewish community in Palestine. After his sarcastic description of the guardsman's memorial service, Brenner added: "The feeling is that some sort of truth, the truth of reality, is hovering over people's heads and hiding behind the accentuated phrase 'Thou hast chosen us', that special Palestinian 'Thou hast chosen us'. . . . It appears that the world does not see that truth, is afraid of it, disregards it, does not wish to know about it—and even has no interest in knowing. But the truth continued to hover, and remained hanging in the breach: volcano, volcano."[110]

The words Brenner placed in the mouth of the wife of Aryeh Lapidot, the mother of the hunchback murdered by the Arab on horseback, disclose the shock felt by the Eastern European Jew, who had hoped to sit beneath his vine and fig tree, when he finally encountered the grim, menacing reality of Palestine:

> "But what is the conclusion?" asked the old woman in a husky voice once, twice. And no one answered her, since they did not understand the question.
> Yet she herself knew what she was asking. Her throat, parched from crying, could no longer shout, "My son! my son!" . . . Her small brain was clear and she knew what she was asking. Aryeh used to say, 'Let's forget Russia, land of blood and slaughter, land of our disgrace.' . . . But it turned out that there's no difference. . . . Exile is everywhere. . . . There is no difference, . . . no security. . . . Are we secure here? The angel of death has eyes everywhere—and what is the conclusion?[111]

The crucial difference between *exile* and *homeland* was the sense of security. Yet it turned out that as the old woman said, there was no security anywhere. The smoldering reality of the volcano cast a shadow of doubt on the usefulness of the Zionist enterprise. Why should so much be sacrificed if in the end, instead of a "safe haven"—that expression which Herzl included in the Basel Programme, the platform of the Zionist movement—a new existential situation is being created, replete with new dangers? "You want to provide refuge for an injured sparrow in a rooster's coop?"—with this question, Brenner challenged the various optimists who, in the manner of Nehama Pukhachewsky, denied that any danger existed.[112]

Brenner's uniqueness lay in his exposure of the quivering nerve of fear as a constant condition: "It was a good moment—the colors of the sky were captivating, and the young girl from the colony said 'Shalom!' with all her charm. But the dread would sally forth, it had to—with what will come—the next moment, tomorrow at dawn, the day after tomorrow toward evening."[113] However, when he had to draw certain conclusions from the shock of that encounter with Arabs, he did not react like many others who, for that same reason, had picked up and left Palestine. Instead, Brenner completed the transference of the model of Jewish–Gentile relations to the situation in Palestine. Not only was the Arab "another kind of Gentile that one had to suffer from." Not only did Jews in Palestine remain in the same weak position they had been in the Diaspora. Not only was existence in Palestine no more secure from the fear of a pogrom than in the Diaspora. Brenner endeavored to explain Arab animosity toward Jews using the same reasons of hatred for the Jewish people that existed everywhere.[114] As a consequence, by dint of that same reasoning, he concluded, "Whatever will be with all the Jewish communities throughout the world, will also happen to us."[115]

This fatalistic conclusion was in total contradiction with the pretension of the Zionists that they could establish another and different existential reality in which the Jew would be the master of his own fate. It stands to reason that Brenner's intention was both to restrain those who praised "lofty heroism" and silence those who believed that acts such as the establishment of an Arab newspaper or any sort of political activity could bring about some change in the state of the core of the volcano.[116] The undermining of Zionist conventions was for him just a by-product.

Brenner was perhaps the only one who gave pointed and pungent expression to the feeling of fear in Palestine. Nonetheless, there is no doubt that he expressed the hidden perceptions of many of the men and women of the Second Aliyah. It was no accident that Berl Katznelson, the most important leader of the Second Aliyah, regarded Brenner's novel *Mi-kan u-mi-kan* as the work that expressed the very essence of that wave of immigration.[117] However, those feelings of insecurity and anxiety surfaced only rarely in the writings of the time. It seems that the immigrants of the Second Aliyah viewed them as a kind of self-evident, concomitant phenomenon that was best not talked about too much. Similarly, they were not overly attracted by the rhetoric of heroism as evidenced by Zerubavel and Poalei Zion. The hero of the Second Aliyah was not the fighter but the worker, who prepared himself for physical labor and sacrificed himself in a daily struggle for survival. Arabs were perceived less as national rivals and more as competitors in the job market. To the extent that there was any thinking about the future of Palestine (and such ideas were rare, as far as can be judged from opinions preserved in writing), those thoughts remained very vague and lacked a sense of reality.

It would appear that A. D. Gordon was expressing the opinion of many when he spoke about competition between Jews and Arabs in terms of peaceful competition: "Palestine will belong to that side that is better able to suffer for it and to work upon its soil."[118] Speaking of Arabs, Gordon said, "They can indeed harm us, but it is not in their power to remove us from the path." In this context, he did not attribute any importance to the power of the fist. The expression he coined that became a popular phrase among the people of the Second Aliyah was "We need valor, supreme valor."[119] Gordon's concept of heroism did not entail physical prowess but was centered on psychological bravery, a courage that did not recoil from difficulties; it advocated taking a strong stance but one not marred by provocativeness. Self-sacrifice, the virtue that was characteristic of the spirit of the Second Aliyah, would ultimately also prove decisive in the struggle with the Arabs. Perseverance, forbearance, the bravery of the worker in his daily struggle—these were the factors that would decide the future destiny of Palestine, not deeds of bravery in the histrionic, exhibitionist sense.[120]

The period leading up to World War I can serve as a kind of laboratory for studying the moods crystallizing in the wake of the encounter of Zionist immigrants with realities in Palestine. The psychological, conceptual, and cultural makeup of those arriving was decisive in determining the way they interpreted that reality. It appears their basic approach was little changed by Palestine; rather, they burdened the facts they encountered with their previous outlook on the world. The models of Jewish–Gentile relations were applied to the realities in Palestine in differing nuances but were linked with the traditional model. On the other hand, the first attempts were made during that period to transfer the new approach to Jewish history, power, and bravery to the situation in Palestine. The application to concrete reality of concepts whose authors regarded them largely as abstract ideas led to both a vulgarizing and a sharpening of those conceptions. The mythological Palestine was supposed to guide the builders of the concrete land. But the truth is that matters were more potential than actual—conceptual kernels of future possibilities.

The Second Aliyah also entered the history of the Yishuv as a period in which the quasi-colonial model was rejected by Jewish settlers in favor of a settlement model aimed at the creation of a separate Jewish community, autonomous, having as few connections with the Arab community as possible. That decision, which ultimately would prove of far-reaching significance for a political solution to the question of Palestine, was more theoretical than actual in the period under discussion. The Jewish community in Palestine was too small for any type of autonomy. Yet it contained a legitimation for preserving and augmenting distance from the Arab community in the personal and national spheres. That distancing was also of great importance in the crystallization of images, stereotypes, and psychological attitudes toward Arabs.

3

The Emergence of the Defensive Ethos

World War I was a watershed in the history of Palestine. Formerly a forgotten and remote province on the margins of the Ottoman Empire, it was now transformed into the focus of diplomatic and colonizing activity—and ultimately into an arena for the struggle between two national movements. Two great powers, England and France, intended to divide the spoils of the Ottoman Empire among themselves. During World War I, Palestine became the subject of high-level political deliberations. After long and complicated negotiations, these ultimately resulted in the famous letter of Lord Balfour to Lord Rothschild, better known by the name of the Balfour Declaration.

The two decisive facts regarding the future of Palestine were the Balfour Declaration and the occupation of Palestine by the British. That declaration created the political framework that enabled the Zionist movement to strengthen its foothold in Palestine and, in the course of time, to bring about a change in the balance of power between Jews and Arabs there. The British conquest and occupation provided the basis on which to implement the latent possibilities in the Balfour Declaration.

The Balfour Declaration allowed Britain to present its wishes for controlling Palestine as being ethically motivated, namely, by the aim to provide the Jews, a people without a homeland, with the possibility of establishing a "national home" in that country. It is not the purpose of the present study to examine in detail the reasons underlying the British decision to advance this particular argument as a legitimation for their aspirations regarding Palestine. Nor is it my intention to probe why they continued to adhere to this line of justification even after the British occupation forces were in control in Palestine and were in a position to determine its fate as they wished. The fact remains that the Balfour Declaration and its specific reference to a "national home" were included in the final act of the San Remo conference (1920) that set out the division of British and French areas of influence in the Levant. The terms of the official mandate for Palestine presented by the League of Nations to Great Britain were worked out to make that objective a reality, which is why this particular mandate differed from all other mandate charters. While other mandates were designed to further the interests and development of the existing population and to lead ultimately to independence, the mandate for Palestine was meant to create the political conditions that might facilitate the large-scale influx of a new population. Its goal was to promote development there that would make it possible to settle that population on the soil.[1] Subsequently, when Britain deemed it wise to retreat from its obligations toward the Jews, there were those who claimed that the mandate contained a double obligation—toward both Jews and Arabs. But a careful perusal of its text reveals that this was not the case: The document leaned quite clearly in one direction, namely, in favor of Jewish interests.[2] Thus, Vladimir Jabotinsky was correct when, after examining the draft of the mandate, he commented that it contained nothing that might make it impossible to realize even the most far-reaching of Zionist objectives, that is, a Jewish state.[3]

From 1917 to 1920 the status of the Zionist movement underwent a sea change. It was transformed from one national liberation movement among many pressing foreign ministries around the globe for a hearing for their claims to a movement recognized by the Great Powers and in international law. The profundity of that change becomes evident when one compares the status of the movement under Ottoman rule to that it enjoyed under British mandatory administration. Muslim dominance in the Ottoman Empire had bestowed a senior status on the Arabs in Palestine. It is true that their status was inferior to that of the Turks; and the Turkish regime surpressed Arab national aspirations with a heavy hand. Nonetheless, there was no doubt that the Arabs enjoyed a higher status than the Jews. Moreover, the Turks were determined not to allow the Jews to expand their hold in Palestine. Difficulties in purchasing land and building houses—not to mention the restrictions on immigration—created daily obstacles that impeded the growth of Jewish settlement. All symbols of Jewish nationalism were strictly forbidden. During World War I, the Turks had doubts about the loyalty of the Jewish community in Palestine. As a result, they issued numerous restrictive laws, extending from the banishment of its leaders to mass deportations. The fate of the Armenians in Turkey, well known in Palestine, generated considerable apprehension within the Jewish Yishuv. Many of its leaders feared that a similar fate awaited the defenseless Jewish minority there as well.

The transition from Ottoman rule to an administration under an enlightened European power was dramatic. The arbitrary character of decisions that had marked the Turkish regime disappeared overnight. Both Jews and Arabs breathed a sigh of relief. Yet that change was even more significant for the Jews: Formerly tolerated infidels, they now acquired a recognized political status—with national rights by dint of the mandate terms—and the right to take action to alter the demographic, economic, and cultural balance of power in Palestine. In basic terms, what they were granted was a major boon: the authorization to change the character of the land from an Arab country to a Jewish one. True, the British occasionally took steps that frustrated the Jews and were interpreted by them as hostile, such as the refusal by the British military governor and members of his staff to stand up during the playing of the "Hatikvah" anthem and the refusal to grant Hebrew equal status alongside English and Arabic. Yet in truth, Jewish exasperation over those minor slights was reflective of the enormous change that had come to pass.

It was an irony of fate that the same processes that assisted the furtherance of the interests of the Jewish national movement also served to augment the strength of the Arab one: The collapse of the Ottoman Empire brought a renewal of Arab national life in its wake. Although the "revolt in the desert," the Arab guerilla movement that Lawrence organized in the Arabian peninsula against the Turks, had little impact on the fate of the war, it made a key contribution to the awakening of Arab nationalism, that centered on the creation of an expansive Arab kingdom. These hopes were focused around the romantic figure of Faysal, the son of Husayn, sharif of Mecca, who was declared king in Damascus in March 1920. At that time, the Arabs of Palestine viewed themselves as belonging to the greater Arab people, and aspired to be part of Greater Syria. In the view of Yehoshua Porath, an expert on the Palestinian–Arab national movement, the Arabs in Palestine wished to be rid of the Zionists even then and regarded them as a potential threat to their hegemony. The fact that they did not make their claims to Palestine a public issue before Faysal's removal from Damascus by the French in July 1920 does not mean that they did not oppose the Zionists. Rather, they assumed there were better prospects of dislodging the Zionists with Faysal's assistance than by raising a separate national claim at the time.[4] Already at that point, the fateful symmetry was evident that would accompany the Zionist enterprise throughout its evolvement: The more powerful the position of the Zionists became in Palestine, the stronger grew the Arab–Palestinian National movement.

The years 1917–1921 saw a burgeoning of messianic hopes that were soon shattered in confrontation with reality. This period witnessed an upsurge in national feeling and its militant expression and also a return to a more moderate stance, cautious and desirous of peace. It saw a welling up of feelings of sympathy and good will toward the British, followed by bitter disappointment. In many respects, these were the pivotal years in shaping the attitudes of the Zionist movement and the central political forces in the Yishuv regarding the feasibility of the Zionist enterprise, the ideal and possible pace of building up the land, and the nature of the political relations with the British and the Arabs. The result was the crystallization of a national ethos based on that interpretation and accompanied by a panoply of symbol and myth. An era that had begun with a blast of trumpets ended with the emergence of a defensive ethos.

The Jewish Legion: The First Debate on the Use of Force

World War I was apparently the last great war in which men rushed enthusiastically to enlist. Romantic notions prevalent at the time about the nature of war as a means for releasing pent-up energies and bringing out the best in men and nations were voiced by many as reasons to volunteer for service. Jews participated in the war by the hundreds of thousands, fighting under the flags of various states, on both sides of the conflict. Jews with a Zionist consciousness, such as Max Nordau, viewed that spectacle with mixed feelings. They were aware more than others of the problem of

Jewish "lost honor"; in his words, the "feeling of responsibility for the reputation of the people of Israel" was one of the factors obligating the mass enlistment of Jews. Yet Nordau was also conscious of the prospect that those who enlisted had no hope of being rewarded for loyalty to their respective fatherlands. The war was accompanied by ugly antisemitic manifestations in the various combatant nations. These outbursts revealed the deep-seated suspicions among the population when it came to Jews: "Even the heroic death of our [Jewish] soldiers they describe as an act of profiteering, one that supposedly reaps enormous profits." While the war raged, the combatant nations began to put forward their demands regarding peace settlements. The feeling among Jews that they, as a people, were also entitled to compensation for sacrifices made was a quite natural consequence of their disappointment over the attitude of the European nations toward Jews who had fought and died for their respective fatherlands.[5]

The war had created instability in the international arena, an opportune moment for anyone wishing to change the status quo. The hopes that had languished in dim obscurity since Herzl's failure to obtain a charter for Palestine were now rejuvenated in the light of the anticipated changes and the new postwar order in the Middle East should the allied powers prove victorious. The Zionist Organization, as an international organization whose members could be found among all the combatant powers, formally announced its neutrality in the war and shifted its central offices from Cologne to Copenhagen in neutral Denmark. Aside from the fact that it suffered from a certain pro-German proclivity due to the preponderance of members of German origin among its leadership ranks, the Zionist Organization was a strong adherent of neutrality for a key reason, namely, its apprehensions regarding the fate of the Jewish community in Palestine. Any identification of the movement with the Allied powers was likely to provide a motive for the Turks to vent their wrath on the Jews in Palestine. On the other hand, it was clear to any sharp-eyed observer that Zionism's hopes depended on an Allied victory, since a German–Turkish victory would not lead to the desired political changes in the Middle East.

For that reason, various persons in different countries began to take steps to further the political interests of the Zionists when the day arrived for a peace conference after the war's conclusion. Beginning in 1915, Chaim Weizmann was tireless in his efforts to acquaint British policymakers with the Zionist movement and its aspirations. Parallel with this effort, Jabotinsky and Joseph Trumpeldor (a Russian socialist who had distinguished himself in service in the czar's army during the Russo–Japanese War of 1905) were active in trying to persuade the British to set up Jewish battalions within the framework of the British army. In the initial stage, they enjoyed only partial success. The British were prepared to set up a Jewish service battalion but not a combat unit. Jabotinsky did not regard such a lackluster battalion as a realization of the dream for a Jewish fighting force and would not have any part of it. But Trumpeldor persevered, and the battalion was set up. It served in Gallipoli, suffering the terrible hardships of that wretched front. Although its official name sounded pathetic (Zion Mule Corps), an important precedent had been established, namely, a Zionist corps in the British military.

Jabotinsky did not despair after his first disappointment, and continued to be active in trying to set up a Jewish battalion made up of Jewish refugees from Russia living in London. The British authorities were unenthusiastic about the idea, as were the Jewish tailors who were meant to provide the reservoir of potential recruits. In the end, however, the thirty-eighth Battalion of the Royal Fusiliers, a Jewish Legion, was set up, and sent for training exercises in Egypt. Parallel with Jabotinsky's activity and in the light of his success, a voluntary movement arose in the United States. Among its founders were Pinhas Rutenberg, a Russian–Jewish revolutionary, David Ben Gurion and Yitzhak Ben Zvi, leaders of the Poalei Zion Labor party in Palestine who had been banished by the Turks during the war. They set up the thirty-ninth Battalion of the Royal Fusiliers, which joined its predecessor in the dunes of Egypt.

Along with the diplomatic and military activity in Europe and the United States, an attempt was made for a similar purpose (though of a different nature) by Aaron Aaronsohn. Aaronsohn came from Zikhron Yaakov, a small village known then only for its vineyards. He later became world-renowned in the field of botanical research in Palestine. Aaronsohn, an impressive and controversial personality, gained the confidence of Jamal Pasha, one of the ruling triumvirate in Turkey, who commanded the Ottoman Fourth Army and was in military charge of Palestine during the war. The close contacts with the Turks and the fate of the Armenians persuaded Aaronsohn that Zionism had no hope unless Palestine changed hands. He set up an espionage organization, the Nili[6] group, which furnished intelligence to the British Army in Egypt.

These initiatives reflected the desire by persons from all bands of the political spectrum to take part in the war effort on the side of the British, who had been viewed with favor by Zionists ever since the broaching of the Uganda Plan. The assumption that participation of any kind in the war granted rights at the peace conference table was a commonly accepted thesis, though untested in practice. It was thought that only the "belligerent parties" would be accorded a seat at the negotiations table, so that the presence of a Jewish fighting force on the right side of the arena would have great importance. This was not an originally Jewish idea: At that same time, fighting units were set up among various peoples in Europe buoyed by hopes of national renaissance upon the ruins of great empires in collapse. One need but recall the Czech Legion, and that of the Poles or Finns. Nonetheless, there was a basic difference between a people settled on its own territory with all the attributes of nationhood except political independence and the Jewish people. In addition to the political hopes pinned on them, the Jewish legions were also an expression of the new status the Zionists wanted the Jewish people to obtain as a result of the war. The symbolic value of the legions was by no means inferior to their actual one.

As mentioned, this was the last war whose recruits flocked to the ranks in fervent, patriotic zeal. This itch for combat was not lost on the Jews either. There was something in the atmosphere of the era that awakened dreams of national grandeur, hopes for exploits of heroism, longing for self-sacrifice. It was a time for the release of pent-up instincts and urges that in ordinary times had been repressed by the rule of reason. In 1916, at the height of the war, Tchernichovsky wrote his poem, "Mangina li" (I Have a Melody), where he rhapsodized:

> When God summoned to death over the golden-grained fields
> And he rained blood on a ploughed furrow, and his harvest is a living soul
> What are you, my blood, teeming in me, O blood of the ancients?
> . . .
> Who are you my blood, boiling within me? The blood of the generation
> of the wilderness? Thus!
> The blood of Canaan's conquerors is my blood, it flows and does not rest.
> Again the mighty song calls me, a melody of blood and fire:
> Ascend the mountain and crush the meadow, whatever you see, overtake!
> . . .
> And conquer the land with a strong hand, hold onto it,
> And you shall build an eternal building for the generation to come![7]

The poem was written in Minsk at a most difficult moment in Jewish history there and at a time of defeat for the Russian army. Yet the poet does not deal with realities around him; rather, he focuses on the mythical reality of Palestine, which he envisions reshaped as a result of the war, and the psychological reality of the Jewish people, which he pictures rejuvenated by that war. The farfetched hopes for Jewish sovereignty in Palestine from the time when he composed "Shadows Are Spreading" now become viable and are seemingly within grasp: "And conquer the land with a strong hand, hold onto it, / And you shall build an eternal building for the generation to come!"[8] Indeed, even in "Shadows Are Spreading," the motif of the use of weapons was present as an element, though kept subordinate to the constructive act. Here, however, the gaining of sovereignty over Palestine is described as the result of an act of conquest, in blood and fire. Tchernichovsky's enthusiasm for this is the mirror image of the disappointment felt by Max Nordau over the attitude shown by the European peoples toward the Jews who shed their blood for their respective fatherlands. If the wars fought by Jews for the sake of others do not gain recognition and respect, what is more natural than the conclusion that Jews must fight for their own land?

This insight was not shared by all. When Trumpeldor tried to persuade Ahad Ha-Am of the importance of setting up a Jewish legion, the latter was not appreciative and failed to be convinced. He was not dead set against the idea of a Jewish legion but doubted that it could have the political importance attributed it by Trumpeldor. "If I understand your thinking," he wrote to Trumpeldor, "your main argument is that the legion will prove to whoever needs such proof that we are capable of fighting, and by inference, that we will be able, when necessary, to defend our land." In Ahad Ha-Am's view, the Jews had already demonstrated their fighting prowess wherever they had fought in the war; thus, there was no need for any additional proof. When Trumpeldor remained adamant in his attempt to convince him of the extrinsic merit of a Jewish military enterprise, Ahad Ha-Am replied that Trumpeldor was probably influenced by his military background, while he himself, unfamiliar with the military science, was not in a position to understand that point of view.[9]

The establishment of the battalions was not accompanied by any basic debate on the question of the use of force. Setting up the British battalion met with strong resistance on the part of Jewish immigrants, but that was due solely to practical reasons: These men simply were not overjoyed to enlist and fight. The U.S. battalion was formed riding on a wave of enthusiasm for enlistment, apparently accompanied by little soul searching. On the level of Zionist leadership, the dispute touched on the question whether the setting up of a legion in the service of Great Britain might not provoke acts of revenge on the part of the Ottoman rulers against the Jewish community in Palestine. However, the basic question concerning the legitimacy of the use of force was not placed on the agenda. Aaronsohn's espionage network met with resistance on ideological grounds, since at that time spying was considered a violation of the accepted code of honor. While a person who sacrificed his life on the battlefield was a hero, the spy was regarded as the scum of humanity, a traitor to the trust placed in him, an immoral person devoid of conscience.[10] In this instance, as well, it was not the use of force as such that provoked opposition but the particular form of its application.

For that reason, the Palestinian Legion—the Fortieth Battalion of the Royal Fusiliers—is of special interest. This battalion was created after publication of the Balfour Declaration and the southern part of Palestine had been occupied by the British. Its establishment generated a heated public debate, whose reverberations were still felt long after the legion was disbanded. For the first time, there was an open debate on the basic principles guiding Zionists in respect to the issue of the use of force; positions were enunciated, stands taken, priorities determined.

The Balfour Declaration and the clatter of Allenby's cavalry in Jerusalem gave rise to messianic hopes among Jews in Palestine. The radical shift from the oppression of the Turks, who had increased their pressure on the Jewish community in Palestine after the exposure of the Nili espionage network, to the great shining hope in the wake of new political changes had a crucial impact on consciousness. It awakened a feeling akin to intoxication in persons who otherwise were quite sober in their outlook. The initiative to set up a Palestinian battalion recruited from Jews in the southern part of the land, already under British occupation, came from a group of students at the Herzliya Hebrew Gymnasia, headed by Eliyahu Golomb. They immediately obtained the support of members of the Poalei Zion party that had remained in Palestine, whose spokesperson was Rachel Yanait. These were joined by individuals from various other groups, ranging from farmers to workers. The battalion was to take part in the conquest of the northern area of Palestine, still under Turkish rule, and in this way would forge a convenant of blood with the land.

The entire phenomenon of the movement of volunteering was made possible by a pause in combat between Allenby's conquest of the south (up to the Yarkon River) in the autumn of 1917 and the conquest of the north in September 1918. From the beginning of 1918 to June of that year, the volunteers from Palestine kept knocking on the doors of the British command demanding to be recruited until they were finally accepted as a battalion. If Allenby had not postponed his attack until the autumn, there would have been no place whatsoever for any dreams that Palestine might be conquered by Jews.[11]

The assemblies of volunteers bore greater resemblance to prayer revival meetings than to any sort of deliberations on a prosaic issue such as recruitment to a battalion in the British army. The topic of blood was repeatedly brought up in the discussions. Some spoke about Jewish blood that had been shed in vain and urged that in order to prevent this in future, it was necessary to gather Jews under one command and one flag.[12] Rachel Yanait proclaimed quite simply, "The primitive truth is that the right to the land is purchased first of all in blood—this truth is being forced upon us at this historical moment."[13] Given the present state of affairs, one person remarked, only one item had retained its value on the world stock market: human life itself.[14] Another explained that "a people that spills its blood proves that it wants to survive."[15] Indeed, the Jewish people had inscribed on its flag "Not by force, not by power, but by the spirit"; however, "We want to prove that there is no effort we will spare at the hour of salvation!"[16]

In the life of a national movement, the import of symbols and symbolic acts often exceeds the value of facts. For that reason, rational considerations in favor of participating in the war played a minor role compared with the exaltation, in the view of some—sheer madness, from the perspective of others—that seized a segment of the modest community of the Second Aliyah. All the hidden longings for manifestations of Jewish power now burst forth. The low-keyed approach that had characterized the majority of the Second Aliyah faded. The idea that a Jewish corps under a Jewish flag would take part in the conquest of Palestine brought tears to their eyes. The fervor of the volunteers for the opportunity to shed their blood for the sake of acquiring their homeland rose to a fever pitch. That irrational emotionalism was especially evident in the comments of Shmuel Yavne'eli, one of the leading figures of the Second Aliyah and an ardent socialist. He declared that Zionist diplomacy ought to be assisted by the instrument of force and that it was that force which the volunteers hoped to create. Yet in order to make sure no one would be so foolish as to assume incorrectly that he was motivated by logical considerations, he went on to explain that "it is not proof that convinces people to volunteer but, rather, the inner spirit of God."[17] Highly popular was the saying by Rabbi Akiva, uttered when he was being tortured by the Romans after the Bar Kokhba revolt: "All my life I have regretted that I did not have the chance to fulfill the commandment 'with all your soul and with all your might'." The opportunity to fight for the land was conceived in terms of Jewish martyrdom, thus achieving the status of the supreme sacrifice for the sake of the Jewish people.[18] There was a sense of coming apocalypse in the air. The expressions "end of days" and "salvation" cropped up repeatedly in every speech and even in private correspondence. Yavne'eli declared: "The creation of a Jewish force is the eradication of the exile, its absolute negation. It means the reestablishment of historical life after a long caesura and the restoration of Judea to its ancient pride." As though that were not enough, he added, "Every person in a Jewish army implements the concept of the messiah." Yavne'eli rephrased the verse from Isaiah (2:5) "O house of Jacob, come ye, and let us walk in the light of the Lord" into "O house of Jacob, let us go and fight."[19]

The debate about the legion introduced a new concept into the political lexicon of the Yishuv: *activism*. The supporters of the recruitment were called *activists*, its opponents, *conservatives*. So great a majority of activists were members of the Labor movement that Eliyahu Golomb, one of the founders of the recruitment movement, announced that volunteering for military service symbolized "a new national morality that began with the arrival of the first Hebrew worker."[20] The concept *activism* had originated in the soil of socialist ideas; activists were those who could not be content with waiting idly by for redemption to come but, rather, strove to accelerate the process by their own action. In other words, activism was the programme of revolutionaries who had no hesitations about transforming the course of history and did not recoil from the idea of using force if necessary to achieve their aims. Ever since the debate about recruitment to the legion, *activism* had been associated with an aggressive response and a resolute readiness to fight. Over the course of years, the term underwent several changes in meaning, along with the evolving situation in Palestine. Yet it generally referred to persons who placed particular value on furthering the military arm of the Zionist movement, preferring it to other aspects of Zionist construction. They also were prepared more quickly than others to point to a need and feasibility for the exercise of force. Within the framework of Zionist terminology, *activism* had a positive connotation as the opposite of *passivity*. The latter smacked of exile, acquiescence in divine judgment, and making peace with one's presumably allotted fate. The Zionist movement viewed itself as revolutionary; as such, it had a decided preference for individuals who dared to take action over those who stood docilely by and waited for events to occur.

The close link between revolutionary ethos and activism was openly broached by the supporters of the legion: "*Activism* was the focal point where all the sparks ignited by the aspiration for revival were gathered together and concentrated." This statement by Rachel Yanait was not a reference to military activity but, rather, to social activism that would come in the wake of the liberation of Palestine. It was obvious to her that "national salvation is the beginning of socialist redemption."[21] Thus, when members of the Poale Zion party worked hard for the sake of the legion, they were also working simultaneously for the creation of a socialist society in Palestine. Associated with this context was the role of Ha-Shomer, the guardsman organization, whose image was now transformed from an esoteric phenomenon during the Second Aliyah to a key link in the chain of Jewish valor that continued on in the legion volunteers. "The blood of the guardsman" was now mentioned as equivalent in value to the "sweat of the worker," a comparison that would have been unlikely to win over many adherents during the Second Aliyah. Recruitment to the legion was presented as *the* revolution—"revolution in the form of war."[22]

Many of the volunteers enlisted only after great hesitation. They were not swept up by the wave of messianic enthusiasm, nor did their hearts beat faster to the roar of the cannon. Some of them had pacifist leanings or at least harbored strong convictions that the war was a major calamity for the entire world. Their decision to enlist despite these misgivings derived from an awareness that the paths taken by history were unfathomable and that on occasion evil ultimately led to good in the dialectic turn of events. The movement in favor of recruitment had triggered a powerful wave of public ardor, of such a magnitude as all the preaching over decades about the virtue of physical labor and the redemption of the land by toil had not succeeded in generating. It was their hope that this spontaneous awakening would lead to a sense of exaltation, to the unity of hearts and purpose necessary for a large-scale, creative enterprise. That idea was essentially no different from the conception of the Russian populists, who, after despairing of any possibility to spark a massive popular awakening as a prelude to revolution, attempted to awaken the spiritual energy slumbering in the people by means of inspiring, exciting deeds. Such acts included political assassinations—meant to shake the people from its passivity and serve as a catalyst in the process of popular uprising.

The hope to turn the movement for enlistment in the legion into a kind of engine to spur significant changes in the Jewish people found expression in the statements of the volunteers who were members of the Agricultural Workers Union on the eve of their recruitment: "We hope and expect that the movement of volunteer enlistment . . . will stir feelings of obligation and honor in people's hearts and a burning desire for redemption and that it will bring to our land an army of volunteers for its liberation and camps of pioneers laboring to establish a working people."[23] A more vulgar and radical version of that same idea was expressed by an anonymous volunteer who said: "We repeatedly called on the people to join together in common labor. The people did not respond. We have come to call upon it once again, now to the field of slaughter. Sweat is an evolutionary process. Blood is a revolutionary process. What sweat is unable to accomplish over generations, blood shed in battle will achieve in the span of a few short years."[24]

This idea was rejected in disgust by those same elements in the workers' camp who were repulsed by messianic, militant rhetoric. "What is happening here?" reflected a person from the ranks of the Second Aliyah, many of whose comrades had gravitated to the camp of the recruits: "Am I indeed a limb hanging loose, detached from the body of the people? And the call of nature, the deep voice of the nation in this critical hour, the voice of the vigorous man—do they not penetrate to me?"[25] Some of those who opposed the legion regarded enlistment as an abandonment of the meager achievements of the workers movement that had been barely preserved during the war. Enlistment was viewed as a step to abandon the rigors of physical labor—so boring and tedious—for the sake of a more exciting way of life. They also felt it might endanger the safety of that remnant of the movement in Northern Palestine still under Turkish rule. Likewise, some claimed that enlistment constituted a violation of the declared neutrality of the Zionist movement in the war.[26] This was basically the view of individuals involved in political activity. But there were other voices, whose position was determined by a profound opposition to any participation in war and the shedding of blood. Their opposition to violence was total. Just as their associates who had enlisted linked war and revolution as two complementary values, they also connected them, rejecting both: "There is nothing good in this world that comes as a result of bad," one of them wrote: "This war will bequeath a legacy of failure and evil to countless generations." He also challenged, "Where, then, is the revolution that has brought true fruits for the benefit of mankind and future generations?"[27]

During this entire debate on enlistment, the topic of the Arab inhabitants of Palestine remained marginal, as though all the turmoil taking place there was of no concern to them. Most of the participants in the debate did not refer, even indirectly, to the natives of Palestine. Only Yavne'eli underscored the importance of the Jewish battalions that under their own flag would pass through all areas of Palestine—places where up until then no Jew had tread. There they could discover what land was not under cultivation, as a prelude to later Jewish settlement. He also considered it important to demonstrate a Jewish military presence throughout the land: "The natives there will recognize our claims and power when they see us, in the broad light of day. That recognition . . . will traverse the conduits of oral legend and remained fixed in the minds of the inhabitants for generations to come."[28] The importance of the demonstration of strength inherent in the appearance of Jewish batallions in Palestine and its impact on the Arab population there was hinted at during this extensive debate but not elaborated on at any point. It would appear that it was thought best not to awaken sleeping bears from their lair.

Unusual was the stance taken by Mordechai Kushnir, a member of the Second Aliyah, active in the circle close to Berl Katznelson, a group that was split over the issue of volunteering for the legion. Kushnir was one of those who rejected the idea. A pacifist by nature, he was opposed to all bloodshed whatsoever. It is true that Judea had fallen "in blood and fire," but this was no proof, he contended, that it would also be resurrected in blood. That sentence—adapted from a poem by Cahan that had served as the slogan of Ha-Shomer—took on the status of a veritable historical necessity during the debate in question. This serves to illustrate the power of a phrase or slogan when embraced by a national movement at a heroic moment. The repeated reference to this slogan during the debate on the battalions was not accompanied by any explanation as to who that war of blood and fire would be directed against. Since the Turks were still in control of the northern areas of Palestine, this lack of clarity left matters open, allowing people to interpret what was intended as they wished. Kushnir did not fall prey to the axiomatic captivation of the phrase "In blood and fire shall Judea rise again." Moreover, he exposed a crucial issue lying beneath the surface of the dispute on the legion: In what way should Jews develop relations with the Arab inhabitants of Palestine? On the basis of an advantage in physical strength or by other methods? Kushnir distinguished between two possible versions. One, dubbed by him "independent life," was based on the presence of a Jewish majority in Palestine, which would develop its own forces for self-defense. The second, which he termed "alien political life" (i.e., something that does not derive internally from the people but, rather, is acquired from the outside), was predicated on a Jewish minority, which would set up a military force to establish its national superiority.

"National defense" and "national dominance" were the two contrasting concepts that Kushnir attempted to sketch. The first path necessitated developing a human relationship with the Arab inhabitants of the land, learning their language and customs. That approach did not close its eyes to the need for a Jewish armed force and regarded self-defense as the lesser evil. The path of national dominance was manifested by domineering, high-handed behavior, provocative acts, and emulation of the aggressive manners of the bedouin. While the path of "national defense" placed limitations on the use of force, the approach of "national dominance" liberated the settlers from restraints. "The historic meeting between us and the Arab tribe," Kushnir asserted, "will not be sealed in blood or in the darkness of night with an armed belt. . . . Rather, [it will be] in the broad light of day, within the framework of an everyday system of cordial mutual relations between simple and honest neighbors."[29]

The enormous enthusiasm about demonstrating Jewish fighting prowess was not accompanied by a concomitant zeal for military symbols and manners. The truth is that there was no battalion more "civilian" in character than the battalion of volunteers from Palestine. Military discipline, ranks, and uniforms were incompatible with the essentially anarchistic nature of the pioneers of the Second Aliyah. They soon became embroiled in confrontations with their British commanders. When the men did not like a particular order, they were quick to organize a strike, as they had done as civilians. Parallel with their Jewish commanders, appointed by the British, they set up a kind of "soviet" of their own. When required to carry out an order not in keeping with their understanding of their duty, they were near to declaring open mutiny. Indeed, His Majesty's Army had never known recruits like these.[30] The difference in style between them and Jabotinsky was very pronounced in this respect.

Jabotinsky came to Palestine together with the battalions from Egypt and was received with great emotion as someone who had been a Zionist leader even before the war—and had authored the idea of the Jewish battalions.[31] His rhetorical skills were enlisted in furthering the cause of recruitment; and at every meeting where he spoke, he awakened urges for blood and violence. This was the first example of masses being swept up by the words of a Zionist speaker. The loss of the individual personality of the listener, the emergence of a kind of regimentation of heart and mind, each person prepared to stand up and enlist on the spot, suggested the presence of a state of consciousness quite distant from that which had characterized the attitudes of the Second Aliyah. In a meeting in Jaffa, Jabotinsky extolled the virtues of blind obedience. He told his audience that once, during his military service, he had been insulted by an officer. He had responded only by replying "Yes sir." As some youngsters left the meeting, they picked up on that curt response, and repeated a spirited "Yes, sir!" The entire atmosphere created the feeling that Jabotinsky belonged to a "different" school of thought and that there was no inner understanding between him and the greater majority of volunteers from the workers' camp.[32] In their perspective, the Jewish battalion marked a deviation from their preferred way of life, whose focus was on productive labor. In Jabotinsky's eyes, the battalion was everything. The external mannerisms, blind discipline, and deadening routine were all acceptable to him as being necessary for the establishment of a genuine military unit. The workers, however, wanted to set up a popular militia whose ranks were manned by citizens recruited for a special assignment, on a temporary basis.

The legion did not realize the high hopes that had been pinned on it. In September 1918, Allenby launched a lightning attack on the north of Palestine; and in a few weeks the war was over. The Jewish battalions did not participate in the conquest itself. Their blood was not shed for the sake of Palestine. Instead of being given an opportunity for acts of valor, they were ordered to guard prisoners of war. The degrading routine of army life was not sweetened by more exalting and adventurous action. Overnight, the legion had changed from the precursor of the coming of the messiah into a bitter disappointment.

At the time of the great ardor and excitement that had surrounded the setting up of the legion, Yavne'eli expressed his hope that it would be the nucleus for a new myth, one that would galvanize the link between the Jewish people in the Diaspora and its heroes in Palestine.[33] On the face of it, the legion, indeed, contained many of the ingredients that myths are made of: It was the first Jewish army in two-thousand years; could boast a flag, an insignia, a partially Jewish command, and Jewish officers; and was part of an army that had conquered Palestine. Notwithstanding these advantages, the unit did not become a myth. Even the "Scroll of the Legion" (Jabotinsky's account of its history) is more along the lines of a necrologue—a gravestone to its memory—rather than an attempt to create a myth.[34] The fact of basic failure—that is, that the legion did not realize the expectations of its members and had not shed its blood for the homeland—is still insufficient to account for the lack of interest in transforming it into mythical material. After all, hard and sobering facts have never stood in the way of the creation of myth. Thus, it would appear that the key to understanding why the legion was not mythologized and did not become a component of the emerging Jewish Palestinian mythos should be sought in another domain, namely, the content of the message the legion communicated. Its message was apparently not in tune with the spirit of the times and the needs of the public.

Signs of a decline in the popularity of the battalions appeared immediately after the occupation of Galilee. As time passed and it became evident that there was little purpose to their military service, the frustration of the recruits mounted. What ideology was unable to accomplish, boredom and difficult conditions of service did. Men from its demoralized ranks began voting with their feet and deserting. Those who had opposed the battalions now found new strength. The return of A. D. Gordon to active involvement (he had been caught up in the recently occupied area) added public weight to the opponents of the legion. He did not attribute any importance whatsover to the legion. In his view, the British would have conquered Palestine anyway, for interests of their own, with or without Jewish assistance. The decisive fact in Palestine, he maintained, was not whether a number of Jews took part in the war for its conquest but, rather, whether Jews were living there, settled on their land, and working its fields. From a moral viewpoint, it was permissible to defend existing possessions but not "to be a wheel—even a fifth wheel—on the chariot of a conquering army of lords and slaves."[35] The best of A. D. Gordon's writing was dedicated to a resolute struggle against adoration of the notion "by blood and fire," and for a return to the former center of gravity of the movement, namely, labor and settlement.[36]

A debate was published in the journal *Ha-Poel ha-Tzair* pro and contra the continued existence of the legion. In this exchange, Avraham Katznelson came out in support of its continuation, while Nathan Hofshi was dead set against it. Katznelson interpreted the decline in the popularity of the legion as symbolizing the difference in the attitude toward power among Jews and non-Jews, to the detriment of the former: "They rely on their strength, and we on our weakness; they count their bayonets, and we our slaughtered."[37] In contrast, Hofshi, with great pungency, set out the position of the pacifists. He described the existence of a Jewish army as "a catastrophe, both a national and human disaster." He argued that it was necessary to negate the slogan "In blood and fire shall Judea rise again," replacing it by the old one, "Our life consists of nothing but labor," since physical toil was the only wellspring for the right to national life: "If the bitter day should arrive when we are convinced that there is no possibility for survival of the people except by the aid of the fist, we shall say, 'It is better to perish rather than to have our hands sullied in blood'."[38] There was something in the tone and content of these words indicative of a change in the atmosphere on the street: The intoxication with the legion was already a thing of the past. A few months earlier people like Hofshi had been derisively labeled "onion scraper" or "vegetarian." Now their opinions were listened to, and their nonviolent perspective, even in the extreme radical version espoused by Hofshi, was felt worth a hearing.[39]

During the entire course of the dispute, Brenner avoided expressing a set view. He did not enlist, and he revealed a bit of what he really was thinking by a sarcastic remark referring to Rachel Yanait's statement to the effect that the land would be purchased by blood. He also voiced his opposition to furthering the myth of the legion.[40] Brenner crowned the description of his meeting with A. D. Gordon, in which the latter had thoroughly lambasted the legion, with a quite meaningful motto. It was apparently quoted from the words of his old friend: "Our faith in the messiah is the fruit of our weakness or, also, the cause of our weakness. In any event, our messiah won't be riding on a stallion when he comes."[41] Brenner had little sensitivity for the kind of great hopes that had quickened the pulse of his comrades who had enlisted. He was too empirically minded—oriented toward experiencing reality—to indulge in visionary flights. Yet he refrained from saying anything in public against the legion. Gradually, his position came to light. When the Hebrew edition of the book by Henryk Sienciewicz, *By Fire and by Sword,* was released by Stybel Publishers in Warsaw, Jabotinsky published a laudatory review, emphasizing the educational value of this action novel: "We need young men who know how to ride a horse, climb trees, swim, use their fists, and fire a rifle."[42] In contrast, Brenner wondered why Stybel had decided to "present us with this stupid and superficial book, this hollow novel by a poet of the Polish aristocracy."[43] When he came to criticizing Jabotinsky, he used Jabotinsky's preference for Sienciewicz over Knut Hamsun to underscore the fact that he did not belong to the common fold.

Jabotinsky's proclivity to use rhetoric and borrow concepts from the world of international politics and his extreme demands prompted Brenner, as early as 1920, to compare Jabotinsky with the pompous hero of Italian nationalism at that time, D'Annunzio, the conquerer of Fiume: "Programs full of people at rigid attention, personal influence, explosive demands in the newspapers, the clashing of swords (of iron or paper?)—in short, the farcical poet and hero with that vaudeville show of his staged in Fiume."[44] Jabotinsky tended to give great importance to the Jewish army and to praise military style and military regimentation (with all that that life entailed) as an ideal for the education of the young. This aroused feelings of both animosity and ridicule in Brenner: "A state we don't have, work we don't have, and he tells us, 'Be militaristic!'?" On the other hand, Brenner was unable to accept the position of the pacifists. For someone like Brenner, who had been brought up under the impact of the experience of Jewish helplessness and who treated self-defense in Eastern Europe as a sacred duty, the idea of negating *any* use of force by Jews (even for self-defense) was unacceptable. During the general euphoria characteristic of the heyday of the legion, the British conquest, and the soaring expectations for immediate redemption here and now, Brenner reported on the arrival of the first ship bringing immigrants to Palestine since the war. The ship was carrying several hundred orphans from the pogroms that had broken out in the Ukraine during the course of the Russian civil war. He ended his report with the following words: "It is good that this small remaining camp has been brought to the safe shore. . . . And in our joy, should we ask, Is it 'safe'?"[45]

The political changes did not alter Brenner's basic feeling that Jews in Palestine were sitting on a volcano. Thus, he replied to Hofshi's demands for total rejection of the use of force by saying, "He who carries coals to our Newcastle and wishes to preach to us about the ideal of the 'ewe', which gives itself up for slaughter out of extreme piety, . . . he, too, is committing a painful error."[46] It is true that a land cannot be colonized by the sword. Yet if in the process of settlement, defenders are needed at the side of the builders, Brenner proclaimed, both will be blessed.[47]

This view gained popularity in the light of the growing frustration with the legion. It became obvious that Jabotinsky's demands for turning the battalions into a Jewish regular army had little chance of being realized. The slogan "Palestine will be built in a military manner or not at all," which had excited many people just a year earlier, was supplanted by an old slogan coined by Nahman Syrkin, the first ideologist of socialist Zionism, namely, that "Palestine will be built along socialist lines or not at all."[48] The antimilitaristic proclivities of the majority of the recruits drawn from the ranks of the workers gathered strength conversely with the waning of the attraction of the legion. Most of them had not given serious thought at the time they enlisted to how long they were volunteering for. After all, who thinks about that at a time of such elation? But now there were more and more individuals—among them organizers of the legion, such as Dov Hoz, a student from the Herzliya Gymnasia and a close friend of Eliyahu Golomb—who emphasized its transitory character. It had always been considered something temporary, for the need of the hour, they stressed. Thus, the idea of reestablishing a permanent army was out of the question.[49] The notion of a popular militia was broached as an alternative to a standing army, a pet conception in Jabotinsky's thinking. It was felt that a professional army devoted to nothing but military life corrupts its members, stimulates aggressive urges, and can even be misinterpreted by neighbors as an expression of belligerence toward them. In contrast, no one can doubt the right of workers to defend themselves and the fruits of their labor. Worker self-defense springing from the midst of sweat and toil, was a version that acquired an ever greater canonical status among the workers.[50]

As noted, the waning of militarism as an idea was due in part to its failure in practice—because of the marginal role assigned to the legion by the British and the depressing reality of everyday barracks life. One of the conclusions drawn from this was that a more modest form of defense was preferable: a popular militia, without uniforms and pretensions but under the rule and command of the Jews themselves.[51] This concept was given public approval in June 1920 when the convention of the Ahdut ha-Avoda party* in Kinneret resolved that the establishment of the

*The Ahdut ha-Avoda party was established in 1919 as a result of the merger between the right-wing faction of the Marxist Poalei Zion party, under the leadership of David Ben Gurion, and the "Non-Affiliated Group," consisting of non-Marxist socialist groups drawn from the Second Aliyah, under the leadership of Berl Katznelson.

Hagana (Defense Force) as a broad popular militia was one of its goals. Theoretically, a conflict could arise between the notion of "defense based on work," which suggests an absolute defensive approach, and that of a broad-based militia, whose nature is not necessarily defensive. However, since none of the founders of the Hagana thought at that time of establishing a permanent force but, rather, were concerned about the immediate protection of life and property, this was not a real contradiction.

Even if it was not the intention of the majority of its initiators, the legion ultimately came to symbolize militaristic tendencies that were alien to most of the Jewish community in Palestine, especially the Labor movement there. The message it communicated was not in keeping with basic conceptions that had accompanied that movement from its inception. Its notion of power based on external attributes of strength and on a professional army under non-Jewish (i.e., British) authority, was alien to the fundamental thinking of the greater majority of those who had supported this activist adventure. The primacy of labor, which appeared to have been momentarily swept under in the great wave of enthusiasm for military duty, returned, regaining its primary role in the ethos of the Labor movement. A land is to be gained by virtue of labor, not by dint of conquest: This axiom expressed the conclusion of all the leaders of the movement. They recognized the need for self-defense but felt it should be limited in scope, temporary, and of a nonprovocative nature. The legion became a symbol of a conception that was basically alien to the movement. If one adds the fact that the legion was unable to point to any impressive successes or acts of great valor, this appears sufficient to explain why it was not mythologized. One of the principal objectives of myth is to propagate a pedagogical message formulated on the basis of what the myth exemplifies. As it turned out, the legion was unable to serve except as a negative example.

Ultimately, the first dispute on the issue of the use of force ended with the retreat of the activists.

Tel Hai as a Defensive Myth

The legion, with its five thousand men, took on a marginal role in the history of the Yishuv, receding ever more into the background over the course of time. In contrast, a small clash between Jews and Arabs in a remote corner of Northern Palestine became a national myth virtually as soon as it occurred, a myth that retained its power over decades. The Tel Hai incident, which ended with the death of Trumpeldor and his comrades, can serve as a paradigm for the development of a Zionist myth, shedding light on the psychological and emotional needs of an entire movement.

In actual point of fact, the Tel Hai incident was not a matter the Jewish community in Palestine should have been proud of. According to the Sykes–Picot Treaty of 1916, the north of Palestine was to be part of the French sphere of influence. There were several Jewish settlements in the region, the northernmost one of which was Metulla. During the war, a few more settlements were established, including Kefar Giladi and Tel Hai, populated by members of Ha-Shomer and other workers. Several dozen persons were concentrated in the two settlements. The area was of major importance from a Zionist viewpoint, since it contained most of the sources of the Jordan River, considered the only serious source of water in Palestine. After the British occupied Palestine and the French established control in Syria, this region became a kind of border area between the British and French forces. Tension there mounted from the beginning of 1920, prior to preparations for the Arab nationalists' crowning of Faysal as monarch in Damascus in the spring of that year. The lack of clear governmental authority in the area led to the emergence of irregular forces, some of which were supporters of Faysal, others simply robbers and brigands.

The decline in security along the northern border triggered a dilemma: Should one remain there or withdraw from the area? The inhabitants of Metulla, level-headed farmers and family men, decided to leave the village, their houses and possessions, and to depart by way of Sidon to wait for better days. In contrast, the young workers in Kefar Giladi and Tel Hai resolved to stay on. They approached the leaders of the Jewish community in Palestine with urgent requests for food and other supplies and, in particular, for more men to come to their assistance. Their requests were answered only to a very limited extent. The Zionist Commission in Palestine, the body representing the Zionist Organization to the British authorities, washed their hands of the entire matter, since it was unclear whether those settlements were indeed located within the designated British Mandate territory. The Provisional Council of Jews in Palestine, a body made up of representatives of the Jewish public drawn from the various political parties and currents, did not show much resourcefulness. Those in the center and on the right viewed the whole affair as some sort of secret plot by the Left to augment its power. Jabotinsky's assessment was that the workers in these two settlements had no prospects for resisting an attack and advised that they be evacuated until the political fog had lifted. Representatives of the workers requested that assistance be sent, but they did not prove any more resourceful in organizing any expedition in time. While the convoy bringing help was on the road, they encountered refugees from Kefar Giladi and Tel Hai who had evacuated the settlements after a clash had erupted on March 1, 1920 between Arabs from near-by Halsa and Tel Hai settlers. It was in this fight that Trumpeldor and five of his men were killed.[52]

The myth of Tel Hai began to crystallize even before the incident had occurred, as if that point in Palestine's wild north had been specially singled out to serve as a symbol over and beyond its practical importance. There was a prescient feeling that it was the fulfillment of some earlier expectation, as in a drama where something alluded to as a possibility in the first act finally occurs in Act III. Some two months before the clash, a worker of Tel Hai, Aharon Sher, one of the most affable of the young members of the Second Aliyah, traveled down to Jaffa and submitted an article for publication to the Ahdut ha-Avoda periodical *Kuntres*. Written in a very simple and modest style, Sher's piece called for assistance for the northern settlements in the light of the mounting tension in the region. Subsequently, that article was completely forgotten, except for one line in it that later became a slogan, a call to battle, a symbol: "A place once settled is not to be abandoned."[53] Sher was killed soon after on February 1, 1920, while plowing in the field.[54] In the deliberations within the Provisional Council on whether to defend Tel Hai and Kefar Giladi or to evacuate the settlements, Labor movement leaders such as Berl Katznelson and Yitzhak Tabenkin voiced sentiments in line with Sher's battle cry. It is true that from a practical point of view, Jabotinsky was apparently right when he asserted that those settlements could not be effectively defended. But they contended that abandoning them would have graver significance than making them the object of a battle. Tabenkin claimed that the Arabs understood only one thing, namely, force and that if the Jews were to retreat in the face of a threat of violence, then they would end up retreating all the way to the desert. The only way Jews could assure their right to the land was by "an obstinate, desperate stand, without looking back."[55]

The report on the Provisional Council meeting in the moderate paper *Ha-Poel ha-Tzair* (the organ of a moderate left-of-center party then opposed to the legion) contained the principal components of the myth. "We are not a people of warriors," said the editorial "and our entire purpose in settlement is to create a national and political position in our homeland on the basis of mutual understanding and amicable relations with our neighbors. *Yet wherever Hebrew soil is drenched with the sweat of Hebrew workers, and with their blood, that place is holy to us, and we have no right to abandon it.*"[56] This appears to be the first time that this concept— linking sweat, blood, sacredness and nonabandonment into one web—was defined as a binding principle.

The mythologization of the event began immediately after the day the clash occurred in Tel Hai, the eleventh of the Hebrew month Adar. There were few factual descriptions published: The details were apparently not known and did not carry weight. What was of significance was that six workers, "loyal and brave, people of labor and peace" (as was stated in the famous "Yizkor" (In memoriam) written by Berl Katznelson after the incident)[57] had "perished while guarding the motherland."[58] Up until that time, the concept *moledet* (motherland) had not been much used in Zionist literature. "Land of our forefathers" had been the more common expression. After the Tel Hai affair, there were more frequent references in the papers to the "motherland" and its defense, perhaps as a secular alternative to the previous concept, laden as it was with religious connotations.

It was known that a battle had been fought in Tel Hai and that Trumpeldor and his comrades had died there while resisting. This was the first time in Jewish history for two thousand years that Jews had preferred to die in battle rather than to retreat. The clash in Tel Hai was viewed by many as proof that Jews were capable of defending themselves and that it was no foregone conclusion that every time they were attacked, they would be beaten. One of the writers of *Ha-Poel ha-Tzair* wrote:

> Since the day we were exiled from our land, the awesome words have haunted us everywhere: "I will send a faintness into their hearts in the lands of their enemies; and the sound of a shaken leaf shall chase them" (Leviticus 26:36). And all our lives we prayed: . . ."Please make us proud and courageous. . . ." Your glorious and heroic death has given us grounds for hope that our people will return to a new life, like that hero of alien lore who, on touching his land—his mother—was rejuvenated.[59]

The connection between bravery, a contact with the soil, and the renewal of the vitality of the people seemed to be obvious. Brenner, full of a sense of impending disaster (as always), was also stirred by the events at Tel Hai: "When the hour of harsh trial arrives, will each one of us—the name of Trumpeldor and his comrades on his lips—stand fast in that place which fate has assigned him?"[60]

The figure of Trumpeldor embodied traits conducive to mythologization. Handsome, a hero in the Russo–Japanese war (in which he lost an arm), Trumpeldor did not have a trace of militarism in his character. When his friend expressed amazement that he had not asked for an officer's rank in the Russian army, he answered that he was planning to immigrate to Palestine to establish a colony there, since "we'll be at home there and not among strangers." And what if anyone were to say to him in Palestine, "Go and be gone from here, contemptible creature. You are a stranger in this land!"? He said, "I will defend by force and by the sword, I will rise up and defend my fields, my rights," adding, "and should I fall in battle, I will be happy, knowing for what I die." Yet he immediately qualified what he had said: "But it is virtually certain that we will not fight or die. There'll be no need for that. There will be a need for labor, and we shall work."[61] From that time on, he made serious efforts to establish an agricultural colony in Palestine, and lived for a time in a commune in Migdal, near the shores of the Kinneret. During the war, he was active together with Jabotinsky in promoting the Jewish Legion. Yet as soon as the revolution broke out in Russia, he hurried there and organized He-Halutz (The Pioneer), an organization of young persons who intended to emigrate to Palestine and to build the land according to socialist ideals. He preceded his comrades and emigrated to Palestine to organize their immigration. Back in Palestine, he attempted to counter particularistic tendencies in the young labor movement, hoping to overcome these by setting up a general organization of workers. While busy with these various plans and efforts, he learned of the desperate situation of the workers in Galilee and hastened to Tel Hai to assist them. Death overtook him there.

According to a story that spread like wildfire across Palestine, he had uttered the Hebrew equivalent of the Roman apothegem "Dulce et decorum est pro patria mori." Jews were not known to say such phrases when dying. A Jew was prepared to die as a martyr for the glory of God's name, but not in a fight for a homeland. Indeed, even in the deliberations preceding the incident at Tel Hai, one of the participants declared that it would be a shame should people die there, since "one soul from Israel is dearer" than any material loss.[62] Just how great the emotional impact was of the report about Trumpeldor's words at his death can be seen from Brenner's reaction. As noted, Brenner rejected the attempt to create a myth surrounding the guardsmen in the book *Yizkor,* viewing this as misplaced pompousness. He ridiculed any exalted tones in respect to supposed deeds of glory. At that time, he wrote a eulogy for one of the legendary figures of the Yishuv, Michael Halpern, and the reader cannot tell what is stronger in his description—his sense of compassion or of sarcasm toward the old man who waxed poetic about his pretended glorious exploits. He ended his eulogy with the words: "Now you, too, are silent at last. . . . That is better. Silence is appropriate."[63] This was not the tone Brenner used in relation to Trumpeldor: "Didn't we all hear the echo of the silent and exalted call of the one-armed hero: 'It is good to die for our country'? Good! Blessed he who dies in this consciousness, Tel Hai his pillow of earth."[64] Despite Brenner's avoidance of flowery rhetoric and any exposure of feelings, the silent pathos of Trumpeldor contained a certain inherent truth that Brenner could not overlook. He was disgusted by the rhetoric of self-sacrifice but paid tribute when confronted with true devotion.

The nature of the myth was fixed quite early. The eulogy delivered by Berl Katznelson on those who had fallen can serve as a model to illustrate the components of the myth. The "Yizkor," a prayer for the memory of the dead, is removed here, as in the book *Yizkor* of the Second Aliyah, from any religious context. Instead of being directed to the God of Israel, the prayer is addressed to the *people* of Israel, who are asked to remember the pure souls of those who had fallen in battle. The "Yizkor" does not contain a jangling of swords or call to vengeance. The fact is underscored that those who were slain were "people of labor and peace"—simple workers who, by their toil, "risked their lives for the dignity of Israel and the land of Israel." The two components of honor and land are interlinked; Jewish honor, a sensitive topic since the inception of Zionism, is being redeemed by the readiness of the young to stand fast and fight back. The land is being redeemed by the work of the young and their defense of the land, in accordance with Sher's principle, "A place once settled is not to be abandoned." It is the soil that creates the psychological and physical attitude necessary for the willingness to fight. Consequently, life on the soil brings about a renewal of Jewish dignity. In the narrow context, Berl deals with the defense by the plowers of Tel Hai of the land they cultivated. But his words can be interpreted as referring to the defense of *all* the land of Palestine, that is, the defense of the right of Jews to Palestine. This fact is linked with the last sentence of "Yizkor," in which its author requests that mourning should continue "until the day Israel returns and redeems his stolen soil." Katznelson did not explicate what the expression "stolen soil" meant, nor was there any need to. The code was understood by his milieu, and the ambiguity was necessary for more than one reason. The text implicitly expressed the claim to Palestine as the birthright of the Jews—against any other possible claimant to the land.

There were two layers—overt and covert—in the "Yizkor." In the overt domain, the message transmitted lacked militancy and aggressiveness. There was not the slightest reference there to the cult of blood or the slightest assertion that shed blood was the source of claims to ownership. Those who had fallen were simple workers defending the fruits of their toil. These were men who had not intended to fight but were ready to defend to the last the piece of land they had saturated with their sweat. This was an antithesis to the slogans during the heyday of the legion, which claimed that a country was supposed to be acquired by blood. Here, one had the notion of a country gained by sweat and that the sweat justifies the fight for it. This was a point the whole movement could rally around. The journal *Ha-Poel ha-Tzair* commented: "It is not with blood that we wish to redeem our land, it is not by the sword that we wish to conquer it but, rather, by physical toil. . . . Yet we will not give up one handful of the soil of our homeland, we will not abandon even one position. And where one has fallen, thousands will come to take his place."[65] In the covert domain, both Berl's "Yizkor" and the pages of *Ha-Poel ha-Tzair* were permeated with the strong conviction that possession of Palestine by Jews would entail not only coping with the physical elements but also with human resistance. What during the Second Aliyah had been only a theoretical discussion on the danger of national conflict or a nagging sense of a constant existential danger now became open Jewish defiance in the face of imminent hostility. The message was, "You will not succeed in deterring us by force."

If one examines the simple facts of the clash at Tel Hai, it is evident that what occurred there was, indeed, a failure. Assistance did not arrive in time, and the defenders were basically abandoned to their fate. As for the principle "A place once settled is not to be abandoned," Tel Hai, Kefar Giladi, and Metulla were, in fact, abandoned. In respect to the criterion embodied in Tabenkin's words "If we withdraw from Tel Hai, we will retreat all the way to the desert"—that is, that it was imperative not to retreat due to the conclusions the Arabs might draw from such a move—there was, in fact, a pullout from the entire area. The political issue involved—fixing of the northern border and inclusion of the sources of the Jordan within the boundaries of the British Mandate—was not raised at all in public discussion at the time and did not play any role in the myth. From the French and British viewpoints, this marginal clash between Arabs from Halsa and the Jews of Tel Hai was of little import in deciding the fate of this region. Ultimately, from a practical point of view, the position of Jabotinsky and the Zionist Commission was vindicated. They had assumed that the critical situation in the region was temporary and that for that reason, it was wiser to withdraw and return later under the protection of the British than to make a hopeless stand. From the operational–military perspective, the clash was grave as far as the number of casualties was concerned. Yet that number bore no relation to the scale of the attack. Rather, it derived from bad luck and the unexpected turn of events not anticipated by either the Arab attackers or the Jewish defenders. All this had no impact on the crystallizing myth.

A year after the clash at Tel Hai, *Ha-Poel ha-Tzair* commented, "A year has passed now, and on the graves at Kefar Giladi [where the fallen were buried] the miraculous buds of a national myth are sprouting"—a myth that was having an enormous impact on Jewish youth in the Diaspora. "The people of Tel Hai are becoming a myth," the writer explains, "because their enterprise is becoming a reality."[66] He was referring to the emergence of the Third Aliyah. Among its immigrants were the members of the Labor Battalion, many of whom had been disciples of Trumpeldor in He-Halutz. Moshe Gluecksohn, later the editor of the liberal daily *Ha-Aretz* and renowned for his moderate views, now wrote that in answer to the slaying of the six at Tel Hai, six thousand pioneers had come to Palestine. In this way, the people of Tel Hai had "in their death, bequeathed to us life." This expression, used by Bialik in connection with Jewish martyrdom, took on another meaning now—concrete, almost palpable.[67] "In their blood, the mountains of Galilee were bought and acquired for us."[68] There now appeared for the first time the notion that the defense of Tel Hai and the casualties suffered there had earned the Jews the right to the northern border—not as a rational explanation of the events supported by facts but, rather, as a sentimental presentation. It was claimed there that the sheer fact that Jews finally did return to the abandoned settlements and that the north of Galilee was indeed included in the British zone proved indisputably that the Tel Hai incident had, indeed, had a major impact.[69]

The growth of the myth surrounding Tel Hai sparked great enthusiasm. One of the spiritual leaders of the romantic youth movement Ha-Shomer ha-Tzair, referring to He-Halutz, wrote: "Like any religious movement, it does not require slogans or paragraphs in a program. What it needs is living and fertile symbolism: *mythology*." And he explained the significance of the myth: "Motivated by this myth, sweet boys and dreaming girls, smiling like infants, march toward the great sacrifice. Motivated by it, thousands ascend the mountain to the hidden temple of revival."[70] Covered by the layers of flowery rhetoric in which the myth was enveloped lay its central core: the model of self-sacrifice. The meaning of sacrifice was now somewhat different from the original example of Trumpeldor and his comrades—a sacrifice not of blood but of sweat. The option of sacrificing blood, however, remained in the background—an undesirable option, but one from which there was no flinching.[71]

A reference to ancient myths soon appeared. The ancient myth intermingled with the modern one, generating a kind of interlocking chain of Jewish valor, stretching from the "generation of the conquerors of Canaan," the Hasmoneans, the heroes of Yodefat and Gush Halav, on down to the valiant defenders of Tel Hai. The enormous impact of Hebrew poetry is evidenced by the use already made of the epithet "conqueror of Canaan" as employed by Tchernichovsky just a few years earlier.[72] Traditional symbols, such as the contrast of the few against the many, the weak against the strong, present in the hymns of Hanukkah, now took on a new vitality. Tel Hai was presented as the symbol of national destiny—the struggle of the few against the many and the weak against the strong and the accomplishment of a pioneering mission. The perseverance of Hasmonean and his sons was compared to that of the fighters of Tel Hai.[73]

The Tel Hai episode was immortalized in a number of poems that became extremely popular. While the Tel Hai myth was centered basically on the principle "A place once settled is not to be abandoned" and presented the tradition of Tel Hai as an obligation for promoting continued immigration, physical labor, and settlement throughout Palestine, the poems focused more on the heroic figure of Trumpeldor and emphasized the element of his bravery and self-sacrifice, along with the dimension of work. The one-armed hero, who plowed the fields by day and carried a rifle at night, became the topic for popular balladry. Even Jabotinsky, who had been opposed to the defense of Tel Hai, paid homage after the fact to the sacrifice of Trumpeldor and his comrades. He wrote a poem about them, and as befits a myth-generating poem, he relied on another myth. In the poem "From Dan to Beersheba" he noted that there was not a square inch of land in Palestine that had not been soaked by Jewish blood. Blood is the principal motif in the poem, the element that provides continuity between past and present. The high point of the poem lies in the declaration that the blood of the conquerors, or tillers, of Tel Hai is purer than any other blood shed in Palestine. Aside from extolling self-sacrifice, the poem lacks any message. In contrast, a poem by the poet David Shimonovitz (Shimoni) deals with the lesson of Tel Hai and can serve to highlight the educational message that the labor movement attached to these events.

> Like a vision of hope,
> Like a redeeming message,

An invigorating melody,
Day of Tel Hai, ring again:
The wonder has not vanished yet,
Even in captivity and prison,
Since the rock is still vigorous,
The rock of Israel!
This day will be remembered in trembling,
By a people longing for redemption.
This day is glowing evidence
That the dignity has not yet departed.
Since the vigor is still fresh,
Despite the draughts of thousands of years,
And the purity of valor still flowers
In faithful hearts.[74]

The basic apprehensions of Zionist thinkers in general, and the Labor movement in particular, regarding Jewish vitality as evinced by deeds of valor melted away in the face of the bravery shown at Tel Hai. The events there were seen as eloquent testimony not only to the fact that the small group of pioneers in Tel Hai were prepared to sacrifice themselves but also that deep in the Jewish soul flowed wellsprings of self-dignity and willingness to sacrifice. These qualities pointed to the presence of that same vital force without which a people cannot survive. Passages and phrases from that poem by Shimonovitz appeared in various contexts in periodicals of the youth movements and other publications. It was enough to mention one or two phrases to evoke the association. The combination of lofty language and an extremely simple national message created a romantic atmosphere that invited self-sacrifice and readiness for self-immolation. In Shimonovitz' poem, the lesson of Tel Hai was transposed from the domain of action—work and defense—to a more exalted, almost metaphysical plane.

Tel Hai also became a site for a national cult. A unique monument was erected near the graves of Trumpeldor and his comrades: a roaring lion, symbolizing the "lion cub of Judah," that watches over the Hula Valley from the hills of Upper Galilee. Transforming a place of burial of heroes into a pilgrimage site and focus for a cult is quite familiar from history. Yet this appears to be the first such instance of the creation of a secular cult at a grave site in the annals of Jewish history, and it remained unique for quite some time. Every year on the eleventh of Adar—Tel Hai Day—members of the youth movements have made a pilgrimage to the monument. The day was integrated into the educational program of the youth movements (especially that of the young workers, Ha-Noar ha-Oved) as a holiday in the full sense of the term. The holiday combined the messages of labor, courage, love of the land, and the principle "A place once settled is not to be abandoned."[75] As the years passed, the more distant the actual event became, the more it took on mythical dimensions in the consciousness of the young. These dimensions were strengthened by the use of phrases and expressions from the poems and songs about Tel Hai that were regularly sung each year and from Berl Katznelson's "Yizkor," which was also recited at every commemoration of the holiday.[76] During the 1930s, the ritualization of Tel Hai Day in the form of a yearly pilgrimage to the site and the reading of the same, almost canonical, texts and poetry and singing of the same songs in a solemn gathering was already an established tradition.

As I have mentioned, Tel Hai had a double message. First of all, there was the element of bravery: The Jews had not retreated but had fought to their death. When Sheikh 'Izz al-Din al-Qassam, a famous Arab terrorist of the day, was killed together with his comrades in 1935 in a clash with the British army in the mountains near Nablus, Ben Gurion described the incident as "*their* Tel Hai," that is, a case testifying to their self-sacrifice and bravery, which also had the potential ingredients of a national myth. On the other hand, Tel Hai had a clearly defensive message: "We have no aspirations for the domain of others or to conquests by the sword. The Hebrew worker came to Tel Hai with the *plough,* was driven out from there by the sword, and returned to Tel Hai with the *plough.*"[77] As Mordechai Kushnir defined it, the basic message was "martyrdom by standing fast."[78] Yitzhak Tabenkin, one of the leaders of Ahdut ha-Avoda, termed this "the apotheosis of labor and the tie to the soil."[79]

A myth is made up of a core story about an event that took place, elaborated by a further layer of legends, messages, and symbols. By using the concept *myth,* we express neither doubt in, nor confirmation of, the truthfulness of the facts on which the myth is based. What interests us are the psychological and public needs that generated a certain story in public imagination and transformed it into something larger than life, giving it a special, almost transcendental meaning. The messages and symbols the myth communicates seem to us far more important than the question, What is the factual core of the story, and what is the mythic sheath in which it is enveloped? The messages and symbols are bound up with an additional question, namely, Why did a special myth emerge at a certain place and time? This question also can be asked in connection with the myth of Tel Hai. What was the reality in 1920 that engendered the need for a legend of the Tel Hai type? In the history of Jewish colonization in Palestine, there had been no precedent for the principle "A place once settled is not to be abandoned." Emphasis on the sacredness of the place that was "conquered" by Jewish labor was likewise an innovation. Right from the inception of the new Jewish settlement—and especially during World War I—settlement sites were vacated and abandoned without attributing any particular importance to such a move. In actuality, even after the Tel Hai incident, Jews continued to abandon places that had been settled earlier.

Tel Hai must be comprehended against the background of events that coincided with it. The end of the war and the first two years after the British takeover were marked by an ever-more-acute sense of struggle between Jews and Arabs in Palestine. Under the Turkish regime, Jews and Arabs did not dare to express national aspirations. Jews sufficed with talk about labor on the land, while Arab national consciousness was as yet in its formative stages. The British occupation opened floodgates and liberated instincts that had been long repressed. The outbreak of Jewish and Arab nationalism was accompanied by a mounting mutual awareness. The Arabs were cognizant of the Balfour Declaration and followed, with lively interest and growing apprehension, any change in the status or behavior of Jews in Palestine. Overnight, the Jews changed from being *dhimmi,* (i.e., tolerated infidels under Islamic rule) to rivals laying claim to the land and exercising considerable influence with the authorities. The Jews now demonstrated growing confidence. In Arab eyes, that new self-assurance was evaluated as a form of insolence. The Jewish sense of ownership of the land, concealed during the Ottoman period, now erupted into the open and functioned to strengthen Arab fears. But the main reason for Arab apprehensions was the basic change that had taken place in their previous status as a predominant Muslim majority. At the time, anti-Zionist feelings were greatly exacerbated by the upsurge in Arab nationalist fervor—focused up until 1920 on the Hashemite Faysal, candidate for the ruler of Greater Syria—and the concurrent apprehensions of the other contenders for Palestine, namely, the Jews, whose position seemed greatly strengthened.[80]

The growing nationalist trend among the Arabs did not go unnoticed by the Jewish community. They reacted with misunderstanding, bewilderment, and mounting anger in the face of the mild British reaction to manifestations of Arab nationalism. Such manifestations included articles of incitement in the press, the appearance of nationalist organizations, and the holding of meetings at which fiery speeches were given and anti-Zionist claims vociferously asserted. The Turks, when they withdrew, left significant amounts of light weaponry, which the Arabs then took. Although the Jews also succeeded to a certain extent in filling their storerooms with arms, the Arabs had a tradition of familiarity with weaponry, and most knew how to use a gun. When the British authorities demanded that they hand over their rifles, the Arabs still continued to keep their personal weapons. The Jews, in contrast, in the first upsurge of trust in the new rulers, handed over a portion of the weapons in their possession. The years 1919 and 1920 were accompanied by an ever-steeper decline in physical security in the frontier areas of the country. Under the Ottomans, the whole country was under the same ruler. Now, the areas on the eastern bank of the Jordan river from the Sea of Galilee northward and all of Northern Palestine were ostensibly under the control of Faysal. Actually, a state of near anarchy prevailed, with gangs of armed men roaming the countryside. A Jew was occasionally murdered while at work in the fields or on the road. There were now marauding attacks by bedouin on colonies and theft of cattle on a scale that had been unknown under the Turkish regime. The decline in security led to the awareness—more a feeling than a rational insight—that the Arabs constituted a genuine competitor for Palestine. Not a *potential* competitor (as was the assessment during the Second Aliyah) but, rather, a second full claimant to the right to the land, expressing that claim principally by massive physical presence and aggressiveness.[81]

During the Turkish period, the question of the borders of Palestine had generated little interest: The Ottoman Empire rendered that issue superfluous. Now it became a matter of political and public discussion. The question focused on the boundaries of Palestine that had been debated at the Versaille conference. Of equal importance was the question of Jewish settlement *within* Palestine. The early days of British rule had spawned hopes and plans about Jewish settlement, systematic and rational, that would ultimately lead to Jewish colonization throughout the length and breadth of Palestine. In the initial stages, Jews were to settle in the four corners of the country, which were the less inhabited areas, in order to avoid confrontation with the Arab inhabitants and also to determine the future borders of the country.[82] Consciousness of the geography of colonization was a part of the new era, generated by its prospects and risks. It was only at this point that the concept of the *sefar* (frontier) emerged in Palestine. Jewish settlement throughout the land acquired an ideological dimension: The Arabs declared that they would prevent Jewish colonization from spreading in Palestine by refusing to sell them land. The Jews interpreted the threat to their tiny, isolated settlements not only as stemming from the insecurity in the new frontier areas but also as an indication that Arabs would attempt to reduce the boundaries of Jewish settlement. The question was whether the Arabs would succeed in restricting Jewish settlement or not. The crux of the matter was no longer the question of financial means or the relationship with the authorities, as in the Ottoman period. The future of the Zionist enterprise now seemed to be dependent on whether the Jewish settler was prepared to endanger his own life and that of his family by locating in regions remote from the main centers of Jewish settlement. Such regions were characterized by dubious government control and considerable Arab presence, both in numbers and fighting ability. This, basically, was the definition of *frontier*.

The slogan "A place once settled is not to be abandoned" became timely and relevant due to the new circumstances that endowed territory and borders with a new importance and placed the burden of Zionist realization at the doorstep of the Zionist settler. The turn to national idealism and readiness to sacrifice was a natural outcome. The search for symbols that would present settlement in frontier areas in particular, and the principle of settlement in general, as sacred was in the air. This was the reason why, during deliberations on the defense of Tel Hai, the representatives of the workers spoke as though they were addressing History personified. By the same token, the idea made its debut in the periodical *Ha-Poel ha-Tzair* regarding the sacredness of a place drenched with the sweat and blood of workers—even before a single shot had been fired at Tel Hai. This also explains why Aharon Sher coined the slogan "A place once settled is not to be abandoned" even prior to the disturbances in Tel Hai.

Tel Hai was not just a story of bravery but of bravery of the "right kind"—bravery that integrates courage, resoluteness, modesty, settlement, physical labor, nationalism, and socialism. This was a civilian sort of courage, without manners or pretensions, without ranks and discipline, devoid of militarism. It served as proof of the advantage of the pioneer who risks his life as contrasted with the "organized" bravery of a regular army. It was also proof of the need and importance of independent Jewish defense, not subject to the British authorities. In more than one sense, Tel Hai was the antithesis of the Jewish Legion. If the legion symbolized the flush of aggressive optimism of the first days under British control, Tel Hai symbolized the return to the older concept that Palestine would not be conquered by the British for the Jews, nor, indeed, by any act of conquest by the sword. The land would be "conquered" by settling it, by making a stubborn stand in each and every place. The self-assured but short-lived aggressiveness was supplanted by a long-termed, obstinant perseverance that made the ultimate success or failure of the Zionist enterprise dependent on the *Jews* and their resoluteness.

One of the features distinguishing the Tel Hai myth is the almost total anonymity of the Arab attackers. Their identity was in fact known: They were neighbors of

Tel Hai and Kefar Giladi, both before and after the incident. Nonetheless, in the descriptions of the clash, the identity of the attackers was not pointed out; and at a later stage in the development of the myth, they were not alluded to at all. It is noted that an attack took place, that Trumpeldor was injured and died and other comrades of his killed (without any indication of the circumstances)—but nothing else. In the mythical narrative, it was not clear where the attackers came from or where they disappeared to. In the "canonical" description of the attack on Kefar Giladi that took place several days later, the story always was that the attackers demanded to check whether there were any French hiding at the place, just as they had requested at Tel Hai a few days earlier. This demand added a foreign, nonlocal touch to the Tel Hai episode, as though it did not derive from the sphere of relations between Jews and Arabs in Palestine. That is possibly the key to an understanding of the anonymity of the attackers in the myth that developed. The question of Jewish preparedness to fight and resoluteness of purpose was an internal Jewish matter that was bound up with the norms of Jewish behavior. The Arabs were marginal to the topic, as though not affecting its core. There was need to educate people in terms of a myth of staunch bravery and self-sacrifice. On the other hand, the self-image communicated by the myth was that of "men of work and peace," who come with intentions to promote peace and development. If the attackers had been depicted in detail, they naturally would have constituted a focus for hatred. Since they remained anonymous—not just individually but even in respect to national origin—it was possible to educate people in terms of a myth of bravery without teaching them to hate. On the other hand, this placing of the attackers in a veil of obscurity also led to the delegitimization of them and their aims. They lost their human shape and form and became stereotypes. While the defenders of Tel Hai took on a dimension greater than life, their attackers were portrayed in flat and nebulous dimensions: a kind of symbol of the force of destruction pitted against the power of creativity and construction.

The 1920–1921 Riots and the Birth of the Defensive Ethos

If contemporaries had been asked whether Tel Hai marked a shift in their conception of Palestinian realities, they most probably would have replied in the negative: When the Tel Hai incident took place, Zionist hopes were still high, there were still expectations for a rapid colonization of Palestine by multitudes of Jews; moreover, there was still a solid trust in the British authorities. The events at Tel Hai were explained as deriving from the political confusion rampant in the region, involved in a struggle between the forces of Faysal and the French in Syria. Nothing of that kind could occur under a British administration—or such was the general assumption. But two events soon transpired that changed the vague, unfocused mood of the previous year into a new understanding of the situation, destined to serve as an emotional, psychological, and rational foundation for the accepted Zionist policies during the next fifteen years. When the shift in perspective came, it found a symbol, a parable, a paradigm in the myth of Tel Hai.

This marked the birth of the *defensive ethos,* a term that here denotes a complex of attitudes, guiding norms, and ethical and educational concepts that shaped the worldview of a substantial proportion of the Jewish community in Palestine in respect to relations between them, the Arabs, and the British. Such an ethos is molded by a certain self-image of the individual in relation to his environment. Yet in a reciprocal fashion, the ethos reshapes that image as well. The dialectical relationship between ethos and reality derives from the constant tension between the principles a person is bound by, and feels committed to, and his actual everyday behavior. While the myth may be the product of a one-time event that affects human imagination and consciousness, the ethos is created slowly, the product of a process of clarification of ideas and fragmentary attitudes that crystallize in the course of time into a system of guiding principles. Such principles make up the implicit—or, at time, partially tacit—foundation of the ideological or political superstructure. The defensive ethos was also formed in this way. It was not explicitly formulated anywhere by any leader. Nonetheless, the ethos was central in the education of an entire generation. It determined social norms and was significantly responsible for the patterns of thought and behavior that evolved and even for the accepted rhetoric of the time.

The years 1920–1921 witnessed two outbreaks of Arab violence against Jews. The first, the disturbances during the al-Nebi Musa celebrations in April 1920, were limited to Jerusalem. A large angry crowd of Arabs surged through Jaffa Gate into the narrow alleyways of the Old City and attacked Jews whom it encountered along the way. There were also attempts by Arabs to assault Jews in the newer sections of Jerusalem. The second outbreak of violence occurred on May 1, 1921, and continued for several days. This time the center of trouble was Jaffa and the surrounding area. Fifteen young pioneers were killed in the Immigrants' House in Jaffa. Jewish passers-by were cruelly murdered. The writer Y. H. Brenner and five persons who were with him (two of them also writers) were murdered near their home in an Arab neighborhood near Jaffa. There was an attempt to attack Petah Tikvah; Kefar Sava and other small settlements were abandoned and set ablaze. Jewish property was pilfered.

The al-Nebi Musa disturbances took place under the unblinking eye of the British military regime that was charged with exercising supreme authority in Palestine until the signing of a peace treaty with Turkey. Modern research on the military regime has shown that its leaders, Field Marshal Edmund Allenby (at that time commander of the Egyptian Expeditionary Forces) and Major General Sir Louis Bols, the chief administrator, were, to put it mildly, quite cool toward the pro-Zionist policies followed by the British government and even tried their hand at various manipulations aimed at bringing about what they considered a necessary volteface. They wished to unite Palestine and Syria under Faysal's crown in order to strengthen the British toehold in the Middle East against the French and, conversely, to rid themselves of the Zionists. There is evidence pointing to the fact that this position on the part of the heads of the army was made known to Arab leaders and was taken into account by them. There was some basis to the Jewish claim that the authorities were hostile to them and were not fulfilling their obligation to stop incitement and nip angry disturbances in the bud. Just before the al-Nebi Musa celebrations, the army had been ordered to leave Jerusalem, a decision described by the Palin report on the riots, an indubitably anti-Zionist account, as a serious mistake. Thus, it is no surprise that the Jews interpreted the attitude of the military regime to be one of support for the rioters and their objectives.[83]

It appears that the British government saw the events in a similar light. A short time later, the decision was made in San Remo regarding the division of the Levant into spheres of influence between Britain and France. Palestine, including its northern section, was subsumed within the territory under British authority; and the Balfour Declaration was incorporated into the agreement between the Great Powers on the future of Palestine. Even though the peace treaty with Turkey had not yet been signed (due to the revolution of Ataturk), the military regime was disbanded. Herbert Samuel, one of the leading figures in the British Liberal party and a proclaimed Zionist, was appointed high commissioner for Palestine in June 1920. For the Jews, this constituted a kind of vindication of their complaints against the military administration and of their expectations regarding the British.

Yet the events of May 1921 erupted less than a year later, under the enlightened administration of Herbert Samuel. They were far worse than those of the previous year in respect to scope and number of victims. Samuel reacted vigorously, calling out the army, making numerous arrests and engaging in collective punishment, particularly the levying of fines on Arab villages involved in the attacks. Yet he also acted to assuage Arab opposition by his declaration of June 3, 1921, whose tone was conciliatory toward the Arabs. Samuel announced that Jewish immigration would henceforth be limited by the economic absorptive capacity of Palestine and that Arabs would be given representation in the legislative body to be set up in Palestine.[84] Samuel's policies were interpreted by the Jews as submission to violence and capped the process of accumulated disenchantent with the British authorities.

Whoever reads the press of that period cannot but be impressed by the intensity of the sense of grievance and anger among broad circles in the Jewish community in Palestine toward the British authorities. The 1920 disturbances called to mind analogies with the pogroms in Russia. "Will Jerusalem Become Like Kishinev?" shrieked the headline in one newspaper.[85] "The pogrom against Israel in Eretz-Israel is still continuing," Berl Katznelson proclaimed.[86] And Brenner quoted a passage from the poem by Bialik "Al ha-shehitah" (On the Slaughter): "The hangman! . . . you have an arm with an axe, and as for me—all the world is my gallows."[87] Following the disturbances in May 1921, Yavne'eli declared that the riots in Jerusalem the previous year were reminiscent of the Kishinev pogrom; and those of May 1921 reminded him of October 17, 1905 in Russia, the day that signaled the outbreak of the cruel anti-Jewish riots as part of the wave of reaction in the wake of the first Russian revolution.[88] Quotations from Bialik's "In the City of Slaughter" in the press strengthened the association with Kishinev.[89] When members of the Hagana were arrested by British officers, an analogy was immediately drawn between these arrests and those by Russian officers of members of Jewish self-defense units during the pogroms in Russia. This analogy occurred quite naturally to those whose youthful experiences were weighed down with painful memories due to the failure of Jewish self-defense efforts as a result of the intervention of the Russian army on the side of the rioters.[90]

At the same time, the paper *Ha-Ivri* (The Hebrew) in the United States published an article that denied any similarity between the disturbances in Jaffa and a genuine pogrom. The article stated that what had transpired in Jaffa was basically a number of skirmishes between Arab rioters and Jews defending their possessions—a depiction that was more suited for Zionist propaganda purposes in the Diaspora. This explanation provoked Kushnir's anger, who called the authors of the statement "charlatans," insisting there had been "a genuine, full-fledged pogrom in Jaffa."[91] Yosef Aharonovitz also rejected any attempt to present the events as some sort of squabble: "In Jaffa, there was a murderous pogrom," he stated, "and it is impossible to turn participation in such riots into a matter of simple theft."[92] The analysis of the events in terms of a model based on Jewish–Gentile relations was shared by moderates and activists alike. M. Gluecksohn responded to the 1921 disturbances with the statement, "This is a 'pogrom' Russian-style, an ordered pogrom organized right from the beginning in all gory details, a pogrom with scores of dead and hundreds of injured, with acts of violence and looting by masses of people, . . . with policemen participating in the acts of murder and pillage,"[93] while the activist Ben Gurion wrote, "We who experienced the pogroms knew quite well that without the wish of the authorities and their open or clandestine backing, actively or passively, the task of the pogrom cannot succeed." He went on to depict the riots as a pogrom, secretly encouraged by a segment of the authorities.[94]

Use of the pogrom model derived initially from the availability of that paradigm to this particular public. Persons who had grown up in the Pale of Settlement knew and understood only one type of majority–minority relationship—a situation of domination in which the majority forces its supremacy on the minority by the use of force. The image of the Jew as victim contrasted with the image of the Gentile as murderer, as in Brenner's "He Told Her," was a constituent part of their self-image. Accordingly, Jewish weakness was the cause of the pogrom: "Wherever our numbers are few among many Gentiles, *we are in exile,* even in the place called the Land of Israel."[95] This was also how they explained the hatred of the Arabs toward Jews: in Palestine, like Europe, antisemitism was due to incitement: "It is a fact that the masses of Russians, Poles, and Arabs are capable of being incited against us and incessantly instigated to commit acts of murder and rape against us, without any limit."[96] The papers were full of reports about the terrible pogroms taking place at that time in the Ukraine, which had cost the lives of scores of thousands of Jews. The new states established after the war, such as Poland, Romania, and Hungary, were quick to express their newly won sovereignty by means of anti-Jewish riots. Quite naturally, it was assumed that what was taking place in the Ukraine, Poland, and Romania—and concomitantly in Palestine—had a common cause: hatred of the Jews, an enmity that bore no relation to Jewish actions or failings. Rather, according to Brenner, its source was that same curse of being a weak minority scattered among the Gentiles.[97]

There was a double conclusion drawn from this analysis. On the one hand, it encouraged the self-image of the innocent victim, the sacrificial lamb. Zionism wished to liberate Jews from their self-image as victims; but in a paradoxical way, the situation that had developed in Palestine did a great deal to fuel that image, since it gave Jews an immanent sense of being the right side. On the other hand, the conclusion drawn was that Jews should do their utmost to liberate themselves from the curse of being a weak minority subject to the whims of the majority. Already shortly after Tel Hai, Shaul Meirov, one of the activist graduates of Herzliya Gymnasia and a central figure in matters of the Hagana, had declared, "We must be a force in the land." He was not referring to military might but, rather, to power in the sense of demography and colonization. Only the immigration of thousands of young Jews could significantly alter the situation in Palestine. The answer to the disturbances was a bolstering of the Jewish community and the expansion of the Zionist foothold in Palestine.[98]

The central component in creating the analogy between pogroms in the Diaspora and riots in Palestine was the stance of the British authorities as perceived by the Jews. The pogroms in Eastern Europe were marked by the fact that they destroyed the sense of security that comes naturally to a person under a stable government. The Jews were not always able to prove that the authorities were really guilty of collusion in planning or carrying out the riots. Yet, from the point of view of the Jewish man in the street, it made no difference if the authorities, for reasons of their own, did not mete out severe punishment to the rioters or hesitated to take forceful steps against them. Nor did it really matter whether some local official, acting on his own or based on a distorted understanding of his superiors' intentions, took steps that could be interpreted as offering encouragement to the rioters—or, indeed, even assisted them. To the Jew, it was ultimately immaterial whether the army prevented Jews from responding against the rioters due to fears that such clashes would get out of hand. The decisive factor was the concrete reality: the fact that he and his family were being exposed to violence and that the authorities did not defend them. Supplement the picture by the arrests and trials of Jews who were found carrying arms or implicated in a fight, and the Jews had no need of any further proof of government policy. It was clear to them that this was an evil-minded, hostile government, which had handed over the Jews to the mercy of the rioters and then was brazen enough to sentence them for the crime of self-defense.

That same logic was applied to the British authorities in Palestine. When the military administration adopted a stance hostile to the Jews during the al-Nebi Musa riots, it became obvious to them that they were facing a familiar situation. First, the authorities reacted with excessive patience to the violent Arab demonstrations in favor of the crowning of Faysal in Damascus, disturbances that developed a strong anti-Zionist character. After that, during the riots, British official behavior was a mixture of indifference and criminal neglect. Finally, they arrested Jabotinsky and his men, who had tried to organize self-defense in Jerusalem. After the riots, they decided to calm the situation and withheld permission for the Jews to put on a large public funeral for the victims. As if that were not enough, most of the rioters were not brought to trial, while Jews caught carrying arms were punished with heavy sentences. Those stiff penalties were canceled only in the framework of a general amnesty that included both rioters and defenders. Thus, it is not surprising that Berl Katznelson referred to the dead victims by the ancient Hebrew expression *harugei malkhut* (those slain by the government). The phrase derived from the annals of Jewish martyrdom after the Bar Kokhba revolt and was used in reference to the Ten Martyrs executed by the Romans. He compared the order issued by the authorities temporarily prohibiting Jews from entering Palestine to the command by the Roman emperor Hadrian forbidding Jews from entering Jerusalem following the Bar Kokhba revolt. The restrictions on Jews after the riots reminded Katznelson and his comrades of the events in Russia in the spring of 1882; after the "hot" pogrom in the south came the "cold" pogrom of the May laws restricting the area of Jewish settlement and heralding the end of the era of relative liberalism toward Jews. When describing the empty streets of Jerusalem during the funeral of the victims, Katznelson added, almost inadvertently, "There was only a Jew-baiting Russian Orthodox family standing on the balcony, looking on."[99]

When even more violent riots broke out under the administration of Herbert Samuel, spontaneous reaction patterns among those who had grown up in the Pale of Settlement were further intensified: Even a high commissioner who was Jewish and a Zionist had adopted policies similar to those of the Russian authorities. Once again, "Arabs murdered and looted, and the Jews are the ones held up as guilty and put on trial."[100] The authorities came out with an explanation that the disturbances had been the result of clashes between Jewish communist and anticommunist demonstrators on May Day. Jews regarded this as sheer nonsense. How could an internal political quarrel among Jews result in horrible murders in a hotel for immigrants in Jaffa? Government communiqués spoke about clashes between Jews and Arabs and tried to play down the fact that the attacks had come solely from the Arab side. Arab policemen had taken active part in the riots and went unpunished. On this occasion as well, the British were quick to arrest Jews who, in defending themselves and their families, had injured their attackers. Stolen Jewish property was not returned, the murderers of Brenner and his friends were not brought to justice. The British put a stop to immigration, and even Jews already on their way to Palestine were returned to their ports of embarkation. Samuel's speech on June 3, 1921 completed the picture: Once again, the rioters were being encouraged by the authorities—violence was rewarded, the victims punished.[101]

There is a debate among historians about Herbert Samuel's policies. Some view his moderate approach as a factor that functioned to reduce Arab militancy and helped postpone the next outbreak until 1929. According to this perspective, his policies were not harmful to the development of the Jewish national home and actually furthered its development by creating a respite period of eight full years of peace—indeed, the longest unbroken span of peace in Palestine under the British.[102] In contrast, others regard his appointment of al-Hajj Amin al-Husayni as mufti of Jerusalem and his attempts to establish a legislative council as vain attempts to appease the Arabs, actually fostering the radical forces among them at the expense of the moderates.[103] In the eyes of Jewish contemporaries at the time, Samuel was viewed almost as a national traitor, who had sold the Jewish birthright in Palestine for a proverbial mess of red pottage.[104]

From that point on, the euphoric attitude toward the British did not reemerge. The view of A. D. Gordon, who right from the beginning had seen them as imperialist occupiers, interested solely and exclusively in what was good for their own rule in Palestine,[105] was shared by many. Again and again, complaints were heard that under the Turkish administration, life and property had been more safe and secure than under the British mandatory regime.[106] The Jews expected that the British would bring home to the Arabs, once and for all, that Palestine was meant for the Jews. Many argued that if the Arabs would finally realize that the authorities were determined to establish a national home for the Jews, they would accept the fact as inescapable and cease their opposition. The unsatisfied Jewish demand for the British to take a "strong hand" constituted an additional source of bitterness and suspicion.

Seemingly, one might have expected that the Hebrew press would be involved in a continuing debate with the Arab claims and arguments against Zionism, Jewish immigration, the Balfour Declaration, and so on. In actual fact, no such discussion developed in the Jewish press. Once again, the Arabs were accorded a marginal role in the great debate being waged in the Hebrew papers, this time with the British. The Arabs were presented in stereotypic fashion, as anonymous figures, a "wild mob," "agitators," or "effendis." There was no Jewish–Arab dialogue and, conversely, no Arab–Jewish dialogue. The two sides in the Palestinian triangle preferred not to establish any direct contact between themselves, but, rather, to communicate by the intermediary of the British administration. The reason was that each of the two sides claimed the land for its own. Any recognition of the adversary and his rights meant giving up the claim to exclusiveness of one's own rights. Yet indirectly, the manifestations of popular Arab nationalism had a significant impact on the Jewish side. As long as the "Arab national problem" existed only in potentia, members of the Poalei Zion party did not hesitate to preach openly and forcefully about the inevitable national clash looming on the horizon in Palestine. But when they were faced with the actual phenomenon, they suddenly stopped acknowledging its existence and began to come up with surrogate explanations for the presence of Arab opposition to the Zionist enterprise.

The early mandate period is characterized by, among other things, the fact that most of the Jews in Palestine shut their eyes to the emergence of an Arab national movement there. Viewing Arab hatred of Jews in terms of a European-style anti-semitism provided a simple and self-evident explanation for Arab manifestations of opposition to Jewish immigration and settlement in Palestine. The claim that anti-Jewish manifestations by large masses of Arabs did not derive from their own authentic interests but were, rather, the fruit of *agitation* (especially by Christian Arabs) was virtually a logical extension of this notion.[107] It was argued that in addition to the Christians, the effendis and the other Arab notables living by exploitation of the Arab masses were also to blame for the agitation. In Russia, as well, enlightened Jews explained the riots there by claiming that the masses had been stirred up by agitation, instigated to violence by reactionary priests and government officials.

The subject of the subliminal Arab–Jewish dispute centered now on whether Jews were causing any real harm and damage to the Arabs. The Jews argued that Arabs were spreading idle rumors about them: contentions that the Jews intended to rob the Arabs of their land, take their property, and even their women. Jewish immigration was portrayed as a project aimed at dispossessing the Arab population; and the Jewish community, which served as a source of income for Arab villages, was depicted instead as a source of exploitation and robbery. That kind of specious argumentation was easy for the Jews to deal with, since any informed person had to acknowledge that Jews investing capital in Palestine were creating new jobs and promoting a rise in living standards there, including those of the Arab population. The credibility of Arab arguments suffered as a result.

Thus, the question apparently boiled down to a quite simple one in the eyes of the Yishuv: Was Jewish settlement harming the Arab indigenous population? It was commonly held that the Zionist movement was doing its utmost to assure that no harm came to individual Arabs. Yet this did not provide an answer to the pivotal issue, namely, To whom did the country rightfully belong? In actual fact, this was the central Arab claim: They demanded the right of possession of the land, including the prerogative to prevent Jewish immigration, which they viewed as a factor that in future might endanger their control of the country.

The Jewish response to that claim was ambiguous. Jews demanded their right to settle side by side with Arabs in Palestine, by dint of their historical claim, their current plight, and the promises they had been given. In 1919, when hopes were still flying high, Jabotinsky gave a speech before the Palestinian council, presenting a plan for a Jewish government in Palestine. He did not hestitate to make clear his conviction that that government would have to be exclusively Jewish. The meeting ended with cries, "It all belongs to us, all of it is ours!"[108] In 1920, Brenner made a distinction between Arab opposition to a future Jewish state—for which he had no satisfactory answer—and opposition to Jewish settlement in unpopulated areas. Brenner regarded the latter opposition as unjustified: "We are in the right here."[109] After the 1921 riots, Mordechai Kushnir, the most moderate of the moderates, wrote: "Whether the Arabs like it or not, Palestine is one of the countries open to European immigration. . . . They won't be able any longer to occupy the land simply by sitting with their legs crossed, under their Ishmaelian garb, smoking their waterpipes."[110]

From the early 1920s on, frequent use was made of the argument that the Jews wished to settle only in the areas not inhabited by Arabs. The Jews were not coming to dispossess the Arab community but, rather, to establish a Jewish community side by side. The land was spacious enough for both Arabs and Jews. Brenner protested, "Are all the expanses of Arab lands—half-deserted—too little for the Arab nation that it cannot tolerate the notion that Jews will come to settle in a land that was once the land of their fathers when, for some of these Jews, that settlement is a question of life or death?"[111] Both Jabotinsky and Brenner shared the idea that the existing world order, including the current division of lands, was not morally binding and was subject to change. The socialist Zionists espoused the notion that just as it was unjust for one individual to have great wealth while others starved, so it was unjust for one people (the Arabs) to have land without end while another (the Jews) was doomed to destruction, lacking any territory it could call its own.[112]

This argument came close to defining the existence of two systems of justice: formal and supreme. It did not negate the Arab point of view (as other arguments put forward by the Jews had) but set out priority scales based on the needs of two peoples. Existential necessity gave priority to the Jewish claim to settlement in Palestine over the Arab claim that it be kept for the Arabs alone. This approach was indicative of a subliminal level in the debate, with Arab arguments familiar from the Arab press. On the whole, the dispute was not carried on directly with the Arab side. Rather, it was an internal Zionist debate on the question of the inherent justice of the Zionist claim to Palestine and whether it did or did not entail encroachment on Arab rights.

The clearer the magnitude of Arab opposition and the sensitivity of the British to that opposition became in 1920–1921, the greater was the tendency to focus Zionist arguments on the socioeconomic aspects of Jewish–Arab relations, disregarding the broader political issues. Characteristically, it was Brenner who gave the most pointed expression to this approach: "Perhaps tomorrow the Jewish hand writing these words will be stabbed," he wrote prophetically: "Some 'sheikh' or 'hajj' will thrust his dagger into that hand in front of the British governor." But Jews who remained alive would recount, "We are the victims of evil, the victims of the wicked desire to augment power and wealth, victims of imperialism. . . . Not ours. We had no imperialist ambitions. We did not want to create governments here. We only wished to settle desolate lands with Jewish immigrants, to establish a Jewish community side by side with that of the Arabs. The Arab laborer is our brother. . . . The day will come when there will be a strong tie between us, the workers of Israel, and them, the Arab workers."[113]

This passage contains most of the main components of the defensive ethos: The Jews have no aspirations to rule in Palestine—they are coming to colonize the wilderness and to develop regions that to date have gone unploughed. They bring tidings of progress and development to the land, for the benefit of all its inhabitants. The clash of interests between Jews and Arabs is not the product of a genuine contradiction in interests between two peoples. Rather, it is the result of agitation and incitement by the reactionary elements among the Arab people, who are motivated by the fear of the progress and change now being ushered in by the Zionist colonization. In addition, the ruling power, guided by imperialist motives, has acted to undermine relations between the two peoples in Palestine: In order to maintain power, it is pursuing a policy of "divide and rule." "Perfidious Albion" is infamous for such policies; thus, it is no surprise that its rule has led to Arab outbreaks against Jews. The likening of the high commissioner to Pontius Pilate put the final touch on this picture.[114] In Palestine, as elsewhere, the Jews remain the weaker element, insulted and injured. But while the strength of antisemitism is growing throughout the world and Jews are losing ground everywhere, there is still hope in Palestine that in the distant future, the Arabs will understand their folly.

The passage highlights the major change that took place in self-image and understanding of the realities in Palestine during the early period of the British Mandate. During 1919 and 1920, Zionist hopes soared. It appeared as though all the dreams of Jewish independence in Palestine were on the verge of immediate realization. Yet it soon became clear that there was another claimant to Eretz Israel, who vented his anger in violent outbursts. These outbreaks exposed once again the true reality, namely, the existence of an active volcano threatening to erupt in Palestine. In his eulogy on the murdered Brenner, Rabbi Binyamin wrote: "Brennerke! The volcano is still smoking, erupting, spewing forth its dark and fuming lava."[115]

The ambiguous stand of the authorities toward these realities also became evident. There was a need to respond to this official stance on two planes: that of action and that of ideas. In the domain of action, the conclusion was "In your blood shall you live!" The defiant slogan "In place of each one killed, thousands more shall come" began to circulate in the Yishuv soon after Tel Hai; it took on added meaning after the riots of 1920 and 1921. Following the 1921 disturbances in Jaffa, a poem by David Shimonovitz was published that gave vent to the action principles of the defensive ethos:

> Do not mourn,
> Do not lament,
> In a time like this,
> Do not lower your head . . .
> Work, work!
> Plowman, plow!
> Sower, sow!
> In a bad moment,
> Double the toil,
> Double the product.[116]

The optimistic aggressiveness of earlier years had vanished. People grit their teeth and braced for greater efforts. Yet this was not a return to the ethos of the Second Aliyah. At that time, no one had thought in earnest about the real possibility of a Jewish state in the near future. Now, in the secret recesses of the heart, hopes stirred for Jewish sovereignty. But the naive candor of the early years of the British Mandate did not return—a self-imposed censorship reigned supreme.

The realization that the establishment of the Jewish state would be a lengthy, tiring, unglamorous process intensified in 1922. The five previous years had been characterized by hopes for a "shortcut." The revolutionary era catching fire then in Europe also cast its shadow on Palestine. Everyone talked in terms of historical breakthroughs. The messianic hopes that had sparked the men of the Jewish Legion were triggered by the belief that, in the course of but a few years, Palestine would become a Jewish state. It was in this mental climate that the aging Nordau suggested the idea of instantaneously transporting half a million young Jews to Palestine, accommodating them in temporary camps, like soldiers, until housing and work could be provided. In one fell swoop, he wanted to transform the demographic balance in Palestine in favor of the Jews, thus paving the way for Jewish sovereignty based on majority rule. Jabotinsky was also thinking along similar lines. When he developed his Plan for Temporary Government in Palestine in 1919, he assumed that the Jews were still a minority there and therefore that the British "trustee" should rule the country in the meantime. However, that arrangement was viewed as a transition phase on the way to full Jewish power in Palestine.[117] His untiring campaign until 1922 for the survival of the Jewish Legion was also based on the hidden assumption that it was possible by a single act to change the balance of power in Palestine and to bring about the immediate establishment of a Jewish state. If an important leader like Jabotinsky, who lived in Palestine and was familiar with the situation, continued to think that it was feasible to change demographic and political realities within the course of a few years, it was no wonder that the Jews of Eastern Europe, who clutched passionately at any hope for salvation, gave the events an exaggerated interpretation. At the 1920 Zionist Convention in London, the first Zionist gathering after the end of the war, representatives from Eastern Europe attended, carrying in their pocket lists of proposed ministers for the Jewish state that they assumed was about to be set up.

Ideas about a shortcut were not limited to the Right and Center of the Zionist movement. They were no less familiar, and perhaps discussed even more often, in the socialist wing of the movement. In their thinking, a nationalist vision was amalgamated with a socialist one: At the beginning of the 1920s, the small Labor movement in Palestine was inspired by an eschatological ecstasy bent on immediate realization of its vision of constructing a Jewish society based on socialism. The central concept of the Ahdut ha-Avoda party was the idea that it was possible to accelerate the pace of historical processes by the energetic efforts of a determined vanguard. A similar concept had been elaborated by Nahman Syrkin since the turn of the century and was current in Palestine already during the Second Aliyah, namely, that the Jewish entity in Palestine could be built up by following a socialist path. The success of the Bolshevik revolution in Russia, which stirred the hearts of socialists in Palestine, provided a model for the implementation of the idea. Socialism and an independent Jewish government were, in their view, two interconnected and inseparable components. The two were to be realized here and now. The dimension of immediacy was immanent to the conception of a shortcut. Just as the revolutionaries in Russia did not wait until the historical process envisaged by Marx had come to fruition but forced the issue, the socialists in Palestine should, it was argued, also serve as the midwives of history and hasten revolutionary change there.

This was the idea behind Ben Gurion's proposal to establish the Workers Company of the General Labor Federation of Hebrew Workers in Palestine as a general commune. The workers would be members in that commune, work within its framework, and their needs would be provided for by the commune in egalitarian fashion. The Workers Company was meant to be a stimulus and lever for building Palestine as a Jewish socialist country. At that time, the He-Halutz comrades of the dead hero Trumpeldor set up a unit named the Brigade for Labor and Defense in Honor of Joseph Trumpeldor. Its objective was defined as that of "building up the land by means of a general commune." They were also certain that their vision could be made concrete reality within the span of a few short years.

In addition to the general enthusiasm for the Bolshevik revolution and the aspiration to emulate the Soviet experience in Palestine, the belief in a socialist shortcut drew its sustenance from the economic fact that private capital remained hesitant to invest in Palestine, an undeveloped country replete with risks and situated far from Europe in the Middle East. The Jewish middle class regarded Palestine as a kind of risky adventure that still had not proved its viability. Consequently, the main human resource available to the Zionist movement was the young pioneer, motivated in equal measure by national and socialist ideals. It was reasonable to presuppose that those young people would attempt to build a society in their own image. The Zionist Organization was preparing to set up a fund for the colonization of Palestine based on the generosity of the Jewish people—the Keren Ha-Yesod (Palestine Foundation Fund). Within a few years, the fund was supposed to raise some twenty-five million pounds sterling. The combination of national capital and young socialists prepared to implement their hopes made the idea of building a socialist society in Palestine—here and now—an option that many considered feasible.[118]

Already in 1920, the sober-minded among the Zionists started to have certain doubts about the shortcut. The May 1921 riots galvanized a change in their thinking. Basically, this was the context of the dispute between Weizmann and Jabotinsky that intensified during those years, touching on the question of the limits of the possible from the Zionist perspective. Jabotinsky still believed that the Zionist leadership could induce the British to pursue policies that would facilitate the establishment of a Jewish national entity in Palestine at an accelerated pace. In contrast, Weizmann felt that the opportune moment from the Zionist perspective had already passed. The frozen sea of international politics (to use an expression coined by Lloyd George), which had thawed during the war, had frozen over once again. British public opinion had increasing reservations about costly policies abroad, resulting from the need to maintain an army and put down local uprisings. British policy in Egypt, Iraq, and Transjordan was aimed at providing a certain degree of independent government in return for guaranteeing peace and quiet and securing British strategic interests. Those interests were principally concerned with safeguarding open routes to India. (Oil did not appear as a central factor until after World War II.)[119] Weizmann believed that under such circumstances, there were no prospects for the Zionist movement to tally up further achievements: Its immediate task was to mobilize its full strength to make the British fullfil their commitments contained in the mandate charter. The center of gravity of Zionist activity would, he believed, have to shift from political efforts to the sphere of settlement so as to provide a demographic, economic, and social base in Palestine. As a disciple of Ahad Ha-Am who found himself implementing Herzl's political program, Weizmann understood relatively early on (and sooner than many of his associates) that the revolutionary moment in the history of the movement had passed and that the time had come to return to the evolutionary modus operandi.

Arab opposition to the Zionist enterprise in Palestine was the central factor in shaping the cautious policy adopted by the British; consequently, it did exercise an indirect influence on Zionist strategy. Yet no less than this, the transition from the shortcut conception to an evolutionary policy was dictated by limitations in human and financial resources and the organizational capacity of the Zionist Organization during those formative years. It had no practical experience in organizing emigration or colonization work; and when it faced the Third Aliyah (1919–1923), it was totally helpless. The new immigrants were unable to find employment in Palestine. After a short time, the Zionist Organization sent a telegram to the Diaspora with the message *Don't come!* The great mountain of the Palestine Foundation Fund had labored and brought forth a mouse: After several years of fund-raising, a total of some two million pounds sterling was collected. Despite its impressive successes in the political domain, the Zionist Organization did not show great competence in mobilizing the Jewish people for the project of building up Eretz Israel. The transition to an evolutionary approach, labeled "one more acre, one more goat," (an expression used derogatorily by some, in praise by others), was due as much to the obvious difficulties inherent in a project of mass immigration and of an urban European people and its colonization in the Eastern Mediterranean as to political problems.

Weizmann's victory in the Zionist Organization over Louis Brandeis and his faction—likewise in 1921—marked the ascendancy of the evolutionary approach. Brandeis and his associates thought in terms of large-scale, carefully planned activities. The first stage was aimed at establishing an infrastructure, only after which the actual colonizing activity would begin. The type of settler Brandeis envisaged was similar to that of the Puritans who had settled North America during the early colonial period. He did not take the constraints of Palestine into account, in particular the problem of timing: Postponement of immigration and colonization to a later date could have run up against unfavorable political circumstances that might have prevented colonization completely. The Zionist Organization had no experienced rural workers at its disposal, as called for by Brandeis. Rather, colonizing work was carried forward by the Zionist pioneers who were available, full of enthusiasm but lacking in experience—experience that could only be gathered by trial and error during the process of colonization. Jabotinsky supported Weizmann in his struggle with Brandeis but soon parted ways with him, unable to accept the latter's step-by-step policy, which he believed conflicted with Zionist interests.[120]

Paradoxically, Weizmann obtained backing from the Palestine Labor movement. The crisis of the Third Aliyah (which peaked in 1923) brought home the realization that hopes for an *immediate* Jewish socialist state in Palestine had no basis. The sense of crisis had begun with Tel Hai and gathered credibility with the disturbances in 1920 and 1921. When organizational and economic constraints were added, many understood that the intoxicating days predicting the dawn of the messianic age were a thing of the past. Now, a gray and tedious period of slow and difficult labor set in, colonizing Palestine by means of a protracted process whose end could not be envisioned. Some were shattered by this realization. The Labor Brigade never recovered from the precipitous descent from the heights of a faith buoyed by the notion of the shortcut to the harsh and sobering realities of the everyday pedestrian problems that the Zionist movement had to grapple with. Others, such as the leaders of the Ahdut ha-Avoda party, adapted to the change with a grinding of teeth. Yet in their secret heart, there continued to burn the hidden ember of hope for the revolution to come—a revolution in both the Zionist and socialist sense.

The evolutionary conception was based on the assumption that time was on the side of the Zionist project and that Zionist policy had to be oriented toward gaining precious time for the purpose of building the Jewish infrastructure in Palestine. The defensive ethos was an integral component of the evolutionary concept: It provided the Zionist enterprise with the requisite breathing space in respect to the Arab problem and the clash with Arab nationalism. The interpretation of the Arab problem based on concepts derived from the domain of Jewish–Gentile relations in Eastern Europe transformed it: From a dispute between two peoples over one and the same piece of land, it was changed into a problem bound up with the backwardness of Arab society. Seen in this light, it was thought that the Arab problem would fade away with further progress and societal advancement. Ironically, the conclusion drawn from this approach was that an Arab national problem did not exist. Hence, after the 1921 riots, most of the editorials in the Zionist press in Palestine and abroad explained the events as the product of incitement.

One exception in this respect was a young leader of the Ha-Poel ha-Tzair party,

Chaim Arlosoroff. In an article published at that time, he noted that the Arab movement in Palestine lacked many characteristic attributes common to national movements in Europe. But, he argued, one key fact should not be disregarded: This was a genuine national movement that had the gift for mobilizing and organizing the masses.[121] Both Arlosoroff and those who denied the existence of an Arab national movement drew a similar practical conclusion, although for different reasons. All wished to reduce tensions and return to a situation of peace and quiet in Palestine. Arlosoroff did not believe in the policy of the strong hand. He regarded a reconciliatory approach as the only effective way to engage in dialogue with the Arab National movement (which is why he had a favorable opinion of Herbert Samuel's policies). The others, in contrast, wanted peace and quiet as a means to settle the land without having to resort to the use of force.

There were several factors underlying the denial of the existence of the Arab problem that was prevalent during the first fifteen years of the British Mandate. First of all, the weakness of the Zionist movement in Palestine played a role. Even in the days of the Second Aliyah—largely a select group of idealistic immigrants— it was difficult for people to accept living in constant conflict with the Arabs. This was all the more true in the mandatory period, when the immigration was no longer composed of young, carefree pioneers but also included fathers of families, especially starting in 1924. The thought of life in the shadow of a volcano may have sounded romantic to youth, but for adults it contained an element that was frightening. At the end of the 1920s, Jews amounted to some 20 percent of the total population in Palestine. Those were not encouraging figures if one lived in the awareness of an unavoidable confrontation with the majority population. It was not farfetched to draw anti-Zionist conclusions from this demographic balance of forces. What was more natural than to suppress the reasons for the danger by presenting the disturbances as resulting from Arab misunderstanding of Jewish intentions, instead of a genuine clash of interests. Given the weakness of the Jewish community in Palestine, the perspective of peace was vital to the survival of the Zionist vision.

Zionist propaganda sought to present the Zionist enterprise to world opinion (particularly British public opinion) as a project of peace that could provide an answer to the injustice done by European peoples to the Jewish people. Accordingly, that solution could not involve large expenditures or unpleasant consequences, such as the oppression of the local population. The propaganda sketched an idealistic picture of a land being built by a unique colonizing enterprise, bringing peace, blessings, and progress to the entire region. Confronting the existence of an Arab national movement would have led to the conclusion that settlement of Palestine by Jews was likely to entail clashes with the Arab inhabitants. Such reasoning might well do harm to the international status and position of the Zionist movement, and reduce its public and political support. The Zionist interest in gaining valuable time necessarily meant avoiding the issue of a Palestinian Arab national movement.

Moreover, the Labor movement in Palestine in the 1920s needed to be reassured by a profound sense of the justice of its way, not only from the national viewpoint but also from the socialist perspective. The magnetic attraction of Soviet Russia was at its high point during that period. Alert and active young Jews in Eastern Europe were attracted by the sun of change rising in the East. In Palestine, the Jewish Labor movement was engaged in a difficult competitive struggle with the Left for the soul of Jewish youth. One of the issues that left-wing opponents seized upon in their attacks against the Zionists was the Arab question: Is the establishment of a Jewish society in Palestine harming the local Arab population? More generally, how does the Zionist movement plan to deal with the existence of an Arab majority in Palestine? On one occasion, a young leader of the underground Zionist youth movement in the Soviet Union met with one of the leaders of Ahdut ha-Avoda, who happened to be in Moscow at the time, and proceeded to bombard him with questions about the "Arab problem." Finally, the latter replied in Yiddish: "Listen, have you already solved the Jewish problem that you're bugging me so much with the Arabs?"[122] If this is how Zionists who risked their lives for their Zionist principles felt about the issue, how much more would others who were on the borderline between Zionism and communism?

The struggle between Zionism and communism also continued among the pioneers who emigrated to Palestine. In the light of the disappointment after the failure of the shortcut approach, all the vulnerable points of the Zionist project were more accentuated, among them the "Arab question." The settlement of the Jezreel Valley, on lands purchased by the Jewish National Fund from the Lebanese Sursuek family, entailed the removal of Arab tenants. This left its psychological traces on the young socialists from the Labor Brigade who had come to settle in the place. The press avoided expressing those sentiments, due to internal censorship; but there can be little doubt that the question was often discussed in the tents pitched in the Jezreel Valley.[123] The boon of material progress Jews were bringing to Palestine could serve as a suitable answer to the embarrassment as long as the national consciousness of the Arab population there was rudimentary. But as soon as the problem could no longer be explained by economic, social, and cultural concepts and had to be faced as an issue of nationalism, the built-in difficulty became far more pronounced. How could a movement aspiring to justice, like that of the Zionists, find itself embroiled in a conflict with another national movement?

In paradoxical fashion, it was their comprehensive belief in the justice of national movements and the right of peoples to self-determination that ruled out the possibility of recognizing the existence of an Arab national movement. Openly acknowledging its presence would have engendered an intolerable welter of internal contradictions. In this regard, the defensive ethos provided an answer to extremely profound psychological needs. That ethos taught that the Zionist project was not one of conquest but, rather, of settlement. It was an enterprise of peace and brotherhood, aspiring to build a socialist society, holding out a hand of friendship to Arabs. For the time being, as Brenner commented, that outstretched hand had been rejected; but in the future it would be welcomed. Objectively, there was a class solidarity and unity of interests between Jewish and Arab workers; but the Arab ruling classes, for class interests of their own, had prevented the simple masses from understanding this fact.

This concept had already been broached by Brenner, on the eve of his murder, in his description of a meeting between himself and some Arabs in the orchards near his home. He describes their appearance as inimical and alien, and they failed to return his greeting. Arabs occupied a low rung on the scale by which Brenner evaluated non-Jews. He certainly preferred Russians or Latvians, placing Arabs on the same level as the "Eastern Poles," whom he despised. Yet he met one young Arab boy, a farm hand; and, in broken language, a conversation had developed between them. Now Brenner's heart longed for that simple young man: "Working orphan! Young brother!" He wanted to have ties with *him,* not with the hostile effendis.[124]

The defensive ethos repressed the basic facts of the existing confrontation between Jews and Arabs, painting it in comparatively optimistic colors. By obscuring the national character of that clash, this ethos proposed other alternatives for the system of future relations between the two peoples, based on economic and social cooperation. It transferred the potential for aggressive feelings from an entire collective to individuals in that community and acted to suppress any impulse for hatred. In a situation of colonization and national confrontation, that ethos advocated a perspective of peace and fraternity. In the eyes of the Zionist socialists, the fact that those who attacked Jews were largely simple workers did not compromise the class explanation, just as the fact that the rioters in Russia had been ordinary people did not prevent Jewish revolutionaries from admiring the Russian masses. The defensive ethos contained a satisfactory explanation for the contradictions of the present and held out hope for a better future.

One of the consequences of this approach was a mythologization of the Arabs. As long as Arabs remained alien to Jews and there was little direct familiarity, that explanation was able to retain its validity. The operative model of Jewish–Arab relations was not based on real, flesh-and-blood Arabs. Rather, it was nurtured by an abstraction, an image of the Arab created by the Jews for their own psychological needs. That apparently helps to account for a paradoxical fact: The Jewish community most distant from, and alien to, Arabs in Palestine was that of the socialist workers.

The defensive ethos blended well with the evolutionary approach in an additional sense, namely, its opposition to setting up an army. Disappointment with the legion had led to antimilitarism. The lesson of Tel Hai was that defense had to spring from labor. The Ahdut ha-Avoda party hoisted the flag of a popular militia, and established the Hagana organization in 1920. Later on, the Hagana was placed under the control of the General Federation of Jewish Workers in Palestine (the Histadrut), founded the end of that year. Brenner, who was present at the Kinneret convention of Ahdut ha-Avoda when the Hagana was set up, waxed uncharacteristically eloquent, using superlatives in his description of the men of the Hagana who had participated in the deliberations (apparently Eliyahu Golomb and Dov Hoz). "Happy the man who was privileged to have been at that occasion," he wrote afterward.[125]

Establishment of a Jewish organ for self-defense reflected a sobering awakening from the illusory hopes placed in the British administration and a return to patterns of traditional Jewish behavior toward the authorities. It also pointed to the fact that the Jews would be a minority in Palestine for a long time to come and would need to be defended against rioters. While Jabotinsky's legion had been designed to demonstrate Jewish superiority in Palestine, the Hagana was meant to conceal the true dimensions of Jewish military capabilities, clothing these in a system of construction and settlement. It constituted a kind of emergency instrument that can prove useful in difficult times but is better if not needed. The legion held out the prospect of a dramatic change in the status of Jews, one that in the end was not realized. The Hagana heralded a new recognition: It was now clear that Zionism would not be achieved by means of dramatic deeds but, rather, by small mundane acts devoid of glory, such as the purchase of land, one acre after the next, and of weapons, revolver after revolver. The barefooted revolutionary and the members of self-defense units from the Diaspora served as models for the Jewish defender in Palestine. The myth of Tel Hai—with its modest bravery, simplicity, and absence of symbols of power— left its impact on the landscape of Palestine and became the prime formative symbol of the defensive ethos.

All this might have been acceptable were it not for one fact: the basic difference between the reality in Palestine and Russia. Despite the minority status of Jews in Palestine, the relationship between them and the Arab majority bore little similarity to that between Jews and Gentiles in the Ukraine. As I have mentioned, the persistent self-image of Jews in Palestine was that they were a nation in embryo, the legitimate lords and masters of that land, aspiring to alter the balance of power there between Jews and Arabs. Although it contained elements similar to clashes between a violent majority and a persecuted national minority, the Jewish–Arab conflict in Palestine was ultimately a clash between two peoples competing for the same country. This fundamental political element was totally lacking in relations between Jews and non-Jews anywhere in the Diaspora. Jews in Palestine were not simply innocent victims and did not view themselves as such. Rather, they conceived themselves as fighters dying in a battle for their homeland. Hence, the model of relations between Jews and non-Jews from Eastern Europe was only externally applicable to realities in Palestine and did not, in fact, provide an answer to the fundamental problem. That was why even Brenner had contradicted himself when dealing with this issue. On the psychological level, there is no doubt that Brenner saw the Arabs in Palestine through the spectacles of the man who had written "He Told Her" and whose sister had been murdered in the 1905 riots in Russia.[126] All his life, he had sensed the dread of the volcano physically. He also despised the Levantine way of life and was anything but enchanted by the so-called magic lure of the East. At the same time, he was cognizant of the fact that in Palestine, Jews saw themselves simultaneously as both a majority and a minority: a majority in their claim for sovereignty, and a minority in their demand for protection. Thus, his explanation that the al-Nebi Musa disturbances were the result of imperialistic machinations by the British demonstrated a surprising lack of consistency.[127] His characteristically open-eyed and sober perspective, devoid of illusions regarding Jewish–Arab relations in Palestine, went through a certain metamorphosis in the last year of his life—as though he, too, had been wooed by the defensive ethos and had embraced it as a factual truth.

For the scholar, the defensive ethos poses certain difficulties. To what extent, for example, did the authors and promoters of this ethos genuinely believe in its fundamental structure? Those structural features included the self-image of the Jew as victim, derived from the analogy to Jewish–Gentile relations in the Diaspora; presentation of the Jewish–Arab clash as a product of class agitation, holding out a positive perspective for the future; and accusations that the British were promoting the conflict for their own sinister motives. The concrete upshot of this was that the clash was accorded less importance and an optimistic belief was cultivated that Jewish settlement in Palestine could progress peacefully. These features appeared in various forms and contexts throughout the entire period of the mandate. At this stage, it is impossible to answer in an unambiguous manner the question to what extent they believed in it. Already in 1920, in his address to the delegation of Brit Poalei Zion, Yitzhak Tabenkin, one of the three leaders of Ahdut ha-Avoda (along with Berl Katznelson and Ben Gurion), used explanations integral to the ethos, such as suspicion regarding the foreign ruler, the negative role of the effendis in the framework of Jewish–Arab relations, and the need for self-defense. Conversely, Tabenkin had certain flashes of insight hinting at a different interpretation, such as the following: "Political necessities are forcing the leaders of Zionism to foster the illusion that we can settle the land peacefully and in agreement with the Arabs."[128] In reference to Weizmann's efforts to arrive at a general agreement with the Arabs, according to which the Jews would recognize Arab sovereignty in Syria in return for Arab abandonment of any claim to Palestine, Tabenkin declared: "I don't believe in a compromise of that kind. Those are false hopes." The frequent use of the concept *false hope* or *illusion* regarding a Jewish–Arab peace agreement is significant. He also added: "There are those who think the problem will be decided by war. But we are not strong enough for that."[129] It would appear that at this point in time, Tabenkin did not share the optimism of the defensive ethos. However, he recognized that the Jews were still weak and rejected the possibility that a violent confrontation at that stage could decide matters in their favor. Consequently, despite his inherent pessimism, he adopted the practical conclusions drawn on the basis of the defensive ethos as an advisable approach, namely, settlement by peaceful means and expansion of the Jewish hold on the land.[130]

These fragmentary comments by Tabenkin suggest the contours of a clandestine debate centered on the key questions of Zionist strategy that was apparently going on at the time, far removed from the limelight of the press. Was it possible to settle Palestine peacefully, or was a violent clash between Jews and Arabs inevitable? In the 1920s, all were apparently in agreement that it was too early to arrive at any conclusive answer. For the moment, the necessity of the hour was to push ahead with settlement of the land; and the explanatory line adopted had to be based on principles of the defensive ethos. There were those who honestly believed its principles, while others accepted only a portion of its elements. And there were some who apparently viewed it as, at best, an expedient propaganda line and an important instrument for education.

II

THE HEYDAY OF THE DEFENSIVE ETHOS, 1922–1936

4

The First Challenge, 1922–1929

After a stormy beginning, the British regime stabilized its position in Palestine. Life entered a certain routine, and the great excitement and agitation that had characterized the early years of British rule abated. It was replaced by the lethargic, slightly soporific atmosphere of a relatively remote colony. The main questions on the agenda were the economy and its development and the absorption of immigrants, while political problems retreated to the periphery of public interest. The stability that prevailed provided a theoretical cast, divorced from reality, to the relatively few deliberations taking place on the great political questions.

That tranquility was suddenly shattered at the end of the 1920s, when the issue of the Wailing Wall burst onto the scene in Palestine, initially in connection with the events of Yom Kippur 1928 and later on in the wake of the August 1929 riots. Those 1929 riots constituted a turning point in the history of Palestine and led to changes in consciousness, psychology, and the accepted rules of the political game. They demonstrated the vulnerability of the Jewish community in terms of both security and politics and highlighted both the strength and the limitations of the Arab National movement. The disturbances also emphasized the erosion that had set in and begun to alter the British conception regarding the pro-Zionist obligations included in the mandate. The disturbances and the political tremors that shook the Palestinian scene stirred a heated political debate in the Yishuv and the Zionist movement and led to an unprecedented sharpening and polarization of positions. Ultimately, the shock waves generated in the wake of the riots subsided; and from the time the Fifth Aliyah commenced in 1932—the largest of the immigration wave down to the establishment of the state—the political dispute began to ease and was once again relegated to the margins of public concern.

In retrospect, these three periods (1922–1929, 1929–1931, 1932–1936) were the heyday of the defensive ethos. It is true that that ethos was the object of contention and attack virtually from the first moment it gained a place in public consciousness. Nonetheless, despite all the attempts to discredit it, the defensive ethos continued throughout this entire era to provide the ideological and political basis for the exposition of the Zionist position on questions pertaining to Palestine. Yet beyond its function as a propaganda device, the ethos played a central role in the crystallization of the consciousness and self-image of the entire Labor movement in Palestine. The defensive ethos generated hopes for a better future, to be achieved in ways that would not contradict the natural moral sensibilities of persons whose worldview was essentially socialist in orientation and who had been educated to an awareness of the sufferings of the weak and oppressed. That ethos fostered a central belief: Not only was Jewish settlement in Palestine fundamentally just, but it could also be implemented without causing any serious injustice or harm to the Arab population. Because of this, it appeared reasonable that such settlement could be realized without having recourse to means of coercion or the use of force.

The influence of the defensive ethos was pivotal in all aspects of the educational system in Palestine. Despite the fact that at times, education apparently proved an inadequate instrument when pitted against everyday confrontations in the street, the open country, or the highway, it played a major role in preventing the emergence of overt expressions of hatred against Arabs among the Jewish community. In mandatory Palestine, hatred of the "natives" among immigrants—a familiar animosity characteristic of colonial countries in which there had been a prolonged and bloody struggle between settlers and the local population—did not surface except among certain fringe groups. To the extent that hatred existed beyond the perimeter of such marginal groups, it was rejected as a norm and relegated to the margins of public consciousness and expression.

The defensive ethos went hand-in-hand with evolutionism: It served as a conceptual ally and a moral buttress for faith in the possibility that Zionism could be made a reality by a gradual process and without historical breakthroughs that by their very nature tend to be bloody. This conceptual complex was bound up with the awareness that the time span at the disposal of the Zionist movement was adequate for effecting the desired transformation in the demographic and economic composition of Palestine and that gradual methods would indeed serve to advance the movement toward its aspired goal. Although challenged, these three elements— the concept of sufficient time, evolutionism and the defensive ethos—held their ground. Consequently, the fundamental assumptions and associated conceptual–psychological superstructure remained intact until the late 1930s.

Opposition to the defensive ethos and its two concomitant basic assumptions was accompanied by the creation of alternative ideological frameworks based on different approaches to force—absolute affirmation or total negation. However, the significant evolutionary developments in the ethos did not take place in the organizations and groupings that were critical of the defensive ethos. Rather, that process occurred within the mainstream current representative of the national consensus at the time, namely, the Labor movement. The central struggle to maintain the defensive ethos or, alternatively, to replace it by another ethos, either militant or pacifist, took place in the labor ranks. The changes that movement underwent in respect to its understanding of reality, and attitudes toward guiding norms and accepted methods of action were ultimately the dominant factor in shaping the relation of the Yishuv to the use of force.

The Impact of the "Years of Small Deeds"

In the annals of the Jewish community in Palestine, the 1920s are regarded as "days of small deeds," and rightly so. The exaggerated hopes of the early years after British occupation of Palestine had resulted in nothing but bitter disappointment. As mentioned before, the ability of the Zionist movement to mobilize the necessary financial resources for an extensive project of settlement proved to be extremely limited. If it had not been for Herbert Samuel, who initiated basic infrastructural development projects in Palestine—in particular the construction of a network of roads, a project that provided the majority of pioneers of the Third Aliyah with gainful employment in 1920 and 1921—most of the young immigrants would have been compelled to leave the country.

This was the nonpromising beginning to a decade that many viewed in retrospect as the decade of lost opportunities of the Zionist movement. After experiencing an economic crisis in 1923, it was soon caught up in a euphoric mood in the face of the first mass wave of immigration in 1924–1925, emanating from Poland. Yet even before that immigration made itself felt, the community was buffeted by the most profound economic crisis in its history, which soon developed into a crisis in Zionist self-confidence. In the 1920s, nobody was certain that this interesting project—Jewish colonization in Palestine—would, indeed, survive. The Jews did succeed in expanding their area of settlement to the Jezreel Valley, and a number of additional settlements were established in the Sharon plain. Yet on the whole, the pace of growth of the Jewish community in Palestine, particularly in economic strength, did not augur well for the future prospects of Zionism. In 1927 the number of those leaving Palestine was approximately double that of those arriving. At the end of the decade there were some 170 thousand Jews in Palestine (150 thousand by other estimates), amounting to some 15 to 20 percent of the population. Leaders like David Ben Gurion and Berl Katznelson and public opinion shapers like Moshe Beilinson, chief journalist at *Davar,* the Labor movement daily, took pains in public to show self-assurance and faith in the future of the movement. Privately, however, many of them suspected that their life project and dream, with which they identified so completely, was now on the verge of collapse.[1]

Given that critical situation, it was doubtful whether the Arab problem, in general, or questions regarding the use of force, in particular, were central in their consciousness as matters of major concern. They were occupied with the problem of finding funds for placing the cooperative workers' enterprise, known as the Ha-Hityashvut ha-Ovedet (Labor Settlement) on a firm footing, providing housing for workers, and creating new sources of employment. All efforts were concentrated on one overriding task: building up the land. Since that project was bogged down and not proceeding properly, such efforts consumed all their energies and abilities. The only years during that decade when there was a serious discussion on the Arab question were 1924–1926, during the brief period of the Fourth Aliyah and the economic boom it brought. The brief respite it created from the elementary problems of survival made it possible for people to dedicate some of their energy to questions of less vital importance in their view—as a kind of luxury.

At the Fourth Conference of Ahdut ha-Avoda held in 1924 in Ein Harod, an important public discussion took place on the Arab question. That party congress can serve here as a kind of laboratory for examining the functions the defensive ethos fulfilled in the reality of the 1920s and investigating the deeper currents hidden behind it. Debate on the Arab issue erupted in the wake of a proposal made by Shlomo Kaplansky—one of the veterans of the Poalei Zion party and among its more important leaders—calling for the introduction of new constitutional patterns in Palestine. Kaplansky had come to the conference from London, where he had been active in Poalei Zion, the party affiliated with Ahdut ha-Avoda. The London office of Poalei Zion had been opened with a specific aim in mind, namely, to foster connections with the British Labour party, regarded by members of the Ahdut ha-Avoda as a sister organization. The situation faced by socialist Zionists in London during the 1920s was not a simple one. The atmosphere in progressive circles was decidedly anticolonial. The future leaders of the national liberation movements in the British Empire were studying at that time at the London School of Economics. Young Palestinian Jews enrolled as students there, such as Moshe Shertok or David Ha-Cohen, wished to establish friendly relations with young socialists from other parts of the world, viewing them as part of the great camp of progress to which they likewise belonged. But it became clear to the socialist Zionists that the world outside saw them differently. The Balfour Declaration and British Mandate served for many as proof that the Zionists were in fact allied with British imperialism. They professed their allegiance to socialism in vain. They were regarded as part of the enemy camp. The contrast between the self-image nurtured by these Palestinian Jews and their image in the eyes of other socialists was a source of much grief and distress for them.

The "Arab problem" played a central role in the rejection of Palestinian Jews by the progressive circles in which they aspired to strike roots and be accepted. Frequently, the question was raised how, in concrete terms, the socialist Zionists planned to solve the problem of relations between the two peoples in Palestine. When the first Labour government came to power in 1924—a party in whose good will the members of the Ahdut ha-Avoda trusted—the directors of the office of Poalei Zion in London searched for a political formula that would make it possible for the Zionists to cast off the image of a movement hiding in the protective shadow of British imperialism. They hoped to effect this change in image by launching an initiative to alter the political system in Palestine in the direction of greater democratization and representation for the local population in the government.

The ideas presented by Shlomo Kaplansky to the party conference in Ein Harod were intended to be a socialist response to the proposals put forward by Herbert Samuel regarding the formation of a legislative council, all of which had been rejected by the Arabs.[2] Samuel's proposals were based on the principle that the Arab majority in Palestine would be properly represented on the envisaged legislative council. But the authority of that council to pass anti-Zionist legislation would be curbed by having the mandate as its binding constitutional basis, not to be deviated from. In addition, British representatives on the legislative council would function to hold the balance of power between Jews and Arabs. Kaplansky proposed that the envisaged legislative council should be more representative and allot the British only a minor role. He recommended the establishment of a legislative body with two houses: The lower house would be based on proportional representation (implying, of course, an Arab majority), while the upper chamber would consist of equal numbers of Jews and Arabs. Any future legislation would require approval by both houses. As an extra precaution, essential issues such as immigration would be removed from the jurisdiction of the proposed council.

That proposal stirred up a storm of disapproval far beyond what might be expected from such a moderate and cautious scheme. The dispute revolved around several fundamental points: At this stage, should the Zionists initiate their own plan to solve the Arab question? Does Kaplansky's proposal protect vital interests of the movement? Is there at present any sense and logic in attempting to find solutions to the Arab question? If so, in what direction should one look? The fundamental assumptions of the defensive ethos were confronted with a concrete political proposal. Kaplansky was well aware of this. Already when he put forward his initial suggestions, he was prepared to defend himself against these assumptions. Indeed, he restated the customary notion that the Arab National movement was undoubtedly led by effendis "who hate us as workers and as bearers of civilization and new ways of life." Yet he qualified that statement by claiming that every national movement starts out in the ruling classes; hence, the Jews should recognize that a great national Arab movement was now making its debut in the East. Apart from that, he declared that his proposal was meant to demonstrate to the enlightened British public that the Jews had their own constructive suggestions regarding the Arab problem, fully compatible with the demands of conscience of the World Socialist movement.[3]

All the leaders of Ahdut ha-Avoda in Palestine were arrayed against him. Ben Gurion, Berl Katznelson, Tabenkin, and Yitzhak Ben Zvi were all adamantly opposed to his proposal. The idea that Jews should actually initiate any sort of political plan was rejected outright. Such a move was viewed as the antithesis of the evolutionary conception of Zionist strategy, which envisioned a gradual expansion of the Jewish foothold in Palestine, postponing the political solution until such a time as the balance of power between Jews and Arabs had shifted in favor of the former. Ben Gurion stated openly that any proposal based on the existing balance of forces would quite naturally prove to be to the detriment of the Jews. For that reason, it was advisable in the meantime to put off political initiatives, concentrating all efforts on practical work in Palestine. Using different arguments, this stance was echoed by his associates in the leadership. Political initiatives were regarded as the antithesis of evolutionism, because they derived from the existing situation and balance of forces, reflecting and consecrating the status quo. In vain Kaplansky tried to prove that his proposal would not be detrimental to the growth and development of the national home. His associates had a telling reply: If it did not harm the Jewish cause, then there was no prospect it would be accepted by the Arabs. And if it was acceptable to the Arabs, there was no doubt that it would be deleterious for the Jews.

There was a kind of symmetry between Arab opposition to the high commissioner's legislative council scheme and Jewish opposition to Kaplansky's proposal. In both instances, based on the perspective of immediate pragmatic interest, it appeared advisable for the two sides to accept the respective proposals. But in both cases, they preferred to forego the tactical advantages for the benefit of the more basic strategic position: Jewish–Arab participation in any kind of legislative council would entail recognition of the mutual rights of the two peoples to Palestine. That recognition was unacceptable to both the Arabs and the Jews (though for different reasons). From the Arab perspective, recognition of the Jews as a people with equal ownership rights to Palestine when Jews made up some 10 percent of the population appeared totally absurd. In comparison, the Jews, although only 10 percent of the inhabitants, felt they were the future lords and masters of the country. For that reason, they regarded abandoning the potential of future growth for present political expedience as a foolish move reflecting a lack of understanding of the historical process—if not worse.

The rhetoric at the 1924 party conference expressed a way of thinking based on analysis of political realities, with a crystal-clear grasp of the basic facts. At the same time, it also contained elements of socialist rhetoric whose connection with reality was at times rather loose, to say the least. The two types of rhetoric were intertwined, and the same person occasionally oscillated freely between one approach and the other. A conspicuous example of this was Ben Gurion. He declared that the Arabs would not be satisfied with Kaplansky's proposal, since they wanted the actual power in Palestine: "Let's not fool ourselves. There's no question here of the *form* of government, regime, or order; rather, it's a matter of who has real power and control"[4]—the power to determine the fate of the Zionist project included. In his view, the dispute was not about appropriate phrasing or constitutional schemes, as Kapalansky and other well-intentioned individuals wished to believe. Rather, the problem involved the very core of Zionist ideology: "We do not recognize their right to rule *the land,* as far as they have not developed it." Latent in this definition was the Zionist claim to the right to change the face of Palestine and the demographic, economic and cultural configurations there by peaceful means. With the same degree of clarity, Ben Gurion proclaimed his opposition to any kind of political decision based on the existing balance of power between Jews and Arabs in Palestine. This was the realistic dimension in his politics.

At the same time, Ben Gurion attributed the absence of any dialogue with the Arabs at the time to the fact that the Arab leadership was made up of effendis, who . despised socialist Zionists not only for national reasons but even more for reasons of social class. Consequently, it was impossible to come to terms, and negotiate, with such a leadership. This argument provided an ideological basis for rejecting the various political proposals, though Ben Gurion had himself shortly before justified that rejection using a realistic line of political argumentation. That composite stance revealed the need felt by Ben Gurion and his associates to find some modus of mediation between their Zionist credo and their socialist outlook. Neither Ben Gurion nor his audience were able to rest content with arguments based solely on national egoism. They needed to account for their motives and aspirations using reasoning borrowed from the socialist, class-oriented arsenal of arguments. Thus, Ben Gurion explained his refusal to consider any political proposals at that point in time by asserting that the current Arab leadership was reactionary. This claim, which (readers will recall) was a part of the system of assertions underlying the defensive ethos, held out a promise for the indefinite future, namely, that it would be possible to converse with the Arab side at some later, unspecified time. Indeed, Ben Gurion added that the potential partner for talks would ultimately be the Arab worker. He waxed poetic when speaking about the natural bond of solidarity between the Arab and Jewish worker: "We, the Jewish and Arab workers, are sons of one country; and our paths of life will be forever linked."[5] On the other hand, Ben Gurion recognized that the process of developing the class consciousness of the Arab worker, still backward and weak, would take considerable time and effort. He contended that Jews had a central task in helping to advance the Arab worker. Two years prior to that, under the impact of the revolutionary fervor that engulfed him in the early 1920s, Ben Gurion declared that the task of the Jewish worker was to "stand at the helm of the movement of liberation and revival of the peoples of the Middle East"[6]—to assume no more nor less than a vanguard role! Now he was careful to avoid such grandiose, farfetched declarations, yet one can still sense in his words the enthusiasm he felt regarding the great socialist mission in Palestine—the challenge of advancing the lot of the Arab worker.[7]

In Ben Gurion's thinking at that time, activity in the domains of class and society was conceived as an alternative to dialogue with the Arab National movement. Ben Gurion, the then incumbent secretary of the Histadrut, invested great energy and considerable human resources in efforts to organize the Arab workers. The 1920s were a decade in which the idea of the "joint union" of Jewish and Arab workers flourished. Yet an examination of Ben Gurion's rhetoric at the party convention in Ein Harod indicates that there were two levels, only loosely interconnected, in his approach. On the first level, he dealt with the Arab problem from a highly realistic standpoint, attempting both to safeguard the span of time necessary for the Zionist movement to settle Palestine by peaceful means and to avoid closing the door on options for future Jewish control of the land. On this pragmatic level, he dealt with the present and not-too-distant future and defined practicable tasks. On the second, more visionary, level, he sketched out a utopian mission whose implications for the immediate present were limited; its implementation, if possible, would occur in the distant future, as a by-product of the realization of Zionist aims.

This argument became quite common currency in the 1920s, due to the difficulty encountered by dedicated socialists in grappling with the unsettling fact that they were locked in a confrontation with another national movement. The mechanisms of human defense against cognitive dissonance facilitated repression of those portions of reality that were likely to disrupt their preferred picture of the world. Harmonization between their socialist consciousness and the actual situation was achieved by giving an interpretation of the Jewish–Arab conflict based on class theories, while disregarding its national contours. Awareness that this was a struggle between two national movements for one and the same piece of territory entailed drawing several painful conclusions—consequences they were unable to deal with at this stage. Their deep-seated conviction that they were not committing any injustice and were embarked solely on a project of building a desolate land for the benefit of all its inhabitants could remain intact only as long as discussion about the problem of Palestine was limited to economic and social spheres. Belief in the possibility of Jewish settlement in Palestine and of changing the status quo there by peaceful means was conditional on the assumption that the Arabs were not national opponents and that, therefore, their opposition to Jews could be placated by economic benefits. But the moment the discussion shifted to a national–political framework, unsettling questions arose that they found difficult to answer.

Second, recognition of the existence of an Arab national movement would, if carried to its logical conclusion, lead to the insight that a violent confrontation between Jews and Arabs was inevitable; that is, it would necessitate coming to terms with the perspective of a future bloody struggle. At that stage in the evolution of the Yishuv, acceptance of such a perspective was inconceivable: After all, the self-image of the movement was that it aspired to peace and progress. Moreover, the balance of power between Jews and Arabs was overwhelmingly in favor of the latter at that juncture. For psychological and ideological reasons, the socialist Zionists needed to suppress and blot out any awareness of the existence of the Arab National movement.

The idea of a joint union and its partial application was the product of this suppression of awareness. Organizing of Arab workers by Jewish socialists looked like a practical answer to the disturbing question, What can be done *now* to help solve the Arab question, given that all proposals for constitutional change are considered invalid? Focus on organizing Arab workers also supported the thesis that it was actually impossible to talk with the current Arab leadership. On the face of it, it was an approach that vaulted national lines, underscoring the superiority of class identity over national identity. It also integrated the situation in Palestine within a global struggle of the forces of progress railed against the forces of reaction, sketching a perspective of peace that would flow from the certain final victory of the World Socialist camp.

The decisions adopted at the 1924 Fourth Party Conference in Ein Harod reflected this thinking: They accused the British authorities of promoting the position of the Arab ruling classes at the expense of the Jews. In so doing, members of Ahdut ha-Avoda complained, the British strengthened the hand of agitators and those fomenting hate between the two peoples. On the other hand, the decisions claimed that Jewish settlement in Palestine would lead to economic development that would redound to the benefit of all its inhabitants, Jews and Arabs alike. They included a declaration that the path to "strengthening the bonds of fraternity, peace, and mutual understanding between the Jewish and Arab peoples" would be tread by advancing the consciousness and organization of the Arab worker and by establishment of a workers alliance of Jews and Arabs.[8]

Yet there was something strange in the way matters were presented at that early stage, even within the narrow framework of the resolutions of the conference. While the Arabs were portrayed as individuals motivated basically by class interests and divided into categories of "good" and "bad," similar class motives were not attributed to members of Ahdut ha-Avoda. The decisions unambiguously emphasize the primacy of Zionist objectives, without dealing with the dimension of class differentiation among Jews. This application of a different yardstick in regard to the national aspirations of Jews and Arabs did not pass unnoticed by the conference participants. At least those at the conference who had come from England, such as Shlomo Kaplansky, Berl Locker (later chairman of the Zionist Organization), and

Zalman Rubashov (Shazar, third president of the State of Israel) protested against it. Rubashov did not hesitate to declare that presenting the clash between Jews and Arabs in class terms was not sincere: If an Arab mass movement with an anti-Zionist platform had appeared, members of Ahdut ha-Avoda would have opposed it, whether socialist or otherwise. He also argued that the demand directed to the Arabs that they have a "progressive" leadership before it would be possible to negotiate with them was unfair: After all, the Zionist leadership also failed to conform with socialist criteria, yet no one doubted their right to represent the movement.[9]

Ben Gurion's tendency to develop renewed fervor from time to time for revolutionary ideas, manifested here in his approach to the scheme of a joint union, did not prove to be contagious. Two of Ben Gurion's associates in the leadership, Yitzhak Tabenkin and Berl Katznelson, were not at all enthused about the idea of a joint union as an immediate solution to the Arab problem. None of them supported this concept at the party conference; and even afterward, as far as is known, they were not among its enthusiastic proponents. Both were frank about their opposition to Kaplansky's plan. Tabenkin asserted that there was no substance to attempts to find a political scheme that would please both Arabs and Jews, because the clash of interests between them was fundamental. "In general," Tabenkin noted, "a political question is not, in fact, a question of the proper program but rather one of power, of the balance of forces."[10] Consequently, he did not regard the concentration by members of Ahdut ha-Avoda on settlement activities in the previous two years as neglect of political activity, as Kaplansky had complained. Rather, he categorized this as an expression of "healthy political instincts," since they were strengthening the real power of Jews in Palestine.

Katznelson spoke in a similar vein. He did not hesitate to admit that he himself could offer no solution to the Arab problem. He felt that the true solution would evolve from work on creating a socialist society of workers in Palestine. In the meanwhile, it was necessary to acquiesce in the need to preserve the political status quo, which was enabling the continued expansion of the Jewish hold in Palestine. Katznelson was not deterred by the stigma of cooperating with British imperialism. "The negative attitude toward the Versailles agreement," he said, "does not need to blind our eyes and to deny the little good that it contains; and the confirmation of our right to Palestine is this good."[11] He thought in terms of expanding self-government on the municipal level as the appropriate way for promoting the political education of both the Jews and the Arabs, to their mutual benefit. But he realized that this was no substitute for political democracy. However, like many of the revolutionaries who had grown up in Eastern Europe, Katznelson at this point in his life did not accord any particular importance to what he contemptuously termed "formal democracy."[12] For that reason, unlike his comrades from the West, he did not feel uncomfortable when he found himself in a situation where he had to defend a regime that did not represent the population.

For the first time, statements were made at a party conference that assumed the existence of an identity between territory settled by Jews and the area over which they should have political control. The concept of "territorial concentration," that is, of establishing connected blocks of Jewish settlement, with territorial continuity, was broached here for the first time in a political discussion. It was suggested by both Ben Gurion and Katznelson as the wise settlement policy that ought to be pursued by the Labor movement. They proposed to set up a Jewish governmental authority in those areas, while the areas inhabited by Arabs would be self-administered by Arabs. This idea of two national autonomous territories is the first example of various plans that were to accompany the history of Palestine from this juncture on. Such plans were all variations on two basic alternatives: division of government or division of territory. It appears that at this stage, not even the authors of these proposals had a completely clear conception. At the level of consciousness, they thought that they would eventually be the rulers and masters in all of Palestine. Yet in the realm of practical action, they recognized the right of the Arabs to govern themselves and to rule over the territory where they lived. Conversely, they wanted to expand the areas of Jewish settlement and to develop the natural wealth and economic resources of Palestine.

The idea of two societies living side by side, interacting but not intermingling (conceived as a possible acceptable social and economic option already back in the time of the Second Aliyah) was given encouragement during the 1920s. It guided the location of Jewish settlements and served as a model for the system of Jewish–Arab relations. Even the proposed joint union was to be composed of two separate organizations, Jewish and Arab, linked together in the Alliance of Workers of Palestine. The national separation was designed to make it possible for the Jewish community to maintain a closed, protectionist economy, with a European living standard and European wages. Without such an economy, there was serious doubt whether Jewish workers would be able to hold their ground in Palestine. Significantly, this contrasted with the practice of hiring Arab workers in the Jewish economy because Arab labor was cheaper. Along with this dimension, there was a tendency to create blocks of Jewish settlement to serve as nuclei of Jewish autonomy and self-rule. Such concentration contrasted with the dispersive approach of promoting Jewish settlement throughout the length and breadth of Palestine, locating settlers within Arab areas and towns. In justifying the need for separation, the economic and political arguments were buffered ideologically by pointing to the existence of two diametrically different cultures: The reasoning here was that for mutual benefit, it was imperative that each sector should develop at its own pace and in accordance with its own individual needs.[13]

Though these evolving ideas had not yet crystallized into a fully coherent concept, they were absorbed almost unconsciously, without further examination and served as practical guidelines for everyday behavior. Zionists regarded the denial of an Arab exclusive right to Palestine as a matter of negligible importance. An anecdote by Shlomo Levkovitz (Lavi), one of the pioneers of the Second Aliyah and a founder of Kibbutz Ein Harod, serves to highlight this perspective. On the Palestinian Railroad, under the Turks, it was customary that if all the seats in third class were occupied, passengers were allowed to enter the first-class compartment and take vacant seats there. On one such occasion, Lavi and his friends went into the first-class compartment, where, according to Lavi, an "effendi" (the stereotype of a well-dressed Arab who looked distinguished) was sitting. When he saw the unwelcome guests enter, he spread himself out over the entire seat to prevent them from sitting down. Lavi was undaunted; he proceeded to push the man's legs off the seat, and he and his friends then sat down. Although he was arrested for this offense and had to pay a fine, Lavi felt he was in the right: A person should not be allowed to monopolize for himself a whole seat with room enough for five to sit comfortably, forcing them to stand. Lavi's moral lesson was: "We have been a people wandering from place to place for thousands of years, and found no repose. Now we have returned to the land whence we were cruelly exiled. With a pure heart, we have the right to tell the inhabitants who took our place: 'Move over a little, come on, move over. There's so much room in your Arab country, and in this land of ours, there's still a lot of room too'."[14]

Lavi and his associates felt that the socialist ideology, which rejects absolute rights of possession, justifying a redistribution of the world's wealth, was a source for legitimating the Jewish demand that Palestine should be redivided among them and the Arabs. Lavi's anecdote depicted the Arab claim to exclusive possession as the caprice of a rich man, backward in his class consciousness, who stubbornly seizes control of space that is not necessary for his existence. Just as the revolutionary is permitted to take from the rich and give to the needy, it is also permissible for the Jews to "move" the Arabs if they do not move voluntarily. This approach naturally harbored an element of aggressiveness: After all, every revolution and redistribution of wealth entailed the use of a certain degree of force. Force was regarded as justified and "proper" if it served a just purpose. In the 1920s the aspect of violent force alluded to by this short anecdote was not directly visible and apparent. *Power* in those years was understood in terms of critical mass—demographic development and settlement. As long as the evolutionary concept prevailed, the idea of using power in the more literal sense was practically unheard-of among the socialist Zionists.

Perusal of the poetry published at that time reveals the extent to which the issue of the Arab in Palestine was suppressed; it also illustrates the predominance of the defensive ethos, with all its concomitant assumptions. In the 1920s, Abraham Shlonsky's first poems appeared in print. Shlonsky had come with the Third Aliyah and was a member of the Labor Brigade. A volume of his poems entitled *Ba-galgal* (In the wheel) describes his experience as a young pioneer in Palestine. A young man is uprooted from the home of his parents. As much as he is involved in, and elated by, the new reality in Palestine, his heart is still torn by longing for the world he has left behind, its beliefs, symbols, and loyalties. Arabs rarely appear in his poems; and when they do, they play a minor role, as mythological figures or as fixtures in the Palestinian landscape.[15] His thoughts do not concern their presence but, rather, are centered on his private world, his personal experiences. Shlonsky's poetic world can serve to illustrate the prevailing separation between Jewish and Arab society: He feels neither hatred nor love for Arabs, almost as though the reality of Arab neighbors did not exist. Yet that can be explained by the personalistic nature of Shlonsky's poetry, which focuses primarily on the realm of private individual experience and does not endeavor to deal with matters of public life. Jewish reality is depicted by him through a highly personal, selective prism. The Arab is not a part of it.

Coinciding with the appearance of the book of poetry by Shlonsky, the full version of Yitzhak Lamdan's poem "Massada" was published after sections of it had appeared in the Labor press.[16] From a certain perspective, Lamdan's poetic creation was the antithesis of Shlonsky's: an expression of the collective experience, so pungent, predominant, and all-encompassing that it does not allow the individual any space for self-expression. It described the essence of the pioneering Third Aliyah, the product of the Bolshevik revolution. Central to the poem's thematics were the destruction of the former Jewish world in Eastern Europe in the wake of the war, the revolution, the ensuing civil war, and pogroms. The hero was the pioneer struggling to migrate to Palestine, the final destination. As Lamdan wrote at the end of the poem: "This is the limit, from here on there are no boundaries. / And behind us, all paths lead to a single dead end."[17] The fortress Massada, the last of the Jewish fortresses to fall in the great revolt against the Romans (A.D. 73), served Lamdan as an allegory for Palestine in the present, the haven to which the Jewish refugee fleeing from the destruction raging in his homeland could aspire. The use of the image of Massada for this purpose was dialectical. Lamdan transformed the symbol of desperate courage into an emblem of rebirth, renewal, and reconstruction: "Again Massada shall not fall." The poem makes free use of an ancient myth that awakens immediate associations of combat, defense, and valor. The new Jew knocking on the doors of the fortress was distinguished by the resoluteness of his decision; and that is how he succeeded in coping with the hardships along his route and the temptations of false solutions (from a Zionist point of view) that lured him on his "ascent" to Palestine. Outstanding among them was the magic attraction exercised by the Russian Revolution. Apart from that, he was distinguished by his readiness to fight for Massada (i.e., for his homeland). There is a great emphasis in the poem on the identity between combat and national revival. But Shlomo Zemach, in his critique of "Massada," was correct in stating that Lamdan failed in his attempt to describe the fortress itself.[18] Indeed, Lamdan's description stops short at the gate of the fortress. He conceived of the fight as a gigantic struggle for the building of the land, and not necessarily as actual military action.

The mythological framework contributes substantially to a blurring of the image of the enemy. It is not clear who is threatening the fortress and against whom the slogan "Again Massada shall not fall" is directed. In terms of the internal logic of the poem, the essence of that call is only declarative and rhetorical, expressing the hope that the enterprise of national revival in Palestine will be successful—and nothing more. The final words of the poem are a traditional phrase that Jews are accustomed to recite at the Torah reading in the synagogue when one of the five books of the Pentateuch is terminated: *Hazak, hazak ve-nit'hazek* (Be strong, be strong, and let us be strengthened!)[19] It would be possible here to interpret this as a reference to strengthening the position of Jews in Palestine. There is also one vague reference to Arabs, wrapped in mythological metaphor. Lamdan makes a comparison between Ishmael, who was banished into the desert but became a great people ("Heavy with schemes, on the humps of his camel, he sways and sings"), and Isaac and his descendants, who were exiled to the desert (in a metaphorical sense, of course) and are fainting from thirst.[20] Yet apart from this brief mention, there is no reference in the work to Arabs. The Arabs are not a part either of the historical framework or the actual pattern of the poem. The enmity of the author, insofar as it exists, is directed toward the peoples from whose midst the Jews have departed.

These peoples are familiar, flesh-and-blood reality, not just mythological figures. The entire poem turns inward, to the Jewish people, trying to persuade it of the greatness of the Zionist idea and its realization by associating present suffering and past valor. The poet uses exalted language, tending toward hyperbole, romantic to the point of embarrassment—a tone that differed from what was usual in poetic diction at the time. The prevailing vogue was a more restrained rhetoric and style. Despite the fact that the poem apparently deals with both the past and future, its focus is on the past, Jewish life in exile, the formative experience of immigration. The Arab, as adversary and challenge, does not exist in the consciousness of the pioneer storming Massada.

The third literary example illustrative of the marginality of the Arab problem in public consciousness during that period is the poetry of Rachel (Bluwstein). One of the most popular if not *the* most popular, of poets among so-called *Eretz Israel ha-Ovedet* (Labor Palestine)—that is, the communal settlements and the workers at large—Rachel published her first book of poems, *Safiah* (Aftergrowth), in 1927. She composed poems of great delicacy, highly lyrical, whose main subject was her store of personal experiences in Palestine: "Only about myself I knew to tell."[21] She had no pretensions about writing poetry that broadcast a national message. The latter type of poetry was considered more important and was at the center of attention of most male poets who were her contemporaries. The critics sometimes voiced their displeasure over the direct and unsophisticated message in her poems and her simple imagery, heavily influenced by the Bible. Yet her poems captured the hearts of many, both young and old, and preserved their freshness for the years to come. A number of her lyrics were set to music by Yehuda Shertok shortly after publication and became part of the legacy of Hebrew popular song.

Two of the best known and most popular of the poems by Rachel he set to music were written in 1926–1927: "El artzi" (To My Country) and "Ve-ulai lo hayu ha-devarim me-olam" (Perhaps It Was Never So).[22] It was no accident that these two poems were specifically singled out to be set to music. Rachel's experience, as described in the poems, were collectively shared by the pioneers of the Second Aliyah. This later became the source of inspiration and model for emulation of all the "graduates" of the school of Labor Palestine. Here was the discovery of the Palestinian landscape and falling in love with it; the attachment to the land, working on it; a world of one-time experiences, characterized by love and modesty, described in low-key and gentle tones. The love of Palestine expressed in the description is depicted using delicate undertones, devoid of flowery phrasing or aggressivity. Rachel did not employ the metallic blare of the trumpet to project her message, but spoke in a voice resonant with silence.

> I have not sung to you, my country
> And I have
> Not praised your name
> With deeds of heroism
> With the plunder of battle
> Only a tree—my hands have planted
> On the quiet banks of the Jordan
> Only a path—my feet have tread
> On the fields.[23]

In a nutshell, this short poem expressed the quintessence of the defensive ethos. Of course, its impact on the public mood is difficult to assess. But it remains a significant fact that this poem was one of the most popular lyrics and was often sung, especially in a choral rendition, in kibbutzim, the youth movements, and by groups of He-Halutz. Messages communicated by such songs are internalized almost imperceptibly, needing no direct indoctrination. This is also the secret of their impact. The message this song imparted was one of patriotism without militancy. The fact that it was so widespread and popular indicates that what it had to communicate was compatible with the ideological–political Zeitgeist and shared popular sentiment.

In an almost dialectical way, this message did not contradict the central myth of valor of the era, that of Tel Hai. The attachment to Palestine and the willingness to sacrifice oneself for the land whether in the line of defense or work were common to both. It goes without saying that in the case of Tel Hai, the rhetoric was far more exalted, though even in respect to Trumpeldor, the tones began to become more muted. The "people of toil and peace" of Berl's "Yizkor" were cut from the same cloth as the poet Rachel. Their attributes of modesty and humility were in keeping with the "days of small, ordinary deeds" of the second half of the 1920s. The poem reflected the public mood as much as it shaped it. The emphasis on the loyalty of the individual and the importance of the small achievements gained a new popularity when the great feats of the movement at the beginning of the decade (also characterized by collective responses) had become a thing of the past. This was the self-image that the movement preferred for itself—simple in manner, modest in expression, identifying with the Palestine landscape, peace-loving and oriented toward a life of physical labor.

It was also the image that took root in the evolving extracurricular system of education by way of the youth movements developing at the time. A style of behavior crystallized that praised and fostered these virtues. All of this culture was turned inward, oriented toward the education of the "new man." The culture of manners that evolved around the songs and the "style" and the self-images derived from them was nonaggressive. Yet, its bearers showed little interest in what was happening among their Arab neighbors. The Arabs remained outside the perimeter of awareness and engagement of the Jews both as individuals and collectively. Just as the Jews in the shtetl lived cut off from the Gentiles and the latter did not leave their mark on internal Jewish life, the Jews in Palestine were also creating a separate entity—to which the Arabs remained external.

In the formation of a national ethos, it is possible to distinguish between *canonical* influences and *marginal* influences. Influences of the first type are beyond dispute, and all agree that they express the consensus. For example, Bialik and Tchernichovsky were canonical for the entire Zionist public. For the members of the Second Aliyah, Brenner was canonical—an attitude adopted later on by the men and women of the Third Aliyah and the disciples of the youth movements. Though with time they were also canonized, Berdichevsky and Ahad Ha-Am were never totally accepted. Some of Ahad Ha-Am's ideas concerning the establishment of a spiritual center in Palestine as well as his positive attitude toward the existence of the Diaspora were welcomed by only a portion of the public and were rejected by many others. Similarly, Herzl was not acceptable to the thinking of spiritual Zionists due to his emphasis on the establishment of a state and because of the poverty of the spiritual content of his Zionism. Rachel and Lamdan were integrated into the Zionist canon immediately, without any objection. Their message was not controversial. On the contrary, it functioned as a kind of accepted cultural common denominator, beyond all differences in political approach and ideology.

The fate of another poet—perhaps the most significant of them in respect to his power as a writer—was quite different. Uri Zvi Greenberg was born in Galicia and immigrated in early 1924 to Palestine. Already then, he had established his reputation as a well-known poet in Yiddish and Hebrew.[24] He immediately became a central figure in the press of the Labor movement, publishing poetry and essays. The Ahdut ha-Avoda weekly *Kuntres* and the weekly paper of the Ha-Poel ha-Tzair party, *Ha-Poel ha-Tzair,* were both eager to have his poems and articles—writings that had an impact and echo within the small world of the Labor movement. When, about a year later, *Davar,* the daily of the Histadrut, edited by Berl Katznelson, made its debut, Greenberg was in the first issue—a special honor that many had apparently coveted.[25] For a number of years after that, down to 1929, he regularly published poetic essays and lyric poetry in *Davar* and *Ha-Poel ha-Tzair.* His ideas were controversial and on a number of occasions provoked stormy polemic. Yet the fact is that during that time, his thinking was not esoteric enough to warrant ostracism and expulsion from the Labor movement. In later years, after Greenberg had begun to identify with the revisionists, the great rival of Labor, he was banned from the fold: In the publications of the Labor movement from then on, there was a veritable conspiracy of silence regarding him and his work. However, attitudes toward him in the 1920s had been quite different. Thus, there is some reason to assume that even if his ideas were marginal, they were not beyond the perimeter of consensus—or at least were not considered to be heresy by the ideologues of the Labor movement.

Greenberg's world was Manichaean. It was based on a constant confrontation between the good and the bad. The respective enemy, against whom a fierce battle was waged, changed with time: Christian Europe, the Arab East, the international and Jewish bourgeoisie, and the Labor movement in Palestine. The good were alternately the Jews, revolutionaries, workers in Palestine—and ultimately, adherents of Greenberg's teachings. Verbal violence was an integral component of his style. He often used expressions such as "carcasses of rotting traitors," "Sanballats," and the like, while the object of his derision changed from occasion to occasion.[26] Use of the term *Flavius* (Josephus) as a cognate for traitor and a person who colludes with the authorities went hand-in-hand with the description of the high commissioner in Palestine as Pontius Pilate. An obsession with treason pervades his writing. It is impossible not to feel his stylistic proximity to intellectual–cultural currents that heralded the coming of fascism.

One of the dominant experiences (if not *the* most dominant one) in Greenberg's work was the generations-old clash between Jews and Christians. The hatred of the European world for the Jewish people was something he regarded as axiomatic. He had a complex attitude toward the Christian world, particularly that of Eastern Europe, in which attraction and repulsion, love and hate were intermingled. In one of his early poems, contained in the first book of poetry he published in Palestine, *Eima gedola ve-yare'ah* (Great Terror and a Moon), he characterized his immigration there as a necessity ("We had been compelled to leave") and expressed what he felt about his native country:

We were compelled to hate even what we loved. We loved the forest, the river, the well, and the mill.
We loved the falling of leaves, the fish, the pail, and the Sabbath bread. And in *secret, secret,* we also loved the sound of their bells,
The little Gentiles with their whitish hair.[27]

The departure from the towns of his native land is depicted as a total and final good-bye, with the foreknowledge that those towns were doomed to annihilation:[28] "Our synagogues—to be set afire. The wretched houses—to be plundered. Hoes—to dig graves in every town."[29] The echoes of the pogrom he witnessed in 1918 in Lvov mingled in his poetry and essays with the horrors of the civil war in Russia and Poland and the Ukraine riots of 1919. Christian symbols—Jesus, the cross, churches, bell towers—appeared in his work as symbols that awakened terror, emblems of an eternal, implacable enemy. Only in Palestine did he break free from his dread of Christianity: "Here the cross does not stab, the peal of bells does not strike fear," he wrote in one of his first poems in Palestine.[30]

In Greenberg's view, Europe was a decadent society, on the verge of extinction. He took the "decline of the West" for granted, beyond dispute,[31] and described Western culture as bourgeois, self-satisfied, smug. In contrast, he identified with the ruffians of the world, the revolutionaries arising to destroy existing society. In 1924, when Lenin died, Greenberg published a eulogy extolling the propagator of the great revolution, venerated by the "kingdom of the barefooted in hunger and plague." For him, Lenin symbolized the ability of the leader to seize the historical opportunity, the power of the *individual* to stamp his signature upon history. "Already now it is possible to believe in miracles and salvation, and in the impact of the authority of the *individual*," he wrote. He ended his eulogy with the declaration, "The Hebrew proletarians stand on the Hebrew island facing Moscow in a salute to Lenin's funeral!"[32] An essay written in response to his eulogy claimed that without Lenin, there would have been no Dzierzynski (first chief of the Soviet secret police) and recalled the bloodbath for which Lenin was responsible. Greenberg was incensed by this criticism. These arguments, he proclaimed, were characteristic of the Jewish democratic press in Palestine, which was bourgeois in its nature: "There is an iron wall between them and the working class when it comes to *thought and perception,* as well."[33]

Greenberg believed there was a common destiny linking all revolutionaries throughout the world with the pioneers in Palestine. In his view, the "divinity of ardor" was what inspired the former to storm the barricades and the latter to live in deprivation and poverty under the scorching sun of Palestine.[34] He saw the workers as the bearers of the new revolution, those whose task it was to make the Kingdom of Israel a living reality, to be established between the desert and the sea. Greenberg had great admiration for the barefooted workers building up the land and compared them to the priests building the temple sanctuary for those who would follow in their footsteps. Self-sacrifice, suffering, and destitution were given exalted poetic expression in his poems:

And we all sit here and write in the night a holy lie (hands now swollen—) to mother and wife:
Fair, fair is the country. The land flows with milk—Wonderful the moon on the sea and the vineyards—
And a son, the poor one, will not write: at night he washes his shirt, and during the day, the burning heat consuming him, he stood and dug."[35]

"A kingdom of the barefooted on the sands" was how Greenberg in 1924 described the image of Jewish sovereignty he aspired to.[36]

The year 1924 marked the beginning of the Fourth Aliyah. Greenberg saw it as an immigration wave of the petty bourgeoisie, individuals coming to Palestine primarily as a convenient destination for migration, with no plans to sacrifice themselves as pioneers on the altar of the homeland. Greenberg treated them with the familiar disdain characteristic of the "negators of the exile" and did not mince words when expressing his disgust. "The 'extensive' immigration is a reaction against our Zionist, revolutionary vision," he stated, adding that "within our liberation movement, the diasporic nightmare rears its head in Zionist form."[37] In contrast with the affirmative symbol, the "ruffians of the human race," bearers of the flag of sacred revolution who sacrifice themselves for the sake of the people, he presented the symbol of negation: "the putrid stench of emigrating Jewry," whose motivating sentiment was pure and simple egoism.[38]

In the 1920s Greenberg still identified wholeheartedly with the Labor movement. When the economic crisis set in during the Fourth Aliyah (from the end of 1925)—a downswing marked by heavy unemployment and emigration from Palestine—Greenberg wrote some of his most impressive poems, including "Ra'av be-Eretz Israel" (Hunger in Palestine) and "Hizdaharut" (Irradiation), in which the settlements in the Jezreel Valley and the suffering pioneers there were endowed with a quality of sacredness.[39] "Yours is the kingdom, the poor in rusty Palestine"[40] he proclaimed, adding that the valor of the hungry who had kept faith with Zionism was greater than the bravery shown at Tel Hai.[41] He already began to single out those he blamed for the situation—such as the Zionist leadership, which he felt had to be replaced. "There will be a forcible changing of the guard at the head of our liberation movement," he stated, with a hint of violence in his words. In keeping with revolutionaries who believe that the situation must get worse before it can improve, he added, "Total crisis will be our salvation."[42]

Shortly after his arrival in Palestine, Greenberg began commenting on the Arab question. In his bifurcated world, the Arab was a threatening factor, frightening and bloodthirsty. As I have mentioned, the first book of poetry he published in Palestine bore the word "terror" in its title. That terror stemmed from the Arab threat. The Muslim East, and the crescent symbolizing it, played a role for him similar to that played by Europe and the cross: an existential danger for the Jews, a constant threat. Just as he earlier had compared the cross to a knife that pierces the heart, he now described the crescent in the same murderous light.[43]

If it is possible to speak of a Hebrew hate literature against Arabs during this period, Uri Zvi Greenberg is its author. In his work, the Arab is depicted as a potential murderer, his knife honed and dipped in poison.[44] Recurrent are the motifs of the knife and blood—the Jew always the victim, the Arab the murderer. The encounter with the Arabs on the highway, or in Jerusalem, is depicted as a kind of obvious situation for murder—one needing no justification or explanation.[45] In Greenberg's world, fear is a constant companion, almost pathological. Immigration to Palestine did not eradicate the feeling of fear that had accompanied him in the Diaspora but only changed the reason for his terror. In Europe, anxiety had been intermingled with a sense of closeness and intimacy. As mentioned, he had mixed feelings regarding his native Galicia. Yet he felt close enough to its people and their culture to declare that the Jewish community in Palestine was the "European Hebrew people."[46] There was no such ambivalence in Greenberg's work when it touched on the Arabs. The Arab was a stranger, an alien not only in the ethnic sense but in a cultural one as well. The mystery of the East frightened him, awakening associations of secret plots, of hatred—simmering and overt.[47] Added to the alienness and the mystery of the Arab, filtered by the alembic of his poetry into the images of knife and blood, was the enmity toward the adversary: a rival people, in competition for the patrimony of Palestine. He soon commented on a topic Jews had kept their silence about up until then: the existence of a Muslim mosque on the Temple Mount: "The *Mosque of Omar* [i.e., the Dome of the Rock] is standing on *our* most holy land: *the site of the temple. On the head of the people.*"[48] He compared Jerusalem to the body of a mother whose head had been severed, the Muslim mosque joined to her body instead. He prayed for an earthquake that would stamp out the shame of Jerusalem, now in thrall to the cross and crescent. The fields near Jerusualem cultivated by Arabs are described by Greenberg as covered with boils. When he visits a Jerusalem under foreign control, he feels disgrace, fear, and contamination, as the "last soldier of the House of David born in Europe."[49]

In Greenberg's work, dread and hate are joined with a powerful feeling of possessiveness over the land. Fear is a necessary product of his conviction that the Arabs will not permit the Jews to settle in Palestine peacefully. For that reason, the encounter bristles with threat, both open and covert. Yet he also invited that threat: From the first moment on, Greenberg averred that it was not his intention in Palestine to ask anyone's opinion or permission in regard to his right to settle there. He defined himself as a man "acting in his own domain" and consequently free from any consideration of what others might think.[50] He soon began to employ the term Canaanites when referring to Arabs. That analogy was not accidental: In the Bible, God had given the land to the Jews to conquer it from the Canaanites. When Greenberg termed the Arabs Canaanites, it articulated his perception that Jews must conquer Palestine from them and also functioned as a delegitimization of Arab rights to the country. Just as the Canaanites had had no right to the land in the distant past, even though they had been settled there for many generations, the Arabs had no right in the present. The following passage discloses key features of Greenberg's attitude toward the Arabs: "And in the avenues of Zion dwells the Canaanite, with his wives, children, camels, / He draws bread from my soil, extracts honey from my trees, fish from the sea, and pierces my night with the sound of his flute."[51] The sustenance of the Arab, based on the produce of the land, is considered a form of robbery: It violates the property of the land's true owners. The cultural alienness expressed in the depiction of the Canaanite and his house takes on a special nuance through a seemingly naive detail: the Arab playing on his flute, a sound that cuts through the night of the Jew. In Eastern Europe, the sound of bells had resounded sweetly in the author's ears; but the wail of the Arab flute is piercing, threatening. The Arab presence in Palestine is depicted by Greenberg as proof of the inferiority of the Jews, who remain unable to stamp their signature on the land, in contrast with their Arab competitor—well-established, posing a threat to the Jewish community by his very existence. This feeling of strength on the one hand, and helplessness and inferiority on the other, mingled with, and cross-fertilized each other in Greenberg's writing and served as the source for both the sense of possessiveness and superiority and the sense of fear and alienness.

As for the issue of the unionization of Arab workers and, more generally, manifestations of class solidarity with Arabs, Greenberg disagreed, right from the beginning, with the position taken by Ahdut ha-Avoda, the party he initially identified with. Greenberg denounced the participation of Jews and Arabs together in a small joint strike organized in Jaffa, immediately hailed by *Davar* as an example of Jewish–Arab solidarity, a ray of hope for the future. He commented that it was better to say as little as possible about the "Arab problem" and especially to avoid talking about "ethical motives," since such motives were likely to arouse uncalled-for suspicions.[52] When the inhabitants of Damascus joined the insurrection against the French authorities that had broken out in the Druze Mountains in late 1925 and were suppressed with a heavy hand, Jews in Palestine organized a fund campaign for the victims of the revolt. This drive was initiated primarily by members of the Labor movement and by intellectuals who had established an association called Brit Shalom (Covenant of Peace). At that same time, *Davar* denounced the festive display of flags of the Jewish legion in a synagogue in Jerusalem, expressing fears that Arabs would view this as a provocation, even though the mandatory court had granted permission for the display.

Greenberg was infuriated over these two incidents. He fiercely objected to raising funds for the victims of the Syrian uprising, arguing that there was a lack of reciprocity: Arabs had not shown a similar sensitivity toward Jews and their suffering either in Palestine or the Ukraine. Regarding the flags incident, Greenberg stated that military exhibitionism was indeed superfluous at a time when there were thousands of unemployed; yet it was inconceivable that Jews should themselves forego an opportunity for a national demonstration after the British had given specific permission for it.[53] In order to underscore the irony of such assistance to Arabs, he described once again the murder of Brenner and Louidor during the May 1921 disturbances, using imagery and expressions designed to exacerbate feelings of animosity toward the Arabs.[54] Beilinson, in his reply to Greenberg, said there was a need for exercising utmost caution in relations with Arabs "as regards the rights, feelings, and even superstitions and prejudices of the other side" and that it was necessary to "teach a sense of respect toward the neighbor dwelling in our midst."[55] Imperceptibly, the expression "dwelling in our midst" reflected the instinctive feeling of ownership prevalent among Jews in Palestine: a reference to the Arab major-ity as though it were a minority living in the dominant Jewish community.

Greenberg saw these matters from a different perspective. In contrast with Bei-linson's call for patience and moderation and an attempt to refrain from causing any injury to the Arabs, he exclaimed, "The very expression of our desire to be an absolute majority in Palestine already contains a demand for our predominance." In his view, this in itself was damaging to Arab interests. Greenberg dismissed off-handedly the ethical behavior that Beilinson had demanded, "The process of our rejuvenation under the duress of our people's plight determines an ethics whose laws we obey"—in other words, common and accepted rules of ethical behavior had been rendered null and void by the ethics of emergency.[56] In calling for frater-nity between nations, brotherhood between Jews and Arabs, Beilinson had stated his conviction that "this is the true path to internationalism." Greenberg dubbed such an approach, which mixed class considerations within a nationalist concep-tion, a "conceptual bastard" of the Zionist idea. "Our nationalism is a historical *imperative* in the blood of the Hebrew race," he proclaimed, calling for an intellec-tual dictatorship that would prepare the masses for the "goals of kingdom and sov-ereignty." The pioneers must receive indoctrination that will make clear to them that they are not simply a proletarian class but, more, "armies of national occu-pation"; and they must be schooled in national romanticism and its symbols.[57] Eighteen months after his eulogy to Lenin, Greenberg asserted that the socialist rev-olution in Palestine would occur "when there was already a kingdom, and thus something to revolt against."[58]

The concept of *malkhut* (kingdom, statehood) is central to Greenberg's thought and appears in different variations. "Crown of the kingdom," "kingdom of the House of David," the "idea of the kingdom," and simply "kingdom" are code words in the Greenbergian opus as descriptors of the Zionist goal, denoting a national political entity that is more than just a state. Greenberg's envisaged entity links past and present, is rooted in Jewish history and imbued with sacredness. Greenberg felt it was debasing and cheapening the vision to describe the right of Jew in Palestine simply as the prosaic right to come and settle there. In place of the official concept "national home," he wanted to foster the use of symbolic concepts, culled from the romantic tradition: These would provide spiritual sustenance for the hearts and souls of those who were conquering the swamps. "The idea of state-hood for the Jewish nation" is what should guide Zionist activity; in essence, Green-berg contended, that was a "messianic idea in the heart of every Jew, even beneath the threshold of conscious awareness."[59] Greenberg gave priority to the "idea of statehood" in its elevated messianic definition (although national–secularist in con-tent) over any other idea, demanding total and complete dedication to it.[60] His use of concepts such as the "cosmic square" to denote the special relationship between Jews and Palestine[61] bestowed a kind of transcendental status on this bond, lying beyond the sphere of human volition.

The late 1920s were difficult years for the Jewish community in Palestine. The economic downswing and the resultant crisis of confidence in the viability of the Zionist project, rising unemployment, and the wave of emigration from Palestine led to dejection in the Yishuv. Those were also years of bitter disappointment for Uri Zvi Greenberg. "Kefitzat ha-derekh" (Shortcut) was the title of one of his first poems written in Palestine.[62] The belief it expressed—that it was possible to realize the Zionist revolution in the immediate future—shattered against the jagged rock of Palestinian reality. Greenberg was not the only one disenchanted: A similar disillusionment was also the main factor underlying the crisis that struck the Labor Brigade and ultimately led to the return of some fifty of its members to the Soviet Union. Others led lives of quiet desperation, leaving Palestine quietly, their hopes in disarray. The majority, however, had come to terms with the fact that the construction of the land would be a very slow process, entailing great suffering and exhausting toil. Greenberg accepted that burden of pain: "Let him come!" With love we accept the birthpangs of the messiah."[63] He elevated physical toil, ennobling it to the level of a sacred act. Greenberg described the work of the stonecutters from the Labor Brigade in Jerusalem in a characteristic image: "Our messianic vision splits asunder with dynamite."[64] But he was unable to accept the snail's pace of change, what he termed the "slow evaporation of our messianism."[65] In the poem *"Hazon ahad ha-ligyonot"* (Vision of One of the Legions), written at that same time, he portrayed the burning disappointment over the failure of the messianic leap forward:

> I bore a vision of a kingdom
> And a crown for the crowning.
> Now I will carry, hidden away,
> The coffin of the kingdom that fails to arrive.[66]

That frustration did not spare the Jewish people, which had not responded to the "historical messianic idea" and had not come to Palestine as expected.[67] It was despondency over the role played by the Zionist leaders—Weizmann in particular—who, in Greenberg's view, had been the root cause behind the waning of "our great messianic vision." Finally, that disappointment came to focus on the established Zionist method of gradualism: acquisition of land acre by acre, acquiescence to the slow pace of the building of the land, making do with the limited possibilities:

> Against our will, apparently, we established the method of reduction, and of "going slowly" in the field of action. Incidentally, we were aware at the time that there was an aspiration for great deeds. We redeemed *one* acre of land; and when we pierced it with the plow, we looked forward with painful love, with a great masculine lust, to the *second* acre. Yet with time, the method of constraint became the law. . . . The method of reduction devoured the final goal.[68]

Greenberg rejected any thought of compromise with present reality. For a number of years, he had been calling for an "intellectual dictatorship," whatever that meant; now his demands became more focused, aimed at changing the movement's leadership, including Weizmann at its head. He blamed the leaders for being prepared to accept a crawling pace of building up the land and the limited economic resources. That leadership took the Arab position into consideration and tried to avoid provocations. They refrained from being carried away by utopian ardor and opposed Greenberg-type messianic–visionary flights.[69] Starting in 1927, he began to identify the leadership of the labor movement with Chaim Weizmann, holding both equally responsible for Zionism's failures.[70]

During this period Uri Zvi Greenberg was active as one of the most outstanding poets and publicists of the Labor movement. Coupled with his considerable poetic abilities was an element of great emotional power and tempestuous pain that spoke directly to the hearts of his readers. The discriminating among them, such as Yehoshua Heschel Yeivin (who, paradoxically, later became his close disciple and sang his public praises) suggested that Greenberg should speak in more delicate tones. He advised him to abandon the clamor of loud trumpets, in pseudo-Wagnerian style, in favor of the tender strains of the violin.[71] However, in the considered opinion of others, loyal members of the Labor movement, Greenberg's poetic exaggeration was a virtue: an expression of the authenticity of the pain, the anguish of his soul, in the style of the biblical prophets. Any criticism of him was rejected out of hand.[72] It is true that Beilinson polemicized against Greenberg, presenting the canonical position of the Labor movement in critique of his views. Yet the public dispute at that time still did not involve any attempt to delegitimate Greenberg or his views. Such efforts did not emerge until 1929.

However, already in 1927 there were some who pointed out just how alien Greenberg's thinking was to the Labor camp. His ideas were branded "intellectual revisionism"—notions that could confound the minds of the members of the movement. Gershon Hanoch, one of the principal educators in Ha-Poel ha-Tzair, commented that in contrast with political revisionism, which made use of simple expressions understandable by all, Greenberg employed messianic conceptions that functioned to obscure his meaning and to conceal his intentions. Concepts such as *kingdom, vision,* and *messiah* lent themselves to a poetic–abstract interpretation but lacked concrete meaning in terms of everyday life. In actual truth, Hanoch contended, Greenberg had developed an outlook that was similar in intensity and purpose to the teachings of false messianism.[73]

The juxtaposition of Greenberg's teachings and false messianism had a sound basis in fact. Greenberg himself had an acknowledged fondness for the figure of Shabbetai Zvi, and portrayed him as an ideal leader, like Napoleon. Beyond his attachment to the mysterious figure of the great false messiah of the seventeenth century, Greenberg viewed persistent messianic fervor as the vehicle through which to mobilize the masses of the Jewish people to the Zionist cause and as an instrument for maintaining those masses' loyalty to the movement over an extended period of time. The distance between wish and ability—that is, between the mentality of "forcing the issue" (a messianic phrase) and practical possibilities—did not appear to him to be a sufficient reason for avoiding an approach aimed at galvanizing and cultivating prolonged mass ecstasy. Somehow, by dint of the sheer fervor of the believers, he envisioned that that ecstasy would smash through the walls of reality and bring about ultimate deliverance.

The attitude of the Zionist movement toward the messianic currents had always been marked by ambivalence. On the one hand, it wished to avoid exaggerated fanciful flights to the realm of vision and endeavored to base its policy and activity on the imperatives and images of the real world. The Zionists believed the messianic movements had failed because they had been divorced from the world of practical action. Therefore, right from its inception, the Zionist movement chose to distinguish itself from messianism. On the other hand, the national movement was sustained, both consciously and unawares, by the same spring of irrational, mystical fervor that wished to subordinate reality to patterns of utopian imagination. Here, perhaps, may lie the key to understanding the tolerance shown by a segment of the leadership of the Labor movement toward Greenberg's visionary ideas. The attitudes manifested in the "shortcut," or "forcing the issue," approach were part of the fundamental makeup of the mentality of Ahdut ha-Avoda. Impatience with the slow pace of the wheels of history and the impulse to take one's destiny in hand and serve as "midwives" for history, were an integral component of the intellectual profile of Berl Katznelson, Ben Gurion, Yitzhak Tabenkin, and their associates. They fervently believed in forcing the issue and wished by decisive action to bring about the Zionist revolution (in both national and socialist spheres) and to do so speedily, in their lifetime. From the standpoint of their psychological cast of mind, there was no essential difference between those who wished to achieve a turning point in the national sphere by means of a historical breakthrough and those who wanted to bring about a major transformation in the sphere of society. Greenberg, like Ben Gurion and Tabenkin, admired Lenin—and for basically the same reasons.[74] Just as the revolutionaries, ready to demolish the Old World to its very foundations, did not recoil from the use of force, the various brands of "shortcutters" in Palestine were also prepared to use it when necessary. For that reason, they were not repelled by the inherent violence of Greenberg's style or even by his maliciously malevolent descriptions of Arabs, although in another context, they would probably have denounced them as incitement to hatred. His unwillingness to accept the given situation; protest against existing reality in the name of an internal truth; and advocacy of the right to act on behalf of a "higher justice," liberated from the shackles of bourgeois morality—all those revolutionary elements struck a sympathetic chord in their hearts. Even if they avoided using these methods in actual practice (and it remains an open question whether that refusal derived from moral considerations or lack of opportunity), there was a special place in their hearts for Greenberg's tenor and style. They felt a kinship with his constant turmoil, his restless ardor that strove to shake people from their stupor and inertia, feelings they themselves shared. Greenberg was the magnified, exaggerated reflection of their own secret desires.

At the end of a highly critical essay in which, in customary fashion, he denounced the enervation of the Zionist vision, Greenberg described a chance encounter with an unemployed and destitute worker who had remarked to him: "If they were to tell us today, 'go to the Horan'—the eyes of the speaker were shining with animation—'we would listen and go. In the ranks of Labor Palestine, we are ready'."[75] The Horan (the present-day Golan Heights) was the great dream cherished by Ha-Shomer members from the days of the Second Aliyah. Only within the ranks of Labor Palestine, among whom the myth of building up the land was a central value, could the idea have arisen of using this old magical place name as an impetus for a settlement initiative that would constitute an answer to the Zionist crisis of the Fourth Aliyah. Consciously, they had made their peace with the fact that the settlement of Palestine would be a step-by-step process, slow and cautious, and a far cry from the dreams of the early 1920s. Yet in their heart of hearts, they still held out a dim hope that the historical breakthrough, momentarily postponed, would eventually materialize. Only in that light, for example, is it possible to understand the motivation behind the accusations leveled by Berl Katznelson and Ben Gurion against Herbert Samuel. After all, Samuel was the high commissioner who had brought stability to Palestine, aided the pioneers of the Third Aliyah in their efforts to find work, facilitated the Fourth Aliyah and helped to lower the level of tension between Jews and Arabs. Between the lines of their words gapped disappointment over the distance between the actual small-scale deeds and their abiding grandiose expectations. It was not accidental that Ben Gurion attacked the slogan being bandied about in circles of the Zionist Organization headed by Weizmann and among the ranks of the nonrevolutionary workers party, Ha-Poel ha-Tzair: "Back to Hibbat Zion!"[76] The revolutionary impulse, the motivating force in their personality, was constantly frustrated by reality. As individuals who recognized the necessity to compromise with reality, they accepted the evolutionary conception and the defensive ethos. But on occasion, in times of decision or great tension, the revolutionary impulse burst forth and directed their actions. For that reason, in their innermost being, they had a profound understanding for the spirit animating Greenberg and his thinking. Consequently, they were unable to reject his severe critique of Weizmann's policies wholeheartedly, even though they were Weizmann's allies and remained cognizant of the fact that their alliance with him was essential for the survival of Labor Palestine—an alliance by dint of which Zionist Palestine *was* being built, even if at a far slower pace than was desired.

Greenberg's style, his imagery mined from the rich quarry of Jewish traditional culture (particularly the historical events that Berdichevsky had utilized and passed on to his disciples in the Labor movement) gave his labor readership the feeling that he was one of them. Not only did his enmity toward the Christian world and, more generally, the non-Jewish world not awaken their disgust, it played on a sensitive chord, extremely taut, in their souls. These were Jews who had grown up in the Pale of Settlement, between the slaughter of Kishinev and the pogroms of the first 1905 revolution—a generation for whom Brenner was the mouthpiece. Only recently, they had followed with heavy heart the bloody 1919 pogroms that ripped through the Ukraine. They were unable to muster feelings of love and forgiveness for the non-Jewish world. Even if, as committed socialists, they professed the brotherhood of all peoples and advocated universalist ideas, still in the Jewish sphere, Greenberg's Manichaean description of the world answered to their "gut perception" of reality. For that reason, they tended to discount his expressions of enmity as poetic license, not to be taken all that seriously. On the other hand, his Zionist–revolutionary maximalism was viewed as being quite commensurate with their own outlook.

The mental junction between socialist apocalypticism and nationalist apocalypticism found its manifest expression in the catastrophe-centered Zionist conception shared by Greenberg and the leaders of Ahdut ha-Avoda: In their view, the Diaspora was doomed to annihilation; and Palestine should serve as a safe haven, a land of rescue. The feeling of imminent catastrophe lent a special urgency to their characteristic impatience, which, by the same token, tended to depict life in the

Diaspora in menacing colors. As individuals who felt they bore the burden of responsibility for the fate of the nation, the state of emergency that they assumed the Jewish people was facing gave them the right to cast aside the rules of conventional morality, rules that under normal conditions they would have been careful to adhere to. Hence, they did not regard Greenberg's eruptive violence as a deviation from their own basic cast of mind and psyche.

It was not accidental that it was someone from the Ha-Poel ha-Tzair party who pointed out that Greenberg's thinking was not in tune with the conceptual framework of the Labor movement. Gershon Hanoch noted that there was a contrast between Greenberg's revolutionary apocalyptic visions and the concrete needs of the movement; for the latter required hard work, devoid of any glamor and visionary flights. This contrast was identical with one that had always separated Zionism from messianic movements. In Hanoch's view, attentiveness to "messianic sound of trumpets" led to a lack of responsibility, oppositionalism, and an inability to face reality and its limitations:

> From time to time, during the short history of our liberation movement, true revolutionaries, living modestly and laboring with great toil, try . . . to cast off the burden of great ideals from themselves and their generation, to extricate the movement from the "all-encompassing embrace" of the Great Revolution, and to bring it closer to the idea of the *small* day of redemption and to the so-very-difficult "minimum." And each time, the waves of cosmic or messianic ideals return—from the "kingdom" in Zion to the "revolution" in Moscow—to inundate the consciousness and will, in the meantime a bit more down-to-earth in orientation. And once again, we are told to force the issue or, in modern phraseology, to "set the psyche in motion," in a blast of abstract redemption.[77]

Against these messianic–idealistic "waves," Hanoch stressed simple labor as an educational and moral value of ultimate importance, at least for the course of that generation. For all practical purposes, the leaders of Ahdut ha-Avoda accepted this educational and political conception sketched by Hanoch—but did so reluctantly, out of necessity, rather than conviction.

The closer one came to the end of the 1920s, the more pronounced were the differences in approach between the Labor movement and its rivals. This process was given impetus as a result of the emergence of Brit Shalom and the Revisionist movement. From both ends of the political spectrum, they challenged basic assumptions of the defensive ethos. Greenberg's attacks against evolutionism developed quite rapidly into forays against the political line pursued by Labor Palestine. Toward the end of 1928, it was already clear that Greenberg's path had parted ways with that of the movement. A short article was published in *Davar* mocking his apocalyptic view of catastrophe: "They threaten with messianism on the one hand, and with diasporic submissiveness on the other. They imagine a beam to be a splinter; and wherever they go, History accompanies them. Flavius is discovered everywhere. Similes are found at every step, analogies wherever one treads."[78] In 1929 Berl Katznelson published the first volume of *Yalkut Ahdut ha-Avoda* (The anthology of Ahdut ha-Avoda), a compendium regarded as the authentic and accepted expression of the party's consensus. It did not contain a single article by Greenberg.

That volume gave appropriate space to the position of the "activists" in the dispute on the legion, and many of the articles in the collection were imbued with a revolutionary spirit. Nonetheless, the defensive ethos predominated. Greenberg was ultimately too much for the movement to digest.

The "fraternity of the extremes," that is, the psychological proximity between the revolutionaries who wished to force the issue and the nationalists who desired that same end, was not lost on contemporaries. When Beilinson analyzed the factors that had induced a group of intellectuals such as U. Z. Greenberg, Abba Ahimeir and Yehoshua H. Yeivin to leave the Labor movement and join its rivals on the right, the revisionists, he was referring to the psychological similarity between the two aforementioned types, who both refused to accept the fetters of reality. In Beilinson's view, both were opposed to the mentality of the Labor movement, conceptually and psychologically. The confrontation with the Right led to a sharpened definition of evolutionism as the path of the Labor movement and to further discrediting of the various currents committed to shortcuts. The latter were increasingly depicted as being out of step with the central thrust of the movement. But was the revolutionary impulse truly repressed or only concealed from view?

Jabotinsky and the Theory of Frontal Confrontation

In 1925 a new political grouping made its appearance in the Zionist arena, the Revisionist party. More than any other political party, it was identified with one dominant personality, the figure of its founder Zeev (Vladimir) Jabotinsky. Jabotinsky had left the Zionist Executive in 1923 as a result of his growing dissatisfaction with Weizmann's policies. During the period 1923–1925, he formulated most of revisionism's guiding principles. Finally, he translated the sympathy he had encountered among groups of young Zionists, especially in the Baltic states, into a political framework and founded the Revisionist party.

Jabotinsky was one of those individuals whose personality awakens either great sympathy or profound dislike. As I have mentioned, members of the Labor movement in Palestine sensed already at the time of the legion that he was not one of them. Later, despite the fact that they had respect for his honesty and dedication, they rejected the position he had taken on Tel Hai. After he was arrested for the supposed offense of defending the Jews of Jerusalem during the 1920 riots, Ahdut ha-Avoda placed him at the top of their list for the Assefat ha-Nivharim (Assembly of Delegates), the legislative body of the Jewish community in Palestine. Nonetheless, he remained alien to the movement. There was considerable similarity between his thinking and that of the leaders of Ahdut ha-Avoda. Like him, they protested against Samuel's policies, rejecting the approach that reduced and belittled Zionist goals in Palestine. The basic difference between them lay in the taproots of their world outlook and its implications for Palestine; there were also distinctions in style, of no less importance than the ideological differences.

Jabotinsky was born in Odessa, a new area of settlement in Southern Russia outside the Pale, a city known for its cosmopolitan diversity. He grew up in an assimiliated Jewish home. His given name was Vladimir, his native language Russian, and he attended a Russian high school. Jabotinsky became involved in Zionism and learned Hebrew only later, as a young man. He had a natural and relaxed attitude both toward himself and his non-Jewish surroundings. His heart was not troubled by the fear of the cross or perturbed by the peal of church bells. Absent in Jabotinsky's experience was the twisted and tempestuous legacy of the Pale of Settlement. There was something non-Jewish, very simple, straightforward, and direct in his attitude toward reality. He did not tend to categorize the world into Jews and non-Jews. Jabotinsky believed that human society was propelled by rational principles (in the European sense) and that justice and morality were what ultimately guided the world.

At the second convention of the Union of Zionists–Revisionists held in 1926, Jabotinsky distinguished between the psychology of the ghetto and his own outlook and totally rejected the notion that depicted Gentile society as a "world of brigands." In his view, that conception was "the fruit of two thousand years of nightmare in Jewish history" but reflected a twisted approach. "The 'Gentile' has the same nobility of spirit and sense of justice that we have," he asserted. Like Herzl, he believed in "the conscience of the civilized world, in the omnipotent power of a just cause."[79]

It is difficult to discern the presence of any element in Jabotinsky makeup—psychological, emotional, or cultural—that had its source in Jewish religion. Unlike the phraseology of many of his contemporaries, his written Hebrew is two-dimensional and lacks the freight of associations, allusions, and imagery that comes naturally to a person brought up in traditional Jewish culture. Even in speeches and articles originally written in Hebrew, the reader has the impression that they were translated from another language into a select, modern, crystalline Hebrew, a diction lacking in mystery. In contrast with members of the Labor movement and with Uri Zvi Greenberg (who in that sense was definitely one of them), Jabotinsky did not bestow the attributes of a secular religion on his Zionist outlook. "Messiah," "end of days," "hastening the coming" (i.e., *forcing the issue*) and numerous other concepts drawn from Jewish eschatology are absent in his writings. Such expressions and images were often employed in the publications of segments of the movement infused with a secular messianic fervor. He likewise had no need for the imagery of Berdichevsky. In fact, Jabotinsky's arsenal of images and heroes was quite limited. Though he recognized the importance of romantic pathos, especially as far as the education of youth was concerned, he made little actual use of it and preferred logical analysis to any appeal to the emotions. Nonetheless, there was some facet of his personality that was in contradiction with the seemingly clearheaded logic of his writings and teachings. His concepts were too simple on the surface: They depicted a picture that was ostensibly logical yet in actual truth was nonrealistic. The formal logic that underlay his arguments was not always compatible with historical logic.

Jabotinsky identified with a world in which Europe was the dominant factor and its word was law. To a substantial extent, this was already part of the world of yesterday by the 1920s. Jabotinsky was aware of the fact that European imperialism was confronted by an upsurge in numerous national movements and would ultimately lose its control of colonies overseas. Yet he regarded imperialism as the historical ally of the Zionist movement and hoped he would be able to tap its assistance during the interim period required by the movement to sink roots and establish itself in Palestine. Oscar Grusenberg, an attorney who had gained fame in 1913 as defense lawyer for Beilis in the blood libel trial in Russia, had advised Jabotinsky to try to come to an understanding with the Arabs. Jabotinsky wrote him: "It is true that Europe can only subjugate the Arabs but is unable to work out an understanding with them on the basis of that subjugation. For that reason, it will, in the span of another 50 or 75 years, ultimately lose those countries inhabited by Arabs—maybe even sooner, say in about 30 years. However, 30 years could be sufficient, under a proper regime, to allow us the opportunity to create a Jewish majority in Palestine."[80]

This was the reason why he was opposed to the evolutionary conception. Time was of the essence. The short span he assumed was available to the movement to acquire a foothold in Palestine required an "activist" policy, that is, one that rejected the moderate British policies, since they allowed only for a slow pace of growth of the national home. Jabotinsky did not believe it was possible to establish a national home or a Jewish majority without the existence of certain political preconditions, the prerequisite for massive Jewish colonization. He termed those conditions a "colonizational regime." According to his estimate, the scope of immigration required in order to reach a Jewish majority in twenty-five years was forty thousand immigrants annually. The Zionist movement, given its modest dimensions and limited resources, was unable to organize an immigration of such magnitude or to deal with its absorption in the Palestinian economy. Hence, Jabotinsky argued, the mandatory government—which, according to the mandate, was charged with the task of encouraging the establishment of a Jewish national home—was obliged to take certain steps in order to advance that objective. First, it should initiate a "land reform," that is, confiscate lands not cultivated by Arabs and place them at the disposal of Jewish settlement. Jabotinsky believed this move was absolutely necessary in light of a salient economic fact: A rise in the price of land in Palestine in the wake of Jewish demand had made it questionable whether the Zionist Organization would be financially able to implement its settlement plans. In order to finance that settlement, the British government should give Jews a loan backed by the collateral of the land that had already been placed at their disposal. In addition, the British mandatory government should institute protective tariffs for the benefit of new Jewish industry. All these conditions would be at the expense of the Arabs not only on the national–collective level but on the individual–personal plane as well. Aside from the central matter of "land reform," the special tariffs would also harm the Arab community directly, since, although the Arabs had no particular interest in developing industry themselves, they did have a practical interest in keeping tariffs in Palestine low, a policy that guaranteed them cheap imports. Jabotinsky believed the clash between Jewish and Arab interests was unavoidable and asserted that the only way to overcome Arab opposition to Jewish settlement was by erecting a military "iron wall" between it and its rivals.[81]

Jabotinsky described his attitude toward the Arabs as "polite indifference."[82] In his writings and speeches, it is difficult to find examples of stereotype of Arabs or any manifestation of hatred (or any other emotional attitudes) toward them. He regarded the Arabs as a "problem" standing in the way of the Zionist movement, an obstacle that had to be dealt with. Jabotinsky was not given to socialist sympathies. Schemes and visions for improving the world and transforming society that so animated his contemporaries left him cold and awakened his suspicions. His political thinking was not softened by the humanistic aspirations that had moved Herzl, for example. Jabotinsky saw himself as someone motivated and propelled by one single and all-consuming idea: Jewish nationalism in its Zionist version. The dominance of the national idea in his worldview was not unique. If one had asked members of Ha-Poel ha-Tzair and even of Ahdut ha-Avoda what the dominant feature in their ideology was, they probably would have answered: Zionism. Yet in their outlook, Zionism was supplemented by the admixture of the socialist–humanist element. Both consciously and unconsciously and, in the final analysis, subordinate to the national component, that socialist element served in their perspective as a kind of valuational filter for national egoism and its implications, mollifying, criticizing, and restraining its excesses. Consequently, the nationalist-minded intellectuals in the Labor camp, such as U. Z. Greenberg, Abba Ahimeir and Y. H. Yeivin, were eventually compelled to leave the movement and seek their political home among the revisionists. In terms of the ethics of action, Jabotinsky had a normative point of origin that differed from that of the leaders of the Labor movement. The latter felt themselves restricted by a given system of rules governing relations between peoples and nations. When they transgressed those rules, they did so with misgivings, hesitation, and caution, with a sense of guilt at violating norms of conduct. In contrast, Jabotinsky felt right from the outset that he was not bound by such norms and their constraints.

Jabotinsky was completely candid and frank in his attitude toward the Arabs, free of complexes and inhibitions. In 1926 he declared, "The tragedy is that there is a clash here between two truths; but the justice of our cause is greater."[83] The absence of stereotypes in his thinking was part of his same, unadulterated basic attitude to the problem: He did not seek justifications for the political line he advocated and thus did not have psychological need for any negative images of the Arab that might function as a palliative to soothe his conscience. For that reason, he did not require any proof that an Palestinian–Arab national movement did not exist. As mentioned, the leadership of the Labor movement was hard put to recognize the existence of an Arab national movement in Palestine. Jabotinsky, for his part, had no such qualms: He had no difficulties accepting as given the fact that such a movement existed, was legitimate, and was equal in its aspirations and intrinsic value to other national movements. It is hard to determine what the clarity of his deduction was based on: Did it derive from an analysis of the existing reality as encountered in the field or from a more abstract conception? As far as is known, Jabotinsky did not have any direct connections with nationalist-minded Palestinian Arabs. In Paris, he had met young Arab nationalists from the Maghreb, Egypt, and Syria— and possibly from Palestine. Most probably, however, his analysis of the situation was based on general assumptions about political developments in the area: Since a nationalist ferment was taking place throughout all of the Arab East, it was reasonable to assume that Palestine would not be spared.[84] There was no country of colonization, he contended, where the natives had welcomed colonization by in-migrating settlers. It was immaterial whether those settlers behaved justly and fairly and were highly moral in their conduct or were simple thieves: The reaction by the native population to their project of settlement had been identical in all instances. Moreover, the opposition of the natives had not been contingent upon the actual concrete prospects for European settlement to reside peacefully, side-by-side, with the indigenous population. Even in places where there were great expanses of un-populated territory and land was in abundance, the natives had risen up against the settlers and defended their right to their ancestral land.[85]

Jabotinsky made use of this argument in order to dispel the covert hope lurking behind the assumptions of the defensive ethos, namely, that Jews could settle Pal-estine without resorting to military force. It is doubtful whether that analysis was based on an assessment of the actual situation of the Arab National movement in Palestine at that time, the level of its conceptual and organizational development, or its ability to mobilize manpower. Rather, Jabotinsky's analysis was founded on a theoretical condition—analogies with other liberation movements and other lands of colonization. From this vantage, he arrived at the conclusion that the Jew-ish–Arab confrontation was not only unavoidable but was already imminent. It is true that an Arab national movement did exist in Palestine at this time. However, it is unlikely that it had reached the stage of development that justified Jabotinsky's analysis.[86] There was an element of self-fulfilling prophecy in his words. Assuming that the confrontation was unavoidable, he did everything in his power to clarify and accentuate it. In contrast with the policy of obfuscation adopted by the contem-porary Zionist leadership, he demanded total candor. One should not only openly enunciate Zionist intentions to establish a Jewish majority in Palestine but also concede that the Arabs were adamantly opposed to Jewish settlement and that it was impossible to arrive at any kind of an agreement with them in the foreseeable future. Jabotinsky contended that such an agreement was impossible until Arabs became convinced that they had no option but to accept Jewish settlement. The only way to bring them to this realization was by establishing a military force in Palestine.[87]

The topic of guaranteeing the peace and security of the Jewish community in Palestine by means of force was at the top of Jabotinsky's agenda from the time of the legion on. There is no doubt that the experience of the legion was one of the formative experiences in his life; it left its imprint not just on his thinking but also on his style of speech and behavior, indicating a quite profound degree of internal-ization. During the early years of the mandate, all his activity was directed toward achieving one paramount aim, that of guaranteeing the continued existence of the legion. After it was disbanded, he focused on establishing a battalion made up largely of Jews within the framework of the British army. This was supposed to be a battalion under British command, with British uniforms. For Jabotinsky, the external aspects of the military, such as uniforms, discipline, and hierarchical struc-ture, had a key educational value. He also regarded these as a potential deterrent for the Arab population. By the same token, he had little enthusiasm for the idea of setting up an underground Jewish militia and was not enamored of the combi-nation of fighter and worker, along the lines of Trumpeldor in Tel Hai. Jabotinsky preferred a professional, well-polished military to a fighting force of irregulars based on improvisation.[88] He also suspected that if the British were quietly to allow the Jews to set up a militia, they would be compelled to follow suit and do the same for the Arabs. Considering the Arab advantage in numbers, this would tip the scales in their favor.[89] Yet he saw no reason why the British should oppose the establishment of a completely or primarily Jewish battalion within the British Army. In order to encourage them in this direction, he suggested that the Zionist Organization should finance the maintenance of such a battalion. He was not perturbed by possible Arab opposition to the formation of the battalion or by the fear that they might regard the unit as some sort of provocation, as the British and the moderate Zionists argued. The reader of Jabotinsky's writings can sense between the lines not only Jabotinsky's recognition of the fact that such a confrontation was inevitable but something else as well: a kind of excitement in anticipation of the coming clash.

Jabotinsky's policy of frontal clash was not in keeping with the psychology of the Yishuv in the 1920s. The notion that there was no way of avoiding a confrontation between Jews and Arabs in Palestine was, to say the least, rather disconcerting at a time when Jews constituted only a small minority of the population. The cruel determinism of that conception was difficult for people to digest, most of whom were antimilitant in outlook. It was hard to come to terms with the awareness that the Jewish community there was destined to live by the sword for a prolonged period—and even harder when it soon became clear that there was no basis for the hope that the British would fulfill the role assigned to them by Jabotinsky. In Jabotinsky's conception, the Jews and the British were two European components on the same side of the arena in a land of colonization. Jabotinsky believed in the identity of Jewish and British interests; and he demonstrated his loyalty to, and friendship for, Britain throughout the course of his entire political career. It appears that not only the British Army but British power in all its governmental forms had left a lasting imprint on his thinking. He saw a Jewish Palestine as the veritable bastion of European civilization pitted against the stormy waves of Arab nationalism.

However, the British thought differently. They believed their interests in the Middle East were allied with those of the Arab peoples. Quite early on, they began to regard their self-incurred obligation toward Zionism as an unfortunate blunder—an error that they should remedy as soon as possible. At best, they attempted to limit their role in the Zionist project to one that was minimal and passive. Moreover, the British did not conceive of the Jews as white European settlers confronting Arab natives. The truth of the matter is that they saw them as another category of native, exceptionally troublesome, with unreasonable demands and pretensions. The British officials in Palestine, trained in a colonialist tradition that it was necessary to preserve the well-being of the natives, openly preferred the Arabs, who were authentic Orientals, mysterious and charming, to the loud and uncouth Jewish immigrants. Not only was there little prospect that the British would actually implement the "colonizing regime" that Jabotinsky advocated, but they even rejected smaller concessions, such as broad Jewish participation in the armed forces and police in Palestine. It is doubtful whether the British at that time accepted Jabotinsky's concept of an inevitable confrontation. What is certain is that as experienced as they were in the ways of government, they did not think there was any reason to hasten the arrival of trouble that could be put off by a policy of caution. Thus, they spurned any proposal that could be interpreted by the Arabs as a provocation. Jabotinsky's theories had no prospect of being tested in the field.

This fact was not overlooked by the Palestinian Jews. Perhaps that is the main reason why Jabotinsky and his teachings met with little success in the Yishuv, particularly in the 1920s. People continued to believe in more optimistic scenarios than that of an immediate and inevitable confrontation. After 1921, as the years passed and calm returned to Palestine, Jabotinsky's crying wolf regarding the riots that would erupt there sounded less and less convincing. People wanted to believe in the defensive ethos; they wanted to have faith in the notion that the small everyday acts they patiently performed would gradually lead to the ultimate realization of the great idea. Only exceptionally enthusiastic young people could be attracted to the romanticism of an army that did not exist. The others sought more concrete paths for their creative energies.

Jabotinsky viewed himself as the spiritual heir of Herzl and Nordau—and to some extent this was true. There was substantial similarity between his logical–formal train of thought and their analytic perspectives. This was the legacy of European enlightenment, unburdened by traditional Jewish complexity. Like them, Jabotinsky was also free of fanciful conceptions about the world of ancient Jewish myth. Like Herzl and Nordau, he was a secular nationalist. He believed, as they did, that politics was the dominant component and that economy, society, and culture, despite their importance, were all subordinate to the political dimension. In his endeavor to act with total and complete candor and always say what he actually meant without any concern about expediency, one can discern something of the legacy of that deep aspiration to restore lost Jewish dignity. As will be recalled, that desire had been one of the chief concerns among Zionists in the preceding generation. The element of *hadar* (roughly, "gentlemanly behavior") in his educational thinking was a direct continuation of the approaches calling for Jewish action that would engender respect, so that Gentiles would no longer accuse Jews of shameful shrewdness and cunning.

Jabotinsky's conception of force is also associated with this. He was undoubtedly influenced by the experiences he had gathered in his efforts on behalf of self-defense units in Eastern Europe. But he attributed much greater importance to the aspect of the military component in fashioning the image of the new Jew. In his book *Samson* (translated from Russian into Hebrew in the late 1920s), Samson sends the Jews his last testament in the final scene where his disciple bids farewell to Samson before his heroic death. Samson commands the Jews to do three things: amass iron, take a king as ruler over them, and learn laughter. That third instruction contains a wry hint at the tendency of loyal Zionists, especially from the Socialist camp, to take themselves and the world too seriously, unsoftened by a grain of humor. The first two instructions reflected that same sphere in Jabotinsky's consciousness that had nurtured a militaristic tendency in him. He saw Jewish weakness as a product of two interlinked facts: a lack of national discipline (manifested in the absence of a ruler able to set in motion thousands of arms by a single word) and an absence of military ability (symbolized here by iron).[90] The military education he wanted to provide his disciples was designed to overcome and remedy these two evils in Jewish existence: Jews should become accustomed to carrying out orders, accepting hierarchy, and obeying superiors. These were traits that Jews traditionally had not held in high esteem. At one and the same time, this also involved getting them used to weapons and creating the physical force that could decide the future fate of Palestine. Right from the outset, such military force was meant to be directed against the Arabs.[91] Its importance was not only practical but also lay in the change in Jewish mentality engendered by the emergence of such a force and by training in military values.

As I have mentioned, Jabotinsky had no prospect of testing his ideas in the practical laboratory of Palestine. But he did apply them in the education of youth. Parallel with the formation of the Revisionist movement, a youth movement called Betar associated with it was also set up. Brit Yosef Trumpeldor (Covenant of Joseph Trumpeldor), the full name of the movement, altered the customary way of writing the name Trumpeldor in Hebrew in order to create the acronym that would recall the name of the fortress of Bar Kokhba, which fell in battle against the Romans in A.D. 135. The Tel Hai story and the figure of Trumpeldor were also adopted by Jabotinsky's disciples as guiding myths: In the Betar version, there was a blurring of the socialist bonds associated with the dead hero and extra emphasis on the military aspects of his personality, his military experience in Russia, his participation in the Zion Mule Corps in Gallipoli, and his role in the battle at Tel Hai. Jabotinsky even attributed to Trumpeldor a definition of "pioneer" that differed from the customary definition popular in the ranks of the Labor movement: according to Jabotinsky's formulation, a pioneer was somebody prepared to carry out any task required of him by the national movement.[92] His definition lacked the usual emphasis on physical labor in general and tilling the soil in particular. Jabotinsky and the Betar movement adopted the myth of Tel Hai and Trumpeldor with a focus on the militant, combatant aspect of Tel Hai.[93] The Betar youth movement was educated in a spirit that gave pride of place to military paraphernalia and values: uniforms, order drills, and absolute hierarchy in the organization of the movement. The uniforms were designed to imitate those of the scouts, yet the use of brown (the color of the soil as Jabotinsky noted) immediately awakened associations with military khaki. Later, in the 1930s, it also seemed reminiscent of the brown shirts of the Nazi storm troopers; but that similarity was unforeseen. With time, Jabotinsky and his associates also attempted to provide Betar with the rudiments of military training.[94]

Whoever reads through the contents of the educational program of Betar, which included studying the classics of Hebrew poetry, finds it difficult readily to pinpoint the differences between it and the Labor youth movements. The nature of the meetings and the poems and passages read from Hebrew literature were, in fact, not essentially different. Yet in Betar, there was no study of certain chapters of world history seen from the perspective of the downtrodden and oppressed peoples and classes, nor was there any attention given to the history of the international and Palestinian Labor movement. The militarist games and the monistic idea of "one banner" (i.e., nationalism alone, unmitigated by any other scales of values) were the elements that made Betar unique. The poverty of the spiritual–intellectual world that was the inevitable result of this self-imposed abstention led to an increased emphasis on elements drawn from the romanticism of various national movements. With time, the impact exerted by Polish national romanticism on Betar became quite pronounced.[95]

An excellent example of this world of values and the problematic orientation deriving from it can be found in the "Betar Hymn," written by Jabotinsky for his youth movement in 1932. The lines that became especially popular were the following:

> In blood and sweat a new race shall arise,
> Proud, generous, and cruel. . . .
> For peace is muddy,
> Sacrifice blood and soul,
> For the sake of the hidden grandeur. . .
>   to die or to conquer the mountain.

As is frequent in poetic products of national romanticism, it is difficult to ascertain the exact concrete meaning of these idioms and phrases. It is not clear what was exactly meant by reference to the race that is "proud, generous, and cruel." It is also uncertain how the hyperbolic figure "peace is muddy" was intended sincerely or was merely for the sake of rhetoric. The expression "hidden grandeur" leaves a great deal to the imagination of the reader. The image of the mountain as a symbol of the Zionist mission had already appeared in several earlier works, as I have mentioned. According to Jabotinsky's son, who was present when the song was composed, his father's guideline was simply to find words that would rhyme with final -ar, such as *Betar, akhzar* (cruel), and *nistar* (hidden). The hymn recalls three heroic debacles from national mythology: Betar, Yodefat, and Massada (in Lamdan's, rather than the regular Hebrew, spelling). The reference to Yodefat had been rare in the previous mythologization of the national past, since the story of Yodefat in Josephus ends with the treason of the author. All in all, none of the symbols recalled here are exceptional within the framework of the accepted system of Zionist education. The hymn is not a particularly outstanding work in the Zionist Hebrew poetic corpus. Jabotinsky's poetry does not contain any residues of Jewish tradition and suffers from a lack of spiritual depth. Indeed, the hymn appears to be a pure demonstration of romantic poetics,[96] devoid of the abysses and peaks prominent in the work of U. Z. Greenberg.

Jabotinsky's style was inseparable from his personality. When one of his disciples, Yeshayahu Klinov, wished to try to bring the revisionists closer together with the camp of Labor, he suggested to Jabotinsky that he should express himself in a more cautious and circumspect way. Jabotinsky replied that his strength as a journalist was not in writing about some objective truth. Rather, he bent the stick, in a figurative sense, all the way to the opposite side in order to accentuate and sharpen the point he wished to emphasize. "This is the only journalistic method I can use," he remarked.[97] Jabotinsky's expressive style and rhetoric had a certain importance in fostering the militant inclinations of his disciples. The concepts he chose, such as "wall of iron," "ethics of the wall of iron," and the expressions employed in the "Betar Hymn," were of major pedagogical significance, even though he himself apparently used them with poetic license, rather than serious intent. The form of expression was important to Jabotinsky, and he purposely chose aggressive for-mulations. For example, in an appearance at Beit Ha-Am in Tel Aviv in late 1928, he spoke about the primacy of nationalism in the colonization era and stated that during that period, "there is no justice, no judiciary, no god in heaven; there is only one single and decisive law to which all is subject—settlement."[98] Addressing a group of Betar youth in Tel Aviv, he called on them to create scandals, in the spirit of "peace is muddy," in order to promote the use of the Hebrew language and the sale of products "made in Palestine." He enjoyed using the expression *hooliganon,* a Hewbrew diminutive of the loan-word "hooligan," and called for nonnormative behavior as the special obligation incumbent on youth in that era.[99]

According to Beilinson's report, Jabotinsky also dedicated a section in his speech to the role of youth in relations between Jews and Arabs. From the restrained tone taken by Beilinson here, it is possible to understand that Jabotinsky spoke on this occasion about the need to give young people military training.[100] It is not unlikely that he utilized concepts no less aggressive in this domain. There was some sort of built-in tension between the proclivity of Jabotinsky toward *hadar,* solid, polite, and restrained quality, and his inclination to break all the rules of the game, utilize extreme language, and encourage others to actions that violated the rules. Ultimately, the element of *hadar* was channeled in the direction of drilling exercises, uniforms, and formal etiquette internal to the movement. But the world external to Betar was treated to a different aspect of Jabotinsky and the education he wished to promote—a conscious subordination of the moral principles to the national cause.

Brit Shalom: The Faith in an Imminent Jewish–Arab Accord

In his diary entry for April 26, 1925, Arthur Ruppin, who from 1908 on was involved in all the Zionist settlement schemes and experiments in Palestine, a member of the Zionist Executive at intervals during the 1920s and 1930s, and even its chairman in Jerusalem for the years 1933–1935, described two meetings that took place at his home in Jerusalem on successive days. At the first, the well-known revisionist and journalist von Weisl was the featured speaker. At the second, Yosef Horovitz, an internationally acclaimed orientalist, gave the lecture. "Horovitz wants Jews and Arabs to cooperate, while Weisl wants to lead Jews, as pioneers from Europe, against the Arabs, who occupy this outpost of Asia"[101]—with these brief words, Ruppin succinctly described the fundamental differences in concep-tion between the revisionists and those circles that a short time later would establish the Brit Shalom.

As is the way of extreme poles that struggle against the center, there was consid-erable common ground between the approach of the revisionists—Jabotinsky in particular—and that of the members of Brit Shalom. Neither camp hesitated in its resolve to face the Arab problem squarely, define its nature, and seek relevant solu-tions. Both camps rejected the principles of the defensive ethos and stressed its lack of credibility and (it should be noted) the element of hypocrisy that they believed it contained. Against the tendency to obfuscate and obscure the nature of the Jewish–

Arab contrast, they chose to speak about it overtly and refer to it directly, without fear or vacillation. While the adherents of the defensive ethos wanted to postpone dealing with the Arab problem to a point as distant in the future as possible, these wished to face up to and grapple with that issue immediately. They had no difficulty in recognizing the existence of a national Arab movement; moreover, they believed that any serious attempt to deal with the Arab question necessitated taking the reality of that movement into proper account. From that point on, however, the paths of the two extreme poles parted. While Jabotinsky assumed that a Jewish–Arab confrontation was inevitable and that it had to be dealt with by military force, members of Brit Shalom believed it was possible to prevent the collision and to arrive at an accord with the Arabs that would facilitate peaceful Jewish settlement in Palestine.

Brit Shalom was established in 1925, and Ruppin was its first chairman. The association included an impressive list of intellectuals, some of whom were associated with the Hebrew University in Jerusalem. Others were outstanding journalists or held key posts in the Zionist bodies and were moderate in political outlook. Their ranks included a large number of persons who had immigrated from Central Europe, from the German-speaking cultural area—such as Hans Kohn, Hugo Bergmann, Ernst Simon, Gershom Scholem, and Robert Weltsch. Numerically, the association never exceeded more than several dozen members and sympathizers. Yet its public influence was incommensurately greater. The leaders of the Labor movement, for example, regarded the organization and its membership as important enough to polemicize against them in the pages of *Davar*. The leadership of the Labor movement in the 1920s recognized the importance of Brit Shalom as an intellectual focus and did not disqualify the association and its views as non-Zionist. They believed that its emphases were mistaken and its methods of action infuriating, but they did not doubt their credibility or loyalty to the Zionist ideal. Labor responses to Jabotinsky and his ideas were far more pointed than to the positions of Brit Shalom. It is very possible that this mildness in response derived from the relative weakness of Brit Shalom among the public at large and from the assumption, correct in itself, that it had no prospect of winning hearts and minds over to its stance. In contrast, Jabotinsky had specific political aspirations and a community of admirers, and these made revisionism a serious potential competitor. Yet it appears that the bond between members of Brit Shalom and leaders of the Labor movement was greater in the 1920s than the proximity between Labor and revisionism. The fact that material by U. Z. Greenberg was published side-by-side with articles by Hugo Bergmann, one of the most militant members of Brit Shalom, was evidence of the political tolerance prevalent during that era. Moreover, it was also proof of the marginality of the Arab problem at that time; in the culture of the Jewish community in Palestine, it was customary to deal tolerantly only with questions that were not felt to be crucial issues related to survival.

Pacifism as a concept did not win many hearts in Palestine, though there was quite substantial admiration for individual pacifists. For example, the figure of Tolstoy was admired and was the topic of endless disputes over the question of whether evil should be opposed or not. A. D. Gordon, even if he did not call himself a pacifist, basically rejected the use of force. At the time, Berl Katznelson admired Karl

Liebknecht for his refusal to endorse German involvement in World War I. The figure of the pacifist George Lansbury, a member of the Labour party in Britain, also aroused feelings of respect and admiration. Nonetheless, pacifism as such was one of the more marginal ideas in the diffuse galaxy of concepts current in Palestine in the early decades of the twentieth century. Here and there some "enthusiastic proponents" could be found. These were drawn mainly from the ranks of Ha-Poel ha-Tzair, and leaned toward the thinking of Tolstoy: figures such as Shlomo Schiller, Nathan Hofshi, Z. Yehuda'i, Mordechai Kushnir, and even several of the founders of Nahalal, the first cooperative moshav. But these pacifists were extreme individualists, who never pretended to represent anyone but themselves. The political and emotional climate in Palestine was not conducive to the spread of pacifist thinking. Even Nathan Hofshi, the vegetarian, faithful from his youth to Tolstoyan ideals, found himself standing guard duty in Metulla in 1920, rifle in hand.[102] The need to defend life and property, one of the basic rules of survival in Palestine, virtually closed the door on any possibility that pacifist ideas would gain currency there. The socialist Zionists, among whom there was a theoretical sympathy for the idea, avoided applying it to the conditions prevailing in Palestine. The majority preferred the revolutionary idea to that of pacifism. Pacifism had a basic element of passivity that was in absolute conflict with the urge for action that animated them. Despite the fact that pacifism was not widespread, there was public sympathy for the idea and its adherents, as a kind of gesture by someone who recognizes the worth of a good idea even though he himself is unable to implement it in practice.

Brit Shalom did not declare itself to be pacifist, although the thinking of a portion of its membership was quite close to pacifist positions. The problem that its members wanted to deal with was (as Ruppin formulated it) how "to settle the Jews, as a second people, in a country already inhabited by another people, and to accomplish this peacefully."[103] Both Ruppin and Jabotinsky shared the tendency to think in concepts borrowed from the arsenal of European colonialism. Yet while Jabotinsky presented the situation in Palestine as analogous to that of other lands of colonization, Ruppin and his associates wanted to create a unique and special state of affairs in Palestine, hitherto unknown: colonizing without the use of force. Jabotinsky saw force as a natural component of political life; in contrast, members of Brit Shalom viewed the use of force as a repelling and deterring element of the same political life that they had undertaken to alter. The belief that it was possible to change reality without resorting to violent means was a basic assumption operative in their outlook. For example, Ruppin wished "to attempt a new social order in Palestine without sudden changes [i.e., revolution] or the use of force."[104] The Bolshevik revolution aroused a substantial degree of sympathy, though people recoiled from its manifestations of brutality. Members of Brit Shalom hoped that it would be possible in Palestine to establish a model society without making use of means of coercion. In Palestine, "it will not be necessary to destroy before one can build."[105] They believed that an accord between Jews and Arabs was not only vital but feasible and urgent. In this point, members of Brit Shalom disagreed not just with the revisionists, who regarded confrontation as axiomatic, but also with the Labor movement. The latter considered such an accord desirable and possible but not in the foreseeable future. While adherents of the defensive ethos believed an accord would be a function of the growth in real Jewish power in Palestine, they did not think it was possible to attain it until after the community there had become viable. Brit Shalom had a different conception. They sensed that with the passage of time, Arab nationalism was growing ever stronger and ever more adamant in its opposition to Zionism. For that reason, they contended, the proper time for an accord was not the distant future but as soon as possible. Moreover, the adherents of the defensive ethos had avoided negotiating with the Arabs and had concentrated their political efforts on negotiations with the British authorities. In contrast, members of Brit Shalom argued that it was crucial to sit down with the Arabs directly: "An immigrant people conducts negotiations with the countries he is emigrating from, and does not negotiate with the population of the country *to which* he wishes to emigrate—all the paradoxicality in our political situation today is expressed in this."[106]

The discussion was being conducted within the framework of the dispute regarding a legislative council. Members of Brit Shalom contended that the Jews should come to an accord with the Arabs on the future structure of a legislative council, instead of attempting to prevent parliamentary representation for the Arabs of Palestine and their participation in the government. In their internal deliberations, Brit Shalom members quickly arrived at what they felt was the crux of the problem: The Arabs were afraid of losing their position as the majority in Palestine; and as long as the Jews aspired to be the majority, the Arabs would not cease in their opposition to Jewish immigration and would not agree to any accord with them. The dilemma became clear: how can one neutralize the problem of majority versus minority within the framework of relations between the two peoples so that Jews need not fear being a minority in a state with an Arab majority, and Arabs would not have to fear the possibility of becoming a minority in a state with a Jewish majority? It was impossible to solve this problem by convenient and pleasant formulas, no matter how much those participating in the deliberations would have wished to do so. There were some who tried to convince themselves that the problem was not really so serious, since even after the Jews would be a majority in Palestine, they would still be but a small drop in the ocean of Arab peoples surrounding them. That fact could potentially satisfy the Arabs and serve as a guarantee that the Zionists, once they became a majority, would indeed institute the equal rights for Arabs that they had kept promising them when they were a minority.[107] Members of Brit Shalom assumed that negotiations between Jews and Arabs would result in working out a constitutional structure that would provide guarantees for the rights of both peoples and defuse the explosive question of relations between majority and minority in the Palestinian context.[108]

In one of the discussions, Yosef Sprinzak, a leader of Ha-Poel ha-Tzair who had pursued university studies in Beirut before World War I and had contacts there with Arab nationalists, broached the idea that the concept *rov* (majority) should be dropped and replaced by the term *rabim* (many).[109] On the whole, there was little sympathy among adherents of Brit Shalom for the Herzlian idea of a state. The version of Zionism they advocated was close to the thinking of Ahad Ha-Am, who taught that spiritual–intellectual revival was more important than political resurgence. In 1925 Shlomo Schiller wrote, "Nowadays, the slogan of a return to a Jewish state is political adventurism" and that it unnecessarily exacerbates relations between the two peoples in Palestine, harming the work of settlement as a result of the tension generated. He went on to note, "A Jewish state, the meaning of which is control by the settlers of the local population (since two states on a single territory is an absurdity), is not alive as an aspiration in the hearts of Jews either in Palestine or the Diaspora."[110] Ruppin viewed Herzl's concept of the state as the product of the latter's disregard for the presence of Arabs in Palestine and his reliance on imperialistic and diplomatic conceptions that had turned out to be a figment of the imagination in the light of prevailing circumstances in Palestine.[111] For that reason, Sprinzak's formula gained currency within Brit Shalom. It entailed renouncing the claim to Jewish predominance in Palestine, underscored by the demand for a Jewish majority; but it did not rule out the possibility that Jews might eventually become a majority there. This constituted an attempt to depoliticize the demographic problem and thus to circumvent the principal question, namely, Jewish immigration to Palestine. At that juncture in time, no one in Brit Shalom was suggesting that limitations should be placed on immigration.

The endeavor to neutralize the question of majority led to the idea of a binational state. In such a state, neither people is dominant and identified with the state, with the other as a minority. Rather, two peoples share state sovereignty, and both have the same right of ownership. This right is not dependent on the numerical relation between them. The idea of a binational state was in conflict with the conception of a Jewish state not only in the domain of politics and sovereignty but in the sphere of emotions, as well. The Jewish state was supposed to liberate Jews from the burden of living in the midst of another people. The idea of a binational polity not only obligated Jews to take the existence of others in their country into consideration but also compelled them to give up the psychological relief associated with liberation from a multinational situation. The Churchill White Paper of 1922 served as the constitutional point of departure for the binational idea. That document was interpreted by Hugo Bergmann and his associates as creating a balance between Jewish and Arab rights in Palestine. In a binational state, each people was supposed to be organized for itself within the framework of two national autonomies endowed with equal rights.[112] Parallel with this, Bergmann hoped that a "Palestinian" citizenship could be created and that loyalty to it would supercede particularistic national loyalties of the two constituent peoples.[113] The radicals in Brit Shalom, such as Hans Kohn and Ernst Simon, as well as the chancellor of the Hebrew University, Judah Magnes, who was basically pacifistic in outlook, probably welcomed Bergmann's statement that "God endowed the people of Israel with a special favor, making its national home the homeland of *two* peoples."[114] It is doubtful whether other Zionists also thought that this was an act of grace. At best, they apparently assumed that this was yet another trial by which the Lord endeavored to test his people. Be that as it may, the binational idea now became the platform of Brit Shalom, designed to serve as the basis for rapprochement between Jews and Arabs.

Despite all their firm belief in the goodness of the human heart, members of Brit Shalom did not put their trust in the good nature of both sides to preserve the delicate balance they wished to create in Palestine. The binational idea was linked with the idea of Palestine's remaining under British control for an extended period. Members of Brit Shalom had an ambivalent attitude toward British imperialism. Most had misgivings about the Balfour Declaration and preferred, instead, a League of Nations mandate for Palestine that would guarantee Jewish rights of immigration and settlement. Yet it would not grant them privileges beyond that, as the British Mandate ostensibly did, stirring Arab agitation without being truly conducive to the advancement of Jewish interests.[115] However, parallel with their grave misgivings about an alliance with British imperialism, they saw the need for a constant presence of a third party in Palestine that could serve as arbiter in the binational state, and would ensure that the rights of both peoples would in fact be respected and preserved. Hans Kohn contended that until nationalism disappeared as a political factor and until all political boundaries were eliminated under the protection of a "genuine" League of Nations, Palestine should remain part of the British Empire; then the question of sovereignty there would not be raised at all. Kohn did not recoil from the prospect of that option; on the contrary, he viewed it as a highly positive eventuality: "The mandatory power and the League of Nations need to bear responsibility to make sure that it will not be possible, now or in the future, to subjugate one segment of the population by the power of the majority." This kind of protectorate was supposed to continue indefinitely.[116] Thus, the binational idea, which had sprung from the aspiration to give political expression to the Arab population while preserving Jewish rights, led, in the final analysis, to a conclusion amounting to an arrangement to prevent either of the two peoples in Palestine from gaining sovereignty.

There were two levels of discussion in the arguments used by Brit Shalom members to justify its political line: the politicial–pragmatic level and the ethical–moral level. In the pragmatic sphere, they attempted to demonstrate that time was running out for the Zionist movement. As proof, they pointed to the national upsurge in Egypt, Syria, and Iraq. They also noted that the level of education among Arabs in Palestine was on the rise and that an educated generation would thus appear on the scene in a few short years, raising extensive political demands. Moreover, they argued, the British, once it was clear to them how powerful Arab opposition was to their pro-Zionist policies, were bound to work out an agreement with the Arabs at the expense of the Jews. The Jews had no army at their disposal such as Jabotinsky had urged, to take Palestine by force. Consequently, they reasoned, it was better for the Jews to arrive at an understanding with the Arabs and conclude an agreement as soon as possible under conditions that would ensure continuing immigration and settlement but that would recognize Arab rights to equal partnership in the sovereignty over Palestine.[117]

Concomitantly, there was a discussion in the sphere of ethics. The key question was, Are Jews who settle in Palestine exempt from the obligation to apply the principles of morality guiding the private sphere to that of politics, as well? Even if members of Brit Shalom tended to frame their arguments as being based on a realistic analysis of the situation, in actual fact, the ethical problem was at the center of their thoughts. The clash between a strict moral ethos that demanded application in the public sphere of the same norms applied in the private sphere and a complex and complicated political reality gave rise to the special composition of Brit Shalom. "Zionism never ceased to rely on the most exalted principles of morality," Gershom Scholem noted: "Why should those principles suddenly be revoked when they are no longer comfortable for us?"[118]

A significant proportion of Brit Shalom members regarded Ahah Ha-Am as their mentor and viewed morality as the essential trait of Judaism. In their perspective, Zionism was a movement of intellectual and cultural rejuvenation that could develop only in Palestine, due to the special bonds between the Jewish people and its land. The intrinsic value of the Jewish entity to be created in Palestine would be evaluated in terms of its moral qualities and substance, not its political or military strength. Hence, the necessity of arriving at an agreement with the Arabs was not dictated by an opportunistic political need but derived from the system of beliefs and ideas that obligated moral behavior at every stage of Jewish settlement in Palestine. For Brit Shalom, the question of the attitude toward Arabs served as the litmus paper to test the toughness of the moral fiber of the movement.

Already at the beginning of 1929, Hugo Bergmann protested against the chauvinism that had reared its head among the younger generation in Palestine and against educating young people "in the ideals of the *biryonim* [hooligans] and the cult of force." He also warned about the emergence of these phenomena among the Arabs, as well, and viewed this development as a threat to the prospects for cooperation between the two peoples.[119] It is doubtful whether such phenomena were as widespread at that juncture as Bergmann portrayed them to be. Rather, it would seem that he wished to warn about an anticipated development, not an actual one. The feeling in Brit Shalom circles that Jewish–Arab relations were progressively deteriorating led them to ever-more-pointed formulations of their principles and goals. On the other hand, the difficulties inherent in implementing those ideas became clearer and clearer. That process brought about a differentiation among the ranks of members of Brit Shalom themselves. There were those, like Bergmann, for whom a Jewish–Arab accord became the crucial goal and who argued that the association should make active efforts to achieve it. Others, like Ruppin, wanted an accord but had increasing doubts about the feasbility of achieving it. They contended that the association should best avoid political activity and limit itself to intellectual discourse. After an illuminating exchange with Hans Kohn and Hugo Bergmann, Ruppin recorded in his diary: "The conversation also revealed in other respects how difficult it is to balance the realization of Zionism with general ethical considerations. It left me rather depressed. Is Zionism really to end up as shallow chauvinism? Is it impossible to provide the ever-growing number of Jews in Palestine with a field of activity without oppressing the Arabs?"[120]

In a letter to Hans Kohn, Ruppin detailed the clashes of interest between Jews and Arabs that could not be bridged: the purchase by Jews of land for cultivation and consequent eviction of tenant farmers; and the immigration of destitute Jews, who supplant Arabs, taking their jobs. In such a situation, Ruppin argued, there is no sense in declaring one's support for a constitution, as Bergmann and Kohn demanded, since any thorough examination of the problem of a constitution "would immediately reveal to the Arabs that the constitution we envisage and which is essential for our survival can be no more than a fiction of a constitution in their eyes."[121] Ruppin had as yet not retreated from the basic assumptions of Brit Shalom. But his words contained the first signs of doubt about the feasibility of finding a way to an accord with the Arabs that would simultaneously protect the vital interests of the Zionist project.

In the public debate that raged during those years between people of Brit Shalom and the leaders of the Labor movement, the former attacked the fundamental principles of the defensive ethos. The decisions of the Ahdut ha-Avoda conference at Ein Harod in 1924, which postponed the issue of negotiations with the Arabs to a distant future, when their leadership would be composed of the "right kind" of people, were severely criticized by Brit Shalom. Hugo Bergmann made the accusation that "a program like this orients itself toward the distant future in order to avoid dealing with the burning problem of the present."[122] A demand for immediate negotiations contradicted the basic assumptions of the defensive ethos. The idea of a binational state was in contradiction with the principles of the Jewish right of ownership to Palestine. It also made reference to Arab nationalism in Palestine as an existing fact. In contrast, Beilinson and his associates—as much as they wanted to take Arab rights into consideration and give the Arabs autonomy "with their own schools, language, and way of life," in accordance with the concept of autonomy in Eastern Europe—were not prepared to recognize them as equal partners to a state but only as a "fragment of a nation."[123] While Brit Shalom regarded the Arab question as paramount, the Labor movement viewed it as one of many questions and not the most important one. Brit Shalom's critique of the defensive ethos was rejected, just as the criticism from the Right was spurned. The more the economic situation deteriorated at the close of the 1920s, the more marginal the discussion of the Arab question became.

Beginning in 1928, there was mounting tension between Jews and Arabs. After years in which the British had imposed impeccable public order and Jews, men and women alike, had been able to walk freely throughout all of Palestine in complete safety and without fear, the situation now changed: There were more and more incidents of rape of young Jewish women in Jerusalem by Arabs and an increasing number of robberies in cities and towns everywhere in the country. Although the background to these incidents was criminal, not nationalist, the fact that the assailants in all these incidents were Arab and the victims Jewish heightened the tensions between the two communities and strengthened the negative stereotypes of Arabs among Jews: They were seen as aggressive, light-fingered with the property of others, with licentious designs on Jewish women.[124] It appears that for the first time there now was a discernable note of animosity among Jews toward the Arabs as a collective. This moved Yitzhak Schweiger, a public figure and writer associated with Ahdut ha-Avoda, to warn about the danger of a new and awakening hatred toward Arabs among the Jews in Palestine.

When Jews from Eastern Europe chose to cite an example from the domain of Jewish–Gentile relations, they were accustomed to make reference to the system of relations between Jews and non-Jews familiar to them from the Diaspora. This was also true in Schweiger's case. He argued that in Europe, mutual hatred had poisoned the life of Jews and Gentiles alike. In contrast, in Palestine "we are happy to say, we harbor no hatred toward Arabs in our hearts." Again, "There is a clear awareness that we always need to be careful, on our guard; that we require our own means of defense and a defense force of our own. Yet enmity is nonexistent!" Schweiger did not advocate love or even special fraternization. After all, in the Diaspora, he argued, excessive familiarity had not prevented hatred. He preferred that Jews should settle separately—"even in specially designated areas." But he called for wise caution in relations with Arabs, since the two peoples were destined to live side-by-side and relations between them had to be guided by the conviction that both peoples had been created in the image of God. Schweiger contended that Jews were still free of the taint of "that leprosy" (as he dubbed national hatred). But he thought it necessary to issue a warning that danger was, indeed, lurking in wait.[125]

Schweiger's article was exceptional within the compass of Hebrew journalism in Palestine at the time. It was extremely rare to pose the question of Jewish–Arab relations in a human context, rather than one involving politics or economics. Schweiger depicted not real flesh-and-blood Arabs but an anonymous collective. Yet his call for relating to the Arab as a human being and his references to the danger of an awakening of ethnic hatred in Palestine were unique. It is impossible to know whether Schweiger had been affected by the articles of Uri Zvi Greenberg, or the burgeoning aggressiveness of the revisionists in Palestine, few in number yet vociferous. Perhaps his ideas had been prompted by reading the sensationalist and biting right-wing press, especially the paper *Doar ha-Yom* (Daily Dispatch). Maybe the attacks in the streets and on the roads had engendered an atmosphere of fear that might deteriorate into hatred. In any event, his article was considered important enough for inclusion in the Ahdut ha-Avoda anthology, *Yalkut Ahdut ha-Avoda*, an indication of the tendency characteristic of the defensive ethos to educate people in the spirit of the ideals of nonhatred and the perspective of peace.

Several months later, the Va'ad Leumi (National Council of the Jews in Palestine)* initiated an information campaign on the Arab question. The context of this decision was a rise in Arab–Jewish tensions due to an incident that set the snowball rolling that ultimately led to the August 1929 disturbances. On Yom Kippur, September 24, 1928, Jews placed a dividing curtain between men and women praying at the Wailing Wall. The British police were quick to remove the partition, seized upon by Arabs as a departure from the status quo at the Wall. The police did not even wait until the end of prayers and hastened, with what appeared to be excessive dedication and alacrity, to carry out their appointed task, seriously offending Jewish religious sentiments. A wave of agitation by both Arabs and Jews inundated the country.

Haim Margolis-Kalvaryski, one of the veterans of the Palestine Jewish Colonization Association (PICA) in Galilee, who was known for his excellent contacts with Arab notables even before World War I and was a member of Brit Shalom,

---

*The Jewish community in Palestine was organized in a legal body known as Knesset Israel (Community of Israel), with which every Jew was automatically affiliated unless he or she opted out. The members of the Knesset Israel elected a parliamentary body known as the Assefat ha-Nivharim (Elected Assembly), from which in turn, a Va'ad Leumi (National Council) was elected. In the National Council all the parties present in the assembly were represented proportionally.

wrote an open letter entitled "To Our Muslim Brothers," published in the Arabic press. He sketched an idealized picture of Jewish–Arab relations before World War I and even in the period after the 1921 disturbances. Kalvaryski wanted to set the events at the wall in proper perspective and asked the Arabs who were true to their own religion to show consideration for Jewish religious sensitivity. The tone of the letter was amicable, affable, and incredibly naive. He depicted the worsening of Arab–Jewish relations as the result of a "misunderstanding" and pointed to Brit Shalom as an expression of the desire among Jews for friendly relations with the Arabs.[126] *Al-Jami'ah al-Arabiyyah,* the organ of the circles supporting the mufti of Jerusalem, al-Hajj Amin al-Husayni, responded to his letter in an article burning with incitement against the Jews. It was alleged they were plotting to take control of the Temple Mount and destroy the mosque there; that they wanted to establish a national home in Syria and Iraq, as well; and that they wished to expel the Arabs from Palestine. The article stated that the Arabs, the majority in Palestine, demanded a parliamentary government with proportional representation and the revocation of the Balfour Declaration. An accord with the Jews was possible only if they would renounce the plan of a national home and the Balfour Declaration and support a government based on majority rule. As far as Brit Shalom was concerned, the article said that the Arabs did not trust the purity of that association's intentions.[127]

Filastin, a Jaffa newspaper owned by Arab Christians and reflecting the views of the opposition to the Husaynis, resorted to similar arguments, adding an additional demand: an end to immigration as a precondition for peace. Beilinson responded to this exchange by reenunciating the defensive ethos: Peace with the Arabs would be feasible only when they were convinced that the Jews were a genuine power. An accord could only be the result of a balance between equals. On the other hand, he rejected any call for the use of physical force. Beilinson warned: "Many, even among us, have recently begun to replace the term 'strength' with the term 'fist'. Yet in actual truth, use of the 'fist' (gaining the edge by physical means) is the most contemptible, cheap, and uncertain element within the complex of 'strength.'" He added, "True strength lies in the creation of values rooted in reality."[128]

It was precisely this antiviolent formulation by Beilinson that illuminated the fundamental differences in approach between Brit Shalom and the Labor movement. Brit Shalom pictured a Jewish–Arab accord as the eventual product of mutual concessions. Far-sighted individuals would arrive at such concessions as a result of their recognition that the alternative to the path of an accord led to bloody confrontation. The heads of the Labor movement, in contrast, believed an accord would be the outcome of a balance in national forces. It would be achieved only after it was clear to those involved that such an accord was inevitable. For the shorter term, both parties wished to preserve peace with the Arabs; yet they differed as to the ultimate objectives of such a peace.

5

The Second Challenge, 1929–1936

The August 1929 riots left a profound impression on contemporaries: They were conceived as a turning point, in whose wake the naive assumption that had been at the basis of the defensive ethos—namely, that it would be possible to establish the Zionist entity in Palestine prior to the eruption of Arab nationalism—lost much of its credibility. From the historical vantage point, it appears that observers at the time were hasty in drawing negative conclusions from those riots: The 1930s were in fact a decade that witnessed accelerated, peaceful growth in the Jewish community in Palestine once the traumatic waves of the August disturbances had subsided, and the intense preoccupation with the Arab question over the two years following those riots had also subsided. From various perspectives, it is possible to view the 1929 troubles as an isolated event that did not ultimately lead to genuine changes in British or Zionist policy. By the same token, those riots did not bring about a significant change in the topic under focus here, namely, Jewish attitudes toward the use of force. After a period of great tension, in which Jewish public opinion gave considerable attention to the Arab question and its various implications, interest shifted to other problems, in particular Hitler's rise to state power in Germany and the absorption of the Fifth Aliyah (1932–1936). The most massive immigration prior to World War II, it put an end to the economic slowdown of the years 1929–1931 and engendered a rising wave of confidence in the future of the Zionist project and in the ability of the Jewish people to implement it. In 1929, however, those developments still lay beyond the horizon. The outbreak of the August riots surprised, frightened, and shocked the Yishuv, causing both an emotional–psychological, and an ideological–political, upheaval.

The 1929 Riots: A Case Study in Jewish–Arab Relations

First of all, the riots were a shock to contemporaries by dint of their very occurrence: The fact that disturbances could break out under the British mandatory regime and that for several days the authorities had lost effective control was cause for great concern among the Jews in Palestine. For the first time since 1921, there was a sense that Jews in Palestine were sitting on an active volcano. At the twenty-third council of the Histadrut, convened in 1929, Meir Ya'ari, head of the Marxist-oriented Ha-Shomer ha-Tzair, a kibbutz movement that had its origins in the idealistic–romantic youth movement, challenged the leadership with a question that preoccupied many: "A hundred and fifty thousand Jews on a volcano. What will come of this? What can we tell the Jewish people?"[1] The paper *Doar ha-Yom,* controlled at that time by the revisionists, published an article with the significant title "We're Sitting on a Volcano."[2]

The riots were accompanied by militant Arab slogans such as "The law of Muhammad is being implemented by the sword," "Palestine is our land and the Jews our dogs," "We are well armed and shall slaughter you by the sword."[3] There were also brutal acts by Arabs for the apparent sake of cruelty, such as the killings in Hebron, where small children were tortured by their murderers before being murdered. The dread that the Arabs were planning to annihilate the entire Jewish community—men, women, and children—in one concentrated burst of violence surfaced for the first time in the wake of the August 1929 disturbances. "Is it possible for us to exist here as long as we are a minority?" asked Ben Gurion: "Is there any security for our lives in Palestine?"[4] In his diary, Ruppin confessed the fear "lest a massive Arab uprising liquidate our entire project."[5] A statement issued by the Labor parties after the riots specifically asserted that the disturbances had had a paramount aim: the annihilation of the entire Jewish community in Palestine.[6] At the founding convention of Mapai, Ben Gurion declared that while prior to the disturbances, only isolated individuals had thought it might be possible to liquidate the Yishuv by a general slaughter of Jews, perceptions had changed: now "The idea of annihilating the Jewish community had gained popularity."[7]

A sense of danger had accompanied life in Palestine, like a hidden leitmotif, throughout the period of the Second Aliyah. With his accustomed straightforwardness, Brenner had given overt expression to those apprehensions. Yet most Jews in the Yishuv had not been endowed with the sharp senses of the writer. Their awareness did not envision the danger in terms of sitting on a volcano that one day could consume the entire community. Rather, it focused on more everyday concerns: the risk that threatened travelers on the roads, farmers ploughing in the fields, families living in an isolated settlement. As long as the Arabs did not show any political intentions or the organizational abilities to mobilize large masses, the danger seemed limited, containable in predictable bounds. Many believed the disturbances in 1920 and 1921 were isolated incidents, uncoordinated and lacking the guiding hand of a national leadership.

Not so the August 1929 riots. These constituted a new phenomenon: For the first time, the Jewish community in Palestine found itself caught up in a wave of violent disturbances that swept with a fury through Jewish settlements and neighborhoods throughout the length and breadth of the country. The danger now appeared to threaten the very survival of the entire Jewish community. "If even in our homeland we must suffer from the terrible curse that is in the reproach 'And thy life shall hang in doubt before thee' [Deuteronomy 28:66], dependent on the mercy of others, . . . what motherland, what sort of safe haven do we have here?" demanded the writer Abraham Schwadron (Sharon).[8]

The natural inclination in the Yishuv was to talk a great deal about the decline in the sense of security and to complain about the British authorities: They had not acted at the proper time and had done too little to stop the riots. There was a traditional Jewish tendency to shout *gevalt* whenever Jews felt threatened by a strong and dangerous enemy. Yet the disadvantages of crying for help were soon evident. It is true that Jews in the Diaspora were deeply upset by the events in Palestine, and there was a powerful awakening of pro-Zionist sentiment among Jews in Poland and the United States. They expressed their outrage over the occurrences, and demanded that the British fulfill their obligation and defend the Jews. A collection fund was also set up to provide assistance to settlements that had been damaged and destroyed, and the Jewish response to this fund drive was relatively generous. Simultaneously, however, the shortcomings inherent in portraying the Zionist project as an enterprise suspended over the abyss became clear: "The simple, practical, and clever Jew will ask whether it is worthwhile and even permissible to risk his capital, his own life, and that of his family in a country on the verge of disaster."[9] The decline in security in Palestine had a negative effect on investments there: Every manifestation of unrest acted to deter Jews from investing funds and restrained Zionist activity.[10]

The "heroic" response to these circumstances was that there was no alternative: The Jews should adapt, and get used, to living in the shadow of a volcano. That perspective had a magnetic appeal for courageous youth in search of some modus of self-sacrifice, as reflected in a popular poem inspired by Tel Hai that gained currency at the time. In that poem, comrades give the final honors to a victim who had fallen in the Ephraim Mountains: "Like you, we, too, shall sacrifice our lives for our people."[11] Yet this consciousness was not a viable option for the masses: "On a volcano, you can't build a permanent structure that can serve as a haven for an entire people," Moshe Beilinson commented.[12] Sober-headed leaders in the Yishuv had no illusions about the potential attraction of the perspective of "By thy sword shalt thou live" (Genesis 27:40) when it came to the Jewish population as a whole. On the other hand, those same segments of the Jewish people (such as idealistic youth) who were undaunted by physical dangers were likely to recoil from, and reject, the Zionist project "due to psychological and ideological difficulties bound up with establishing a Jewish homeland under the pressure of incessant war against the Arabs (or the imminence of such a war)."[13] Ben Gurion was quick to recognize the potential danger: "The awareness that the Jews are sitting on a volcano is likely to undermine the foundations of the entire Zionist movement."

The theory of the volcano was diametrically opposed to the defensive ethos. Indeed, even at the time of Tel Hai, the idea of sacrifice had been integrated into the complex and had become a part of that ethos. However, there was a natural limit on the level of tension and intensity of confrontation that the defensive ethos was able to absorb while still remaining intact. It should be recalled that this ethos rested on a fundamental supposition, namely, that realization of the Zionist project would not require the use of force. Nonetheless, despite the fact that beginning in 1929, the "yishuvist" psyche became permeated with the fear that there could be a total annihilation by the Arabs, that dread did not lead at this stage to abandoning the defensive ethos and its tenets. It appears that the basic confidence in British protection, though undermined, remained intact in the aftermath of the disturbances. The weakness of the Jewish community in Palestine, numbering then some 170 thousand, may also have contributed to repressing the calamitous conclusions that suggested themselves in the wake of the riots.

The 1929 troubles constituted a crossroads in respect to cooperation between Jews and Arabs. The hardest-hit localities had been Hebron and Safed, mixed towns where Jews had lived together with Arabs for many generations. This fact was mustered in support of arguments calling for separation between Jewish and Arab communities. Moreover, the communities in those two towns were of the "old Yishuv": deeply religious, non-Zionist Jews. They did not carry weapons or know how to protect themselves; nor did they believe their neighbors would harm them. In the aftermath of the riots, the surviving remnants of the old Jewish community in Hebron left the town. The Jews who were evacuated from Gaza during the riots never returned there. Parallel with these events, a boycott movement developed among the Arab community against the previously prevailing custom of renting apartments to Jews in mixed towns. Significantly, Arabs had not ventured to launch attacks in the areas where Jews were concentrated in larger numbers. This gave added impetus to the colonization approach based on contiguity, namely, the creating of a continuous stretch of Jewish territory, while not settling in those parts of Palestine where it was difficult to locate settlements linked into a connected strip. Thus, the 1929 riots exercised a major formative impact on the future map of Jewish colonization in Palestine. That configuration would serve as a basis when the day arrived for a partition plan.[14]

The riots and everything connected with them were given heavy coverage in the press. The time-worn concept *pogrom* took on a renewed prominence in descriptions. Terms such as "slaughter" and "butchery" were very frequent in characterizing the attacks that had been perpetrated against Jews, especially in Hebron. The paper *Ha-Aretz* headlined its report on the bloodshed in Hebron "In the City of Slaughter," writing that "the Arabs of Hebron carried out a genuine slaughter against the Jews there, like those of Gonta and Petlyura."[15] The paper *Davar* stressed even more the analogy with pogroms in Russia, describing the flight of Jews in Hebron from their murderers and how they had hidden in filthy holes—scenes lifted straight from Bialik's classic poem "In the City of Slaughter."[16] *Doar ha-Yom* filled its pages with descriptions of atrocities and pictures of those butchered.[17] The "old Yishuv," that had "gone to the slaughter like sheep" (a phrase used by *Ha-Aretz* in describing events in Safed),[18] not attempting to resist, awakened feelings of revulsion and disgust among the new, Zionist Yishuv. The helplessness of the yeshiva students and the cowardice displayed by the religious Jews, who had not adopted the new national ethos, were depicted as the opposite of the stance of courage shown by the new Yishuv. The fall of Kibbutz Hulda after a battle with attackers was held up as the positive antipode to the shame of Hebron and Safed.

The press made a custom of presenting one or two descriptions of "like sheep to the slaughter," stressing their negative attitude toward this kind of behavior, contrasting it with a positive example of Jewish self-defense. Writing in *Davar,* Beilinson emphasized the valor of the defenders: "Overnight, all the young people were transformed, as though they were made of iron."[19] *Doar ha-Yom* described Jerusalem preparing to defend itself: "In the eyes of its sons . . . flashes the metallic light of 'we shall not surrender', . . . the same metallic light that was in the eyes of Elazar ben Yair at Massada."[20] Uri Zvi Greenberg wrote:

> This night they are shooting at your gates, my holy city!
> And your defenders had drawn a belt of defense round about you
> . . .
> A Jewish soldier prays with a *rifle* for your safety,
> May the rifle please you better than the sound of a harp![21]

The readiness to defend the community and take a courageous stand—this was now accepted as an identity symbol of the new Jewish Yishuv. What had been largely a set of educational values in the past—fostered by tales of valor, the revival of national–historical myths, and emphasis on the sense of national dignity—now became an imperative for practical action. The principal of the Herzliya Hebrew Gymnasia in Tel Aviv, Haim Bograshov (Boger), wrote in *Ha-Aretz:* "Over the course of an entire generation, we educated our children and pupils that they should not hold out their necks to the slaughterers, that they should not die like the dead of Safed, perish like the butchered of Hebron. . . . It is over. The time of riots has passed for us and will not return, for we shall not let ourselves be killed without resisting."[22]

Almost imperceptibly, a powerful identity was generated between self-defense, demonstration of force, and national revival. To a certain extent, the process occurring here was that the basic ideology contained in Bialik's "In the City of Slaughter" and Brenner's "He Told Her" from the time of the Russian pogroms was being applied to the situation in Palestine. In the perspective of that ideology, a lack of self-defense was viewed as a moral failing. It demanded of the Jew that he demonstrate his intrinsic human value by a readiness to risk his life by standing up to and resisting his assailants. Abraham Schwadron wrote, "The saints of Hebron, of blessed memory, who in 1929, some twenty-five years after the beginning of the movement of self-defense among Jews, did not attempt to defend themselves, and did not manage to kill even one of their butchers died a death that was absolutely immoral."[23]

The events of August 1929—characterized by phenomena reminiscent of pogroms—and the two types of response that became apparent for the first time in Palestine posed once again the issue of the proper physical response to attack as a crucial question of the national ethos. The difference between the traditional Jewish response and the national stance was repeatedly underscored: A person who defends himself fulfills the commandment of the national ethos. Anyone who fails to do so is not a participant in the emerging national entity. What had been conceived in Tel Hai as a first outstanding exploit now became an order binding on all. On Tel Hai Day 1930, the first commemoration after the riots, Tel Hai was portrayed as the first link in the chain of valor that had inspired the steadfast stand of the Jewish community in the dark days of 1929.[24]

The 1929 disturbances caught the Yishuv and its leadership by total surprise.

"What was most disturbing about the Arab uprising," wrote a member of Kibbutz Ein Harod, "was our lack of knowledge about it until the large gathering in the mosque and the attack on the Jewish neighborhoods of Jerusalem."[25] The Hagana, a body that had existed in theory since 1920, was poorly organized, untrained, and not properly armed. Although in Jerusalem it succeeded in putting a halt to attacks on Jewish neighborhoods, the Oxford students (then in the city) mobilized by the mandatory government as an auxiliary force until the arrival of regular troops from Egypt proved more effective than the Hagana in stopping the Arabs.[26] In village areas, an extremely rudimentary form of Hagana was organized. Many youngsters who reached maturity in the late 1930s could readily recall the experience of hiding secretly in the barn loft, under the bed or in the water tower when their parents departed for guard duty during the summer of 1929.[27] Heroic self-praise was meant to bolster the spirit of the Yishuv in confronting a danger it was not prepared for, either psychologically or physically.

It is not surprising that in this situation, tendencies appeared for taking vengeance (or, as the preferred phraseology put it, *exacting retribution*). There were certain acts of revenge that came upon the heels of the 1921 disturbances, but these were directed against persons known to have been involved in the killings. The first recorded documentation of an injury to an Arab by a Jew based on revenge motives occurred in 1922 and was publicized thanks to a response by Ahad Ha-Am. A rumor spread that young Jews had killed an innocent Arab boy. In its wake, *Ha-Aretz* published an article denouncing the act. Ahad Ha-Am, living in Tel Aviv, where he spent the final years of his life, was shocked by the story and wrote a letter to the editor of the paper strongly condemning all acts of vengeance: "Is *this* the dream of the 'return to Zion', . . . that we would come to Zion and befoul its soil by the shedding of innocent blood?" He interpreted this as a renunciation of the vision of the prophets and the fundamental moral principles guiding the Jewish people. Do we come to Palestine, he asked, "only in order to add another small nation of new 'Levantines' in one corner of the Orient, who will compete with the Levantines already there in all those corrupted qualities—lust for blood, vengeance, competition, etc.—that are the content of their lives?"—reverting to stereotypes about the peoples of the Middle East that were widespread in Eastern Europe. He ended his letter, as usual, with a memorable formulation: "If that's the 'messiah', may he not come in my time!"[28]

The press did not comment openly on the topic of Jewish revenge against Arabs in the aftermath of the 1929 riots. One can surmise the reasons for this caution. First of all, any story about Jewish retribution was likely to encourage the British authorities to take action against the perpetrator, so that the revelation in the press could be interpreted as an act of informing. Second, the Jewish political line was to present the disturbances as an Arab attack against peaceful Jews. In contrast, the mandatory government portrayed the events as a clash between two peoples. For that reason, maintaining the image of the innocent man who defends himself and does not seek retribution against his attackers was important both for political and internal moral reasons. Third, there was an element of incitement in the very description of acts of vengeance, which most of the leaders of public opinion wanted to avoid. For that reason, the existence of acts of revenge can only be inferred from fragmentary comments in the press. In his diary, Ruppin mentions several "isolated incidents in which the Jews went beyond plain self-defense in a shameful manner."[29] *Mi-Bifnim,* the publication of Ha-Kibbutz ha-Meuhad (United Kibbutz movement), complained about "mischievious pranks and wild actions" committed by Jews against Arabs and expressed concern about the educational implications of such actions.[30] Incitement to vengeance came from circles of the revisionist Right. From a certain perspective, that fact made it easier for proponents of the mainstream current in the Jewish community to identify the agitators with the principal political opponents of the Labor movement. Moreover, that identification made it easier to portray opposition to vengeance as being the trademark of Labor.[31] Yet there is no doubt that similar tendencies toward revenge were alive in the Labor camp. It was not coincidental that *Davar,* on the morning after the riots, began a regular column entitled "Lights from the Darkness." That column reported on cases where Arabs had aided Jews in danger, concealing them and saving their lives. A week after the disturbances, Beilinson, the senior journalist at *Davar,* published an article in which he made a distinction between Arabs guilty of riotous acts and those who were innocent. He urged his readers not to make all Arabs collectively responsible for the criminal acts of a few. "If this view gains the upper hand in the community," he warned, "it is likely to lower us to the same level as the assailants and robbers."[32] The public statement made by the labor parties after the riots was also careful to underscore that the Jews were not at war with the entire Arab people and had no interest in vengeance. It also suggested the necessity to be on guard against the spread of the kind of chauvinist thinking being propagated by the revisionists.[33]

The desire to take revenge sprang from the feeling of weakness and helplessness, a widespread sentiment in the Yishuv in the aftermath of the disturbances. Vengeance was the other face of the Hagana's failure. It expressed the spontaneous response of young people who had no institutional path for their desire to act. Consequently, vengefulness was more prevalent in circles outside the established frameworks of the labor movement, which provided safety valves that facilitated a checked release of the psychological pressure generated by the disturbances.

Ideas of vengeance were in contradiction with the defensive ethos that still predominated. Apart from the open appeal to the use of physical force, these ideas clashed with the traditional self-image of the Jew, internalized in the defensive ethos: that of the eternal victim of the aggression of others. Jews defend themselves but do not attack; they seek peace and thus do not plot to take vengeance. The Jew reacts to riots with constructive actions: If Jews wanted true revenge, it was argued, they should act to strengthen the Jewish community in Palestine, accelerating the pace of building the country.[34] A well-known poem by David Shimonovitz dealing with the aftermath of the 1921 riots but still relevant and popular in 1929 expresses the characteristic response:

> Do not mourn,
> Do not lament,
> In a time like this,
> Do not lower your head . . .

> Work, Work!
> Plowman, plow!
> Sower, sow!
> In a bad moment,
> Double the toil,
> Double the product[35]

On this occasion, Shimonovitz composed another highly popular poem, "Nevertheless, and Despite Everything—Eretz Israel!"[36] "No mercy, no help, no soldiers, just construction and builders"—that is how the editor of *Ha-Poel ha-Tzair* defined the needs of the day.[37]

Vengeance was in contradiction with the basic Zionist interest in preserving peace and tranquillity, and lowering the level of Jewish–Arab confrontation in order to facilitate the continued strengthening of the Yishuv. Zionist policy did all it could to present the disturbances as the product of agitation and not as expressing the true feelings of the Arabs in Palestine against Jewish colonization. So Zionist leaders claimed in testimony before the British investigative committee sent to Palestine and headed by Walter Shaw. That agitation, according to leaders on the left, was rooted in two causes: the designs of the mufti in Jerusalem and his associates, who maligned the Jews as schemers planning to take control of the mosques on the Temple Mount, and the provocations of the Betarists, especially the procession by Betar members to the Wailing Wall on the fast of Ab 1929. In retrospect, that procession actually appeared like a provocation that had played into the hands of the agitators. In both cases, the disturbances were analyzed as phenomena that were not immanent to Arab–Jewish relations. Acts of vengeance were in total contradiction with this sort of explanation.

Beyond any political considerations, the defensive ethos taught a philosophy of tolerance; and it was that approach which was on trial during the disturbances. The thorny question of how to inculcate the educational values of tolerance and non-hatred when reality teaches a different lesson presented itself now for the first time with an acuteness and urgency previously unknown. What should one tell a child who had spent the night in the loft of the kibbutz barn and had seen the flames rising everywhere on the horizon from the burning granaries of nearby kibbutzim when that child was well aware that Arabs had set the fires? The answer to the dilemma at this stage still remained within the ideological framework of the defensive ethos: We reject aggression, but the obligation of self-defense is a moral duty of the first degree. We do not educate for militarism. Tabenkin, leader of Ha-Kibbutz ha-Meuhad and one of the most important educators of the Labor movement, asserted, "The soldier and the defender are different types, and different educational paths lead to them."[38] "We will never sing a hymn of glory to guns and weapons of destruction. We shall never express a fondness for the knife and the dagger," wrote a member of Ha-Kibbutz ha-Meuhad. He voiced apprehensions about the potential negative educational impact of acts of violence and vengeance: "A generation has grown up in Palestine. That generation sees, hears, and understands. We will not spoil it. It should know to defend its own life, but it will be exceedingly difficult to teach this generation not to overstep the limit, . . . not to be swept up by the current of hatred inundating everything."[39]

Education for socialism was designed to provide an answer to that dilemma. It stressed the components of love for one's fellow man, equality, ethics, and a humane approach to all creatures. Yet it also taught that one should not accept evil and that it was incumbent on a person to act for the sake of creating a better world. In other words, it preached activism. Making a distinction between effendis and fellahin, agitators and agitated, guilty and innocent, "good Arabs" and "bad Arabs" made it possible to continue to espouse humanitarian socialism without disregarding the surrounding realities. Hate was reserved for the class enemy, the reactionaries—blurring the contours of national enmity.[40]

One of the most pithy expressions of the defensive ethos appeared in a lullaby by Emanuel ha-Russi, which was written in the wake of the 1929 disturbances. The song "Sleep, My Son, Lie Quietly" enjoyed great popularity and entered the canon of the Hebrew popular repertoire. In the song, a mother puts her boy to bed after his father has gone out to stand guard duty. The father plows during the day and stands guard at night. Nearby, "The granary of Tel Yosef is aflame, / And smoke is also rising from Beit Alfa." But the son can sleep secure, because his parents are guarding him. When he grows up, the song states, he, too, will go out with his father to plow and stand guard. This was an updated version of the Tel Hai myth: the interlinking of work and guard duty. Guard duty is meant to protect the fruits of labor. The song does not contain even a hint of aggressiveness. But it does express acceptance of the fate both father and son must bear: to dedicate their lives to work and defense. To witness the fruits of their labor going up in smoke and then to start all over again.[41] Just as the anonymity of the attackers is preserved in the Tel Hai myth, here, too, aside from the flames rising from the granaries, there is no reference whatsoever to the enemy against whom one must defend oneself. The nonidentity of the attackers released the song text from any obligation to relate to them and, consequently, from expressions of hatred. Yet such anonymity did interject an element of hypocrisy. In the case of Tel Hai, there was a dimension of alienation, deriving from the geographical distance and the mythical dimensions attributed to the event. In contrast, here the reference was to occurrences that had taken place in immediate time and space, and the disregard for the identity of the attackers in this case actually did not blur their identity. Aside from a depiction of the atmosphere prevailing in the summer and autumn of 1929 in the frontier areas of Jewish colonization, the song is characterized by an element of resignation: The disturbances taught that the building of a Jewish Palestine will entail long years of sacrifice, loss of the hard-earned fruits of labor, and a need for self-defense. Another layer was added to the evolutionary approach: a heightened awareness of the length of the process and the dangers it embodied emanating from the Arabs. Yet Labor circles had not yet voiced any objection to the conception itself.

Even if the Labor press did its utmost to avoid any inflammatory rhetoric, quite a few stereotypes of Arabs appeared during that period. They expressed the feeling of futile rage and fear and internalized the enmity that had emerged in the wake of the riots.[42] The Arabs were depicted as vicious, wild, and bloodthirsty sons of the desert. In Yeivin's characterization published in *Doar ha-Yom,* they lacked an elementary sense of ethics and were like a predatory animal that when devouring its prey, does not feel that it committed any transgression.[43] Expressions such as "murderers," "bands of robbers" and "bloodthirsty rioters" were frequent appellations, even in the moderate paper *Davar*.[44] Distinctions were often made between the Jews as a cultured, European people and an Oriental race of desert savages.[45] The public statement issued by the major two labor parties right after the disturbances noted, "We were faced with an outburst of the worst instincts of savage masses— religious fanaticism coupled with a lust for robbery and plunder and a thirst for blood."[46] In internal political discussions, the Arab leadership was dubbed a "ruling gang." Puritanical labor figures regarded the apparent willingness of Arab leaders to take bribes as proof of the worst kind of moral degeneracy. The fact that Arab leaders became wealthy from land sales to Jews and had no compunctions about playing a double role—taking money from the Jews while simultaneously agitating against them—was interpreted by the Labor leadership as a financial ploy: using political agitation in order to drive up the price of land. In general, it was common thinking among Jews that mendacity, a lack of probity, corruption, and a lust for profit were traits characteristic of the bulk of the Arab leadership. A sense developed that Arabs could not be trusted: Even when he showed a friendly face toward Jews, it was contended, the Arab intended to do them harm. Efforts by Arabs to learn European culture from Jews were depicted derogatorily as attempts to ape foreign ways and smacked of assimilationism. George Nasir, an Arab Christian who was a member of the Left Poalei Zion (an orthodox Marxist party that made its appearance in Palestine in the 1920s) and who remained loyal to the Jews during the disturbances, was scornfully depicted as a person who had merely been "bought" by the Jews.[47]

Two main categories of stereotypes emerged: those of the simple Arab masses and those of the leadership. No term of contempt was spared to characterize the leadership. They were the agitators and instigators, who by lying and deceit whipped up the masses into a religious frenzy and stirred uncontrollable urges. They were the hypocrites who tried to play both sides of the fence, enjoying profits from land sales to Jews, while inciting Arabs against them in order to strengthen their hold over the masses. The simple people, in contrast, were divided into various categories. There were the desert savages, easy to incite and uninhibited by civilized restraints, who murder, rape, rob, and pilfer. Yet there were also fellahin and Arab workers: These were the potential allies of the Jewish workers, and Jews had an obligation to be active in their ranks. However, it was generally acknowledged that it had been the fellahin and workers who had rioted against the Jews. The fact that they had preferred to side with their leaders against the Jews during these disturbances was not overlooked. "Yet most days here in Palestine," Ben Gurion noted, "are not days of riots, so that we must join in common cause with the exploited fellah and the worker."[48] In contrast, the Arab leader, motivated by narrow class interests and political considerations, was thought to be incorrigible; and negotiation with them was deemed pointless, if not impossible.

The 1929 riots damaged the attempts that had been made in the 1920s to forge an alliance between Arab and Jewish workers. There were only a small number of Arab workers who preserved labor solidarity during the disturbances. On the other hand, now more than ever in the past, Jews sought to be active in the Arab sector and made efforts to find ways to establish ties and advance cooperation. Socialists found it natural to channel the desire for action among Arabs by trying to organize Arab workers. In the 1920s, when the concept of organizing Arab workers enjoyed relative popularity, it had been incorporated as part of the platform of Ahdut ha-Avoda, the main party at that time. In contrast, a process now set in that can be termed the "shift of consensus": The general consensus veered to the right, and a conception of action that had been popular in the 1920s within a major segment of the Labor movement shifted to the margins of interest among Mapai in the 1930s. The Zionist radical Left embraced it as a political plan; at that time, this included the Left Poalei Zion, a small party lacking any influence, and Ha-Shomer ha-Tzair. The latter had a certain significance, since it was an important kibbutz movement and boasted a large youth movement in the Diaspora. In Mapai, a small number of dedicated activists continued to work toward organizing Arab workers; but the party leadership had lost interest in the matter. The days when Ben Gurion had been the tribune of the joint union and had declared that it is incumbent on the Jewish worker to "stand at the head of the movement of liberation and revival of the peoples of the Near East" receded into the past.[49] Now the joint union became the banner of the left opposition to Mapai in the Histadrut and a topic for the mockery of Berl Katznelson. Groups of young workers, laboring in the colonies alongside Arabs, were serious about the idea of brotherhood among workers and had been educated in this spirit. This aroused the concern of the movement leadership: That sense of fraternity could act to weaken their dedication to the struggle for "Jewish Labor" being waged at that time in the colonies. Consequently, Katznelson launched an attack against the supposed "sentimentalism" shown by those workers in their attitude toward Arabs.

Whenever the leaders of the Labor movement wanted to cite some evidence pertaining to social or political matters, they customarily referred to their experiences in the Pale of Settlement. Berl Katznelson contended that just as young Jews there had been lured by the ideology of "going to the people" and had romanticized the Russian peasant, young Jews in Palestine were behaving in a similar way in their attitude toward the Arab worker: "That same muzhik, the stench of whose tar-covered boots the young Jew found it difficult to stand, they described to themselves as though he were a person of great refinement and endowed with a deep soul, to whom it was possible to pour out all those sentiments of pity and feelings of brotherhood which that same young person was unable to reveal to those close to him: his father, his mother, the storekeeper, and the [Jewish] artisan."[50] The identification between the rioting Gentile in Russia and the rioting Arab in Palestine reappeared in Katznelson's comments. All the Jewish attempts to woo the muzhik and forge bonds of solidarity with him had not helped the Jews when they were in distress, and there would be a similar response by the Arab worker in Palestine. It was mistaken to expect that organizing the Arab worker would prevent him from joining the effendis, who were fellow Arabs, at a time of unrest. This position was generally accepted then by the bulk of Mapai's leadership; it viewed efforts to organize the Arab worker as quixotic romanticism, doomed to failure from the start.

That stance was associated with a question of definition that played a key role in the public debate after the riots: Were the disturbances an uprising or a pogrom?[51] This distinction was not just semantic but expressed differing evaluations of the nature of the riots and suggested different conclusions to be drawn from them. Whoever described the riots as an uprising or revolt tacitly signaled a belief that the Arabs of Palestine were rising up against the mandatory regime and the Balfour Declaration, that is, that their motives were national in nature and that the riots pointed to the existence of a national Arab movement. Those who held that the riots had been a pogrom claimed that they had been provoked by incitement, the absence of preventive action by the authorities, and Jewish weakness. Such a perspective effectively denied the presence of internal developments within Arab nationalism. These two estimations of the nature of events had central implications for policy formation in the Labor movement after the riots.

Positions were formulated in terms of one's attitude toward the broader question: Was it necessary to try to reach a general agreement and come to an arrangement with the Arabs? Those who contended the riots were a genuine revolt implicitly held the view that a political agreement was imperative. Those who considered the events a pogrom let it be known by such a contention that they did not believe any kind of agreement was necessary. Thus, for example, Beilinson rejected the arguments put forward by members of Brit Shalom that the Jews in Palestine were faced with a national uprising. He explained the riots by reference to "religion and blood," that is, the religious incitement focusing on the al-Aksa Mosque and the baseless rumor that Jews had been killing Arabs. The riots were not the outcome of a national movement, Beilinson contended, and were not even the fruit of hatred toward Jews. Rather, they had been planned by a gang headed by the mufti of Jerusalem, al-Hajj Amin al-Husayni. Beilinson stressed that such a conspiratorial gang should not be given a prize in the form of political concessions. He outlined his position in an important series of articles published in *Davar* in October 1929 entitled "Summing Up the Riots." Yet the real reason for his avoidance of any assessment that contained even the slightest element of recognition of an Arab national movement in Palestine was revealed shortly thereafter. The occasion was a meeting of the leadership of the two Labor parties, Ha-Poel ha-Tzair and Ahdut ha-Avoda, preceding their eventual unification, a merger that resulted several months later in the establishment of Mapai, the Palestine Workers party. In that meeting, Beilinson explained that he was opposed to any proposal that recognized the Arab right to Palestine: "For my part, I still am unable to give up the idea of Palestine as a Jewish state." He went on to note that the right of Jews to Palestine had priority over the right of Arabs.[52] Beilinson's opposition to viewing the riots as a revolt derived from his fears about this perspective: Such an approach gave a kind of tacit recognition, however indirect, to the existence of another contender for the right of sovereignty over Palestine.

Tabenkin and Katznelson, two of Ben Gurion's key associates in the leadership of the movement, also shared Beilinson's view that the riots were a pogrom, and for the same reasons. Tabenkin not only portrayed the riots as a pogrom but used that categorization as an argument for rejecting any constitutional framework that would allow Arabs to participate in government. "Any people that shows that it cannot impose political order except by rioting against another minority people has no right to demand sovereignty," he asserted. In principle, an agreement could not be reached with a people "that seeks freedom by means of pogroms." The riots, in his view, revealed the lack of political maturity on the part of the Arab community. For that reason, it was forbidden to agree to any "central government" as opposed to national autonomies. He stressed the feudal nature of Arab society as an additional argument against giving them any form of self-government.[53] Berl Katznelson, embroiled in a dispute with Zionists in Germany who leaned toward the views of Brit Shalom, emphasized his opposition to defining the disturbances as an uprising. "The word *revolt* serves only as a glorifying euphemism for the riots, to whitewash the 'heroes' of the riots and minimize the image of our sufferings," he complained. In his view, the existing Arab movement was not entitled to the appellation National, since its aspirations and goals were only negative.[54] He, too, was consistently opposed to any constitutional changes.

That position, denying the very existence of an Arab national movement and its manifestations in order to oppose the need to share Palestine, derived from a twofold need among socialists: Not only did they want to do what was politically correct, they also felt it was necessary to be able to claim that absolute justice was on their side. Brit Shalom or Jabotinsky could afford to recognize the existence of an Arab national movement in Palestine and infer the necessary consequences, in keeping with their political perspective. Recognition of a clash in Palestine between two kinds of justice did not disturb Jabotinsky's sleep. But Berl Katznelson, Tabenkin, and Beilinson, who educated their disciples in the principles of humanism and morality, found moral ambivalence unacceptable. "We will be able to fulfill this [educational] mission only if we imbue the young with the conviction that absolute justice is on our side," Katznelson asserted.[55] That statement reflected the central dilemma faced by those who were simultaneously both educators of the youth movement, preaching its absolute values, and political leaders, who recognized the necessity on occasion of avoiding total candor and making concessions. The fear of "internal confusion," conceptual and psychological,[56] the loss of confidence among idealistic youth in the justice and righteousness of Zionism, ultimately induced them to advocate positions that were tinged with ambiguity.

Beilinson coined a formulation that later became an educational slogan: "Who does Palestine belong to? The Jewish people and the Arab community living there."[57] This slogan recognized the right of the Arabs living in Palestine to be citizens enjoying full equality but did not concede a single inch when it came to the rights of the Jewish people. Beilinson defined those rights as "independence of the Jewish people, control over its own destiny, the redemption of Israel in its land."[58] That definition was opaque enough to conceal the problem regarding the future political status of the Arabs once those three objectives were realized. Beilinson spoke about an "Arab program" of the Labor movement that would act to promote a comprehensive agrarian reform. Such a reform would break the hold of the effendis on Arab society and lead to a rise in Arab living standards in Palestine. Yet he did not raise or even hint at the question of Arab participation in government. The vague contours of his definitions allowed idealistic young people, who were in a state of confusion following the riots, to identify with Zionist objectives without any guilt feelings.[59]

From the Jewish perspective, the disturbances were a wicked act perpetrated by the strong against the weak, an attack that any government faithful to preservation of law and order was obliged to prevent. Hence, they were quick to criticize the British administration for not having prevented the riots or, at least, for not having suppressed them in time. The truth was that both the Jewish community and the mandatory government had been lulled into a false sense of security by the period of eight peaceful years beginning in 1921. The riots caught them unawares; in particular, there were insufficient troops on hand to quell the unrest. Most of the killing had taken place before the army arrived. Feelings that Jews had once again been the innocent victims of violence and that the authorities, knowingly or unknowingly, had aided and abetted the attack reinforced the old stereotype that had accompanied all past outbreaks of enmity toward the Jews: the Jew as victim, the Gentile as murderer, and government authorities supporting the violence. The self-image of victim exempted most from the need to grapple with the question of justice, since it formulated the situation in black-and-white clarity: peaceful individuals attacked by merciless murderers. This was the thinking and perception of the man in the street. Only relatively small elites understood at that stage that the analogy with the situation in the Diaspora and with age-old hatred of the Jew was not necessarily applicable in the case of Palestine. As we have seen, the leadership did not abstain from appealing to the "gut feeling" of its constituency of supporters by recurrent use of such familiar analogies. But those analogies conflicted with the emphasis on the new image of the Jew, proud and courageous, ready to fight back. The contradictory messages of victim and hero were still bound together within the framework of the defensive ethos, which fostered the image of the defender, rejecting that of the soldier. Nonetheless, the confusion felt in the ranks of youth, so worrisome to Katznelson and his associates, was evidence of a basic incompatibility between these two messages.

The Political Debate, 1929–1931

The 1929 disturbances sharpened sensibilities and led to a focusing of the public debate on the Arab question. The revisionists interpreted the unrest as final proof corroborating the position that only by the strength of an "iron wall" would it be possible to guarantee the safety of the Jewish community in Palestine. They stepped up their verbal attacks against the British authorities, since they held the key to Palestine's future. The revisionist hand was strengthened by the anti-Zionist policies of the mandatory government in the period prior to the MacDonald Letter of February 1931. They rejected any attempts at compromise and reconciliation with the Arabs and argued that an increase in Jewish pressure on the mandate authorities was the only proper response to the disturbances. It was also at this juncture that the ideology of violence reached fruition within the maximalist wing of the Revisionist movement.

At the same time, this was likewise the finest hour of Brit Shalom. The question of how Jews and Arabs might live together over the longer term had become a pivotal issue in the wake of the riots. Members of Brit Shalom regarded the riots as the realization and embodiment of all their worst fears, past predictions, and warnings. They contended that the more time passed, the harder it would be to arrive at an agreement with the Arabs. What Arabs had been willing to agree to before the 1929 riots was now no longer acceptable to them. In their view, the riots served as proof that Jewish–Arab accord was a question of life and death for the Jewish community, making it imperative to arrive at an agreement as soon as possible. The more explicit the Arabs became in their uncompromising enmity toward Zionism, the more members of Brit Shalom insisted upon greater concessions on the part of the Zionists. Up until 1929, they had not considered a Jewish majority in Palestine to be a necessary objective, but did not reject it as an eventual development. The notion "not a majority but many" did not negate the potential possibility of a Jewish majority, even though it abandoned the idea of that majority as a condition sine qua non. Now Brit Shalom members began to raise more unambiguous demands, calling for an explicit abandonment of the idea of a Jewish state and of a Jewish majority. They argued that it was not quantity that mattered, but quality. Although they adhered to the idea of "binationalism," in the sense of two peoples sharing sovereignty, they now assumed it was obvious that the Jewish minority status was an unalterable factor.[60] In the publications of Brit Shalom, members of the movement were cautious about their statements. But in closed meetings and internal discussions, they made explicit reference to the need to reach an accord with the Arabs on the basis of restriction of immigration. They argued that Arabs were fearful of a large Jewish immigration to Palestine, since it would lead eventually to a loss of their status as dominant majority. Thus, if Jews wished to come to a peace agreement with the Arabs, there was no alternative but to fix a top ceiling for the number of Jews in Palestine.[61]

These remarks had a considerable impact within Mapai. As mentioned, Mapai had been set up in 1930, and one of its constituents was the former Ha-Poel ha-Tzair. That party had been distinguished, among other things, by its moderate, antiactivist leanings. Alongside those who rejected the existence of Arab nationalism and defined the disturbances as a "pogrom," other voices also began to make themselves heard within Mapai. Already at the beginning of October 1929, an essay was published in *Ha-Poel ha-Tzair* in which its author, a leader of Ha-Poel ha-Tzair and later in Mapai, declared that although incitement had played a role in the disturbances, "behind the agitators stands a national movement with certain aspirations that are in opposition to ours."[62] Michael Assaf, who subsequently became one of the most important scholars of the history of Arabs in Palestine, declared unreservedly his belief that the Zionists were locked in a struggle with a national mass movement. Moshe Shertok (Sharett), later foreign minister and Israel's second prime minister, explained Arab apprehensions about the immigration of Jews by reference to their sense of national identity. Ben Gurion gave the most succinct definition, which was characteristically pungent and cutting: "The debate on whether there is or is not an Arab national movement is a useless verbal dispute. The essential matter for us is that the movement is mobilizing the masses." The following remark sounded reminiscent of his previous position: "We do not regard it as a movement of revival, and its moral fabric is questionable." But he qualified this by adding: "Yet in the political sense, this is a national movement."[63] That position expressed the thinking of substantial segments of his young party, especially those from Ha-Poel ha-Tzair. Already in the 1920s, two of its leaders, Chaim Arlosoroff and Yosef Sprinzak, had demonstrated their sensitivity toward Arab nation-alism. At the time, Arlosoroff had viewed the 1921 disturbances as manifestations of a national movement,[64] while Sprinzak was involved in the deliberations of Brit Shalom from its inception and was considered the originator of the formulation "not a majority but many."

The debate soon centered on the question whether the Jews should initiate a plan for constitutional changes in Palestine. That was a kind of second act to the drama that had been staged in Ein Harod in 1924; but this time one of the main actors, Ben Gurion, had changed the script. As will be recalled, the classic positions of the defensive ethos had been victorious at Ein Harod, that is (1) there is no Arab national movement, nor should any constitutional changes be initiated; and (2) it is necessary to try to postpone proposals for political changes to the most distant possible time; what matters is the creation of faits accomplis, crystallization of gen-uine Jewish power in Palestine. Consequently, there is nothing to talk about with the effendis, the current leaders of the Arab movement. The only proper partner for negotiations is an Arab movement led by the workers, and that will probably not develop until the distant future. We have already noted that this had been Ben Gur-ion's position; he had felt that any plan that proposed to determine the future char-acter of Jewish–Arab relations in Palestine was a major mistake, since its reasoning would be based on the existing balance of power, which patently was not to the benefit of the Jews. Now, after 1929, Ben Gurion accepted the basic conception of Brit Shalom that the time was ripe for an agreement: Jews had better initiate a plan of their own for constitutional changes and take action to achieve an accord with Arabs based on that plan. This should be done before the British, for their part, instituted a plan for a legislative council, which would be more detrimental from the Jewish standpoint.

As the riots receded into the past, it became clear to Jews that world public opin-ion in general—and British public opinion in particular—did not view the distur-bances as wicked attacks by violent rioters against peaceful citizens. Not only did it refrain from accusing and denouncing the rioters and the British administration, as Jews had expected, but there was renewed public discussion overseas about the entire question of Palestine, the Balfour Declaration, and the mandate; soon the Jews found themselves on the bench of the accused. That tendency emerged prom-inently in testimony presented to the committee headed by Walter Shaw and was even more pronounced in the conclusions of the committee, which laid the blame for the disturbances at the door of the Yishuv, contending that their root cause should be sought in the economic and social changes that Jewish colonization was bringing about in Palestine. The committee's report drew special attention to the eviction of fellahin from land purchased by Jews. This hostile tendency was strengthened in the wake of the conclusions of John Hope-Simpson, sent to inves-tigate the capacity of the economy for absorbing new immigrants in Palestine. In his final report, he made future Jewish immigration contingent upon a develop-ment plan by the government. The tendency reached its apogee in the White Paper of Lord Passfield, which accepted the negative conclusions of Hope-Simpson regarding the current limited absorptive capacity of Palestine but did not include his recommendations for a development plan. The Passfield White Paper restricted future immigration on the basis of political criteria, placed limitations on Jewish purchase of land, and concluded that a representative government had to be set up, that is, a majoritarian legislative council. Passfield's wife, Beatrice Webb, announced that there was no room in Palestine even for another cat.[65]

The hostile tendencies on the part of the British administration in Palestine, seconded by various politicians in the Labour government then in power in Britain, did not go unnoticed by the Jewish leadership in Palestine. Ben Gurion, a leader with a sharp sense of politics, responded to them quite early on: He abandoned the position he had advocated six years before and now, for all practical purposes, embraced the views of Kaplansky and his associates.

At the end of November 1929, Ben Gurion presented the leadership of his party with a plan, the Establishment of a Governmental Regime in Palestine. Its weighty title already hinted at the change: The concept of a Jewish state, which had been frequent in Ben Gurion's remarks at Ein Harod, was absent here. In its stead appeared the vague conception *mishtar mamlakhti* (governmental regime), which could be interpreted broadly or narrowly, depending on interest. Ben Gurion's plan created a direct link between three components: development of the Jewish community in Palestine, the relations between Arabs and Jews there, and self-government. It envisioned three stages in the development of Palestine. The present stage, which would last some fifteen more years, was characterized by a Jewish position of numerical inferiority to the Arabs, Arab attempts to liquidate the national home, and the first beginnings of governmental institutions common to both Jews and Arabs. During this stage, the government would remain basically in the hands of the mandatory authorities. The second stage would be characterized by the growth of the Jewish community: it would increase to some 40–50 percent of the entire population. The Arabs would recognize the fact that they could not dislodge, and dispose of, the Jewish community and would resign themselves to its existence. The institutions of self-government would then be expanded from the municipal to the district level, and the mandatory power's authority would be reduced. In the third stage, Jews would reach at least numerical equality with the Arabs, thus completing, according to Ben Gurion's definition, the establishment of the national home. A federal state would be set up in Palestine, based on national cantons, and the power of the mandate would expire. The country would be governed by the council of the federal union, made up of two houses: the House of Peoples, in which Jews and Arabs would be represented in equal numbers, and the House of Residents, where representatives of the cantons would sit, their number being determined in accordance with the size of the respective population. Decisions would be dependent on the approval of both houses.[66]

Ben Gurion's proposal sparked a debate on several levels. Did Jews have to initiate a proposal of their own at this stage? Was Ben Gurion's suggestion likely to prove acceptable to the British and the Arabs? Everyone would have preferred for the status quo to continue, with no changes in government in Palestine until the "transition period" (a term coined by Arlosoroff), in which Jews were in an inferior position, came to an end. However, the deterioration of the political situation, especially in the light of the anticipated British positions, rendered that option unrealistic in the eyes of the majority of those participating in the discussion. The question whether the Jews should put forward a proposal of their own in respect to the question of government was answered in the affirmative, though without much enthusiasm. There were heated discussions about the acceptability of the proposal to the British and Arabs. Arlosoroff contended that the British would not understand a structure as complicated as that proposed by Ben Gurion, which was unprecedented in the history of the British Empire. In his view, it was wiser to propose a plan for a legislative council, along the lines of the scheme presented a few years earlier by the then high commissioner, Herbert Samuel, but with added restrictive clauses that would prevent it from becoming an institution hostile to the Jewish community. The main attraction of Ben Gurion's plan for the Arabs presumably lay in the idea of participation in the executive power: From the first stage on, Jews and Arabs would participate in the executive institutions. No one could guarantee that such a plan, which did not give the Arabs an advantage over the Jews at any stage, would indeed be acceptable to them. Ben Gurion, for his part, believed that an agreement was feasible. His associates expressed their doubts.

But over and beyond this, objections were voiced by the Jewish side regarding the acceptability of the plan. Though it neither acknowledged the sole right of Arabs to sovereignty in Palestine nor the right of the current majority there to determine its future, the plan clearly abandoned the idea of any exclusive Jewish right of sovereignty over Palestine in the present and future. This concession, even though it had merely theoretical importance at the time, was a hard morsel to digest for an ideological movement; after all, the idea of a Jewish state had been central to its thinking and education. For that reason, Berl Katznelson suggested that far-reaching political proposals should be avoided and that Zionist efforts should be concentrated on the demand for the democratization of the regime in Palestine from the local level on up, that is, beginning with the municipal administrations. Katznelson sketched a plan according to which two national autonomies would eventually be set up, each of which would develop according to its own needs and at its own pace. That plan avoided definite proposals regarding the form of government to be operative in the future in Palestine, based on a covert assumption that it would ultimately be determined by the balance of power then in existence. At the same time, it also nullified the possibility of Jewish–Arab participation in the central executive bodies (at the expense of the authority of the mandatory power)—a positive component from the point of view of the two parties, found in both Ben Gurion's and Arlosoroff's plans.[67]

The debate raged in Mapai on this issue for over a year. The more the political situation deteriorated, the more the position of those advocating an upcompromising line (Katznelson, Beilinson, Yosef Aharonovitz, Tabenkin) was weakened. The political crisis was accompanied by a period of slowdown in the economy and immigration. The years 1929 to 1931 boasted few Zionist achievements in the building of a Jewish infrastructure in Palestine. Doubts reigned from within, and the faith in the righteousness of the Zionist path weakened. Attacks by Brit Shalom and the revisionists became more intense. The undermining of positions was expressed by a new terminology: In the past, the question had been whether Palestine was the land exclusively of the Jews or whether Arabs also had a patrimony there. Now a new note was heard: "The Arab community is not the only master of this land. Palestine also belongs to the Jewish people," Beilinson wrote. Ben Gurion added, "The right of the Jewish people [in Palestine] is no less than the right of its inhabitants."[68] The tone of self-defense became more strident as the hostile stance adopted by the Labour government became clear. Members of Brit Shalom and their sympathizers followed the developments in Mapai with sympathetic interest. It appeared that the wind was blowing in the direction of the moderates. In the central committee of Mapai, there was a majority for proponents of a Jewish legislative initiative—whether in Arlosoroff's plan of an improved legislative council or Ben Gurion's Jewish and Arab participation in executive bodies. This initiative conflicted with the defensive ethos: It did without the self-image of the just and persecuted and abandoned the juxtaposition of Jews over against Gentiles. It accepted the basic principle of discussion with Arabs in the present and raised no difficulties regarding the nature of the partner for talks. It replaced the perspective of an accord that would come as the product of a change in the balance of power in Palestine in favor of the Jews with another option: an accord as a result of Jewish weakness.

While the Labor leadership, active at the political front and aware of pressures and dangers, expressed a willingness to come to an accord on the basis of conceding the principle of Jewish sovereignty in Palestine, the rank and file were not prepared to follow suit. The response on the street to the August 1929 riots was in the spirit of the defensive ethos: They will not intimidate us! It is necessary to grind our teeth when faced with Arab threats and to continue to create the Jewish power base. It is impossible to reach an accord from the negotiating stance of weakness, because the opposing side will not agree. "The strong will want us—and want peace with us—when we, too, are a power." This statement by Yosef Aharonovitz articulated the thinking of the rank and file at the grass-roots level.[69] Among the sympathizers of the movement, the position advocated by Beilinson and Katznelson and expressed with acuity in the pages of *Davar* was very popular. The tolerance shown by *Davar* in the 1920s toward the views of Brit Shalom and Uri Zvi Greenberg was now supplanted by fierce enmity, manifested in refusing to publish the public statement of Brit Shalom and disqualifying its members and their views. In an internal discussion, Berl Katznelson dubbed them "uprooted," hinting at their central European origin and their assimilationist background. He indicated that their political views were the product of their alienation from Eastern European Jewish culture. Katznelson's statement was reiterated in similar form by his followers.[70] The man in the street had no sympathy for the position of Brit Shalom. Even before the riots, Ruppin learned from his son that a fellow pupil at school had told him he should be ashamed that his father was in Brit Shalom.[71] After the disturbances, negative attitudes increased; the public regarded the ideas advocated by Brit Shalom—especially the public struggle conducted by members of that association on behalf of those positions—as an act bordering on treason.[72]

A showdown took place in the Mapai Council of February 1931 between proponents of the hard and soft lines. It was on the eve of the MacDonald Letter, a document that revoked the anti-Zionist clauses in Passfield's White Paper and gave the national home a new lease on life, ultimately fateful for its development. That fact was still hidden in the nebulous future; but it was already known that the political struggle in London, under the leadership of Chaim Weizmann, president of the Zionist Organization, who had resigned in protest over the White Paper, had met with success. The feeling of urgency that had accompanied the internal political discussion since the riots was somewhat lessened. Berl Katznelson presented the classic position of the defensive ethos: We must reject any proposal to change the government in Palestine. The scheme of a legislative council is objectionable because it contains an element of recognition of majoritarian rule by the present Arab majority. Katznelson illustrated his views by quoting the old story about a Jewish man who, under constraint, had promised a bullish landlord he would teach his bear to read the prayer book within three years. When asked how he would accomplish this feat, the man answered that by the time he would have to prove his ability, either the landlord, the bear, or the Jew would probably already have died. The name of the game was to gain time. In the end, the council rejected the proposals made by Arlosoroff and Ben Gurion and accepted the plan of municipalities put forward by Katznelson, associated with a scheme for parity: the principle of equality between Jews and Arabs in governing Palestine. The new slogan was "Not to rule, not to be ruled."

In the light of the "dovish" plans that were current within Mapai in 1930, the proposal of parity (ultimately accepted as the guideline of the party) represented a kind of retreat. The demand for equal representation in government by a minority that numbered some 20 percent of the population was far from "minimalist" in the British or Arab perspective. Yet it should be remembered that this was in large measure the essence of the proposals made by Brit Shalom prior to the August 1929 riots—a form of government that removes the thorn from the question of majority by recognizing equal rights for the two peoples in Palestine as two peoples sharing the right of sovereignty in Palestine. From the Zionist perspective, this constituted a gargantuan concession. It was the first time the Zionists had initiated a proposal acknowledging the equal right of the Arabs to Palestine. The parity plan presented the vision of two autonomies, developing separately, side by side. Proponents of the proposal contended that equilibrium between the representatives of both peoples in the executive would compel them to eschew radical policies, forcing them ultimately to cooperate.[73]

It is doubtful whether Katznelson and his supporters truly and sincerely wanted parity as the future form of government in Palestine. Even though it left open the possibility for achieving a Jewish majority in Palestine in the course of time, the Zionist concession the plan contained was difficult to stomach. Apparently, this proposal was meant as a response to British proposals regarding the legislative council. It contained a formula that was advantageous for the Jews in the present and did not foreclose on future development of the national home, especially as far as immigration was concerned. After the British rejected that plan (presented to them unofficially) and, for all practical purposes, permanently shelved it, no one was especially sorry. Nonetheless, the parity plan remained the platform position of Mapai on the Arab question down to 1937. Although it was never approved as an official proposal of the Zionist Executive, in actual fact, it was regarded as a formal policy position during that period. It appears this was the most radical proposal ever adopted as a platform position on the Arab question by a key Zionist body.

The Seventeenth Zionist Congress took place in Basel in 1931. The debate between the revisionists, who demanded that the struggle against Britain be intensified, and members of Brit Shalom, who demanded that the Zionist leadership should dissociate itself, openly and in public, from the idea of a Jewish state and a Jewish majority in Palestine, was channeled into a polemic over the question of the *Zielsetzung* (final goal) of Zionism. The dynamic clash between the two poles led to extreme positions. Not without some justification, Ben Gurion accused Brit Shalom people of having put the question of the final goal on the public agenda. Statements by Chaim Weizmann were fraught with ambiguity on the question of a Jewish majority in Palestine and prompted Jabotinsky to initiate a discussion in the congress on the question of the final goal. A storm erupted when Weizmann gave an interview to the Jewish Telegraphic Agency (JTA), in which he stated that he had no sympathy or understanding for the idea of a Jewish majority in Palestine and that the Arabs would interpret such majoritarian demands as aggression directed toward them. On the face of it, Weizmann adhered to the formulas regarding parity and the notion "not to rule, not to be ruled," which had been adopted by Mapai. In truth, however, Weizmann at that time was leaning toward positions similar to those advocated by Brit Shalom and interpreted the idea of parity as a formal abandonment of the possibility for a majority. In contrast, Mapai was barely able to make its peace with the idea of equal rights for Jews and Arabs in the ownership of Palestine and did not even come close to abandoning the idea of a Jewish majority. Although there were a number of former members of Ha-Poel ha-Tzair who did support the Brit Shalom approach, they were far from the consensus. At the congress, Mapai found itself maneuvered into a situation in which it was called on to forsake its ambivalent formulas (chosen with great care in order to blur its positions) and declare openly whether it supported the idea of a Jewish state. A public declaration at that moment in favor of a state as the aim of Zionism was viewed by circles in the center and on the left as politically unwise, since it was likely to inflame the political climate once again, without resulting in any political profit whatsoever. In the end, the congress avoided a discussion on the question, utilizing one of the euphemisms the Zionist movement used externally when it wished to sidestep far-reaching political pronouncements.[74] Indeed, Gershom Scholem was right in his contention that it had become clear at the congress that the majority of the movement wanted a state but were afraid to admit it openly. Scholem challenged the members of Mapai, arguing that their rejection of an open declaration on the final goal was motivated by strategic reasons only: "It was not their heartfelt belief but, rather, their political acumen and anxiety about the fate of the Zionist enterprise that spoke from the mouths of the majority of those opposed to the declaration."[75]

Members of Brit Shalom estimated that the Labor movement was shifting in a "dovish" direction and hoped that tendency would continue. But in actual fact, the decision taken in the Mapai Council in February 1931 marked the limit of concessions that the central current in the Zionist movement was prepared to make. After the repercussions of the August 1929 riots and the anti-Zionist turn in British pol-

icies, the situation returned to stability following the MacDonald Letter. Berl Katznelson's view, which advocated gaining time and postponing political settlements
as long as possible, was reinstated as the position of the movement.

Violence as a Political Method: The Emergence of an Extreme Right

The most vicious attack on the defensive ethos in the wake of the 1929 riots was
launched by a troika that already then was regarded as the maximalist faction in
the Revisionist movement, namely Uri Zvi Greenberg, Abba Ahimeir, and
Yehoshua Heschel Yeivin. The three, all gifted intellectuals and very eloquent writers, had left the Labor movement about a year previously, veering right to its political rival, then on the rise. Ahimeir stood out as the leader of the group at the beginning of the 1930s. He demonstrated abilities as an educator and took on the halo
of a leader. The disturbances were proof, legitimation, and encouragement for them
to advance an ideology that held up force, especially political violence, as a preferred method of action.

Whoever searches for new components in that ideology will be disappointed.
Virtually all the basic ideas that the three preached could be found in the teachings
of earlier Zionist thinkers. Justifiably, Ahimeir believed the spiritual roots of Betar
lay in modern Hebrew literature, from Y. L. Gordon, Bialik, Berdichevsky, and
Tchernichovsky to Zalman Shneour and Yaakov Cahan.[76] In an anachronistic
manner, he noted that "Hebrew culture is permeated with the ideas of Betar to a
far greater extent than the Zionist public sphere or Jewish youth."[77] However, the
selection of ideas and motifs of the writers he chose to highlight was not accidental:
He made use of elements in their writings that were conducive to his approach, at
the expense of other aspects he preferred not to mention. It appears that Georges
Sorel, a French anarcho-syndicalist thinker who preached the creed of violence, to
whom they did not acknowledge their debt, had indirectly, through the writings of
others, exercised a decisive impact on their intellectual world.

Ahimeir's point of departure was the absolute primacy of the nation. As mentioned, the monistic idea of "one banner" was already present in Jabotinsky's
thinking. Yet it was Ahimeir who thought it out to its radical conclusion. He wrote:
"Zionism is an aim in itself. All means for its realization are legitimate in our
eyes. . . . Other ideals interest us only to the extent that they assist us in learning the
weakness or strength of the enemy."[78] Not only did he preach the priority of
national interest over against moral principles. He even held this up as an important
pedagogical principle. A frequent term of abuse in Ahimeir's writing is "vegetarian." In the first editorial to appear in the paper of Betar in Palestine, *Tel Hai,* he
wrote: "*Tel Hai* . . . shall remove the fig leaf from the vegetarian opinions of Bub-
erism and Borochovism, revealing them in all their nakedness." In one brief sentence, he made short shrift of both Brit Shalom and the Left, categorizing them as
cowardly pacifists.[79] As I have mentioned, there were only few pacifists in Palestine;
but the adherents of the Labor movement cherished a certain respect for them,
mixed with a drop of compassion. In his youth, Ahimeir had been attached to the
ideas of Tolstoy and was even an admirer of A. D. Gordon. Now he fervently

espoused the opposite gospel, railing against them. He rejected the concept of pacifism, regarding it as an expression of a psychological constitution unsuitable for a mentally healthy people. "Among us, there is far too much ostentatious exhibition of naive humanism and vegetarianism," he complained.[80] He praised the fostering of a cult of militarism, compared Tel Hai to Thermopylae, and made Trumpeldor into a symbol of military virtues and a promoter of their advancement. Ahimeir viewed militarism and aggressiveness as manifestations of national vitality, the *healthy* (one of his most popular adjectives) antithesis to the delicate and tender vegetarians, always concerned about ethical considerations and plagued by other inhibitions that had no place in the new Hebrew nation.[81]

Ahimeir believed it was his task to direct the education of the generation that would be prepared to fight the war of independence of the liberation movement. Consequently, one of the targets of his attacks was the sort of education a young man was currently receiving in Palestine. He complained that Palestinian reality, marked by harshness and cruelty, was not being properly depicted by the educators. "The murder of a Jew in Bethlehem, attacks on the soil of Eretz Israel—Does pedagogy prohibit talking about these matters?"[82] Education in Palestine was bland and devoid of character: Instead of teaching children about acts of bravery, self-sacrifice, heroes of the past and present, educators endeavored to present the child with symbols and figures that were neutral from the national point of view, and were unable to arouse the patriotic passions of the child. Ahimeir seized on the children's paper edited by Yitzhak Epstein as an example. In it, the dove was presented as the symbol of the people. Instead of describing the feats of one of the heroes of the Bible, that paper printed a tale about a rabbit. On Lag Ba-Omer, children were not told about the exploits of Bar Kokhba, lamented Ahimeir, but rather about Hibbat Zion (the lackluster movement that had preceded Herzl). Ahimeir compared the bloodless pallor of stories about Palestine to the educational heroism infused in the young heroes of Enrico d'Amicis. The children of Italy are nurtured on tales of valor, he complained, while children in Tel Aviv are taught not to take risks and to value a life of peace and contentment.[83]

The dialectical relation between myth and reality, between interests anchored in the real world with its constraints and national romanticism with its symbols, was developed by Ahimeir ad absurdum. Where it was necessary to choose between genuine interest and romantic symbol, he preferred the symbol over the actual achievement. That approach is reflected in the following lines: "Those who constitute the vegetarian segment of the public in Palestine are of the opinion that increasing Jewish population there has priority over everything else. . . . We believe that the honor of Israel is paramount."[84] As will be recalled, the topic of "Jewish honor" had accompanied Zionist thinking right from the beginning. Yet it was precisely in Palestine, that the topic of national dignity detached from the concrete problems and genuine achievements of survival had ceased to be of central concern. Ahimeir revived the issue and raised it to the level of a cardinal value for which interests could be sacrificed.[85] In his eyes, the defense of Jewish rights at the Wailing Wall justified even the shedding of blood. "For the sake of doubtful interests of Rabbi Israel [i.e., the Jewish people], we are prepared to sell Israel's dignity," he charged: "They created an exaggerated cult of the life of each single soul of Israel."[86] He contrasted "political romanticism" with "diasporic rationalism." The latter, he asserted, gives preference to interest, the former to the brave gesture that stirs the imagination of children and teaches them to value heroism. A diasporic people, Ahimeir claimed, is unable to comprehend the psychology of those who conquer the North or South Pole, heroes of aviation who risk their lives. It is likewise unable to fathom the willingness of a people to sacrifice hundreds of thousands of their sons, as the French did at Verdun. Heroism, Ahimeir contended, is the character of a state-centered people, while martyrdom is the mark of a people in exile.[87] Ahimeir acknowledged the fact that the romantic heroes often failed. The Poles, in all their galant revolts, suffered disaster after disaster. Neither did the heroes of the Jewish pantheon of Ahimeir, the fighters of Yodefat, the Temple Mount, Massada, and Betar redeem the people but, rather, ended their heroic stand with downfall and destruction. However, he noted, "thanks to the heroes of Massada, the mark of eternal life was imprinted on the brow of the Jewish nation."[88] A national movement has its own logic, based on psychological motivation rather than rational thinking. For that reason, it is unable to denigrate itself, even for the sake of its own survival. The willingness to lower one's head until the storm has passed is a feature characteristic of Jews in the Diaspora who grew accustomed to suffering all sorts of indignities for the sake of survival.[89] The most important thing is not the political gains but, rather, the nurturing of a new national mentality, characterized by the readiness for total self-sacrifice in defiance of the established political order and by a disdain for the moral inhibitions typical of simple mortals.

Ahimeir was well versed in Jewish sources but, by the same token, was also familiar with Russian and German culture. The fear of the Gentile world, one of the central components in the intellectual world of Uri Zvi Greenberg, was not part of his mental makeup. He measured the Jews by the yardstick of the Gentile world and believed they were able and obliged to play according to the same rules that were standard in the world at large. He used images borrowed from the realm of ancient Jewish myth (as had Berdichevsky and his disciples). Yet for him, they became identified with heroic deeds to be imitated in the present or symbols of identity and identificational codes. For example, he often utilized images from the Jewish War against the Romans: Massada, Betar. But his approach, in the final analysis, lacked the eschatological ardor of Uri Zvi Greenberg and was oriented more toward the modern world and innovative methods of political action. His attachment, for example, to the Nili group and its heroes, in particular the figure of Sara Aaronsohn, who committed suicide while being interrogated by the Ottoman authorities during World War I, was reflective of the limitations of his mythology. He preferred modern heroes, who identified with antiestablishment groups, symbolizing the willingness of the individual to break free from the conventions of society and to rise to heroic heights. The examples of heroes he used also reflected his preference for modern secular romanticism over a traditionally Jewish-oriented romanticism.[90]

Ahimeir considered the willingness to use violence as the supreme test of the revolutionary, the fighter, the terrorist. He recorded in his notebook: "I was quite satisfied in my last class for Betar members. I asked what the true and proper criterion was for evaluating events. One person answered: the quantity of blood that had been shed. That is the true Betarist answer."[91] The figures of political murderers from the past exercised an especial fascination on him. He dedicated his *Megilat Sikarikin* (Scroll of the Sicarii), a study of the political murderer, to the memory of Charlotte Corday, Marat's assassin, and Fanya Kaplan, who had attempted to kill Lenin and wounded him. On the surface, it appeared to be a neutral work of research on a philosophical topic. But Ahimeir did not conceal his positive attitude toward the assassins. The name he used as an appellation, the sicarii, disclosed his position; Ahimeir viewed the biryonim, sicarii (those who secretly carried a *sica,* or knife, to murder collaborators with Rome), and other remorseless Zealots during the war at the time of Second Temple as his venerated heroes. It was not by chance that he used the pseudonym Abba Sicra and dubbed the organization he founded Brit ha-Biryonim (Covenant of Hooligans). It should be recalled that the renewed legitimation of the Zealots from the period of the great rebellion against the Romans (A.D. 67–70) had already been initiated by Berdichevsky. But it was Ahimeir who utilized the Zealots as a central symbol, transforming them into a guiding myth. Treating failures as victories was an inseparable component of national romanticism, professing a perverted love for the "twilight of the gods."

Ahimeir wrote, "The sicarii view history as the doing of negative heroes, not the sons of God, but the sons of Satan."[92] Faithful to his amoral conception, he declared that it was not the righteous who were the makers of history but rather those who revolted against the establishment and its rules, those who dared to dictate the rules of the game themselves. For that reason, the terrorist is the true hero of history. He characterized the terrorist as an idealist, who sacrifices his life on the "altar of the life to come." Marxism rejects personal terror, because "it looks askance at the heroic deed of the individual."[93] Yet even those who defend the existing order, he wrote, know in the secrecy of their hearts the superiority of the political killer over the simple murderer. The decisive question is, "For what purpose was the murder committed?"[94] That short study was published during the Biryonim trial in 1934, when Ahimeir was accused of having set up a terrorist organization. The manuscript was confiscated and presented in court as evidence. It is generally assumed that Ahimeir wrote the *Scroll of the Sicarri* about 1926.[95]

Although he had a liking for concepts and symbols from the Jewish War against the Romans, it appears that to a great extent, Ahimeir took his ideas from the Russian populists, who had not hesitated to kill Alexander II and many others in the leadership of the czarist establishment. The concept of the avant-garde, a small minority that views itself exempt from the restrictions of conventional morality, was among the commonly accepted notions in the cultural–political climate of Palestine. Persons from the Labor movement were probably more vulnerable to ideas of that kind than followers of the school of Jabotinsky. It was not accidental that Ahimeir and his associates were soon involved in a direct clash with Jabotinsky. While the latter was an adherent of the parliamentary school of thought of the nineteenth century, a firm believer in law and legalism, they were disciples of the revolutionary–ruffian current typical of the twentieth century. Jabotinsky thought in terms of an opposition that sought to replace the government by the democratic process. In contrast, the thinking of Ahimeir and the maximalists centered on bloody revolution that does not hesitate to use violence to achieve its aims. The slogan they coined—"To invigorate the movement in spirit and blood; to replace the *oppositionary* means by *revolutionary* means, action instead of talk"[96]—was directed against Jabotinsky and his methods. Yeivin demanded that the revisionists should start behaving like a true national liberation movement. They should no longer restrict themselves to parliamentary methods but had to storm barricades and to take action, by blood and fire, to establish a Jewish state. The twentieth century, he declared, is characterized by ideologies that know no mercy: Communism replaced social democracy, fascism supplanted conservatism. Zionism was obliged to get used to that new reality, or it would fail.[97] "Creation of the race of *biryonim*"—thus Yeivin defined the desired psychological essence of the new Jew.[98]

Even before the 1929 riots, Ahimeir had wished to enlighten the public to the fact that universalistic, humanistic concepts would not lead to the creation of the Jewish state. "The messiah will not come in the figure of a poor man riding on a donkey," he wrote in one of his essays: "The messiah will come, like all messiahs, riding on a tank, delivering his orations to the people."[99] In the aftermath of the riots, he undertook to dispel the illusions still current regarding the possibility of realizing Zionist aims by peaceful means. "When the messiah comes," he declared, "all of us will follow him over a bridge of paper. But as long as he has not arrived, the path of redemption leads . . . across the bridge of iron."[100] Attacking Jabotinsky's legalism, he scorned the idea of a petition, a pet notion of his. Jabotinsky believed that the British government would change its policy in favor of the Jewish national home if it were presented with a petition signed by millions of Jews. Ahimeir and his associates depicted the petition as a bridge made of paper, a pathetic, anachronistic illusion belonging to another era. They contended that a bridge of iron would be constructed by way of violent action—deeds that would arouse the attention of the entire world.[101]

Ahimeir and his associates had a deep hatred of the Soviet Union. Since his experience in Russia during the civil war, Ahimeir had nurtured a profound enmity toward the regime there. Yet that fact did not prevent him from admiring Lenin and the methods of the Bolsheviks, like his colleague Uri Zvi Greenberg. Their thirst for power and lack of inhibitions won his admiration, as the welcome model of leadership, one that is not choosy about the means it uses in order to defeat its opponents.[102] Contrasted with the Nietzschean greatness of the Bolsheviks, Zionism appeared in his eyes to be of minor stature and meager exploits. In the twentieth century, the fate of millions had been decided by the wave of a hand, such as the slaughter of the Armenians, the exchange of population between Turkey and Greece, collectivization in the Soviet Union, and the parades of hundreds of thousands in Nuremberg and Moscow. And at such a juncture, he complained, the Zionist movement was wasting its time trying to obtain several thousand wretched certificates for immigration.[103]

Ahimeir and his colleagues applied the patterns of European national liberation movements to the Zionist movement. The peoples from which they had borrowed educational models were the Poles, Czechs, Italians, and Irish. In general, the European liberation movements engaged in struggle against foreign rulers governing their homeland. In their eyes, the counterpart in Palestine to the foreign ruler was the British administration. The "Hebron government" (the term used by Ahimeir and his associates for the mandatory regime) was presented as a regime planning to treat the Jews as "natives" in their own homeland; to place them at the mercy of an Arab government; to leave Palestine to languish in desolation; to close the gates to immigrants; and numerous other evil plots and designs—all of which justified the label *the British oppressor.* In the first issue of the magazine *Brit ha-Biryonim,* organ of the militant organization he established in 1932, Ahimeir called on Palestinian youth, spelling out his plan of action against Britain: "We speak clearly: There is a need to fight. *Really* to fight, as all oppressed people have fought to achieve freedom for their homeland." For that reason, he wrote, "you must be a soldier, a loyal soldier, fighting for the honor of your people."[104] The definition of the British as "foreign ruler" gave the Jews the guise of a "local" population, conveniently solving, as if by chance, the problem of the right to Palestine: It was obviously intended for the natural sons of Palestine, namely, the Jews. Accusations leveled against the British that they were to blame for the 1929 riots ("a government of pogroms" was a widespread epithet) was an integral component of the romanticism of the concept *foreign ruler* and sanctioned the enmity toward him. Accusing the British of all the pains suffered by Zionism except for those attributed to the Zionist Executive was also a reasonable tactic for mobilization.

The problem of the relevance of European models applied to the situation in Palestine did not trouble Ahimeir, Yeivin, and their disciples. Educational romanticism was more important than mundane reality. The question what would happen to the small Jewish community in Palestine if the British should actually decide, as the Biryonim demanded, to pull out, was not on the agenda. Expressions such as "path of suffering and defiance," "prisons and torture," "foreign oppressor," "hands of traitors," and "British antagonist" created an intellectual climate in which rational considerations retreated in the face of romantic emotionalization. The propagators of "revolutionary Zionism" (another code name for the maximalists) encouraged the young to embrace the notion that the central problem on the national agenda was the removal of the foreign ruler—once this had been accomplished, everything else would work out.

The surprising feature was the little attention they paid to the Arab problem. The maximalists had no special love for the Arabs. "Desert savages" was one of the epithets reserved for them. U. Z. Greenberg's poems, referring to the August 1929 riots, contained descriptions of atrocities in Hebron in which Arabs were mentioned as murderers. The reality of the volcano was also emphasized.[105] "Packs of wolves from Arabia," "Arabia and Edom"—these expressions used by Greenberg contained mythical motifs, depicting the Arabs as "haters of Israel," in the same category as Gentiles in Europe. In his writings, the Arabs underwent a process of demonization and were not related to as real human beings. In contrast, Ahimeir and Yeivin rarely referred to Arabs. After their immediate reactions to the 1929 riots, cast in the spirit of Greenbergian hate-literature, they seldom made any reference to them. Among the competing components of the Palestinian drama, this was one that received their least attention. At times, one has the impression that they were not even cognizant of its existence. The patterns they adopted from European liberation movements did not contain a suitable slot for categorizing the Arabs without doing damage to the perfection of the model. Those liberation movements freed peoples that were settled on their own land. They were not asked to deal either with the problem of a people 'in formation" or that of a second local population with aspirations of its own regarding the future of the country. Consequently, Ahimeir and Yeivin solved the problem by turning their back on its existence. This approach had additional advantages: The question of who had a legitimate right to the country did not perturb them at all, and they were certainly not apprehensive about the emergence of an Arab national movement. In their image of reality, the competition in Palestine was between the Jews and the British; there was no third party.

In principle, it was the British who were the great adversary. In actual fact, most of the animosity and hate literature created by the group of "revolutionary Zionists" were directed toward the "enemy within," namely the Zionist leadership. From the end of the 1920s on, the alliance between the Labor movement and Weizmann had been one of the basic political facts in the Jewish community and within the Zionist movement. That alliance closed the door for the revisionists to Zionist positions of leadership. The three who had abandoned the Labor movement (the so-called renegades, as Katznelson termed them) had no doubt that this movement was the focus of power in the Yishuv. They knew that anyone who wished to change the political system had to lash out at the Labor movement, and undermine its legitimacy, credibility, and position among the public. Yet beyond the political–rational arguments, that group nursed a pathological hatred for the Labor movement's values, symbols, and cultural codes. It is difficult to account for that hatred without resorting to psychological explanations. It appears that a familiar phenomenon was operative here: apostates who demonstrate their new fidelity to excess by piling abuse on their previous beliefs. Jabotinsky never showed the crudeness and hatred evinced by this troika, men who only shortly before had been allied with the Labor movement. The paper *Hazit ha-Am* (People's Front) published a novel in installments by Heschel Yeivin entitled *Jerusalem Is Waiting.* With great talent, the author integrated fragments of reality with half-truths and demagoguery, supposedly depicting the hidden truth about the Labor movement leadership. The leaders of the Labor movement were portrayed both as men who, weak in character, failed to act and, conversely, as evil, demonic figures impelled by dark motives, bereft of personal or social morality, and embezzlers living at the expense of the national funds.[106] Immediately after the riots, Greenberg blamed them for the disaster: You are guilty of the shedding of blood in Zion because

> You told the small Hebrew tribe to live in peace
> To plow and toil . . .
> And not to think of the volcano under their feet.[107]

The accusation leveled against the leadership of the Labor movement, holding them responsible for the riots, was not presented as stemming from any actual facts but was based on ideological considerations. Since the Labor leaders had deceived the Jewish community into believing in the possibility of peace in Palestine, they were to be blamed for the tragedy that had transpired. During the years of British–Zionist confrontation in 1929–1931, Labor people were accused of having failed to stand up to the British and of sycophancy toward the foreign ruler. They were presented as traitors in the tradition of Josephus Flavius, who had sold the dignity of the people and its interests for a cup of tea at the house of the alien ruler. An epithet current at the time was "agents of the enemy regime."[108]

Eventually the maximalists devoted most of their time and efforts to denouncing the leaders and the policy of the Labor movement. Jabotinsky, and even some of the members of Brit ha-Biryonim, demanded that they direct their revolutionary zeal against the British—in vain. Hence, the leadership of the Labor movement and its values remained the preferred target for their unbridled attacks.[109] Aside from the psychological motives for that preference, it was also rooted in the simple tactical fact that launching an attack against other targets entailed risks they could not take. Incitement against the British authorities beyond a certain limit could lead to the closing down of the paper, the disbanding of the organization, and even arrest. Attacks against Arabs were totally out of the question. In contrast, possibilities for slandering the leaders of the Labor movement were, for all practical purposes, unlimited, since the British showed little interest in internal Jewish verbal squabbles as long as public peace was preserved. In a way, the selection of Labor as the main target for vilification reflects the inherent weakness of the maximalist faction.

This fact casts revealing light on the dichotomy between words and deeds that was so characteristic of Ahimeir and his colleagues. Intellectuals, not men of action, they were in love with the magic of extreme phraseology, enchanted by the theater of reality. Their aggressiveness, as radical as it was, remained basically verbal. Brit ha-Biryonim, an ephemeral movement whose membership did not encompass more than a few dozen isolated individuals, succeeded in carrying out only three actions: a demonstration against the visit of deputy British colonial minister Drummond Shils in Palestine; a demonstration against the census administered by the mandatory government at the end of 1931, interpreted by the maximalists as a design to stress the minority status of the Jews; and disruption of the lecture by Norman Bentwich, a British Zionist who was dismissed by the mandatory government from his post as attorney general, due to complaints by Arabs about his supposed pro-Zionist leanings. He had been appointed professor to fill the Chair of Peace at the Hebrew University in Jerusalem; and the Biryonim protested against the pacifist tendencies of the chair during his lecture of February 1932. If we include the actions of Betar activists on the periphery of Ahimeir's influence, one can add to this list the blowing of the shofar near the Wailing Wall at the termination of Yom Kippur (an act that had been prohibited by the British following the report of the International Wailing Wall Committee appointed by the League of Nations in 1930) and the removal of the Nazi flag from the German consulate, first in Jaffa and then in Jerusalem. All those actions were more symbolic than violent in the true sense. The Biryonim had a fondness for scandal, for the dramatic scene that attracts the media. They also did not shrink back from engaging in moderate actions of hooliganism, such as the disruption of a lecture. But they did not go so far as to carry out any genuine acts of violence.[110]

Of course, there remains the question of the murder of Arlosoroff, at that time head of the political department of the Jewish Agency in Jerusalem. He was shot under mysterious circumstances on June 16, 1933, while strolling along the beach in Tel Aviv. This shooting took place following a campaign of vilification and character assassination against him by the paper *Hazit ha-Am*. In the trial two revisionists, close associates of Ahimeir, were indicted, and Ahimeir was accused of incitement to murder. Ahimeir was soon released; and the two others, after being found guilty in the first instance, were released due to a lack of evidence in the second instance. Was this murder in fact the liberating act of the terrorist, so admired by Ahimeir? He and his associates repeatedly denied any connection with the murder, with an insistence that contradicted the teachings of violence they preached. That denial, of course, proves nothing. However, the fact that Ahimeir emerged a broken man from his experience in prison and did not return to the helm of leadership of any group suggests that the great priest of violence as a political method was personally not cut out to lead the life of a terrorist. There was a certain incommensurability between Ahimeir's personality as a sensitive human being, apparently unable to harm a fly, and his uninhibited message of aggressive violence. Was this lack of correlation between the aggressivity of the message and the mildness of the deed the product of psychological recoil or actual weakness? Did he cease his activity because of alarm over the possible implications of his sermonizing or because he was restrained by the police and the Jewish community from acting? Such questions must be left to the judgment of future scholars.[111]

On the historical balance, the phenomenon of Ahimeir and his comrades (indeed, Uri Zvi Greenberg spent most of the 1930s in Poland) was marginal within the broad spectrum of beliefs, ideologies, and opinions current in the Yishuv. Nonetheless, it had a certain importance and influence. Although the number of Ahimeir's followers was quite small, there was always the fringe of Betarist sympathizers. Jabotinsky rejected the message of violent revolution and on several occasions had strongly criticized statements made by this group in favor of a party led by a "dictator," a role they cherished for Jabotinsky. He was also opposed to the demand to remove the British from Palestine. On the other hand, Jabotinsky was unable to rid himself of the Biryonim completely. He was alternately attracted and revolted by their aggressive message. Of course, he also had certain political considerations. They were the most active and impressive group within the Revisionist movement in Palestine; and as Yeivin told him in defiance, it was easier to expel the Revisionist movement from them than to expel them from the Revisionist movement.[112] But beyond this, there was some sort of psychological link between the relatively moderate verbal violence, acceptable to Jabotinsky, and the wild form that the Biryonim preferred—between the mild adventurism that Jabotinsky advocated and the violent scandals that they preached. Although he rejected their proposals to crown him "il Duce," in actual fact, he led his party like an autocrat. There was a profound proximity between the militarism he advocated and that professed by Ahimeir and associates. He distanced himself from the rough revolutionary tendencies that were incompatible with his bourgeois cultural background and tastes. But in regard to political methods, they serve as a kind of antilegalistic mirror image of himself. Jabotinsky's inability to cast off this group derived not just from his political need for them but also from his awareness of a psychological—and to a certain extent, cultural—bond between him and them. In their radical consistency, they took the internal logic of the teachings of revisionism to its final conclusion. That link between them and the Revisionist movement transformed them from a marginal phenomenon to a persistent current in the political life of the Jewish community.[113]

The Labor movement did not view Ahimeir and his associates as an accidental phenomenon. The vigorousness of the response they stimulated testified to the existence of a raw nerve in the Labor movement that vibrated to the frequency they were sending on. Violent revolution as a preferred means for changing the human condition; the revolutionary, who prepares for sacrifice for the sake of the people and who therefore is exempt from the bonds of morality; the avant-garde, the select few who are the bearers of the mission of history—all these ideas derived from the thinking of the Left. From the cultural viewpoint, the revolutionary–ruffian conception of these three thinkers was in keeping with the revolt against convention and bourgeois niceties, which remained an integral part of cultural codes on the Left. But beyond all this, there was also a covert understanding of their violent message, as well. The intellectual world to which a great part of the Left felt attached was not that of social democracy but, rather, the violent revolutionary ideology nurtured in the Pale of Settlement. Its symbols and models were not drawn from the movements of reformist socialism but principally from those of Bolshevist Russia. Their worldview did not reject violence as a means of action out of hand. The more the Labor movement became integrated within the Zionist establishment and gained hegemony in the Zionist Organization, the more it came to accept the parliamentary rules of the game, embraced Western democratic principles, and abandoned the path of revolution. In the period under discussion (the first half of the 1930s) that process was well under way. But the detachment from the intellectual and psychological world of East European revolutionary fervor was gradual and tortuous. The admiration for the revolutionary path and disdain for social democracy remained deeply rooted in the mentality of many of the rank and file of the Labor movement and an important segment of its leadership.[114] Hence, their understanding of the cultural code communicated by this ideological triumvirate was exact and incisive. Their alarm and disgust with "revolutionary Zionism" derived from the fact that here was a frame of mind familiar to them from their own conceptual–psychological sources.

Moreover, this was a period marked by an ongoing fierce struggle between fascism and socialism in Europe. The phenomenon of defection from the Socialist movement to the fascist camp was a familiar one. Ahimeir, Greenberg, and Yeivin were regarded as the Palestinian version of that international turncoat phenomenon. Since the end of the 1920s, the Left had viewed the revisionists as akin to the European Fascist movement. That identification bestowed Manichaean dimensions on the struggle in Palestine between the Right and the Left, conceptualizing it as part of the global struggle between the forces of light and darkness. The defeat of German social democracy without a fight at the hands of the violent Nazis had a traumatic impact on the Palestinian Jewish Left. The fact that the largest of the Social Democratic parties (which could boast an outstanding political legacy) had had misgivings about violating the rules of the democratic game and, instead of fighting in the streets, had preserved formal legality and given in was perceived in Palestine as a negative lesson. One should not surrender without a desperate struggle; one should not allow the forces of fascism to rear their head; one should not attach undue value to formalistic legality. On the other hand, one is obligated to defend the intellectual, social, and political assets of the movement and of democracy, no matter what the price. In this way, the failure of social democracy in Europe served as a legitimating argument for the use of force in Palestine.

The years 1932–1934 were marked by internecine conflict in the Yishuv in which the political struggle spilled from the conference halls onto the street. Clashes between Labor movement people and Betarists became commonplace. For the most part, such confrontations were initiated by the Left, which was the larger, better organized, and stronger of the two camps. At first, they were directed against Betarists who had broken strikes organized by Histadrut members. After that, their purpose was to prevent Betar from demonstrating their presence in the streets. Finally, they attempted to prevent them from carrying out any political action whatsoever. Usually, a large crowd of workers and youth would gather together in advance in order to disrupt demonstrations or meetings of the Right. The use of force by workers to gain control of the street and to curb the influence of the opposing camp was considered a justified means in the struggle against fascism. Berl Katznelson, the most outspoken opponent of the use of violence by the Labor camp, branded this development "the fascist transformation of the Labor movement." However, most of the rank and file responded positively to the "demonstration of muscle" by the workers. The analogy between the domestic Right, symbolized by the figure of Ahimeir and his colleagues, and European fascism gave vent to an accumulation of pent-up frustration among workers, which was discharged in outbreaks of violence.[115]

The murder of Arlosoroff, the ensuing trial, and its aftermath provided an inexhaustible source for mutual incitement and tension. The Jewish community was split into two camps: those who believed in the charge that the revisionists were guilty of the murder and those who did not. The first camp was made up largely of the workers. There was a widespread belief that a secret group of conspirators probably existed among the revisionists, a cell that had adopted the tactic of political murder as a method of action. It supposedly drew political sustenance from Russian revolutionary traditions—either in the "positive" version associated with Narodnaya volya or the negative, degenerate version, associated with Nechaev or Dostoyevski's *Demons*.

As a matter of fact, there had already been a precedent in the Yishuv for a politically motivated murder of a Jew by another Jew. In the early 1920s, Yisrael Yaakov de Haan, a Jew of Dutch background, at first a Zionist and later ultraorthodox, was found murdered. Haan had been involved in anti-Zionist agitation and was suspected of conspiring with the Arab Executive Committee against the Jewish community. The murder was carried out at the initiative of the Hagana command and under its authority.[116] Beilinson severely criticized that action, and Hagana members identified with the Left never made use of that weapon again. Yet Haan's murder proved just how close the Left was to employing such methods of action. The murky existence of sects of mysterious conspirators who decide on carrying out acts of terror for idealistic reasons and then implement them without recoiling was part of the living legacy of revolutionary romanticism they had been educated in.

Consequently, the idea of a political murder was not totally alien to their thinking. In the light of the gospel of violence being preached by the Ahimeir group, Arlosoroff's murder appeared to be a predictable incident.[117]

The struggle between the Labor camp and the revisionists in the first half of the 1930s revealed the dichotomy inherent within the Labor movement: At one and the same time, it carried aloft the banner of the defensive ethos, suppressing the aggressive tendencies of its members, and retained its identity as a revolutionary movement that fostered militancy. The chanelling of aggressive urges in the early 1930s toward a struggle with the revisionists took place in a period in which the Arab problem had receded from awareness and shifted to the margins of public interest. In that struggle, a tendency emerged among a broad public to condone the use of violence. Up until that point, this element had been absent from the system of external relations, that is, those between Jews and Arabs. The question of the correlation between the use of force in internal versus external relations is complex and cannot be unambiguously resolved. Can a society isolate the element of aggressiveness in its culture, restricting it to one sphere alone? Or is it impossible to limit and isolate violence? Is leakage from one sphere of relations to the other bound to occur? Can a society remain humanistic and democratic over an extended period of time while simultaneously engaged in a continued external conflict? Can a society exhibit violence in internal relations yet avoid using it externally? The history of the twentieth century—the Age of Violence in the terminology of the historian Jacob Talmon—is rich in examples of regimes that were violent within and then drifted into violence in external affairs, as well as others that did not. Some democratic, enlightened governments have stood the test of a prolonged external conflict, while others were unable to preserve their internal strength.

In the case of the Jewish community in Palestine, it appears that the question is even more complicated, since the Arab problem was both "internal" and "external." It had an internal dimension because relations between Jews and Arabs were quite intimate in some parts of the Jewish community, and the web of life was a single weave; it was an external problem, because the Arabs constituted a separate national entity, situated outside the perimeter of Jewish society and alienated from it. Is it possible to make any inferences from workers' willingness to use force against the revisionists as to their possible readiness to use force against Arabs?

It appears that the psychological potential and physical readiness to make use of force were indeed present in the community. Jewish society in Palestine was a frontier society in the sense that it did not hesitate to take drastic steps if it felt threatened. The commitment to self-defense as an essential instrument of survival exempted it from the cultural refinement of an established society that by its very nature has greater inhibitions regarding the use of force. That fact was prominent in the reaction to the demise of social democracy in Germany and in the struggle against the revisionists. That same principle was also applicable in respect to the Arab question. From this perspective, it was possible to discern some sort of shift in the direction of a greater readiness to use force.

Ahimeir's ideas did not disappear with the decline of his personal influence. At the end of the 1930s, they were embraced by the underground organizations of the "dissidents" from the Hagana. They became the conceptual foundation of those who viewed themselves as an "alternative society" beside the organized Jewish community in Palestine.

Initial Doubts Within the Political Leadership

The Seventeenth Congress was one of the dramatic events that accompanied the history of the Zionist movement—events in which the movement was called upon to take stock of itself, to reexamine its goals and methods of action. Yet that congress was also one of the most irrelevant when measured in terms of the historical context. The substantive question of whether the evolutionary method of action would lead to the establishment of a Jewish political entity in Palestine by peaceful means was not debated. In the absence of an acceptable alternative, the defensive ethos remained the guiding creed. The revisionists and their supporters rejected that ethos but did not propose any other acceptable method of action in its stead. However, the first reflections and objections regarding its vitality began to appear among the leadership of the main current. One of first to express his doubts was Arthur Ruppin. At the beginning of 1931, Ruppin raised for the first time the issue of the paradoxicality of the hoped-for accord with the Arabs: "What we can get [from the Arabs] is of no use to us, and what we need we cannot get from them."[118] The Arabs were only prepared to grant the Jews minority rights; and for minority rights the Jewish people would not invest its blood and capital in the building of Palestine. In February 1931, Ruppin still believed that it was possible to arrive at an agreement with the Arabs on the basis of a binational Palestine and Jewish support for a Greater Arab Federation. Yet by December of that year, he already despaired of any such possibility. The conclusion that had begun to crystallize in his letter of 1928 to Hans Kohn regarding the existence of unreconcilable contradictions between Jewish and Arab interests now took on fuller form: It was impossible to work out a formula that would preserve the vital interests of the two partners. Not explicitly stated was the conclusion that an Jewish–Arab clash had become inevitable. At this stage, however, Ruppin did not pursue the line of logic he sketched. He continued to participate from time to time in meetings of Brit Shalom or in discussions with Judah Leib Magnes. Magnes, a principled pacifist, also attempted to work out formulas for resolving Jewish–Arab contradictions. It was clear to Ruppin that those formulas had no prospect whatsoever of being accepted by both parties to the conflict.[119] As a matter of fact, he was swept up by the mode of thinking of the central current (which still adhered to the defensive ethos) while praying inwardly that the realization of Zionism would precede the eruption of Arab nationalism. Even though he recognized the inevitability of the conflict, the idea of the use of force was still alien to him.

Chaim Arlosoroff was the leader who arrived at far-reaching conclusions regarding the relation between Zionist aims and methods of implementation. Born in Eastern Europe and educated in Germany, he was the rising star of Zionist diplomacy. In 1931, at the age of thirty-two, Arlosoroff was elected to the key post of head of the political department of the Jewish Agency in Jerusalem. Moderate and a realist, he was the right man to rebuild the network of relations and mutual trust between the mandatory government and the Jewish Agency. That network had been completely undermined as a result of the policy of John Chancellor, the high commissioner during the 1929 riots, who was responsible to a substantial degree for the anti-Zionist slant in British policy after those disturbances. That same summer of 1931, when Arlosoroff began his tenure as head of the political department, Sir Arthur Wauchope—general, statesman, and experienced administrator—took over as high commissioner in Jerusalem. In subsequent years, Wauchope was considered the "best of the high commissioners" by Arlosoroff and Ben Gurion, both of whom had the opportunity to work closely with him. And indeed, the years of his tenure (to 1938) were a period in which the national home reached a takeoff point from which there was no return. Cooperation between the high commissioner and the head of the political department of the Jewish Agency endowed the alliance between Britain and the Zionist movement with a new content. For that reason, there is special significance to the fact that it was Arlosoroff, the architect of cooperation, who was to raise the most serious and severe doubts about the evolutionary methods adopted by the Zionist Organization and, consequently, about the defensive ethos.

A year after he had commenced in his new duties, Arlosoroff expressed his misgivings in a letter to Weizmann, whom he regarded as his teacher and mentor. Weizmann at that time was without formal status, since he had not been reelected as president of the Zionist Organization at the Seventeenth Congress due to the fallout from that unfortunate interview with the Jewish Telegraphic Agency. Arlosoroff was troubled by what he saw as an emerging dilemma: Would continued pursuance of Zionist policy based on evolutionary methods be able to advance it to the next stage in the development of Palestine? At the moment, the Arabs were unable to annihilate the Jewish community in Palestine but believed they had sufficient power to establish an Arab state there without taking Jewish claims into consideration. The Jews could preserve their present positions but were unable to ensure an uninterrupted immigration and colonization process along peaceful lines. The next stage, Arlosoroff reasoned, would arrive when the Jews were strong enough to be able to prevent the creation of an Arab state and the Arabs were incapable of halting the accelerated pace of immigration and colonization. In the end, the hoped-for equilibrium between the two peoples would be achieved. This, in turn, would lead to negotiations and eventually to a solution. Negotiations and peace would come as a result of the crystallization of Jewish power, in the sense of a critical demographic mass in Palestine.

Arlosoroff's analysis led him to conclude that the evolutionary method was no longer conducive to advancing the Zionist movement to the anticipated next stage. He had arrived at that conclusion on the basis of experience gathered in the political department of the Jewish Agency, grappling on a day-to-day basis with the myriad difficulties being placed by the British administration in the path of the national home. The basic reality in Palestine (in particular the existence of an Arab majority) induced the British civil service (by default as it were) to act primarily in accordance with the interests of that majority. For the Jews, promoting the national home called for the introduction of an active, pro-Zionist policy that was incompatible with the tendencies of the mandatory government. To this was added the temporal issue, How much time was left for the Zionist movement to realize its goals? Arlosoroff watched the termination of the Type A mandates and the establishment of independent Arab states in Iraq, Transjordan, and Syria. That process, together with the rapid progress of the Arab National movement in Palestine ("In the meantime, the Arab movement in Palestine has been successful in adapting for itself all the tricks of Zionist diplomacy") signaled that the Zionist hourglass was running out. Over and beyond the constraints deriving from the Palestinian context, Arlosoroff predicted the outbreak of a new world war in the near future. He did not know who the antagonists would be in that conflict but had little doubt that within five to ten years a global conflagration would erupt in which the British Empire would be involved: "When the war breaks out, the Mandate system will collapse and the League of Nations will go on summer vacation."[120]

Given the short span of time left the Zionist movement, he believed there were four options. One was to continue to tread in the shallow waters of the evolutionary method, while slowly accumulating strength, in the hope that some imponderable factor would change the rules of the game. He recalled in this context the old anecdote I have mentioned about the Jew and the bullish landlord. Either the bear would die, or the landlord—an approach reminiscent of Katznelson's stand. Arlosoroff rejected that approach, viewing it as an antithesis to Zionist political activism, a new version of traditional Jewish fatalism. The second option was simply to recognize that under the present circumstances it was impossible to make Zionism a reality and to give up the struggle.

The third option was to limit the realization of Zionism to only a portion of Palestine, in which Jewish sovereignty would be formally established, and "to make that region a strategic basis for possible progress in the future." Basically, Arlosoroff was favorably disposed toward such proposals: "They include the ingredients of territorialism and political self-determination, which embody the basic truth of Zionism." But he thought they were impracticable because Palestine was so small. There was also the problem of Jerusalem and the numerous difficulties inherent in the fact that Jews were settled primarily in the valleys, areas difficult to defend. Moreover— and decisively—even in those settled areas, the Jews still constituted a minority.

Arlosoroff's fourth option derived from a totally different universe of thought: "Under the present circumstances, Zionism cannot be realized without a transition period in which a Jewish minority would govern by an organized revolutionary regime." A minority nationalist government would be set up to exercise control over the nerve centers of state power, especially the armed forces. During the transition period, a systematic policy of immigration and colonization would be in force. That policy would lead to a change in the balance of power between Jews and Arabs in Palestine. When faced with the alternative of abandoning the Zionist dream or giving up "formal" democracy, Arlosoroff chose the second option. The dictatorship of the people (a version of the concept of proletarian dictatorship) was meant to help grapple with the problems of the transition period in which the principle of minority–majority rule collided with what he regarded as historical justice: "About one matter I feel very strongly: that I will never accept a defeat for Zionism until an attempt has been made, commensurate in magnitude and seriousness with the desperate struggle we are waging for the renewal of our national life and the sacredness of the trust the Jewish people has charged us with."[121]

This was the first time a Zionist politician from the top echelons of leadership had raised the possibility that Zionism could not be realized by the customary evolutionary methods and that its implementation would ultimately necessitate the use of armed force. Arlosoroff's view differed from that of Jabotinsky, who conceived the military force that would erect the "wall of iron" as a product of a proposed Jewish–British alliance, a factor accompanying the regime of colonization he wanted the British to institute. Arlosoroff, in contrast, spoke about a situation in which the British were completely excluded from the picture and the problem of Palestine would be decided by the Jews themselves, using their own forces: "Everything I am demanding is based on the genuine strength of the Jewish community itself."[122] The idea that a Jewish takeover in Palestine should *precede* the establishment of a Jewish demographic and settlement infrastructure, rather than being its product, was new. The link between that idea and the sense that time was running out was clear and explicit: The use of force would grow from the necessities of an emergency situation that grants legitimacy to the use of means normally considered invalid and objectionable.

Arlosoroff utilized language borrowed from the world of revolutionary socialism. Even though he was not a proponent of Marxist doctrine and rejected Bolshevism as a method of action, Arlosoroff was under the influence of both. Consciously or not, he internalized the basic conception embodied in such revolutionary doctrine that validates the use of force for a sacred purpose. The concept of an avantgarde entrusted with realization of the historical goals of the nation gave Arlosoroff and his colleagues a feeling of high mission and great responsibility far more powerful than that associated with action within parliamentary frameworks. The readiness to use force was part of an extraparliamentary approach, an expression of despair and frustration with bourgeois legalism, and release from conventional inhibitions in those crucial periods when the fate of the people is at stake.

Despite the psychological readiness to take radical steps, as required by an emergency situation, it was specifically the dispute with the revisionists, who on the surface appeared to be fostering that same approach, that made clear the basic differences between the camps. The conceptual proximity had a negligible impact in the political sphere due to differences in the accepted level of violence, its timing, and its limits. The revisionist disdain for the defensive ethos transformed it into a code of identity associated with the Labor movement.

Arlosoroff's letter to Weizmann went unanswered, a brilliant intellectual exercise by a leader in an hour of despair. In 1933 Ben Gurion replaced the murdered Arlosoroff as head of the political department of the Jewish Agency. He brought with him a fresh enthusiasm for exploring new avenues of negotiations with the Arabs, a line he had been advocating since 1929. The aspiration to come to some kind of an accord with the Arabs integrated well with the efforts by Mapai to ensure continuation of Jewish colonization along peaceful paths. One of Ben Gurion's first actions after taking up his new post was to try to initiate discussion with Arab leaders. The person he attempted to establish contact with was Musa Alami, a young educated Arab who had served for a certain time as secretary to Wauchope and who also had close relations with the mufti in Jerusalem. Ben Gurion's inclination at that time to believe that basic differences could be resolved by the method of heart-to-heart discussion with leaders of the opposing camp—given dramatic illustration a short time later in the agreement between him and Jabotinsky—also manifested itself in connection with the Arab issue. Right at the outset of their talks, Ben Gurion was surprised by Alami's response after the former had given a "Zionist" speech, in which he had expounded on the impetus of development Jews were bringing to Palestine, changes from which the Arabs also benefited. Alami replied that he would prefer Palestine to remain desolate for another hundred years if necessary, until the Arabs were themselves able to develop the country. That answer, which made it clear to Ben Gurion that his interlocutor was motivated by nationalist sentiments, did not deter him from continuing the discussion with Alami. The year 1934 was marked by Ben Gurion's attempts to negotiate and reach an accord with Arab leaders. One of the arguments in favor of the possibility of an agreement at the time was the acceleration that had taken place in the process of building the national home—a fact that in the view of the Jews, at least, made such an agreement worthwhile for the Arabs, as well. The talks did not advance beyond the early stage and failed to evolve into genuine deliberations with the Arab leadership in Palestine. Ben Gurion emerged from these conversations disappointed and more soberly realistic than he had been before.[123]

On April 16, 1936, a few days before the outbreak of the Arab Rebellion, a discussion took place in the Central Committee of Mapai on the issue of the legislative council scheme. The British parliament had recently rejected the proposal to institute such a council. From certain perspectives, that discussion symbolized the end of an era: It reflected the change that had taken place in Ben Gurion's stance regarding the Arab question since his 1934 attempts to reach some sort of an agreement with them. Ben Gurion was the Zionist politician whose changing views best reflected realities in flux. The man who had refused in 1924 to deal with the Arab question in its political aspects changed in the early 1930s into a great believer in the possibility of reaching an accord with the Arabs. Now he altered his views once again. He had come to the conclusion that any agreement with the Arabs was dependent on reaching a prior understanding with the British; and such understanding on the part of Whitehall would not be forthcoming until Jews constituted a major force in Palestine. The man who had delivered a classic Zionist address in front of Musa Alami two years earlier now ridiculed the possibility of proving the righteousness of Zionism to the Arabs or of teaching them about the "advantages" Zionism was bringing to Palestine for all to enjoy. "It would be extremely naive to assume that Arabs would determine their attitude toward us from the standpoint of abstract justice," he noted. The Arabs claim that "this country is an Arab country, and they wish it to remain so. That is quite elementary!" Ben Gurion was not infected by any hatred of Arabs or by the inability of the fanatic to understand the opposing side. But it was precisely his clear-sighted analysis of realities that prompted him at this stage to despair of any prospects for reaching a workable accord. The amateurish views of Brit Shalom members, who tended to believe that what was desirable was also possible, held no attraction for him. As soon as he concluded that an accord was not feasible, he promptly revised his thinking and abandoned any attempts to work out such an agreement. Ben Gurion returned once again to the fundamental position of the defensive ethos: An accord would be a product of the formation of substantial Jewish strength in Palestine, not a precondition for it. The main question on the Zionist agenda was not the Arab question but, rather, the British one: British–Zionist cooperation would offer the key for establishing the necessary power base. Indeed, Sprinzak protested against that approach. "I'm against the view that the Arab issue is not the central factor at any given time," he stated: "It is the fundamental factor at all times, in all spheres." But Ben Gurion's view in this instance reflected the consensus of his party. Basically, Ben Gurion returned to the positions that had been popular before the 1929 riots.[124] It appears that he ultimately reached the same clear and sober conception advocated in 1931 by Ruppin, despite the difficult implications it entailed: What the Arabs are prepared to give the Jews, the Jews don't need; what the Jews need, the Arabs are not prepared to give. On April 16, 1936, members of the Mapai Central Committee were still working under the assumption that it would be possible to push ahead with the creation of a Jewish infrastructure in Palestine by peaceful means and without the Arabs being able to prevent it.

The Hour of Mercy, 1932–1936

The year 1932, when Arlosoroff gave up hope on the defensive ethos, was a transitional period in the history of Zionism. In January 1933 Hitler assumed power in Germany. Overnight, the set of priorities for the movement changed. Manpower and financial reserves that were now at the disposal of the movement made Arlosoroff's first option of biding time ("Either the landlord will die, or the bear") the most germane and applicable one. At the end of 1931 Ruppin, who was considered the principal expert on Zionist colonization, asserted that Jews ought to be able to become a majority in Palestine within two generations. His conservative estimate then was that the Zionist movement could not settle more than fifty-five thousand families over a period of twenty to thirty years.[125] In 1933 he revised that assessment dramatically: Thirty-five thousand immigrants arrived that year, and an economic boom set in that was unprecedented in Palestine. "If we could work at this pace for another five years, we would reach the figure of almost five hundred thousand," he wrote at the end of 1933.[126] The country revealed an economic absorptive capacity that exceeded all the expert predictions. People reacted with dubious caution to this economic miracle, especially in the light of the economic crisis buffeting Europe and the United States at that time, and suspected that the economic bubble would soon burst. In April 1934 the Levant Fair opened its doors on a new site in Tel Aviv, a symbol of the accelerated development of industry. "Perhaps it's only a bluff," the president of the Manufacturers' Association said to Ruppin during a visit to the fair's pleasant pavilions: "But at least it's a bluff made of concrete."[127] Yet all gloomy predictions to the contrary, the high tide continued four years. In 1935 sixty-two thousand Jews arrived in Palestine, a number that far exceeded the rosy predictions of the most enthusiastic Zionists. In the course of four years, the Jewish population in Palestine had doubled, rising to more than a third of the country's total population. From the economic, cultural, and political point of view, the Jewish community underwent a process of crystallization and substantial strengthening.

This era was the finest hour of the defensive ethos. It appeared to many that the hope to establish a Zionist hold in Palestine by peaceful means was being realized. More than ever in the past, cooperation between the mandatory government and the Zionist Executive was vigorous and fruitful. The evolutionary process, that only a year or two previously had seemed to be leading to a dead end, received new impetus in the ferment generated by the Fifth Aliyah. As far as the crucial factor of time was concerned, the present leadership had not come to any conclusions different from those of Arlosoroff. However, a new optimism prevailed regarding the pace of building and the possibilities inherent in it. More than at any time in the past, it was necessary to preserve peace in Palestine. Every day that went by in tranquillity, more Jews were added, and the strength of the community was enhanced. In those circumstances, ideas about a takeover of Palestine by force were considered adventurous, superfluous, even dangerous. All were busy with the task of construction, and only a minuscule number gave any thought to the Arab problem during those years. It was once again shunted to the periphery after having occupied the center of public attention in the years 1929–1931. Indeed, Brit Shalom continued to assert both that the Arab question was the central question for Jews and that Palestine was unable to serve as an answer to "Jewish plight" by means of mass immigration.[128] Yet the majority of Jews thought differently. Other questions were on the immediate agenda: organizing the immigration, absorbing it, creating and promoting industry, expanding the various systems of services, and increasing the area of Jewish colonization.

The extent to which confidence in the eventual triumph of Zionism in the race against the hourglass of Arab nationalism had increased was reflected in the poor condition of the Jewish organ for self-defense, the Hagana. After all the high-flown talk in the aftermath of the August 1929 riots on the need to reorganize and strengthen the organization by allocating resources and obtaining weapons, the Hagana remained one of the most underdeveloped institutions of the Jewish community. Although a group of activists headed by Eliyahu Golomb continued to bear the burden and even to import weapons by various paths and means, the Hagana did not go through a fundamental change in the wake of the August disturbances. It underwent a split in 1931, when a faction headed by Abraham Tehomi left and set up Organization B, a more right-wing body, a rival of the left-wing Hagana under the auspices of the workers' Histadrut.[129] The entire topic of an armed force remained at the margins of public interest. During the years of propserity, the hopes for a quick building up of Palestine blocked from sight the smoke rising from the volcano.

The optimism and accelerated pace of construction found expression in the poetry of the era. One of the characteristic songs of the time was that by a young poet who was later to enjoy a brilliant future, Nathan Alterman, entitled "Morning

Song to the Homeland." This was a hymn to the building of Palestine by peaceful means:

> From the slopes of Lebanon to the Dead Sea,
> We will traverse you with plows.
> We will plant and build you,
> We shall beautify you mightily.

The lyrics speak about trailblazing in the desert, draining swamps, spreading carpets of gardens, and clothing the homeland in a "dress of concrete and cement." The last stanza speaks about the dangers lurking along the way. ("If the path is hard and treacherous, even if more than [a certain] one will fall dead. . . .") It is not spelled out whether the dead person is a victim of malaria or has been killed in a clash with the enemy. The last line contains a more specific hint: "We are yours in battle, yours in toil!"[130] Yet this statement is marginal in the poem, an expression of willingness to make the supreme sacrifice, not a concrete reference to an actual danger. It appears that this was a kind of ritual repetition of two components of the Tel Hai myth: labor and defense. There is no doubt that in 1934, when the poem was written, the scale leaned toward labor. These tendencies were prominent in another of Alterman's poems, also written that same year, later to become one of his most popular, "Song of the Valley." Its subject is a night in the Jezreel Valley: "Rest comes to the tired, / Calm to the toiler." In this poem, along with the restful contentment, the praise of labor and agricultural creation, a shadow of threat appears: "Who fired, and who fell / Between Beit Alfa and Nahalal?" Yet the central motif once again combines labor with guard duty: "Sleep, valley, magnificent land, / We are your guard."[131]

Another highly popular poem during that period was one by Rachel, entitled "Perhaps," set to music like the two poems by Alterman. This song, an ode to labor and love of the land, does not even contain the minor element of defense found in the poems by Alterman:

> Perhaps it was never so.
> Perhaps
> I never woke early and went to the fields
> To labor in the sweat of my brow.
>
> Nor in the long blazing days
> Of harvest
> On top of the wagon, laden with sheaves,
> Made my voice rise in song
>
> Nor bathed myself clean in the calm
> Blue water
> Of my Kinneret, O, my Kinneret,
> Were you there or did I only dream?[132]

Most of the songs current at that time were happy, devoid of any militant overtones.

In the early 1930s the poet Tchernichovksy arrived in Palestine. He belonged to the vitalist school, and admired pagan passion and creativity. From 1932 on, his poetry depicted the Palestinian landscape and its life-styles as reflected in the eyes of a newcomer. In contrast with earlier poems, this work lacked his characteristic aggressiveness. One of his more important poems from that period, "The Vision of the Prophet of the Ashera," contrasted the destruction and desolation that covered the Jezreel Valley in the past with the blessing of productivity that began with the advent of the pioneers. "Zion will be redeemed by the hoe, its fields by work," wrote Tchernichovsky.[133] Two years afterward, in 1934, he described in his poem "I Loved To Wander on the Road" the beat of vitality he encountered around Palestine. The refrain was "The song of work that lasts forever!"[134] One of his poems, "Song of the Guardsman," spoke about the growth that had occurred in the Jewish community in that period and the threat of danger emanating from the Arab, depicted as a person busy sharpening a knife.[135] But even here, the delight in battle that marked his poems composed in the Diaspora was absent. Another lyric from that time, written during the period of the pickets on behalf of Jewish labor in Kefar Sava in 1934, pictured the Arab as a rival in the past, who was likely to attack once again.[136] However, the moral was not directed against the Arabs; rather, it was aimed at strengthening the demand for employment of Jewish workers. These two poems contain a sense of the presence of the smoking volcano yet without drawing any further inferences. The conclusion remained within the bounds of the defensive ethos: Hasten ahead with construction, with creating.

Nonetheless, beneath the surface, feelings of enmity and resentment smoldered. They found expression in the stereotypes current in the public, as exemplified in an article published during that same period by Eliezer Yaffe. Eliezer Yaffe was the author of the idea of the moshav—an avowed anarchist who had dropped out of political activity. As a moral figure, his words carried special weight. The article he published in 1934 was called "And To Ishmael I'll Say." Despite its title, the essay was addressed to Jews, not Arabs. It contained a kind of digest of the various conceptions current in the Jewish community regarding their right to Palestine in the face of the Arab claim. Yaffe did not object to the presence of Arabs in Palestine and even declared, "I shall not envy your hold here, come let us sit together!" But he went on to contend, "You and your ancestors felt yourselves to be strangers here, guests; and you have desolated my land." The fact that Palestine was desolate under Arab rule became proof for Yaffe that they were not the legitimate owners of the country. He argued that Arab opposition to Jewish colonization was of marginal importance, due largely to matters of "convenience." In contrast, for Jews, that question was vital, existential. He sketched a parable. A man who flees to his home because of predatory animals has the right to break into that house even if a stranger is currently dwelling there. He does not wish to drive the stranger out and even brings him benefit. And that stranger is already rich, an owner of many lands. In his depiction, the Arabs were a historical enemy: "You trampled my peace for many generations, as savages of the desert, who live by the sword, by robbery." At the time of the wars against Assyria and Babylonia, the Arabs gave succor to the aggressors. And when the children of Israel returned from Babylonian captivity, they attacked them once again. Only the Maccabees succeeded in restraining them: "And you retreated to your deserts, like jackals in the morning light." When Rome attacked Judea, "once more you came out from your holes and attacked us, you wagged your tails before pagan Rome." While the Jews fought bravely to protect Palestine, the Arabs collaborated with the conquerors. During the Islamic conquests, the Arabs burst forth from the desert "only in order to bequeath the religion of Muhammad to others by the sword." In the present, the Arab was conspiring to disrupt Jewish colonization; but "all of your evil designs and those of your guides will be of no avail." Yaffe suggested to the Arabs that they make their peace with the Jews and benefit from the advantages of civilization: "Extend your hand and be a good neighbor *in my land!*"[137]

Yaffe's vision was one of peace, buoyed by feelings of superiority of the industrious colonizer toward the backward and retarded native. If someone had remarked to him that his essay was replete with stereotypes—of Jews, Arabs, and the relations between them—and that he seemed to show a considerable amount of enmity toward the sons of Ishmael, he probably would have been unable to comprehend the criticism, reacting with insulted astonishment. It can be assumed that Yaffe would have been magnanimous enough to be willing and ready to share his country with the Arab foreign invader. He would have stressed the benefits that Jews were bringing to the Arabs in Palestine. As far as all the negative characteristics he attributed to the Arabs are concerned, he would not have seen that as a biased view but, rather, as the plain and simple truth. After it became clear that historical right and the right to Palestine based on labor were in themselves insufficient as arguments in the struggle for world public opinion, it became popular in the 1930s to maintain that the Arabs in Palestine had forfeited any right to the land because they had neglected it, allowing it to become a desolate wasteland. But Yaffe's assertions were not meant as propaganda. They expressed the internal truth of a socialist—a man known to be sensitive to moral issues, with pacifist leanings. The obvious lack of sensitivity he showed when it came to Jewish–Arab relations (although it was not accompanied by explicit expressions of aggressiveness) indicated that at a certain psychological level, the defensive ethos was functioning as an incubator of enmity and alienation.

Yaffe's words illustrate the gap that had begun to appear between the growing sophistication of the approach taken by the political leadership to the issue of Jewish–Arab relations in Palestine and the outlook of the rank and file. The memory of the August riots did not fade. A residue of animosity and suspicion regarding Arabs remained. Although those years were relatively quiet, here and there a murder took place that appeared to stem from nationalist motives; and such incidents stirred up dormant feelings of suspicion once again. The central myths (such as that of the building of Palestine) received further encouragement in the period of accelerating growth. The Zionist prognosis on the existential necessity that Palestine would assume for Jews as a haven took on a dramatic new dimension in the 1930s in the light of Nazi persecution in Germany and the deterioration in the situation of Polish Jews with the upsurge in antisemitic tendencies in the government there. Increasingly, the man in the street accepted myths and stereotypes as proven facts. The message they communicated was unambiguous and simplistic, lacking any understanding of the position of the other side. It was not tainted by aggressiveness or militant pathos. But the level of animosity toward Arabs that that message contained was unmistakably on the rise. Already at the beginning of the era, after the

1929 riots, there were some who had voiced warnings about the gap between the guiding political conceptions and "the actual attitudes and psychological preparation of the young Yishuv in regard to the whole complex of relations with Arabs, and political maturity in general."[138] In time, the widening gap between the leadership and the rank and file regarding their respective understanding of the nature of the Arab question, Jewish–Arab relations, the complex of problems associated with the Palestinian triangle, and their respective differing perspectives would deepen.

III

THE SHIFT TO AN OFFENSIVE ETHOS, 1936–1947

6

The Arab Rebellion

The Arab Rebellion erupted on April 19, 1936. This was the first campaign in the violent struggle between the two peoples for supremacy of Palestine. Its intensity and the pitch of emotional and political reactions it provoked far exceeded the extent and scope of anything previously known in the conflict between Jews and Arabs. The patterns of Jewish–Arab relations, their respective image of each other, and the possible political alternatives—all these were now highlighted in sharper contrast against the background of violent physical confrontation. The Jews were compelled to reconsider both their assumption that Zionist aims could be realized by peaceful means and the evolutionary conception derived from that assumption. They were also called on to examine their position on the use of Jewish force in response to Arab violence and the associated implications.

A new option was placed on the agenda during this agitated period: the partition of Palestine into Jewish and Arab states. Aside from the stunning effect of the proposal itself, which for the first time raised the possibility of establishing a Jewish state as a feasible political option, it posed once again the fundamental question of Zionist desiderata. The stormy public dispute on the issue revealed a panoply of attitudes and opinions on basic questions: What were the aims of Zionism? What spans of time were deemed available for their realization? What was desirable, and what practicable? In addition, a new factor appeared on the scene during that era: Jewish Palestinian youth. Its education, world outlook, and attitude toward Arabs and the use of force now became decisive components in the formation of a new ethos, that of the fighter. The Jewish warrior—as a cultural and social model and as a fact of life—emerged during the Arab Rebellion.

At its inception, the Arab Rebellion did not seem to differ from earlier waves of Arab violence. Following false rumors about Arabs who had allegedly been assaulted in Tel Aviv, Arabs in Jaffa rushed to attack Jewish passersby. On "Bloody Sunday," April 19, nine Jews were murdered there, and another ten were injured. The unrest soon spread to other mixed towns. At the same time, preparations were made to organize an Arab general strike. After a few days of trouble in which the initiative was in the hands of young Arab radicals, who enjoyed immediate, spontaneous support among broad segments of the Arab population, the Arab leadership responded to the popular rising tide and established the Arab Higher Committee. That marked the turning point from a violent protest movement to an organized rebellion, aimed at political objectives even though it did not shrink back from the use of violence. The goals of the rebellion were formulated as demands addressed to the British authorities: a halt to immigration, prohibition of land sales to Jews, and the speedy establishment of a democratic government—namely, relegation of state power to the Arab majority. An end to the general strike was made contingent upon the fulfillment of these three demands.

The Arab economy was on strike for some six months, during which it absorbed heavy financial losses. Sales of produce from Arab villages to Jews were ceased. Arab shops in towns were closed. Arab workers stayed away from their jobs in Jewish orchards. The tendency toward separation of the Jewish and Arab populations, a trend that had developed in the wake of the 1929 riots, was now greatly strengthened. In fear for their lives, Jews abandoned their homes in mixed neighborhoods, now termed "frontier neighborhoods," and fled to areas inhabited solely by Jews. The Jaffa port was in effect closed to Jews, since travel to it was extremely dangerous for them. The lack of proper supplies of fresh fruit and vegetables and dairy products forced the Jewish·economy to develop and maintain branches of production that previously had been mainly in Arab hands. This fact enhanced the trend toward economic autarchy and was seen by a large segment of the Jewish community as a vindication of their demand for "Jewish labor" and "Jewish produce"—demands that in the early 1930s had been at the center of a stormy public dispute.

The Arab Rebellion differed from prior outbursts in several key respects. First of all, the Arab community's depth of involvement and the readiness on the part of broad segments of the lower classes to make economic sacrifices and even to sacrifice their own lives, if necessary, were unprecedented. This was a national uprising, with all the accompanying manifestations associated with a popular rebellion, incidents of courage and cruelty. Second, this was an organized political action, under a central command; and the majority of the Arab population exhibited the requisite discipline. Third, the length of the strike and unrest during the first stage, which continued until October 1936, underscored the determination and staying power of the leaders of the rebellion. Although they terminated the strike without having achieved a British commitment to fulfill their three demands, the prestige of the rebellion leadership was maintained, since the decision to terminate the strike came after a request by Arab kings to halt the action so as to permit a royal commission to investigate the reasons underlying the disturbances. The ability to combine political action (the strike) with violent acts that disrupted the patterns of normal life was indicative of a degree of maturity and sophistication previously unknown in the Arab National movement in Palestine.[1] The renewed upsurge in violence after the publication of the findings of the Peel Commission in the summer of 1937 and the intensification of the violence in 1938 strengthened the first impression that this was a durable political phenomenon enjoying broad public support.

The political maturation of the Arab National movement was the product of a number of factors. The most significant of these was the spurt in the growth of the Jewish national home during the years 1933 to 1935. The Arabs followed the rising tide of immigration and the demographic and economic development of the Jewish community in Palestine with growing concern and apprehension. There was a process of radicalization in the Arab population, marked by the appearance of groups that viewed violent means as essential to stop the growth of the national home. From the early 1930s on, bands of Arab terrorists began to appear. Three members of the Kibbutz Yagur were murdered, a father and his son in Nahalal, and a number of others. In 1935, in the wake of the feeble British response to Italian aggression in Ethiopia, Britain's prestige was severely damaged. Italy's standing and status rose dramatically in the Eastern Mediterranean as a result of the Italian victory over Emperor Haile Selassie and his dismissal, while the British responded with verbal protests only and took no action. Developments in the Arab countries in late 1935 and early 1936 demonstrated the decline in the image and influence of the imperialist Great Powers Britain and France. In Syria, after a prolonged strike of the population, the French gave in and agreed to negotiate with the Syrian national leadership on a new treaty patterned along the lines of the treaty signed in 1930 between Iraq and Great Britain. That treaty had granted Iraq its independence. Disturbances erupted in Egypt, forcing the British to sign a new treaty favorable to Egyptian independence.[2] These successes, all of which were the product of a combination of both political and violent action, left their imprint on the Arabs of Palestine. During that same period, in March 1936, Wauchope's attempt to set up a legislative council failed after a proposal on these lines was defeated in the British Parliament. As mentioned, during the incumbency of Herbert Samuel, the Arabs had been opposed to establishment of a legislative council. Now it became the touchstone for the possibility of chalking up political gains. Even those among the ranks of Arab leadership who persisted in their opposition to the idea viewed its defeat in the House of Commons as a kind of incisive proof of the ineffectualness of cooperating with the authorities. When it was added to the list of events in neighboring countries, the rejection of the scheme for a legislative council was like the straw that broke the camel's back. Once the disturbances broke out, the Arab leadership was quick to ride the wave of popular opposition to the Jews and British in order to induce the latter to put a halt to the growth of the national home.

From "Riots" to "Rebellion"

The first reactions by Jews to the 1936 outburst were quite similar to responses to earlier waves of riots. The surprise effect was repeated. It goes without saying that people had been cognizant of the rising tension in Palestine since the autumn of 1935, when Sheikh 'Izz al-Din al-Qassam and his band were trapped by police and wiped out in the Jenin Mountains in a clash with British police and military forces—an event that, as I have mentioned, Ben Gurion had dubbed "their Tel Hai." People were also aware of developments in neighboring Arab countries. Nonetheless, when the riots broke out, they were an unsettling surprise, completely unanticipated; and no one had made preparations for their eventuality. A member of Ha-Kibbutz ha-Meuhad commented, "From our perspective, what is most alarming about the recent bloody occurrences is their total unexpectedness and that we were unprepared for such events."[3] There were those who explained the unforeseen nature of the unrest by noting that despite cognizance of the seriousness of the situation, it was impossible to predict either the timing of their outbreak or their scope and characteristics.[4] Others inferred from this fact that it would be impossible to foresee in future when terror might erupt again.[5] That old feeling of a volcano (as a kind of submerged consciousness that surfaced after each wave of unrest) was once again in clear evidence: "The soul caught in the pincers of suffering and torment is the soul of people sitting on a volcano bubbling with noxious vapors beneath the calm crust."[6] "I don't understand the people who can't sense this Vesuvius we're sitting on"—marveled a member of the Ha-Noar ha-Oved youth movement—"that after each eruption, we return to plant and to build."[7] Added to this were apprehensions due to the tense international situation: What would occur should a world war break out? The fear that the Jewish community in Palestine might be cut off from Jewish centers around the world and left on its own to face millions of Arabs "who smell the blood of war" stemmed from a deepening realization that the Yishuv was living on the edge of an abyss.[8]

The feeling that clashes with Arabs were inevitable, that there was a cyclical pattern—waves of violence interspersed with periods of quiet and construction—began to penetrate into public consciousness. Such a perception is present in the words of the youth quoted above, who regarded it as obvious: Just as villagers living at the edge of a volcano return to their homes and fields after the lava has cooled, Jews return and continue to build their settlements after each wave of unrest. A few days after the outbreak of the riots, Arthur Ruppin wrote in his diary: "I have remained exceedingly calm and cool during this time. I have adopted the theory that under the circumstances, it is natural that the antagonism of the Arabs to Jewish immigration should find release in periodic outbreaks; that we are living in a sort of latent state of war with the Arabs that makes loss of life inevitable. This may be unacceptable, but it is a fact; and if we want to continue our work in Palestine in spite of the Arabs, we will have to expect such losses."[9] There was an element of fatalism and determinism in this approach, which predicted a future of repeated clashes between Arabs and Jews until the day Arabs finally acquiesced and accepted the presence of Jews in Palestine. The perspective of recurrent waves of violence, a prospect that Jews had not been able to face either during the period of the Second Aliyah or in the 1920s, now became a conscious component of the mentality of the Yishuv. A member of Ha-Shomer ha-Tzair noted in sadness, "This idea is current among wide segments of the population, in cafés whose customers have not yet heard a single shot fired, . . . as well as in the hut of the worker, whose legs totter after months of toil by day and standing guard at night."[10]

The readiness to confront the terrifying prospect of a war without any end in sight had several attitudinal dimensions. First of all, there was a sense of despair over the possibility of arriving at any kind of an accord with the Arabs in the present period. Second, it contained the implicit recognition of the fact that the latent conflict between Jews and Arabs over dominance in Palestine had become active: The national Arab movement had reached maturity before completion of the establishment of a Jewish entity. Third, it also expressed the perception among Jews that although they had not yet arrived at the stage where they had sufficient power to deter Arabs from waging war against them, they were already strong enough to be able to stand their own in a confrontation. The Zionist enterprise, which in the 1920s had been considered an interesting experiment (albeit with a dubious future), became in the 1930s a genuine force to be reckoned with. For that reason, people were more willing than in the past to accept the existential threat as an inseparable part of reality of life in Palestine. The slogan *We have no choice* began to appear frequently in connection with the Jewish–Arab struggle. "There is no other resort, no refuge, no choice. The commandment of history will be fulfilled" is the final sentence in the book by a Beracha Habas, *Me'ora'ot 1936* (The 1936 Disturbances), a volume that expressed popular conceptions in the Labor movement, especially Mapai.[11]

Not everyone was willing to accept the "decree of destiny" that stated, "You shall live by your sword." Those educated in socialist concepts of human brotherhood between peoples flinched from the "lesson of catastrophe accepted by broad segments of the Jewish community in Palestine," whose meaning was "force arrayed against force, a struggle between forces." Recognizing the need for self-defense, a member of Ha-Shomer ha-Tzair at the same time urged, "It should be proven to one and all that there is no historical necessity that 'this is the way we shall live and advance'."[12] In particular, it was difficult for people to accept the notion that there was no prospect of an accord between Jews and Arabs.

Recognition of the Jewish–Arab clash as predestined, a "historical necessity," did not necessarily contradict the defensive ethos. The self-image of "In your blood shall you live" served as an important component, a kind of link connecting the fate of Jews in the Diaspora (who were constrained to endure persecution and disaster and nonetheless survived) with the fate of Jews in Palestine. The latter had no choice but to stand like a solid rock against the waves of Arab assault. Yet concurrently, the open and persistent confrontation led to a slow shift in the meaning of the concept *power* from the sense of a "critical mass" to physical–military power. Moreover, even if initially there had been no contradiction between the defensive ethos and the idea that Jewish–Arab confrontation was immanent, they were not compatible over an extended period of time. Life in the shadow of constant tension and the recognition that there was no solution for the situation except a confrontation between forces necessarily led to the erosion of the faith in the possibility of establishing a national home by peaceful means. It was that faith that had given moral justification to the defensive ethos. Its undermining undoubtedly had a deleterious impact on one of the main pillars of this ethos.

Yet such an assessment contains an element of prescient wisdom. The first immediate reaction to the disturbances was very similar to Jewish responses in the wake of the 1929 riots. The statement of the Mapai Central Committee on the occasion of May Day was in the old spirit of Tel Hai: "We come with true aspirations for peace, dignity, and mutual assistance," it stated: "We do not come as conquerors but as builders. Yet we shall not retreat in the face of bloody attacks." After stressing the constructive role of Zionism in the development of the country, it added, "Only narrow, reactionary chauvinism is unable to see the blessing [that] our project has already bestowed and that it will bring in the future to the Arab people in Palestine as well." The statement emphasized the three traditional foundations of the defensive ethos: "labor, peace, and self-defense." Along with forceful remarks regarding the resoluteness of the Jewish decision not to retreat under any circumstances, it was careful to distinguish between "good" Arabs and "bad": The Arab people as a whole was not responsible for the disturbances; rather, "those who misled and incited it" bore responsibility. In line with the tradition of "Lights from the Darkness" (the series of anecdotes published by *Davar* after the 1929 riots, about Arabs who had saved Jews) and in the spirit of the joint union, the statement made favorable mention of Arab workers—members of "Alliance of Workers in Palestine," an organization of Arab workers initiated by the Histadrut—who aided Jews in "fleeing from the claws of the predatory animals that had risen up against them" and who, "together with us, called for peace and reason."[13]

The 1936 disturbances revived once again the old debate about the existence of an Arab national movement. Once more, the question was broached as to whether the riots were a rebellion or a pogrom. The truth is that the term *pogrom,* in common currency during earlier disturbances, was rarely employed this time. Only Berl Katznelson spoke about the "pogromist Arab movement"; and in his eulogy on Beilinson in November 1936, he stated, "A man who himself had never witnessed a pogrom until 1929 was unable to keep from his mind the horror of a pogrom sweeping over us."[14] The term that replaced *pogrom* was *disturbances.*

The late 1930s witnessed the outbreak of frequent pogroms in Poland. It was apparently problematic to place the events in Poland and Palestine on a similar plane. Here and there, attempts were made to see an analogy between the stance taken by Jews toward the rioters in Poland and the position of Jews in Palestine. That analogy served Berl, for example, in his argument against publishing a paper in Arabic: The great number of Jewish papers in numerous Gentile languages in Europe, he said, had never served to curb antisemitism.[15] The analogy was in keeping with the defensive ethos because it created an identity between the weak Jew who was in the right in the Diaspora and the weak Jew who was likewise in the right in Palestine. The self-image of the underdog was nurtured by the identity between Jewish fate there and in Palestine. The deterioration in the situation of Jews in Poland after the death of Marshal Pilsudski and the upsurge in Polish antisemitism ostensibly supported the argument that Arab opposition to Jewish colonization was rooted in the soil of the same dark motives. On the other hand, that analogy was in contradiction with another component of the defensive ethos: the conception that attributed different weight to the death of a Jew in defense of his land and the death of a Jew in a pogrom. This component, which had already appeared during the Second Aliyah, grew stronger, bolstered by the myth of Tel Hai: It underscored the superior value and the meaningfulness associated with a Jewish sacrifice in Palestine as contrasted with a meaningless death by violence in the Diaspora.

An example of this juxtaposing can be found in a poem by Fanya Bergstein, written during the 1936 riots:

> I am the daughter
> Of generations of Jews, bent down, crouching,

> The fear of every *strazhnik* and bully in them.
> Fearful of the bark of the neighbor's dog,
> Stepping aside for the smallest of street hoodlums,
> Quick to greet the villain and the drunk.
> Quaking like a leaf in the storm,
> With the echoes of riots and murders.

In contrast,

> I am a sister
> To all who face death every day
> And know not if these are his last. . . .
> To all who lay at the feet of sweat-soaked
>   boulders
> And at the heads of plant-covered mountains
> —Their lives, their pure souls—
> I am a sister.[16]

In his preface to the volume *Me'ora'ot 1936,* Berl Katznelson made it a point to create an association between the Jew—the victim in the Diaspora and in Palestine—by utilizing the phrase from Bialik, "The entire world is my gallows," applying it to both types of sacrifice. Nonetheless, even Katznelson was careful to stress that "this generation, that is turning the gallows into an arena of battle, swallows its tears and won't shed them."[17] The analogy between Jewish weakness in Palestine and in the Diaspora was disturbing for the self-image of the Yishuv as being differentiated and set apart from the Jews of the Diaspora by its bravery and as symbolizing a new type of Jewish response. This is perhaps one of the reasons why the word *pogrom* was relatively rare in the literature of the period.

The term *disturbances* had already appeared in the early 1920s. It did not have any heavily weighted connotations like *pogrom* as was also neutral in respect to its attitude toward the question of the existence or nonexistence of an Arab national movement. In 1936 it became the key concept distinguishing between those who saw the Arab outburst as the expression of a national movement, calling the events a *rebellion,* and those who denied its existence. The latter used the word *disturbances,* and this was the expression commonly employed by the Hebrew press. When the publishing house of *Davar* issued a book at the end of 1936 that summed up the canonical explanation of the events, it was quite naturally entitled *1936 Disturbances.*[18]

The Hebrew press now adopted what Ernst Simon, a member of Brit Shalom, had dubbed "the politics of quotation marks." Already at a May Day gathering some ten days after the riots had broken out, Berl Katznelson spoke about "this so-called 'rebellion'."[19] Beilinson was always careful to put the expression Arab Rebellion in quotation marks in his articles in *Davar,* and Tabenkin did likewise in his contributions for *Mi-Bifnim.* That citational policy was also applied to expressions such as "Arab National movement" and (Arab) "leaders." Similarly, the Arab Higher Committee was likewise duly referred to in qualifying quotation marks.[20] In a response to criticism by Shlomo Kaplansky, who protested against this policy, Beilinson stated that "a legend about an 'Arab Rebellion', whose existence I deny" had taken root in Palestine. He made a distinction between the external dimension of the uprising and its internal aspects. Arabs were acting as though they were rebelling; but in actual fact, he contended, they were not rising up against the state, as proven by the fact that the mandate authorities were not taking action against them.[21] Tabenkin criticized the tendency toward "idealizing the movement of the Arab 'rebellion'." He presented the Jewish inclination toward viewing the uprising as a rebellion as something pathological: an expression of a characteristic Jewish disease, whose essence was self-disparagement in the face of bravery by others. The truth of the matter, said Tabenkin, was that this movement was not directed against Britain but, rather, was a reactionary movement, "feudalist–imperialist," marked by its brutal approach to minorities—like the Iraqi movement in its attitude toward the Assyrians and Kurds, the Syrian movement in dealing with the Maronites, and the Saudi movement in its attitude toward foreigners and foreign culture in general.[22]

The use of quotation marks was meant to awaken doubt among readers about the credibility of the term so circumscribed and hesitations about its legitimacy. It was designed to convey to the public the awareness that this was actually a pseudorebellion, not a bona fide popular uprising. Its causes were not rooted in Arab national interests but derived from other dark motives.[23] The advocates of this approach explained the outbreak of the "Arab Rebellion" by British policy: If the authorities had adopted stiff measures as soon as trouble had broken out, the whole "revolt" would have petered out in a few days. The mild response of the government, and a lack of resoluteness on the part of High Commissioner Wauchope were the factors that helped transform a marginal event into a sequence of major disturbances. There were certain differences in the sophistication of placing blame on the British. Tabenkin, for example, recognized that Arab opposition to the impressive growth of the Jewish entity in Palestine was a central factor in the disturbances. Yet this fact did not induce him to believe that the revolt was directed essentially against British policy in Palestine, since he systematically refused to acknowledge the British role in the development of the national home. He contended that the growth in Jewish power in Palestine had taken place *despite* British policies, not by dint of them. Tabenkin presented the riots as the product of a British–Arab alliance. "The government in Palestine is responsible for the disturbances, their outbreak, timing, and purpose—and not just for their continuance and the form they adopted," he stated vehemently.[24]

Katznelson was more cautious. "There can be no doubt that a formidable Arab factor does exist," he conceded: "But whether it really has an impact on the British or merely serves as a card in their hands is not as yet clear to me. However, I am unprepared to concede that the 'fear of the Arab' is the factor determining the attitude of the high commissioner toward our project."[25] In general, Berl had been very circumspect in his statements about the Arab question and did not tend to express utopian hopes regarding the possibility of arriving at an agreement with the Arabs, either in the left-wing version of Ha-Shomer ha-Tzair, or the Brit Shalom version, or even the version of his close associate Ben Gurion. Now, however, he accused Britain of not having seriously tried to bring Jews and Arabs together to sit down and talk peace: "Compromise with the Arabs is dependent on the wishes of the British, and they have never truly wanted to bring us to a compromise with the Arabs."[26] Aside from the accusation that the British stirred up contention and strife, along the lines of "divide and rule," which was always identified with "perfidious Albion," there was another element operative here: the readiness, frequent since the 1920s, to attribute to the British, the symbol of authority and Western imperialism, devious motives as far as Jews were concerned. That assertion was taken for granted not just by most Mapai members but also by the entire Right in Palestine, including the Jabotinsky camp and especially the followers of Abba Ahimeir, who never doubted its conclusions. They regarded the failure of the British to quell the uprising by force simply as an evident expression of Britain's anti-Zionist policy.

Groups to the left of Mapai, such as Ha-Shomer ha-Tzair or Left Poalei Zion continued, like Tabenkin, to attribute the Jewish–Arab clash of interests to opposition by the Arab effendis to the socioeconomic progress that Jewish community development was bringing to Palestine. In their eyes, the reason for the rebellion was incitement by Arab leaders, various religious leaders, and other reactionary elements attempting to inflame the Arab masses. Yet they, also, did not hesitate to blame the British: They charged them with fanning the flames of the rebellion and at the same time demanded they take stricter measures to quell the disturbances. They still believed that the organizing of the Arab worker was the magical prescription for Jewish–Arab relations. However, aside from accusing the Histadrut leadership of failing to take action along these lines, they did not perceive any connection between the Jewish situation in Palestine and the Arab Rebellion. This was indeed a classic position from the standpoint of the defensive ethos: It did not attribute the reasons for the violent events to the concrete conditions prevailing in Palestine but, rather, to global processes in which the Jewish role was quite marginal and which would ultimately end in victory for the forces of progress. Concurrently, it continued to present the Jew as an innocent victim of abuse and brutality by the authorities.

That view was not shared by all. The more a person's position exposed him to the complexity of political decisionmaking, the more understanding he showed toward the British and Arab positions. The approach of Ben Gurion and Shertok, members of the political department of the Jewish Agency, and of Arthur Ruppin was marked by the attempt to empathize, trying to get into the shoes of the opponent.

From the very first discussions in the Mapai Central Committee on the Arab Rebellion, Shertok explained the disturbances by pointing to Arab fears about the growing strength of the Jews. "Fear is the main factor in Arab politics," he remarked.[27] In contrast with the view that denied the very existence of an Arab national movement, Shertok contended: "There is not a single Arab who has not been hurt by the entry of Jews into Palestine; there is not a single Arab who does not see himself as part of the Arab race. . . . In his eyes, Palestine is an independent unit. Previously it had had an Arab face, and now it is changing."[28] Ben Gurion considered the Arab uprising to be a Palestinian expression of nationalist trends along the lines of those that had led to uprisings against the regimes in Syria and Egypt: "I cannot disregard the fact, even if it is bitter and terrible . . . , that in Palestine today there is an Arab uprising and a bloody war *against the government and against us.*" Although it was possible to prove that the majority of the Arab people did not want the rebellion, it is a characteristic of national revolts that they are always led by an "energetic minority full of initiative." That minority imposes its will by force on the "inert majority." Ben Gurion demanded that his colleagues acknowledge "the existence of an Arab war against us as an independent fact, self-sustained and nurtured by inner sources."[29] While Ha-Kibbutz ha-Meuhad and Ha-Shomer ha-Tzair still adhered to traditional explanations, there were new approaches in the third kibbutz movement, Hever ha-Kvutzot. One of the members of the movement wrote, "An Arab national movement has been discovered, a mature and militant movement." He warned: "Let's not make it easy for ourselves [by claiming]: these are young hoodlums, the actions of hooligans. . . . Such political thinking is counterproductive."[30]

The willingness to admit the existence of an Arab revolt deriving from immanent Arab motives was linked with a readiness to appreciate the difficulties faced by the British in suppressing the uprising. Comments by Shertok reflected the extent of popularity of the tendency to accuse the government. He felt it necessary to state in the Mapai Central Committee that based on the information available to him, he could "assert that the government did not wish to have any disturbances in Palestine and, in any event, had no interest in seeing them spread." There was also a widespread claim that the British failed to quell the revolt because its victims were Jewish and they were unconcerned about possible Jewish deaths. In response, Shertok explained that although the authorities had made mistakes in putting down the revolt, those errors had been made by the British in other areas of the empire as well—where there were no Jews: "For that reason, you cannot explain British errors by asserting that the high commissioner does not care whether trees are uprooted, orchards destroyed, or some Jews are killed."[31] Characteristically, Ben Gurion replied with especial acrimony: "There are comrades who see only one enemy— the government. . . . [They claim] that even what the Arabs do to us is just the product of a government that plots and schemes against us. I cannot share that view. Nor can I explain to myself how those comrades arrived at such astounding blindness."[32] Eliyahu Golomb, head of the Hagana, mocked the current Jewish tendency to try to prove that from the vantage of pure British interests, the British should make common cause with the Jews: "The English," he remarked, "do not always understand their interests the way we understand them or would like them to understand [them]."[33]

During the entire span of the Arab Rebellion, a stormy debate raged behind the scenes regarding the public stance toward the government. While Ben Gurion and his associates thought it was supremely important to avoid useless attacks against the authorities, the press of the Labor movement continued to attribute almost every possible outrage to them. They accused the British of failing to fulfill their obligations and of putting Jewish lives at risk. "When it is a matter of criticism of the government, we are not obliged to tell the truth," stormed Ben Gurion in the wake of a distorted report in *Davar:* "Aside from a few cases, I have not seen criticism of the government that is not exaggerated." Ben Gurion (while actually directing the arrows of his criticism at Katznelson, the paper's chief editor) added that "even Beilinson" (who was in charge of writing *Davar*'s editorials), "one of the most ethically minded persons in our ranks, did not take pains to be precise when criticizing the government."[34]

It would appear that there was no topic in connection with which *Davar* enjoyed greater popularity among the broader public than its nonsophisticated, one-sided presentation of the triangle of relations in Palestine. Beilinson, until his death in November 1936, bore the Zionist propaganda campaign on his shoulders. While he normally directed his criticisms at negative internal phenomena, in periods of political tension (as after the 1929 disturbances and during the Arab Rebellion), he applied his formidable talent to what was called "standing fast." Beilinson was largely responsible for the fact that the conception that denied the existence of an Arab national movement and accused the British of fostering the Arab revolt, was widely accepted in the public, and shaped the outlook of that generation. "Standing fast" did not mean to argue with the British or to convince the Arabs. Rather, its impact was directed toward the internal front. It was motivated by a need to strengthen the conviction about the righteousness of the movement against all its contenders, to preserve the sense of inner truth. This policy was apparently based on a hidden assumption that any kind of recognition of the Arab National movement or of the government's difficulties putting down a popular revolt and inability to prevent acts of terror might wreck the entire structure based on the assumptions of the defensive ethos. It would also damage the self-image of Jews as a people unjustly persecuted in Palestine, as elsewhere throughout the world.

For that reason, Beilinson, Tabenkin, and Katznelson dedicated considerable efforts to undermining the image of the Arab movement as a legitimate entity. In the past, it had been easy to deny its very existence because outbreaks of violence had been sporadic and occasional. Now, when the intensity of the violence was clearly visible, even those who had wanted to disregard it were forced to recognize its power. From this perspective, the use of the quotation-mark method of reference constituted a half-hearted admission that there was no longer any possibility of avoiding its existence as a fact of life. The new method was to deny its right to exist and its basic legitimacy, arguing that it was a movement lacking moral standards.

The tactics utilized by the organizers of the Arab revolt were those of terror: ambushes that injured the weak and defenseless. There were relatively few attacks against the British army. Instead, passersby or workers in the fields were assaulted; hand grenades were tossed from a moving train in Tel Aviv or at the entrance to a movie theater in Jerusalem. There was an incident involving two Jewish nurses who came to care for Arabs at the hospital in Jaffa and were murdered by Arab terrorists. There was also the case of a worker in the field who was asked by an Arab acquaintance for a drink of water; when he turned to fulfill the request, he was shot and killed. There was a terrorist outburst in the Jewish quarter in Safed, resulting in the murder of a father and his three children. Incidents like these strengthened the image of the Arab as a bloodthirsty desert savage, who does not shrink from the most brutal of acts and lacks all moral inhibitions. One of the actions often engaged in by Arabs was the setting of large fires that destroyed the work of years. In addition, they cut down thousands of fruit and shade trees planted by Jews. The planting of trees was one of the symbolic acts of the ethos of "making the desert bloom," one of the most important components of Zionist ideology. It appears that the Arabs, either consciously or unconsciously, aimed their activity at one of the typical and visible signs of the change taking place in the Palestinian landscape as a result of Jewish colonization. The pain over sections of forest that had been destroyed was at times as great as the sorrow over loss of human life. "Of course, human life is more precious to us than any gravestone," wrote Katznelson after desecration of graves in the Jewish cemetery in Safed: "But the destruction of plant life and stone is instructive regarding the nature of the destroyer and his dark urges; it teaches us [about] more than bloodshed."[35]

Arab acts of terror were interpreted as proof of the absence of any moral foundations to their movement. "The means used by a movement always attest to its purpose and content," Tabenkin wrote: "The murder of children, women, and the elderly, [the destruction of] trees and fields, attest to the nature of that movement. . . . There is no faith in the word, pledges, oaths."[36] An educated Arab, in a letter to the *Palestine Post,* complained about the fact that the rebels were termed "rioters" and "robbers" in the press, while in actual fact they were just defending their rights. He also likened their struggle to that of Judah Maccabee and George Washington. Berl Katznelson replied sarcastically that presumably, according to the concepts of the Arab Liberation movement, these historic figures had also murdered by ambush, attacked infants, uprooted trees, paid for a glass of water with a bullet, and so on. And he added, as a conclusion: "Even if the so-called lovers of freedom who demand justice will rise again and again in defense of our torturers and those who despicably shed our blood, we will persevere as ever and shall not acknowledge either the love of freedom or the righteousness of the war that claims Jewish children as victims [and destroys] Jewish trees and gravestones."[37]

Depicting the Arab National movement as being immoral nurtured the self-image of the Jew as an innocent victim of Arab violence. "You paragons of morality," inveighed the poet S. Shalom: "Why were you able to move the whole world when it came to Sacco and Vanzetti; but for people who build their homeland by pure and sacred means, who are murdered in brutality by the dozens, for these you don't even lose one word?"[38]

The depiction of the Arab movement as unethical was a kind of line of retreat clung to by those who rejected the existence of Arab nationalism in Palestine after the fact of its existence became difficult to deny. To a certain degree, it was the continuation of the argument that had been repeatedly advanced since the days of Ein Harod Conference in 1924, namely that it was impossible to talk with the leaders of the Arab movement, since they were reactionaries. Even in 1924 the argument was voiced that it was not a genuine national movement because it had no positive cultural attributes and its content was nothing but anti-Zionism. Now another argument was added: The acts of terror perpetrated by that movement had undermined its legitimacy as a national liberation movement. Accordingly, it did not represent anything but the forces of darkness and the primitive urges of desert savages.

A new element was integrated into this web during the 1930s—fascism. The Labor movement in Palestine followed the rise of fascist forces in Europe with growing apprehension. As was already mentioned, the fact that the Socialist movement in Germany had been defeated without a battle engendered feelings of deep shame among socialists in Palestine. They followed with bated breath the desperate struggle of the Schutzbund in Vienna in 1934 against the battalions of Dollfuss, the right-wing Austrian prime minister. The struggle of the Schutzbund became one of the guiding myths in the youth movement of Ha-Kibbutz ha-Meuhad at that time. With the rise of the antisemitic right-wing forces in Poland during the 1930s, the situation of Jews there also deteriorated. All these events exposed the weakness of civilized conventions and norms. They also demonstrated once again the vulnerability of the Jews, whose standing in European society only yesterday had seemed so secure. In that period, a marked identity emerged between the fate of Jews and that of the Left: In the same places where the Left was suffering from persecution, Jews were likewise hounded. Against the vehement antisemitism of the majority of fascists, socialism offered an alternative that abrogated the importance of the national or racial reference group and advocated brotherhood between nations, all sharing the fate of the wretched and the oppressed. From the vantage point of the Labor movement in Palestine, the world during those years appeared polarized between the forces of light and darkness, the camps of progress and reaction. Their own identification with the camp of progress was uncontestable. As socialists and as Jews, they viewed themselves as belonging to the camp of those active in the fight against fascism.

The rise in the fortunes of fascism was welcomed by the Arab camp. Fascist Italy and Nazi Germany appeared to be threatening the position of the imperialist powers in the Middle East. The more they challenged the Western powers without the latter's responding with adequate force, the more their prestige increased throughout the Arab world in general and in Palestine in particular. The antisemitism of the Nazi regime was not viewed as a drawback in the Semitic East. There was also genuine cooperation between the Arab rebels in Palestine and the Italian government. It would appear that Italy directed funds to the Arab Higher Committee, and thus assisted in fanning the flames of the revolt.[39] Swastikas appeared in Arab towns in Palestine, and shops decorated their show windows with portraits of Hitler.[40]

The manifestations attesting to sympathy for the fascist powers and Arab rebels' self-identification with them were regarded by the Zionist Left as corroborating their intuitive feeling that Arab opposition to Jewish colonization in Palestine derived from the same psychological disposition and social and political conception that had spawned fascism. Just as that was based on hatred, animosity for all humanist ideals, and opposition to the equality and brotherhood of nations, so, too, was the Arab National movement. The celebrations for May Day 1936, which took place in the shadow of the Arab revolt, served as the first opportunity for underscoring the identity between the international antifascist struggle and the struggle of the Jews against the Arab revolt in Palestine—between persecution of Jews by fascists around the world and Arab attacks on Jews in Palestine. In a leaflet issued by Mapai, the fate of Jews in Poland and Germany was compared with their fate in Palestine. Just as the Jews in Palestine defend themselves and stand fast in the face of enemy attacks, so do they in the Diaspora: "There too, the National and Socialist movement taught our people a lesson in self-defense and battle." The leaflet also stated, "An alliance has been forged between the Jewish worker in Palestine and the creative forces, thirsty for freedom, throughout the world." The identity between the Zionist struggle in Palestine and the global antifascist struggle was stressed in statements such as the following: "We see our mission here as combined and interwoven with the great war being waged along the entire front of civilized humanity— for the freedom of peoples and the equality of men."[41]

Tabenkin, in his May Day speech, went far beyond the generalizations contained in the Mapai leaflet. In his view, there could be no doubt that the rise of fascism expressed the fears of "militant nationalism" concerning an upsurge in socialist revolutionary forces. The Old World, despairing of maintaining its positions through democratic means, turned to the use of violence and terror "as the last means in a desperate war." "The twentieth century," he proclaimed, "begets both revolution and the fear of it, the readiness to implement it and the decision to revert to the Middle Ages, to forms of war and a civilization of murder, hatred between peoples and the subjugation of races." The use by Arabs of terror against Jews identified them as belonging to the Fascist camp. What is happening in Palestine, claimed Tabenkin, is one battle in the war of Nazi terror. "The swastika that has been unfurled over Hitlerite Germany, and the green flag, the Arab 'national' flag, hoisted now by the reactionary leadership of the Arabs in Palestine—these flags are one and the same: the banners of hatred between peoples," he proclaimed.[42] Meir Ya'ari, the foremost leader of Ha-Shomer ha-Tzair, also viewed the leading elements in the Arab community as commensurate with forces of fascist reaction. "As far as prominent young elements from the 'intelligentsia' were concerned," he noted, "they are fascist elements." There had been no genuine process of differentiation among the Arabs, and reactionary circles still continued to dominate. Yet now they had learned terrorist tactics from European fascists. Although fascism on the whole is a "manifestation of modern imperialism" argued Ya'ari, the Marxist, in hair-splitting fashion, "A Fascist movement can also arise in a backward country."[43] Identifying the Arab movement with fascism abrogated any need for its recognition. As a movement belonging to the forces of reaction, it was by definition devoid of any positive attributes and quite naturally could not be a legitimate partner for negotiations. The fact that it made use of terror as a means for struggle was proof for him that it was identical with the forces of darkness.

The Arab revolt took place simultaneously with the shocking occurrences in Europe. The analogy between those events seemed almost self-evident to persons whose psychological identification with the Jewish fate and the Socialist camp was total. "Our struggle is a part of the world struggle, a world war," Tabenkin commented in a meeting of the Ha-Kibbutz ha-Meuhad secretariat. One must always remember "that the redemption of our people is part of the redemption of mankind that will come as the result of a persistent struggle."[44] The analogy with Spain, where workers were fighting against fascists, and Palestine, where Jewish workers were struggling against Arab terror, was repeatedly raised. "I would like us to feel the internal connection between those wars," Tabenkin noted, "between the struggle of our people . . . and the struggle of the worker and the world war in Spain, China, Russia." Socialism's defeats and the rise of fascist power indirectly strengthened the hand of socialist Zionists: Just as justice ultimately would triumph on the global scene, despite temporary setbacks, likewise in Palestine "the force that was oppressed is the rising force."[45] Their place in the camp of justice gave them moral strength, bolstered the weak in faith, and removed doubts and misgivings. It also did away with the need to make any reference to the concrete situation in Palestine. There was an element of mythologization of reality here, its explanation by reference to events beyond the perimeter of the present time and place, its interpretation as a part of global processes that it was impossible for human beings to prevent or halt. At the same time, there was an element of promise that victory would ultimately be forthcoming; and an explanation was given why that victory was slow and entailed such suffering.[46]

The analogy with the European situation was also applied in explaining the position taken by the British. The late 1930s were not the best years for the European democracies. Their weakness in confrontation with the fascist powers was repeatedly manifested: noninterference after the Japanese invasion of China, the acceptance of the entry of German troops to the Rhineland in 1936, the policy of nonintervention in Spain, acceptance of the Anschluss, the Munich accords that became a symbol of the appeasement policy, and acquiescence in the "swallowing up" of Czechoslovakia by the Germans. What was more natural than to explain British policy in Palestine by using those same idioms and phrases, those identical models of action (or inaction) that accounted for the stand of that power against the fascist forces? British reluctance in Palestine to respond with force to Arab violence was explained as a Palestinian version of the policy on nonintervention in Spain.[47] Later, in 1938, when the change in British policy (from support for a partition scheme to a pro-Arab stance, given formal expression in the May 1939 White Paper) became apparent, Britain's retreat was explained as part of her global surrender to the forces of violence. Just as Britain had chosen to appease Hitler even at the price of sacrificing an ally, it also preferred to sacrifice the Jews and appease the Arab terrorists. Even Robert Weltsch, whose approach to the Arab question was in the spirit of Brit Shalom, used the term Jewish Munich to refer to a possible British abandonment of the Jews. In his estimation, it was an era of "exploitation of the small peoples as pawns in the chess game of the great powers."[48] The identification between Britain's treacherous betrayal of her allies and her attitude toward the Jews in Palestine was not only limited to ardent Zionists. During the days of Munich, Jan Masaryk, the Czech ambassador in London, in bitter sarcasm suggested to Weizmann, president of the Zionist Organization, that he should buy a three-storey building in London. On the first floor would be Haile Selassie, the exiled emperor of Ethiopia; on the second would be Masaryk; and the third floor would be saved for Weizmann.[49]

The events during the late 1930s in Palestine and elsewhere were interpreted as being part of a single fabric in which the weak were plundered by the strong, might was right, and the forces of justice and morality stood helpless before the terror of the violent. The world was divided among the violent (who rejoice in battle), those who are trampled under foot by them, and those who appease (coming to terms post factum with the victory of violence). This picture of the situation significantly shaped public consciousness among Jews in Palestine.[50] Many believed that in the clash between the forces of good and evil, human dignity obligated one to fight to the end and not to submit without a struggle. For that reason, great importance was attached to the desperate battle of the Schutzbund in Austria. Likewise, the civil war in Spain awakened feelings of solidarity. Czechoslovakia was the example of what should not be done. Resolutely confronting the aggressors and fighting back against all odds now became central values.

Self-Restraint and Response

A few days after the disturbances erupted, a new concept made its appearance in the political lexicon in Palestine: *Havlaga* (self-restraint). It is not known who coined this concept in the particular context of the time. In the years to come, it would serve alternately as a term of abuse and an expression of praise, depending on the attitude of the speaker. To be self-restrained means intentionally to avoid any response in kind to a negative act perpetrated against you. This is a limitation of one's own behavior not as being *unable* to respond, to pay back an attacker double in kind, but rather as *choosing* not to. *Havlaga* was the declared policy of the institutions of the Jewish community in the face of the severe Arab provocations.

The need to establish a policy of self-restraint derived, first of all, from the circumstances of the outbreak. Several days prior to April 19, two Jews had been murdered by Arab bandits while traveling on the Nablus–Tulkarm Road. During the funeral of one of them, held in Tel Aviv, the crowds accompanying the funeral grew unruly; and several Arabs who happened to be in the vicinity were beat up. At the same time, two Arabs were murdered near Petah Tikvah. Although it was not known who had commited the murder, the general hypothesis was that it was an act of vengeance by Jews. When the riots erupted in Jaffa, the leaders of the Yishuv were quick to proclaim a policy of restraint in order to try to prevent the situation from deteriorating into general clashes between the two peoples in Palestine. The leaders of the Jewish community wished to prevent the British from having any opportunity to present the disturbances as clashes between two ethnic groups, as they had the August 1929 unrest. One of the things that most roused the Jewish community (which was considered by the leadership as a political disaster) was the fact that the authorities had blurred the distinction between the attacker and the victim. For that reason, they were later able to lay the blame for the 1929 disturbances at the door of the Jews. Having learned their lesson, the leaders tried this time to stress that the Arabs had been the violent party, the Jews, only the victims. In this way, they wanted to compel the British authorities to fulfill their role as the ruling power in Palestine to protect the security, life, and property of the inhabitants. Beyond this, they appealed to the high commissioner to protect the rights of law-abiding citizens against efforts by lawbreakers to change the prevailing political situation by force. Against the three demands of the Arab Higher Committee to put a halt to immigration, stop the sale of land to Jews, and institute a democratic government, the Jews demanded the continuation of immigration and of the process of building the national home, without any changes in the political status quo. They justified these demands by the argument, among others, that violence should not be rewarded and that the authorities should not submit to force. Self-restraint as a policy was designed to demonstrate to the world at large that the Jews were a people desirous of peace and that even when faced with severe provocations, they could exercise restraint and avoid violence.

The notion of self-restraint combined a mixture of moral principles and political–pragmatic considerations. It is difficult to determine the relative importance of these two components. In retrospect, one can easily conclude that the political considerations were the decisive element, especially since even those who initiated this policy and attempted to maintain it tried to explain and justify its motives by arguments drawn from the domain of pragmatic utility. Although moral arguments were also advanced, most of these had a tone of apology or embarrassment, as though they were not the really decisive ones. "We live in a world where morals are good for preachers," Ben Gurion explained: "But people do not live by morals. Even the Jews have stopped abiding by them. We will not persuade the Yishuv by using words of morality alone—unless we can prove that this [policy of revenge] also promises a political disaster for the Jewish community."[51] As time passed, and the use of force was gradually accepted as a legitimate instrument in the Zionist arsenal, the tendency increased to justify the policy of restraint by pragmatic arguments. Moralistic reasoning was associated with various types of "self-righteous" behavior and was rarely pressed.[52] Nonetheless, it appears that the tendency in the Jewish community at the beginning of the unrest to adopt a policy of self-restraint, which was widely and unequivocally accepted, is indicative of the fact that this was primarily a spontaneous response of a people desirous of peace, recoiling from bloodshed and wishing to avoid it. Of course, there were other minority views, especially in the ambience of the Irgun Zevai Leumi (IZL), the faction headed by Abraham Tehomi that had split off from the Hagana and was politically oriented toward the revisionists. Yet aside from a few exceptions, the greater majority of the community, on both the left and right, accepted and maintained the policy of self-restraint. This was the era before public opinion surveys. However, from literature, the press, and political deliberations, it appears that the generation of the leaders of the movement, people from the Second and Third Aliyah, regarded self-restraint as a self-evident policy under the circumstances. A correlation existed between age-group and attitude toward restraint: The younger the person, the greater his or her reservations about self-restraint.

The policy of restraint was a rationalization and politicization of the age-old Jewish repugnance for the spilling of innocent blood. There was a fundamental difference between the stance of being on guard and defending oneself against any attacker and acts of retribution for terrorist actions. In the first—an attitude that had been accepted in all previous waves of unrest—there was no doubt about the identity of the assailant, and the counteraction was aimed directly at him. In the case of terrorist activity, the attackers would lie in ambush along the road, attack, and then quickly make their getaway. There was no way of identifying the culprits. The option for response was either to engage in random attacks against Arabs, wherever they might be found—terror in answer to terror—or to avoid any action whatsoever, aside from direct self-defense. The distinction between "guilty" and "innocent" Arabs was one of the fundamental assumptions of the defensive ethos. It harbored a persistent hope that a common denominator for peace could be found. That ethos also stressed that not all Arabs were hostile toward Jews—only those who had been incited and led astray by their leaders. If there is no automatic identity between "Arab" and "enemy," one can raise the moral question, How is it possible, by a premeditated act, to attack and injure innocent persons? The injuries inflicted on Arab passersby in Jewish areas (a milkman in Haifa, a peddler in the Rehavya neighborhood in Jerusalem, and Arabs in Tel Aviv) not only did not provide a sense of satisfaction for vengeance taken but even awakened feelings of shame and disgust.[53]

There was no issue in which the lack of symmetry in respect to Jewish–Arab relations was so pronounced as the issue of self-restraint. In Arab eyes, every Jew, by dint of being a Jew, was regarded as an enemy; right from the outset, the struggle had been viewed as total. From the Jewish perspective, an intellectual, psychological, and political effort was made to maintain a differentiated image of the Arab. It is thus not surprising that while terrorists were praised on the Arab side as national heroes, and no moderates spoke out against acts of murder and brutality, similar outrages by the Jewish side met with shock and profound misgivings among the Jews.

This lack of symmetry preoccupied contemporaries. Ben Gurion commented on it on several occasions: The means employed by the Arabs are appropriate for their purpose, and the means used by Jews must likewise suit their purposes. The objective of the Arabs is to foment unrest and to make it impossible for Jews to come to Palestine. In contrast, the Jewish interest is to guarantee peace and quiet and prevent disturbances on the way to the building of Palestine. Thus, it is in the Arab interest to murder and burn, while Jews have no interest in taking such action.[54] Moreover, while Arabs can, by utilizing terror, persuade Britain to change its policies to their benefit, Jews will not be able to win Britain's good will by terrorist methods. Consequently, "Arab terror is directed toward achieving the Arab objective. Jewish terror contradicts the Jewish objective." Commenting on the wave of terror by IZL in 1938, Ben Gurion said, "Terror brings advantages to the Arabs; but terror will destroy Zionism and the Jewish community in Palestine."[55]

As I have mentioned, the provocation was extremely serious. In order to stand up against it and maintain the policy of self-restraint over time, it was necessary to erect psychological barriers to restrain the natural and growing urge for vengeance. One of the ways to do this was to prove that the Jewish policy of self-restraint was effective and that Arab acts of terror were not effective—did not stop the growth of the Jewish community. The reorganizing of the Jewish economy to respond to the challenge of separation from the Arab economy by an autonomous supply network was presented in the press as an appropriate response to the Arab strike. The opening of the jetty in Tel Aviv made banner headlines as a constructive reaction to the closing of the Jaffa harbor to Jews, and as an example of the "conquest" of new positions as a result of the Arab Rebellion. Jewish drivers who risked their lives by continuing to drive on the roads of Palestine in order to guarantee deliveries and keep connections open with small and remote settlements became the heroes of the day. Simultaneously, the figure of the guardsman was lavishly praised. The biblical verse "Every one with one of his hands wrought in the work and with the other hand held a weapon" (Nehemiah 4:16) often appeared as a slogan and challenge meant to strengthen the hand of the guardsmen who went out night after night to stand watch, after a day of exhausting toil in the fields.

The papers repeatedly stressed that not a single settlement was abandoned because of the riots. Fields that had been devoured by fire were once more put under the plow. Viewed as the crowning accomplishment of these efforts was the fact that immigration had not been halted and that the high commissioner even approved a new schedule—the six-month labor immigration quota—an act unheard of during earlier disturbances. New settlements were established in areas of high risk, such as the Bet Shean Valley; and a novel settlement type was introduced and developed, the "stockade and watchtower." This form was designed to permit colonization in frontier areas while safeguarding the settlement from attack. Moreover, for the first time in the history of the Jewish community in Palestine, thousands of Jews were enlisted as auxiliary police and guards to assist the British army in protecting Jewish settlements.

The thesis that each wave of disturbances ultimately led to a strengthening of the Yishuv was fondly cherished.[56] From the perspective of the defensive ethos, that thesis had many virtues; it bolstered the self-image of the Jewish community as one that was bravely facing its attackers, along the lines of the myth of Tel Hai. It also served as proof for the effectiveness of self-restraint, since it ultimately functioned to foil the chief objective of the insurgents, namely, to disrupt the pattern of normal life in Palestine. As long as the building of Palestine continued and there were even new "conquests" credited to the account of the Yishuv, there was no reason to call into question the wisdom of the evolutionary conception. The continuation of building the country and its fortification were considered the appropriate and genuine response to the Arab Rebellion and terror. Such constructive action was also presented as the mature antithesis to the childish eruption of urges for revenge.

An additional psychological barrier erected to serve the needs of *havlaga* was the self-image of the Jews as a people that hated violence, contrasted with the image of the bloodthirsty Arab. Everyday, Jewish–Arab relations suffered a severe blow as a result of the Arab revolt. Long-standing friendships were shattered, bonds between acquaintances and neighbors were severed. Encounters between Jews and Arabs virtually ceased. Eliyahu Golomb, commenting on the rupture, noted a remark of Chaim Sturman, one of the veterans of Ha-Shomer, who served as liaison with the Arabs for the settlements in the Jezreel Valley and was killed by a mine in September 1938, who said that in a short while he would forget how to speak Arabic.[57] Instead, a sense of mutual distrust mounted, fear of any nonroutine movement, along with profound lack of confidence and deep animosity.[58] One of the poems expressive of the spirit of the era was Tchernichovsky's "On Guard." The refrain in the poem goes, "This night, too, we will give up sleep!" The poet describes the Yishuv mobilizing to guard its elderly, its children, its property, and the fruits of its labor. The Arabs are not mentioned by name in the poem; but they are referred to as those who wage a "holy war," against which the guardsmen stand resolute watch. They are described as "savages"; an Arab is "a man of the desert, hungry for spoil, thirsty for blood."[59] Tchernichovsky also wrote a new lullaby that told about a child who "was conceived to the sound of jackals, born to the sound of bombs, the son of pioneers."[60] In the press, Arabs were described as "highway robbers," "treacherous murderers," "barbarian, savage, shedders of blood":[61] "They are bloodthirsty savages, who perpetrate their deeds in darkness, and all their courage is from ambush."[62] Such descriptions were repeated endlessly. On the face of it, it might appear that the press gave license to these responses; but this was not the case. Arrayed against the desert savage was the moral paragon of the Jew, who does not attack the innocent. "They were afraid to confront us face to face," a member of Mapai remarked in comparing Jewish and Arab behavior: "We did not wish to stoop to such moral degradation as to fire bullets at the innocent."[63] A. Z. Rabinovitz, one of the respected elders of the Yishuv, wrote: "We will not follow in their steps nor commit deeds like theirs. In the heart of Israel dwells the idea of prophecy, the indwelling spirit of mercy and love." For that reason, he continued, "even in a time of brutal attacks on our lives and property, we are strong enough to overcome hatred and revenge."[64] Beilinson used the same contrast: "Only in one area have the attackers shown their strength: murder from ambush, murder of individuals who are completely innocent and without sin, the murder of women and children. We must leave that field to the Arab murderers. We shall not follow in their wake."[65] Ben Gurion noted that the Yishuv had exhibited "not just a strong tie to the land but also its moral superiority. . . . It defends itself with bravery . . . but does not exceed its bounds, nor does it stoop to the level of its attackers."[66]

The self-image of the Jew as a man of morality—an image that the national movement inherited to a significant degree from Ahad Ha-Am and his disciples—was an integral component of the guiding myths of the Jewish community in Palestine. It both nurtured the policy of self-restraint and was in turn nurtured by it. As I have mentioned, self-restraint answered to psychological needs and expressed a spontaneous response by broad segments of the Jewish community who were deeply averse to bloodshed.[67] It served as proof of Jewish superiority over the Arabs not by might nor by power but by the strength of morality. It bolstered Jewish confidence that they were in the right and underscored the moral hollowness of Arab claims. The prominence given to the contrast between Jewish and Arab methods of action served the policy of self-restraint. The use of terror was identified with everything negative, despicable, and immoral. In a dialectical fashion, the popular stereotype of the immoral Arab was used to delegitimate the unchecked use of force against him.

Yet, at the same time, self-restraint undermined another sacred tenet of the national movement, namely, the principle that the Jew was obliged to defend his life and dignity. The revolutionary difference between the new and the old Jew derived initially from the differing attitude of these two human types toward the issue of self-defense. One of the principal differences between Palestine and the Diaspora was based on the certainty that in Palestine a Jew would defend himself and that his blood could no longer be shed at will. Yet that certainty was now compromised by the policy of self-restraint: It transformed the Jews once again into the "insulted who do not insult," the injured who do not injure in return.

Negative responses were soon in coming. Only a week after the outbreak of the disturbances, David Shimonovitz penned a poem of defiance that became a classic in the repertoire of the youth movements. The poem begins, "No! We shall not allow our blood to be shed in vain." It goes on to explain that human life is indeed sacred but that our blood is also sacred and will not be abandoned. The second stanza brings the problem to a head:

> Our blood is like water on all the lands of the earth . . .
> But *here* we will not be like a wilted leaf,
> Like a leaf scattered by every wind that blows—
> *Here* we shall not meet death like sheep!
> *Here* our faces shall not be struck by the whip;
> We will challenge death—and live!

The emphasis is on the uniqueness of the situation in Palestine, fundamentally different from that in the Diaspora. The contrast between "here" and "there"—Palestine and the Diaspora—is defined as a contrast between a life of passive resignation in the shadow of constant fear and life in the shadow of danger met actively, head on.[68] Shimonovitz was ambivalent in pointing out the implications of his poem. Obviously, a person who was active, as Shimonovitz was, in the Labor movement, found it difficult to launch an open attack on the policy of restraint. But his making Jewish identity in Palestine dependent on a courageous response to Arab outrages, especially his call, "We shall not allow our blood to be shed in vain," the poet signaled that passive self-defense was not enough, that it was necessary to respond in kind.

One of the more refined writers, Yaakov Steinberg, published an article in which he attacked the pretense and self-deception inherent in the defensive ethos and in the notion of restraint. In the Diaspora, Jews learned to exercise self-control and avoid taking revenge. Yet in Palestine, what point is there in continuing the pretension, the source of which lies in constraints of diasporic Jewish existence? "What is the sense of healing our blood by that bleeding medicine whose name is self-restraint, when we are full to overflowing with it? All concessions are permitted to a Jew in Palestine, except the conceding of a small degree of valor, namely, to stand up in self-defense." In the Diaspora, the Jew never spoke of "enemies"; all he had were "disasters" and "troubles." But in Palestine, a Jew is free of those inhibitions; and the time has arrived for him to stop splitting hairs and call an enemy an enemy, like every people does in a time of danger: "Instead, we were fed all day long with the stale old topic of agitators and adversaries and foreign leaders who are unqualified for leadership." And the Jewish community was nurtured with half-truths that, instead of clarifying the frontline, blurred it.[69]

Steinberg gave a literary expression to the feeling of betrayal experienced by Jews who came from the Diaspora, buoyed by the expectation that in Palestine they would find a way of life liberated from the need to "understand" the alien and "take him into consideration" that characterized Jewish life in the Diaspora. Yet in Palestine, he found himself drawn once again into adopting attitudes that lacked the simplicity and directness of a normal people. This was a repetition, in another form, of Brenner's sentiments when he first encountered Arabs in Haifa: "So . . . once again . . . there's *another* sort of alien in the world that one must suffer from." Restraint was conceived as one additional form of Jewish self-control not rooted in an authentic Jewish need but rather a product of the constraints associated with living in close proximity to another people. Steinberg's article, later included in the anthology *Me'ora'ot 1936,* was a kind of outer limit still barely acceptable to the thinking of the Labor movement. Not by chance, a reply accompanied the article, objecting to the use of the term *enemy* in reference to Arabs. The reply then went on to praise all the old socialist ideals of brotherhood.[70]

Jabotinsky was in basic support of the policy of self-restraint but aware of the predicament it entailed: "That trial will lead to a severe psychological crisis for our people. The idea of 'defense', the message of Bialik in 'Masa nemirov' ['In the city of slaughter'], which is basically the matrix of our regeneration and the renewal of a healthy youth—that enormous and important foundation of our national movement—is today discredited in everyone's eyes."[71] That psychological crisis was not limited to the borders of Palestine. Polish Jewry reacted with surprise, disappointment and protest. Ezriel Carlebach, in later years a senior journalist in Israel, published an article in *Heint,* the paper of the progressive Jewish mainstream in Poland, against the policy of restraint and announced that he was ashamed of the Yishuv. More articles in the same spirit were published in the Jewish press in Poland.[72]

The sensitivity of Polish Jews to the issue of self-restraint was understandable. In the pogroms perpetrated in Poland with rising frequency in the late 1930s, young Jews had made attempts at self-defense, though with but limited success. Polish courts responded with harsh verdicts against the defenders, who had killed rioters. These desperate acts were a projection of the ideology of the new Jew, who attributes an intrinsic value to the act of self-defense, even if its actual impact is minuscule. And in Palestine, where the model of the new Jew was meant to be transformed into an unquestioned and self-evident pattern of behavior, the Jews had chosen to react in a manner that appeared to belong to the category of hesitant response characteristic of the diasporic Jew. In their vale of tears, the Polish Jews had not only regarded the Palestinian model as worthy of emulation but also cherished it as a source of hope and pride. This accounts for their bitter disappointment.

Characteristically, the leaders of the Labor movement considered Jewish reaction in the Diaspora to be not merely a painful misunderstanding but, in part, a manifestation of objections abroad to the seniority and centrality of the Palestinian leadership with respect to the Diaspora. Berl Katznelson criticized these tendencies, deriding the tendency of diasporic Jewry to demand that Jews in Palestine should possess all the good virtues that they themselves were sometimes lacking. A diasporic Jew "can be a coward, but we have to be brave. He heard that there are guardsmen here, heroes, riding on horseback, victorious, sparking fear in the hearts of Arabs—and, lo and behold, a sudden disappointment! Are we not permitted to disappoint his idealistic conceptions [of us]?"[73] Katznelson justified self-restraint by claiming that it was actually based, in large measure, on concern about Jews in the Diaspora. The leaders of the Yishuv could put a stop to the riots with a single blow were they to agree to but one thing—a halt to immigration. But since their first concern was for the fate of the Diaspora, they were adamant in their rejection of this idea. That was the real reason for self-restraint, Katznelson stressed. In this light, the "ingratitude" on the part of the Diaspora was even more pronounced.

In contrast, Binjamin Lubotzky (Eliav), from the ranks of the revisionists, published an article attacking self-restraint and tried to explain the short circuit that had been created between the Diaspora and Palestine. In his view, the problem was not the images and expectations Jews in the Diaspora had of the community in Palestine. Rather, the problem lay in the fact that Jews had clearly understood that the objective conditions in Palestine were no different from those in the Diaspora: "It is becoming evident that Palestine is also the exile!" In Lubotzky's eyes, the inclination of leaders of the Yishuv to claim their innocence and to prove their virtues were the obvious characteristics of a persecuted minority. In his view, "diasporicality" meant self-effacement at the feet of a ruler and an absence of "manifestations of bravery, unity and pride, holding one's head high."[74] Y. H. Yeivin also regarded restraint as an expression of the "ghetto in the soul" and the renewal of the "old deformities of the Diaspora." It was no accident that he referred here to the old Berdichevskian concept of *change of values* as what was actually needed.[75] Abba Ahimeir developed a similar tack. In his essay "Alcazar and Self-Restraint," he juxtaposed the courage of the commander of Franco forces in the fortress at Toledo in the famous episode during the Spanish Civil War to what he termed the "swamp of self-restraint." Following Berdichevsky, he described Jewish history as the chronicle of the constant repression of Jewish heroism in favor of the conquest of impulse. "Zionism inherited self-restraint from the concepts of the shtetl in the Diaspora," he argued; and it is marked by an expectation that the "Shabbos goy" (i.e., the British) will fight for the Jews instead.[76] When Jabotinsky, in the summer of 1939, agreed to the IZL's discarding of the policy of restraint, he also felt it necessary to use the image of the Diaspora: "The blackest of all the attributes of the Diaspora is the tradition of leaving Jewish blood defenseless—blood that can be shed with impunity and for which no tax is paid."[77]

In the dispute on self-restraint, self-images deeply rooted in the new national ethos were articulated. It was agreed by one and all that the diasporic Jew was cowardly, helpless, and submissive. In contrast, the community in Palestine was supposed to be brave, masculine, bold, and uncompromising. In this categorization of the Diaspora versus Palestine, there was an element reminiscent of the division of the sexes. The Diaspora took on a feminine image, with all its implications, while the Yishuv was attributed a masculine image. Expectations were different for male and female; what was considered natural for her was, for the male, a betrayal of his very essence. The clash between images and reality, between the real world and myths, engendered tensions that were often unbearable, and that ultimately acted to destroy the policy of self-restraint.

Parallel with the undermining of the image of the Yishuv as that of the New Jew, the foundations of education for self-defense given to youth in Palestine were also shaken. A member of the Hagana complained: "At various times, in the pages of this paper and on other occasions, you who are our leaders have taught us the lessons of life in this country. You've explained to us the characteristic traits of this 'noble people' [the Arabs] and have never ceased to emphasize that the Orient knows only one master—the fist—and respects the philosophy of 'might is right'. And just look, now you've come and turned things upside down!"[78] Acceptance of the policy of self-restraint required a different level of sophistication from that taught in the Hagana. For that reason, the Hagana leaders found themselves in an uncomfortable situation, exposed to pressures from the rank and file to allow them to take acts of revenge. Since the Hagana was a disciplined body, the number of cases in which its members acted on their own were limited and did not amount to a new approach in the organization. Yet these pressures from below did not slacken until an alternative channel of action evolved and facilitated the release of internal pressures.[79]

The severe challenge to the policy of self-restraint came from the side of the IZL. In 1937 there was a split in the group; and one faction, under the leadership of Tehomi, returned to the ranks of the Hagana. Those who remained outside the Hagana set up the revamped IZL as an organization controlled by the radical circles in the Revisionist movement. The IZL accepted the leadership of Jabotinsky in principle (and at times in practical terms, as well); but its teachings were principally derived from rightwing radical circles in Palestine. They drew inspiration from the ideological triumvirate of Uri Zvi Greenberg, Abba Ahimeir, and Y. H. Yeivin. Soon they developed a philosophy of action that challenged not only the view current within the Labor movement but those of Jabotinsky, as well.[80]

On the whole, the IZL embraced the popular romanticism of the national movement, especially that of Poland, supplemented by Jewish historical myths that had been popular since the beginning of the century. Ahimeir's perspective affirming the use of force was fused to that of U. Z. Greenberg, which gave a mythical–symbolic interpretation to the world and reality and regarded historical fact as secondary to residual historical perception. On the face of it, the conceptual sources from which the Labor movement and the IZL drew sustenance were basically the same. Both borrowed the idea of the avant-garde that sacrifices itself on the altar of the people from the Russian *Narodnaya volya.* All the heroes of the people (Judah Maccabee, Bar Giora, Yohanan from Gush Halav, Elazar ben Yair, Bar Kokhba) were part of the Zionist historical pantheon. Until quite a late stage in the IZL's development, Trumpeldor and Ha-Shomer were considered modern heroes. It is true that David Ha-Reuveni and Shlomo Molkho appeared principally in Greenberg's writings and did not function as symbolic figures in the Labor movement. Moreover, holding up the Nili group as a model (a trend started by Ahimeir) was not current in the Labor movement. The tendency to attribute every virtue and quality to Nili was rooted in the simple need of a besieged and oppressed group, such as the IZL, to find intellectual parents in a nonestablishment group similar to itself. For that reason, Nili was the chief link in the chain of valor in modern Palestine that claimed the achievement of the Balfour Declaration (among other exploits) to its credit. Basically, however, the differences between the IZL and the Labor movement were not in different guiding myths but in their dosage (so to speak) and the degree of commitment to them. In the Labor movement, the historical symbols were designed to augment the spirit of patriotism and national romanticism, no more. In the IZL, those myths took on the importance of an obligatory commandment. Like Ahimeir before them, IZL members also attributed a special value to the exhibition of national aggressiveness. The value of an act was not measured by its actual achievement but, rather, by the residue it left behind in the national myth. The fact that the overwhelming majority of heroes (particularly the most revered among them, such as Elazar ben Yair, Bar Kokhba, and the Nili group) ended their lives in failure and death did not perturb them. On the contrary, it added to the attraction of the figures. In the ideational universe of IZL members, life was not acted out on the plane of mundane reality, with all its limitations and constraints, but took place in some unspecified locus in the twilight zone, where words determine the importance of deeds and symbol outweighs fact. In that universe, decisive importance was attributed to *how* at the expense of *what*. Consequently, drawing sustenance from the same conceptual sources and common shared myths did not lead to cooperation between Labor and the IZL, since reality was assessed and interpeted in the two movements on two totally different levels, leading to diametrically opposed conclusions.

The policy of self-restraint accentuated the contrasts in the approaches to both reality and myth. While the Labor movement fostered the self-image of the Jew as a man of morality and in this way came nearer to certain features of the conception of Ahad Ha-Am, the IZL drew closer to the opposite pole of the pristine Jew, liberated from all commitments and moral restraints and motivated only by national interests—a conception reminiscent of certain aspects of Berdichevsky's vitalist thinking. Avraham Stern (Yair), one of the radical youth in the IZL, and in later years the founder of the even more radical Lehi group, began his career as the author of the IZL anthem "Anonymous Soldiers." Written in 1932 under the influence of the 1929 riots and their aftermath, it is replete with conventional nationalist romanticism. Similarly, the objectives mentioned in the song "Defense and Conquest" do not differ in essence from those in other songs of sacrifice of that era. The wish of the fighters to "die for their country" often appeared as a motif in such songs. The atmosphere is more compressed and somber than in related poems of the time. Stern speaks of "terror and dread," "dark nights of despair," "cruel fate," and "prisons." Yet it is possible to attribute that somberness to the poetic rhetoric of the author, not necessarily to any exceptional ideas he may have had. However, faced now with the Arab Rebellion and the policy of self-restraint, Stern proclaimed: "Power is always decisive in the life of conquerors of lands and fighters for freedom. Power always has forged the fate of peoples. Power has always had its effect through resolute decisionmaking and the readiness to go all the way by war and conquest. . . . That power was created clandestinely by dreamers and fighters, breakers of oaths, those who cast off the yoke of treaties and opponents of the law, national revolutionaries."[81] The key phrases in this passage are "power" (repeated in an almost hypnotic rhythm), "war and conquest," and "national revolutionaries." One major source of inspiration for that grouping was Uri Zvi Greenberg, who wrote a poem at that time entitled "One Truth and Not Two":

> *Your teachers have taught: the Messiah will come in future generations.*
> Judea shall arise without fire and blood.
> It will arise with every tree, with every additional house.
> And I say: If your generation holds back
> And does not hasten the end
> And does not test the shield of David by fire
> And in blood the knees of his horses do not wallow—
> The Messiah will not come, even in a distant generation
> And Judea shall not arise.[82]

The belief in power as the sole arbiter in the fate of peoples and nations went far beyond the conception of Jabotinsky, who attributed great importance to world public opinion, world conscience, diplomatic give-and-take, and the impact of masses in distress. This divergence led to a collision that came to a head at the Betar World Convention held in Warsaw in September 1938, when Jabotinsky, under pressure from younger members, was forced to change the Betar oath and to add to the line "I shall not lift my arm but in defense" the words "and for the conquest of my homeland." There was poetic irony in the fact that Jabotinsky now confessed that when he had written the Betar hymn six years earlier (with phrases such as "in blood and sweat," and "to die or conquer the mountain"), he did not understand what he had written. Never before was the magic effect of words so evident as in the demand presented now to Jabotinsky to treat his own text at face value and implement it.[83] Stern and his associates dismissed all the liberal legacy that was part and parcel of Jabotinsky's teachings and embraced, without any filtering, Ahimeir's philosophy of power, pure and simple. In the case of Ahimeir, those ideas remained restricted to the sphere of ideology—aspirations that he had no power to realize concretely—and for that reason, perhaps, he did not hesitate to carry them to the extreme. But the IZL was an underground organization and had dangerous toys at its disposal. It did not shrink from translating into action the extreme conception of power preached by its mentors.

Circles of the radical Right inveighed against the policy of self-restraint as an approach that was undermining the very foundations of Jewish existence in Palestine. Not only was Jewish blood being shed without provocation, but the Arabs could walk unmolested in the Jewish areas while the Jews had to avoid the Arab areas for fear of death. Not only did the Arabs interpret the policy of self-restraint as a manifestation of weakness and cowardice on the part of the Jews, but the British authorities likewise had no respect for those whom they had to protect, who failed to respond to attacks in kind, who failed to establish their right to sovereignty over Palestine by the use of force. That, in the IZL's view, was the reason for the conclusions reached by the Peel Commission, which recommended partitioning the country into a Jewish, and an Arab, state. They argued that only because of the fallacy of self-restraint did the British dare to present this plan, aimed at depriving the Jews of the right to Palestine.[84] The IZL's infringement of the policy of self-restraint was geared to provide an answer to the psychological need for revenge. But beyond this, it had symbolic importance as a demonstration of Jewish strength in the face of the "impudent courage" of the Arabs and offered proof that they were not the only ones able and ready to use force. The IZL reprisals were intended to have far-reaching results. By means of violence, they wanted to bring about a shift in the public climate in the Yishuv, destroy the power of the "defeatist" circles, and give rise to a new leadership.[85]

In 1937 Uri Zvi Greenberg, who had returned from Poland to Palestine the previous year, published one of his most influential books of poetry, *Sefer ha-kitrug ve-ha-emuna* (The Book of Indictment and Faith). Some analysts contend that this volume played a crucial role in undermining the legitimist approach that had been pursued up until that time by the revisionists.[86] No other single written source could claim to have served as inspiration and goad to action and to have shaped the world-view of young men eager for the fight as much as this slim book of poems. Greenberg did not spare his criticism of the leadership of the Yishuv. The Labor movement had no more bitter enemy than this poet who had deserted its ranks and now raged:

> Five murderous months passed in smoke.
> And lower than grass are those who remained alive on the blood.
> A quiet like this prevails only in the cowshed after the butcher.
> Such degradation, such quiet cannot be found among any nation in the world.[87]

His settling of accounts with his past comrades did not end with the months of self-restraint. He castigated:

> Those who taught: There was no need to train young people
> As battalions for a battle with the Arab on the day of wrath—
> But simply to live, without God, kingdom, or defender.
> Without national parades, raucous with joy, and heavy beats.[88]

The intentionally low-key tone of national pathos in the Labor movement was separated from the heights of Greenbergian messianic pathos by an abyss of symbol, emphasis, and image. He wished to impart to youth what he perceived as the correct national spirit, acquired by means of nationalist symbols of identification, such as mass parades, along the lines of those organized by the fascist regimes. Just a decade earlier, Greenberg had seen the poetry and valor reflected in the life of the pioneers in the Jezreel Valley. Now he spoke differently: "A people that has no soldierly singing among its men is laid waste"; he proclaimed that a people's dignity was wrought upon the field of battle.[89]

The most famous poem by Greenberg was "Judea Today—Judea Tomorrow—Prophetic Burden of Sorrow and of Joy." After a description of the situation in Jerusalem, where Britain had allowed "the Arab dogs to wag their tongues at the sons of King David!," Greenberg sounds a prophetic note, envisioning a Nazi attack on Great Britain and the decline of the British Empire in India and around the world: "The day of your kingdom leans toward evening." Then he describes the British departure from Palestine, envisioning the suffering that will befall the Jews: "I hear much wailing, I see the murdered and butchered, conflagrations." It is impossible to determine here whether he was referring to events in Palestine or the Diaspora. The words of the following passage, often quoted since then, became a kind of cult text in right-wing circles in Palestine:

> I see thick prisons, gallows, in Jerusalem, in Jaffa, in Acre—
> And the faces of Jewish sicarii, condemned to the gallows.
> I see how they walk to the gallows,
> The dawn of Jerusalem reflected in the pallor of their faces.

The poem closes with a prophecy of comfort and victory:

> And already I behold a formation of my aircraft,
> Flying over the Temple Mount on a joyous day
>
> . . .
>
> David's banner fluttering on high from his tower.[90]

If it is legitimate to speak about cases in which life mimics literature, this is one of them. The poem was published about a year before the first "gallows martyr" (another emotional epithet from the same school of pathos) was sentenced to death by the British authorities. There is no doubt that this poem had an enormous impact in right-wing circles no longer satisfied with radical talk and itching for action. Shlomo Ben Yosef, a member of the Betar group in Rosh Pina that attacked an Arab bus, was sentenced to death under the emergency laws introduced by the British because of the Arab Rebellion, although he had injured no one. He became the martyred saint of the movement, a pedagogical symbol. Songs were sung about him, and young people were taught to follow in his footsteps. Jabotinsky, who had opposed reprisals, felt it necessary to affirm the actions of Ben Yosef, who had acted in violation of orders, by giving him a corresponding order after the fact. In a letter to Ben Yosef's mother, he wrote: "his disciples, more than mine, will show the way to this generation."[91]

In the IZL's eyes, the example of Ben Yosef sanctified the use of terror as a method of action by which a certain group in the community is singled out to become a standard-bearer of history. Terror was no longer perceived as just another means to deter Arabs from attacking Jews or to pressure Britain into not withdrawing from the national home. Rather, it was an identifying code, conferring on its adherents special rights and an exalted role in the national hierarchy. The use of force ceased to have a functional importance and became a value in its own right. The objective of force was "the conquest of the homeland Israel by the sword of Israel." A homeland was not earned except by the right of conquest, it was argued. The war for the conquest of the homeland was already being waged: "And we swear to continue in this war of valor and will not lay down the sword—once more unsheathed from its scabbard, after 1,800 years—until we complete the liberation of our homeland."[92]

The question still remained: Who was the enemy from whom the land must be conquered? On the one hand, all of the IZL's actions before World War II were directed against Arabs. On the other hand, the British were presented more and more as "foreign occupier," an expression coined by Abba Ahimeir already at the beginning of the 1930s. The IZL depicted British policy since the outbreak of the disturbances as a constant betrayal of its obligations toward the Jews. As will be recalled, the partition plan was presented by them as part of the anti-Jewish trend among the British. It was self-evident that Britain's concrete retreat from its obligations toward the Jews, embodied in the White Paper of Malcolm MacDonald, published in the spring of 1939, was seen as an act of deceit justifying a declaration of war against the British. But Jabotinsky, despite all his criticism of the mandate government and all his attempts to exert pressure on it by threatening to replace it with another power, was not prepared to give Britain a bill of divorce. Until his dying day, he supported a pro-British orientation, regarding Britain as the "lesser evil" among the Great Powers that might rule in Palestine. Moreover, in spite of the elevated pathos of the underground movement, its actual strength was quite limited. To oppose British might was a task beyond the realistic capabilities of the organization. For that reason, even when fury against the British reached a highpoint, such as after the hanging of Ben Yosef, the Arabs were the target they singled out for acts of reprisal. This also was what occurred after the publication of the White Paper in 1939. That ambivalence in defining the enemy was ultimately what led to a split in the IZL. Lehi, founded under the leadership of Avraham Stern, would later, indeed, seek out candidates for allies alternative to the British. Meanwhile, the statements about a "war of bravery" and "the conquest of Palestine by the sword" should be interpreted as rejecting the evolutionary method in the building of Palestine and repudiating the defensive ethos bound up with that approach, proclaiming loud and clear that only conquest by force would bequeath a right to the land.[93]

The rejection of the defensive ethos also meant that those who were identified with it were no longer qualified to stand at the helm of the Yishuv. From its inception, the delegitimization of the leadership of the Labor movement had been a central leitmotif of the radical Right in Palestine. Greenberg gave it the most forceful and vehement expression, characterizing the leaders as "scoundrels," "traitors," and "Flavians." The press of the IZL in Palestine and Poland heaped scorn upon the leaders of the Left. The more confident the IZL became in its activist policy and its uninhibited use of terror, the more it took on the aura of an alternative to the defeatist leadership of the Jewish community in Palestine. As someone who had been elected by history to bring about the kingdom of Israel, IZL's leader considered it self-evident that "in the light of the confusion and perplexity of those who pretended to be its 'leaders', I found it necessary, in my capacity as head of the *true* leadership of the Yishuv, . . . to say the following to you."[94] At the end of that same document, he explained that he had taken upon himself to judge and execute Jews, justifying this by virtue of his being "the person who, by token of his job, bears responsibility for the fate of the Yishuv and for the future of the war of liberation."[95]

Labor movement leaders were quick to realize the dangers immanent in the IZL. They viewed the acts of terror initiated by the organization as sheer insanity: Not only did they fail to stop Arab terror, they even threw oil on the fire, pushing the Arab population to rally around the Arab terrorist gangs. They feared that this policy could likewise undermine the position of the Jewish community in Palestine in world public opinion, especially in Great Britain. In their eyes, British public opinion was a kind of supreme court of appeals regarding the decrees of the British Mandate authorities. Although some on the left criticized Britain and did not spare accusations and abusive language, the position of Weizmann, Ben Gurion, and Shertok was ultimately the one that shaped the political orientation. In their perspective, Britain was the only ally of the Jews at that juncture, though not unconditionally so. In its actions, the IZL seemed to strive to liquidate any remaining British obligations to the Jews. Moreover, the mass indiscriminate killings of the aged, women, and children by the IZL awakened disgust and grave misgivings. The basic problem with the IZL was not in the organization itself, they contended, but, rather, in the public periphery that gave it support. In any discussion on terror aimed at expressing public repudiation of those acts, all the forces in the Jewish community interested in stemming the power of the Left and nurturing a grudge, for whatever reasons, against the established leadership immediately rallied to the cause of the IZL. The IZL became a focus of identification for any embittered individual who had a grievance against the hegemony of the Left. This included groups from the right, and even the center, of the political spectrum; they were joined by various rabbis and even a segment of the religious Zionist Mizrahi party. The latter, allies of Labor in the political arena, shrank from accusing a Jew of bloodshed, especially in view of the fact that such an accusation was made to the authorities. In Jewish tradition, that was an act that smacked of "informing," that is, open calumny against Jews. The tradition among Jews to preserve solidarity in the face of the rest of the world led to a closing of ranks: The leaders of Mizrahi chose to cover for the IZL. Yet it appears that among most of those who decided to defend and protect the IZL, the main consideration was to preserve it as a political option against the Labor movement.[96] The attitude toward the use of force became one of the central topics in the power struggle within the Yishuv. That process evolved in the wake of the riots and was to a substantial degree the product of the policy of self-restraint, which created an identity between the attitude toward force and the opposing political camps.

Within the Labor movement itself, there was considerable worry about the IZL's influence on Labor's younger generation. The tool mobilized in the struggle against the IZL and its values was the branding of the IZL as a fascist grouping. Identifying the revisionists with fascism had begun in the late 1920s. Now that perspective was provided with practical evidence (not just ideological arguments) to bolster its position. Unbridled nationalist ideology joined with the sanctification of violence as the exclusive political method and generated an image of a movement suggesting the presence of fascist characteristics. The IZL continued its line of unlimited enmity toward the Labor movement. Uri Zvi Greenberg's vilifications were added to those by the IZL leadership, describing the Labor leaders as traitors, and their social–political system as surrender and appeasement. The left was incessantly denounced by them as being motivated by class interests and derided as the bootlickers of communist Russia. In such a situation, it was not difficult to associate the IZL with Nazism or fascism, since one of their identifying marks was an unremitting war against the Left, its symbols, its images, and its identifying codes. The fact that Ahimeir had identified with Franco in Spain and that the IZL had also expressed its sympathy for the Right in the Spanish Civil War likewise left its imprint on consciousness. At a time when the world was bifurcated into left and right, the Jewish Left in Palestine was totally identified with one camp. In contrast, the IZL, even if it had criticism for Hitler, whom Greenberg had dubbed Amalek, did not shrink from finding positive points even about Nazi Germany, not to speak of Mussolini's Italy. Like Brit ha-Biryonim in its beginnings, their criticism of Nazism was not total and absolute but limited solely to the racist antisemitism of the regime. The IZL conducted an ongoing flirtation with the right-wing, antisemitic regime of the colonels in Poland, considered fascist in Palestine. Just as the Palestinian Labor movement had no doubt about its allegiance to the camp of the international Left, the IZL did not doubt that it was part of the international radical Right. Its press had little praise for democratic ideals or governments.

Consequently, it was self-evident that the Labor movement would mobilize its symbols of collective identity in the war against the IZL. The suspicion that the IZL would attempt to take control of the Yishuv was not farfetched. The history of Europe during that period was rich in examples of a small and violent minority seizing control of a large and passive majority. Although there appeared to be little likelihood of such a takeover in Palestine under the British Mandate, people in such cases tend to think in absolute categories, not in pragmatic terms. Even if a genuine takeover was difficult to implement, the apprehensions about intimidation, bank robberies, kidnappings, extortion of funds, and even executions of enemies of the IZL were not unfounded. The IZL executed Jews suspected of informing, even though some of these persons were totally innocent. The memory of Arlosoroff's murder, for which the Labor movement continued to hold the revisionists responsible, fed the fear that the IZL might harm Labor leaders. The declaration quoted above by Avraham Stern that he was the genuine leader of the Jewish community and that it was his right to pass judgment pointed in that direction. The feeling that the IZL was the sworn enemy of the Labor movement and that a war should be waged against them as a class adversary and part of world fascism complemented the political and moral opposition to terror.

The collective identity of the Labor camp as a left-wing movement, arrayed against the forces of fascism, was mobilized for the struggle against the IZL. Among Jewish Palestinian youth groups, the labels "fascists" or "Nazis" created an instinctive opposition to them and everything they stood for. From that moment on, it was not so very important what they said but, rather, how they were identified. Just as branding the leaders of the Arab Rebellion as fascists functioned to delegitimate them and discredit them for any role in negotiations, the same was attempted with the IZL. That was also part of the tack taken by Labor to delegitimize the unlimited use of force. Since the IZL's uniqueness and strength were principally associated with its terrorist activities, discrediting the organization necessitated a fundamental repudiation of its methods. In this way, the IZL's identity as a fascist organization was mobilized as a weapon in the struggle against the powerful lure that indiscriminate force had for certain youth groups. The phrase "fascist approach" was repeatedly used to describe their actions. Thus, the inclusion of the dispute about the use of force within the boundaries of the overall confrontation between right and left ultimately led to the identification of the unrestrained use of force with one camp and its discrediting with the other.[97]

Simultaneously, the policy of self-restraint underwent various modifications and changes over the course of the three years of the Arab revolt. These shifts did not go as far as the two radical conclusions of the IZL, namely, that only armed force can bestow a right to the land and that to achieve such a sacred objective all means are legitimate. Nonetheless, the meaning of self-restraint changed from the beginning of the period to its close.

When the policy of self-restraint was proclaimed immediately after the outbreak of the disturbances, it was interpreted as passive defense. On the basis of experience with earlier riots, the expectation was for mass attacks by Arabs on Jewish settlements in an attempt to storm them. Residents would set up a heavy guard along the perimeter fence of the settlement; and when there was an attack, they would return fire. Yet this time, the attackers utilized another method. Perhaps it was because Jewish settlements had grown stronger in the meanwhile, and it was harder to destroy an entire site in one blow than it was in the past. Or perhaps it was that attacks of that kind were suitable for spontaneous violence spawned by the passions of the moment as a one-time assault but remained inappropriate for a prolonged struggle led by regular fighting units. Whatever the reason, the Arabs changed their tactics from frontal attack to ambush. The Jewish community, particularly its defense forces, had no proper response to this new approach. The pressure from the ranks for acts of vengeance expressed the frustration of young and energetic Jews, ready for sacrifice but unable to find a way to channel their urge for action. Passive guard duty behind a perimeter fence stirred feelings of rage and helpless wrath when the fields beyond the fence went up in flame and thousands of trees were destroyed. There was as yet no adequate tactical response to attacks from ambush on workers in the fields, vehicles, and passersby. The truth was that the British Army had no proper answer at this stage, either. When an incident occurred, it dispatched a police or army unit to the scene; but the gang had generally disappeared before help arrived. The initial response was to increase the number of police by recruiting supplementary Jewish police officers to the British force, dubbed *notrim* (supernumerary constables). These Jewish policemen were trained to serve as an auxiliary security force. As *notrim,* thousands of Jewish young men received their first taste of military training. The architects of self-restraint, especially Eliyahu Golomb and Moshe Shertok, repeatedly cited this fact as one of the fruits of that policy.

However, other forms of response slowly began to crystallize."Getting outside the fence"—the designation for the new method of settlement defense—integrated several components into a military method better known today as "commando action" or "antiterror tactics." The method was based on small, well-trained, mobile units, familiar with the terrain and capable of lying in wait for Arab gangs. The transition from regular to small-scale warfare, from daylight to nighttime combat, and from fighting near buildings or crossroads to combat in the field marked the emergence of a military doctrine that turned a new leaf in Jewish defense in Palestine. The beginnings of that revolution lay in local initiatives, the so-called wandering mobile defense units. They were distinguished by the fact that they had a vehicle at their disposal and were independent in their activities. With time, they evolved into a separate military unit, termed FOSH (field squads). The person whose name is closely associated with their formation was Yitzhak Sade, one of the more colorful figures of the Labor movement. Sade received his military training in the Russian Army during World War I and fought with the reds in the civil war there. He migrated to Palestine with Trumpeldor's He-Halutz and was one of the founders of the Labor Brigade. A stone-quarry worker and wrestler, Bohemian in life-style, a lover of books and writers, Sade's personality expressed the inner contradictions of the Labor movement. A revolutionary socialist to his dying day, he was one of the originators of the notion of an independent Jewish military force in Palestine. Up until then, the Hagana had been one of the less developed institutions in the Yishuv. It was basically a federation of associations of guardsmen, in a situation where each settlement was responsible for its own defense. In contrast, the field squads scheme was the first attempt to set up an organization that was subject not to local, but to centralized, control. Recruits to these units were on regular duty, not mobilized just for emergency service, as had been the previous standing practice. The organizational changes reflected a new awareness of the importance of military force and an attempt to exploit the legal umbrella supplied by the British to the auxiliary police for the establishment and training of a skeleton Jewish military force.

The transition from a method of defense to one of attack involved psychological changes, reflecting a new stage beyond the boundaries defined by the myth of Tel Hai. As will be recalled, Tel Hai symbolized the notion that "a place once settled is not to be abandoned." The application of this principle was now expanded from the boundaries of the Jewish areas to encompass all open territory in Palestine. This was the first time that Jews did not suffice in simply defending their settlements but also initiated offensive actions in areas inhabited by Arabs. The action in the field increased the sense of ownership of Palestine, raising it from a theoretical to a practical level. The young people who moved at night, armed, through the heart of Arab areas, felt they were indeed the lords and masters of the land, as their fathers never had. Moreover, up until then, the hostile encounter between Arab and Jew had usually been initiated by the Arab side. Now the Jews began to carry out such actions on their own. Although ideology continued to distinguish between "good" and "bad" Arabs, the encounter in the field, or in Arab villages, was a confrontation between Jews and Arabs, a fact that underscored the totality of the national conflict in Palestine.[98]

One of the most crucial factors in respect to the development of a Jewish military force was the encounter with Wingate. Charles Orde Wingate was a British officer from a distinguished Scottish family with a long tradition of military service. The Jewish leadership had difficulty in assessing him. Wingate was one of the few British officers who was completely dedicated to the Zionist cause, for reasons of religious conviction. He initiated the revolution of commando action from the British side: the deployment of small units, active in the field, exploitation of the factors of night and surprise, the indirect approach—all these were applied by him to protect against Arab attacks the oil pipeline from Iraq passing through the Jezreel Valley to the refineries near Haifa. After that, he set up the Special Night Squads (SNS) utilizing the same tactics against Arab insurgents in the Bet Shean and Jezreel Valleys, and in Lower Galilee (1938). He recruited the cream of the youth in the field squads to his units, and they learned combat techniques under his command. Wingate was a professional soldier, unperturbed by pangs of conscience that troubled socialists who suddenly found themselves in the thick of battle. Among his troops, a remark circulated that was attributed to him: It claimed that Joshua's mistake had been that he had failed to properly clear out the area.[99] Wingate employed methods of intimidation and considerable brutality against Arab villagers. Rumor had it that he used to line up in a row villagers suspected of murder and then select every tenth one to be executed. In reports by members of the field squads under his command, one can find a mixture of admiration, intermixed with misgivings about the merciless raids on bedouin encampments, attacks that entailed humiliation of inhabitants and damage to property. This was the first time men trained in the Hagana had encountered such a form of military comportment. It was incompatible with what they had been taught by their commanders in the Hagana or their counselors in the youth movement. Yet on the other hand, Wingate was a revered commanding officer, especially popular with persons from labor settlements. His base was in

Ein Harod, and Chaim Sturman was his good friend. Participation in one of his raids was considered a special privilege. It stands to reason that elements of the set of norms adhered to by Wingate and his officers penetrated the ethos of the Jewish fighter that was beginning to crystallize at that time.[100]

The ideology of self-restraint, when applied to the new aggressive methods, stated: "We do not harm the innocent, and our weapons will remain pure. We attack armed bands and their bases in the villages." From a field ambush, it was possible in most cases to distinguish between an armed band and simple passersby. But when a raid was organized on a prominent building in an Arab village, the matter was more complicated. Efforts were undertaken to evacuate residents from structures marked for demolition, as a warning or in reprisal for attacks against Jews in the same area. Yet on a number of occasions, innocent bystanders were also, inevitably, injured. A new definition of the "guilty" was created. Indeed, collective guilt should not be applied to the Arabs, an argument that had been used by the IZL to justify its mass injuries. Yet if a village had served as a hiding place for an Arab gang, it was permissible to place collective responsibility on the village, along the lines of "blood revenge" common in Arab society. According to that code, all the tribe members were held responsible for a murder perpetrated by any one of them. It appears that this was the approach prevalent among the ranks of the field squads.[101] "Purity of arms" remained a central value in education. Its practical meaning was that an accidental passerby should not be injured. But if one jeopardizes one's own safety and penetrates an Arab area, taking that risk grants one immunity from guilt (so to speak), for the fighter cannot always be successful in pinpointing the members of the bands. The matter was tackled on two levels simultaneously. One was conceptual–political: Here, the attitude toward "purity of arms" was the criterion distinguishing the policies of the IZL from those of the Hagana. The second was the practical level. It remained rather vague and intentionally blurred as far as the boundaries of the permissible and nonpermissible were concerned. Delicate questions, such as the use of a rifle or a grenade, distinguished at times between preservation and nonpreservation of the "purity of arms." (A grenade injures indiscriminately, while the rifle strike is more accurate.) The awareness of these fine distinctions indicated that the accepted norm demanded caution in the use of weapons and that a violation was associated with a recognition that there had been a deviation from that norm. Along with this, there were some who noted that what distinguished between the method of the Labor movement and that of the IZL was no longer a difference between self-sacrifice in work and defense and self-sacrifice in war and bloodshed, as in the past. Rather, now it became a fine distinction between two types of war and bloodshed: Though one was more "civilized" than the other, they did not differ in essential respects.[102]

The transition from methods of defense to those of offense was not accepted as self-evident by persons living in labor settlements. Precisely those who were hit hardest by the armed bands had their reservations about Jewish participation in raids on nearby villages. "Such actions are appropriate for the British army that is here today and tomorrow will leave Palestine," argued men of the Hagana units in the settlements: "But they are not suitable for us, because they will serve to ruin our relations with our Arab neighbors."[103] A substantial amount of persuasion was required in order to convince people in the settlements to agree to give Wingate a quota from the ranks of their own people. The thinking of these people was still limited to the bounds and needs of local defense. The aggressive mentality of a combat based on mobility and firepower was alien to individuals who had been educated by the Tel Hai myth.

The central myth of the new era was Hanita. The establishment of this settlement point on the Lebanese border in Western Galilee was the symbol of the adaptation of the defensive myth to the new circumstances. It marked a further application of established concepts regarding colonization and the building of Palestine as the proper response to Arab attacks; at the same time, all aspects of this settlement operation pointed to the change that had taken place. The location of the new settlement was a symbol in itself: Situated in the heart of an Arab area, on the route taken by the armed bands filtering down from Lebanon to Palestine, the establishment of Hanita at the very high point of the riots was like placing a bone in the throat of a lion. The "ascent" to Hanita was part of a widespread settlement operation that was worked out during the course of the Arab Rebellion and gained momentum in the light of the Peel Commission partition scheme. Settlement efforts were concentrated mainly on two sections of the country that had been largely empty of Jews up until that point, namely, the Bet Shean Valley and Western Galilee. The method of settlement at the frontier, or "stockade and watchtower," that had evolved during the disturbances (i.e., the immediate setting up of a fence and a guard tower to protect against nighttime attacks) was still in keeping with the spirit of Tel Hai. Hanita represented a new stage in the process. On the surface, the situation appeared identical: A settlement is founded and then goes about organizing its own local defense. Yet Hanita's distance from any other point of Jewish settlement and its location in an area of danger necessitated another form of organization and a heightened level of defense. Initial settlement in Hanita required the mobilization of manpower, organizing ability, and finances of the magnitude of a military operation. The large numbers of volunteers who came to assist with its establishment combined with units of the field squads, whose function was to defend the place from expected attack. Such an attack took place the very first night, March 25, 1938. All the important figures in the Hagana were on the scene at the time. Although that attack failed, it claimed two lives and revealed the deficiencies of the static methods of defense that were employed that night. The following morning, Yitzhak Sade was given the opportunity to put his mobile guard units into action; the next attack ended in a major victory for the field squads.

Twenty-five years later, the author of the *Sefer Toldot ha-Hagana* wrote, "Hanita became a fact; and the Arabs learned once again, after the lesson of Tel Hai, Hulda, and Tirat Zvi, that a place where the foot of a Jewish settler has tread, where the blood of a Hebrew defender had been spilled, will not be abandoned by its builders and defenders."[104] This statement, whose historical accuracy is open to debate, is indeed the epitome of the defensive ethos, from the days of Tel Hai on, internalized in the "official" history of the development of the Yishuv. In actual truth, the presentation of Hanita as one more link in the chain of valor in the old style was no longer in keeping with the concrete circumstances. The balance between the two components in the myth of Tel Hai—work and defense—changed, in favor of the latter. In descriptions of the establishment of Hanita, the role of men of the Hagana, especially of the FOSH, was given special prominence. Their feats were depicted as a genuine military achievement, indicating the maturing of the Hagana both organizationally and militarily. In contrast with other settlements where the colonizing element was the crucial one, here the primary feature associated with the "conquest" of the place was its political significance. The land was purchased despite its poor agricultural quality; and for more than half a year after Hanita was formally established, it continued to be manned by Hagana personnel. Only later on did the first group arrive that was actually supposed to settle there.

Even at that stage, force was not presented by members of the Labor movement as the sole means for strengthening the Yishuv; rather, it was conceived as one element in a broader array of means and methods. Settlement, especially in new and peripheral areas, was stressed as a Zionist task of no less importance than the bearing of arms. Yet there can be no doubt that the prestige of bearing arms was enhanced. For the first time, the type of the fighter, whose only craft is warfare, as distinct from the worker in the fields, appeared. The circumstances in Hanita were special; and in other settlements of the stockade-and-watchtower type, the integration of warrior and worker was maintained. However, from that time on, the awareness that the fighter's role was no less important than the worker's was prevalent.

The ethos of the fighter emerged slowly. In the numerous poems and songs about Hanita, little reference was made to physical labor; in contrast, the elements of heroism and bravery were stressed. One poem referred to Hanita by stating:

> You are the wall of steel,
> In nights of siege,
> And you embody the dream of hope,
> For generations to come.

In another poem the poet asks, in the repetitive form of the biblical question, "What of the night in Hanita? In Hanita, what of the night?" And he replies, "There's a guard in Hanita, all night long, all the night." But there were other poems, as well. One of those more often sung was the "Song of the Five" (a group of five workers killed in the Jerusalem hills in 1937). It began, "Five men went forth to build a homeland." Set to music, the poem was popular in the youth movements and contained no reference whatsoever to defense. The song "This Is the Way—and No Way Else!" was steeped in the love of the homeland. It speaks about the plow, siege, and guard duty and is no different in kind from songs at the beginning of the 1930s. A song that maintains the equilibrium between the sword and the plowshare in exemplary fashion is a poem about Zeid, written in 1938 after Alexander Zeid, one of the veterans of Ha-Shomer, was killed in Sheikh Abrek: "Again and again, sword and plow, bridle and clod, hands embrace." He goes on: "Night, saddle, day, plow" and continues in that same spirit, closing with the line, "Seven times to build, one to die, this is the sign, this the destiny." One of the more popular poems in that period was written specifically for the occasion of the opening of Tel Aviv Harbor:

> Boats go forth to distant lands,
> a thousand hands unload and build.

> We conquer the beach and the wave,
> we are building a harbor here.[105]

At that same time, a poem appeared that was to become the poem of the era. It was written by Nathan Alterman, the same young poet who five years before had composed "Morning Song to the Homeland" and "Song of the Valley," two odes to the building of the land. Now he wrote "Zemer ha-Pelugot" (Song of the Squads), a poem that to a significant degree marks the borderline between the defensive ethos and the ethos of the fighter:

> Wait for us, my land,
> In the spaces of your fields.
> Wait for us in the broad fields of bread.
> Your boys once brought you peace by the plow.
> Today they bring you peace by the rifle!

The poem is dedicated to the field squads:

> Squad, rise, climb the mountain,
> Squad, you will be the one to conquer;
> Where no man has yet trodden,
> There the squads will ascend.

This was probably the first poem from the school of the labor movement dedicated completely to the glorification of a fighting unit. It appears that the poet was well aware of the traditional stand of the national ethos, since he emphasized—and not by chance—that peace in the past had come by the blade of the plow and was now being brought by rifles. Alterman's friendship with Yitzhak Sade was instrumental in transferring the meaning of the change from the limited circle of the military elite to the broader public. The poem played a key role in fostering the self-awareness of the Fosh and their ésprit de corps, as well as in the struggle against the IZL's influence on the young. Yet beyond all that, it highlighted the beginning, almost unawares, of a slow shift of the center of gravity of the national ethos.

It was necessary for a recognition of the importance of Jewish power to become crystallized before the ethos of the fighter could be born—*power* not in the sense of a critical mass (as had been usual up until then) but in its literal, physical meaning. The Arab Rebellion exerted a major impact on this process. The duration and intensity of the unrest had greater influence than any ideological development. It should be recalled that until military experience was gained in the ranks of the auxiliary police and Wingate's Special Night Squads, it was by no means commonly recognized that Jews were, indeed, capable of setting up and operating their own military force. Consequently, service in Wingate's units in particular—and in the auxiliary police in general—was of major importance in advancing the idea that the possibility of an independent Jewish force should be taken seriously. The expert opinion of Wingate, a British officer, that the young men of the Jezreel Valley had excellent fighting potential played a vital role in convincing the leadership. In the summer of 1938, an essay appeared by Eliyahu Golomb, openly explaining the need for an independent Jewish force: "We need force, and it is not important what it is called—a Jewish force, ready, equipped, fit, and trained to fulfill more decisive roles in more decisive times." Between the lines he hinted at the type of tasks that force was meant to perform. Although it would not be able to defeat a European power, it would be capable of standing up to the Arabs of Palestine and perhaps to the Arab states.[106] This appears to have been the first time that one of the leaders of the Yishuv spoke explicitly about the eventuality that the fate of Palestine would be decided by a Jewish force or that it would at least entail the use of Jewish military force. Golomb thought in terms of creating an independent Jewish fighting arm by exploiting possibilities that had opened up under the aegis of Great Britain as a result of cooperative efforts during the Arab uprising. Yet there was a hidden cognizance (that perhaps had not yet even penetrated the consciousness of the author) that in the end the Jews in Palestine would have to face the Arabs and the sovereignty issue be decided by the point of the sword. In contrast with the IZL, which held that a military struggle had already begun (though it was still unclear who the adversary was), Golomb acknowledged that this option was still quite distant. Nonetheless, he viewed preparation for it as a central task on the public agenda.

The years of the Arab revolt sharpened the feeling among Jews of dependence on the British and, by the same token, led to the realization that the Jews needed to break free from that dependence. The limited scope of Jewish military ability, coupled with the endeavor to remain within the sphere of legality, underscored Jewish need for protection by the British police and army. On the other hand, there were differences in outlook between the British and the Jews regarding the desired methods and options, as well as the desired timing, for quelling the riots. These differences, understandable in the light of differing perspectives, illuminated the fact that this relation of dependence restricted Zionist options in Palestine and was probably harmful to the security of life and property. That dependency was also seen as a political obstacle, since the British would ultimately demand and collect the price for their protection. A rise in enmity toward the British, generated in the main by the gap between Jewish expectations of the British and what the latter were prepared to do, enhanced frustration in the Yishuv. A paradoxical situation evolved: While in the political sphere—and even more, in the operative domain—cooperation between the Jews and British seemed to peak, in the sphere of public consciousness, Jewish animosity toward the British deepened, taking on previously unknown proportions. Indeed, it was an ungrateful task that the British had undertaken. The aspiration to establish an independent Jewish force that would be capable of standing up on its own to the Arabs—or at least able to plug up the breaches left by the British Army, was a natural desire under the circumstances. Added to this was the new option of a possible partition plan. The idea of a Jewish state had suddenly become a concrete possibility. Within the framework of ideas on a future Jewish state, discussions also took place on the plan of defense for such a state. Here for the first time, leaders of the Yishuv confronted the issue of responsibility for security, bound up with the gaining of independence. The security complex was a political problem they had not had to deal with seriously up until then.[107] Finally, one of the characteristic features of the Arab revolt was the increasing involvement of Arab states in the entire question of Palestine. As noted, it was intercession by the

Arab kings that had made it possible to end the general strike and facilitate the coming of the Peel Commission. From that juncture on, the Arab states showed ongoing interest in Palestine. Hence, for the first time, apprehensions arose that they might eventually intervene in the case of a Jewish–Arab clash in Palestine.

This apparently provided the background to the first signs of a new approach to the question of power. One of the leaders of the National Council of the Jews in Palestine, Avraham Katznelson, a former member of Ha-Poel ha-Tzair and a moderate, responded to Golomb's article. Like Golomb, he was an ardent proponent of Jewish–British cooperation. Yet he welcomed Golomb's idea about setting up an independent Jewish force, which he defined as an expression of the "aspiration of the Jewish community for emancipation in the field of security." He pointed to the arms race in the Arab states and suggested two ways of solving what he called the "security problem": immigration and "militarization of the Yishuv." Recognizing the novelty inherent in his call for "militarization," he felt it necessary to point out that even if pacifist sentiments might be offended, the matter was too serious to be postponed. He called for obligatory military training for the entire Jewish community. In order to make sure his concept of "militarization" was not mistaken for the position of the revisionists, he stressed it would be "not a professional military faction but a people—ready to fight, trained and equipped for the task."[108]

The Coming of Age of Palestinian Youth

The years of the Arab Rebellion were a junction where local events crossed with global developments, the fate of the Jewish community in Palestine, and the Diaspora—along with ideological and political changes. That crossroads was also the point of intersection between a changing reality and a new generation, one that had been educated in Palestine or born there. From this juncture on, the members of that generation were the ones who would be responsible for the implementation of Zionism in respect to the use of force. Although they did not mold policy, they carried it out. Ultimately, their view of the world and psychological makeup, the boundaries of what was "permissible" and what was "prohibited," would be the factors shaping the approach of the Yishuv to the use of force—if not in the realm of ideas, then at least in practice.

With a mixture of love, hope, and admiration, the fathers of the movement watched the growth of a Palestine-bred generation. They expected that generation to be born in the image of the New Jew, liberated from the constraints of the Diaspora and its complexes, a free man, a true reflection of his homeland. They recognized only too well that despite the mental effort they invested, their *own* bond to the land of Palestine remained primarily intellectual. Who knew better how difficult it had been for them to break free from their love for their former homelands' climate and landscape. They eagerly awaited the coming of age of a new generation whose loyalty to Palestine would not stem from internal conviction but would be natural and instinctive. They had a fervent wish for muscular, suntanned sons, light-footed and self-confident, courageous and straightforward. The physical dimension was extremely important. It will be recalled that decades earlier, Herzl's eyes were filled with tears when he witnessed a demonstration of equestrian abilities by the youth of Rehovot.

The fathers of the movement chose not to leave things to nature. They did not assume that the bond with Palestine would automatically nurture a generation whose relation with the land would be direct and unmediated. Rather, they invested considerable thought in the education of the young in order to impart to them that powerful bond with the homeland. In the elementary schools, a subject was introduced called *Moledet* (Homeland). That subject included an outline of the geography of Palestine and its characteristic climatic features, recognition of flora and fauna, and the forms of settlement. It also encompassed the learning of songs of the homeland, the drying of wild flowers, and various other activities designed to acquaint the children with Palestine and foster their love for the land.

One of the instruments for inculcating love for the homeland was the Bible. Since the very beginnings of modern Jewish colonization in Palestine, the Bible had occupied a central position in secular education. In the Herzliya Gymnasia in Tel Aviv, the first Hebrew secondary school in Palestine, Bible studies were designed to familiarize the pupil with the early history of the people, nurture love for the homeland, and implant a bitter enmity toward the Diaspora and its disgraces.[109] These objectives remained operative throughout the entire period of the mandate. In a book on secondary education in Palestine edited by H. Y. Roth, the Bible was described as "national literature," accepted as such by all segments of the population, from right to left. The Bible "brings us back to the homeland, to the Palestine soil, to its natural and human features."[110] A Bible lesson had to be saturated with "the fragrance of the Palestinian soil." Those who had immigrated during the Second Aliyah used to hike around the country with their Bible in hand, identifying names of places mentioned in Scripture. Their children embraced the idea that the Bible was the guidebook to Palestine, its flora and fauna. In addition, the Bible was the "textbook for national history."[111] The story of the emergence of the Hebrew people is narrated in the Bible with great poetical power; this narration assisted greatly in illustrating the process of the genesis of a people, its settlement in the land, and the difficulties of governance there. Teachers preferred to stress Bible stories and the early prophets and placed less emphasis on the latter prophets. One of the educators inquired skeptically: "Is it really all that worthwhile to occupy the intellect and imagination of children for so much time with discourses and stories on the exploitation of the weak, injustice, fraternal hatred, prostitution, fornication, and the like? Isn't it possible that the great and never-ending wrath of those divine demagogues may disturb the psychological composure of our children?"[112]

These words were written in the late 1930s; but already at the beginning of that decade, Ernst Simon had complained about the dominant trend in the teaching of the Bible. In comparing the approach of Ahad Ha-Am to the Bible, who stressed the Jewish moral principles it contained, and Berdichevsky, who called for purifying the Bible from the dross of the prophets who transformed it "from an ancient heroic epic to a vision of peace and love for one's fellow man," Simon argued that in the school curricula, Ahad Ha-Am had retreated and Berdichevsky reigned victorious. The Bible was being presented as a heroic epic. As an illustration, he mentioned the example of Jeremiah. In the schools, pupils ask whether Jeremiah was in fact a true prophet, as the Bible assumes, or actually a defeatist, who weakened the resistance of the people at the time of siege—or perhaps even a "traitor" after the manner of Josephus. The child identifies with the heroes of the Bible but not with the moral pathos of the prophets.[113] Simon contended that the majority of teachers were close to revisionism in their thinking. But even setting that hypothesis aside, it appears likely that the basic impact and influence of the Bible was not as an instrument to impart the moral teachings of the prophets but to inculcate the sense that the Jewish people had a claim to ownership of the land and to strengthen the bond with it.

On the other hand, throughout the early 1930s, one could seldom find any special emphasis on historical symbols or early historical myths within the youth movements attached to Labor Palestine. Of course, everyone learned about the heroic struggle of the Hasmoneans and the Jewish War against the Romans. Yet it was not the practice of the youth movement in that period to stress those aspects of the national tradition. In 1931 a youth gathering was held in Ben Shemen for the advancement of world peace. Disciples from all the youth movements affiliated with the Labor camp in Palestine participated; they listened to recitations, took part in folksinging and dancing, and visited an exhibition whose topic was "Never Again War." Some of the leading figures of the generation, such as Zalman Rubashov (Shazar), Ernst Simon, and Yitzhak Tabenkin gave speeches in support of the struggle for peace.[114] The popular symbols of heroism at the time did not have a national character; rather, they were socialist, stressing the bonds with the international proletariat struggling against the forces of fascism.[115]

On the whole, the world of the Palestinian youth was focused on the immediate environment, the life of the Jewish community in Palestine and its problems. Anything beyond that was strange to young people and failed to engage their attention. Already at the beginning of the 1930s, the fathers of the movement had been concerned about the distance between Palestinian Jewish youth and the life of the Diaspora. At the end of the decade, one of the teachers defined the educational dilemma as follows: "The Hebrew [Zionist] teacher generally does not know what he should do: Should he try to endear the Diaspora to his pupils and teach them about Jewish life there, or is it better if he deflect their attention from that way of life and inculcate a hatred for the Diaspora?"[116] The dominant ideology in the Yishuv believed in the Negation of Exile; that is, it viewed the reality of Jewish life there as doomed to ultimate destruction. This historical conception, depicting Zionism as the only answer to the plight of the Jewish people, was imparted to the young through the writings of Mendele and Brenner. Their bitter critique of Jewish life in the Diaspora was interpreted by those in Palestine as an accurate and unadorned description of things as they really were. Undoubtedly, the "fathers" were also steeped in this literature, and were radical in their negation of the Diaspora. Yet they knew the concrete reality of the Diaspora from their own experience. When they revolted against their parents and everything they represented and abandoned their homes, families, and towns to emigrate to Palestine, they inoculated themselves against the lure of the past by portraying it as despicable and doomed. The Zionist revolution, like all revolutions, demanded the burning of bridges to the past. But engraved in their hearts was the genuine picture of Jewish life in Eastern Europe, vivid both in its light and shadows. Most important, their hearts were filled with a love for the particular Jews to whom they themselves belonged, whom they knew from experience, and with whom they identified. The situation was different when it came to the young who had been educated in Palestine. When they read Brenner and Mendele, the picture that remained engraved in their minds was this sarcastic caricature. They did not relate to these writings as creative fiction but rather as a documentation of living reality. The severity of the criticism was not tempered by the mitigating input of direct experience. Parents did not tend to speak with their children about life back in the old country. There were but few families in Palestine where the grandfather and grandmother were also present. Had they been a part of the family environment, their bond with the life-styles of Eastern Europe could have served as counterevidence to muster against the ideological aggressivity of modern Hebrew literature. Ernst Simon warned about the "lack of any knowledge whatsoever among youth in Palestine about the life of the Jewish masses; moreover, they lack any psychological possibility of understanding, if nothing else, the conditions of existence of the Jewish masses in the Diaspora."[117]

A similar phenomenon of alienation and lack of understanding was also prevalent among that generation when it came to Arabs. Apparently, one would have expected to find a reverse symmetry between the generation of the fathers and that of the sons—the fathers unfamiliar with the Arabs but knowing Jewish life in the Diaspora, the sons distant from the Jews of the Diaspora yet familiar with the Arabs in Palestine. However, such symmetry was not the case. Most of the young in Palestine had grown up within a framework of Jewish existence in which the Arab was an external, accidental, marginal element. There were extremely few points of encounter between Jewish youth and Palestinian Arabs. In the old colonies where Arab workers were employed, Arabs had been part of everyday life. But these colonies were a segment of a Palestinian reality whose relative importance in the Jewish Yishuv was on the decline. In contrast, the role played by patterns of living based on a separation between the Jewish and Arab communities was gaining momentum; there was Tel Aviv, the Jewish city, separate Jewish neighborhoods in mixed towns such as Haifa and Jerusalem, labor settlements, and the new colonies based on Jewish labor. The Arab appeared in this ambience as a peddler or a seller of dairy products or vegetables but not as an integral component of everyday life.

There was extremely little curiosity about the other people in the land. Jewish children disliked learning Arabic—perhaps because the teachers were not gifted enough or because children preferred French as a second foreign language, after English.[118] There were very few efforts in the schools to impart a knowledge about Arabs to the pupils or to familiarize them with Arab life-styles. This policy was not limited to the schools: The socialist youth movements also adherred to it. In the educational program of Ha-Noar ha-Oved there were some twenty topics to be covered, but only one was devoted to the Arab community in Palestine. That theme was not accorded any special attention, and it appears to have been treated in an offhanded manner. In the chapters of the program dealing with modern Jewish colonization and settlement in Palestine, Arabs were not mentioned except in connection with the problem of Jewish labor.[119] It is doubtful whether closer familiarity with Arabs would necessarily have led to relations of friendship and brotherhood, as contended by Brit Shalom and groups close to that organization. One notable exception, the principal of the agricultural school in Ben Shemen, Dr. Siegfried Lehmann, did everything in his power to bring his pupils closer together with the Arabs living nearby. He initiated visits to bedouin encampments, and Jewish pupils from Ben Shemen would bring small presents for the Arab children. But the pupils did this to please Lehmann, who was a distinguished educator and an admired personality. They did not feel any genuine closeness to those children and among themselves used to make fun of the practice of bedouin parents, who would take the candy they brought to the bedouin children for themselves. There was a gap between the approach of Lehmann, trained in German humanism, and the pragmatic, "earthy" approach of his pupils.[120] They loved him but saw him as a visionary, cut off from reality. Despite Lehmann's educational efforts, the friendship forged between Ben Shemen and its neighbors did not prevent acts of violence against the youth village during the riots.

Generally speaking, these young people did not harbor any hatred toward the Arabs. Among their fathers, animosity toward non-Jews had deep psychological roots, the product of boyhood experiences and the legacy of age-old persecution. In contrast, those young men and women had no firsthand experience of antisemitism, and related to non-Jews with a naturalness uncomplicated by complexes. They had a pride bordering on conceit in their conviction that the world was theirs, waiting for them to take. The loaded concepts of their parents, such as *pogrom,* did not awaken any identification in them; rather, young people felt a kind of revulsion, intermingled with pity. Consequently, they did not view the Arabs as another kind of non-Jew they had to suffer and put up with, as Brenner had written. They did not think of them in terms of historical forces, anti-Jewish currents from the time of Pharoah and Amalek to Haman, the Crusaders, Chmielnicki, and Petlyura. Rather, they saw these non-Jews in a Palestinian context, as a local problem with real, concrete, not mythical dimensions. They had been educated to believe that the Zionist project in Palestine was an enterprise of peace and progress, bringing benefit to all its inhabitants. They also accepted uncritically the thesis that Arab opposition was an expression of the backwardness of Arab society and that the path to coexistence in peace was the building of a joint union.

The primary instrument with which the principles of morality and humanism were imparted to pupils in Palestine was socialist education. Although that education was quite naturally limited in scope and only reached the left and its periphery in the Yishuv, there is no doubt that it had considerable influence among broad circles of the population, particularly the leading youth elites. Socialist education was the conduit through which these youth were introduced to the world at large, learned about other peoples and countries, became familiar with government systems and social institutions, and acquired their emotional attitudes toward what was good and bad, just and unjust, right and wrong. Their education was narrowminded but not necessarily provincial. Their view of the world was bright and clear. The planet was divided into two camps: that of progress and justice and that of reaction and oppression. Between these two camps were various strata and classes destined to disappear from the world's stage. In the struggle between good and evil, good would ultimately prevail. They identified with the World Socialist movement as the representative of the camp of justice. They admired the socialist myths of the era, such as the struggle of the Schutzbund, the civil war in Spain, and the rising sun of Soviet socialism, almost blinding in its attraction. In the late 1930s, Soviet Russia was not yet a central educational model in the youth movements; but there is no doubt it was a topic of interest, curiosity, and identification. The socialist literature they read taught them to be sensitive to acts of injustice and discrimination and outraged at the oppression of the weak by the strong. They felt sympathy for the struggles of liberation movements across the planet, from Europe to China and South America. They read about hungry children in India and Africa, child labor during the industrial revolution, and exploitation of the labor of one's fellow human beings and learned to identify with the weak and defenseless. They saw Jews as part of the wretched of the earth, whose deliverance would come with the victory of Zionism and socialism.

Just as their knowledge of diasporic Jewry was intellectual, abstract, and not internalized and did not become part of their own lives, socialist education likewise remained external. They identified with the World Socialist movement but did not apply the moral pathos that they acquired from reading literature to the social phenomena they encountered in everyday life. Their fathers had experienced the pain of Jewish deprivation and poverty in Eastern Europe and knew what discrimination and exploitation really meant. For them, socialism was a liberating faith, a ray of hope in the dark valley of life, the redemption of human dignity. In contrast, the youth of most of those brought up in Palestine was not spent under the duress of social deprivation. Although those educated in Ha-Noar ha-Oved were exposed from an early age to poverty more often than others and at times even carried the burden of supporting their families, most Palestinian Jewish youth were familiar with deprivation and want only from descriptions in literature. Living standards in Palestine were quite low; but since poverty was accepted as a feature characterizing the entire Labor movement, it was not thought to be a stigma or form of suffering.[121] The idealists among them aspired to live a life of equality and cooperation not because those are the responses to injustice in the world, but because that is the way to create a healthy and just society and to rebel against the petit bourgeois life-style that was common in most of the homes of members of the Labor movement.

Already at the beginning of the 1930s, one of the founders of the first agricultural cooperative, Degania, made some sharp observations about the characteristics of the young people born and raised in Palestine. "Our children are pragmatic, and, perhaps, put even more accurately, they are prosaic," noted Yosef Baratz. They become excited about national public events, such as the terrorist murder of a father and his son in Nahalal or Arlosoroff's murder, he pointed out; yet "in contrast, they lack tenderness and a human attitude toward the elementary phenomena of everyday life. What is their attitude toward the poor, the aged, the Arabs, the sick? And from where should they in fact know how to relate differently?" The founding generation viewed directness and simple manners as virtues of the natural man, contrasted with the psychological distortions of those who had been educated in the Diaspora. However, the characteristic Palestinian forthrightness, and a lack of sophistication when it came to human relations, were at the expense of traditional Jewish compassion, which was an obvious "diasporic" character trait.

In their crystallizing system of values, nationalism was at the top of the scale for these young people. "Generally, it seems to me," wrote Baratz, "that the national element is more developed than the social element." While the workers of the world remained a distant phenomenon for them, one that they read about or heard stories about from their parents, "the 'homeland' is not an abstraction for them. They are deeply attached to it." Their approach to the homeland was simple, "without any psychological or ideological complexes of the kind that occupy us," he added. They follow events in Palestine closely and respond with great alertness: "Their love for this endangered homeland is increasing and at times awakens excessive patriotic instincts."[122]

Ernst Simon sketched the symmetry between the attitude of Palestinian youth to the Jew in the Diaspora and to Arabs in Palestine. Youth tended to act as though the Jewish community in Palestine were the majority of the Jewish people and the Jews of the Diaspora unimportant in comparison; similarly, they tended to act as though Jews were the majority in Palestine, and the Arabs an insignificant minority.[123] The source of that symmetry lies in the externality of these two phenomena to the true life experience of a young man who grew up in Palestine. Viewing the Yishuv as the hub of the world was one of the self-defensive psychological ploys adopted by the generation of the fathers against the lure of the greater world outside. They also operated this way in regard to their children's education. The result was a focus on, and preoccupation with, themselves; among other things, this was characterized by a loose linkage to the world at large and a lack of appreciation for its importance. "There is something disturbing in our encounter with Palestinian youth," remarked Tabenkin, "since there is always a feeling in our talks with the young here that the events that occurred in Palestine are separate from the entire world and from the situation of the Jews in the world."[124]

The Palestinocentrism of the sons was not an ideology they had acquired. Rather, it was a reality of life, a psychological disposition, a kind of congenital trait. Socialist education was apparently meant to act as a sort of serum against self-preoccupation and also to function as a window to the world. But the bond with the Socialist camp was theoretical, a kind of ideological abstraction to which they felt attached. Hence, it did not collide with the conception that attributed a unique value to them and their small world and did not force them to venture forth from the tiny shell of their immediate milieu. The Arabs were not part of that shell.

When the Arab Rebellion erupted, the conflict between ideology and reality became much more pronounced. The encounter with fields in flame, trees felled, gunfire, and victims as an everyday experience in whose shadow they had to learn to function left a powerful impact on children and youth. There was fear in the children's houses in kibbutzim during nights when shots rang out and children were ordered by their nurses to hide under the beds. Life changed: The fields were considered off bounds, dangerous; it was forbidden to go for walks or hikes beyond the perimeter fence. Weapons became the daily topic of conversation among the children, war games a popular diversion: "It appears that all the children's thoughts have been reduced to one thing: 'The Arabs are bad'."[125] Reading the papers (where there were daily lists of the dead framed in black and reports on attacks and damage on the front page) became a virtual obsession among the young.[126] With great sensitivity, Eliezer Steinmann described the relations that had developed between him and his young sons in the shadow of the disturbances. Steinmann, who had been educated in the ideals of humanism and socialism, explained to his sons that the riots were isolated incidents, the acts of a "small group of troublemakers," and would soon pass away. Yet with each additional day of destruction and murder, the father's credibility was further eroded. While he had difficulty accepting the facts of life in Palestine, his sons were already drawing their lessons from those facts. In the eyes of his children, he could read, "Life, father, in this country and anywhere else, involves a revolver, a knife, a bomb, murder." If one wishes to live in this country, there was no option but to use the same methods against the neighboring people that they themselves use. "We presented this cruel world in a special edition for the sake of our children—sweetened, slightly softened. For the sake of the infants, we composed an imaginary reality, in which people sit together in the splendor of love," bewailed Steinmann. This saccharine description was based on a failure to tell the truth: "Won't we have to account to our children in the future for our actions, for the way we deceived them?"[127]

The picture of the world in the heads of children living in a society fraught with a high level of ideological tension is generally the reflection of the world picture of adults but purified of the compromises that adults naturally make when reality does not conform with the ideology. Youth education involved imparting unambiguous truths and absolute values. Consequently, the awakening of youth to the existence of an Arab problem was associated with a conceptual crisis threatening to undermine the bases of their world. The roar of bullets shattered the walls of their shell and led to their awareness of the fact that the Arabs would not accept the colonization of the Jews in Palestine. In first discussions after the outbreak of the riots, there was a pronounced tendency by adolescents to embrace the views of the adults, according to party affiliation: A member of Betar quoted Jabotinsky, someone from Ha-Shomer ha-Tzair spoke about the joint union, a member of Ha-Noar ha-Oved commented on the need to build and fortify the country, and so forth. Yet among the flowery platitudes, comments were interspersed that hinted at the existence of a crisis in ideas. A feeling of guilt appeared, accounted for in various ways. One contended that the Jews were ultimately to blame for the riots, since they had not taken steps earlier to prevent incitement and to bring Jews and Arabs closer together. Another thought he was to blame for having neglected the association of Arab workers, which could provide an organizational means to prevent the effendis and agitators from gaining and maintaining control over the workers. Someone commented that during an outing with members of his youth movement group, Arab children had thrown stones at them: "We felt that they were not to blame, but, rather, that we were. There is a need to inform them, explain to them, make them understand our way."[128] The radical conclusion derived from these views (not uncommon among Ha-Shomer ha-Tzair and among the disciples of the youth movements Ha-Mahanot ha-Olim and Ha-Noar ha-Oved) was a questioning of the very right of the Jews, from a moral perspective, to colonize and settle in Palestine.

Such heresy was voiced by members of the youth movements, and their comments greatly troubled their instructors. Yet only a small number of these young people became true heretics. Those who did generally joined the Communist party, which had an Arab orientation; its members, predominantly Jewish, were all adamantly opposed to Zionism. Among others, paradoxically, the feelings of guilt acted to reinforce the old view. The disturbances were presented as a result of serious Jewish oversights. If Jews were genuinely able to explain the purity of their intentions to the Arabs, the situation would be different. Everything was due to misunderstanding, amenable to correction. Not only had it been possible to prevent clashes in the past, it was also feasible to prevent them in future. Idealistic young men found it hard to cope with a reality that signaled that the Jewish–Arab confrontation had, indeed, become an integral part of their lives. "As a result of these riots," remarked a teenager from Jerusalem, "I fear that young people now might get a wrong understanding of things—as if there actually exists here a war for survival between the two peoples." In December 1937 a young member reported that there were those who claimed "this is a war waged by one people against another" but he had a different opinion: "That's not right, it's a war between Arab terrorists and Zionism."[129] One girl made it a point to stress that despite everything, "the basic Zionist–socialist foundations have not been undermined."[130] In the face of the soul-searching of some youth, others demanded that there should be an end to the inappropriate splitting of hairs and that attention should be devoted to pressing existential questions. "The most important and profound elements in our attitude toward the Arabs don't have to be articulated at the present moment," commented Shmarya Gutman, one of the best-known veterans of the Ha-Noar ha-Oved: "It's necessary to concentrate on the existing situation."[131] That situation was one of flying bullets and exploding bombs.

One of the problems that concerned youth was the appearance among Jews of signs of hatred toward Arabs. "What worries me is that these riots may generate a very undesirable attitude among the young toward the people in whose midst we live," noted a concerned young man from Jerusalem. Many members of the movement, he contended, made no distinction between accusations leveled at effendis and simple folk and, "in blind hatred, include the entire Arab people."[132] The increase in the level of enmity between Jews and Arabs hardened the hearts of young Jews toward Arabs injured in the unrest. In Jerusalem in particular, there was a marked phenomenon: an inclination among youth and children to treat the fact of Arab injuries and deaths lightly. One of the young men reported about an argument in his school concerning the question, How many Arabs have to be killed if one Jew is murdered? The mentors of the youth movement and their disciples were shocked when, during a day of terror staged by the IZL in the city, children danced around the body of a murdered Arab.[133] A letter from a young member of the revisionist youth group Brit ha-Kanaim (Covenant of Zealots), to his friend, describing in detail the maltreatment of Arab peddlers by children belonging to his movement in Jerusalem, awakened horror and disgust.[134]

The confusion of these youngsters was not accidental. Their teachers had not come to any agreement on how the situation should be assessed or even what line of explanation should be taken. In the words of Ahuvia Malkin, one of the leaders of Ha-Mahanot ha-Olim, it was possible already in May 1936 to find a mixture of the old arguments mingled with a realistic assessment of the situation. Along with sharp observations on the link between events in Palestine and strikes in Egypt and Syria, the decline in prestige of the League of Nations and Great Britain, and the defeat of the legislative council scheme in the British Parliament, he continued to distinguish between the interests of the effendis and the fellahin and pointed out that the Arab movement was reactionary.[135] In Tabenkin's view, what was happening in Palestine could be explained by global events: the undermining of the situation of Jews in Palestine as a result of the decline in the world situation in the wake of the rise of fascism, a movement that focused on persecuting aliens and the weak. It was leading to "a war between classes or a war between peoples, and the war in Palestine is a part of the war between peoples."[136] At the same time, Eliyahu Golomb sketched a different perspective: "We are in a country where there is a war on between two peoples." The struggle between Jews and Arabs revolved around the question, "What will the nature of this country be?" If the problem were just incitement and class conflict, it would be easier to solve. But the truth of the matter was that the Arab fellahin also wanted the country to remain Arab. "We speak about gangs as if they are only murderers," Golomb continued: "But there are also those among them who are sacrificing their lives for their nationalist aspirations."[137]

As months passed and the riots worsened—especially in November 1937 and the summers of 1938 and 1939—self-restraint became the central topic of discussion within the youth movements. This issue was ideally suited for generating an open-ended discussion in the youth movement. There was the moral dimension, the dilemma for which there was no clear-cut answer, and the possibility to go on at length without exhausting the topic. But beyond that, the young people pressured their instructors to keep on addressing the issue because they had trouble internalizing the views of the leadership. On the one hand, the leaders preached to them about their duty to practice self-defense and the importance of continued efforts in the construction of Palestine. One the other, they cautioned restraint; and, at least during the first phase of the riots, the leadership resigned itself to the loss of hard-won property, contradicting all the principles it had espoused.

The entire gamut of possible views was manifest in discussions on self-restraint: from the notion that the Arabs were enemies and that everything was permissible in the struggle against them to views that were fundamentally opposed to any bloodshed whatsoever. One girl complained that although it was well and good to say it was forbidden to kill innocent Arabs, it was also forbidden to allow them to murder Jews, who were most certainly innocent of any crime, without responding to those killings. Another commented that the time had arrived for Jews to be "a little bit egoistic" in matters affecting their survival. One boy asserted that the strength of Zionism derived from the moral conviction it infused its followers with and that any undermining of moral principles was tantamount to undermining Zionism. The two slogans expressing the poles of opinion in the discussion were "Thou shalt not kill" and "Whoever comes to kill you—kill him first."[139]

It is difficult to pinpoint the true mood that dominated those meetings. It appears that most of the young people were fed up with all the talk about self-restraint. There were some who responded with laughter when hearing about injury to Arabs; on the other hand, they were shocked about the Jerusalem incident, where children had danced around the body of a dead Arab. A young woman who took the minutes of one of the long discussions indicated graphically what she thought about the deliberations by doodling in the margin: a figure of a girl with a big yawn on her face.[139] The discussions were not marked by a particularly high intellectual level, and their reasoning was certainly not original. Nonetheless, the arguments articulated there reflected the feeling of a "typical youth" facing events that by definition contradicted everything he had been taught. "We live in a world of destruction, of fraternal war, with no thought about morality or the principles on which our movement is founded," commented one nineteen-year-old.[140] Most of the members attempted to find a compromise between the worldview they had acquired and the hard facts visible from their very window, staring them in the face. They rejected pure moralistic views, but also repudiated the approach of the IZL. They embraced the teachings of their instructors that for Jews to use methods identical with those of the Arabs would play into the hands of the latter and amount to an adoption of traits associated with the enemy. They rejected terrorism on the ground that it was counterproductive and undermined confidence in the moral rightness of the movement.

However, these talks had a significant impact in respect to their approach to the use of force. "Nowadays, the moral person is the one who has power," proclaimed one of the young men. "Our entire survival in Palestine is based on power," another remarked. Here and there, some expressed old notions of power in the sense of the creation of a critical mass in Palestine and presented the continuation of the development of the Yishuv as the proper answer to Arab terror. Yet others began to deal with the problem of power in its physical sense. "If we could conquer Palestine without bloodshed, then it would certainly be a good thing," one said: "But we are operating under circumstances where occasionally our blood must be shed and also, in given cases, where we must shed the blood of others." The feeling *There is no alternative* appeared between the lines in other remarks: "The situation now is such that there is no alternative except war. We are *compelled* to take up the rifle." From here, it was not far to the conclusion, "There is no possibility of building Palestine without waging a war for every inch of its soil."[141] Tabenkin expressed the feeling of many when he stated in the council of Ha-Noar ha-Oved that "we are involved in a battle because we have no other choice."[142]

The conclusion that suggested itself then but became more explicit with time was that idealistic youth was obligated to take up the task of fighting for the sake of the entire people. Tabenkin laid the ideological foundation for integrating youth into the defense forces. As was customary in his presentations, he spread out the broad panoramic view of a worldwide struggle between the forces of light and darkness, including the struggle of the Zionist Labor movement as an integral part of it. Tabenkin noted that the movement taught its disciples to strive for peace and brotherhood between peoples as its final goal; yet its duty was also to inculcate the necessary traits to achieve that goal: "It is inconceivable that our people will not be taught to defend themselves as Zionists and socialists." In the parallelogram of forces in which the Fascist camp was aiding the Arabs, "this means that we must prepare our people for participation in this war: a war on behalf of humanity, on behalf of the workers, on behalf of the Jews."[143]

Tabenkin's words symbolized a fundamental change in the teachings of the movement. The slogan of the movement since its inception had been "For labor, defense, and peace"; but "defense" had been interpreted at most along the lines of the stand at Tel Hai. "The fighting factor as an element in the building of Palestine was not prominent in our education" is how one of the girls tried to account for the failure of young people to respond actively after the outbreak of the riots.[144] The youth movements in Palestine did not emphasize physical might, and most certainly did not train their members for a life as fighters. The goal the movement aimed at was "living up to one's ideals," expressed in a life of cooperation and equality in a kibbutz. Physical labor was the supreme value and the preferred way of life. Thus, an unfamiliar element—even repellent to many—now entered the world picture of the youth movement.[145]

That shift did not affect the ideology of just the youth movements but had an impact on the thinking of the entire Labor movement. A movement that was adept at training its pioneers to be settlers and workers of the soil prepared, if necessary, to defend themselves was now required to revamp its worldview, accommodating it to the fact that they also had to be fighters. In talking about the "image of man that embodies the value of life," Tabenkin noted, "We have to develop his spirit and body for the task of being a settler, enterprising in labor. But that is not enough. The ideal man we envision requires one additional virtue; he must be a *defender*. He must do whatever is necessary for organizing self-defense and do so consciously, in terms of a carefully thought-out plan."[146]

Only now did the cognizance of just how central defense was in the life of the Yishuv begin to penetrate into the consciousness of the members of the movement. Israel Galili—one of the founders of Ha-Noar ha-Oved and a kibbutz member, as well as one of the key figures in the Hagana from the mid-1930s on (later an influential minister in the Israeli government)—wrote to his father: "Perhaps, dad, you'll be surprised about the spirit of militarism that's taken hold of me. It's not so. The love of life, the urge to act constructively and a love of freedom are what have induced me to regard the recruitment of Jews for defense as the principal focus for the present. Our social, cultural, and collective efforts in Palestine will not slacken. . . . But in addition to our work of colonization, we are now called upon to demonstrate our loyalty to ourselves and to our project by a massive mobilization for the police force and other security tasks."[147] Members of the movement had to be reeducated in order to take on the job of fighter as a part of their accepted and agreed-upon missions. In the summer of 1937, a seminar was held by Ha-Kibbutz ha-Meuhad at which Galili gave a long lecture on the Hagana—the need for it, its history, and sources. It appears that this was the first time a lecture of this type had been presented in the framework of a kibbutz organization.[148] That lecture signaled that the topic of fighting was being integrated within the value system of the Labor movement.

The penetration of the idea of the need to fight into the consciousness of adults was a kind of preface to efforts to inculcate this realization among youth. From a certain perspective, it was easier to introduce the concept to young people than to adults. Youth, as I have mentioned, was less prone to the influence of socialist ideology and more given to input and feedback from everyday reality. There was an adventurous magic about the fighter that had a greater attraction for young people than for adults. Yet in order to attract those considered to be the cream of the young, namely, those who had been brought up in the youth movements, a program of information and persuasion was necessary. Golomb, Galili, and Tabenkin did not spare efforts and spoke to their disciples in the youth movements. Each in his way underscored the vital importance of mobilizing members of the youth movements to the Hagana. Golomb stressed the gravity of the national conflict between Jews and Arabs in Palestine and the weakness of the government's response, which necessitated the creation of an independent Jewish force. Tabenkin praised the internal value of education for self-defense: "There is no socialist morality that can do without defense. It is a moral injunction for a people and the individual to defend themselves." He spoke in favor of "defense without uniforms," in which all the members of the movement would participate, both men and women.[149]

Youth movement members generally had a positive reaction to the new message. Thought about an effective response to Arab attacks, going beyond the perimeter fence, and organizing a nationwide defense system based on new methods stirred considerable enthusiasm in response to the feeling of strangulation and frustration generated by Arab terror and the policy of self-restraint. *Active defense* was the new concept that now emerged. One of the young men described the transition to active defense as a transition "from a feeling of exile to a feeling of homeland, in which we are more at home than the Arabs."[150] Yet many had grave reservations about the new direction. The change that had taken place in the scale of preferences of the movement awakened annoyance and concern. "Our members now are often no longer attracted by toiling on the soil," complained one young kibbutz member: "There's concern that we could lose our deep-rootedness. . . . All of Palestine is Hanita for us, but we should not let a temporary need bedazzle us."[151] People were apprehensive lest the new tendency lead to a growth in chauvinism and the emergence of a new style of life in which the prestige of the man who bears arms would be greater than that of the settler. There was also concern over exposing members of the youth movements to the tedium of military barracks and all the deadening external aspects of force and militarism, ranging from drilling exercises to uniforms and ranks. Yet over against all such misgivings, there was the dominant feeling of "We have no choice."[152]

Israel Galili was the man who led the youth movements to take on the burden of defense. A youth movement member since early adolescence, he endeavored to introduce this special idealistic element, previously lacking, into the framework of the Hagana. When he encountered criticism by members of Ha-Noar ha-Oved regarding the recruitment of its members to the Hagana, Galili replied: "The movement should not evade the tasks imposed on it by the circumstances. . . . There was a time when the only people who were preoccupied with such matters were those poor in spirit. Yet ever since *this task has become a central one in our lives,* we must send better emissaries [to the Hagana], . . . comrades who are rich in spirit." He demanded "that this task be added to the general action program of the movement."[153]

Several more years were to pass before the youth movements would find the appropriate framework that would allow them to be recruited to the forces for defense. Yet the basic psychological and moral decision was made at the time of the Arab Rebellion. This was the time when Jewish youth in Palestine took up the task of fighting as the special and distinctive mission of the generation. Just as the ideology of the Labor movement in Palestine and its central role in the process of colonization were shaped by their fathers, the sons took upon themselves the mission of molding the military might of the people. The decision contained a tacit recognition that at a certain point, youth would be called upon to decide the fate of Palestine by force.

The years of the Arab revolt sharpened and heightened the special relation that youth in Palestine had with the country. While educated to cherish and love the Jewish people, Zionism, and socialism, young people in Palestine reserved their true love for the country itself, the homeland. It was a possessive love, almost sensual, conscious, and without shame. One of the graduates of Kadoorie Agricultural School wrote to his mother in 1938, while stationed on the northern border, not far from Hanita, "If I were able to love my country even more, [I would do it now] when I pass along her border, acquainting myself with her beauty."[154] This love of the land had a major impact on the individual and was even more predominant in the domain of shared experience of the age-group. Members of the youth movement had their most formative experiences during trips and treks around the country. Already in the 1920s, the Herzliya Gymnasia in Tel Aviv had initiated a tradition of school trips; and the various youth movements followed suit. In the early 1930s Ha-Mahanot ha-Olim began to organize excursions throughout Palestine. They crossed over the northern border, going as far as Damascus on their trips. In 1934 they circled the Dead Sea and discovered the splendor of the desert. Excursions had always been a popular activity of youth movements everywhere. This was the origin of the German *Wandervogel*. The romanticism of an excursion to the bosom of nature combined with the challenge of physical effort, the ideal of simple life, mutual assistance, and the formation of a group of friends. In Palestine, this educational method was applied in order to impart a love for the land. The dynamics of youth movement life generated a desire for a group to join together in the open countryside, pass tests of physical endurance, and cope with the challenges of facing both nature and self. With the outbreak of the disturbances, such excursions took on a new importance. They were no longer naive outings by wanderers and hikers but constituted a comprehensive strategy designed to provide an answer to Arab terror while maintaining the policy of self-restraint. The excursion to all parts of the country was intended to familiarize youth movement members with every clod of earth, every hidden glade and grove. They had to learn how to move freely in Arab areas of the country, as well. In the Diaspora, Jews had been afraid to roam about in rural areas where they were few in number. That apprehension reflected the Jewish sense of alienness and nonbelonging. Free movement by Jews in mountainous areas inhabited by Arabs was a kind of mirror image of that old fear: It symbolized their right of patrimony to Palestine. This was a demonstration of Jewish presence, along with education for bold action and overcoming one's fears.[155]

During the dispute over partition, the intensity with which youth identified with Palestine was revealed. The 1937 partition plan put forward by the commission headed by Lord Peel proposing the establishment of two states in Palestine—one Jewish, one Arab—was in any event rejected out of hand by the Arab side. They still viewed themselves as the exclusive owners of Palestine and hoped to be rid of the other claimant to that right. Among Jews, however, a stormy debate developed. Chaim Weizmann, David Ben Gurion, and many others saw the partition proposal as a historical opportunity presented to the Zionist movement. Other leaders, such as Menahem Ussishkin, Yitzhak Tabenkin, Zeev Jabotinsky, Berl Katznelson, and Meir Ya'ari, were opposed to it—some for fundamental reasons, others for pragmatic reasons. The debate on partition exposed the presence of various layers of attitude relating to national myths, along with mature political understanding by a national movement that had descended from the heights of messianism to the solid ground of political reality. The topic of the use of force was marginal in this dispute. Both those who supported the partition plan and those who rejected it emphasized their desire to avoid the need for the use of force and saw their position as a derivative of that desire. Those in favor of partition viewed the state that would be established with British blessing (and, most probably, assistance) as a means to overcome the opposition among Arabs to Jewish colonization. They hoped that Arab fears regarding a Jewish majority would be mitigated when Jews were limited to the area of their own state. Partition could make it possible for a Jewish state to be established peacefully.

On the other hand, those opposed to partition, particularly Tabenkin and Ya'ari in the left-wing camp, argued that partition would stir a never-ending temptation and urge to take control of all of Palestine among both peoples and would necessarily augment militarism and chauvinism. Instead of reducing the friction between the two peoples, as hoped by the proponents of partition, it would increase tensions and lead to rising militancy. But it appears that the issue of the use of force did not serve as a genuine reason to oppose or support partition. Rather, it was the sort of argument people conventionally voice in favor of peace and against war. At least a segment of the proponents of partition saw the creation of a Jewish state as a bridgehead for continuing the expansion of Jewish settlement in Palestine. A large proportion of partition opponents were motivated not by fears about growing Jewish–Arab enmity but primarily by the covert hope that postponement of the establishment of two states in Palestine would make it possible for Jews eventually to take control of all of the country. The debate did not touch on the essence of the defensive ethos. Rather, it involved a question that had accompanied that ethos from its inception: Was time on the side of the Zionist project, and should political decisions therefore be postponed as much as possible? Or was time no longer favorable for Zionism and the time thus arrived for historical decisions? In 1937 opinions on this issue were still divided.

The proposal on partition triggered an upsurge of feelings of love for, and solidarity with, their homeland among the majority of Jewish youth in Palestine and impassioned opposition to any idea of sharing it with another people. This stand was accepted by the preponderant majority of the youth movements except, perhaps, the Gordonists. It was also in keeping with the psychology of youth, the inclination at that age to think in terms of absolute categories of good and evil, and instinctively to oppose compromises seen to be unaesthetic and a manifestation of inexcusable weakness. In the summer of 1937 Ha-Mahanot ha-Olim, the most "Palestinian" of the youth movements, held a camp at Kibbutz Gevat. That camp functioned to crystallize the educational myths of the movement under the sign of opposition to any partition of Palestine. The young disciples went on many outings to the mountains of Galilee. They learned the map of Palestine and its geography and history—in particular the maps of the Kingdom of Israel at the time of the First Temple and the Hasmonean Kingdom at the time of the Second Temple. They read biblical and literary texts that exalted the grandeur of the land and internalized all this as a single, interconnected web.

For these Ha-Mahanot ha-Olim disciples, the mutual relation between themselves and the land was a psychological, cultural, and physical symbiosis. These young men and women attributed an intrinsic value to the bond between those who had been born and raised in Palestine and their homeland. It was believed that Palestine inculcated a distinctive way of behavior, life-style and outlook on life in its native children. Signs of a "native-born" mentality began to appear. In the booklet concluding the summer camp, significantly entitled "In Your Covenant," there is repeated use of the expressions "natural feeling," "native of the land," "people of the land," "spirit of Palestine," "a boy born in Palestine," and "native son." The distinction between those born in Palestine and those who came from the Diaspora is stressed. In a description of new immigrants in the kibbutz, a young girl wrote: "The smell of the Diaspora still exudes from them. A doubt arises in me whether the kibbutz will know how to educate them and to implant in them the spirit of Palestine."[156] The Diaspora is described as "life without a homeland, separation from the soil, physical and mental debility." In the modern period, "the image of man was lost. . . . [There was] antisemitism. The bread of affliction steeped in sighs, drenched with tears, towns filled with filth and abomination, ghettoes, . . . acculturation, assimilation—the massacre of Kishinev—cities of slaughter."[157] Just as the people in the Diaspora suffered from a loss of its human image, likewise Palestine, after having been abandoned by that people, turned into a wasteland and lost its fertility: "summer droughts, desolation of generations, eternal swamps."[158] There is a mystical bond between the people and the land, expressed in mutual loyalty between the two over many generations; the rupture of that bond led to degeneration.

"A covenant between us and the land" was the final conclusion of the seminar.[159] It was accompanied by a powerful feeling of being masters in the land, a feeling that was not theoretical or ideological but, rather, almost physical in nature: "I simply love this land, without any second thoughts. I love its landscape, feel its beauty; and I do not want to give it up," one of the young women stated. Another spoke in more mythical concepts: "One cannot divide up the homeland. One cannot cut up the mother's bosom. . . . How to educate the young generation? Will it yearn for a split plot of land, a mutilated body?" Another wrote: "A man is the image of his homeland's landscape. What shape will you have, my child, if your landscape is decapitated?"[160] During trips in the surrounding area, the feeling of ownership of Palestine returned with new strength. When the signs of a Jewish village appeared in the landscape, they noted, "How good . . . to feel that the soil we are treading on is *ours* and the forest is *our forest*"—then exclaimed, "Can anyone uproot the feeling of unity and wholeness of the land, planted in the depth of the heart? Is it possible to eradicate from one's heart the sense of the homeland living within us, people of the land, within the depths of the soul? Can an imposed border split the mountain chain, sunder *our fields,* tear apart *our forests?*"[161] One of the most pointed expressions of the strong sense of ownership is contained in the following passage: "A story was told in these days about a youth who cried when he saw the map of the Royal Commission. Then I understood: This is the immediate reaction, the intuitive response of a native son."[162] Someone born in Palestine is expected to react differently to the partition plan than a person who was not brought up in Palestine, who did not drink in its landscapes, did not feel himself to be a part of its past and future. The Palestinian, native-born identity of the generation of the sons and daughters was marked by an immediate, direct bond with the country. Even the way they related to it through the prism of the Bible and Hebrew literature was different from that of the Jew for whom Palestine was an abstract love. Among those young people, every idiom and phrase was linked to the landscape, to everyday experiences, to chapters of living reality.

During their excursions through Galilee, it was impossible for those young people not to encounter Arabs along the way. But to read their descriptions, it would seem as though they did not see any Arabs at all. They were expert at spotting ancient Jewish settlements from the biblical and postbiblical eras. The myths of Gush Halav, Yodefat, and Zippori spoke to them directly. When they gazed at the landscapes of Galilee, Gilboa, and Bet Netofa Basin, they were impressed by the desolation or the sight of Jewish settlements. But the Arab villages and bedouin encampments dotting these areas awakened in them only an extremely superficial response. Yosef Braslavsky's article "Do You Know the Land?" included in the Ha-Mahanot ha-Olim *In Your Covenant* booklet encouraged the young people to study also their neighbors in Palestine. That acquaintance was not meant to serve the objectives of "Know thy enemy." Nevertheless, its goal was not friendship and fraternity along the lines of Ziegfried Lehmann in Ben Shemen. Braslavsky understood this to be part of becoming acquainted with the land of Palestine as a whole. In the view of those youngsters, the Arabs were part of the Palestinian landscape, a stone among its stones. They seldom described any visits to Arab villages within Palestine. In contrast, they were generous when it came to descriptions of the welcoming of guests among Arabs beyond the borders of Palestine—as if the border of Palestine were the boundary of competition. In the light of an expression of friendliness in one of the villages on the Lebanese side of the border, the young men remembered that "in the past, as well, there was an alliance between us and the state of Tyre."[163] Here and there, one can sense the feeling of tension and an incipient awareness of the Jewish–Arab conflict. But this was not the central motif. They had no doubt that all of Palestine was their country, that they had no intention to share it with anyone else, and that ultimately they would control the entire length and breadth of it. When they passed the fields of the Arab village of Manara high in the

Naphtali mountains, someone commented that this land had been "redeemed" and that a Jewish settlement would soon be established there. When they gazed from there down to the Hula Valley, "there was a pervading silence, and a whispering wind whispered: 'Step by step, we will also conquer the mountains, the mountains of Galilee, the Golan and Gilead, the mountains of Ephraim, and the bare hills of Judea'."[164] It appears that they regarded these areas, most of which were densely populated by Arab villages, as though they were empty of inhabitants.

In the final party of the summer camp, a program with a potpourri of passages from the Bible was put on, quoting the divine promise of the land of Israel to the people of Israel, the story of the spies, and the positive conclusion of Caleb: "Let us go up at once and occupy the country; we are well able to conquer it" (Numbers 13:30). From there they passed on to passages describing the Jewish people in the ancient past as agriculturalists. Passages from Bialik's "Scroll of Fire" marked the war of destruction of the Temple. The exile was described with references ranging from "By the Rivers of Babylon" to "Zion, Do You Not Ask About the Welfare of Your Captives?" and the climax of Bialik's "In the City of Slaughter." From there they went on to a description of the rebirth, "Comfort Ye, Comfort Ye My People," and modern poems. The most popular of the poets was Rachel, with her modest, simply crafted poems about toil. At the end, the Arab plotting against building up the land was described, utilizing passages from Ezra and Nehemiah, telling how the Jews had managed to overcome the scheming of neighbors against the Return of Zion in ancient times. The ensemble of passages was concluded by a few lines that served as a kind of digest and reduction of the world outlook of those young persons, making use of phrases lifted from Shimonovitz' poem "Like a Vision of Hope": "Ours is a war against nature, a war against the cutting down of the homeland, against a difficult enemy [the Arabs], against the indifferent, mocking stranger [the British]. As *then,* so it is now: *That* is our convenant with the land. Since that time, its taste has not turned stale, it was not parched dry by centuries of drought. It is vital, a flame still blazing in the faithful heart."[165]

There was a pathos in these words, and they contained references to historical symbols and ancient myths to an extent previously unknown within that youth movement. On the whole, their national feeling did not nurture a romantic, messianic mysticism of the kind that inspired Avraham Stern and his associates. It was founded primarily on a direct physical bond between the sons of Palestine and its open spaces. The myths were meant to encourage this instinctive bond, nothing more. This was the essential difference between their nationalistic leanings and those of the generation of their fathers, in general—and the Palestinian Right, in particular. The references in the booklet *In your Covenant* to the heroes of the past, Simeon the Hasmonean, Yohanan from Gush Halav, and the glories of the days of the First and Second Temple certainly did not deviate from the accepted norms of cultural reference in the Labor movement. The somewhat dry account of their ascent to Massada ("All the way we walked and thought: It was here! On the top of that fortress, our ancestors fought to protect their freedom")[166] had nothing in common with the obsession with the glories of the past characteristic of Abba Ahimeir or Uri Zvi Greenberg. But this time those past glories were underscored by the fact that they were presented alone, without the mitigating balance of socialist myths that had been so prominent in earlier years. This new emphasis hinted at a change in the current, in the direction of enlarging the nationalist component at the expense of the socialist component within the emotional and intellectual education of youth movement members. Socialism was their fathers' ideology. The land was theirs, theirs alone. This feeling was accompanied by a fierce sense of possessiveness, of joyous anticipation of the fight for it.

At the close of this era, Eliezer Rieger, one of the veteran educators in Palestine, postulated that there were four different approaches among Jewish youth to the Arab question: the "primitive approach," the "approach of self-disparagement," the "approach of dismissal," and the "fatalistic approach." He attributed the primitive approach to persons from Islamic countries, contending that they transferred Arab treatment of the weak in their countries of origin to the system of Jewish–Arab relations in Palestine. In Rieger's view, this perspective was neither widespread nor popular. Those with the approach of self-disparagement argued that Jews must work out a general accord and compromise with the Arabs or face destruction. Fears of a "massacre of Saint Bartholomew" and of the "ocean of Arabs" engendered defeatist thinking within such groups. This approach, he suggested, could be found among the Orthodox Jews of the old Yishuv and among immigrants from Germany; but "among those born in Palestine and in the new Yishuv, there are, for all practical purposes, no examples of this type." The two final categories of approach were widespread among youth. Those who adhered to the approach of dismissal disparaged the Arabs as a people. They regarded them as backward and inferior to Jews in ability and talent, education and idealism. In their eyes, a genuine Arab national movement did not exist. Rather, there was a kind of substitute, ersatz movement, an artificial construct inflated by the British bureaucracy and emissaries of the fascist powers. According to proponents of this perspective, "a club and a strong hand" was the way to solve the problem. The fatalistic approach, in Rieger's analysis, was especially current among youth but could also be readily encountered among adults. According to this approach, both Jews and Arabs lay claim to Palestine. There was an inherent and unbridgable clash of interests between them. One justice clashed here with another; and only a "slash of the sword" could cut this Gordian knot. Consequently, "from this perspective, a bloody decisive battle between them and us is inevitable"; and "however bitter that destiny may be for the transitional generation, necessity is a cruel master."[167]

Such an angle of vision was the evolutionary product of the approach common in the Labor movement in earlier years. At least in part, it would appear to be reminiscent of the early conceptions of Jabotinsky, who viewed Arab opposition to Jewish entry into Palestine as a constant factor unamenable to change, one that necessitated an "iron wall." Yet the truth of the matter is that this was the conclusion of people who had been educated to believe that it was possible to colonize in peace. Three years of Arab revolt, however, had convinced them of the seriousness of Arab opposition and of the inevitability of an armed clash. It was not incidental that this view was especially current among the youth. It reflected a frame of mind natural to those who had grown up in the shadow of a national confrontation. The second generation in the process of colonization, who felt that they were the natural sons of Palestine, were more tough and ready to face reality—a reality their fathers had tried to avoid confronting.

"Thus, we adopted the cult of force even before we adopted force itself" is how Rieger defined the attitude of youth toward the Arabs.[168] That definition would appear to express ideas that were quite prevalent among young people who had come of age during the years of the Arab Rebellion but did not reflect the educational ideal in the Yishuv during that period. Despite serious tensions deriving from the character of the era, the defensive ethos continued to be the guiding ethos of the preponderant majority of the Jewish community in Palestine, including the Labor movement. Its erosion at that time was a product of three factors: (1) the pressures of the international situation, which glorified heroes of physical might; (2) the pressures generated by the Arab Rebellion, which called into question the reasonableness of the hypothesis that it was possible to establish the national home without resorting to force; and (3) British policies, manifested in the White Paper of 1939. The White Paper was interpreted by contemporaries as marking the end of the alliance between the Jews and Great Britain. This had a direct implication for the temporal question, Was time working in favor of, or against, the national home? If it was no longer possible to promote immigration and Jewish settlement in Palestine because of British policy, then the entire evolutionary conception was undermined—and with it the defensive ethos. The Zionist movement had finally attained a point that Jabotinsky believed it had reached some fifteen years previously. It had achieved major progress during that period and had no reason to regret the fact that it postponed the confrontation as long as possible and did not hasten its coming. But in 1939 the question still stood: Was there any sense in continuing a policy that was aimed primarily at gaining time?

Radical circles concentrated around Lehi were of the opinion that the moment was ripe for an armed confrontation. Yet the overwhelming majority of the Yishuv, especially its leaders, did not cast off the defensive ethos and the evolutionary approach. In this way, a situation was created in which both a defensive and an offensive ethos existed side by side. In the conscious sphere, the defensive ethos continued to reign supreme, especially in the light of the appoaching world war, a crisis that produced a kind of moratorium on the Palestine question. Simultaneously, in another sphere, the ethos of the fighter continued to evolve. It was nurtured by a growing recognition of the ineluctability of the imminent confrontation, a sense that Jewish military might was on the increase, and the consciousness that in the end it was likely that the problem could be solved only by resorting to force. The sense of frustration over the standstill in the progress of the national home and chagrin about British policy helped explain and legitimate the ongoing erosion of the defensive ethos. On the other hand, the existence of that ethos continued to provide a source of self-justification for the Zionist movement—which still envisioned itself as a movement of peace.

7

Consolidation, 1939–1947

The nine years between September 1939 and May 1948 were perhaps the most traumatic in Jewish history. World War II, the Holocaust, the problem of the Jewish
refugees, the struggle to establish a Jewish state, and, ultimately, the emergence of
that state were a series of events that left contemporaries stunned by their magnitude and breathless by their rapidity. If someone in the Jewish community in Palestine had prophesied in 1939 that Jews would have a state of their own within nine
years, he would have been branded a visionary. There was no one who even imagined that the Jews of Europe were facing imminent destruction. Those who pon-
dered the approaching war and its conjectured impact on the Jews in Europe
thought in terms of previous conflicts and familiar types of calamity: hunger, refugees, the hardships of warfare, pogroms. Human imagination did not extend
beyond that perimeter of possible catastrophe. The Holocaust and the establishment of the State of Israel, the two foci of the era's ellipse, were conceived as the
pole of destruction and the poll of redemption. "You are a last true kindness for
those who lie still / And a grace of a first smile for those who survived, empty," wrote
Nathan Alterman, describing the "morning star," that star of hope that would rise
after the night of the slaying of the firstborn, in "Poems on the Ten Plagues," his
first response to the Holocaust.[1]

Between these two momentous polar events lay a series of other significant
developments. Rommel's forward drive in the West Egyptian desert (spring 1941
and 1942), a campaign that prompted the British authorities to make plans for a
total pullback as far as Iraq, had a profound impact on the psyche of the Jewish
community in Palestine. The Yishuv feared the worst and felt it was faced with a
harrowing possibility: total physical annihilation, either by the future German
occupiers or at the hands of the Arabs in Palestine, who were expected to cooperate
with the Germans. At this same time, there were several key episodes in attempts
to immigrate to Palestine: the cases of the refugee boats *Patria, Atlantic,* and
Struma. Each in a different way, the fate of these ships reflected the absolute help-

lessness of the Jews. Another blow was the policy of the Labour government that had come to power in Britain in the summer of 1945. That policy was the total reversal of the pledges the party had made when it had been on the opposition benches; it disappointed the excessive expectations the Yishuv had entertained about the possible revocation of the White Paper in the wake of British victory in the war. Other salient factors in the evolving situation were the struggle against the British, acts of terror and British reprisals, the encounter with the remnant of European Jewry, and illegal immigration to Palestine.

Each of these individual events was powerful enough in its own right to stamp its imprint on an era. Yet now, in an extremely brief and concentrated span of time, all merged together. The 1940s had been marked by a succession of traumatic developments, creating an apocalyptic atmosphere, rich in messianic expectations. That mood was permeated by a mystic faith that the millions of victims and all the unspeakable suffering and anguish could not have been in vain: Some court of higher justice must duly recompense the Jewish people for its supreme ordeal.

The Zionist leadership was faced with a complicated mission: to convert those apocalytic expectations into hard political cash. More than in any other period, the people were ready to dedicate themselves to the struggle and make the requisite sacrifices. One of the pivotal questions of the era was, How can this readiness be directed into channels conducive to achieving political gains? As we shall see, the diverse interpretations as to the best way for advancing the Zionist cause led to bitter disputes, many of which have a relevance for what is the central topic here, namely, the use of force.

Time, Evolutionism, and the Final Goal

It is in the nature of war to disclose aspirations, desires and aims that otherwise lie buried in the deepest recesses of the human heart. That could be seen in the case of the Zionist movement during World Wars I and II. As will be recalled, World War I transformed the Zionist enterprise from one of dozens of ephemeral currents aspiring to realize nationalist goals into a recognized national movement, an ally of Great Britain in its takeover of Palestine. At that time, there were those in the Zionist movement who believed that the historic opportunity should be seized: It was necessary to create political faits accomplis as soon as possible in Palestine. The feeling that the war offered a special opportunity for accelerating the process and taking advantage of historical shortcuts was a natural conclusion, since the war had reopened discussion more generally on questions of government, sovereignty, and national borders. As I have mentioned, a messianic fervor had prevailed in Palestine during the recruitment campaign for the Jewish legion. The war created exaggerated expectations regarding the nature of the national home and the possible pace of its development (see chapter 3).

Zionism as a political movement was comparatively young, with little historical memory prior to the decade of World War I. That era was the matrix for Weizmann's leadership, who continued to serve as president of the Zionist Organization during World War II. Those years were also a formative period for David Ben Gurion, Berl Katznelson, and Eliyahu Golomb, who enlisted in the Jewish Legion. Consequently, it was only natural that when they turned their attention to the possible impact of the new war on the fate of the Zionist project, they thought in concepts borrowed from their experience in World War I. Moshe Shertok, Golomb, Ben Gurion, and Weizmann carried on an untiring campaign to set up a Jewish unit within the framework of the British Army. Initially, it was supposed to be a division; but ultimately, after relentless Jewish pressure and unbelievable difficulties raised by the British authorities, the Jewish Brigade was organized in 1944. The stress on the importance of the participation of a Jewish combat unit, under a blue and white flag emblazoned with the Star of David, was a return to the old pattern of thinking that assumed that whoever participates in the war as a belligerent party would be entitled to a seat at the peace deliberations table. Their experience with World War I taught them that it was doubtful whether that principle would actually be applied in practice. Despite this, when they found themselves in a similar situation, they hurried to adopt the same instrument, hoping with its aid to spur change in the system of political forces. The truth of the matter is that they also had other objectives in mind, such as Jewish participation in the war against Hitler, or provision of military training for Jews from Palestine. Yet those objectives were obtainable by simply joining the British Army, which is what most of the recruits did in the early years of the war. However, the leadership attached paramount importance to the achievement of the desired status of a belligerent party and devoted an enormous amount of time and energy to its attainment. In the end, the Jewish Brigade participated in the Italian campaign on the River Senio. Yet its true importance would lie in another field: the encounter after the war with survivors of the camps in Europe. Meeting with the brigade members gave those survivors a sense of pride and national identity, firing them with the burning hope for speedy redemption in Palestine. As to the political hopes the leadership pinned on the brigade, these did not prove any better founded than hopes attached earlier to the Jewish Legion.

Though their historical experience led them to think in terms of World War I, the realities of the new war weighed down upon them, blocking out excessive hopes. The difference between the situation faced by the Jewish people during World War I and the present was enormous. At that time, both sides had courted the Jews as a potential source of political power. That had given the Zionist movement a certain latitude for maneuvering, and it proved able to exploit this to its benefit. However, in World War II there were no options for engaging in such maneuvers. Like it or not, Jews were obligated to give unconditional support to the Allied camp, since the adversary was the greatest enemy of the Jews of all time. Even in their own camp, the Jewish position was quite weak, as manifested by publication of the White Paper in May 1939. That document placed severe restrictions on immigration and land purchase by Jews in Palestine and stipulated that after a ten-year period, a Palestinian state was to be set up, based on majoritarian rule. It was clear that this proposed state would have an Arab majority. Right down to the outbreak of the war, there were angry protest actions in the Yishuv against the White Paper. With the eruption of hostilities, Ben Gurion coined the slogan "We must help the British in their struggle as if there were no White Paper, and we must resist the White Paper as if there were no war." In practical terms, however, the Zionist leadership aban-

doned the fight against Britain and dedicated itself to promoting maximum participation of the Jewish community in the war effort.

Nonetheless, one of the lessons learned in World War I was clearly applicable
to the catastrophic circumstances of the new war, namely, the urgency of defining
national goals and objectives. Shortly after the beginning of the war, ideas were
expressed about the need for the Zionist movement to declare its war objectives.
The first public discussion on these questions took place at the end of 1940, in a
Mapai gathering at which Berl Katznelson gave the principal address. During the
debate in 1937 on the partition plan proposed by the Peel Commission, Katznelson
had been one of its outspoken opponents. He had contended that it was a mistake
to push forward with the establishment of the Jewish state prematurely, since such
an untimely birth was likely to be abortive. He had called for adherence to the mandate: As long as it was possible to progress in line with the accepted evolutionary
method, one should continue with the work of building the land, and attempt to
postpone final decisions on the fate of Palestine.[2] This had been a continuation of
the line pursued by the Labor movement almost since the beginning of the 1920s.
As I mentioned earlier, that line was manifested in the confrontation with Jabotinsky in 1931, when he had tried to push the Zionist movement to declare its final
goal. Katznelson at that time was one of those bitterly opposed to any declaration
of supposed final goals. He felt such a declaration had no practical value; rather, it
was a superfluous provocation of the Arabs. Now, in December 1940, Katznelson
came out in favor of declaring the final goal, namely, a Jewish state in Palestine.
Concealing the banner of the Jewish state in previous years, he contended, had
never meant the abandonment of that goal. Aside from a small number of Zionists
who truly began to believe in the declared minimal objectives, no one, either Arab
or British, ever thought that the Zionist movement would be satisfied with anything
less than a Jewish state. Rather, it was the weakness of the movement and the lack
of an international opportunity that dictated restraint in declarations. Now, he continued, two things had taken place that obligated the movement to speak up loud
and clear. One was the White Paper, which effectively curbed the possibility of
future evolutionary development; the other was the world war, which had reopened
the account books of international politics. In the past, it had been possible to utilize
all sorts of camouflage methods: "In political life, there are situations in which one
acts according to the saying 'Everyone knows why the bride gets married, but [who-
ever mentions it talks dirty.]'"[3] But now, from the very day the Peel Commission
declared that a Jewish state was a viable possibility, the Zionist movement was pre-
empted from declaring any goal that fell short of it.[4]

Katznelson's speech was in effect the death knell of the evolutionary conception. He and his associates still preferred to keep on progressing at a slow pace in
line with the evolutionary method. But international events and the development
of the Arab national movement compelled them to make an early decision, which
they thought they were not as yet ready for. The feeling was that time was no longer
on the Jewish side; that the previous method had exhausted itself; and, most fundamentally, that a revolutionary situation had reappeared, offering an opportunity
that the movement was obligated to seize by the horns.

At the 1940 Mapai conference, there was no discussion following Katznelson's iconoclastic statements. However, there can be no doubt that his comments had an impact. Ben Gurion spoke in a similar vein on various occasions; and his views ultimatley crystallized into the Biltmore Program, adopted by U.S. Jewry in 1942 as the war aims of the Jewish people. The program spoke about establishing Palestine as a commonwealth, opening up the country to unlimited immigration after the war, and giving the Jewish Agency the authority to administer matters of immigration and the development program for Palestine. Its essential importance was that it presented a Jewish state in Palestine as the war goal of the Jewish people.

In November 1942, a few days before the terrible reports about the Holocaust were confirmed, there was an extensive discussion in the Inner Zionist Actions Committee in Jerusalem on the Biltmore Program. The deliberations touched on the basic questions of Zionist policy—namely the problem of time, of evolutionism versus revolutionary shortcuts—and ultimately arrived at the issue of the Arab question.

The preponderant majority of participants supported the Biltmore Program. Three were opposed to it: Meir Ya'ari, the Marxist leader of Ha-Shomer ha-Tzair; Shlomo Kaplansky, who had been an opponent of Labor leadership when it came to the Arab question ever since the conference at Ein Harod in 1924; and Sally Hirsch, the representative of Aliyah Hadasha (New Immigration), a moderate, liberal party with dovish views, whose electorate was composed mainly of voters of Central European origin. The opponents to the Biltmore plan represented only a small fraction of the Yishuv. But since what was at stake here was approval of a national program intended to serve as a symbol of national resolve, directed to the world at large, the debate was conducted as though two equal camps were involved, as if it was still possible by verbal persuasion to convince people to change their minds.

The dispute with Ha-Shomer ha-Tzair touched basically on the question of a shift from the evolutionary to the revolutionary method. The Biltmore Program assumed that immediately after the end of the war, there would be a massive wave of unlimited and nonselective immigration to Palestine. Since details about the extent of the Holocaust were as yet unknown, there were expectations that millions of refugees would seek a haven in Palestine and the possibility to begin a new life. Ya'ari viewed that as a departure from the method of limited and selective immigration, which had been pursued by the Zionist Organization since the mandate. In his eyes, the new method was dangerously close to revisionist thinking. As an example of the perverted thinking of the shortcut, he referred to the Nordau plan proposed in the early 1920s: It had envisaged the immigration of a half million Jews within the course of a year. The idea of abandoning the slow method of "acre by acre" in favor of the final goal, realized here and now, was something Ya'ari totally rejected. In its place, he proposed continuing on with the old system but pressing ahead more energetically. He was disturbed by the radical political declaration and the quick pace of implementation; in his view, this entailed abandoning humane and educational qualities. Ya'ari elaborated the point that a transition from evolutionary to revolutionary Zionism contradicted the aims of the Labor movement. But the main issue which all three principal opponents of the Biltmore Program agreed upon was the Arab question.

Since the suppression of the Arab Rebellion by the British in the summer of 1939, the Arab question had disappeared from the agenda of the Yishuv. The Arab community was busy nursing the wounds it had suffered over the course of three years of violent unrest. The mufti of Jerusalem, al-Hajj Amin al-Husayni, the principal leader of the Arabs in Palestine, had fled the country; and the leadership of the Arab National movement appeared to be weak and inactive. It went on record as opposed to the White Paper on the grounds that that document did not unequivocally prohibit immigration and spoke about the establishment of a Palestinian state only after a decade. Another uprising was out of the question, both for political and military reasons. It appeared that the British were coming closer to the Arab point of view. Although they were still quite far from meeting the Arab demands, the process was proceeding in a positive direction from the Arab perspective. On the other hand, Arab losses had been heavy, and time was necessary in order to recuperate from them. The war period, in which a large British army was stationed in Palestine and nearby, was not the proper time for an uprising, which would have been quenched immediately by heavy force. When the front approached Palestine and it looked like the British were going to lose the battle, panic spread among the Arabs who were British sympathizers; and support for the Axis powers rose. These matters were especially pronounced in connection with the pro-Nazi revolt of Rashid Ali al-Gailani in Iraq in 1941. On the whole, however, the Arab community in Palestine remained a passive element in the occurrences both during the war and afterward. The years 1939–1947 were apparently the longest continuous period of quiet and relative tranquillity in Arab–Jewish relations in Palestine since the 1920s.[5]

Just as the Arab question had been marginal and was only discussed sporadically prior to the rebellion, after it subsided the question was once again shunted to the periphery. Attention was focused on the difficult and demanding problems of the hour. As usual after a series of disputes, it seemed as though the subject had been exhausted and there was nothing new to add on the basic questions. Moreover, the White Paper effected a major shift in the front of struggle: from Jews against Arabs to Jews against the British. The Arabs were again relegated to a secondary role in public awareness and interest. Among the so-called mainstream of the Labor movement, there was a mounting sense of resignation; people accepted the notion that the riots had done much to instill, namely, that an irreconcilable clash of interests existed between Jews and Arabs in Palestine. Acquiescence in its presumed irreconcilable nature was one of the factors that served to lessen interest in the Arab question beyond the functional sphere of security at that time. There were no longer discussions about the nature of the Arab problem and the question of what should be done to break down barriers between Jews and Arabs, whether it was possible to arrive at an accord, and so on—issues previously high on the Mapai agenda. It would appear that the general consensus regarding the dispute had abrogated the need to talk about it.

Our information on this point is derived principally from Ha-Shomer ha-Tzair sources that voice protest about it. Members of Ha-Shomer ha-Tzair repeatedly called on people to reject the fatalistic view that "as far as the bloody riots are concerned, there is an absolute law of necessary periodicity."[6] Ha-Shomer ha-Tzair activists warned against the view (which they claimed was quite common among the Mapai leadership) "that there is a clash between two national movements in Palestine, one that cannot be bridged by any sort of accord."[7] They complained about the dangerous similarity they discerned between the views of the revisionists and those of the Labor movement: "The revisionists talked about the *sha'atnez* [the impossible mixing together of socialism and nationalism]; and in our own ranks, what has been victorious is the theory of the unresolvable clash."[8] The decline in interest in the topic of a joint union was symptomatic. That idea, initially promoted within circles of the Labor movement mainstream, had already changed in the 1930s into a cause espoused mainly by the Left within the Histadrut. Mapai had also invested a certain amount of effort in the idea, though it had kept a lower profile and, unlike Ha-Shomer ha-Tzair and Left Poalei Zion, had not pinned extensive hopes on the scheme. Now the idea of a joint union became identified as an issue exclusively of the Left, a remnant from an earlier period in which people had believed in class explanations of the Arab question and had placed their hopes in the general advancement of society, expecting that progress would eventually eliminate the unfortunate misunderstandings between Jews and Arabs in Palestine.

Awareness of the existence of an irreconcilable Jewish–Arab conflict contained a subliminal assumption that this was a Gordian knot and could only be cut by the sword. That fact was increasingly evident in discussions on the Biltmore Program. Significantly, that program itself made no mention whatsoever of the Arabs. It presented Jewish claims to Palestine as though the country belonged to the Jews exclusively and the Arabs had no part in its future. All the compromise formulas from the congresses of the 1930s were cast aside. These had attempted to placate the British and Arabs when it came to the aims of the Zionist movement in Palestine. In the decisive moment of truth, the movement stated its position openly and without diplomatic motives. "Ben Gurion's proposal completely disregards the fact that a million Arabs live here together with us—as if they did not exist at all," a shocked Ya'ari wrote in the internal organ of Ha-Shomer ha-Tzair.[9] It meant that the leadership was prepared for the possibility that the Jewish state would materialize against the will of the Arabs. Ya'ari, Kaplansky, and Hirsch found it hard to come to terms with that option, rejecting it principally on moral grounds. The idea of one people ruling over another was deducible from the Biltmore Program, since if it were realized, there would, at the very least, necessarily be a large Arab minority in the Jewish state. They viewed this prospect as aggressive, unethical, and at odds with the traditions of the Zionist movement. Ya'ari reminded Ben Gurion of his earlier proposals, presented publicly with much enthusiasm during the years when the latter believed in the feasibility of a Jewish–Arab accord.

The ethical considerations of the opponents of the Biltmore Program were mixed with practical ones. It was inconceivable, they argued, that the nations of the world would support the establishment of a Jewish state that would rule over Arabs. On the whole, it would be better if the British remained for a prolonged period in the land as a guarantee against Arab aggression on the one hand, and the potential injustice of a Jewish regime that would dominate Arabs on the other, emphasized Sally Hirsch. In his view, the Zionist movement was bifurcated into two opposed camps: "One camp aspires to peace, understanding, and consideration of the other side" while "the second camp genuinely believes the problem can be solved by force."[10]

Unlike previous exchanges on the same matter, the discussion on this occasion was distinguished by its total candor and sober-headedness, devoid of any illusions. Katznelson seized on Ya'ari's comments, who claimed the Biltmore Zionists had a moral blind spot, since they wished to rule over another people: "It is possible that the desire to be a majority in a country in which another people is already the majority is foul. . . . If that is so, then we are foul" because beyond all the rhetoric that obscures the issue, the crux of the problem is that the Jews do not intend to deprive the Arabs of any rights as human beings, but they do wish to alter their political status in Palestine into that of the majority people. If there is a moral defect in this wish, then Ya'ari cannot wash his hands of it either, Katznelson argued, since he also wants a Jewish minority in Palestine. Katznelson was also at odds with the claim that the Labor movement had always valued evolutionary methods and opposed revolutionary steps. Not only did Ahdut ha-Avoda not reject Max Nordau's plan at the time, it even took pains to publish the proposal in its periodical *Kuntres*. Berl reminded his listeners that conceptions requiring shortcuts had been supported by the movement at the beginning of the 1920s. Sadly, the movement had given them up—because it was too weak to realize them, not because it thought they were defective. Now, since the "heavens"—frozen since the Balfour Declaration—had "opened up," the time had come to return to plans that had been stashed away for safekeeping. Now the movement and the moment were ripe to implement them, he contended.

Ben Gurion replied to the challenge raised by Hirsch regarding the use of force. "We are not yet living in the end of days, and require force to defend a good thing," he responded: "You can't disqualify force just because it's possible to put it to bad use." The battle of El Alamein had just been concluded: It had barely saved the Yishuv, preventing a German conquest of Palestine. In the Soviet Union, the cannon were thundering in the battle for Stalingrad. Ben Gurion's words had a special resonance in those days. He gave Hirsch a lesson on the history of Jewish colonization in Palestine: "When we came to Palestine, we didn't come to fight, kill, and be killed. We were idealists like you, and I think we have remained idealists. . . . We didn't come here to shed blood; and we saw that we had to, because we didn't want to be wards in Palestine." If the Jewish community in Palestine had no power of its own, he contended, the Arabs would obliterate it from the face of the earth. The crux of the matter was that there were no Arabs ready to accept any Jewish immigration to Palestine, no matter what its scope. The Arabs rejected the binational formulas of Ya'ari and his associates as much as the maximalist formulas espoused by the Biltmore proponents: "You are facing a situation you don't dare to look at realistically. There are no Arabs willing to agree to Jewish immigration, and we say to the world: Decide."[11] Ben Gurion and his associates assumed that after a horrifying world war, the victors would indeed be prepared to cut Gordian knots. By means of imposed decisions, they would resolve problems that were unamenable to solution by a negotiated accord. Palestine was one of the problem areas that required an imposed solution.

One of the topics raised during the debate on the Biltmore Program was the issue of population transfer, that is, the transfer of the Arabs from Palestine to one of the Arab countries. The topic had been first raised by the Peel Commission, which proposed an exchange of populations between Arabs who were living in the parts of Palestine designated as part of the future Jewish state and Jews from the areas set aside for the Arab state. The issue took on renewed relevance in 1941 after the publication of the platform of the British Labour party, then in opposition: It proclaimed the intention not just to rescind the White Paper but even to evacuate Palestinian Arabs to one of the neighboring countries as part of a comprehensive solution to the Palestine problem.

The transfer conception was based on what was assumed as positive experience in exchange of populations between Turkey and Greece in the aftermath of World War I. Other examples mentioned in the debate included the transfer of the Volga Germans by the Russian government during the war and the removal of the Tartars from the Crimean Peninsula. A slightly different case was that of Birobidzhan, the Soviet attempt to set up an autonomous Jewish region in Asia, which also involved population transfer. The lesson of the 1930s was that states should aspire to ethnic uniformity, since ethnic minorities with bonds to related ethnic communities beyond the border were a recipe for certain trouble. Everyone assumed that in the wake of the war, there would be population exchanges on a massive scale: The Czechs would demand the removal of the Germans from the Sudetenland, the Poles would evacuate Germans from the area of Danzig, and so on. The transfer concept was one of the ideas often raised in connection with the revolutionary changes that were expected to be acceptable to the international community in the aftermath of the war.

Berl Katznelson favored transfer as an integral part of an international agreement that would redraw borders between peoples and states in the postwar era. He emphasized that this would be a peaceful transfer of population based on a mutual agreement. In the wake of the riots against Jews that took place in Baghdad during the pro-Nazi uprising in 1941, a linkage was made between the idea of transferring Palestinian Arabs to other Arab countries and the transfer of Jews from Arab countries to the Jewish state. Ben Gurion's stance was more reserved. In 1937, he had been attracted by the proposal of the Peel Commission, among other things because it recommended transfer. However, in the 1940s Ben Gurion firmly opposed the idea of an imposed transfer plan. And since he did not believe the Arabs of Palestine would willingly agree to any large-scale transfer of population, he thought such schemes were nothing but castles in the air. The position of Mapai on the transfer issue was determined by pragmatism, without moralistic undertones. In contrast, people from Ha-Shomer ha-Tzair considered the idea of transfer morally objectionable and rejected it out of hand. According to their perspective, transfer was an act of compulsion, since there was no prospect that Palestinian Arabs would willingly agree to exchange a relatively developed country for one that was considerably less developed.[12]

It is possible to assume with a high degree of probability that if one of the Great Powers had volunteered to carry out a transfer of the Arabs of Palestine, very few of the Zionist leaders would have opposed such a move. Yet the distance between being prepared to accept such an eventuality and the formal adoption of the transfer plan by the Zionist Organization was enormous. The traditional approach was that there was enough room in Palestine for many millions of Jews and one million Palestinian Arabs. This line was pursued not only in propaganda policy for external consumption but internally, as well. Unlike Ha-Shomer ha-Tzair, most Jews in Palestine were not opposed to transfer on principle. Nonetheless, it was not thought to be an absolute necessity. The mainstream viewed it as a good thing that one could, if need be, do without.[13]

The Biltmore Program sought to gain international approval and legitimation for the establishment of a Jewish state in Palestine. It was clear to all that even if approval could be obtained from that "world court of justice," the Arabs in Palestine would not acquiesce in its establishment. Consequently, immanent in the acceptance of the Biltmore proposals was the recognition that a war between Jews and Arabs was inevitable. However, matters were not yet completely clear; and perhaps some of the participants in the deliberations still had a spark of hope that if there were an international decision favorable to Zionism, the Arabs would abide by it. The large majority supported the Biltmore Program with the understanding that in order to implement it, the use of force would be necessary. In contrast with World War I, in which the idea of Jews engaging in force stirred deep emotions and brought tears of joy to the eyes of many, this time it was a decision made with heavy heart but unflinchingly. The romanticism of the use of force, a feature that had characterized Zionism in its early period, gave way to a down-to-earth political attitude: Force was conceptualized, coolheadedly and soberly, as one of a gamut of means utilized by a political movement seriously intent on realizing its objectives.

As details about the Holocaust became known, the end of the war drew closer; and the widely accepted assumption that the war would give birth to a new world order seemed on the verge of realization, there was a feeling that the moment of truth was indeed at hand. In early 1944 Moshe Shertok, head of the political department of the Jewish Agency, published an article in which he sketched the policy of the Zionist Organization for the years to come. He described the contacts that had recently taken place with Arab leaders and the negative approach adopted by most of them in rejecting any agreement. Those few who did agree to talk with him said, "Let's fight, and we'll see who is victorious." Hence, he argued, the main Zionist effort should not be focused on the Jewish–Arab arena but on the international stage. The time had come for a major Zionist offensive: "Today the entire world is searching for big solutions . . . and people are preparing psychologically for broad conceptions, far-reaching conclusions, great efforts."[14] Moshe Sneh, a leader of liberal Zionism in Poland, who fled to Palestine when the war broke out and was integrated into the political–military elite of the community as the chief of the Hagana National Command, wrote in 1945: "If not now, when? If our national freedom in the land of our fathers is not restored to us even now, . . . from where can we draw the hope that this will ever materialize?"[15]

The end of the war did not lessen the sense of urgency. Alongside those for whom the victory by the Soviet Union was a harbinger of a new socialist world order, there were others who deduced different lessons from the upheavals of recent history. The tragedy of the Jews had been that they believed in progress: "All those millions who died on the stake were victims of the illusions with which Jewish history has been replete over the course of recent generations." The first beginnings of the Cold War awakened fears of World War III. The Jews had no chance of surviving, contended Pinhas Lubianiker (later Lavon), a member of the Histadrut Executive and a prominent leader of Mapai, if they embarked upon that future war without a state. Consequently, "our very physical survival as a people may be decided in one generation, over the next 10, 15, [or] 20 years." The component of time became vital: "It appears that history's Master has given us very narrow and extremely tight limits for saving the Jewish people."[16]

It was significant that Lubianiker, one of the most important among the moderates in the Mapai leadership, also recognized the urgency of the moment. Although there were differences of opinion on the methods the movement ought to pursue, there was no difference when it came to an assessment of the concrete situation: The hour was fateful, and there was a limited amount of time at the disposal of the Zionist movement to translate plans into reality. Even those in whom every fiber revolted against forcing the issue by revolutionary means found themselves compelled to accommodate to a policy that was motivated by a sense of the necessity for immediate revolutionary change. Only relatively marginal groups, such as Ha-Shomer ha-Tzair, still believed in the old evolutionary methods, without final goals or shortcuts.[17]

The change in the concept of time was bound up with a transition to other methods of action. Quite naturally, this led to a new attitude toward the use of force. Up until World War II, the Zionist leadership had viewed physical power as a tool designed to provide an answer to the challenge of Arab militancy. They regarded it as a means to curb and prevent Arab action but not as a way to advance Jewish initiatives or to create new facts. There was already a certain ambivalence in this matter at the time of the Arab Rebellion. The ascent to Hanita and its settlement could not have taken place without the threat of force by the Jews. In other words, in this instance, force also created facts on the ground. Yet on the whole, matters were still blurred—ambiguous—and it was doubtful whether they were clear even to those directly involved. Up until the world war, the only organization that regarded physical force as a decisive factor in the "conquest" of Palestine was the IZL. Yet in 1944 Moshe Shertok proclaimed, "There was an era in the history of Zionism when we were unfamiliar with the language of force and its substance."[18] According to the principles of the defensive ethos, Jews were involved in the work of building the land and defended themselves if attacked. Now a new conception emerged: It is not enough to protect the existing Zionist achievements; it is also necessary to defend Zionist prospects in Palestine. The White Paper did not undermine "what we have now, but rather what can be in the future. For that reason, defense is not just of what exists. . . . The war is for the continuation of the Zionist enterprise."[19] Shertok described it in dialectical fashion, "When our fundamental concerns in Palestine are imperiled, uprising is a form of defense." He elaborated, "protecting immigration is defense; preventing Arab rule in this country is defense."[20] Golomb remarked unpretentiously, "The task of Jewish defense is to facilitate the continuation of the Zionist process, to ensure immigration and settlement, even if we should need to use force against the Arabs or against the authorities."[21] Sneh noted, "Our forces must be arrayed in such a way that their first priority is the task of defending Zionism, while defending the country is of secondary importance."[22] In the framework of the refashioning of the objectives of the use of force, Golomb now defined "self-restraint" in a novel way: "Its meaning is, beside responding in kind to a blow we have received, also to have preventive means at our disposal."[23]

Salient changes occurred during the war years: The conception that viewed power as the guardian of the existing Yishuv receded, giving way to a new and broader one that viewed power as a legitimate means for ensuring the further development of the Zionist project. Force was to play a central role in realizing the political aims of the Zionist movement. The leadership of the Yishuv and the Zionist movement, at that time identical with the Mapai leadership, saw three possible lines of action that when combined, could hopefully guide the wrecked ship of the Jewish people to the safe shore of the state: continuation of the process of immigration and settlement, the struggle for world public opinion, and the establishment of a fighting force. "The combination of these three factors can lead to victory," said Moshe Sneh, commenting on what were, from that point on, the three principal weapons in the Zionist arsenal.[24]

The idea of the use of force to further Jewish interests in Palestine was not easily accepted. It sparked stormy discussion in the ruling party, Mapai, where the crucial decisions were actually made. From the beginning of the war, two central currents had emerged into prominence within Mapai, differing in respect to the question of the limits of the use of force. Paradoxically, the debate did not touch on the question of the employment of force against Arabs. As mentioned, that problem had been shunted aside and had been a peripheral issue since the outbreak of the war. Yet the Hagana and the Palmach were trained to prepare a fighting force oriented mainly toward engaging in operations against the Arabs. The Palmach, set up in 1941 within the framework of Jewish–British cooperation and under the shadow of imminent danger—namely, an invasion by Rommel—became the regular elite unit of the Hagana. Their training exercises were aimed at teaching recruits how to reconnoiter and move around in the Arab areas in Palestine, familiarizing them with their geography and topography, and teaching them how to prepare intelligence material on this terrain. Though there was an atmosphere of constant tension, the situation did not deteriorate into actual clashes with the Arabs. Instead, the basic physical might of the Yishuv was mainfested in confrontations with the British authorities.

After publication of the White Paper in 1939, there were a series of demonstrations that got out of hand, turning into bloody clashes with the British forces. During the war, brutal British searches for weapons in Jewish settlements, such as in Ben Shemen, Ramat ha-Kovesh, and elsewhere, were a common occurrence. An especially traumatic event at the beginning of the war was the episode with three boatloads of illegal immigrants—the *Milos,* the *Atlantic,* and the *Pacific*—ships that arrived at the shore of Palestine in November 1940. The heads of the community and the Jewish Agency beseeched the authorities to allow the Jews to stay in Palestine, even if in detention, until the authorities were convinced that these people were, in truth, genuine refugees and not dangerous spies, as the British alleged. Their pleas were in vain. The high commissioner, Harold MacMichael, was determined to send them to Mauritius in order to set an example for all to see: The intended message was that there was no sense in continuing with illegal immigration. The passengers onboard the *Milos* and the *Pacific,* and some of those on the *Atlantic,* were transferred to the deportation ship *Patria.* Hagana members decided to prevent the sailing of the *Patria* by planting a bomb aboard that would cause damage to the ship. They hoped that the delay this would create would facilitate a change in decisions in London. The result was disastrous: The blast was much larger than expected; an enormous hole was blown in the ship, and nearly three hundred passengers perished. After intervention by Churchill, the high commissioner agreed that the survivors from the *Patria* could stay in Palestine. The rest of the *Atlantic* refugees, who were interned in the meantime in Atlit, were brought by force aboard two deportation ships and sent on a long journey to Mauritius. Their evacuation was accomplished by a show of brutal force that made even many of the British police officers flinch. General Nim, with whom Shertok had discussed the matter, expressed his shock that the Jews could dare to damage a much-needed ship like the *Patria* during time of war. Yet significantly, he was not perturbed in the least by the allocation of ships and other resources for sending refugees to Mauritius. This episode sheds light on the distorted attitude of the British in the Middle East at that time toward the Jewish question, in general, and the problem of Jewish refugees, in particular.[25] In any event, a major debate evolved in Mapai on the *Patria* and *Atlantic* episodes between what were dubbed the "activists" and the "moderates."

The concept of *activism* appeared for the first time during the debate on the Jewish Legion in World War I. The activists were Jews who wanted to take immediate action, rather than wait for events initiated by others. In a practical way, they were the ones who looked forward to the use of force and relished its prospect. That concept now reemerged, but in a slightly different meaning. The feeling was that the British had respect for Arab power yet disregarded the Jews, since they had no fear of them or their potential response. Already at the London conference in the winter of 1939, Ben Gurion had made statements designed to imply that the Jews were ready to make trouble for the British if they damaged Jewish vital interests. British behavior during this period only strengthened the activist faction in its belief that if Jews did not adopt a resolute and courageous position, the British would crush them completely. The actual ability at that stage to use physical force against the British was quite limited. It was manifested in violent demonstrations, in the determination to settle without a proper permit on land that had been purchased by Jews, and in the dogged struggle for continuing immigration during wartime. A difficult question was the proper response to searches for weapons in Jewish settlements, conducted energetically by the British in the early years of the war as if it was the principal military mission of the hour. Should the Jews resist the confiscation of their weapons, by force if necessary, or make do with passive resistance to the searches? On the whole, the limits of the use of force were still very narrow: The Jews did not use weapons against the British, and all victims killed during the aggressive searches were Jewish.[26]

The principal question was whether the Jews should continue the struggle against the White Paper regulations or announce a moratorium until the end of the war in the hope that pro-Arab British policy would change after the war. In the view of the moderates, British policy derived from the exigencies of the hour (which required reconciliation with the Arabs) and was likely to be altered once circumstances had changed. "This White Paper emanates from a certain political constellation (Arab united front, Britain's fear of the Arabs) and will be equally short-lived," wrote Arthur Ruppin in his diary in May 1939.[27] The moderates demanded that tension with the British be reduced; Jews should be unconditionally loyal until the end of the war, assuming that the British government would ultimately change its policy.[28]

On the other hand, the activists viewed the policy of the White Paper as the result of a British assessment that the Jews had no choice but to resign themselves to an anti-Zionist policy, because they needed British protection against the Arabs. In their view, the only way to bring about a change in British policy was by ample demonstration of Jewish power and willingness to fight and suffer losses. This would make it clear to the British that to implement their policy would make it necessary for them to carry out acts of suppression on a large scale, and it was doubtful whether the British government would approve. The activists wished to pursue a policy of confrontation with the British on such crucial Jewish issues as immigration, settlement, and defense, in order to send them a clear message about what the absolute limits were, limits beyond which they were prepared to die and even to kill.

The moderates viewed the *Patria* episode as a manifestation of a lack of responsibility and the product of activist extremism: After all, it was argued, the government had wanted to send the ship to Mauritius, not back to Europe; and if Jews went to that island, they would probably survive.[29] In their eyes, the decision over the life and death of others seemed objectionable from a moral perspective, and they did not hesitate to cite it as an example of what the policy of force pursued by the activists could lead to. The activists, however, regarded the sending of the *Atlantic* refugees to Mauritius as the greater tragedy, since the Jewish community in Palestine had not resisted that action and had left the illegal immigrants without any support in their desperate struggle against the army and the police. They saw the *Patria* episode as a heroic tragedy, typical of the calamities that befall every movement of national liberation. In contrast, they viewed the *Atlantic* incident as an example of dishonorable behavior and national weakness that could generate additional brutal acts of suppression.[30]

The moderates belonged for the most part to the same circles that had earlier opposed the Jewish Legion. They had a moderate view of the Arab problem and were convinced proponents of the evolutionary approach. Politically, they were identified with the former Ha-Poel ha-Tzair. Outstanding among them were Yosef Sprinzak (later first speaker of the Knesset), Eliezer Kaplan (treasurer of the Jewish Agency and later minister of finance), Yitzhak Laufbahn (editor of the party weekly

Ha-Poel ha-Tzair), Pinhas Lubianiker (leader of the youth movement Gordonia and one of the heads of Hever ha-Kvutzot, later secretary general of the Histadrut and minister of defense) and Avraham Katznelson (one of the heads of the National Council). David Remez (secretary of the Histadrut and later minister of transport), who had been one of the leaders of the former Ahdut ha-Avoda, was also in the moderate camp. Against them stood a gallery of Mapai leaders who had formerly been members of the more militant party, Ahdut ha-Avoda, including Berl Katznelson, Yitzhak Tabenkin, Eliyahu Golomb, and Moshe Shertok. Ben Gurion, who was in the United States at the time (late 1940), gave them his unlimited support. Basically, the differences manifested here in temperament and psychological makeup were the same that had caused a rift between the two workers' parties in the 1920s, preventing them from finding a common language until 1930. The exmembers of the Ahdut ha-Avoda preserved the revolutionary spark of their youth. Activism for them meant not just the readiness to take action but also the bond with the world of messianic revolutionaries along the lines of the Russian *Narodnaya volya,* characterized by their willingness for self-sacrifice, a life in constant psychological tension, and a readiness to carry out the decisive revolutionary act. At the same time, members of Ha-Poel ha-Tzair were repelled by revolutionary ways; recoiled from any forms of violence; and regarded the slow, stable, quiet path as the one that would lead with certainty to the final objective while preserving the humanistic character of the movement and the desired ideal type of human being the movement wished to nurture.

In those years, an elite group was formed that believed the fostering of an independent Jewish military force was an objective of supreme national importance. That group included political leaders such as Berl Katznelson, Golomb, Tabenkin, Shaul Meirov (Avigur, head of the Mossad le-Aliyah Bet), along with men from the Hagana who enjoyed personal and political status, such as Moshe Sneh and Israel Galili. They constituted a significant pressure group for advancing the cause of a Jewish fighting force. The leaders of the Jewish Agency—Ben Gurion and Shertok—gave them their backing. Ha-Kibbutz ha-Meuhad, under the leadership of Tabenkin, provided the activists with encouragement and support and served later on as the political basis of broader activist circles.

Katznelson died in 1944, Golomb in 1945. A split shook Mapai in 1944; and the left wing, in which the dominant element was Ha-Kibbutz ha-Meuhad, left the party. As a result, the standing of the activists in Mapai declined significantly. Ben Gurion found himself the leader of a party with a strong moderate wing at a time when the policy he wished to apply was unmistakably activist in orientation. This was the background for the second great dispute between the activists and the moderates.

In the summer of 1945, when most of the world was celebrating the Allied victory over the Germans, the Jewish people was shocked by revelations about the true magnitude of the calamity that had befallen it. Members of the Jewish Brigade met with concentration camp survivors, and the first wave of those survivors began arriving in Palestine. The problem of the Jewish refugees—so few measured against the millions envisaged by the Biltmore Program but so many compared with the number that the mandatory government was prepared to let into Palestine—soon became the central political question. The *displaced persons* issue was the battering ram with which the Zionist leadership would attempt to smash through the walls of the White Paper. Yet in the summer of 1945, matters were still enveloped in the uncertain fog of the future. It became clear that the British Labour government, which had issued exaggerated, radically pro-Zionist declarations when in opposition, was meanwhile unprepared to change the policies laid down in the White Paper. To a remark by Barbara Gould, a member of the British Parliament, that if bloodshed could not be avoided, then, for God's sake, it should be shed in the cause of justice and not injustice, Herbert Morrison, a Labour party leader, replied that in the case of riots, it depends on who can be placated more quickly.[31] These remarks made it clear to Ben Gurion and his associates that the court of justice whose verdict they expected would not be impartial. The official declaration of Foreign Secretary Ernest Bevin was published in November 1945; but it had been clear to Ben Gurion (in London at the time) already at the end of the summer that the hopes the Zionists had pinned on the new Labour government were unwarranted.

On October 1, 1945, Ben Gurion sent instructions to Moshe Sneh, chief of the Hagana National Command, to prepare for armed struggle against the British. In contrast with previous policy that limited itself only to defense of immigration, settlement, and the weapons of the Hagana, this time the struggle was supposed to lead directly to a shift in British policy. That would be effected by impressive acts of sabotage, meant to awaken world public opinion to the problem and even to signal to the British that the Jewish people were no longer prepared to acquiesce in the polices of the White Paper. "The White Paper is a declaration of war against the Jewish people. And our people, without its own government and oppressed, must fight—using all possible means," wrote Ben Gurion. He instructed Sneh to avoid casualties as much as possible and to abstain from personal terror but to retaliate for every person killed by the authorities.[32]

This was the beginning of the Hebrew Resistance Movement, the united underground movement of the Hagana, the IZL, and Lehi, which cooperated from October 1945 to July 1946. The first action associated with it was the freeing of the illegal immigrants imprisoned in the Atlit camp. That action was not a matter of controversy between the activists and the moderates. The latter now considered a "linked struggle" as the proper path. That expression denoted active mass opposition to any step by the authorities aimed against Jewish immigration and colonization. Attacks on British military installations involved in actions against illegal immigration, such as police boats or the radar station, were also considered permissible. However, on November 1, 1945, the Hebrew Resistance Movement for the first time carried out a military action that was not connected with illegal immigration. In that action, known as the Night of the Trains, railroad tracks were blown up at 153 points throughout Palestine. This was a show of force—of tactical capability to take action and military organizing talents—with an evident political purpose in mind. It raised the debate between the moderates and activists to new heights of intensity.

The person who initiated the shift in policy was Ben Gurion. In an impassioned speech he gave in Palestine at the end of November in response to the declaration by Bevin, he stated: "Like the British, there is also something that's dearer to us than life itself. I want to let Bevin and his associates know that we are prepared to be killed, and won't give up three things: the freedom of Jewish immigration, the right to build our desolate homeland, and the political independence of our people in its own land."[33] This tone and policy struck a sympathetic chord with wide strata of the Jewish public in Palestine. He gave voice to the heartfelt sentiments of thousands when, in reference to the Holocaust, he said, "If [the Germans] had known that the Jews have power too, not all of them would have been slaughtered." His explanation of British policy as based on speculations about Jewish weakness and the consequent necessity to prove Jewish strength by a show of force found favor with a substantial segment of the Jewish community in Palestine.[34] One result of this policy was an increase in Ben Gurion's status as a national leader, also recognized by groups on the Right. There is no need to stress that he was backed in this matter by the entire active cadre of the Hagana and the Palmach, and by members of the Ha-Kibbutz ha-Meuhad, who supported the activist policy unanimously. Moshe Sneh, the Hagana chief who implemented that policy, enjoyed great popularity among the younger generation. In Mapai itself, the leadership was split on this question: and although it appears that the activist position won broader public support, there was stubborn resistance to it within the party bodies. After the Night of the Trains, the moderates did not hesitate to air their objections and opposition to the new line.

The most prominent leader identified with nonactivist views was Chaim Weizmann, president of the Zionist Organization. He was not informed about the change in policy; and after learning of the attack on the railroad lines, "Chaim was stunned, and a heavy depression descended upon him."[35] In his meeting with Bevin the morning after, he halfheartedly defended the position of the Jewish Agency, contending that the British policy had brought the Jewish community to the brink of despair and that this had served to weaken the Jewish Agency's hold over the community. In a letter addressed to the Yishuv, he was far more unambiguous in his criticism: "I must register my complete disapproval of violence as a means of attaining our legitimate ends." He called for continuing the struggle, using the means of "persuasion, negotiation, and constructive efforts" and for urging people to have faith that the moral impact of the Zionist cause would ultimately lead to victory.[36] In contrast, Harry Sacker, one of the members of the Zionist Executive in London, who had been known in better days for his moderate views, now stated that under the present circumstances, a bit of lunacy would not hurt, provided it was limited.[37]

In Palestine, *Mishmar,* organ of the party Ha-Shomer ha-Tzair, published a biting critique of the railroad raid; the article was described by the Hagana leaders as a "stab in the back."[38] Meanwhile, the official paper of Mapai, *Ha-Poel ha-Tzair,* carried an editorial that stated, among other things, "The use of violence and destructive force is not among the signposts of Zionism in the past, present, or future." Hence, "if those events on November 1 did in fact take place . . . , their meaning is that the alien forces plotting against us . . . have brought the Yishuv such disappointment that it is unable to maintain control of those among its ranks who are now wild with despair."[39] Actually, the paper's editor, Yitzhak Laufbahn, was far more critical of the policy of force pursued by the movement; but he tried to give a balanced expression to views within his party. But this is not how the article was understood. The rage of the activists against him surged, since the expression "wild with despair" was reminiscent of terminology they themselves had used to describe the IZL and Lehi in a negative light. In addition, he portrayed the event as if it had taken place without the authorization of the party and proclaimed that the Labor movement rejected the use of force and violence on principle. The activists' campaign was piloted by Shaul Meirov; Eliezer Liebenstein, editor of *Milhamtenu* (Our War), the organ of the activist faction within Mapai; Levi Shkolnik (Eshkol, later prime minister of Israel); and members of Ha-Kibbutz ha-Meuhad who had not seceded from Mapai in the 1944 split. At the head of the moderates stood Pinhas Lubianiker, a brilliant debater, who acrimoniously attacked the tendency of his associates to romanticize the heroic struggle and rejected their argument that Mapai had forfeited the trust of youth because of the article denouncing the use of force. "Somebody thinks we may have to pay because of that article—I think we'll have to pay for the deeds," he challenged.[40]

After the Night of the Bridges in mid-June 1946, in which the bridges connecting Palestine with neighboring countries were blown up, Weizmann's patience snapped, and he wrote to Shertok, threatening he would resign if the leadership of the Jewish Agency did not cease the campaign of violence. It is true, Weizmann noted, that British provocations were extremely serious, indicating that the authorities had decided to abandon moral considerations and to rule Palestine by the power of the sword and the hangman's noose. Yet, he wrote, "it is not for us to imitate its methods. Our only force is moral force." Jews should not behave like other national movements, Weizmann argued, for both ethical and practical reasons. Consequently, if terror actions did not cease and no attempt was made to establish control over the dissenting factions (the IZL and Lehi), he would resign immediately.[41] The letter was delayed due to Weizmann's poor health; and two days after it was written, Operation Agatha took place, nicknamed by the Yishuv Black Saturday—a large-scale British attempt to suppress the Jewish community by force. It encompassed a series of repressive measures: the detaining of leaders, curfews, extensive arrests of young men, searches in the offices of the Jewish Agency and confiscation of documents, and searches for weapons and their confiscation. The British activity was violent and brutal. Weizmann vetoed any proposal to respond in force to British actions.[42] The blowing-up of the King David Hotel in Jerusalem, headquarters of the Palestine government and the military command—carried out by the IZL and costing many lives—was, for all practical purposes, the final exploit of the united resistance movement. Sneh called for a renewal of the armed struggle against the British. In vain activists of the Hagana and Palmach fulminated about the cessation of military actions. Even the fiery speeches of Ben Gurion at the Zionist Congress in Basel in December 1946 did not change this fact. Indeed, Weizmann's speech at that same congress, in which he severely criticized the use of terror by Jews, was, in effect, his swan song. Among other things, he stated, "I warn you once again against taking short cuts, against following false prophets and will-o'-the-wisp generalizations and against the falsification of historical facts."[43] He was not reelected as president of the Zionist Organization. Yet his policy rejecting violent struggle was adopted by the congress. Sneh, who symbolized the policy of the resistance movement, resigned from his post as chief of the National Command of the Hagana. Public pressure in favor of violence did not result in its renewal. From that point until the beginning of the War of Independence, the Hagana and Palmach limited themselves to actions connected solely with illegal immigration and settlement.

What had led to the ban on violence? Black Saturday made it clear to the leaders of the Yishuv that if clashes were to continue between the authorities and the Hagana, they would ultimately lead to the annihilation of the Jewish military force by the British. The reaction of the government proved that if the activists were gambling on British misgivings about applying their full might against the Jews, they were mistaken. The activists continued to contend that this was a natural stage in a national struggle, familiar from the history of other struggles, such as that of the Irish or the Boers—where, in the end, Britain had been compelled to sit down and talk. The moderates, however, rejected this argument, claiming that the activists were unable to point to a single political achievement that was the fruit of the use of force. On the other hand, it was alleged they were bringing about the destruction of the Jewish community.[44]

In the meeting arranged between the heads of the Hagana and Ben Gurion in Basel, during the Zionist Congress, Ben Gurion explained to them his motive for bringing to a halt what, by association with the European resistance movement, had been dubbed the "active resistance." He felt that the moment of truth for Jews and Arabs was fast approaching and prophesied that in that confrontation not only would the Arabs of Palestine take part, but the Arab states, as well. He argued that the defense forces had to be prepared for any eventuality. For that reason, it was permissible to annoy the British but "not to utilize means that would jeopardize the survival of the Yishuv, its growth, and the furthering of the constructive enterprise. This is the absolute limit." In respect to the principle of purity of arms, he stressed: "The end does not justify all means. Our war is based on moral grounds." He presented military force as a factor of secondary importance to building the land.[45] The need to preserve strength for the future confrontation with the Arab states and to prepare forces for such an eventuality was a concept still strange and seemingly unreal for the activists. Yet it appears this was the central consideration in Ben Gurion's thinking.

As was usual with persons motivated largely by moral considerations, on this occasion, as well, the moderates were careful not to use arguments drawn from the realm of justice to justify their position. Rather, they claimed that their motives were pragmatic, based on considerations of profit and loss. Weizmann was the only leader who, without any sense of shame, could announce he was disgusted by violence. As a convinced adherent of the teachings of Ahad Ha-Am, Weizmann believed moderation, a slow pace of construction, and moral qualities were the forces destined to lead the wrecked ship of Zionism to the desired shore. This was also the outlook of most of the other moderates. On this psychological foundation, a complete superstructure was erected: It consisted of proofs and arguments geared to persuading people of the utility of moderation when compared with the harm done through violence. Basically, what is evident here is a manifestation of a Jewish cultural tradition whose sources predated Zionism. That was one of the components shaping the approach adopted by the Zionist leadership to the issue of the use of force.

The resistance movement marked the end of one era and the beginning of another. Even if the Zionist movement retreated from the use of force (as at the end of 1946), the fact had been established that force was one of a series of means available to the movement; and the use of such force was deemed legitimate. The debate between activists and moderates on the resistance movement was the last debate concerning the issue of the use of force. The closer the moment of decision came, the fewer moral scruples and objections were voiced to force as a legitimate means.

In January 1947, a month before the British government decided to bring the Palestine question before the United Nations, an anonymous article was published in *Alon ha-Palmah,* the official organ of the Palmach. The article, written apparently by one of the heads of the Hagana, was entitled "Values in the Thinking of the Hagana"; and it summed up the substantial changes that had occurred in the objectives of the Jewish defense force since the end of the war. The aim of defense in the past had been to protect the Jewish community from rioters. Later, the objective had changed from an orientation that was mainly physical to a political one: "to protect and defend the value of 'nationhood', epitomized by the concept *independence.*"

The underlying reason for this shift was largely a change in what was assumed to be the balance of power, meaning the strength of the Yishuv: "[That strength]— and today this means, among the *principle* factors, our armed force as well—does not justify our giving up [any] additional development of the Jewish Yishuv and its growth in ways which appear proper to the community." This style was typical of the change that had occurred. The legitimation of the use of force went hand in hand with the actual growth of the military arm and the deepening awareness of its potential impact as the hour for political decision approached.[46]

Educating the Young in Turbulent Times

The 1940s witnessed the coming of age of the sons and daughters of immigrants who had arrived during the Third and Fourth Aliyah and children who had come to Palestine during the Fifth Aliyah. Both socially and politically, this generation came of age under the fiery sign of Mars. Their childhood was spent in the shadow of the Arab Rebellion, their youth in the flash of the cannon in a world at war. As soon as they reached maturity, they were called upon to join the struggle for the establishment of the state and, later on, to fight the War of Independence. Their worldview and psychology were essentially shaped by these events.

Yitzhak Tabenkin was preocuppied with the question of how to educate youth under wartime conditions. Tabenkin, the founder and leader of Ha-Kibbutz ha-Meuhad, the largest of the kibbutz movements, had enormous influence within the ranks of youth. He had emerged victorious in his struggle for the soul of the younger generation with Berl Katznelson during the late 1930s. Tabenkin's influence was not limited to Ha-Kibbutz ha-Meuhad. It also encompassed youth organizations associated with the kibbutz movement, such as Ha-Noar ha-Oved, the largest of the youth movements in Palestine, and Ha-Mahanot ha-Olim, composed of secondary school students, the most original and "Palestinian" in character of the Yishuv youth movements.

During the 1940s Ha-Kibbutz ha-Meuhad adopted the Palmach. It agreed to deploy Palmach units in its member kibbutzim, and was always prepared to protect the interests of this organization in the political bodies of the Labor movement. Over the course of the years, the Palmach was labeled "Tabenkin's salvation army," after "Timoshenko's salvation army," the nickname of a famous Russian unit during the war. The Palmach became one of Tabenkin's most important channels of influence among young people. Tabenkin was undoubtedly one of the educators who succeeded in shaping the image of youth at the time.[47]

A member of the Ahdut ha-Avoda party from the 1920s, both a Marxist and an anarchist, dogmatic in respect to his path yet at the same time free from any loyalty to a single dogma, Tabenkin combined ardent Zionism with a revolutionary socialist outlook. This amalgamation was of key importance in molding his attitude toward power. At the beginning of the 1930s, Ha-Kibbutz ha-Meuhad, like other left-wing groups around the world, viewed itself as part of the global pacifist movement, wishing to put an end to all wars. But the lesson of the 1930s had been bitter disappointment: States that had lost their fighting spirit and wished for nothing but peace and tranquillity found themselves face to face with aggressor nations. The latter exploited their longings for peace to further their own designs. The weakness manifest by the Western powers in confronting the Axis powers before the war and in its early stages seemed to Tabenkin irrefutable proof that pacificism had been a delusion. In the early war years, Tabenkin made considerable efforts to sever the bonds between his movement and the pacifist tradition. He contended that pacifism "was not motivated by love for humanity—rather, it wished to protect itself by sacrificing others." In his view, it was a bourgeois movement that wanted to ensure the peace of strong states at the expense of the weak. Its aim was to sanctify the existing social order and "formal" political democracy. Pacifism, Tabenkin challenged, wished to function as a kind of substitute for socialism: It was content with the survival of the capitalist order and for the sake of peace was prepared to give up social revolution. It had been born within the context of a decadent European civilization that for the previous two decades had fervently wished for nothing but peace and calm. Pacificism, Tabenkin argued, was synonymous with the unwillingness to fight for values. Pacifism encouraged people to abandon the conviction that there are certain things a man must simply fight for: "In this way, we arrived at a psychological state of mind that fostered nonopposition to evil." That psychological state of mind was not the product of ethical exaltation, Tabenkin contended, but the product of mistaken hope that evil in this way would befall others, rather than us. As proof of the moral limitations of pacifism, Tabenkin pointed to the fact that the pacifist movement had never undertaken to defend Jews.[48]

In Tabenkin's words, one can hear an echo of the atmosphere prevailing during the period of the Munich crisis in 1938 and the summer of 1939, when the question was asked in the press, Should one "die for Danzig"? The war-weariness of Europe's peoples after World War I was one of the decisive factors in strengthening the pacifist currents. Those currents, in turn, had created a highly influential movement opposed to rearmament. As a result, with the rise to power of the dictators in the 1930s, the major Western powers were unable to respond in kind to the German threat. They preferred to retreat from their obligations toward their weaker allies, avoiding at all costs involvement in a war. This is how Tabenkin interpreted the Japanese invasion of China, the civil war in Spain, the Munich agreement, and the White Paper of 1939. All those events had been chains in a great world drama, in which the democracies preferred the disgrace of a cheap peace to the dangers of war. Yet in the end, they lost the peace anyway and went to war unprepared psychologically or militarily, lacking the conviction that one should fight to uphold basic values essential for a people's survival. For that reason, Tabenkin waged a war against pacifism, which he regarded as a false and misleading concept. Tabenkin began his reckoning with pacifism in June 1940 after the fall of France, when England was fighting for its survival and the fate of the world hung in the balance.

His approach to pacifism had implications for the Palestine arena as well. He felt that Brit Shalom and the organizations that had followed in its path were the local, domestic Palestinian version of the seductive delusion of pacifism. To assume that it was possible under the current circumstances to arrive at a peace accord with the Arabs was erroneous, Tabenkin argued. As a socialist, he wished to formulate a doctrine that took into account the possibility of a peace accord with progressive forces in the Arab world; yet he simultaneously assumed that under the given circumstances, such an accord was beyond reach. He thought that the world war was strengthening the hand of reactionary forces among the Arab population in Palestine and in the Arab world, since all parties to the conflict were wooing them, competing for their support. For that reason, the war would not lead to an increase in progressive forces among the Arabs; rather, the conservative camp would be strengthened, and they would attempt to take control of Palestine in the wake of the war. Parallel with this, the process in Palestine of a radicalization of the worker and the fellah was moving forward at a snail's pace. Until it reached maturity, the Yishuv faced constant clashes with the Arabs. Tabenkin drew certain educational conclusions from this assessment of the situation: "One should not educate Jews in Palestine in the illusion that in a world that lives by the sword . . . they might be able to avoid having to defend their enterprise, immigration, and, indeed, their very lives."[49]

Tabenkin's militant conception was an integral part of his socialist outlook. He believed in a socialism whose realization necessitated revolution, that is, war and bloodshed. As an educator, he was faced with a dilemma: How can one educate young people in the ideals of a militant socialism when the moment for revolution was not yet visible on the horizon? On the other hand, as a socialist Zionist whose goal was to establish a national home for the Jewish people in Palestine, he wanted to channel all the creative energies of youth into the activity of building the land. A kibbutz member, he wished to direct those youthful energies toward the task of building up Palestine along socialist lines. It would appear that this was constructive socialism at its best. Yet from his early youth, Tabenkin had been faithful to a more militant conception: the imminent revolution. In his eyes, revolution was not a distant ideal or a messianic dream but a genuine existential entity whose realization in the near future was beyond doubt. He remained loyal to that concept all his life.[50] In order to resolve the contrast between revolutionary consciousness and the desire to educate young people in its spirit with the necessity to build the land and channel youth toward the path of constructive socialism, Tabenkin denied the existence of any contradiction between those two fundamentals. He argued that they were not alternatives: Rather, they were components that combined, leading *together* to the desired future order. The dialectical concept with which he resolved the inherent opposition between the two was *process.* "Socialism is not an act. It is a process," he stated: "It is a revolutionary process, not an evolutionary one—but it is not an act." Tabenkin was never in the least perturbed by a lack of consistency in his views. He did not feel obliged to espouse any specific paradigm. Rather, he borrowed eclectically from various different ideological frameworks, creating his own philosophy of life in keeping with his inclinations—and did not feel inferior to the great social theorists. The notion of a "revolutionary process"—which probably sounded like the proverbial squaring of the circle to orthodox Marxists—was, in Tabenkin's eyes, the bridge between the reality of creating in Palestine what was dubbed "constructive socialism" and his profound psychological affinity with the socialist revolution he anticipated.[51]

As Tabenkin saw it, socialism would be realized as a result of struggle and even war. Comparing the education received by middle-class circles in Palestine with that of the youth associated with him, he said: "We educated the young in socialist values that cannot be attained without a war. Maybe at the [Herzliya] Gymnasia there was education for evolution, but there was no socialist education. That's not how we educated." Socialism, in Tabenkin's view, was one of the concepts for which a man had to be ready to fight. "We endorse the use of force to defend our honor and values. For an idea, a person has to stand steadfast and employ force and even to be killed," Tabenkin proclaimed at the beginning of 1940 speaking at the convention of Ha-Mahanot ha-Olim. Attending a performance of the play *Jeremiah,* he felt a sense of alienness, since the drama expressed support for pacifist ideas and presented Jeremiah as an "ideologue of cowardice." He defined the education of his movement using the biblical phrase "Love thy Lord . . . with all thy soul and with all thy might" (Deuteronomy 6:5). He viewed this kind of education as the antipodal antithesis of pacifism and commented, "A man has to fight for the right to live—by means of information, understanding, using a rifle, devotion, everything."[52]

Tabenkin distinguished between the use of physical force and violence: All violence was a (negative) use of force, while not every use of force was violence. He regarded the use of force as one of the legitimate means of social struggle. When one of the members of Ha-Tenua le-Ahdut ha-Avoda (the party Tabenkin founded after he split from Mapai in 1944) proclaimed that the Labor movement was against violence, since it was pacifist in essence, Tabenkin hastened to set things right: "I do not belong to a pacifist movement in any way. I support the use of physical force. I want the realization of ideas. . . . I don't regard peace as a goal and main value. There are values more important to me than peace. And I want our physical strength to serve as the basis for all our values." The role of physical force would, he argued, come to an end only after the achievement of socialism around the world and the realization of Zionism in Palestine.[53]

On the basis of the experience of World War I, Tabenkin understood that war on such a scale leads to traumatic social tremors in its aftermath. He expected that this would also be the case following World War II. Thus, Tabenkin envisioned a prolonged period of wars, which would come to an end only after the final destruction of the capitalist system. The conclusion that he drew from this prognosis was that not only the generation then coming of age would still have to be prepared to fight but even their grandchildren. For that reason, it was not enough to educate the young, as past wisdom had assumed, to be good workers, diligent and creative: Now they would also have to be trained to be warriors. Characteristically, he found a dialectical definition for that: "Socialism has already come to the conclusion that constructive socialism must also be a fighting socialism."[54]

This, on the the plane of thought, was a translation of the transformation of the defensive ethos into another ethos—a kind of admixture of the old stance with the new offensive ethos. The new man Tabenkin wished to create was supposed to be *"a working man and a fighting man."* Tabenkin did not intend to neglect the component of work: That was the factor which would build socialism. Yet the element of fighting was necessary, since "our creation will not last for even 24 hours unless every day of building is accompanied by fighting prowess."[55] Tabenkin was well aware of the dangers of militarism and was careful to stress the difference between "fascist education" and "militant socialism." As contrastive examples, he cited Horst Wessel and Trumpeldor. For him, heroes like Garibaldi and Thaddeus Kosciusko were exemplary fighters; and he underscored their international ideals.

In this instance as well, Tabenkin utilized a dialectical formulation in order to prove that education for war was in fact education for peace. "Education for war, as contrasted with pacifism," he contended "is a war for a world without war, an antimilitaristic world." He characterized his demand as "militant antimilitarism." He claimed that the difference between his views and those of the revisionists, who were always in favor of military education, was that his pedagogical conception was not intended to teach young people to hate. The school must integrate Jewish and general humane values within a program of educational preparation for fighting: "The school must sow the seeds of hatred for the murderers of Tel Hai; but it also is obliged to teach about the Arabs, their faith, ideas, and language."[56] Just as he rejected the dichotomy of constructive versus revolutionary socialism, Tabenkin denied that there was a dichotomy between humanistic education and education for war. The dialectic resolved all contradictions.

Beyond formulas and definitions, he wanted to educate the young to be strong and courageous fighters, trained physically and mentally for the rigors of battle. He even spoke favorably about Spartan education. There was a considerable difference between that pedagogical ideal and the educational ideals of the 1920s, and even of the 1930s. According to the original myth of Tel Hai, the "people of work and peace" stood steadfast to defend the fruits of their labor; and their fight was meant to protect values acquired by the sweat of their brow. In Tabenkin's current conception, this was not enough. Fighting was indeed necessary in order to preserve what had been achieved but was even more necessary in order to progress on to the next stage of the war of liberation and beyond. That war would be both nationalist and socialist. The examples of Garibaldi and Kosciusko, which Tabenkin cited, were not accidental. They symbolized international socialism, which supported wars of national liberation. Translated into concrete concepts of the time and place, this meant a war for control of Palestine by the Jews. The potential objects of such militance were the Arabs in Palestine and neighboring Arab states. His attitude toward Arabs was ambiguous: He declared his desire for peace; but he also, in a much more forceful manner, stressed the readiness for war and the need to prepare for such an eventuality. In calling for the preparation for war of the coming generation in Ha-Kibbutz ha-Meuhad, he was not referring to a conflict against Hitler: Rather, he meant the future war for Palestine that would come in its wake.

The model that served as a paradigm and source of inspiration was the Soviet Union. The attachment between Ha-Kibbutz he-Meuhad and Soviet Russia had developed in the 1920s. Admiration for Leninism, with its activist message and the legitimation of the use of force for the sake of a lofty goal that it bestowed were deeply implanted in the consciousness of the movement. Tabenkin admired the constructive impetus in the Soviet Union and had a tendency to close one eye to the deficiencies of the system there. The debate between him and Berl Katznelson in the 1930s revolved to a large extent around their differing assessments of the Soviet Union and its brand of socialism. Right from the start, Tabenkin's approach was lenient: When trees are felled, the chips will fly. For that reason, his attitude was relatively indulgent when it came to Stalinist tyranny. During the purge trials in the Soviet Union at the end of the 1930s, there was no genuine criticism voiced in the printed media of Ha-Kibbutz ha-Meuhad on events in the land of revolution.[57] The Molotov–Ribbentrop pact of August 1939 taxed the loyalty of Tabenkin's associates to the Soviet Union. Yet Tabenkin himself soon enough found explanations for the motives that had prompted the Soviets to sign the agreement and to justify the Soviet invasion of the tiny state of Finland, whose brave stand awakened sympathy in the hearts of young idealists. Tabenkin argued that the policy of the Western powers had pushed the Soviet Union into signing an agreement with Nazi Germany. Instead of working out a true alliance with the Soviets and embarking on a joint war against the Nazis, they attempted to divert Germany to attack in the East and spare the West. Tabenkin had no doubt that the war would eventually evolve into a confrontation between the Nazi forces of evil and the Soviet forces of light. But until the anticipated confrontation, the Soviets had to gain time in order to prepare for war and achieve control of strategic areas bordering on the Soviet Union. The vital national interests of the Soviets were what had prompted them to sign the otherwise inconceivable pact.

The idea that a socialist country was obligated to defend the interests of its people and land was two-edged: While sanctioning Soviet political–pragmatic behavior, Tabenkin was also giving his approval to the same kind of behavior in the Palestinian arena: "The fate of Russian socialism is bound up with their loyalty to the interests of *Russia*. We, too, in our own lives, do not see the connection between socialism and nationalism differently, or between a socialist and his people." He added, "Would we consider someone a socialist who says he behaves in a socialist manner at the expense of his people, to that people's detriment?"[58] Just as Russia gave primacy to its national security over socialist values, socialists in Palestine should do the same. The concept of socialism in a single country, which posited a separate path to socialism for each people according to its specific circumstances, was a line propagated not only by Stalin: Tabenkin was likewise enamored of the idea. He forgave all of Stalin's brutalities on the grounds that a state struggling under difficult conditions to implement socialism, while a hostile world is lurking to foil its efforts, is bound to make mistakes; yet those errors ultimately lead to greater progress. They are "human sacrifices for the elevation of mankind." It is true that the Zionist Socialist movement took a different path; it was able to afford those moral luxuries because it dealt with a small and select population and was not responsible for running a state. The inference was that the establishment of a state obligates one to make use even of immoral methods where deemed necessary.[59]

When the Germans invaded the Soviet Union in June 1941 and the war on the Eastern Front began in earnest, Russia's adherents breathed a sigh of relief. Solidarity with Moscow could now finally be freed of the burden of having constantly to apologize for Soviet policy. From that point on, the Soviet Union was the model for the way a people should act in wartime. Its total commitment to war and the willingness of its population to endure unlimited suffering and sacrifice, stirred Tabenkin's admiration. He was enthusiastic about the fact that the Russians had not shrunk back from blowing up the dam on the Dnieper River—one of the symbols of the construction of the new socialist Soviet Union. In contrast, he had nothing but contempt for the shameful handing over of Paris by the French to the enemy to prevent the destruction of the city at any price. In Tabenkin's eyes, the awe-inspiring readiness to sacrifice everything for the battle appeared to be a function of the vitality of regime, able to mobilize all the people's physical and mental powers for the sake of the supreme effort. This, in his view, was something the governments of neither Poland nor France had been able to achieve. It moved him deeply; and he thought it proper to inculcate the Yishuv, whose fate then lay in the balance, with a similar spirit.[60]

The war between Germany and Russia captured the imagination of the Jews in Palestine, especially youth. The majority of adults were from Eastern Europe, and a significant percentage had been born in czarist Russia. In their hearts, they had a warm corner of sympathy and affection for their country of birth, despite all the bitterness of their life there. Aside from sentiments about the past, there was the prosaic fact that Russia served as a land of refuge for hundreds of thousands of Jews who had fled there from Poland and the Baltic states. Solidarity with the Soviet Union against the Nazis came naturally. It encompassed very broad segments of the Jewish public in Palestine, even those who were hostile to the Soviet regime. The identification with the Soviets was especially strong among the same groups on the Palestinian Left who saw Russia as the land of the great revolution and remained faithful to it even after the difficult ordeals it subjected its faithful to. Now that Russia had joined the front ranks of those in the coalition against Hitler, the admiration and sympathy for the Soviet Union swelled to unprecedented proportions. The preponderant majority of the Left saw the Soviet Union as a paradigm, a model for imitation, and a source of legitimation. In the political domain, that admiration was expressed in the hope that the enmity on the part of the Soviet Union toward the Zionist project (which still characterized that regime) would disappear and the "partition" dividing the Zionist Left and the Soviet Union fall away. Tabenkin made predictions in this spirit as early as the summer of 1942, during the great defeats of the Red Army. Individuals from Ha-Shomer ha-Tzair and Left Poalei Zion harbored similar hopes. Things reached the ultimate in absurdity in the spring of 1942, when in the convention of the Histadrut, Ya'ari, leader of Ha-Shomer ha-Tzair, raised the problem of the future political orientation of the Zionist Organization and called for an *orientation* toward the "forces of tomorrow" instead of Britain. His comments led one of the participants to remark (paraphrasing the Creator's reply to Moses and the children of Israel's song in praise of God after Pharoah and his soldiers had been drowned [Exodus 15]), "My deeds are cast into the sea, and you sing about orientation."[61]

The tendency was to find analogies between Russia at war and the struggle in Palestine. For instance, Tabenkin lectured teachers in Ha-Kibbutz ha-Meuhad that they should emulate the Russians, who had resurrected the old Russian myths and national heroes, such as Dimitri Donskoi and Alexander Nevski, and taught about the history of its wars against the Tartars and the Teutonic knights, topics that had been buried away since the days of the revolution. Tabenkin called for educating children and youth in that same spirit, inspired by the romanticism of ancient heroes and exploits of valor, drawn from biblical tales, Josephus Flavius, and others. Education must inculcate knowledge of the geography and history of Palestine, utilizing heroic myths. The new Bible study, according to Tabenkin, should be in the spirit of Tchernichovsky, Berdichevsky, and Brenner, that is, the study of the Bible as a history book and a heroic myth. In addition, there should be instruction on the history of revolutionary wars of liberation fought by other peoples around the globe.[62] The policy of "transfer" carried out by Russia in the case of the Tartars of Crimea and the Volga Germans served as a corroboration that this method of action was a legitimate means to resolve national and ethnic problems. There was also an expectation that after the war, Russia would resolve the ethnic problems on its western border in a similar manner. This too was conceived by analogy as a kind of license for a similar solution in Palestine.

The image of the Soviet fighter was mobilized as a model for the image of the fighter in Palestine. In the summer of 1942 the Hagana was beset by a financial crisis that threatened the existence of its regular standing force, the Palmach. Initially, back in the spring of 1941, the Palmach had been supported by the British Army. Yet from the very beginning, it had been clear that this support was temporary and limited. In the summer of 1942, when the outcome of the battle between Rommel and the British Eighth Army in the western desert was still undecided, the future of the recruited Palmach forces was in doubt. Circles from the Center and Left in the Yishuv did not recognize the importance of the existence of an independent Jewish force and refused to allocate it the necessary funds. Discussion was about a force that amounted to some one thousand persons. This fact illuminates a salient aspect of public consciousness, namely, just how far a substantial segment of the Jewish population in Palestine was from actually thinking in terms of power and an armed force. In any event, Ha-Kibbutz ha-Meuhad volunteered to give the Histadrut a loan for the purpose of maintaining the force and proposed ensuring its continued existence by absorbing units of the Palmach in the kibbutzim. The Palmachniks were required to divide their time between work and training exercises (nine days a month), and in this way to maintain themselves as a unit. This original arrangement sparked considerable opposition in the ranks of Palmach members: They were anything but enthusiastic about the idea of dedicating a large chunk of their time to working in agriculture. In the discussions, Tabenkin and his associates repeatedly referred to the example of Russia in order to foster the sense of legitimacy of that arrangement. Analogies were made with Cossack villages, which had served as a standing source of recruitment for the army during the czarist period: men who were working their fields and could be mobilized quickly when needed. Comparisons were also made with experience gathered during the Russian civil war: Some units of the Red Army had maintained themselves then by supplementary labor. Those units were dubbed the "working army." As an illustration of the importance of agricultural labor for the war effort, examples were cited from the Soviet Union: Exceptionally industrious workers there were singled out for praise; women who cooked oatmeal for the soldiers were given special recognition; and even an actor who put on a performance for soldiers on the field of battle had been lauded for that action. The demand to include women in the ranks of the Palmach was legitimated by the fact that there were thousands of female soldiers serving as recruits in the Red Army. Tabenkin understood the importance of propagandistic–literary material for the war effort. "Work, weapons, and books" was the slogan he coined, citing Stalingrad, fighting for its life, as an example of the proper application of these three components in concrete practice.[63]

During the war and after, Russian literature was in vogue in Palestine: scores of books were translated from Russian to Hebrew. They enjoyed great popularity among young people in general and members of the Palmach in particular. This was literature that dealt with the Bolshevik revolution (*A Lone White Sail on the Horizon*), the growth of the new society in the Soviet Union (*Pedagogical Poem*), and the war (e.g., *Rainbow in the Clouds*, *The Young Guard*, and *Panphilov's Men*, sections of which were serialized in the Palmach bulletin). The Palmach bulletin published numerous war stories and even chronicles about the exploits of partisans in the Soviet Union and Yugoslavia. The Russian war films communicated a message of popular heroism and told of simple people going forth to defend their homeland and the achievements of socialism. The figure of the partisan was a prime source of inspiration in the Palmach. The Russian army, though greatly admired, was not a suitable paradigm for emulation: The Palmach, after all, was an army without uniforms and poorly equipped and maintained itself by supplementary labor in various kibbutzim. There was no similarity between it and a regular army. In contrast, the myth of the partisan, the warrior without uniform, was especially appropriate for the situation of the Palmach and its state of mind.

The Palmach was an army with a civilian mentality. It was an army of volunteers, based on the idealism of its members and on its social cohesion. To a great extent, the Palmach embraced the social, cultural, and even educational patterns of the youth movement in Palestine. Its life-style and experience were quite similar to those of a group of young people living in a kibbutz, plus the added component of training exercises. In its daily life and routine, there was no particular emphasis on the military nature of the organization. On the contrary, the network of relations between the commanders and the ranks rested largely on the prestige of the former: Only rarely did they have to resort to formal discipline. The absence of uniforms and formal ranks also functioned to underscore the "civilian" character of the relations. The importance of shared experience and of the cultural component in the life of the Palmach units likewise pointed to the transfer of patterns from the youth movement to the army unit. Among other things, that atmosphere was meant to shield youth from the deficiencies of the *soldateska*—an expression used by immigrants from Eastern Europe to denote the negative traits and features of army life and barracks realities.

During the war, the Hemingway novel *For Whom the Bell Tolls* (1940, Hebrew translation 1942) was extremely popular. Its figure of the fighting guerilla in the Guadarrama Mountains of Spain conquered the hearts of the young in Palestine. The tactics of guerilla warfare were also a suitable paradigm for the underground nature of the Palmach and its limited means, and these were the fighting methods its members were trained in. The ideal of a popular yet resolute army, courageous and well prepared as fighters, focused on the partisan as its model. During the evenings around the campfire, which became the symbol of Palmach social camaraderie, Russian songs in Hebrew translation were often sung, including many partisan songs. Indeed, Russian songs were the most popular genre among Palmach members.

The aspiration to emulate the Russians did not result in slavish imitation. Components that proved unsuitable to conditions in Palestine in the eyes of the Palmach and its commanders were rejected. For example, the reintroduction of ranks and epaulettes in the Russian Army did not awaken any similar inclination in the Palmach. The iron discipline of "Panphilov's men"—whose commander had the power of life and death over his troops and did not hesitate to exercise it—was likewise not emulated in the Palmach, despite the fact that the novel about Panphilov was almost sacred literature among Palmach ranks. In the same way, education to inculcate hatred of the enemy was also rejected. In Russia and other countries with an active anti-Nazi underground, education to implant hatred of the foreign occupier was a pedagogical instrument designed to bolster the spirit of the underground. But the situation in Palestine was more complex: There was no debate about the need to teach hatred for Nazism and love of the motherland, along the lines practiced by the Russians. It was also clear that just as the Russians cultivated the consciousness in their fighting men that their cause was just, a similar consciousness should be fostered among Palmach fighters. But the Nazis were far away, a distant danger; the real enemy against whom the aggressive feelings of the young had to be channeled were the Arabs and British. Education aimed at instilling hatred for Arabs was likely to act as an impediment on the path to peace in Palestine: "No annihilation of the Arabs and no abysmal hatred for them; likewise, no annihilation of the British and cultivation of hatred for them either—these are the orientation of the Hagana." This fact also limited the possibilities for action open to partisans in Palestine. While their Russian or Yugoslav brethren, fighting against fascism, were allowed to use any means deemed necessary, the situation in Palestine differed. Due to moral and political considerations, their scope of action against the Arabs and British was circumscribed.[64] These directives, published in the Palmach bulletin, give the reader the impression that Palmach members were carrying the analogy too far: Their conclusions based on the analogy of the partisans were somewhat extreme, and even came dangerously close to the views held by members of the IZL and Lehi. For that reason, the Palmach leadership acted quickly to curb the application of the Soviet analogy.

The best example regarding the limit of Soviet influence is Tabenkin's opposition to sending young Jews to assist the Soviet Union during the war. In the first upsurge of enthusiasm for the Soviet Union after the German invasion in the summer of 1941, there were individuals on the Zionist Left who proposed that young people should be sent to assist the Soviet Union in its war against the invaders. Tabenkin replied succinctly that the place of those young people was at home, defending the front in Palestine. The Labor movement, which had looked askance at young people from Palestine volunteering for the civil war in Spain, took the same view in the case of Russia.[65] The attachment to the World Socialist movement, in general, and the Soviet Union, in particular, was secondary to the primacy of Palestine. If Tabenkin had been asked how this was ideologically compatible, he probably would have answered that this was in fact how the Soviet Union acted when it came to its own affairs.

The synthesis between nationalist activism and revolutionary socialism that Tabenkin preached captured the hearts of the young. During the world war, with the Muses silenced, diplomacy hamstrung, and the fate of peoples and countries left to be decided by the sword, it was difficult to expect young people to demonstrate pacifist leanings. The lesson that Palestinian youth had learned from the history of the 1930s was that it was possible to build socialism only by the use of force: "We will conquer this world not by parliamentary means but by force." There was bitter disappointment with evolutionary socialism: "I was educated that the change would come as a result of growth, influence, achievements—not as a result of violence and bloodshed. I don't believe in this now. I don't see any other way except by the use of force." This was a discussion, held in the council of Ha-Mahanot ha-Olim under the shadow of crisis in the wake of the Molotov–Ribbentrop pact and the Russian invasion of Finland. There were some disciples who had reservations about the Soviet regime and serious misgivings about the attack launched by the giant Soviet Union against tiny Finland. Yet the preponderant majority were agreed that the actions of the Soviet Union were not in contradiction with the moral code acceptable to the movement, namely, that there are situations in which the strong, by dint of necessity, are compelled to act against the weak. As an illustration, one of the young people mentioned the example of the strong hand taken by the Histadrut against all sorts of unions weaker than it. Basically, there was general agreement that the use of force was normative and that "power leading to socialism is moral." Consequently, it was easy to arrive at the conclusion, as did one of the participants, that "any assessment that advocates realization of socialism without force and without revolution is unethical, since it delays socialism. Nothing will be realized without the use of force."[66]

When adult ideas and states of mind are appropriated and internalized by young people, there is a tendency to adopt them in a one-dimensional manner: Their borrowed contours are circumscribed, clear-cut, and simple, lacking in sophistication or depth. This was also the case with Tabenkin's ideas. Tabenkin wished to impart an awareness of the legitimacy of the use of force as a means to realize ideas. The emphatic version of those concepts, devoid of mitigating nuances, as expressed in the comments of his pupils, was the product of a process of simplification and radicalization which this idea underwent from one generation to the next. Nonetheless, these young people also felt the pain inherent in shifting from a belief in the brotherhood of peoples, love of man, and the hope of peace to a bald and brutal recognition that only by means of force was it possible to attain the cherished visions. The war led to ideas in strict opposition to the image of the world that had been inculcated in the youth movement even a decade earlier.[67]

The socialist revolution was still a distant dream. The immediate problem young people were faced with—and to which the aggressive lessons of the war were applied—was the future of Palestine. The leaders of the movement did not keep their assessment a secret: Following the end of the world war, there would be a decisive war for control of Palestine. In seminars with leaders of the Labor movement, young people were taught stark realities: "We are heading toward a war between two peoples." Should the Biltmore Program actually be realized and millions of Jews come to Palestine, "there is no doubt this will not be accepted quietly by the other people in the land." There was some reticence within the youth movement about teaching the perspective of a future war between Jews and Arabs. Yet there was something in the entire ambience of the war that opened the door to such observations, unacceptable in the past. This was an atmosphere that demanded clear-headedness, discarding any illusions, while faced with the wholesale undermining of all foundations of human society.[68]

The link between socialist activism and nationalist activism was almost taken for granted by Tabenkin's disciples. Actually, Tabenkin never distinguished between the two: Zionist socialism of the Ahdut ha-Avoda type always regarded the socialist and Zionist components as compatible and to be realized simultaneously. Among youth associated with Ha-Kibbutz ha-Meuhad, an identity was forged between the two: Whoever was opposed to the Soviet system and repelled by revolutionary socialism, was apparently also opposed to Zionist activism, that is, to clashes with the authorities, illegal immigration, and (particularly) the existence of an independent Jewish defense force. In the struggles between the left and right wings within Mapai, the moderates were classified as belonging to the forces on the Right. Indeed, there were some activists, such as Berl Katznelson, Golomb, Meirov, and Ben Gurion, who were in the so-called right-wing camp. But the young people considered them to be moderate leaders acting to curb the drive for action so characteristic of youth. "Moderation" was associated in their eyes with social democracy, a synonym for weakness and failure; with opposition to the cherished Soviet Union; with a faith in treacherous Britain. All these elements were contemptible in the eyes of the majority of the young. Not in vain, one of the youngsters in Ha-Mahanot ha-Olim commented that the moderate youth movement Gordonia had no prospect of attracting young people in Palestine since its educational orientation was not compatible with the spirit and mood prevalent among the youth there.[69]

In the autumn of 1943 a month-long seminar was held at Kibbutz Gevat for the "seniors" (eighteen-year-olds) of Ha-Mahanot ha-Olim. The speakers were the most prominent instructors and educators, as well as key political personalities. Apart from Tabenkin, Katznelson, Golomb, and lesser luminaries, the participants included Eliezer Liebenstein, formerly a member of Ha-Kibbutz ha-Meuhad and now an activist on the right in Mapai, as well as Ernst Simon. Simon, along with other former members of Brit Shalom, Ha-Shomer ha-Tzair, and Left Poalei Zion, had established the group Ihud, another attempt to create a pressure group in the Yishuv for the cause of a Jewish–Arab accord. The confrontation at the seminar between Simon, Liebenstein, and the disciples was highly instructive regarding the thinking and outlook of the young people. Liebenstein and Simon presented the positions of the Arabs and the British to them. Liebenstein tried to explain that "acquiring a country of one people by another is a tragic affair for the Arab people. That has to be understood." He described the feeling of the Arab when a Jew acquired his land, comparing it to the feelings of a Jew when his land is transferred to Arab ownership. Simon attacked the Biltmore Program and in that connection stated: "We are entering a country populated by another people, and are not show-ing that people any consideration. The Arabs are afraid we may force them out of here. They hear ideas about transfer. And there is justified apprehension." He predicted that the Biltmore Program, if made a reality, would lead to war between Jews and Arabs, challenging the idea that it really meant the adoption of Jabo-tinsky's program by the Labor movement: "In the field of visionary politics, Jabotinsky articulated at an early juncture what most other Zionists were only thinking."

Simon's words provoked sharp reactions from the young seniors. They responded with animosity to his charge that the Jews, by coming into Palestine, were causing injustice to the Arabs. They asserted that Jewish settlement had led to a rise in the living standards of the Arab population and in so doing had spurred the development of their national consciousness. Simon's reply that economic ben-efits were no compensation for political damage did not seem to impress them. In contrast, they showed considerable interest in the idea of transfer. Simon rejected population transfer on ethical grounds and also did not think it was a practicable solution. One of the graduates responded with the question, "Which is more ethi-cal, to leave Jews to be annihilated in the Diaspora or to bring them against oppo-sition to Palestine and to carry out a transfer, even by force, of Arabs to Arab coun-tries?" When Simon presented his view that acquisition of land from Arabs was only permissible if it did not involve eviction, one of those present shouted that Bet ha-Shita, the model kibbutz of Ha-Mahanot ha-Olim, was located on lands where Arabs had previously been settled and that they had not received alternative land. Yet where only a handful had lived before, there were now three hundred people. As to Jabotinsky, they argued that the difference between him and the Labor move-ment was not in the approach to the use of force but in the method of building up the land.

Liebenstein explained British policy in a sophisticated way. He presented the British Empire as moderationist: It tried to rule by a minimal use of force and thus pursued a line of compromise and concession. British policy in Palestine was not anti-Jewish, he contended—quite the contrary. That policy facilitated the devel-opment of the national home. The unfortunate matter was that from the moment it ran up against Arab opposition, British policy had searched for ways to arrive at a compromise. Their desire to appease the Arabs derived from the strength shown by the Arabs in Palestine and especially from the massive Arab presence in the region as a whole.

Liebenstein's comments were given a cool reception. One of the young people asserted that his depiction of the British as sympathetic to the Zionist cause and the claim that they had a tendency to compromise was detrimental from the point of view of morale and education: It functioned to weaken the animosity toward the British, against whom it was necessary to struggle. The young men reiterated the view presented by Tabenkin and his associates: Britain was an imperialist power, part of the forces of the past, devoid of any virtue. Liebenstein tried to give the disciples a more complex picture of reality, one in which good and bad were intermingled. There was a need to fight against the White Paper but not to hate the British. If they had so wanted, the British could have suppressed the Jewish community in Palestine completely. "You have a sick attitude toward England," he declared. Simon likewise tried to impart a more balanced attitude to the British: "Among all the peoples, the British have done more for us than any others," he argued. Yet neither of them succeeded in persuading their youthful audience.

While Simon was looking for ways to avoid Jewish–Arab confrontation, Liebenstein felt it was unavoidable: "In the course of the coming years, it will become clear who owns the country." He presented Zionist policy as one that intended to create counterpressure to neutralize Arab pressure on the British. To that end, it would utilize an array of means, one of the most important of which was underground military power. Yet he stressed that this was not the only instrument. Though his conclusion was in keeping with the mood of the young people present, Liebenstein's explanations were at odds with their assumptions about the British. His level of sophistication was too complex, not compatible with their one-dimensional view of the world, a result of education and age.

Simon was bombarded with questions about his attitude toward the Hagana. He replied that he did not reject the use of force in principle. But he distinguished between defense and militarism, stating, "We're approaching the limit beyond which defense changes from a necessary evil into a complete ideology" and "From a situation where defense is seen as an indispensible necessity, we shift to one where it is viewed as a blessing in itself." As an example of this change in values, Simon referred to Tabenkin's approach.

There was a gaping abyss between Simon, the humanist faithful to European civilization of the era before World War I, and the young Palestinians, schooled in revolutionary socialism in the context of a country of colonization. A kind of double dichotomy emerged. When it came to the local arena, members of Ihud expressed their doubts about the ability of the Jewish people to solve without allies (i.e., without Great Britain) its gargantuan problems whenever the war ended. Yet they were optimistic when it came to the international arena. Every dark period in human history, Simon argued, had brought a counterreaction in its wake. Consequently, the world after the end of the war would be better than that which had preceded it. The young people, in contrast, expressed great optimism regarding the strength of the Yishuv and enormous confidence in its ability to decide the fate of Palestine by dint of its own power. Yet they were extremely pessimistic when it came to the world at large. "On what basis can we assume that the new world will be better than that between the wars?" one of them challenged: "I fail to see any reason whatsoever that would warrant such hopes. . . . I have no faith at all in a liberal world that will supposedly arise on the ruins of this one." They repeatedly claimed, "We must be a power," referring to physical might.[70] The somber pessimism of the young and the rationalistic optimism of Simon and his associates were generations apart. They were separated by different cultural traditions and by the impact of reality as a formative factor.

On the declamatory level, the policy of rejecting education aimed at inculcating hatred for Arabs was still valid. Yet at the same time, there was increased reference to the struggle for the future of Palestine as an inevitable conflict. The gap between the peace declarations and the emphasis on the likelihood of war did not escape the attention either of the educators or their pupils. More and more, reference to the aspiration for peace and the desire for Jewish–Arab friendship became a kind of ritualized convention, repeated without any deep conviction.

Toward the end of the war, Shlomo Drexler (Derekh), one of the central figures in Ha-Kibbutz ha-Meuhad, summed up the dominant approach in his circle regarding the use of force in the following words: "The problem is not a theoretical, moral one. . . . In reality, there is no question about the use of violence or not. The problem is, Revolutionary or counterrevolutionary violence? In literature, in university lecture halls, in various kinds of frameworks divorced from real life, there is room for a philosophical discussion about violence or nonviolence. Within the social struggle, there is only one problem: What kind of violence?"[71]

Massada as a Myth of Heroism

One of the methods for probing changes in ethos is to examine changes in the body of myths in whose spirit youth is educated. The mythos that became central during the war years and was dominant even after its end was an ancient story of heroism: the myth of Massada.

As I have mentioned, Jewish tradition over the centuries had not looked favorably on the Massada myth. The tale is told by Josephus in *The Jewish War* and was not absorbed into Jewish traditional texts. It ended up in a reworked version in the *Book of Josippon* and did not enjoy particular popularity in rabbinical literature. The episode contained elements that were considered foreign to the spirit of traditional Judaism. The idea of dying for freedom, not to mention the killing of women and children for its cause, was not acceptable in Judaism. It was Rabbi Yohanan ben Zakkai who was depicted by tradition as the rabbi who saved Judaism, not Elazar ben Yair, the commander of Massada, who remained external to that tradition. In the Middle Ages, there had been examples of family murder and suicide as martyrdom; although these were not normative from the standpoint of Jewish halakhah, they were accepted by the rabbinical sages because of the state of mind of "with all thy soul and with all thy might" that they manifested and that the sages could not denounce.

At the beginning of Jewish historiography in the nineteenth century, Massada was rediscovered by the Jews. It was given favorable mention by Berdichevsky and entered the pantheon of Ahimeir. During the 1920s there were several excursions by students from the Herzliya Gymnasia to Massada, but these apparently did not leave any lasting impression on the behavioral norms of youth in general in Palestine. The popular central myth of heroism in the Yishuv was that of Tel Hai— which, as I have mentioned, was embraced as a symbol by both the Right and the Left, each side emphasizing different elements.

In 1927 there was a watershed event in the evolution of the myth: the publication of Lamdan's poem "Massada." As I have noted (chapter 4), Lamdan used Massada as a symbol of salvation, an allegory for Palestine, to which pioneers from the lands of exile, beset by toil and torment, set forth. Massada (only at the end of the 1930s did the more accurate term Metzada (Fortress) become popular in Hebrew) was depicted as the last haven to which refugees flee, those who have escaped the hangman's noose in countries around the globe. Beyond the efforts that Massada necessitates, the conclusion is optimistic: "Go up the flame of dance / Again Massada shall not fall." Lamdan depicted the heroic epic of the Third Aliyah, Massada serving as the thread linking the destruction of the past and the hope for the future. From the time it was published, sections of the poem were a literary commodity much in demand in readings of the youth movements—all in the heroic–optimistic spirit of its author. The dialogue between the refugee and the guards upon the wall of Massada, that begins with the words: "Open, Massada, your gate; and I, the refugee, shall enter!" was meant to underline the tragedy of Jewish existence in exile, in contrast with the exaltedness of the last refuge. As Lamdan writes: "This is the limit. From here on, there are no boundaries."[72]

The year 1933 saw the publication of research by A. Schulten, the German scholar who had pioneered new directions in investigation on Massada. Yosef Klausner and Y. Bar Droma published a book in Hebrew entitled *Metzada ve-Giboreha* (Massada and its heroes) in 1937, and a trend began to integrate the Massada tale in stories for children. Nevertheless, the legend had still not taken on mythic proportions; nor was it incorporated within the educational context. In excursions now and again up to Massada by the disciples of the youth movements of Labor Palestine, there was a mixture of love for the land, the desire to discover the desert, the challenge of a trip to an unknown region, love of adventure, and the collective experience. There is no evidence of any special effort during that period to impart historical values associated with the site. Massada was a difficult destination in physical terms; and whoever made it to the top, was proud of scaling its heights and enthused about the awe-inspiring natural panorama that unfolded before him from its ramparts. Halfhearted attempts to read the ritual sections from the "Massada" could not compete with the desire to sleep of most climbers who reached the fortress—due to their sheer exhaustion.[73]

In the program of readings put on in the summer of 1939 in Ha-Mahanot ha-Olim, long sections of the poem were quoted, along with selections from *Bi-Vritekh* (In your Covenant) the 1937 booklet of Ha-Mahanot ha-Olim, and other literary works. Lamdan's "Massada" was quoted in connection with the topic of illegal immigration. The influx of illegal immigrants was a central educational theme during that period, and sections from the poem were meant to highlight the resoluteness of the refugees yearning for the secure haven.[74] At this juncture, Massada was still an allegory for Palestine and its development.

At the Twenty-first Zionist Congress in late August 1939, a new tone was heard for the first time. In a version that anticipated the debate between the activists and the moderates, within a discussion on illegal immigration, Shertok lashed out at Rabbi Solomon Goldman from the United States. The latter had spoken in favor of Yohanan ben Zakkai and against Rabbi Akiva, one of the leaders of the Bar Kokhba revolt. Shertok referred to the great revolt and stated: "If our state was destined to be destroyed by Rome, it is preferable that this destruction came after a revolt. Blessed is our history, that gave us this dignity, this pride . . . as evidence that we are a people that will not surrender without a fight, a people prepared to shed its blood for its independence."[75] Up until that time, the positive presentation of the heroic failures of the Jewish war against the Romans had not been popular among Labor movement circles. Not that it was completely absent: Berdichevsky was regarded by Katznelson, Tabenkin and their pupils as one of their mentors, much more so than Ahad Ha-Am. But the fact was that these events were little discussed and certainly not in a positive light. Ever since Uri Zvi Greenberg and Abba Ahimeir had seized upon the myths of the destruction of the Second Temple and made them central components of their historical and political conception, the heads of the Labor movement had been careful about appropriating them for their own purposes. Moreover, those myths were not compatible with the defensive ethos, the urge to build the land, and the evolutionary perspective that dominated Labor thinking. Only after the cannon of World War II began to thunder, and the widespread feeling took hold that the White Paper had cornered the Zionist movement with its "back against the wall" (to allude to a famous article by that title that Katznelson wrote at the time), did the myths of desperate heroism begin to penetrate public consciousness and seep into the educational system.

The first two years of the war brought a series of traumata that had a major impact on education. The *Patria* episode stirred stormy debate among adults between activists and moderates. Young people, however, saw it as an example of desperate courage whose positive value was beyond any doubt. In February 1942 the refugee ship *Struma* sank in the Black Sea, where it had been sent by the Turkish authorities after all efforts to make the British agree to transferring these refugees to Palestine had proven fruitless. The turning away of Jews seeking asylum in Palestine was viewed by youth as not only a manifestation of inhumanity but a national humiliation, as well, requiring a response that was "not selective in its means." For example, members of Kibbutz Gennosar complained bitterly to the Histadrut that it had not activated them before the *Struma* disaster: "We would have been ready to sacrifice our lives in order to prevent that fate and that disgrace."[76] Thousands reacted like them, demanding that they be given the order to take action.

From the perspective of the adults, the most difficult trauma in those years (before the information on the Holocaust was verified) was the fear of a British withdrawal from Palestine. The first wave of such apprehensions swept the community in the spring of 1941, when Rommel was advancing in the North African desert. It was repeated, perhaps even with greater intensity, in the spring and summer of 1942. In the light of the rapid advance of German units in Russia and the pullback of the British to Alamein in Egypt, there appeared to be a realistic possibility that the British could pull back as far as Iraq. The British officers with whom members of the political department of the Jewish Agency were in contact did not conceal the sense of panic spreading through their ranks. The question what the Jewish community in Palestine would do in such an eventuality was painfully difficult. The idea of a total or partial evacuation was not realistic. In the hasty confusion of a withdrawal, no one would devote the necessary logistic means for that purpose. There were those in the community who, in conjunction with Jewish leaders throughout Europe, thought in economic terms: They reasoned the Germans would like to exploit the productive capacity of the Jewish community in Palestine, and that if Jews would behave properly, toe the line, and not indulge in provocations, they might make it through a German occupation unscathed. Others, however, especially those identified with the activists, did not harbor any such illusions. Information from the Russian front on the inhuman behavior of Germans toward the Russian and Jewish population hinted at the fate awaiting the Yishuv if the misfortune of an occupation should befall them.[77]

In the ranks of the active leadership elite, concentrated in Mapai, the top echelon of the Hagana, and Ha-Kibbutz ha-Meuhad, ideas began to surface about a desperate last stand, the "final battle," whose negative outcome was certain. That last stand was destined to generate the myth of the Yishuv's heroism, a community destroyed in the fury of battle. That myth, in turn, would nourish the spirit of Jews for generations to come and serve as a source of pride and national vitality. In the dramatic discussions that took place at the beginning of July 1942 in Ha-Kibbutz ha-Meuhad, in which participants avoided looking each other in the eye, Galili spoke about the desire "to be a kind of Musa Dagh in Palestine, a sort of Massada," in the hope of "demonstrating Jewish dignity and avoiding a death in disgrace."[78]

The first book by the new publishing house Am Oved of the Histradut came into the shops in early 1941. Berl Katznelson, the editor of the new house, chose an anthology about Jewish heroism over the centuries. This is not one of the outstanding titles ever published by Am Oved, but its purpose was didactic: It was intended to teach young people that Jews in the past had found themselves ensnared in impossible, desperate situations and had died a heroic death. "Jewish heroism since the days of the destruction of the Second Temple," Katznelson wrote in his preface, "was heroism without any prospect for victory—the heroism of believers to whom God had hidden his face."[79] He ended his remarks with an attempt to distinguish between the tragic heroism characterizing Jews in the Diaspora and victorious heroism in Palestine, like that at Tel Hai. Though it might lose a battle, it would win the war. Yet it was doubtful whether that optimistic conclusion could be inferred from the book and stand up under the stress of those hard times. Galili considered this volume on heroism to be quite important and made sure that at meetings of the Hagana, sections from it were read aloud. He defined its topic as "Massada throughout the generations" and contended that it contained important educational values when perceived against the background of the era and the "days to come."[80]

Education glorifying heroic death was not popular within the ranks of the Labor movement, in contrast with the tradition espoused by Ahimeir, Greenberg, and their disciples. The lesson read in the fate of Trumpeldor and his comrades was "in their deaths, they bequeathed us life." The Zionist enterprise was not meant to be one more abortive heroic escapade of fasle messianism. Rather, it was a constructive project, nurtured, to be sure, by mystical ardor but making use of rational means. The preservation of strength and care not to squander it in lost battles were central values in the conceptual framework of the Labor movement. However, in light of the expected German conquest, all rational considerations paled; and the moment of truth arrived when the Yishuv would have to cease thinking in terms of utility and come face to face with tragic Jewish fate.

The book on Jewish heroism contained illustrations of martyrdom over the ages. Yet the concept of martyrdom as such found little echo among Palestinian youth. It dealt with events affecting Jews far from Palestine, in the Diaspora. Their motives were principally religious, despite the fact that the book tried its best to stress the national character of Jewish–Gentile confrontations. Martyrdom underscored Jewish weakness and helplessness and did not stir any empathetic feelings among Palestinian youth. In contrast, the Massada legend possessed all the necessary attributes for youth movement education: an impressive and remote site, distant from any populated area, inaccessible and requiring a long and arduous journey. It was a narrative about true warriors, men and women who had preferred death over surrender. It was a Palestinian heroic myth, interwoven with the cruel landscape of the Judean desert, awakening rich associations with the Bible.

At the end of 1941 a group from Ha-Kibbutz ha-Meuhad, distinguished by a number of men who in their youth had been the founders of Ha-Noar ha-Oved youth movement, made an excursion to the desert, placing special emphasis on Massada. This was not the first time that Shmarya Gutman, a member of Kibbutz Na'an and the animating spirit in the group, had scaled the Massada. While Massada had interested only a small number of dedicated enthusiasts in the 1930s, now a conscious attempt was made to transform it into a pilgrimage destination for youth groups, "in order to generate contact between Jewish youth and the fortress, whose educational value is inestimable."[81] This pioneering group initiated a second, longer ascent. January 1942 witnessed the first institutionally organized ascent to the Massada by members of the youth movements. The initiative and most of the young people (numbering nearly fifty) came from Ha-Noar ha-Oved. Yet from the very beginning, an attempt was made to transform the matter into a project involving all the youth movements of Labor Palestine. Thus, participants in this historic ascent were also drawn from the ranks of Ha-Mahanot ha-Olim and Ha-Shomer ha-Tzair. Before the excursion, participants attended a five-day preparation course. That course, besides concentrating on the route and topography, inculcated the teachings of the Massada legend. The excursion itself was brief, in contrast with previous trips to the desert, in which ascent to the Massada was the supreme achievement after a lengthy and arduous trek. This time, the emphasis was on Massada itself and its antiquities and on improving the trail by hewing out steps in its upper section. The excursion was thought to be historic. There was mention that the participants had brought "the good tidings of Massada." The trip symbolized that "the chain of Massada had not been sundered," a nebulous paraphrase of a line from the Lamdan poem. It was decided that they would bring out a special booklet to immortalize the excursion. This constituted the first step in transforming the ascent to the Massada into a tradition in the youth movements.[82]

Right from the start, there was an element of ambivalence in the pedagogical message of Massada. Massada taught the grandeur of heroic death, the preference of voluntary death to a life in bondage. Despite all its romanticism, this was not a message the youth movement could utilize for educating its members. One of the blessings of youth is its inherent optimism. In the conditions of 1942, when even many adults found it difficult to face the dread of annihilation, young people found the idea of death and failure intolerable. Thus, already, the very first references to the ascent of the Massada were ambiguous. Among them was an article accompanied by a photo of the site in the journal of Ha-Noar ha-Oved, *Ba-Ma'ale,* on the eve of Passover 1942. (The ancient Massada suicides had taken place on the first day of Passover, and Ha-Noar ha-Oved had specifically picked that particular holiday for the yearly ascent to its top.) The paper spoke about the fate of the fortress defenders and the global struggle underway against fascism, stressing that Jews were always its first victims. Yet it also proclaimed, "Don't despair, members of Ha-Noar ha-Oved!"—adding, "Massada speaks to us today, too, since for us, all of Palestine is now a single Massada." This was a paraphrase of a line coined by Katznelson after Tel Hai: "All of Palestine is Tel Hai for us, *ancient mounds that live*" (emphasis mine). There was an inclination, in naming Jewish settlements in Palestine, to emphasize the symbiosis of destruction and rebirth by combining the word *tel* (ancient mound) with such words as *hai* (living), *aviv* (spring), and similar expressions. That symbiosis was now implied for Massada, as well, using the phrase by Berl Katznelson. In this way, it was transformed from a symbol of destruction to one linking a glorious past and a shining future. While reminding the reader of the dreadful times, the proclamation ends on the note of triumph: "The Massada camp will gird us for a life of labor, defense, and freedom. *Massada will not fall again!*"[83]

The piece "The Massada Message," which the participants read in the youth camp on the summit of the fortress, was in a style far removed from the low-key tradition of the Labor movement. A lofty tone predominated. The flowery language helped to blur the lack of clarity of its message. The Brennerian phrase "the last ones on the wall"—originally a reference to the last of those faithful to the Hebrew language—was applied here to the defenders of the Massada. The young people of Ha-Noar ha-Oved imagined themselves to be those last ones on the wall, but it was not clear which wall. They tried to mix the message of heroism coming from the war front, especially the Russian front, where Jewish partisans were also fighting, together with the tradition of heroism of Massada. Massada for them meant just a myth of heroism. The component of a community going down in flames was apparently at the back of the minds of the adults who propagated the myth in 1942 but definitely far removed from the youngsters' consciousness.[84]

Ha-Mahanot ha-Olim followed in the footsteps of Ha-Noar ha-Oved. They chose to ascend Massada during Hanukkah, in remembrance of the valorous deeds of the Maccabees, a more optimistic symbol of a heroic war. It is also possible that they were influenced by the fact that the relatively cool weather during Hanukkah is more suitable for an ascent of Massada in the scorching Judean desert. In December 1942, when some 250 youths from Ha-Mahanot ha-Olim scaled the Massada, the news trickling in about the ongoing Holocaust was uppermost in the public consciousness. In a symbolic spirit, the young people brought a stone monument up with them to the summit. It contained the inscription "If I forget thee, Diaspora" and "In memory of the Diaspora, rolling in its blood," as reported in an article written after the event. Like Ha-Noar ha-Oved, Ha-Mahanot ha-Olim did not draw conclusions of despair from Massada. Lamdan's poem, with its positive messages, was the centerpiece of the "Massada ceremony" conducted at the site, which was concluded with the hora dance "God Will Build Massada." Even when the "Yizkor" prayer was being recited for the Diaspora, the conclusion was, "Every drop [of blood] that has survived is to be preserved for these hills and valleys—until the tree of Israel is planted once again in our land." The youths spoke about "constructive vengeance," not about the "final battle."[85]

The other youth movements soon followed suit. Ha-Shomer ha-Tzair and Gordonia, two groupings that represented antiactivist currents in the Labor movement, also fell under Massada's spell. On one of the first excursions of Ha-Shomer ha–Tzair to that region, grenades that had been placed in one of the backpacks as a precaution exploded, killing several youngsters. From that time on, the excursions to Massada by that movement were dedicated to the memory of the dead disciples. The excursion organized by Gordonia in 1945 fell victim to an attack by two armed Arab robbers who assaulted the defenseless convoy. Young men were killed, and property stolen. In response, the Youth Department of the Jewish Agency banned excursions to Massada that year. This was viewed by the young people as an affront to national honor and sparked strong protests.[86] Yet that prohibition was only temporary. The ascent to Massada was incorporated in the educational program of every youth movement within Labor Palestine.

Two components struggled for predominance: heroic pathos and the collective experience. There is no doubt that the importance of heroic pathos was on the increase. Comparing the low-key description in *Bi-Vritekh* with the experience depicted by later classes, there is no doubt that the latter had profound emotional experiences—expressions of solidarity with the heroes of Massada and with the historical romanticism of the site.[87] To the same extent, another significant dimension involved was the "togetherness," the "camaraderie," the dynamics of a group of youth under great tension, facing a test of their mettle. "It seems as though everything that is beautiful, social, and faithful, hidden in the heart of the 'group', a social body, has been revealed to us for the first time," one of the participants recorded after the journey and ascent to Massada.[88] First and foremost, it was the youth movement experience that prompted even the moderate movements to adopt Massada as the object of their excursions. There was no youth movement that could resist this social attraction. Ultimately, the trek served as a means for mobilizing the dynamics of the youth group to the communication of a national message. The psychoerotic experiences of youth blended with the historical–romantic impact of the site.

From 1943 on, Massada and Tel Hai became the two principal educational foci in Ha-Noar ha-Oved. The two were so closely intertwined that in one of the issues of *Ba-ma'ale,* dedicated to the yearly excurions to Massada and Tel Hai, there was a large photo of Massada and, in a small circular inset, a photograph of Tel Hai. The caption underneath read, "The chain has not been severed—from Massada to Tel Hai." The spring was dedicated in the youth movement to extensive discussions on the topic of Jewish heroism in past and present. One theme included in these deliberations was Jewish settlement in Palestine and the central role of the Hagana. The stories of Massada and Tel Hai were the focal symbols in the educational program. Tel Hai changed from an emblem of steadfast defense of the soil to a symbol of the bravery necessary for the acquisition of a homeland. Massada, in contrast, also had certain political undertones, a dimension of struggle for national independence that had been absent from the humbler goals of the Tel Hai myth in the past. Massada and Tel Hai transmitted the message of activism according to Tabenkin: It was better to die than to live a life of bondage. He who fears and capitulates, like France, earns the disdain of the world. In contrast, "whoever endangers all and fights without temporary reservations, enjoys the taste of victory."

Despite the fact that Massada and Tel Hai ended in defeat, as symbols, they were meant to spark hopes of victory. Around these two myths, an entire web of allusions and tales of heroism was woven. That web of tales was created from stories about Jewish and Russian fighters in the world war, along with firsthand narrations of Hagana exploits in Palestine. This was also an opportunity to remind young people that when the world war was over, there would be a struggle for the homeland. All this was associated with the drive in the youth movement for recruitment to the British Army and, in particular, to the Palmach.[89]

Toward the end of the war, the issue of the struggle against the British became acute. During Passover 1944, a trip was organized to Massada dedicated to the struggle for "the liberty of Israel and its independence in a Jewish labor homeland . . . on the eve of the difficult and desperate struggle of those who wish to implement that document of treachery and deceit, the White Paper." Parallel with this, an excursion was organized to Tel Hai that according to the report, united the young disciples "into one camp, loyal and prepared to carry out the order of the hour."[90] In that same period, there was a renewal of another tradition of heroism, connected with the festival of Hanukkah, now termed Festival of Hebrew Bravery—the yearly pilgrimage to Modi'in, the home village of the Hasmonean family, including a visit to the graves of the Hasmoneans and explanations about the wars of the Maccabees.[91] A tradition of the Herzliya Gymnasia since the twenties, it was now also adopted by the youth movements. In 1945 leaders of Ha-Noar ha-Oved waxed poetic about Massada: "What else could the Jewish exiles take with them on their path of sorrow except the memory of Massada?" Actually, they knew that the Jewish people had forgotten Massada and for centuries had had no use for its memory. In fact, this is what made Massada the symbol of the new generation, "the great-grandchildren of its warriors, its heroes," who felt they had little affinity with Jews in the Diaspora, because the latter lacked any tradition of heroism and bravery.[92]

While in Ha-Noar ha-Oved, the Massada cult of heroism was characterized by an extremely high level of pathos, it was integrated in Ha-Mahanot ha-Olim within a methodical program of education, aimed at inculcating patriotism, along the lines of *Bi-Vritekh*. At the festival of the movement held toward the end of 1944, there were pronounced motifs of heroism from the days of Ezra and Nehemiah, the Hasmoneans, Gush Halav, and Yodefat, as well as Massada. By the same token, maps of the movement's trips and exhibits underscoring the role of the movement in settlement activity were also prominent.[93] Along with this there was a special educational program entitled "A Hebrew Boy in the War of National Liberation." This program surveyed all the Jewish myths of heroism, from the heroes of the Bible and Massada, on to Trumpeldor and those who were killed at Kibbutz Ramat ha-Kovesh during a brutal British search for weapons in 1943. Jewish passive bravery over the centuries was also recalled, in the spirit of the *Book of Jewish Heroism*. The struggle of pioneering youth in the ghettos was given prominence. But the heart of the program dealt with the role of youth in defense. Emphasis was placed on the combination of elements of work and defense, and the Palmach camps in the kibbutzim were held up as the desirable model.[94]

The various educational plans, programs, excursions, readings, ceremonies, and parties were not marked by any tone of nationalist aggressiveness. Nevertheless, the massive rise in the component of heroic myths in youth education was significant. The personal diary of one Palmach member depicts how the myth became a central component within the consolidation of group cohesion and ideological indoctrination: "Now I remember the first party. The Hanukkah party. They talked about our role. Our mission. They spoke about bravery, dedication, self-sacrifice. They praised the Maccabees. Warm feelings flooded your heart when you saw how people who were still strangers just the day before were coming closer together, feeling the common bond of responsibility."[95]

Up until the world war, the dominant mythos had been that of the pioneer and worker. That myth expected young people to be faithful workers on the soil of the homeland and to defend it if necessary. Now the message was communicated that the role of the worker continued to be important but was secondary to the role of the fighter. The message imparted by the heroic myths stated that youth was destined to carry to completion the Jewish struggle in Palestine—to fight a war of national liberation—and that this was the first national priority. Occasionally those two messages were combined together, as in the Birya episode in March 1946: The ascent to Birya by disciples of the youth movements, in defiance of British orders, emphasized both the value of the fighter and that of the settler. The clashes with British security forces helped to illuminate this aspect. Similarly, the eleven settlements that were established in the Negev in October 1946, whose defensive value was indisputable, also underscored the interdependence of the fighter and the pioneer. Yet even in these events, there was some shift in the center of gravity: Their chief importance lay not in the colonizing aspect but in their military–occupational value. This is how they were perceived by the young.

The central role of heroic myths among Palestinian Jewish youth is evident in a comparison of the educational programs of the youth movements with educational materials prepared at that same time, apparently by adults, for the Histadrut festival in December 1944. The old slogans, in the spirit of the defensive ethos, reappeared in the adult materials: "Our song is not blood, not battles, our song is life and creativity!" and "One doesn't [re]build ruins by swords!" The hero was the pioneer; and the quotations from the fathers of the movement underscored the importance of immigration and settlement and disregarded the issues of defense and fighting. This program contained no manifestation of the pulse of the time and the events of the era and was in stark contradiction with the predominant trend in the youth movements.[96]

The penetration of historical romanticism into the educational fabric of the youth movements augmented the similarity between the educational content of Betar, the IZL, and Lehi on the one hand and that of the youth movements associated with Mapai or Ha-Tenua le-Ahdut ha-Avoda on the other. I have already noted that the literary and cultural sources were shared by both sides to a significant extent. Tchernichovsky, for example, enjoyed general admiration; and his poem "I Have a Melody," with its message about the "blood of the conquerors of Canaan" and the "melody of blood and fire" stirred strong emotions in both camps.[97]

Nonetheless, there was a key difference between the romanticism of the IZL and Lehi and that of the left youth movements. The romanticism of the Right was to a large extent abstract, out of touch with reality. In contrast, myths on the left were translated into terms that were palpable, visible, amenable to experience: concrete sites, landscapes, places of settlement. Concomitantly, there were two different types of the sense of ownership. One had its source in the romanticism of the past. The second derived from the reality of the present, in which the past served as a backdrop, a strengthener, a supplement to the basic feeling of actual ownership, deriving from the direct attachment to the land. When the poet A. Hillel described the generation of the Palmach, he depicted them all as adoring one beloved, a love that evoked no jealousy among them: "That beloved was the homeland, the country, the soil—*in its simplest meaning.*" The feeling of concreteness is conveyed in the following description: "They are waging the war for their love; out of true love—of the kind that is sucked with the thumb, absorbed with the songs of pioneers, stuck with the briar thorns in the bare leg!"[98] It was not by mere chance that they chose to make so many treks and excursions throughout the length and breadth of Palestine. They developed a new area of studies whose very name hinted at the erotic connection between them and Palestine: Yediat ha-Aretz (Knowledge of the Land).[99] It is doubtful whether these excursions began as part of an intentional plan to impart a sense of homeland; yet it is clear that in the 1940s, that educational effect was already taken into account in the Palmach and the various youth movements. The symbiosis between historical myth and concrete landscape resulted in a unique emotional bond between youth and the land.

Holocaust and Power

Beginning with the end of 1942, the Holocaust became a dominant element in the public agenda of the Yishuv. This does not mean that it penetrated consciousness, became a formative psychological or ideological factor, or shaped value orientations. Even more doubtful was people's actual ability to cope with the reality of the

Holocaust and internalize it. The attitude toward the Holocaust was manifested in two parallel domains: the sphere of principles and theory (grasping as a fact that one-third of the Jewish people was being annihilated) and the human–pragmatic sphere (meeting survivors in Palestine). Between these two domains lay a third, serving as a bridge, namely, the attitude toward what were termed "Jews of the Diaspora."

In a society with a high level of ideological tension like the Yishuv, it can be assumed that such a traumatic experience would leave its imprint on every mode of thought, worldview, and understanding of reality. Indeed, on the rhetorical–declarative level, there was not a speech that did not mention the Holocaust as a formative factor impinging on the consciousness of the generation. However, it is difficult to find an area where it actually functioned as a catalyst for a fundamental change, a different approach, a major shift in behavior. In the political sphere, the goals of the Zionist movement were defined and shaped well before reports about the Holocaust had been verified. When the Biltmore Program was approved, millions of the Jews it had envisaged absorbing into Palestine were already dead. The fact that the disaster became known did not lead to changes in existing plans. Rather, it led to growing pressure for their immediate implementation. The gap left by the murdered Jews was symbolically filled by the She'erit ha-Pleta (surviving remnant)—survivors from the camps and forests, repatriated returnees from Russia, and Holocaust survivors in the Balkans. They were soon joined by Jews from the Muslim countries.

The network of relations inside the various political parties in Palestine or between them and their rivals, does not suggest that any "earthquakes" occurred, either in the political–conceptual sphere or in the realm of human relations, preferred priorities, and norms. The Holocaust did not lead to a major change in worldview, relevant models, or basic ideological attachments. Whoever was "on the left" remained there, as did those "on the right." The cases of a major political or ideational shift as a consequence of grappling with the reality of the Holocaust were few and isolated. Moreover, they generally had to do with the experience of the individual, rather than with the collective. The split within Mapai, evident as early as October 1942, was not halted as a result of the Holocaust. When Mapam (United Workers party) was formed in January 1948 as a result of the unification of Ha-Tenua le-Ahdut ha-Avoda and Ha-Shomer ha-Tzair, its founders made it a point to depict the new political party as a product of the solidarity between the followers of both movements—a bond they said had emerged during the war and was manifested in the uprising in the Warsaw ghetto. But the actual truth was different: The unification was the result of circumstances and developments in Palestine whose connection with events in the Diaspora was rather vague.

An examination of the methods of action of pioneering groups in Eastern Europe, especially in Poland after the war, reveals changes there in attitudes and methods of action. The attempts by leaders of the remaining youth movements in Poland to create new political frameworks, based on the lessons of the Holocaust, met with energetic opposition by the mother movements in Palestine that had remained faithful to older patterns of organization and ideology.[100] Indeed, certain adjustments were made in methods of Zionist action in the wake of the Holocaust:

Illegal immigration, which before the war was on a relatively small scale, now assumed a far greater importance and new proportions. Interest began in the immigration of Jews from Muslim countries, communities that up until the Holocaust had been at the periphery of Zionist activity. Nonetheless, it appears that the answer to the question whether and how the Holocaust changed the world of the Jewish community in Palestine between the years 1942 and 1948 is evident: It altered very little.

In order to internalize historical phenomenon on such a scale, time was needed to create the necessary distance for perspective. For matters to permeate from the external–declarative domain to the internal sphere and then (hopefully) to be translated into ideological and operative conclusions, it was necessary for years to elapse. The events of the 1940s followed each other in such rapid succession that no time was available to digest their import, and responses were nothing but external and shallow.

During those years, utilization of the Holocaust was designed to strengthen and encourage ideologies, views of the world, and self-images that presaged it. The concept *Negation of Exile* was one of the dominant components in Labor ideology in Palestine. A revolutionary movement's need to repudiate everything that had preceded it, to burn bridges to the past in order to gather together the necessary psychological strength for a revolutionary shift, was expressed in the total rejection of Jewish patterns of life in the Diaspora. The negation of exile negated two things: the status of Jews as an eternal minority within a majority people and the economic, social, and political structure of Jewish society (together with the social–psychological traits of the Jew as an individual). Zionist thinkers, beginning with Nahman Syrkin, Ber Borochov, and others of lesser importance, had been convinced that if the Jewish people did not undergo a process of regeneration in Palestine, it was doomed to destruction. That destruction had been expected to occur as a result of revolutionary changes in European countries. Such changes, it was envisaged, would lead to the expulsion of Jews from existing European society and to their erosion in the anticipated social and political struggles. "Catastrophic Zionism" (i.e., the awareness that Zionism had to be achieved quickly, since disaster was imminent for the Jewish people in Europe) was an accepted concept within the ranks of the Zionist movement right from its inception. The view of antisemitism as a dynamic and growing movement had been one of Herzl's conceptual innovations. The conclusion was that it was imperative to act speedily to remove Jews from the Diaspora before the catastrophe occurred.

The conception of catastrophe was opposed to the evolutionary view, which regarded the Zionist project as a slow-paced process, subject to the political and economic constraints placed upon it. There was a wide gap between the down-to-earth realism of the evolutionists and the messianic tension inherent in the catastrophic conception. Yet here, as in other cases, persons were compelled to come to terms with contradictory conceptual frameworks. The same circles of the Zionist–Socialist movement that accepted the catastrophic version (such as Ahdut ha-Avoda in the 1920s and the majority of Mapai until the split in 1944) accepted the evolutionary method as inevitable but did not abandon the catastrophic perspective. Catastrophe consciousness expressed the inner fears felt by the movement concerning the fate of the Jewish people. In the face of events in the 1930s, this approach became more and more relevant. Leaders like Katznelson, Ben Gurion, Tabenkin, and many others articulated this sense of urgency. Significantly, however, the catastrophe they envisaged was not the Holocaust. They expected an increase in phenomena such as pauperization, starvation, lack of hope among youth, and the crumbling of Jewish society. No one thought in terms of actual physical annihilation.[101]

One of the outstanding features of the Palestinian Jewish community was its Palestinocentrism, that is, its tendency to perceive the Zionist project in Palestine as the center of creation. That conception derived from the fundamental Zionist creed that the haven being built in Palestine would ultimately bring the redemption of the entire Jewish people. The ongoing focus on the problems of this small community—to the point of disregarding other burning issues of the Jewish people— found its moral justification in this assertion. Consequently, when the war broke out, the first concern of Jewish leaders in Palestine was how to protect their own flock from the imminent storm. Concern for European Jewry was secondary. They assumed that the dangers facing the Jews there were no greater than those threatening the Palestinian Jews. The threat of a "night of Bartholomew" at the hands of the Arabs in the aftermath of a British defeat seemed more realistic and likely than a slaughter of the Jews of Europe. As long as Rommel's tanks were pounding on the gates of Egypt, the immediate danger threatening the Yishuv was at the top of the list of concerns of Jewish leadership; and the press reports about what was happening in Europe did not penetrate their consciousness.[102] After Rommel was defeated at Alamein and a German invasion averted—and reports on the Holocaust finally verified in November 1942—a slow process of accommodating the reality of the Holocaust to the framework of current ideas and terms of reference in the Yishuv began.

One of the commonly voiced responses was that the catastrophe had been anticipated from the start, that it was a more rapid and brutal realization than expected of catastrophic Zionism. One leader (presumably Moshe Sneh) claimed that "Hitler for me is no surprise. . . . He did not shake my Jewish and Zionist equilibrium one bit. Hitler was expected, he is law for the diasporic Jewry." He contended that the plight of Polish and Romanian Jewry before the war, the assimilation demanded of Jews in "countries of freedom," were in fact equivalent to their annihilation in the gas chambers![103] In contrast, Tabenkin blamed himself for not having been more alert to the handwriting on the wall, despite the awareness since the earliest period of Zionism "that Jewish existence would collapse during revolution. How is it that we did not preach catastrophic Zionism constantly and make it our slogan?" In 1946 Tabenkin already understood the chasm between what had been foreseen and what had taken place: "Apparently, we envisaged the catastrophe. But there were differing degrees of catastrophic prophecy among us and still are. We were probably most sensitive to the certainty of the Jewish catastrophe. We were unable to be calmed by the patience that was incessantly preached to us. Nevertheless, all of us, including those who felt it necessary to force the issue and the restless were cheated; we were led astray."[104] The view that saw the Diaspora as doomed to decline and the perspective that anticipated a physical annihilation were separated by a different approach to the element of time: In the first instance, what was involved was a slow process; in the second, a sudden disaster. People were prepared psychologically and intellectually only for the first eventuality. Hence, the attempt to use familiar concepts to explain the Holocaust soon proved inadequate.

The leaders held up the old Zionist message as the sole viable answer to the Holocaust. Tabenkin stated: "Nothing else will save [Jews] other than this enter-prise. . . . The only program is the Zionist one. Independence of this people in its own land, by its own labor, economy, weapons."[105] Galili told members of Ha-Noar ha-Oved: "We search in vain for new answers to the Holocaust of the Diaspora. The answers are inscribed on the banners of our movement and are established in its decisions and commandments. The answers were carved from the deep recesses of the life of the people and the land."[106]

Golomb posited the appropriate response to the Holocaust in another domain of action: recruitment to the British army. Such enlistment had been his special concern since the beginning of the war. Galili's solution was to advocate joining the Palmach. Tabenkin, in contrast, stressed the need for a broader approach: readying oneself for Zionist missions of any kind, with special emphasis on recruitment to all the branches of the security forces. Ben Gurion, since 1937 under the spell of the idea of a Jewish state, proclaimed that the Holocaust had been possible because "the Jews do not have any status in respect to statehood. There is no Jewish army, no Jewish independence, and no secure and open homeland." He regarded indepen-dence as the recompense for the historical injustice perpetrated against the Jews.[107] A radical expression of Palestinocentrism can be found in the following comments: "The question facing us is whether we will recognize that to fight for Zionism is a commandment no less [important] than to fight against Hitler—and indeed even greater."[108]

The spontaneous response in Palestine to the Holocaust was the impulse to go to Europe to come to the aid of the Jews there. Golomb raised the idea of "platoons of ghetto destroyers." The plan was that young people from Palestine would be par-achuted into occupied Europe or make their way to the Jewish communities there through other avenues. They would bring a message of encouragement from Pal-estine and assist Jews in organizing for self-defense. There were two hidden assump-tions underlying this idea: that Jews from Palestine were in fact able to accomplish what Jews in the Diaspora could not do by themselves and that the action would be carried out in cooperation with the British. The scheme proved abortive because the British had grave reservations about such adventurous ideas, which strength-ened the Zionist claim that there was an inherent linkage between the distress of the Jews in Europe and the problem of Palestine. In Golomb's thinking, this pro-posal was linked with other attempts to strengthen relations with the British and deepen Jewish participation in the war.[109]

Their desire to aid the Jews of Europe notwithstanding, it became clear that it was not in the power of the Jews in Palestine to provide the assistance needed. The possibility of getting to Europe was conditional on British help, and all plans and ideas foundered on that practical necessity. The British had other priorities: They did not regard saving the Jews of Europe as one of their war aims and refused to allocate resources, even symbolic, for this purpose. Of all the proposed plans, the modest one that was finally put into practice in 1944 involved sending in about thirty parachutists, meant to forge a link between underground fighters in the Balkans and the British, while establishing contact at the same time with Jewish survivors. The value of the parachutists was more symbolic than practical. A profound sense of helplessness predominated—of inability to provide a real answer to the burning question of the era. "Every response we have made," Tabenkin said, "all of them, taken together—one big, awful helplessness."[110]

It was natural for that helplessness to be projected onto the Allies. They were the only ones from whom assistance and salvation, if any were possible, might be forthcoming. The restrictions of the White Paper took on a sinister meaning: At best, that document was an expression of the lack of concern by the British for the massive murder of Jews; at worst, it constituted a manifestation of the close emotional proximity between British and Nazi attitudes when it came to antisemitic biases. Tabenkin asserted bitterly: "That is the same Pontius Pilate who washes his hands, claiming they've shed no blood. . . . No door was opened. No gate was opened. Palestine was not opened, England was not opened. America was not opened."[111] A poem by Alterman entitled "From All the Peoples," written at the end of 1942, began with the lines, "While our children were crying in the shadow of the gallows, / We did not hear the wrath of the world." It ended with the prayer of the murdered children before the lord of the universe, who collects their blood, "since no one cares to collect it apart from you." The final lines read "And you will demand it from the murderers, / And from those who were silent, as well."[112]

The fact that what was termed "the enlightened world" showed so little interest in the fate of the Jews served as a renewed and contemporary bit of evidence in support of Jewish skepticism about the non-Jewish world. The spontaneous attitude of Jews from Eastern Europe toward the Gentile, characterized at best by caution and suspicion and at worst by a sense of constant confrontation between the Jewish and Gentile worlds, was now enhanced, corroborated, and intensified. The feeling of total Jewish isolation, facing a world divided into persecutors and the indifferent, was the natural, almost self-evident result:[113] "The delusion from the era of the emancipation, namely, that members of the enlightened human species are responsible for each other and are also responsible to a certain degree for the fate of the defenseless Jewish race, has evaporated."[114]

Yet here, too, perspectives split along lines of ideological affinity and political loyalty. When Tabenkin set about to consider the Holocaust, he took pains to distinguish between the world of the "forces of tomorrow," which held out hope for the future of humanity, and the indifferent world of the Western democracies. For the believers in the Soviet experiment, the fact that hundreds of thousands of Jews who had fled to the Soviet Union to escape the advancing German armies had, indeed, found refuge there was an additional proof of the superiority of the Soviet system over the Western democracies. On the other hand, those who had been hostile to Bolshevik Russia ever since the 1920s did not change their attitude in the light of events. They stressed the fact that the Soviet Union had not allowed Jews from outside Russia to provide assistance to their brothers there except on a small scale. They underscored the destruction the Jewish community had suffered under the Soviet regime, both physical and psychological. The reality of the Holocaust did not change the basic approach of any of them but served as a factor to bolster and encourage existing positions. This fact was highlighted after the war, when the leadership of Ha-Shomer ha-Tzair dismissed the firsthand evidence presented by its members who had spent the war in Central Asia and in the forests of Belorussia— regarding the extent of antisemitism in the Soviet Union and the horrors of the Soviet system in general.[115]

The sense of Jewish helplessness and frustration repeated again and again in comments by leaders of the Yishuv, supplemented by the feeling that the Gentile world had looked on indifferently as Jews were slain, were channeled into two complementary approaches. One presented the Jew as a sacrificial lamb, the perennial innocent victim of the violence of human society. The second was predicated on the belief that Jews could trust and rely only on themselves.

The Holocaust significantly enhanced the conviction that right was on the side of the Jews in the struggle for Palestine. It proved what happened to a people without a physical basis for its existence, whose voice is not heard in the council of nations, whose members cannot find safe refuge, a people without an army, without physical might. When juxtaposed to the tragedy of Jewish refugees—survivors of glorious Jewish communities that had gone up in smoke—the legalistic demands of Palestinian Arabs regarding their right to protection of their majority status rang hollow and seemed trivial by comparison. In a sarcastic poem that Alterman wrote about the last remaining certificate, according to the White Paper rules, left for the Zionist Organization, the poet called the reader's attention to "how a people, after the demise of the executioners, was dying at the hands of the bureaucrats" (the British). He commented ironically on Arab opposition to granting additional certificates:

> And how Arabia, in broad daylight,
> without even blushing, was quick to warn that the expanse
> between Iran and Saudi Arabia is too narrow
> to accommodate her.[116]

Indeed, this view had also been heard on occasion in the 1920s and 1930s. Yet now, in the light of the Holocaust, it seemed self-evident. The sensitivity for the needs of the other side and its rights weakened or, more accurately, became less important under the pressure of current events. Even on this issue, one can find the same camps as before the Holocaust. Ha-Shomer ha-Tzair continued to show sensitivity for the rights of the Arabs, as did Ihud. The Holocaust had no impact on their approach to the Arab question. The majority, especially the large camp of Mapai, also basically adhered to positions on the Arab question they had supported in earlier years. The difference was that the degree of attention and intellectual and emotional alertness directed toward the Arab question were now far more limited. The disaster of European Jewry and revelations of the Holocaust and the political struggle against the British following the war had drained consciousness and emotions and hardened people. The virtues of mercy and charity—up until then a part of their worldview—paled in the face of staggering events. The perspective of the Jew as victim functioned as a license for giving priority to the national interest over other considerations.

The Holocaust underscored the isolation of the Jew: The civilized world divorced itself from the last vestiges of justice and humaneness, and no power had come to the aid of the Jews in their hour of despair. Consequently, the Jew should not expect help. He had better do everything "by his own hands" (as in the subtitle of Moshe Shamir's *Chapters on Alik,* which presented his brother, Alik, as a model of a young Palestinian boy). "If you want the truth, we have nobody except ourselves!"—Tabenkin muttered in a moment of anguish.[117] During his May 1947 visit to Displaced Persons (DP) camps in Germany, he remarked, "We will shape our fate by our own strength only." Yet this did not prevent him from speaking in the same breath on behalf of educating the young in the spirit of internationalism.[118]

Alterman expressed widespread public opinion on the matter in his poem dedicated to a baby girl born on a ship of immigrants en route to Palestine. In commenting on the governments of the world, he noted:

> Their hands did not assist her.
> The heavens will testify.
> She even stopped asking about them.
> She was born on her own, and arrived on her own.
> In short, she took care of everything—on her own.[119]

This idea, likewise, was not new. Its source can be found in Pinsker's "Auto-Emancipation" of 1882, which recalled an ancient slogan coined by Hillel—"If I am not for myself, who will be for me?"—and called for its adoption for the present. The idea hinted at by Alterman—that the British not only did not promote the national home but even restricted its steps and curbed its development—was commonly accepted in the 1920s and 1930s. The concept of the Hagana, as an underground organization, was the product of the notion of self-reliance: Jews had no one to rely on except themselves. Nonetheless, the Holocaust affected this matter greatly.

One of the central lessons deriving from the experience of isolation and helplessness was that it was forbidden for the Jew to be weak: "We feel ourselves to be sons of a miserable people, murdered because of its weakness," commented Moshele Tabenkin, Yitzhak's son and a poet in his own right.[120] The weakness took on dimensions of an amoral attribute: "A powerless people in the physical sense has no biological right to exist; a people devoid of defense that does not carry weapons to protect itself, should not expect assistance from other quarters; a frivolous people that puts its trust in the moral calculations of humanity and the world is commiting suicide," wrote one of the members of Ha-Kibbutz ha-Meuhad: "The millions of Jews who were thrown into the furnaces paid for the sin of the weakness of *all* Jews: both those who were ensnared in the nets of death in the regions where Nazis carried out massacres and those under the rule of 'enlightened' humanity."[121] The conclusion derived from all this was simple, direct, and oriented toward force: "From the crematoria and graves a command bursts forth, for all Jews—*to become a power*— what the Holocaust has commanded us is to become a *Jewish power in Palestine.*" In so stating, Galili was not employing the term *power* in the restricted sense. He was referring to all components of Zionist activity in Palestine: "Land, settlement, defense, labor, and immigration—that is the guarantee for the Jewish future."[122]

But he made these remarks in the context of recruitment for the Palmach. The association was clear. Years later, in an encounter with Zivia Lubetkin, one of the leaders of the Warsaw ghetto uprising, Tabenkin declared: "Our dreadful fate compels us to be strong. To be weak, without power—that is something familiar to us from time immemorial; now we have no alternative but to strive to be powerful."[123]

Power was not meant as an answer to feelings of frustration and the desire for revenge, despite the fact that someone asserted: "We have no language to censure our murderers except for the language of vengeance and power."[124] The revival of a people, proud and free, in its land" was supposed to be the true revenge.[125] It appears that from the first moment the reports were verified, the leaders made conscious efforts to direct the feelings of enmity and rage into constructive channels and to guide youth toward finding satisfaction in the military frameworks within the community. This was conceived as a substitute for revenge aimed at the Germans, a desire for vengeance that was beyond the realm of attainment. The Palestinian arena was meant to absorb the psychological energy generated by the information on the Holocaust and to direct it into the struggle for gaining Jewish sovereignty over Palestine. There was some fear about nihilistic inclinations, likely to attract many young people to the organization of the "dissidents" (the IZL and Lehi), as a desperate response to a world casting off moral values—a world in which, in order to survive, one has to be rapacious, a wolf among wolves. For that reason, constructive activity was depicted as the true victory over the destructive forces that Hitler had unleashed against the Jewish people. The need for a powerful, positive ideal transformed the slogan coined by Ben Gurion and his associates—Jewish independence in Palestine as the war aim—into the pole of hope of national revival, the opposite of genocidal destruction.

The animosity toward the British, an integral part of the complex network of relations between the Palestinian Jewish community and the authorities, was exacerbated, taking on new and unprecedented strength and depth, in the wake of the Holocaust. All the frustration, despair, humiliation, and helplessness that marked the Jewish collective response to the Holocaust found an outlet in hatred for the Gentiles who were closest at hand, namely, the British. The charge that the policies of the mandatory government had led to the destruction of Jews or, at least, that those policies did not permit the saving of many who could have been saved, was not groundless. Apprehensions about an invasion of Jewish refugees flooding into Palestine, that would jeopardize the policies of the White Paper, played a paramount role in the insensitive attitude of the government to the plight of the refugees. In the domain of public opinion, what was decisive were the infuriating facts, such as the *Patria, Atlantic,* and *Struma* episodes and reports about relatives and friends who were desperately trying to reach the shore of Palestine while the British refused to permit their entry on the grounds that they were "nationals of enemy countries," likely to be Nazi spies. Within the circle of leadership, there were even more shocking experiences: endless negotiations to save children by bringing them to Palestine—discussions that in the end led to nothing. Heartlessness was demonstrated in connection with the *Struma* affair, British efforts to hinder the Yoel Brand mission to save Hungarian Jews, and other incidents.[126]

Despite all the mitigating assumptions historians are required to put forward in assessing government actions and shortcomings under the pressure of wartime, it is nonetheless difficult to find many points that speak in favor of the Palestine government. The accusing finger pointed at the British was not exclusively the product of the hysteria of a helpless public that had a psychological need to direct its anger at the most proximate authorities. Rather, it was based on hard facts.

From the end of the war on, as it became clear that the British had no intention of revoking the White Paper and allowing Holocaust survivors to enter Palestine, rage against them surged, reaching previously unparalleled proportions. In the drama of the mid-1940s, the Arabs of Palestine played a quite marginal role. They dwelt somewhere in the background, necessitating a modicum of attention in the operative sphere, a domain toward which the various groups in the Jewish community still had differing attitudes. In contrast, the British were on a direct collision course with the Jewish community. It goes without saying that there was a certain difference in the phraseology used by the Hagana and Palmach in referring to the British as contrasted with the terminology customary in Lehi and the IZL. The latter were radical in voicing their hatred for the British, whom they tended to blame for the destruction of European Jewry. Likewise, they did not hesitate to make analogies between the Germans and the British, seeing a common basis to their actions. Such extreme statements were rare among Hagana and Palmach circles. Yet beyond certain differences in expression, manners, and a dispute on ways and means, the hatred of the British and the struggle against them gained a widespread following in the Jewish community in Palestine—most especially among young people, both on the right and on the left.

Nonetheless, it is doubtful whether the Holocaust contributed to a fundamental change in approach regarding the issue of the struggle against the British. Two conceptions developed, not necessarily contradictory. One, characteristic of the IZL and Lehi, as well as the youth groups associated with the Labor movement, described the conflict in Palestine in terms of the anti-imperialist struggle of the oppressed peoples (India, Indonesia) or else the European national liberation movements (Ireland, Poland, Italy). In that context, the Holocaust was of secondary importance. The second conception, current among leaders in the Yishuv, stressed the uniqueness of the Jewish fight for independence of a people not settled in its land. In this conception, there was more room for inclusion of the topic of the Holocaust. Yet both apparently conceived the struggle against the British as a struggle whose focus was in Palestine, driven by motives and interests that were basically Palestinian. From the Holocaust, it derived legitimation, emotional strength, and moral indignation that helped crystallize a national consensus around it. But the struggle was against the White Paper and on behalf of a pro-Zionist solution in Palestine. The British opposed these two objectives. The conflict was waged over these two issues, not over the emotions generated by the Holocaust.

One of the central lessons of the Holocaust was the very fact that it had happened. Among the factors underlying individuals' difficulty grappling with and coming to terms with the reality of the Holocaust was the absence of any historical precedents for the event. But once it had transpired, it created a new point of reference. Prior to Auschwitz, it had been an inconceivable idea. Now it became an integral part of the conceivably possible, a component within the psychological and social fabric of individuals and peoples. The grave lesson drawn was that if it could happen once, it could happen again: "Therefore, our historical experience tells us today: It is possible to annihilate us, even in Europe, even in the proximity of all the civilized peoples, even when we are a concentrated population."[127] The Holocaust was not explained by supposedly "racial" traits of the German people but by the deeds of the fascist regime, the root cause of evil in the world, leading entire peoples to destruction. The view of the Holocaust as part of the world apocalypse made it easier to cope with. It was not only Jews who had been victims of fascism: Everything that was good and enlightened in the world fell victim to the forces of darkness. This view of the tragedy contained an element of slight comfort, and held out hope for a better future. Yet it simultaneously suggested a chilling prospect: that under certain circumstances, the Holocaust could reoccur. At times of revolution, for example, when institutions crumble and frameworks collapse, the forces that make the Jew, the eternal alien, into the scapegoat of a society in crisis could resurface. If the Holocaust did not derive from a unique constellation of circumstances but, rather, from the development of a social–political system subject to rational explanation, then the chance of another Holocaust could not be ruled out. When Tabenkin surveyed the postwar world in 1946, the tensions between the blocs, and the prosepcts for revolution and upheaval in Eastern Europe, he anticipated the possibility of additional cataclysmic convulsions. Given the danger of World War III, considered a realistic option by the Left, the fear of a reoccurrence of the Holocaust became a decisive component in the world picture.[128]

Although those who feared World War III had in mind a clash between the imperialist West and the forces of revolution, the idea of total annihilation was also applied to the Palestinian arena. When Ben Gurion, speaking in the Zionist Actions Committee in the summer of 1947, on the eve of the imminent political decision, discussed the threat of an attack on the Yishuv by the Arabs of Palestine together with the Arab states, he said, "At present, we are not facing acts of robbery and terror designed to disturb our work but, rather, a plan to uproot the Yishuv and liquidate the Zionist 'danger' by annihilating the Jews of Palestine." He added even more pointedly: "And let us not be frivolously optimistic. And let us not say what happened to six million Jews in Europe cannot happen to 650 thousand Jews in Palestine. . . . What happened in Europe can happen in Palestine, and in the near future." In recalling the slaughter of the Armenians during World War I and the killing of the Assyrians in Iraq in the 1930s, he argued that the philosophy of violence was not the exclusive legacy of the Germans and that there were precedents in the Middle East.[129] The impact of these analogies on the speaker and audience can only be surmised; but it is likely that in that particular historical context, it was enormous.

The fear that the Arabs in Palestine were plotting to annihilate the Jewish community there had surfaced for the first time in the wake of the 1929 riots (see chapters 4 and 5). The small size and weakness of the Yishuv at that time, amply evident in the riots, and the merciless killings in Hebron, Safed, and Motza, as well as various statements by Arabs, awakened the feeling that Arabs were planning one day to rise up and annihilate the Jews. Such fears were not voiced during the Arab Rebellion of 1936–1939, the most serious confrontation with Arabs prior to the war of 1947–1948. There were reasons for that: The Yishuv had grown in size, had become far more self-confident, and was better equipped to defend itself. The fact that the British also protected the Jews quite effectively likewise contributed to allaying fears that the community might be totally wiped out. During World War II, however, such apprehensions were revived in the light of the open delight of the Arab community over British failures during the tense days that preceded Alamein. Arabs were not cautious in expressing their intention to settle accounts with the Jews in Palestine. It should be recalled that up until 1947, the Jews had not faced the Arabs without the British, who functioned as a buffer defense. Fears about what might happen should the British withdraw were not unfounded. Apprehensions returned about the possibility of an Arab "night of Bartholomew."[130] Thus, it was not the Holocaust that generated the anxiety of annihilation within the top leadership echelons of the Jewish community. Nonetheless, there is no doubt it served as an illustration and historical lesson that was not to be forgotten, a reminder that the nightmare that had terrified them was not the product of a sick imagination but had a harrowing and recent precedent in the expanses of civilized Europe.

Reports on the destruction of European Jewry spoke about millions who had gone to their death without resistance. The first witnesses to come from the field of slaughter were a group of women and children, Palestinian citizens, exchanged for a group of German citizens. They arrived in Palestine in November 1942, followed by a handful of members of the Polish He-Halutz, who came to Palestine in the course of 1943. Not only did they describe the cruelty of the Germans, but they also detailed the absolute helplessness of the Jews and the fact that they had not rebelled against their bitter fate. From the very first moment, Jews in Palestine found it very hard to digest this fact of Jewish passivity. The more distant they were from the realities of Jewish life in Europe, the younger their age, and the greater their involvement in military activity in Palestine, the more difficult it was for them to comprehend the situation of the Jews during the Holocaust.

The expression "like sheep to slaughter" was first used in connection with Jews in Nazi Europe going to their death in a leaflet published by Abba Kovner in the Vilna ghetto, where Jews were murdered as early as 1941. In that leaflet, he called on the Jews to resist—not to go passively like sheep to slaughter but to rise up against the Germans. In Palestine, the expression apparently began to appear in print in late 1942. In December of that year, a few days after the atrocities became known, Tabenkin appeared in the Histadrut council and expressed his stupefaction over the absence of manifestations of Jewish self-defense in Europe. The story of the destruction of the Jews of Radom was published in the press at that time. The report was based on the testimony of a witness who had come to Palestine and described how Jews were handed spades and ordered to dig their own graves. The question why that Jew, who knew that his fate and that of his family had been sealed, did not lift up his spade and strike the German soldier guarding him was repeatedly asked even by persons rooted in the reality of Jewish life in Eastern Europe and well aware of the abysmal isolation of the Jews at the hour of their death, separating them not only from their murderers but also from the whole non-Jewish population.[131] As time passed, the question accelerated: The death machine had been operating for more than two years. Jews should have been able to prepare for self-defense, to find a way to defend themselves![132] Such "queries" plagued many of the veterans in the community in Palestine; but they were always careful to state that those Jews should not be judged. They even pointed to an analogy between the helplessness of the Jewish situation in the Diaspora and the sense of impotence that afflicted the Yishuv in the summer of 1942, when faced with the prospect of an occupation of Palestine by Rommel's divisions.[133] But as deep as their solidarity with the condemned Jews was, it was not total: "At that same council, we were tormented by the question, Why did the Jews act this way? And that left a shadow of terror," Tabenkin remarked in reference to testimony by a member of He-Halutz from "over there" presented at the convention of Ha-Kibbutz ha-Meuhad in 1944.[134]

From its inception, the Zionist movement had cherished the image of the "new Jew." Schooled in Bialik's "In the City of Salughter" and Brenner's "He Told Her," the prime characteristic of that new Jew was his readiness to fight for his life and for the abstract value of "Jewish honor." The willingness of Jews to go "like sheep to slaughter" was such a profound blow to the self-image of the Yishuv that doubts arose as to whether the Zionist movement had actually succeeded in fashioning another type of Jew, different from the "old," traditional Jew.

> That experience of annihilation without resistance bored in our hearts, ate away at us: Hadn't we started a new chapter in Jewish history? Hadn't we created a new type of Jew? Is there really no hope for the people, no hope for a change in values? Is this people really sentenced to eternal exile and slavery for ever, with nothing but its superiority of spirit and conscience?[135]

The entire structure of ideas that had been built since Bialik, Berdichevsky, and Tchernichovsky—from the time the great shift began, moving from a spiritual to an "earthy" Judaism—appeared like so much foam on churning waters in the face of the inconceivable submission of millions of Jews to their fate.

The expectation of manifestations of heroism from "over there" concealed feelings of guilt (almost unmentioned) over the failures of the Jews "here": The Jewish community in Palestine had proven incapable of infiltrating even a single Jew into Poland during the years of mass annihilation. There were only extremely loose and sporadic contacts between the Jews in Palestine and in Eastern Europe. An enormous gap had existed between the relatively tranquil life in Palestine during the later years of the war, the unprecedented economic prosperity there, and the ruin and destruction that had simultaneously ravaged Europe. Guilt was also felt because there were so few opportunities for deeds of valor in Palestine during the war years.

If this is the way veterans thought and spoke—men whose total identification with the Jewish people was beyond doubt—how must the young have felt? Right from the beginning, they had lacked empathy for the Jews of the Diaspora and any sense of spontaneous solidarity with them. The concept Negation of Exile that they were taught in school and in the youth movement was not interpreted and appropriated by them as a rejection merely of the minority status of the Jew or an opposition to the existing frameworks of Jewish life in the Diaspora. Rather, it was a rejection of the Jew himself—his characteristics and traits, traditional life-styles, and attitudes toward his surroundings. When referring to European Jewry, the young Jews in Palestine tended to prefer abstractions, (as in the slogan "If I forget thee, Diaspora!)" to describing real flesh-and-blood persons. They were not referring to the Jews of Brest Litovsk, Psheitik, or Bendzin but to an abstraction—alien and not really the object of sympathy.[136] The expression "diasporic Jew" transmitted a whole complex of features that were regarded as objectionable in the eyes of Palestinian Jewish youth: distance and alienation from labor and nature and, most particularly, weakness and lack of physical abilities. It symbolized everything that youth in Palestine did not want or need to be.

The syndrome of "like sheep to slaughter" was more widespread among youth than adults. The former internalized the fact that those who had walked unprotesting to their death had been members of their own people. Their rage, humiliation, and pain existed on an abstract plane of national solidarity. They expressed these emotions in numerous statements and speeches on the external level of declaration. But when they left aside these generalizing exaggerations and penetrated to the plane of their concrete, deeper attitudes, they voiced negative criticism, repugnance, and even disgust: Those Jews had not acted in accordance with behavioral codes acceptable to Palestinian Jewish youth. "There are forms of abuse against which response is justified—without weighing the consequences," declared Moshele Tabenkin, contrasting those brought up in Palestine with the stereotype of Jews in the Diaspora: "I believe that there are . . . some psychological traits that are special to us, the generation of the Jewish Hebrew worker, raised and educated here in Palestine, . . . that would have placed each of us in the camp of the avengers, without further considerations or thought, even without any purpose."[137] Moshele Tabenkin presented the contrast between those educated in Palesine and in the Diaspora in terms of the spontaneously violent reply of the former in the event of abuse and the passive acceptance of judgment by the latter.

In a talk with members of Ha-Noar ha-Oved, Galili warned about the fact that "among Palestinian youth, there is a prevalent sense of superiority to young Jews from the Diaspora. There is also highflown rhetoric depicting youth in Palestine as the progeny of Judah Maccabee and Shimon Bar Giora." He challenged his young audience: "Has youth in Palestine already withstood those trials to which Jewish youth in the Diaspora has been subjected?" He demanded of them not to judge their brothers until they had stood in their place. Yet in the depths of his heart, Galili also shared the expectation that Jews would prove themselves and their mettle by engaging in armed struggle.[138] When, several years later, Yigal Allon summed up the experience of the Palmach, which he described as a "Palestinian product par excellence," he noted with caution, "Over a great many years, many of those born and raised in Palestine were affected by a lack of understanding when it came to the problems of the Diaspora and even by some sort of feeling of superiority toward its Jews."[139] The connection between the "feeling of superiority" and the fact that the Jews in Europe had failed to resist and fight becomes clear from his later comments.

It was natural that the same feeling of haughtiness and alienation found only rare expression in writing at the time.[140] Nonetheless, it was undoubtedly widespread. In later testimony by survivors, there is repeated mention of the sense of humiliation felt during the encounter with the disdainful approach shown by young

Palestinians, who did not hesitate to confront them with accusations about victims who went "like sheep to slaughter." Moreover, the majority of the survivors who appeared at various forums and spoke about their experiences found it necessary to comment on that question in apologetic tones. There are also traces of this in the belles lettres of the period, for example, in the description by Moshe Shamir in *Pirke Alik* (Chapters on Alik) of the protagonist's desire to join the British Army: "Something has to be done about the annoying matter of Hitler and his brownshirts. . . . We'll chop them down to size; so that they should know that Jews . . .—yes, there are also other kinds of Jews in the world, Jews who may even cut down mechanized Prussians." The legitimiation for this approach, even in a later era, is highlighted by the fact that this passage was included in the *Sefer ha-Palmah,* the canonical version of the Palmach experience, published in 1952.[141]

There was no particular "chemistry" generated in the encounter of Palestinian Jewish youth with the so-called She'erit ha-Pleta or, thereby, with the experience of the Holocaust. Ha-Mahanot ha-Olim, for example, did not initiate even a single meeting with survivors who managed to get to Palestine during the war.[142] One of the first female members of He-Halutz to make her way to Palestine and tell her story was Reniya Hershkovitz. She was invited to speak at youth meetings and gatherings of the Palmach and in kibbutzim. According to her own account, one Friday evening after she had finished speaking about the most horrible of history's many tales, the kibbutz members promptly got up, pushed the tables and chairs to one side, and, as though nothing had happened, started to dance.[143]

In 1946 a literary collection appeared, entitled *Yalkut ha-Re'im* (Friends' Anthology). It claimed to represent the spirit of the new Palestinian generation. One of the stories in the anthology was by Moshe Shamir, entitled "The Second Stutter" (Ha-gimgum ha-sheni). It was apparently the first literary reaction by a young Palestinian Jew to the destruction of European Jewry. The journal *Ba-Ma'avak,* periodical of the Circle of Young Palestine, praised the story, claiming that it gave an honest portrayal of the atrocities in the concentration camp from the perspective of the "Palestinian Jew, free, proud, healthy, who despises all sickliness." That young person "sees the sick sadism of the Nazi torturer—but also the bent-down, sick nature of the tormented victim." The salvation of the diasporic Jew comes when he is absorbed into a kibbutz in Palestine and becomes a new man. "Indeed, this is the most magnificent victory of the Palestinian generation," the article's author proclaimed, "to witness the healing and straightening of Diaspora Jews when they are absorbed in its life-style *and are assimilated to it.* This is a new meaning for the concept *immigration* [*aliyah,* 'ascent']. They are 'ascending' to us, to our level of internal health and freedom—without our having to 'descend' to the subjugation and servility of the Diaspora."[144]

It is difficult to overlook the internalizing of certain antisemitic concepts in this passage: "health" is to "sickliness" as "Palestine" is to the "Diaspora," and use is made of the same adjective to denote the diapsoric Jew and the Nazi. The Palestinian stereotype of the Jew in the Diaspora depicted the latter not only as inferior to the Palestinian Jew, but also as a pathological individual, plagued by physical and mental problems. This was the conceptual basis for the demand of "assimilation" among "healthy" youth in Palestine.

This radical attitude toward European Jewry was certainly not shared by everyone. Yet there can be no doubt that it was widespread among Palestinian Jews as a kind of emotional and psychological basis (not always fully conscious) and shaped to a significant degree their attitude toward the surviving remnant of Europe's Jews. One of the most famous sketches published during that period was by Yitzhak Sade, entitled *"Ahoti al ha-hof"* (My Sister on the Beach). It appeared several times in the Palmach bulletin and was subsequently included in *Sefer ha-Palmah*. One can view the piece as expressive of the "canonical" attitude toward the survivors. The sketch describes an encounter on the beach in Palestine between Sade and a young girl. She has a tattoo that reads "Only for officers." Afterwards it becomes clear that the girl was also sterilized by the Germans. She weeps, repeating over and over again: "Why did they bring me here? Do I deserve that young healthy men should risk their life for me?" Sade answers her in a tone of affection and encouragement: "Our love for you is true, you will be our sister, bride, mother." He ends the sketch with the words: "For the sake of my sisters, I am strong. For the sake of my sisters, I am brave. For the sake of my sisters, I will also be cruel. For your sake, everything— everything!"[145]

Symbolizing the Holocaust by means of a girl who was forced into prostitution was not accidental. Although such prostitution was marginal among the complex of atrocities of the Holocaust, it embodied a highpoint in degradation and perversity, especially in the eyes of young men, sensitive to sexual matters. It also symbolized the impotence of Jewish males in the Holocaust, their inability to protect their females. This image was in accord with the stereotypic analogy that preceded it, namely, that the Diaspora is feminine and weak while the Jewish community in Palestine is masculine and strong. The girl is the wretched opposite of the young, healthy men who risked their lives for her when they helped her descend from the illegal immigrants' ship at the shore. She is passive, they active. She receives, they give. She requires legitimation; and Sade, who here symbolizes the Palestinian Jewish community, provides her that legitimacy from the generosity of his heart. Her inferiority to those born in Palestine is manifest. The final chord is also important: Ultimately, the tragedy of Europe's Jews allows the young man to break free of accepted moral constraints: "For the sake of my sisters, I will also be cruel." It is likely that Sade simply wanted Palmach members to show more compassion toward the survivors. But the result was an additional confirmation of accepted stereotypes and moral justification for the offensive ethos so popular among youth.

After the close of the Twenty-second Zionist Congress, which was held in Basel in December 1946, Israel Galili and Yigal Allon wished to check on the *bricha* (escape) operation among refugees in Europe, and were accordingly smuggled into Poland. Galili was deputy chief of the Hagana National Command, and Allon was commander of the Palmach. They visited Auschwitz and He-Halutz training centers in the area and returned along the same route they had taken. In later years Allon showed interest in the life of Jews in the Diaspora that extended beyond the accepted general slogans of solidarity.[146] On a number of occasions, Galili spoke out in talks to trainees of Palmach and Ha-Noar ha-Oved against the contempt shown for the Jews of the Diaspora. In light of their positive attitude, the reaction of these two leaders of Palestinian youth to the reality of the destruction of European Jewry is puzzling; for in their writings, it is impossible to find anything indicative of their immediate, spontaneous response to their encounter with the field of slaughter. Indeed, one can surmise that the evidence in Auschwitz was so depressing that their immediate reaction was silence. However, the fact that even after much time had passed, they never chose to comment on it, points in another direction. Many years later, Galili spoke about an intensification of their hatred for the Nazis after the visit. But aside from that, he did not mention a single impression—no episodes, no encounters with human experience. According to the testimony of their escorts, the two were extremely interested in the *technical* details of the *bricha* operation but in little else.[147] The actual experience of the Holocaust remained alien. It was absorbed in external fashion, on a rhetorical plane, but was not internalized and made a component of the collective identity of Palestinian Jewish youth.

In his last encounter with youth in the summer of 1944, Berl Katznelson made reference to this phenomenon: Young people were alienated from diasporic Jewry and unable to identify with it. Palestinian youth, Berl noted, showed an interest in partisans fighting in the forests of Russia. They were able to develop profound empathy with a story from the days of Ha-Shomer or a tale about the field squads or Wingate. They identified with stories from the time of the riots, attacks by Arabs, Trumpeldor, maybe even Bar Kokhba. But "the Palestinian young man is incapable of experiencing the general Jewish fate." As the greatest mentor of his generation, Katznelson had no illusions: "Our child," he stated, "grows up as the son of a new people, a special people. That which was written and spoken decades ago, in pride and haughtiness, is now coming true: that no desert generation and no offspring of the Diaspora will blossom here. Rather, what is being developed here is a new man."[148]

All the examples of topics mentioned by Katznelson that stirred the hearts of young people and generated emotional identity were centered on one key focus: fighting. Most of them touched upon events that had taken place in Palestine, generally within frameworks related socially and ideologically to those in which the young people were active. The only deviant example is connected with partisans in Russia. However, they were already identified as created in the image of the men of the Palmach, with the same value systems and patterns of response. When Ruzka Korchak, one of the fighters in the Vilna ghetto and also active as a partisan in the forests, met Yitzhak Sade in January 1945 in Palestine, he told her: "We'll be friends, I'm a partisan too."[149] Thus, it is not surprising that the only topic associated with the Holocaust that young Palestinian Jews could identify with was combat: the revolt in the ghettos and fighting in the forests.

On the eleventh of Adar 1943 Ben Gurion made an uncustomary appearance at the annual youth rally in Tel Hai. He began his address with the words, "Once again, we have gathered together at *Massada*—this Massada not of the latter days but of the pioneers." The description of Tel Hai as Massada was questionable, and Ben Gurion surmounted the logical refutation by the use of an idiom that sounded proper yet remained nebulous. All his comments had a double message. He spoke about the need to be prepared to die a Massada-like heroic death, yet emphasized that the aim was not a beautiful death but a beautiful life, in the spirit of Tel Hai. At that meeting, between descriptions in superlatives of the heroism of the leaders of Tel Hai and Sejera, the settlement where Ha-Shomer was founded, Ben Gurion reported for the first time that news had been received about an uprising in the War-saw ghetto (presumably the clash with German forces in January 1943). Referring to the rebels, he declared, "They learned the new philosophy that the leaders of Tel Hai and Sejera commanded us to fulfill—heroic death."[150]

Thus, from the very first moment, the ghetto uprising was drawn into the prev-alent myths in the Yishuv. It contained all the components necessary to transform that uprising into a Palestinian tale of heroism. An awesome story of human glory, and the dearth of information about it (derived from German sources, Radio Lon-don, Kuybyshev, and channels of the Polish underground) did not detract from the exaltedness of spirit it engendered. It moved the veterans to the point of tears and provided a feeling of satisfaction and pride to the young. "We were thinking about a stand of that kind when the possibility of an invasion of Palestine was on the agenda," Golomb responded to the news, creating an identity between "there" and "here."[151] The telegram sent by the pioneering movement in Poland stated, "Men and women of the movement who are still alive are continuing to fight for the dig-nity of the surviving Jewish remnant in Poland." It touched a highly sensitive chord: National dignity, measured by the readiness to fight, a value that had been trampled under foot by Jews who went "like sheep to slaughter," was finally redeemed by the ghetto uprising. The contrast was stressed: The former were indeed deserving of pity, but they did not win external glory like the Jews who stood on the ramparts fighting for their dignity. The link between the rebels and He-Halutz pio-neering movement added another layer of solidarity. It is no accident that *these people* had reacted differently. After all, they were the brothers of the movement in Palestine, deriving from it their strength, education, and inspiration. In referring to He-Halutz House in Warsaw, Lova Levita, an intellectual leader of Ha-Kibbutz ha-Meuhad, noted, "Here a different life and different dreams were formed, *here they died differently*"[152] These fighters were depicted as Palestinian Jews who had not yet arrived in Palestine, not as the offspring of Jews of the Diaspora.

The bravery of the ghetto fighters provided an answer to the problem posed by the gravediggers in Radom. A statement by the Palmach command on the occasion of the victory over the Nazis on May 8, 1945 noted: "This we know: not all Jews dug their own graves. And the pioneering movement was the one to hoist the flag of revolt."[153] The ghetto uprising was lauded as the first battle in the war of the Jews, which would continue after the world war was finished and would end with a battle for Jewish independence.[154]

The revolt was integrated as a link in the chain of age-old Jewish heroism. The ghetto fighters were compared with the warriors of Massada and those of Betar. The symbolism of the fact that the revolt erupted on the first day of Passover, the same day Elazar ben Yair and his fighters on Massada had committed suicide, was emphasized. Beyond general reports and the telegram quoted, no one as yet had had any direct contact with the rebels. Nevertheless, their aims were explained to youth in the following way: "To avenge the blood of Israel, to establish the Jewish homeland, to build up Massada—symbol of Jewish heroism throughout the ages."[155]

The ghetto revolt underwent the reversal process characteristic of the treatment of myth in the youth movements: From a symbol of destruction, it was transformed into one of revival and resurgence. The slogan "To build up Massada," (or, in its more common formulation, "Massada shall not fall again,") used often and liberally to summarize the lesson from the desperate battle of the ghetto, also hinted at the limits of the identification by young people with that battle. They were happy to identify with that courageous stand, but they did not understand or identify with the tragedy.[156] Youth rejected the message of despair, embracing only the content of heroism. In this way, even that tragic stand was incorporated as part of the ethos: "In their death they bequeathed us life."

The distinction between a worthy and a meaningless death, between falling in battle in the liberation war of the people and being a purposeless victim in the Diaspora, had been a frequent motif in the defensive ethos from its very inception. Now it served the tendency to set apart death "here" from death "there." On the first page of the January 1946 issue of *Mi-Bifnim,* organ of Ha-Kibbutz ha-Meuhad, a passage was published from Yitzhak Katzenelson's "Poem of the Murdered Jewish People." The essence of this passage lay in the lines:

> O Lord in heaven, I cried in trembling:
> Why and for what did my people die?
> Why and for what did it die in vain,
> Not in war, not in battle?

Later in the issue appeared Tabenkin's eulogy for eight men from the cooperative settlements who were killed when the British opened fire while searching for illegal immigrants and weapons. "If we are destined to die prematurely, by the hand of man—*this is the way to die,*" Tabenkin announced.[157] The contrast between the two types of death gave a justification and meaning to the latter. In a eulogy in the Palmach bulletin on those killed in the attack by the Hagana on the British camp in Sarona of February 1946, the bereaved parents were told, "Your sons were not led helpless to the slaughter by oppressors" and that they died "so that crematoria will never again be built for the people of Israel."[158] The Palmach bulletin published a ballad by Alterman on the suicide of Saul defeated on the Gilboa. Its moral was, "A people defeated *on its own land/*will rise once again seven times over."[159] Every word penned in that period was loaded with associations to the Holocaust, partly intentional and partly unconscious. Underscoring the difference between a victim in the homeland and one in the Diaspora, as in the poem by Alterman, was significant, just as the publication of the ballad in the Palmach organ was significant.

Starting in 1945, a trickle of survivors of the ghetto and forest fighters slowly began to make their way to Palestine, people such as Ruzka Korchak, Eliezer Lidovsky, Abba Kovner. In August of that year, the first meeting took place in London between the leaders of She'erit ha-Pleta and the Zionist leadership. Zivia Lubetkin arrived in Palestine in the summer of 1946, Yitzhak Zuckerman (Antek) a year later, both leaders of the Jewish fighting organization in the Warsaw ghetto. From the very first moment of the encounter, a conscious effort was made by the activist elite to create empathy and a sense of solidarity for the ghetto fighters among Palestinian Jewish youth. Tabenkin set the tone for them, in his opening of the platform of Ha-Kibbutz ha-Meuhad, especially for Zivia, whose testimony at the Yagur convention in June 1946 became the "canonized" version of the Warsaw rebellion. She and Antek were revered and admired as symbolic figures. Yitzhak Sade and Yigal Allon met with them for long, soul-searching discussions; and found a common language, especially Antek and Allon. They invited the fighters to appear at Palmach meetings at all different levels.[160] Quite consciously, the legend was fostered of the fraternity of arms among the fighters "there" and "here." They were presented as Palmachniks by natural affinity:[161] "That was a meeting between brothers, a meeting of fighters; and one heart recognized its like."[162] Allon, commander of the Palmach, called it a meeting of "brothers in arms and ideas."[163] The Palmach bulletin published articles on the ghetto rebels, along with the song of the Jewish partisans, and stressed the close emotional affinity with them: "We will learn a great deal from them—and they also have something to learn from us."[164] The massive effort to impress on youth that these fighters were truly "our own flesh and blood" indirectly strengthened the contrasting widespread view that the *others* from "there" were *not* "of our kind."

Despite the pronounced fraternity and camaraderie, tensions were not lacking. The Palestinian Jews expected that the newcomers would recognize the superiority of the Palestinian ethos and conform accordingly: "When they speak *in this spirit, the partitions separating us crumble*"[165] stated the Palmach bulletin, impling that sometimes they don't and then the partitions remain. One issue carried an anonymous sketch, supposedly straight "from the mouth of an illegal immigrant." The piece portrayed a romantic picture of the encounter between two groups of fighters: On the shore, after the illegal immigrants had disembarked from the ship with the help of the local fighters, the convenant between them was forged.[166] It appears that this article was written by the bulletin editors in response to the accusation contained in the words of Zivia Lubetkin in Yagur (paraphrased in the sketch) to the effect that the emissaries of the Yishuv had not broken through to the Jews in Poland during the war. That accusation, previously voiced by Antek in the 1945 conference in London, was seldom referred to, if at all, by the young people.[167] The encounter on the shore was meant to symbolize that helping the illegal immigrants disembark and taking care of them removed this blemish from the shining armor of the fighters of the Yishuv and had opened a new chapter in relations between fighters "there" and "here." The ghetto rebels likewise resented talk about "like sheep to slaughter." They refrained from pointing an accusing finger at Jews who had chosen not to fight the oppressor and objected to the tendency among Palestinians to attribute a presumed moral superiority to those who chose to fight in the forests as compared with those who chose to stay and die with their people in the ghetto.[168] It appears that the common denominator between the Jewish fighters from Poland and Palestinian Jewish youth lay in the shallow layer of narratives about brave exploits and heroism, avoiding reference to such highly charged experiences as *Aktion, Umschlagplatz,* and liquidation.[169] In the last resort, even the rebels were affected by the feeling that the love they lavished on the Yishuv was not reciprocated.[170]

As any other topic associated with the Holocaust, the ghetto revolt was also presented as evidence in internal political debates in Palestine. One of the central lessons the activists drew from the fact that some fighters in Warsaw, Vilna, and Bialystok had survived was that he who dares to fight has better chances of surviving than someone who fears for his skin and submissively accepts his fate. Tabenkin had asserted this even before the revolt as a reason in favor of Jewish self-defense.[171] Totally disregarding the unique circumstances of the Holocaust and the fact that ultimately, it was only due to chance that some of the leaders of the rebels survived, he drew an analogy between the supposed lesson of the ghetto uprisings and activism in Palestine. Even earlier, as in connection with the *Patria* episode, the activists argued that in the long run, taking risks prevents calamities, while passive acquiescence in one's fate eventually leads to greater disasters. Now the revolt was cited as conclusive proof of the thesis of resistance: "He who flees from danger—danger pursues him and catches up with him. He who faces danger—overcomes it."[172] This lesson was mustered as evidence to justify the position of the activists in the dispute between them and the moderates on the question of armed struggle. Fighting was presented not only as an obligation of honor and an instinctive, natural response of Palestinian youth but also as the effective path that would ultimately lead to victory.

The attitude of Palestinian youth to the uprising and the rebels symbolized the limits of its ability to identify with the Jewish people in the Diaspora. "The Jewish suffering in the ghetto is incomprehensible to us," Berl Katznelson noted bitterly. The revolt "brings the man of the ghetto closer to us, in line with our own terms of reference; it allows us to find some formula to hold on to, or, as someone said, to find relief—since this whole thing is so alien to us."[173] The traditional Jewish responses of acceptance of judgment and martyrdom in the effort to preserve humanity even under impossible conditions were incompatible with the self-image of the new Jew. For that reason, only the rebels were granted entry into the Palestinian pantheon. They were integrated within the offensive ethos and fructified it, as symbols and foci of emotional identification.

In 1945 a dispute on the Holocaust erupted within Ha-Mahanot ha-Olim. It appears this was the most serious debate held at the time in the Jewish community in Palestine on the question: Is it necessary to derive certain pedagogical implications from the Holocaust? On the face of it, the dispute centered on two alternative educational programs. In actuality it constituted a preparatory stage anticipating the breakup of Ha-Mahanot ha-Olim along the fracture lines of the split between the political parties Mapai and Ha-Tenua le-Ahdut ha-Avoda. Yet despite the political connotations, the debate was in keeping with youth movement tradition, an ambience in which educational values were taken very seriously. Discussions revolved around two educational conceptions. The first, prevalent in Ha-Mahanot ha-Olim since the late 1930s, proceeded from a socialist point of departure. It surveyed the development of human society in line with the *Communist Manifesto,* described the present and future in accordance with Marxist doctrine, placing the proletariat and the presumably forthcoming revolution at the center of attention. It then went on to examine the national question around the world, finally arriving at the Jewish question. Eventually it presented the inevitable conclusion, given the socialist and national perspective—Zionist Palestine as the answer to all problems, reconciling all contradictions. The second pedagogical conception started with an analysis of the present, focusing on Jewish history and Jewish nationalism. A large chapter was dedicated to the Holocaust. After that, it proceeded on to the pressing problems of the day (the struggle for Palestine, the Jewish refugees, and the like). There was only marginal mention of socialism.

On one side of the arena were the conservatives. They contended that the Holocaust did not necessitate any revision in basic approach and worldview. The teachings of socialism had passed the test of events, proposed an explanation for the phenomenon of genocide, and even proved that the only hope for Jewish redemption lay in the socialist world order. They explained the Holocaust as resulting from the fascist regime, against which all the forces of socialism were locked in struggle. They claimed that the behavior toward the Jews of Soviet Russia during the war gave ample evidence that the world was not divided up according to conflicting nationalisms but, rather, according to principles of class. By giving the Jewish refugees a haven in its expanses, Soviet Russia proved the superiority of class solidarity over the principle of nationalism. On the other hand, the challengers argued that socialism had lost its relevance in the face of the cataclysmic events that had occurred. These days, every nation was focusing on its own affairs. Even Russia underwent change when confronted with the reality of the war and had resurrected long-forgotten national heroes and cultivated national myths, giving no heed to their "class value." The Jewish people had gone through a trauma that would continue to pursue it and whose implications must be taken into account. The first of these was that "the world closed its doors to us"—the solidarity of labor had proven to be impotent on the day of reckoning. Consequently, they asserted, we must turn to concentrate on ourselves, study our national culture, and make it the Archimedian point for comprehending the world. The old internationalism should be replaced by a new Jewish solidarity aimed at identifying with the fate of the Jewish people; conclusions should then be drawn about the pressing tasks that youth would have to carry out. The affinity for Russian (Gentile) culture, much in vogue among youth, was exaggerated and false: For example, everyone sings gustily about "Cossack horsemen," disregarding the fact that those same Cossacks abused Jews.

A substantial part of the dispute revolved around the question of instructing the young about the concept *negation of exile.* The "conservatives" did not see the Holocaust as a reason to change their attitudes toward what was regarded as negative in Jewish history and were opposed to romanticizing the shtetl and patterns of Jewish life destroyed in the Holocaust. National self-identification was not supposed to be founded on forgivingness, leniency, and softness, they argued, but on a clear and penetrating view of the shortcomings of Jewish society and the demand to change them in a revolutionary way. Moreover, one should not base attitude on national criteria but on class criteria: There are good and bad Jews, and the Holocaust had not altered that fact. On the other hand, those who demanded change contended that in the face of the destruction of European Jewry, the rejection of, and lack of understanding for Jews of the Diaspora had to change. While avoiding idealization, the time had nonetheless come for a more balanced attitude, presenting the history of the people and its relations with the surrounding world as the core of the educational agenda. By the same token, the matter of universal processes should be given marginal importance.

One of the focal points in these discussions was the topic of myth and symbol. Those who demanded change included discussion of Yavneh and Massada in their new curriculum plan, based on the contention that these were the two pivotal historical symbols that had nourished the spirit of the people in its exile. In this dispute, Massada played a role similar to that played in the past by the myth of Betar or the war against the Romans—indicating that it had indeed become the predominant myth of heroism. Proponents of the prosocialist program of studies opposed mentioning the two in the same breath. They ardently espoused the view that there was a fundamental and profound difference between them. Yavneh symbolized diasporic heroism, now flawed, while Massada was the positive symbol of activism and revolt against submissiveness. The attempt of those demanding change to suggest that the myths of Yavneh and Massada complemented each other was rather questionable. It appears that the authors of the educational program wished to legitimize the traditional forms of Jewish response, symbolized in Yavneh, as part of the broader framework of legitimation they wanted to impart to the diasporic history of the Jewish people. On the other hand, conclusions drawn from the Holocaust and the ghetto uprisings were not conducive to docile resignation as at Yavneh. Hence, a strange compound was fused, one that made no sense historically and was flawed by an internal contradiction.

Two sources feeding the offensive ethos emerged into clarity in the course of these discussions: the socialist–revolutionary and the Zionist–activist. The former described the struggle of the Jewish people for freedom in their own land as being one front among many in a powerful global battle being waged between the declining forces of capitalism and the rising forces of tomorrow. Symbols of Palestinian heroism were interwoven and integrated with socialist symbols: the red flag, May Day, Vienna 1934 in struggle, Madrid under siege, Stalingrad and the heroic Russian war. Local activism was conceived as part of a global movement altering the face of the planet. That movement provided the legitimation for the Jewish struggle in Palestine. The second described the civilized world as having turned its back on the Jews. Consequently, the Jews must tend to their own interests even at the expense of neglecting broader fronts. The symbols it wished to promote were Jewish par excellence, expressive of the age-old conflict between Jews and the Gentile world. Its legitimation for Zionist activism was derived from Jewish fate, the need to ensure that the Holocaust would not be repeated, and the immediate task of saving the surviving remnant of the Jewish people.

These diverse sources of sustenance did not lead to different operative conclusions. It is true that here and there someone warned about chauvinistic tendencies as a result of isolationist inclinations. Even these sporadic expressions did not refer to the Palestinian situation and Jewish–Arab relations; rather, they made reference to the tendency for cultural seclusion from the Soviet Union and the world of tomorrow that had surfaced in the discussion. Though divided in philosophical perspective, they did not differ in the domain of present-oriented activism. There was no difference whatsoever in positive attitude toward the offensive ethos between the disciples of Tabenkin, who stressed the socialist approach, and those of Katznelson, who stressed the nationalist one.[174]

The Holocaust played a secondary role in the formation of the offensive ethos. This ethos began to emerge during the Arab Rebellion and crystallized during World War II and its aftermath. It grew in the light of events in Palestine and evolved in the shadow of the anticipation of further occurrences. Its character was shaped by the awareness of the inevitable clash with the Arabs and the ongoing confrontation with the British. The "native" Palestinian identity of the youth that emerged in the second half of the 1940s appropriated the offensive ethos as its most pronounced trait and gift. If there was any event outside the boundaries of Palestine that had a decisive impact on the growth of this ethos, it was first and foremost World War II, which gave enormous impetus to the emergence of power-oriented concepts.

The further one gets from the Holocaust, the more it appears as an event of such magnitude that everything in its wake seems dwarfed by its shadow. For example, there is a tendency to describe the very establishment of the State of Israel as a direct result of the Holocaust. There is no doubt that in the political struggle after the war, the Holocaust had a major impact on U.S.–Jewish and world public opinion. Yet the argument that it was the dominant factor in the establishment of the state is not corroborated by the facts. It is sufficient to recall that a state had been proposed to the Jews in 1937 as part of the Peel Commission recommendations; and even before anything was known about the Holocaust, there was a proclamation that a Jewish state was the chief war aim of the Jewish people. It is also possible to imagine that if the Holocaust had not occurred, the pressure of the many more millions of living Jews would not have been inferior to the moral weight of the martyred dead. The tendency to explain phenomena by using the Holocaust is likewise a familiar argument in connection with formation of the offensive ethos. But a careful examination reveals that all of its Holocaust-associated components existed prior to that event. The Holocaust catalyzed an acceleration and intensification of certain states of mind, psychological proclivities, and approaches to reality but did not generate any new ones. It was central in providing moral justification for the power struggle by reinforcing the self-image of the Jew as eternal victim. The conclusion drawn that Jews must never permit themselves to get into a similar situation in which they are powerless was paramount in bolstering the claims in favor of a state.

The majority of the Palestinian Jewish community found it difficult to identify with Jews who had gone to their death "like sheep to slaughter." This was a blow to the self-image of the Jew that could not be coped with and resolved. A partial substitute lay in identification with the symbols of armed struggle in the Diaspora, namely, the ghetto uprisings. Parallel with this, psychological energy generated by the Holocaust was turned outward. The "externalization" of the Holocaust began—an open and unending account between Jews and other nations. The Holocaust did not foster a new human sensitivity or a different relationship between Jews among themselves. It did not lead to changes in worldview or fashion a new social or national conception. All these would have required an internalization of Jewish experience in the Holocaust; but this internal processing was not forthcoming, at least over the short term. Feelings of rage, frustration, and guilt were channeled into rhetorical statements, a conception of international relations based on sheer force, and a struggle for the fate of Palestine.

Activism as a Characteristic of Palestinian Identity

The last stages of World War II and its aftermath witnessed the emergence of a new consciousness: that of the Palestinian generation. This was a generation that took pains to distinguish itself from its fathers. It seemed different in its gait, characteristic movements, style of clothing, and hair. The fluent Hebrew it spoke was marked by a guttural accent, which emphasized the generation gap. Its idioms and slang were the product of a spoken language and local needs. The differences between the generations were not only external. When the parents took a good look at their sons and daughters, they perceived several features that gladdened their hearts, since the founders of Zionism had hoped and prayed for the advent of such a generation. These youngsters had a liberated attitude toward nature and were comfortable in its midst. Their bond with the land flowed from an instinctive identification with the homeland. They were happy to engage in physical labor and undertook it naturally, without much ado. For them, socialism or kibbutz life were something self-evident. The expressions "simplicity" and "naturalness" were frequently used to characterize this youth, while the generation of the fathers had been plagued by psychological complications and hangups. That generation was torn between attachment to its native land and loyalty to its adopted home, Palestine. It was beset by doubts about its abilities when it came to manual labor, and about its socialist perceptions. In contrast, the sons accepted the realities of their life with great simplicity, without complexes or the burden of excessive self-questioning. Life in Palestine, with the kibbutz experience as a part of it, came to them naturally. They had not been required to struggle for the values they accepted. These young people took for granted the teaching of their fathers and had no desire to revolt against it. That fact awakened mixed feelings among the adult generation. Although they were pleased to have successors, they would have preferred for their sons to have acquired their way of life by a process of struggle, assessment, and discovery, internalizing the values they adopted as their own. They were cognizant that an absence of such struggle and the acceptance of their parents' values in literal terms were phenomena characteristic of a postrevolutionary generation. Nonetheless, they were troubled by a certain sense of dissatisfaction, afraid the younger generation had acquired those values mechanically, without any profound inner conviction.[175]

Among the manifestations of the simplicity of youth was an abhorrence for high-sounding phrases, flowery rhetoric, and a brand of pathos that had been a characteristic mark of the older generation. They had a disgust for any display of emotions and asserted themselves by using simple, direct language and discarding conventions of politeness. On occasion, this degenerated into crudeness and arrogance. Their penchant for simple, unadorned behavior included an aspiration for honesty and sincerity in interhuman relations: They wished to tear down the barriers deriving from the duplicity of civilization. Pleasant manners were considered to be a false veneer used by bourgeois society to cover over its ailments and thought proper to be tossed onto the garbage heap of history. The type of the "tough guy," the sabra (a cactus tough and thorny outside but savory and sweet inside), became the ideal paradigm for Palestinian youth. That young person had nothing but disdain and contempt for "ideologies." He perceived them as characteristic of the older generation, originating in the Diaspora—and thus of no consequence in Palestine. Ideologies were marked by much talk and little action; their time had ended, and now action was the order of the day. Soviet Russia, fighting heroically against the Nazis, became a model for this generation: an example of the superiority of deeds over words. It was much more interested in Stalingrad and the exploits of the partisans than in the intricacies of Marxism. "Ideology had been the yardstick of truth for the previous generation. The yardstick for the new generation is the task to be performed," stated Uri Avneri, editor of the journal *Ba-Ma'avak,* seen by many as a kind of manifesto of the new generation.[176]

The collective identity of Palestinian youth was marked by two outstanding characteristics: a "native" mentality and militant activism. "The special thing about this youth is that it is *Palestinian.* It was raised in this country, absorbed its spirit—and the country became part of its very essence," one commentator stated in a lecture entitled "The Floor—to the Palestinian Generation!"[177] The "Palestinian spirit" was believed to nurture physical and mental abilities, a new psychological structure, a different attitude toward reality. "The Palestine movement is . . . a movement creating its life in the land, from the land, through life in the land—not by means of instruments borrowed from other locales and conditions," asserted one of Tabenkin's disciples.[178] The Palestinian identity was marked by a strong sense of repulsion toward Diaspora Jews, coupled with a sense of alienation toward the older generation. The title of this lecture was not accidental. It was a paraphrase of a line penned by a very popular young poet, a member of the Palmach, named Chaim Guri, one of the typical representatives of the new generation. The original read, "The Floor—to Comrade Mauser." That idea was not restricted just to youth. Adults in those days also felt that the time for talking had passed and that might alone would bring about the desired change. From 1942 on, Nathan Alterman played a role in the Hebrew press that Beilinson had filled during the 1930s, that is, the role of the spokesman for the activistic Zionist consensus. As the Soviet tanks rolled across the Prussian border, he wrote,

> Those same cannon,
> In their booming voice,
> Easily teach the Herr Baron
> What all the treasures of ethics and poesy together
> Were unable to impart to him.[179]

Thus, it is not surprising that young people thought accordingly, infected by what Dov Stock (Sadan, an important writer and journalist) dubbed the "hubris of youth."[180]

"Our generation is a generation of struggle," Uri Avneri proclaimed: "We were raised and educated in the struggle of the riots. We grew to maturity in the struggle against the White Paper. And the struggle for control of Palestine is our principal pioneering goal."[181] Moshele Tabenkin admitted it was "true that ideological matters and abstract questions do not hold interest for each and every one of us. . . . But the affairs of Zionism and its realization, the question of our constant dignity and our steadfastness in the campaign—all these are imprinted upon our soul and in our blood."[182] The alert and activist segments of youth viewed activism as their ideal. They saw the Yishuv as divided between the "good" (supporters of an active struggle against the British) and the "bad" (various types of weak-kneed individuals from the Right and Left, nurturing an "immigrant" mentality, lacking the true Palestinian spirit).

The militant mood was inculcated to a significant degree by the youth movements but especially by the organization that in the course of the 1940s became the focus of Palestinian youth: the Palmach. There was no framework that had a more decisive impact on the shaping of the image of youth than the Palmach. It was an organization of fighters, and it wished to be actively involved in battle. Its predominance was pronounced even in groups that were subject to opposing educational influences. Young people from Ha-Shomer ha-Tzair, schooled in humanistic traditions and the fraternity of all peoples, adopted to a significant degree the approaches prevalent in the Palmach. With sorrow and concern, mentors of Ha-Shomer ha-Tzair noted that the process of the struggle had enhanced "the feeling of alienness and animosity toward our neighbors" in their boys, while military training in the framework of the Palmach "created a certain experience . . . that was not conducive to advancing youth and strengthening those ideals that we had inscribed on our banner."[183] In the battle between ideology and reality as factors molding youth, there was no doubt about which was the stronger element at the end of the 1940s: Reality had gained the upper hand. Veterans of Ha-Shomer ha-Tzair noted with dismay that the dialectic expression they had coined, "militant humanism"—a kind of oath to keep away the evil spirits of the age—could not hold its own against the upsurge of deep-set impulses, the exaltation of power, and the decline in the role of ideology.[184]

The blatant activism of youth was one of the reasons why it followed Tabenkin. The divisions in political life in the Yishuv were not structured in terms of political issues. The great disputes on the Arab question or on partition cut right across the ruling party, Mapai, and the debate was conducted internally within party ranks. The question of activism had a similar fate in internal party disputes in the 1940s. The split in Mapai, already visible in 1942 and a fait accompli by 1944, came about as a result of a complex party dynamics, in which the attitude toward activism played a secondary role. The line that divided the two parties did not run between activists and moderates. To be sure, Ha-Tenua le-Ahdut ha-Avoda was militantly activist, but Mapai was only partly moderate. Youth found this ambivalence hard to digest. Ever since Ha-Kibbutz ha-Meuhad had stood by the Palmach in 1942 and saved it from disbandment, and increasingly so after it provided housing in its kibbutzim for Palmach units, Tabenkin and his associates came to symbolize true activism in the consciousness of youth. They were highly suspicious of activism along the lines preached by Berl Katznelson or Ben Gurion—a stance allowing room for considerations of political utility. Due to the special circumstances in Palestine, the antiestablishment attitude so natural to young people took on the guise of an eagerness for battle. Added to this was the component of revolutionary socialism as an ideology of action. Activism in this version became a code of political identification.

The days of action of the Hebrew Resistance Movement were a time of exaltation and excitement for youth: at long last, the "old man," Yitzhak Sade, had given the order, as recalled in a song of that era. Yet there were also elite groups within the ranks of youth that had reservations about armed struggle. A group of youth instructors in the boy scouts turned to Chaim Weizmann, who visited Palestine in the winter of 1946, with a request for encouragement and assistance for taking action against the new political line: "We are opposed to acts of terror [of the sort] that have recently been carried out in Palestine for purposes other than that of defending immigration and settlement." These young men, who were members in the Palmach, sought an avenue to influence their disciples in the youth movement toward the moderate direction they espoused.[185] Yet these were but a minuscule minority in their age group. The preponderant majority relished the prospect of armed action. It was a shining era that ended in bitter disappointment. The resignation of Moshe Sneh and the cessation of activity indicated that the moderates had the upper hand, to the deep dismay and sorrow of the Palmachniks. They felt they had been deceived, and that their cause had been betrayed. Beginning with the autumn of 1946, Palmach publications were interspersed with a number of critical comments on the dominant trend of moderation in the Yishuv. When the first buds of independent political consciousness emerged among the young—expressed, among other things, in the pages of the periodical *Ba-Ma'avak* (whose name, "In Struggle" was likewise not accidental)—they were linked with a demand that the fighters be given power, since they were the native sons and would be called upon to battle for independence of the homeland when the moment arrived. The moderates were asked to pass on the reins to persons who had grown up within the framework of the Hagana. "All Authority to the Defenders of the Yishuv" was the title of an article attacking the policies of Weizmann and his moderate associates after Black Saturday.[186]

During the world war, the militant attitude that was widespread among the youth groups associated with the Labor movement veered closer to views espoused by the IZL and Lehi. It is difficult to find any essential changes in the attitudes of the latter two organizations regarding the use of force when compared with their thinking in the late 1930s. Avraham Stern and his associates had been proponents of the concept of unlimited force even before they split from the IZL and set up Lehi, also known as the Stern Gang. In the first years of the war, this organization made a semantic distinction between "enemy" and "oppressor." Hitler was classified as an oppressor, while the British were enemies. They saw Hitler as one link in a long chain of persecutors of the Jewish people throughout the generations. In their view, a victory over Hitler would not solve the central problem of the Jewish people, a "lack of political status": "For that reason, we are not prepared to lose our forces on that nondecisive front of battle."[187] In contrast, the British stood directly in the path of the Jewish people leading to sovereignty in their own land. It followed that the principal means of struggle had to be directed against the British in order to dislodge them from Palestine. Stern, Israel Eldad-Sheib, Nathan Friedman (Yelin-Mor), and their associates carried the reasoning of Ahimeir, who saw the British as "alien occupier," to its logical conclusion. This was an extreme position in the line of Palestinocentrism: They held that it was of no importance to participate in the war against Hitler. Moreover, in line with the principle "My enemy's enemy is my friend," there was an additional avenue worth exploring: One could try to gain assistance from the Nazis against the true enemy, the British. That position led directly to attempts by Lehi to forge contacts with the German authorities at the end of 1941.[188] This aspect of their approach was obviously in total opposition to the conception of Ahimeir and Uri Zvi Greenberg, whose commitment to the Jewish people was never in question. The attempt by Lehi to court the Germans proved abortive and led to nothing but casts revealing light on the psychological makeup of that group's leadership, and the contortions of morality they were drawn into as a consequence of their conception of power, in which the ideas of both Darwin and Nietzsche intermingled.

In the 1940s the Arabs played a secondary role in the thinking of Lehi. At the start of that decade, they considered Arab power negligible and asserted that Jews would have no trouble in countering any opposition on their part. In the second half of the 1940s, when Lehi embraced an anti-imperialist stance, they argued that there was no real conflict of interests between Palestinian Jews and Palestinian Arabs and that all the clashes that had occurred were the product of British agitation. They contended that when the Arabs came to realize that Jewish power was not directed against them but against the oppressive imperialist regime, they would cease being hostile. This conception was part of a broader change in orientation that began to make itself felt at that time in Lehi: a shift from attempts to forge an alliance with the Axis powers to a new reliance on the Soviets. Yet a certain ambivalence toward the Arabs remained: The covert assumption was that the Arabs were not a genuine adversary, since they were not truly a people: For that reason, they should not be regarded as a factor in deciding the future fate of Palestine. On the other hand, it was self-evident to Lehi members that if the Arabs nevertheless put up resistance, they would be suppressed by the Jews without hesitation and with a heavy hand.[189] The "minorization" of the Arab problem must be seen against the backdrop of the intensity of what, in Lehi's eyes, was the pivotal issue: British "foreign rule" in Palestine.

During the course of 1944 a process of shifting the emphasis from the Arab problem to the struggle against the British also occurred in the IZL when Menahem Begin, its commander, proclaimed a "revolt" even though the world war was still raging. The IZL was more moderate than Lehi in its attitudes toward the British: It called for a war not against the British people but against British policy, in order to effect a change in that policy. In contrast with the relative indifference of Lehi members toward events in Europe, Begin and his associates linked the "revolt" they had proclaimed to British behavior in the face of the destruction of European Jewry. The intensity of their hatred toward the British was explained by them as a response to the intolerable stand taken by the British toward the Jewish people during the war. On that point, the IZL's position was in harmony with the feeling of broad circles within the Jewish population in Palestine, which had strongly resented the British policy of closing the gates to Jewish refugees. Nonetheless, the principal reason for the IZL's attacks against the British starting in 1944 was not the situation in Europe. Rather, it was the feeling that nothing whatsoever had changed in British policy in Palestine and that it was therefore necessary to fight in order to bring about such a change.[190] The anti-imperialist ballast of Lehi did not win hearts and minds in the IZL ranks. The latter organization remained firmly planted in the ideological soil of revisionism, and was right-wing in its general world outlook.

The perception of the British as enemy number one of the Jewish people was

not an alien idea to the Palestinian Jewish youth affiliated with the Labor movement. At a convention of activists, Eliyahu Golomb, to his annoyance and surprise,
encountered a position that he had been confronted with on occasion during his
drive to persuade young people to enlist in the British Army. The Hagana and Palmach members stated their view that the war being fought by Britain in Europe was
not the concern of the Jewish community in Palestine, since Hitler was fighting in
Europe, and this did not affect the Jewish community here. As far as the danger of
an Arab uprising was concerned, there was no need to prepare for such an eventuality, since they had already learned what was necessary during the Arab Rebellion.
The central task on the immediate agenda, they asserted, was to prepare for war
against the British.[191]

Hatred of the British and the struggle against them created a broad common
denominator among Jewish youth. In the autumn of 1943 an ephemeral organization named Am Lohem (A Fighting People) was founded. Its membership
included activists from the IZL, Lehi, the Hagana, and Palmach. Its importance
was not in the domain of action, since the organization broke up before it had carried out its plan to kidnap High Commissioner Harold MacMichael. Rather, the
significance of the grouping lay in the very fact that a basis could be found for a
consensus between groups that were diametrically opposed from the educational
and ideological point of view.[192] The more the IZL and Lehi intensified their war
against the British, the greater was their prestige in the eyes of Palestinian youth. In
a convention of youth groups affiliated with Ha-Tenau le-Ahdut ha-Avoda in 1944,
Moshele Tabenkin spoke on behalf of the brave fighters of the IZL and Lehi, claiming that the young people in Ha-Tenau le-Ahdut ha-Avoda shared more ground
with the IZL and Lehi than with the "moderates" in Mapai.[193]

The IZL and Lehi rejected the authority of the executive of the Jewish Agency,
the body representing the Zionist Organization. The executive was certain that the
separatist activity of these organizations was endangering its political strategy.
While the main dispute with the IZL in the late 1930s had centered on the question
of the limits on the use of force (which had a direct bearing on the question of
restraint), the heart of the matter now was the issue of authority and discipline. For
that reason, it proved possible in the autumn of 1945 to find a common basis for
action within the framework of the Hebrew Resistance Movement. Even within
this framework, the Hagana acted with far greater restraint than the two other organizations. The guideline in the Hagana of avoiding loss of life whenever possible
was unacceptable to Lehi, while the IZL did not regard it as a reason to change plans
for action. This became evident in the blowing up of the King David Hotel in Jerusalem in July 1946. The more intense the struggle became, the greater was the willingness of those two organizations to attack British soldiers and kill them, with or
without a direct reason. The Hagana was strongly opposed to attacking British soldiers indiscriminately.

The activist leadership of the Labor movement found itself walking a thin rope.
On the one hand, it wished to maintain the militancy of youth and inculcate a mar-
tial spirit, since it was apparent that at some stage in the political struggle for Palestine, it would be compelled to employ its military prowess. On the other hand, it
recognized the pedagogical and political dangers inherent in the power-oriented

mood of the young. Moshe Shertok gave a definition of the situation that well expressed the dilemma and its resolution: "We must reject the notion that opposes the use of force; likewise, we must repudiate the view that advocates placing all our trust solely in the use of force. Limitations are an important factor in the efficiency of power."[194] Ben Gurion added: "We have to realize that there are limits to our force, and we must also realize that we need our power—not only for resistance. We emphatically reject the anti-Zionist concept of 'Only this way'."[195]

Against the IZL slogan, "Only this way," the activist leadership of the Jewish community advanced the slogan "Also this way". That distinction contained a renewed emphasis on the importance of constructive action. "Immigration and settlement are the two tablets of our covenant with Zionism," wrote Galili in a letter to a friend, responding to propaganda by the IZL and Lehi. The latter, in the wake of the establishment of the Hebrew Resistance movement, had proclaimed that for all practical purposes, the Hagana had adopted their program. In response to that propaganda, the struggle for immigration (both legal and illegal) and settlement (with or without a permit) were presented as specific traits of the Hagana and Palmach, distinguishing them from the other organizations.[196] "There is a world of difference between a movement created for building up the land, for labor, for constructive purposes, forced to fight *as well* and a movement whose be-all and end-all is the use of arms," proclaimed Yitzhak Sade, a model figure for youth.[197] Along with the declaration that there would apparently be no way of avoiding the use of force if the Arabs attacked the community or if the British prevented the Jews from exercising their right of free immigration to Palestine. The leadership made clear that this was a necessity, nothing to take delight in and look forward to: "There is no need for a positive attitude toward terror in order to make use of force, to fight and to utilize terror *as a means*." These remarks by Eliyahu Golomb expressed the de facto acceptance of the use of force, along with the desire to restrain and curb the excessive enthusiasm regarding its employment spreading among the ranks of young Jews in Palestine.[198]

The instrument that was singled out to highlight the difference between the IZL and Lehi on the one hand and the youth affiliated with the Labor movement on the other was socialist identity. As during the years when dispute raged on self-restraint, now, too, this was the main vehicle utilized to curb the attraction of those organizations for young people. The historical link between them and the Revisionist movement, famous for its antisocialist policies (expressed in the slogan "Yes, break it up," coined by Jabotinsky in reference to the Histadrut), served as proof corroborating the fascistic character of the IZL and Lehi. Their terror acts were depicted as equivalent to those of the radical Right in Europe, especially the Nazis—as actions designed to take control of the Yishuv and institute a fascist regime there. "The hand that knew how to fire at Lord Moyne [British minister of state in the Middle East, murdered in Egypt by Lehi in 1944] was trained previously in the pogrom against the workers' club, against the kiosk and printing house of Yiddish papers, against the red flag and the hymn of the International," Tabenkin noted. In his analysis, the murder of Moyne pointed to a coming campaign of terror within the Jewish community, leading to the killing of its leaders, along the lines of the murder of Arlosoroff. "Gangs like that, if they are not stood up to, will come into our homes and take control of us from within," he predicted.[199] This position was reiterated on innumerable occasions by leaders of all the left and center movements in Palestine, extending from Ha-Shomer ha-Tzair to Aliyah Hadasha. It functioned as a crucial component in the delegitimization of Lehi and the IZL and in portraying them as bodies beyond the pale of the Zionist consensus. The extortion of funds and acts of robbery perpetrated in the Jewish community in order to finance their actions, attacks against British without any consideration of possible injuries to innocent bystanders, and the murder of British in cold blood—these acts gave credibility to the thesis that these were organizations dedicated solely to the brutal use of force and whose ultimate goal was to take control of the Palestinian Jewish community.

On two occasions in the history of the struggle against the British, Ben Gurion and the leadership of the Jewish Agency did not shrink from using force against these organizations. The first such instance occurred in the autumn of 1944, in the wake of the murder of Lord Moyne. Alarmed that that assassination would slam shut the door on any prospect for a pro-Zionist solution initiated by Winston Churchill, the Zionist leadership did everything in their power to underscore their disgust with the deed. This was the source of the detention action against members of Lehi and, particularly, the IZL, which was the larger of the two groups and enjoyed broader public support. In a number of cases, the action—nicknamed by the IZL and Lehi the *Sezon* (hunting season)—even led to the handing over of underground members to the British security police. The *Sezon* was repeated in 1947. Palmach members were positively inclined to take action against the two underground groups. Schooled in Tabenkin's revolutonary socialism, they felt it was a sacred task to strike out at the fascists within the Jewish community. Their only reservation had to do with cooperating with the British security police, and the handing over of IZL members to them. When the leadership decided to terminate the *Sezon,* having become convinced that it had not led to a positive change in British policy, the Palmach was incensed that the action had been canceled before completion. There was a special mixture here of animosity toward the fascist "dissenters" and a naive belief that it was possible to solve complex political and social problems with a simple but powerful demonstration of resolve if only the leaders would act decisively. Galili noted a tendency among youth to look for simple, quick solutions: "Young comrades have pretensions about clear solutions and clear-cut policy. In all matters, what they basically want is a decisive battle—whether against the government, the 'dissenters', or the Arabs." He tried to convince his audience that the Zionist movement was not capable of effecting such decisions in any of these domains: "Young people are laboring under the illusion that a Jewish state already exists. From the rock of that illusion, it hews its conceptions of dignity, national tactics, and tactics of struggle, its conception of the national capability for action and the might of national authority." He stressed: "Youth does not have a true assessment of our strength, neither in itself nor in relation to other forces. It is attracted by the false glitter of erroneous concepts of national dignity."[200]

The propaganda against the IZL and Lehi raised, once again, a line of argumentation derived from the defensive ethos: The advantage of the constructive deed, of immigration and settlement as against the use of force. Galili's remarks indicate that the same young people who had embraced the teachings of socialism and constructive principles and lived by their guidelines felt deep down that they were only of secondary importance. The Zionist order of priorities adhered to by the adults in the movement, to which they remained faithful until death, was not internalized in a similar manner by youth. They recognized the importance of settlement, especially if it entailed physical danger and risk. They acknowledged the significance of immigration, particularly if it was illegal and involved a demonstration of force. Yet their true enthusiasm was for fighting. Any talk about the limits of Jewish power in Palestine—requiring consideration of political factors and even of the other people in the land—were viewed by them as evidence of the flaws that marred the "desert generation." They thought they were in no need of allies or the support of world public opinion. They had no doubt that they were capable of conquering Palestine.[201] Confidence in the ability of Jewish power to tip the scales in favor of a pro-Jewish solution in the event of an armed struggle for Palestine was a predominant feature of youth right across the political spectrum.

Affected by the "hubris of youth," those young people were certain they were destined for great things. They had an inexhaustible faith in themselves and their ability to conquer the whole world and to decide the fate of Palestine. Their hands had not yet been scorched in the flames of reality, and they believed nothing was beyong their grasp. They viewed their fathers as a generation that had finished its role: Now it was their turn to leave their imprint on Jewish history. They did not regard themselves as trailblazers in the field of ideas. In that sphere, they had nothing new to add. Moreover, they were not plagued by moral dilemmas: Discussion of Dostoevsky's Grand Inquisitor had ceased to stir any interest, even among the more intellectual Ha-Shomer ha-Tzair members.[202] They followed world events and took in their significance, but in a selective manner. Their universe was ultimately quite narrow and limited, restricted to the confines of Palestine.[203] They were men of action, without intellectual pretensions. Their intellectual simplicity joined with a power-oriented conception devoid of illusions. "If we have no strength, then all the other demonstrations, including our protest about the injustice done to us, will be of no consequence," proclaimed one of the leaders of Ha-Mahanot ha-Olim.[204] "This we know: in this world, sentiment and humanism have virtually no value," commented one young man from Ha-Noar ha-Oved on the eve of his recruitment to the Palmach.[205] A teacher in Ha-Shomer ha-Tzair voiced his worry about the relativistic outlook that had spread among youth, affecting its moral fabric.[206] Still, the socialism they had been educated in served as a barrier against inordinate chauvinism. But reality placed the humanist principles under a difficult test of credibility. In this context, revolutionary socialism in its Tabenkinian version gave a dimension of moral legitimacy to aggressive feelings and the eagerness for battle.

In the wake of the *Patria* disaster of 1940, Dov Stock wrote a letter to Berl Katznelson dealing mainly with the reaction of the young people to the occurrence. Stock was deeply shocked by the sheer callousness shown by young people toward the tragedy of nearly three hundred killed. One of the young men commented to him: "Look, what can be done? Accidents will happen." One of the instructors wrote a letter full of praise for the "clean job" that had been done and took no pains to add "a few crumbs of sorrow for the dead, the injured, and shocked." Faced with the "hardening of the hearts, especially among youth," Stock felt "that Hitler has already been victorious in depth, if not yet in breadth."

Citing a line by Bialik—"Apparently you have oppressed us so greatly that we turned into wild animals"—he commented:

> This coarseness is the greatest of all tragedies, i.e., the point where the essential dif-
> ference is canceled out between the oppressor and the oppressed and the soul of the
> oppressed [becomes] like the soul of the oppressor. I am fearful there are but few
> among us who can see this awful calamity coming; and most fail to sense that what
> they have fought against until now has begun to infiltrate their souls, is growing,
> ramifying and [that] one cloudy morning they'll discover to their chagrin that
> they've become the captives of "cruel spirits."

He ended his letter with the words, "My heart is like a wound, and I see that the last threads [of communication] have been severed."[207]

It is doubtful whether such a cutting judgment was appropriate and justified in the case of Palestinian Jewish youth. Yet there were components in that youth's makeup in contradiction with age-old Jewish traditions of love for man, mercy, and compassion. The horizons of that youth were narrow: Its limited field of vision excluded all those who did not belong to the familiar circle of experience and way of life in which it had been raised. These young people had profound friendship for persons close to their heart, showed a special gift for comradeship, were capable of devotion, and willing to sacrifice themselves in the hour of need. But when dealing with people outside that magic circle, the Palestinian youth was unable to apply those human feelings and humane virtues his father's generation had tried, with only partial success, to impart to him. If he harbored any feelings of tenderness, he did his best to conceal them. Externally, he manifested an attitude of objective func-tionalism and regarded the exhibition of human emotions as a contemptible weak-ness. His fanaticism and fighting spirit were vital factors in the decisive period of the birth of the state. Yet it was doubtful whether this was the ideal young man the Zionist thinkers had envisaged. "We don't want Jewish *shkotzim* [young, Gentile bullies]. We want a generation that will be able to carry upon its shoulders the spir-itual burden of our socialist pioneering enterprise," proclaimed a key educator in Ha-Shomer ha-Tzair in January 1947. However, even he was aware of the internal contradiction between this lofty ideal and the aspiration for a "youth more healthy, simple, and rooted," fulfilling the national goals.[208] The synthesis between the demands of the time and the lessons of the age on the one hand and the phenom-enon of a "native" generation on the other nurtured a new Jewish species: a Pal-estinian tribe, with a mental and psychological makeup that differed significantly from that of their fathers.

8

Conclusion: The Birth of the State

A night of straits, a night of trial.
And you ready, experienced.
I saw you desperate, I saw you armed.
My last remnant, and a brazen brow.

I saw you and understood
How short the distance is
Between the verge of catastrophe
And the eve of jubilation.

NATHAN ALTERMAN, *Night of Siege*

Meeting in Lake Success, New York, on November 29, 1947, the United Nations General Assembly passed a resolution on the partition of Palestine and the establishment of two states between the Jordan River and the sea. This decision was received with an unparalleled outburst of jubilation among Jews in Palestine, while profound mourning spread through the Arab community there, coupled with a firm resolve to fight to resist the partition.

The Arabs were uncompromising in their unwillingness to come to terms with the existence of a second national community in Palestine. The early expectations of the Zionist leaders that the Arabs, in the course of time, would recognize the advantages the Zionist enterprise was bringing for them and would reconcile themselves to its presence proved to have been illusory. Likewise, the hope that Jewish strength, in the broad sense of the term, would persuade the Arabs that it was necessary to share sovereignty in the country with the Jews revealed itself to be irrelevant, given the realities of 1947. With a population of 650,000 Jews in the land, the Arabs continued to maintain the same stance they had adopted in 1920, when the Yishuv had numbered only some 56,000. In retrospect, that appears to have been a fatal, yet inevitable, error on their part. The possibility that the Palestinian Arabs would accept Jewish colonization and settlement in Palestine and would peacefully

353

renounce their sovereign rights to a part of the country, was incompatible both with their self-image as the exclusive proprietors of Palestine and with their assessment of the situation. The Arabs in Palestine, who outnumbered Jews by nearly two to one and who had been promised assistance by Arab states in the event of war had all the reason in the world to trust in their ability to decide the issue by sheer force. Yet after the smoke and dust of battle receded, the Jews controlled territory extending beyond the boundaries that had been allocated to them in the UN partition resolution, and nearly 600,000 Arabs had gone into exile—some by choice, others by force. This Jewish victory was not won easily. More than 6,000 Jews had fallen in the war (about 1 percent of the total Jewish population at the time), a figure nearly equal to the number that were to die in the subsequent forty years of continuing hostilities. The feeling of self-confidence and exaltation generated by the victory was tempered by a sense that a great miracle had occurred.

On May 14, 1948, Ben Gurion recorded the following entry in his diary: "At four in the afternoon, Jewish independence was proclaimed, and the state established. Its fate lies in the hands of the security forces."[1] This was both a description of the situation, prosaic and sober, and a summation of a chain of developments extending back some fifty years. Ben Gurion perceived reliance on military forces as an integral component of the establishment of the state; he accepted it—unjubilantly, yet without protest. It was simply self-evident. The use of physical might to achieve political goals became one of the accepted means in the arsenal of the Zionist movement.

If someone had predicted to Herzl that the state he had envisaged would ultimately be established in blood and fire and that its fate would rest on the point of a sword, the author of *The Jewish State* would undoubtedly have been repulsed and would have rejected the implications of this prophecy. His ideas about the establishment of a Jewish state were shaped by conceptions of progress in a global community of enlightened peoples, a world in which problems were solved by reason and common agreement. The ethos of the Zionist movement in the first half of the twentieth century was a strange mixture of ideas and concepts, imbued with a unique psychological and emotional tenor. The accumulated impact of diverse sources (e.g., ancient Jewish tradition, nineteenth-century humanistic and liberal enlightenment thought, and twentieth-century nationalism and socialist–revolutionary ideology) gave rise to a complex and varied collective personality, in which the desire for justice and sovereignty, moral elevation and physical power, the fraternity of man and national greatness were all intermixed.

This old mentality not only rejected the use of force as being "non-Jewish" but ascribed an ethical value to abstaining from power and its exercise. The fact that it rationalized weakness (as opponents were quick to point out) did not render it less influential. It remained deeply rooted in Jewish sentiment, even when Jews expressed pride in their emancipation from its fetters and declared their loyalty to a more aggressive credo.

On the other hand, from the very beginning, the evolving national ethos contained undertones of admiration and longing for power. The Jews were presented as powerless and without a homeland—two essential deficiencies that the national movement aspired to remedy. The romanticism of power in the early stages of the

Zionist movement gave vent to Jewish longing for national grandeur, dignity, and an equal status among the nations of the world. It answered to deep psychological needs of an oppressed, humiliated, and persecuted people. That romanticism rejected Jewish religion—depicted as the source of Jewish misery—and sought the roots of the Jewish people in ancient Hebrew myth, striving to mold a new Jew, liberated from the shackles of religion and the strictures of morality and motivated by instinctive and creative vitality.

From its inception, the aspiration for the renewal of the Jew and his image was bound up with the hope for achieving a land of his own. The yearning for a homeland reflected the Jewish aspiration to adopt the same components of national identity as other European peoples—traits that the Jews had been prevented from acquiring due to their dispersion among other peoples. Even though they were not initially aware of this, the idea of a homeland entailed the use of force. The homeland would serve as refuge and protective haven for Jews; as such, it would have to be able to make use of military might when necessary. In contrast with various concepts of Diaspora nationalism, the national territorial concept contained a nucleus of the idea of Jewish independence. In order to gain a country of their own, the Jews had to be prepared to enter into confrontation with another people and to demand their national rights, even at the point of a gun. Aggressiveness was thus an integral component of the process. The ongoing deterioration in the situation of the Jewish people in Europe during the first half of the twentieth century imbued this process, first, with a sense of urgency, later, with a sense of tragic loss, transforming the desire for a homeland from abstract wishes for national renaissance into an imperative for survival.

In many respects, Zionism was unique as a national movement. One of its (presumably singular) characteristic features stemmed from the fact that it was a national liberation movement that was destined to function as a movement promoting settlement in a country of colonization. This incongruity between the liberating and progressive message internally and the aggressive message externally acted as a central factor in the shaping of self-images and norms—and, in the end, also patterns of action—in the Zionist movement. Zionist psychology was molded by the conflicting parameters of a national liberation movement and a movement of European colonization in a Middle Eastern country.

The Zionist movement was a decided latecomer on the colonial scene: Movements of colonization by Europeans were common up to the late nineteenth century. By the end of World War I, when the Zionists first succeeded in gaining international recognition, the right for self-determination for the peoples of Asia and Africa was already regarded as sacred among progressive circles around the world. The Zionist movement (in particular, its socialist variant) viewed itself as belonging to the forces striving for a better world and could not accept the fact that the framework of its activity was determined by the contours of a country of colonization.

The encounter between the Second Aliyah, the dominant group in shaping the mentality of the Yishuv, and the reality of Palestine, was traumatic. Though extremely individualistic and diverse in their approach, the immigrants of the Second Aliyah nonetheless shared a common conviction, namely, that the world operated according to ethical rules and that justice would ultimately prevail. Their moral pathos imbued them with confidence in the righteousness of their path. Their need to feel that they were on the side of justice derived from the emotional and conceptual foundations of their worldview. For that reason, the socialist settler flatly rejected the self-image of a European who was usurping the rights of the native population. Furthermore, he was unable to make peace with the prospect of unending war. Consequently, he created a model that interpreted this reality differently, making use of a complex amalgam of ideas and behavioral patterns that have been termed here the "defensive ethos."

The defensive ethos blurred the fact that there was a basic clash of interests in Palestine between the Jewish immigrants and the people already settled there. It also suggested an explanation for Arab opposition to Jewish settlement that made it possible to disregard the fact that what was involved was a fundamental clash between two national movements fighting to gain sovereignty and control over the same country. On the other hand, the ethos did contain a recognition of a potential Jewish–Arab confrontation. This recognition, however, did not envision an inevitable, head-on collision. On the contrary, it strove to lessen the tension between the two peoples as much as possible in the hope that it might ultimately be possible to establish a Jewish entity in Palestine peacefully, without having to resort to the use of force. By the same token, the defensive ethos justified avoidance of any attempt at negotiating with the Arabs. No confrontation and no compromises was the concrete conclusion drawn from the defensive ethos.

That conception remained strong during the 1920s and the first half of the 1930s. It was attacked by critics who had few misgivings about the image of the Jew as colonialist settler, such as Zeev Jabotinsky, who wished to implement fully the model of a colonization country in Palestine. At the same time, it was also criticized by those who accepted the existence of a national Jewish–Arab conflict, such as Brit Shalom. Wishing to cast off the stigma of the linkage between the Jewish Liberation movement and imperialism, Brit Shalom members called for direct Jewish–Arab talks, without British mediation. Yet, just as Jabotinsky failed to prove to the British that their interests were commensurate with unlimited British support for Zionism, members of Brit Shalom were unable to convince Jews (not to speak of Arabs) that an agreement protecting the basic interests of both sides was indeed possible. "Has the Zionist movement missed opportunities?" asked Gershom Scholem retrospectively: "I am doubtful today if much would have changed at the time had we done one thing instead of another."[2]

The defensive ethos was distinguished by two parallel approaches to the Arabs. One related to the Arabs as individuals, while the other viewed them as a people. The existence of those two approaches helped fashion a distinction between relating to the Arab as a human being and, contrastingly, seeing him as a member of a people vying for control of Palestine. While in the first domain, Jews were obliged to adhere to the acceptable canon of ethical tenets in interpersonal behavior, in the second sphere, the constraints of national interest served to release persons from compliance with those rules. Thus it was argued that one should act to promote the rights of the Arab worker and better his lot and avoid placing him at any disadvantage. Yet at one and the same time, it was permissible to demand of the Arab that he renounce his exclusive claim to Palestine. It was prohibited to expel the fellahin;

but it was perfectly alright to purchase land from the effendis, even if that involved eviction of fellahin from the soil. This tendency was also evident during the War of Independence and in its wake. The leadership of the young state was shocked by revelations of maltreatment of Arabs, plundering and robbery. Leaders insisted on preserving the so-called purity of arms and did not hesitate to declare publicly their revulsion at abuse of Arabs and denounce incidents of murder and rape. On the other hand, no equivalent legitimation was given to pursuing a public debate on the expulsion of Arabs. At the time, S. Yizhar, in his story "Hirbet Hiz'ah," was the only writer who dealt openly with the matter.[3] There was an internal logic in this sort of differentiation. Harm to Arabs as individuals was enjoined; yet expulsion, an act on the plane of national confrontation, was permissible. The formula used by Clermont-Tonnerre in respect to Jews in the debate on Jewish emancipation during the French Revolution may be adapted to the present situation: To Arabs as individuals, everything; to Arabs as a people, nothing.

The tendency to speak in two voices, reflecting the presence of an overt, and a subliminal, layer in relating to the Arab question, was integral to the defensive ethos. The relationship between those two layers is a problem that continues to confound the historian, due to the lack of direct documentary evidence. At what point did the leadership become aware that there were fallacies in the logical structure of the defensive ethos and that the Zionist movement would not be able to avoid a head-on collision with the Arab national movement? By the nature of things, doubts about the validity of the central ethos of that era could not be raised in any public discussion. It is likely, though, that those questions were often broached in tête-à-têtes between friends and private conversations among the leadership. Hence, ideas on this theme found no expression in the source materials of the era. In addition, there was an almost hypnotic power in the ritualistic repetition of accepted truths: It served as a means by which these aspects of reality, so difficult to cope with from the intellectual and psychological point of view, were shifted to the margins of consciousness both of the individual and the collective. Presumably, although people like Berl Katznelson, Yitzhak Tabenkin, and Moshe Beilinson were well aware of the logical fallacies—a dimension hinted at here and there in their writings and statements—they were, indeed, able to come to terms with the gap between the truth they described and imparted to their followers and the truth whose existence they admitted only to themselves. The human soul is complex; and the leadership of the Second Aliyah showed a particular aptitude for accommodating itself to internal contradictions, not wasting its energies in fruitless pursuit of conceptual perfection yet maintaining its faithfulness to basic principles. This was a special feature of its extraordinary vitality.

In retrospect, the Jewish–Arab confrontation in Palestine takes on the dimensions of Greek tragedy. From the very inception of Jewish colonization in Palestine, the course of ultimate confrontation was inherent in the situation. Specific commissions or omissions by the Jewish side were marginal to the thrust of its development. Precisely because the great questions were beyond resolution, it was especially important to be able to live with the problem on a long-term basis. In this context, the inner conviction of being on the right side assumed a special importance, along with the ability to preserve one's humanity and ethical values in the shadow of a prolonged national confrontation. The defensive ethos proved decisive in this context. That ethos taught faith in the possibility of peace and preached a philosophy of nonhatred toward the Arabs. It demonstrated the importance of the spoken and written word in public education, even when not everything being said was believed by everyone all the time. These attitudes were repeatedly articulated in the media, in speeches by leaders, and in lectures and study seminars and left their imprint on consciousness. Indeed, beneath the layer of public rhetoric, in which empathy and understanding was voiced for the problems of the Arab worker and fellah, lay a hidden layer of fear and suspicion. Yet the facade of hope for peace and brotherhood was maintained and cultivated. It left a considerable residue, especially since this was a highly self-conscious public, attempting to live in accordance with its beliefs. The more threatening the realities in Palestine turned, the more pronounced the gap between the message of the defensive ethos and the demands of reality and the stronger the objections and challenges to the humanistic values that the educational system was endeavoring to impart to its students. Yet up until 1936, at least, the defensive ethos, despite its weaknesses, proved able significantly to curb any tendencies toward enmity and aggressiveness.

Another ethos, termed here the *offensive ethos* made its debut during the Arab Rebellion and was augmented in the 1940s. That ethos was rooted in the growing consciousness of an inevitable confrontation between Jews and Arabs that emerged during the 1936–39 disturbances. The old models for explaining Arab animosity toward Jewish colonization, namely, "imperialism" or the hostile "Gentile," were acceptable only as long as manifestations of Arab hatred remained sporadic and could be explained by marginal motives. Beginning with the 1940s, the message communicated by the leaders to the public (particularly youth) stressed that the Jews should prepare themselves for the historic clash with the Arabs of Palestine. Recognition of its unavoidability was not easy to digest for a movement that had been educated to believe that Arab enmity would ultimately dissipate, going the way of all prejudice. The traumatic reality of the late 1930s and 1940s—which undermined the credibility of the system of ethical values in general, generating patterns of thinking marked by cynicism and sober pessimism—played a decisive role in this remolding of outlook and stance.

The perception of the existence of an essential and polarized conflict between the two peoples did not develop overnight. The old formulations of the defensive ethos continued to appear during the course of the 1940s both in public declarations and in private conversations. Yet parallel with these, other elements emerged indicating the formation of a consciousness of confrontation. Awareness of the clash was associated with the undermining of the belief that it might be possible to continue to postpone the anticipated confrontation. The sense that the hourglass of Zionism was running out derived from the show of force by Arab nationalism in Palestine. This feeling of urgency was intensified as a result of the political climate at the end of the war, when the "frozen sea" of the international order seemed to be melting again (to use Lloyd George's metaphor). It was nurtured by the general awareness that this was a fateful moment in Jewish history, in the wake of the Holocaust and in the face of the acute problem of Jewish refugees. The new ethos reflected the impatience of contemporary youth with the old evolutionary methods. It demanded a showdown.

Impatience and the eager anticipation of a confrontation typified the young, but the educational message communicated by the leaders was tempered by a mitigating element. Although now imbued with the recognition that the moment of truth was close at hand, their message was careful to emphasize that there was in fact no choice. The concept of "no choice" *(eyn brera)* implied that the educational orientation acknowledging the superiority of peace over war was, indeed, still a salient factor.

It is true that the idea of "no choice" had been incorporated within the defensive ethos. But "no choice" then had referred to defending the existing foothold, along the lines of the biblical injunction "In thy blood, live" (Ezekiel 16:6). The modern interpretation of this verse was that sacrifices are essential for national rejuvenation or (as Alterman put it), "No people will retreat from the foxholes of its survival." Now, however, it referred to a military decision in a battle for ultimate sovereignty in Palestine: no longer a steadfast resistance unto death but an offensive to be launched with the aim of attaining Jewish rule in Palestine. The slogan "no choice" served simultaneously as an explanation of the situation and a justification for fighting. It placed the burden of guilt on the opposing side and hinted that although war was not something to look forward to, necessity knew no law. *Eyn brera* expressed an orientation that rejected any veneration of war or the fostering of a cult of militarism yet nonetheless provided legitimation for engaging in battle.

The Arabs had repeatedly declared their intention to uproot the Jews from Palestine. Thus, the perception of confrontation was accompanied by a fear of total annihilation of the Jewish community in Palestine. Apprehensions regarding a new Holocaust that would extinguish the remaining hope of the Jewish people were a constant component of the sense of no choice during the 1940s. In addition to the impact of the Holocaust, fear stemmed from the awareness that the approaching clash with the Arabs would take place in the absence of the third party to the Palestinian triangle, namely, the British. This was to be the first face-to-face collision between Jews and Arabs. The dread of annihilation strengthened the sense that there was no choice, while altering its context: Now the Jews were looking forward to a showdown, and they were also prepared to risk the life-or-death war that it entailed.[4]

The willingness to embark on a decisive war had its origin in another constituent element of the offensive ethos: the confidence that now the Yishuv was capable on its own of tipping the scales of power in Palestine. Until 1945 the belief that Jews were strong enough to conquer Palestine was professed mainly by a marginal circle outside the mainstream of public opinion in the Yishuv. When Ahimeir, at the beginning of the 1930s, declared the British to be "foreign occupiers" who should evacuate Palestine, this was little more than verbal posturing. Statements in the late 1930s by the IZL that voiced ambitions to conquer Palestine seemed like empty rhetoric, based on wishful thinking. And when Arlosoroff, in 1932, advanced his notions about a Jewish revolutionary minority taking control of Palestine, it was little more than a pipe dream.

Now, however, things had changed. Once it became clear that the British were consistent in their anti-Zionist policy, Zionists geared their efforts toward bringing about a radical solution that would compel the British to leave Palestine. This policy was coupled with the awareness that the Yishuv would have to face the Arabs on its own. That prospect was viewed by the leadership with a mixture of defiance and anxiety. It now accepted the necessity for an independent stand and took the necessary measures to prepare the Hagana for the military conflict on the near horizon. Yet it did not have total confidence that the Yishuv would, indeed, gain the upper hand in the ensuing clash, particularly if the Arab states were to come to the aid of Palestinian Arabs. Though the leaders were plagued by doubts, these were rare among the younger generation. Since the early 1940s, the IZL and Lehi were sanguine and certain that the Jews could defeat the Arabs handily. They did not take the military might of the Palestinian Arabs seriously; and since they downplayed its danger, they concentrated their efforts on the struggle against the British, perceived as the real adversaries. In their view, the war of national liberation should aim at a British decision to leave Palestine. A British evacuation would be sufficient, they believed, to guarantee Jewish control of Palestine. On the other hand, members of the Hagana and Palmach continued to view the Jewish–Arab confrontation as the crux of the matter. Yet in contrast to previous occasions, they, too, were now persuaded that the Yishuv was strong enough to stand on its own against the Arabs. They had no doubt that it was in their power to bring about the historical breakthrough. Despite their identification with the Left, they tended to spurn the "Natives." Similar to their opponents in the organizations of the "dissenters," they also simultaneously embraced the image of anti-imperialist fighters and the mentality of the native settler. The inclination of Ben Gurion and his associates to seek the support and assistance of the international community as a supplement to the independent might of the Yishuv (a residue of the defensive ethos) contrasted with the younger generation's blatant reliance on military might.

The 1940s witnessed a collision of momentous events in Europe and in Palestine with the coming of age of a Palestinian Jewish generation. The qualities of the warrior distinguished this generation from the preceding one, and endowed it with a special standing. The life-style of the fighter became the key formative experience for its members. Juxtaposing the thinking of the fathers and sons, one can note profound changes in their attitudes toward the physical and social environment, as well as in their conception of nationalism, their psychological makeup, and their guiding norms.

On the whole, it is possible to discern a process of reduction, concretization, and demystification. What for the fathers was an exalted myth, a grand ideal, or a distant dream became for the sons prosaic reality, something three-dimensional and palpable. For the fathers, the myths of Berdichevsky and Tchernikovsky generated the pseudoreality of Palestine, which they had clung to, drawing from it vital sustenance. Even when they encountered Palestine in the flesh, the images of that land and its symbols, rather than its concrete reality, continued to infuse them with enthusiasm and motivation. The myths of Palestine were intertwined within their national conception, which was basically oriented toward Jews and Jewish experience in the Diaspora. A few of them developed an enthusiastic love for the Palestinian landscape, traveled frequently, and even fostered customs of pilgrimage to given sites, such as Modi'in. The men who proved an exception in this regard within their age group served as the link connecting the generation of the fathers with that of the sons. For the latter, Palestine was extremely concrete, identified with the landscape, experiences of youth, hardship, sweat, and thirst—and was an integral part of their self and being. "We are your harvest, beloved homeland, paying tribute to you till the end," wrote one contemporary, Zvi Guber, who fell in the War of Independence: "To us, you are like the soil to trees, the nest for the bird, like water to seedlings on a hot summer day."[5]

This difference in relating to Palestine also had implications for the sense of dominance in the land. The fathers had a theoretical feeling of ownership, based on historical rights and a sense of belonging, the product of cultural–historical ties. It had been powerful enough to bring them to Palestine, and endowed them with the mentality of being lords and masters there, even when they had constituted no more than a tiny minority. Yet simultaneously, they were conscious of being strangers in the land, plagued by their alienation from its landscape and climate and the entire Palestinian experience. Their argument that concrete labor bestowed a right to the land derived from their unshakable belief in the intrinsic ethical value of manual labor, coupled with their consciousness that the historical claim alone had a questionable validity. Hence, they recognized the importance of international legitimation, and were reluctant to renounce the Balfour Declaration and the mandate: they viewed these as valuable links in bolstering the Jewish claim to the country. In contrast, the sons regarded Palestine as their own, a patrimony that could not be questioned. It was theirs not by right of legend or ancestral burial grounds but, rather, by dint of the fact that they had been born in the land (or, at least, raised there). The country was an inseparable component of their personality. They did not have the slightest doubt that this was their land and that none beside them had any part in it. "No stranger will own it. It's mine, mine!" wrote one of the young men fervently in commenting on Jerusalem: "This land will be ours, ours!"[6] There was an enormous distance between the sentiments of Tchernichovsky—who had written "This will be our homeland" (see chapter 1), expressing a wish, a dream, and a hope—and the feeling of concrete ownership that beat in the heart of that young man. The sense of "native" ownership had emerged for the first time among the youth in the colonies of the First Aliyah and had been accompanied by a certain haughtiness and arrogance toward Arabs. The subsequent generation of the Second Aliyah and its successors introduced different norms of behavior. Now, however, their own sons embraced norms that were basically quite close to those that had guided the natives of the old colonies and to which they had objected: the sense of "chosenness," a condescension toward the newcomers, and contempt for the Arab natives.

The fathers had burdened the complex of Jewish–Arab relations in Palestine with all the imported freight of the age-old confrontation between Jews and Gentiles. The admixture of a sense of superiority and inferiority that was an integral part of these relations in the Diaspora was transferred by them to the situation in

Palestine. The fear of the Arab went hand in hand with scorn for him. Concurrently, the Arab problem became part of an all-embracing socialist perspective; in its framework, the Arab in Palestine and his contemporary relations with Jews were viewed as the product of existing social circumstances. That perspective held out the promise of a shining future of peace and cooperation for the world in general and the two peoples in Palestine in particular. It is true that socialism had, to a large degree, fostered a sense of patronage with respect to the "natives." But that patronizing attitude was instrumental in impeding the rise of animosity and aggressiveness.

It was the fathers who decided on the form that Jewish settlement would take in Palestine, forging a separation between the Yishuv and the Arab community by means of the ideology of "Jewish labor." This division answered to a deep psychological need on the part of the fathers to live among Jews and to be free from any dependence on another people. On the other hand, it generated alienation and distance between Jews and Arabs and impeded the formation of dialogue on a person-to-person basis between them. The Arab remained external to Jewish Palestinian experience. The friction zones between Jews and Arabs in Jewish areas became fewer and fewer. In Jewish eyes, the Arab slowly lost his reality as a living human being. He was viewed as an abstract concept, without concrete form and face, located beyond the perimeter of the Jewish settlement. Hatred toward Arabs was not a prevalent phenomenon at the time; manifestations of enmity toward them were usually associated with specific incidents and did not express a general attitude. However, neither was there any particular active interest in Arabs. The socialist settlers were preoccupied principally with their own affairs. They had a total lack of curiosity when it came to their Arab neighbors. It is true that the "Arab worker" was viewed with sympathy; yet this was a sympathy for the abstract Arab and was not translated into a relation with a living, flesh-and-blood human being. Parallel with the rise in hostile actions by Arabs, the sense of alienation from them grew stronger among the Jewish community. The dispute was increasingly mythologized as an expression of the age-old enmity toward Jews. These latter factors, which strengthened the tendency toward dehumanization of the Arab, ultimately proved instrumental in legitimizing the use of force against him.

The younger generation was free from the ideological ballast that had burdened their fathers. Their attitude toward the Arab was simple, direct and without qualms, devoid of myth and mystery. They neither loved nor hated them. They showed no sympathy for, or particular confidence in, the idea of a union for the Arab worker. Though born in Palestine, they did not excel their fathers in the meager interest they showed in the Arabs, their language, and their culture. By the time they reached maturity, the glass wall separating Jewish and Arab society was already a fixture, firmly in place. During their excursions and trips around Palestine, naturally, they encountered Arab villages everywhere. Yet that fact had no impact on their sense of being masters in the land. They regarded those villages and their inhabitants as part of the Palestinian landscape, as a segment of the various natural difficulties that would have to be surmounted in the course of colonizing the land. They did not share the sense of anxiety that had accompanied their fathers in Palestine. They had no fear of the Arabs; though they did not disregard the dangers inherent in Jewish–

Arab confrontation, they believed they would be able to overcome them. They viewed the approaching armed conflict between themselves and the Arabs in terms of a struggle for Palestine—a country that the Arabs were trying to steal from the Jews. The issue of confronting a competing national movement, which had been a considerable worry for their fathers, was unimportant for them. They were impervious to the positions of the other side and invulnerable when it came to simple human emotions. The condition of "numbness of the heart," described by Stock, in which a kind of coarseness seemed to have enveloped their feelings and sensibility, was a characteristic feature in the personality of the young Palestinian Jew.

The world of imagery of their fathers had been stamped by the dualistic self-image of victim and hero. The weakness of Jews in Palestine with respect to the Arabs was perceived to be the local version of a universal phenomenon. It served to strengthen the analogies between the situation of Jews in Palestine and Europe, and added a mythical dimension to Arab opposition to Jewish colonization. The catastrophe of European Jewry enhanced this tendency, endowing it with a new saliency. The world became a debtor owing an obligation to the Jewish people. In the polarized logic of such a perspective, the victim is the opposite of the violent attacker. For that reason, it was presumed as self-evident that the Jews were the seekers of peace. This was an additional way of eluding the dilemma of the socialist in a land of colonization. The self-image of the few pitted against the many—the weak against the strong—was a common motif. It was cultivated before the War of Independence and retained its importance ever after. Ben Gurion and others were always careful to stress Jewish weakness when it came to the balance of power with the Arab side. Ben Gurion, who already in 1929 had made a distinction between a numerical balance of power and the balance of power in actuality, referred shortly before the War of Independence to two estimations of the situation. One was based on the comparative analysis of strength of the small Jewish Yishuv as compared with the total of all Arab states; and it was this evaluation that was stressed in all appeals to public opinion. The second rested on a realistic estimate of the power the Yishuv could actually muster as compared with the forces the Arab side could bring into play on the field of battle; and that analysis was meant principally for internal consumption. The vulnerability of the Yishuv, the modern incarnation of the "eternal victim," was a moral justification for war and victory. In this way, the victory in the War of Independence was not viewed as the natural result of the balance of forces but, rather, as some sort of miracle: It could only be explained as a prodigious overpowering of the stronger by the weaker side, a manifestation of the superiority of right over might.[7]

Among the sons, the dualistic pattern in the identity of the fathers was replaced by their adoption of the self-image of the hero and the concomitant projection of the image of the victim onto the Jews of the Diaspora. The hero defends the victim and avenges him yet is also distinguished from the victim; in no case does he wish to be identified with him. Unlike their fathers, the sons did not feel they were engaged in a battle against the entire world. They were only involved in a struggle for Palestine and its control. Their enemy (British or Arab) was defined and concrete. They also did not feel any need to justify their war, having no doubts or hesitations that it was, indeed, just. Free from the psychological and ideological complexities of the preceding generation, they did not hesitate to cast off the halo of the victim, sufficing with the nimbus of the warrior.

The nationalism of their fathers had been enveloped in a sheath of socialist concepts. Socialism placed a limit on national egoism, moderating and subjugating it to a universal ethical system. On the other hand, socialism also served for many as a permit for the use of violence. Violence was reasoned to be a legitimate means if the end for which it was used was just. Making socialism a reality justified a violent revolution. According to that same line of reasoning, the realization of Zionism also justified the use of force. Could there be any cause of greater justice than to ensure the survival of the Jewish people, the proletarian among the world's peoples?

Given the prevailing conditions in Palestine, a violent revolution was both impossible and absurd. Consequently, the Zionist socialists did not direct their revolutionary zeal toward the destruction of society but, rather, toward the rebuilding of Palestine. They accompanied their constructive project by militant explanations that gave it an aura of revolutionism, but without the stain of bloodshed. However, revolutionary violence continued to be considered legitimate and in certain circles was even glorified. The distance between its application for the sake of realizing social desiderata and for implementing national goals was minimal, especially in the case where national and social objectives were so closely interwoven as to be virtually indistinguishable.

Their fathers had romanticized about power. They dreamed of courageous Jews, marked by valor and bravery. They fostered the veneration of heroes of the past, revering the symbols of power and sovereignty. However, most of them were unable to transfer their notions from the realm of declaration to that of action. In their everyday lives, they were incapable of resorting to violence and had a heartfelt repugnance for force. Brenner's writings are testimony to the tension that existed between the rhetoric of bravery and the disappointments of reality. The sons, however, refrained from rhetoric about bravery, avoiding flowery talk and demonstrative posturing. The romanticism of force gave way to a simpler attitude; it was factual and treated force as a natural component of the social fabric. Instead of verbal aggressiveness and the cult of heroism, there was simply the concrete act of fighting. This juxtaposition was not true of the IZL and Lehi, groupings that continued to cultivate the romanticism of power, regarding it and the psychological climate it generated as no less important an element in the national ethos than the actual use of force.

The fathers were conscious of the dichotomy between their ambition to educate their sons to be bearers of the same ethical burden they had shouldered and their wish to let them develop free from distress and doubts. In the depth of their hearts, they knew they were educating a generation of warriors whose destiny it would be to ultimately decide the battle for the fate of Palestine. For that purpose, they had to be loyal, simple and straightforward, tough and strong, and have an unlimited love for their country. The mental and spiritual complexity of the fathers, the product of a reality rich in ambiguities, could not be the lot of this new generation, raised in a land caught up in an ongoing process of colonization. Instead of constituting a source of creativity (as it had for their fathers), this complexity for them would only have become an impediment in the struggles the future held in store. Nevertheless, the fathers wished to inculcate humanistic values in their sons' education, to forge barriers to hold aggressive urges in check. That humanistic approach involved a critique of militarism and resolute opposition to all its forms. Yet this opposition to militarism was not accompanied by opposition to the use of weapons as such. Trumpeldor was considered to be the positive antithesis of the professional soldier; a brave worker, who had stood at the head of his men to protect his home in the hour of need, without a uniform or any orders. The ideal was that of *fighters,* not that of soldiers. Only Betar and the IZL revered the ideal of the soldier in its literal sense. Concurrently, in the Labor movement, another ideal type of warrior was cultivated: fighters who took their cue from the models of antifascist underground groups—guerrilla units—from the Russian and Yugoslav partisans striking the German Wehrmacht from the rear. The style emulated was that of the revolutionary fighter, unencumbered by the symbols and imagery of the regular army. That type of fighter was supposed to be more sensitive to humanistic values and less subject to a framework demanding blind discipline. The Palmachnik, who lived by his labor in the kibbutzim, became the symbol of the fighter–citizen.

It is doubtful whether those external differences in framework and patterns of behavior were sufficient to create a different attitude toward fighting or to develop "civilian" barriers to military callousness and insensitivity. It is true that the social atmosphere in the Palmach put pressure on the isolated individuals who deviated from the prevailing norms that educated its fighters in the spirit of "purity of arms" and avoiding any harm to the innocent. The fact that women also served in the units functioned to mitigate military coarseness to some extent. However, when confronted with the supreme test of actual fighting, the Palmach, like any other combat unit, proved itself capable of superb examples of human kindness alongside acts of harsh brutality. The Jewish warrior revealed himself to be loyal and brave, dedicated and persevering. When it came to the enemy, Chaim Guri probably expressed the dominant feeling prevalent among his comrades:

> Were we better or worse than others? Perhaps better, because our war was more just. Because all we had was one choice. Actually, we really had no choice. As events developed, there was a natural accommodation with death, losses, and suffering. We were not more cruel than others. Nor were we any more compassionate. We were not thirsty for blood and did not turn death into a moral value. We were efficient based on a sense of conviction. We were enthusiastic and able to muster double the strength, in times of success as well as in times of failure.[8]

The Palmach left behind a corpus of songs that became popular folk songs with the passage of time. In years when the Palmach had no assignments for action, it had sung "The Floor—to Comrade Mauser." But the songs of the War of Independence, in which the Palmach constituted the veritable spearhead of the Israeli army in the making, are replete with the romanticism of the fighter who longs for home and hearth, dreaming about peace and quiet. Significantly, Arabs do not appear in any of the songs. Reference to "the enemy" never identified the latter by name. In the literature of the Palmach generation, in contrast, the figure of the Arab appeared

quite frequently, especially in episodes describing the young Jewish fighter, caught
in the dilemma of the captor in charge of a helpless Arab prisoner of war. Here and
there, one can find expressions of empathy for the suffering of the innocent. That
empathy is on a personal basis, one human being to another. There was no empathy—or even understanding—on the national plane. For that reason, S. Yizhar was
the only one among the writers of the so-called generation of the War of Independence who dealt with the experience of the expulsion of Arab population—an event
some of those writers participated in, or at least were witness to.

In 1948 Pinhas Lubianiker depicted the native sabra as a generation infected by
primitive and crude nationalism.[9] There were those who viewed the Palmachnik as
the realization of the model of Amram, Brenner's hero in *Mi-kan u-mi-kan*.
Amram is the son of the hunchback who was murdered by an Arab and the grand-
son of Arye Lapidot, who demanded that Arabs be treated with justice and morality. In the novel, Amram neglects his scholastic duties, to which he is indifferent,
but feels at home in Palestine, exhibiting the traits of a man of action, excelling in
physical abilities and in the knowledge of how to pay back the Arabs double in
kind.[10] In both Lubianiker's and Brenner's depiction, the features characterizing
that youth were clear to contemporaries: down-to-earth, physically adept, eager to
use arms, and very aggressive. These young people showed contempt for the external trappings of the soldier but were enthusiastic for battle. In addition to their preference for national goals above all others, they were distinguished by a simplistic
division of the universe into two camps ("for us" and "against us") and a self-confidence bordering on impudence. All these were vital components in the psychological makeup of young people who had been groomed for the moment of truth.
This generation constituted what Alterman dubbed the "silver platter" on which
the state was presented to the people. They carried out what their fathers had been
unable to.

Does the image of youth as outlined on the eve of the establishment of the state
and during the War of Independence point to a process of brutalization and vul-
garization typical of the second generation in a country of colonization? One should
distinguish between temporary shifts and more lasting transformations. The erotic
passion for the land was unique to this generation. To be sure, love for the homeland and patriotism remained constituents in the guiding norms of youth in later
years; but they were marked by a reduced intensity and ardor. The willingness to
sacrifice one's life on the field of battle was integrated into the national ethos, and
each generation cherished that value of supreme devotion in its own way. But the
acute sense of being the sole masters of the land ceased to be a driving force among
Israeli youth during the years 1949 to 1967. When the War of Independence ended,
residues of the socialist education imparted to disciples in the youth movements
proved to be more effective than could have been anticipated. A significant proportion of ex-Palmachniks settled in kibbutzim. Aggressiveness lost its grip and,
with it, the lust for battle. The aspiration for peace returned, becoming an ideal, a
fervent desire, a value propagated in education.

Nonetheless, a distinction should be made between the short-term and long-
term impact of the process of colonization. The first seventy years of the new Jewish

colonization in Palestine took place in the shadow of an ongoing conflict between a "Diaspora" mentality (i.e., a deeply rooted Jewish psychology and socialist ideology) and the evolving Palestinian realities. The dominant process was one of slow but constant erosion of the mental layers whose source lay in the Diaspora. The story of "the fathers" is a tale of efforts to set up defenses in their psyche against being eroded by that reality. They did this by means of ideology, an entire system of credos and norms, indoctrination, and a blocking from consciousness of the portions of reality that were incompatible with their beliefs. Despite this, reality prevailed. It challenged their good will and purity of faith and their myriad attempts to elude a confrontation—and eventually won out. The importance of indoctrination was especially pronounced in the case of the second generation. Though it had manifested traits that were opposed to those of the preceding generation in its youth, it ultimately accepted and internalized significant segments of their teachings. This does not mean to imply that ideas or education can overcome the impact of reality in the long run. Indeed, the process of slow erosion accompanied every generation from that juncture on; hence, the point of departure for each successive generation when it came to the use of power was progressively less ambivalent than that of its predecessor. Mutations in national mentality do not occur overnight: They require generations to take hold. Nonetheless, it is arguable that the contours of the process were already evident during the 1940s, even if that process has not yet been fully completed, half a century later.

The process of the erosion of the mental inhibitions typical of the generation of the fathers took place parallel to the erosion in socialist faith. Though it legitimized the use of violence for the sake of just causes, the socialist credo, by dint of its universalistic moral commitment, served as a damper on excessive nationalistic ardor. The early 1950s witnessed the decline of socialism as a guiding ideology in Israel. No other humanistic conception with equivalent strength and attraction arose to take its place. As a result, Jewish national identity in Israel lost its link with a universalistic worldview. In the past, that universalism had been an integral component of both Jewish faith and the socialist credo. The confluence of the erosion of traditional Jewish loyalties and the waning of socialist loyalties led to a victory: Reality in Israel triumphed over the conceptual and mental barricades that had been set up and arrayed against it.

The War of Independence was the conflict in which the offensive and defensive ethos interfused, meshing their strands to the point where it was difficult to distinguish one from the other. In the fury of that war—which appeared to threaten the very survival of the small Jewish community in Palestine and in which the Jews were attacked and forced to defend themselves—the fundamental values of the defensive ethos provided a justification and explanation for the concrete fighting. Old and young used identical concepts. True, older people stressed the "miraculous" element in the Jewish victory, while the younger generation tended to underscore the motifs of bravery and willingness for self-sacrifice of their brothers-in-arms. Yet both young and old spoke in terms of the defensive ethos, even when they acted according to principles of the offensive one. The integration of both the defensive and offensive ethos in the traumatic event of the War of Independence—a conflict that was protracted, laden with hardships, and costly in lives—had a major impact on shaping the educational values in the State of Israel for more than a generation.

With its inception, the state took charge of all defense matters. The question of the use of arms was removed from the context of moral and philosophical debate and transferred to the realm of state sovereignty. It now became one of a series of obligations that independence imposed on those who had reaped its benefits. As long as others bore responsibility for government, the Jews were able to continue to search their souls when it came to the question of power. The previous sensitiveness many had shown regarding security questions was a reflex of the fact that the British had had the thankless task of dealing with such matters in Palestine. Now the Jews themselves were responsible for their own protection and survival. They lacked any tradition of governance. The priority given to "raisons d'état" in European countries since the seventeenth century over considerations of morality or religion was a new doctrine for them. Nonetheless, all agreed that the Jewish state should behave in accordance with international norms when it came to such issues, adopting criteria like those followed in the democratic countries. People also tended to agree that moralistic considerations should be applied when it came to the individual but that they were not always applicable on the level of the state. "You can't build a state wearing white gloves," Alterman wrote: "The job is not always clean and morally attractive."[11] From this juncture on, discussion revolved around the question of what was obligated by the interests of state and, thus, permissible and what those interests did not necessitate and was, therefore, prohibited. The practical aspects of the use of power were relegated from the sphere of society to the state. Questions of the extent of aggressiveness and its forms ceased being a matter for public discussion and were compartmentalized, becoming an issue for deliberations mainly in the top echelons of government and the army. Tactics and strategy stopped being the reflection of a system of values and became a function of ability and utility. The maintenance of an army and its nature was no longer a question of the national ethos and became one of the "services" provided by the state. That phenomenon was characteristic of Israeli society during at least the first thirty years of its existence.

A distinction emerged between the use of force—now a matter in the hands of the state, legitimate and accepted—and the national ethos. Components of the offensive ethos were internalized within the national ethos. The idea that Jews had to fight for their homeland was accepted as the norm, and few challenged its predominance. The centrality of the role of the fighter was an additional legacy of the offensive ethos. The image of the warrior became a pedagogical model promoted on all levels of Israeli society. While the stereotype of the pioneer–worker was shunted more and more to the margins of national consciousness, that of the warrior filled the gap. It created a common denominator around which the Right and the Left—and all strata of society—could unite and rally. The matter of "security"—a concept that in the 1940s had replaced the more modest one of "defense," and that denoted the complex of roles associated with the power-related aspects of the Jewish–Arab conflict—became the focus of national interest. The enormous prestige of the security system shielded it from normal public scrutiny and granted its members partial immunity from the law, unlike mere mortals. Security became the sacred cow of the young state.

Yet components of the defensive ethos also continued to fulfill an important role in shaping public consciousness. Presentation of Arab enmity toward Israel as another variation of antisemitic hatred remained widespread, in varying degrees of sophistication. The fact that the Arabs adopted the stereotypes and symbols of traditional hatred for Jews—and ultimately became contaminated with antisemitism—helped to implant that notion, blurring the different context of the dispute in Palestine. The waves of mass immigration in the wake of the establishment of the state led to a decline in the "native" tendencies among youth, previously quite popular. The bond with the Jewish people and Jewish history was endorsed by the overwhelming majority of the public as part of the national ethos. This identification with the Jewish past acted to strengthen the self-image of the victim.

The numerical balance of power between the Arab states and Israel did not improve over the years to the benefit of the Jews. Although a Jewish critical mass was created in Israel, Jews remained a small minority in the Middle East, with their backs to the sea, facing millions of Arabs threatening to destroy them. The military ratio of forces was likewise not to the benefit of the Jews: The more the Jews bolstered their forces, the more the Arabs augmented theirs. Consequently, the awareness of being weak in the face of the more powerful adversary remained operative. Although the Jews proved their ability to defend their lives, the recognition that their survival hung by a mere thread resurfaced after 1949 on at least two occasions, namely in 1967 and 1973. The consciousness of the Holocaust slowly penetrated the national psyche and, with it, the growing anxiety in the face of possible annihilation. The fear of destruction became a central factor in bolstering the self-image of the Israelis as weak—victimized but righteous.

The volcano continued to smolder, accompanied by a recurrent motif of Jews on the defensive, faced with aggressive Arabs. This served to nurture a psychology commensurate with the defensive ethos. The sense that there had been no choice was a key justification advanced in all the wars fought by the Jewish state up until 1982. Though it is possible to dispute whether all of Israel's wars have indeed been wars of *eyn brera,* the fact that leaders felt it was necessary to present them in this light is significant testimony to the enduring strength of the defensive ethos.

Realities in Palestine, which proved their potency in altering and reformulating norms relating to the use of force, did not have the same impact as far as self-images were concerned. The self-image of the just Jew was interwoven with that of the weak and defenseless potential victim. Hence, the change in the actual balance of power was not accompanied by a parallel change in the Israeli *consciousness* of power. The more pronounced the gap became between the self-image of the victim and Israeli military ability, the greater became the pitch of professed self-righteousness. This had been present in the defensive ethos since its very inception.

This existence, side-by-side, of the predominant offensive ethos, along with mentalities left over as a residue from the defensive ethos, is not surprising, considering the fact that the process of the erosion of old norms was extremely slow. That ambiguity is manifested on occasion in times of crisis: The phenomenon of hesitation, doubt, and self-criticism, both before the actual confrontation and in its wake, points in this direction. The suspicion of Gentile plots and designs and the belief—at times hidden, at times overt—that "the whole world is against us" constitute another dimension of that ambiguity. The strange admixture of a sense of power accompanied by a willingness to defy the entire world with the sense of helplessness and profound apprehension is also part of these same psychological patterns. Indeed, it is evident here how consciousness has lagged behind reality.

The longed-for "normalization" of Jewish life appeared to be on the way to becoming a reality in the Jewish state. The attitude toward the land gradually lost its "conceptual" dimensions and became more "down-to-earth" in nature. The number of Israelis born in the country increased dramatically, and their attitude toward their homeland became one of "natural" patriotism. Soul-searching regarding the question of the legitimate right to the land was no longer on the agenda for the mainstream and remained a topic that was of interest principally to marginal groups. A new type of Jew came into being, one for whom the use of weapons was natural. Yet to a certain extent the old Jewish mentality, with all its ambivalence toward the use of force, was still alive. That mentality did not prevent the army from acting in accordance with state interests, nor did it curb political leaders in their decisionmaking when this involved the use of force. It also did not hinder brutal decisions. Yet it did make it easier for the leaders to arrive at moderate decisions that were at odds with the wishes of the militants. The making of manifestly "difficult" decisions by the leadership, such as those involving withdrawal and territorial concessions, was facilitated by the fact that a large segment of the public continued to abhor the notion of being a nation of conquerors. In so doing, the leadership relied on a broadly based layer of public opinion, conditioned by the defensive ethos to view peace as a most desirable national goal, second only to survival. Thus, although unable to prevent war, the defensive ethos undoubtedly remains a vital and resilient component on the road to peace.

Notes

Chapter 1

1. George Mosse, *Germans and Jews* (New York, 1970), 61–76.

2. Gershom Scholem, "Im Gershom Shalom" (With Gerhsom Scholem), in *Devarim be-go* (Explications and Implications) (Tel Aviv, 1976), 11–16.

3. Theodor Herzl, *The Complete Diaries of Theodor Herzl,* ed. R. Patai (New York, 1960), 1:4–7.

4. Jonathan Frankel, *Prophecy and Politics: Socialism, Nationalism, and Russian Jews, 1862–1917* (London, 1981).

5. Leo Pinsker, "Auto-Emancipation," in his *Road to Freedom: Writings and Addresses* (New York, 1944), 74–106; Herzl, *Complete Diaries;* see also Theodor Herzl, *The Jewish State* (New York, 1946), 75–78.

6. See Moses Hess, *Rome and Jerusalem* (New York, 1956); Yaakov Katz, "Le-verur ha-musag mevasrei ha-Tziyonut" (On Elucidating the Conception of the Heralds of Zionism), in *Shivat Tziyon* (Jerusalem) 1 (1950):91–105.

7. See Mosse, op. cit., 3–33; Shmuel Almog, *Tziyonut ve-historia* (Zionism and History) (Jerusalem, 1982), 13; Yehoyakim Doron, "Ha-Tziyonut ha-merkaz-europe'it mul ideologiyot germaniyot bein ha-shanim 1885–1914" (Central European Zionism Confronting German Ideologies in the Period 1885–1914), Ph.D. diss., Tel Aviv University, 1977, p. 14.

8. Herzl, *Jewish State,* 70.

9. See Mosse, op. cit., 77–115; Doron, op. cit., 12ff.; Almog, op. cit., 14ff.; Hans Kohn, *The Idea of Nationalism* (Toronto, 1967).

10. Ahad Ha-Am (One of the People) was the pen name of Asher Zvi Ginsberg.

11. Mosse, op. cit., 82–92; as an illustration, see Martin Buber, *Bein am le-artzo* (Between a People and Its Land) (Jerusalem, 1984), 9–14.

12. Theodor Herzl, *Old–New Land (Altneuland)* (New York, 1960); see also Ahad Ha-Am, *Al parashat derakhim* (At the Crossroads) (Berlin, 1930), 3:143–59.

13. Herzl, *Jewish State,* 87–89.

14. See Michael Heymann, *The Uganda Controversy,* 2 vols. (Jerusalem, 1970, 1977); David Vital, *Zionism: The Formative Years* (Oxford, 1982), 267–364.

15. Herzl, *Jewish State,* 83, 93.

16. Ibid., 94–95.

17. See Almog, op. cit., 85.

18. Herzl, *Jewish State,* 147.

19. Idem, *Diaries,* June 6, 1895, 1:33.

20. Ibid., June 7, 1895, 1:40.

21. Ibid., June 14, 1895, 1:101.

22. See, e.g., Pinkser, op. cit., 94–95; Herzl, *Jewish State,* 95–96.

23. Herzl, *Jewish State,* 95–96.

24. Pinsker, op. cit., 87.

25. Herzl, *Diaries,* June 12, 1895, 1:96; see also Doron, op. cit., 154.

26. Doron, op. cit., 113.

27. Pinkser, op. cit., 86.

28. Doron, op. cit., 113.

29. On the question of antisemites, see Herzl, *Diaries,* June 12, 1895, 1:84–85; the quotation is from June 15, 1895, 1:103.

30. Ibid., June 16, 1895, 1:106–07.

31. The story can be found in Ahad Ha-Am, "Medinat ha-yehudim ve-tzarat ha-yehudim" (The Jewish State and the Jewish Plight), in his *Al parashat derakhim,* 2:32–33.

32. Herzl, *Diaries,* June 9, 1895, 1:58.

33. Ibid., June 7, 1895, 1:38.

34. Ibid., 39.

35. Max Nordau, "Ma hi mashma'uta shel ha-hit'amlut le-gabeinu ha-Yehudim?" (What is the Significance of Gymnastics for Us Jews?), in his *Ketavim tziyoniyim* (Zionist Writings) (Jerusalem, 1960), 2:82–86; for the German original, see Max Nordau, *Max Nordaus Zionistische Schriften,* 2d ed. (Berlin, 1923), 427–33.

36. Max Nordau, "Yahadut ha-shririm" (Judaism of the Muscles) in his *Ketavim tziyoniyim,* 2:188; for the original German, see Max Nordau, "Muskeljudentum," in his *Max Nordaus Zionistische,* 424–26.

37. Max Nordau, "Ha-Yehudi ha-tza'ir" (The Young Jew), in his *Ketavim tziyoniyim,* 2:140.

38. Pinsker, op. cit., 87.

39. Herzl, *Jewish State,* 156–57.

40. Max Nordau, "Ha-ma'apilim shel 1881" (The Pioneers of 1881), in his *El amo: Ketavim mediniyim* (To His People: Political Writings) (Tel Aviv, ca. 1936–37), 1:7; see also his "Yahadut ha-shririm," 187.

41. Herzl, *Diaries,* June 13, 1895, 1:131–32.

42. *Voskhod,* October 8, 1882; also in *Ketavim le-toldot Hibbat Tziyon* (Documents on the History of Hibbat Zion), ed. A. Druyanow, vol. 3 (Tel Aviv, 1932), 451–57.

43. Ha-Rav Kalischer, *Derishat Tziyon* (Seeking Zion), quoted in Hess, op. cit. 106.

44. Herzl, *Jewish State,* 100.

45. Idem, *Diaries,* June 12, 1895, 1:88–89.

46. Idem, *Jewish State,* p. 76.

47. Ahad Ha-Am, "Ha-kongres ve-yotzro" (The Congress and Its Creator), in his *Al parashat derakhim,* 3:56.

48. Ibid.

49. Micha Yosef Berdichevsky, *Ba-derekh* (On the Road); vol. 3: *Am ve-eretz* (People and Land) (Leipzig, 1922), 112.

50. Many essays were written on this matter. See, among others, Micha Yosef Berdichevsky, "Al parashat derakhim" (At the Crossroads); Yehoshua Tohn, "Sifrut leumit" (National Literature); Mordechai Ahernpreis[?], "Le'an?" (Where To?)—all in *Ha-Shilo'ah* (Berlin) 1 (Heshvan–Adar II, 1897); Micha Yosef Berdichevsky, "Tzorekh ve-yekholet be-sifrutenu ha-hadasha" (Need and Ability in Our Modern Literature), *Ha-Shilo'ah* (Berlin) 2 (Nisan–Elul 1897). See also Micha Yosef Berdichevsky, "Mikhtav el ha-orekh" (Letter to the

Editor); Shimon Bernfeld, "Heshbona shel sifrutenu" (An Account of Our Literature)—both in *Ha-Shilo'ah* (Berlin) 3(Tevet–Sivan 1898). My thanks to Shulamit Laskov, who called my attention to these articles.

51. Ahad Ha-Am, "Shinui ha-arakhin" (A Change in Values), in his *Al parashat derakhim*, 2:71–73.

52. Idem, "Medinat ha-Yehudim," 29.

53. Idem, "Shinui ha-arakhin," 74.

54. Idem, "Basar va-ru'ah" (Flesh and Spirit), in his *Kol kitvei*, 3:230–31.

55. Idem, "Pitz'ei ohev" (A Lover's Wounds), in his *Kol kitvei*, 1:20.

56. Idem, "Tehiyat ha-ru'ah" (The Revival of the Spirit), in his *Al parashat derakhim*, 2:117.

57. Idem, "Ha-Kongres ha-Tziyoni ha-Rishon" (The First Zionist Congress), in his *Kol kitvei*, 3:53–54; idem, "Medinat ha-yehudim" 29–31.

58. Idem, "Ha-Kongres ha-Tziyoni ha-Rishon," 56.

59. Idem, "Ha-musar ha-leumi" (National Ethics), in his *Kol kitvei*, 3:86–89.

60. Ahad Ha-Am stated as follows: "Let us therefore assume that as [Nordau] says, there is nothing in the spirit of Jewish ethics basically opposed to such marriages" (ibid., 89). In my opinion, Ahad-Ha-Am's formulation hints that though disagreeing with this assumption, he prefers not to become involved in any dispute about it; in contrast, he would rather emphasize the moral obligation of the nationally minded person to be solicitous about the continued existence of the people.

61. Micha Yosef Berdichevsky, *Al ha-perek* (On the Agenda) (Warsaw, 1899), 72–75.

62. Idem, *Mahshavot ve-torot* (Thoughts and Theories), vol. 1 (Leipzig, 1922), 31. Unless otherwise indicated, emphasis in quoted material is in original source.

63. Ibid.

64. Berdichevsky, *Ba-derekh*, vol. 2 (Leipzig, 1922), 77.

65. Idem, *Mahshavot ve-torot*, 32–33.

66. Ibid., 34–38.

67. Idem, *Ba-derekh*, 2:53.

68. Ibid., 62.

69. Idem, "Mi-shnei avarim" (From Two Sides), in his *Mahshavot ve-torot*, 1:34.

70. Idem, "Hirhurim" (Reflections), in his *Ba-derekh*, 2:61.

71. On this and other topics related to the national conception of Ahad Ha-Am, see the important essay by Baruch Kurzweil, "Ha-Yahadut ke-gilui retzon ha-hayim ha-leumi ha-biologi" (Judaism as the Manifestation of the National Biological Urge to Survive), in his *Sifrutenu ha-hadasha: Hemshekh o mahapekha?* (Our New Literature: Continuity or Revolution?) (Tel Aviv, 1959), 190–224.

72. Berdichevsky, "Tziyunim" (Remarks), in his *Ba-derekh*, 2:72.

73. Ibid., 77.

74. Idem, "Hirhurim," 61.

75. Ibid., 58.

76. Idem, "She'elot ve-he'arot" (Questions and Notes), in his *Ba-derekh*, 2:81.

77. Idem, "Hirhurim," 61.

78. Idem, *Ba-derekh*, 2:80.

79. Ahad Ha-Am, "Shalosh madregot" (Three Steps), in his *Al parashat derakhim*, 2:65.

80. M. M. Feitellesohn, "Batala ve-avoda" (Idleness and Work), *Ha-Zman* (Vilna) 1(January–March 1905).

81. S. J. Ish-Horowitz, "Le-she'elat kiyum ha-Yahadut" (On the Question of the Survival of Judaism), *Ha-Shilo'ah* (Krakow) 13:(January–July, 1904), 303.

82. Feitellesohn, op. cit.

83. Ish-Horowitz, op. cit., 303.

84. Feitellesohn, op. cit.

85. Ish-Horowitz, op. cit., 303.

86. A. Tziyoni, "Mehapsei hekhsherim" (Seekers of Permits), *Ha-Zman* (Vilna) 2(April–June 1905):.

87. Moshe Leib Lilienblum, "Zekhut ha-kiyum ve-hoser ha-matara" (Right of Existence and Lack of Purpose), *Ha-Shilo'ah* 13(January–June 1904).

88. Ibid. Tziyoni, op. cit.

89. Tziyoni, op. cit.

90. H. N. Bialik, "El ha-tzippor" (To the Bird), in his *Kol kitvei* (Complete Works) (Tel Aviv, 1961), 1–2.

91. Shaul Tchernichovsky, "Shir eres" (Lullaby), in his *Shirei* (Poems) (Tel Aviv, 1968), 19. My thanks to Chanita Goodblatt for her assistance in translating the poems in this chapter and in locating English translations already in print.

92. Idem, "Ani ma'amin" (I Believe), in his *Shirei*, 9–10.

93. Idem, "Le-nokhah pesel Apollo" (In Front of the Statue of Apollo), in his *Shirei*, 24–25; translation by Maurice Samuel in *The Menorah Treasury*, ed. Leo W. Schwarz (Philadelphia, 1964), 682.

94. Shaul Tchernichovsky, "Be-En-Dor" (In En-Dor), in his *Shirei*, 7–8.

95. H. N. Bialik, "La-mitnadvim ba-am" (To the Volunteers among the People), in his *Kol kitvei*, 27–28.

96. Idem, "Metei midbar" (The Dead of the Desert), in his *Kol kitvei*, 92–95; translation from Ruth Nevo, *Chaim Nachman Bialik: Selected Poems*, (n.p., 1981), 112.

97. Yaakov Cahan, "Anu olim ve-sharim" (We Ascend and Sing), in his, *Kol kitvei* (Complete works) (Tel Aviv, n.d.), 20.

98. See, e.g., the words of Yosef Klausner regarding the war of the Hasmoneans in "Yesod ha-tenua ha-hadasha be-Yisrael" (The Roots of the New Movement in Israel), *Ha-Shilo'ah* (Berlin) 2(Nisan–Elul 1897). He develops the idea there that a cold, logical view of the situation would have induced the Hasmoneans not to fight against the Syrians and that Judaism would have been destroyed and disappeared. Yet spiritual force prevailed over physical force.

99. Yaakov Cahan, "Biryonim," in his *Kol kitvei*, 86–87.

100. Ibid.

101. Moshe Leib Lilienblum, *Derekh teshuva* (The Path of Repentance) (Warsaw, 1899), 38–39.

102. Ben-Zion Dinur et al., ed., *Sefer toldot ha-Hagana* (History of the Hagana), vol. 1, pt. 1, (Tel Aviv, 1954), 154–70, esp. 166.

103. Zalman Aranne, *Autobiografia* (Autobiography) (Tel Aviv, 1971), 11, 33–34.

104. Y. H. Brenner writes, "The complete and final development: in the 1880s, flying feathers and cracked skulls by the hundreds; at the beginning of the century, the torture of virgins and the killing of people by the thousands; and now, we are sitting in blood, my brother, soaked in blood" ("Mikhtav arokh" [A Long Letter], in his *Kol kitvei* [Complete Works] [Tel Aviv, 1927], 6:42).

105. H. N. Bialik, "Al ha-shehita" (On the Slaughter), in his *Kol kitvei* (Tel Aviv, 1961), 41.

106. Y. H. Brenner, "Mi-toch ha-pinkas" (From the Notebook), in his *Kol kitvei* 6:54; idem, "Mikhtav arokh," in his *Kol kitvei*, 6:42.

107. Ahad Ha-Am, "Megilat setarim shel Ahad Ha-Am" (The Secret Letter of Ahad Ha-Am), in his *Kol kitvei* (Tel Aviv, 1961), 501–2. My thanks to Shulamit Laskov, who provided me with additional materials associated with this matter. Ahad Ha-Am complained about

the fact that the leaflet had ultimately been published without mentioning the names of its authors. This had been done due to fear of the censorship authorities, but had detracted from the significance of the document. See Ahad Ha-Am, *Igrot Ahad ha-Am* (Letters of Ahad Ha-Am), 2d ed., vol. 3 (Berlin, 1924), 240, 250–51.

108. H. N. Bialik, "Be-ir ha-harega" (In the City of Slaughter), in his *Kol kitvei,* 97; translation by Abraham M. Klein in *Complete Poetic Works of Hayyim Nahman Bialik,* ed. Israel Efros, vol. 1, (New York, 1948), 139.

109. Shaul Tchernichovsky, "Barukh mi-Magentza," in his *Shirei,* 144–154.

110. Y. H. Brenner, "Hu amar la" (He Told Her), in his *Kol kitvei,* 6:29–33; idem, "Mikhtav arokh," 42.

111. Brenner, "Mikhtav arokh", 42–44.

112. H. N. Bialik, "Al ha-shehita," 41; translation from Nevo, op. cit., 34–36.

113. Dinur et al., op. cit., 1:160–61; see also Anita Shapira, *Berl: The Biography of a Socialist Zionist* (Cambridge, 1984), 14–15.

114. Lilienblum, op. cit., 46; quoted in Ahad Ha-Am, "Shetei matzevot" (Two Monuments), in his *Al parashat derakhim,* 4:185–87.

115. Micha Yosef Berdichevsky, "Min ha-mahane" (From the Camp), in his *Ba-derekh,* 3:89 (quote from an essay by Max Mandelstamm).

116. Ahad Ha-Am, "Emet me-Eretz Yisrael" (Truth from Palestine), in his *Al parashat derakhim,* 1:29.

117. Ahad Ha-Am, "Shalosh madregot" (Three Steps), in his *Al parashat derakhim,* 2:64–65.

118. Cf. Shulamit Laskov, *Ha-Bilu'im* (The Bilu Group) (Tel Aviv, 1980).

119. Frederick, the Grand Duke of Baden, one of Herzl's earliest supporters, was greatly influenced by the preacher William Henry Hechler, who was a pastor with the British Embassy in Vienna and wrote *The Restauration of the Jews to Palestine, According to the Prophets;* see Alex Bein, *Theodore Herzl,* (Cleveland, 1962), 190–92.

120. Cf. Ahad Ha-Am, "Emet me-Eretz Yisrael," 34, 36, 43.

121. One example of such literature is the journal *Luah Eretz Yisrael* (Palestine Calendar), edited by Avraham Moshe Luncz and published yearly (Jerusalem, 1885–1915). See, e.g., the poem by Lilienblum from his play *Zerubavel,* published in a translation by Israel Teller in the *Lua'h Eretz Yisrael,* issued in 1898. See also Israel Teller, "Tmunat ahat ha-moshavot be-Eretz Yisrael" (A Picture of One of the Colonies in Palestine), in *Lua'h Eretz Yisrael,* 1898. Several years later, David Ben Gurion complainted about the nonrealistic writing on problems in Palestine appearing in the Hebrew press in the Diaspora ("Le-verur matzavenu ha-medini" [On Our Political Situation], *Ha-Ahdut* [Elul 1910]).

122. Ahad Ha-Am, *Al parashat derakhim,* 1:28.

123. Ahad Ha-Am, "Shalosh madregot," 64.

124. MD'D [pseud.], "Me-Eretz Yisrael" (From Palestine), *Ha-Shilo'ah* 2 (Nisan–Elul 1897): 452–57.

125. In respect to the bedouin, MD'D specifically states (ibid.) that he derived a portion of his facts from an article by A. Sapir.

126. A. Sapir, "Ha-sin'a le-Yisrael ba-sifrut ha-aravit" (Hatred of the Jews in Arabic Literature), *Ha-Shilo'ah* 6(July–December 1899).

127. Yitzhak Epstein, "She'ela ne'elama" (A Hidden Question), *Ha-Shilo'ah* 17(November–April 1907/8).

128. Menahem Ussishkin, *Our Program* (New York, 1905), 13.

129. Micha Yosef Berdichevsky, "Me-Eretz Yisrael le-Eretz Stam" (From Palestine to Just Any Country), in his *Ba-derekh,* 3:80ff.

130. Hillel Zeitlin, "Ha-mashber" (The Crisis), *Ha-Zman* 3:(July–September 1905).

131. Epstein states in the essay: "There had already been an incident with a writer whom the 'Zionists of Zion' always eulogized; and when he dared to tell the bitter truth in the meeting of 'Ivriya,' namely, that it was impossible now to buy land in Palestine and dispossess the Arabs from their holdings, to drive away Arabs who were toiling on their lands, one of those who adhered to 'Jewish morality' jumped up to prove that on the contrary, the Jews were justified and the Arabs were a disgrace" (op. cit.). I was unable to establish whom he was referring to here; perhaps he was hinting at one of Ussishkin's followers.

132. This topic is mentioned several times in Zeitlin, op. cit. See also Zeev Jabotinsky, "Tziyonut ve-Eretz Yisrael" (Zionism and Palestine), in his *Ketavim tziyoniyim rishonim* (First Writings on Zionism) (Jerusalem, 1949), 121–25.

133. Zeitlin, op. cit.

134. References to Borochov are based on Matityahu Mintz, "Ha-Aravim ba-prognozot shel Borochov" (Arabs in Borochov's Prognoses), *Molad,* Adar 1972. The quotation is on p. 480, from Borochov's "Le-she'elat Tziyon ve-teritoriya" (The Question of Zion and Territory). On Borochov and his relations with Ussishkin, see Matityahu Mintz, *Ber Borochov: Ha-ma'agal ha-rishon, 1900–1906* (Ber Borochov: First Circle, 1900–1906) (Tel Aviv, 1976), 87–151.

135. Borochov's "Ha-platforma shelanu" (Our Platform), quoted in Mintz, "Ha-Aravim ba-prognozot," 481.

136. Ibid., 482.

137. Ahad Ha-Am, "Higi'a ha-sha'a" (The Hour Has Arrived), in his *Al parashat derakhim,* 4:75–76.

138. Moshe Smilansky [Ha-Mashkif (The Observer), pseud.], "Hashkafa ivrit" (Jewish Outlook), *Ha-Shilo'ah* 18(January–June 1908).

139. On the incident itself and the factors involved, see chapter 2.

140. The first report on the incident in Petah Tikvah was by Shmuel Hirsch to Leo Pinsker, dated April 4, 1886. See Alter Druyanow and Shulamit Laskov, eds., *Ketavim le-toldot Hibbat Tziyon vi-yishuv Eretz Yisrael* (Documents on the History of Hibbat Zion and Settlement in Palestine), rev. ed., vol. 4 (Tel Aviv, 1987), doc. 791, pp. 117ff. Items 796, 798, 803, and 807 also deal with the matter; but the most important are 791 and 807. The matter of "thunder" is referred to in doc. 807, p. 156, with press response on p. 157.

141. Ibid., doc. 791, p. 118 and doc. 807, p. 157, for the topic of religious and nationalist hatred.

142. Epstein, op. cit., 196.

143. Ha-Mashkif, op. cit.; Elazar Rokeach to Zalman David Levontin, quoted in Druyanow and Laskov, op. cit., vol. 4, doc. 807, p. 157.

144. Zeitlin, op. cit.

145. Yosef Klausner, [Ish Ivri (Hebrew Man), pseud.], "Hashash" (Suspicion), *Ha-Shilo'ah* 17(July–December 1907).

Chapter 2

1. David Ben Gurion to his father, Petah Tikvah, November 8, 1906, *Igrot David Ben Gurion* (Letters of David Ben Gurion), Vol. 1 (Tel Aviv, 1971), 82.

2. See Ahad Ha-Am, "Emet me-Eretz Yisrael," in his *Al parashat derakhim,* 1:26. Y. H. Brenner, "Bein mayim le-mayim" (Between the Waters), in his *Kol kitvei,* vol. 4 (Tel Aviv, 1927), 66. On the aspect of trauma, see Berl Katznelson, *Igrot* (Letters), vol. 1 (Tel Aviv, 1961), 125, n. 2: "All the fear and trembling of a man who is suddenly hurled from the zenith of the Zionist vision to the nadir of the colonist situation. . . ." The expression "soil of the

vision" appears in his writings. The phrase "legendary kingdom" can be found in Ben Gurion, "Bi-Yehuda u-va-Galil" (In Judea and Galilee), in *Luah Ahiever* (Ahiever Calendar), vol. 2. (New York, 1921). A marvelous description of this image of Palestine can be found in the first pages of S. Y. Agnon, *Temol shilshom* (Bygone Days) (Tel Aviv, 1947), 7, 28. See also Berl Katznelson, "Darki la-aretz" (My Road to Palestine), in his *Ketavim* (Collected Writings), vol. 5 (Tel Aviv, 1948), 376.

3. Brenner, *Mi-kan u-mi-kan* (From Here and There), in his *Kol kitvei,* 4:153.

4. See, e.g., Agnon, op. cit., 38–39.

5. "Zikhronot Rabbi Yosef Reuven Paicovitch" (Memoirs of Rabbi Yosef Reuven Paicovitch), recorded by Menahem Ben Aryeh, Rosh Pina, AKM,* sec. 15—Allon.

6. On Ben Gurion see his letter to his father, Petah Tikvah, October 1, 1906, *Igrot,* 1:75; see also Shabtai Teveth, *Ben Gurion and the Palestinian Arabs: From Peace to War* (Oxford, 1985), 7; on Katznelson, see Anita Shapira, *Berl: The Biography of a Socialist Zionist* (Cambridge, 1984), 25–26.

7. Brenner, *Mi-kan u-mi-kan,* 4:153.

8. Ibid.

9. Brenner, "Bein mayim le-mayim," 4:73.

10. Vladimir Dubnow to Simeon Dubnow (Petersburg), Jaffa, October 20, 1882, in *Ketavim le-toldot Hibbat Tziyon vi-yishuv Eretz Yisrael* (Documents on the History of Hibbat Zion and Settlement in Palestine), ed. Alter Druyanow and Shulamit Laskov, rev. ed., vol. 1 (Tel Aviv, 1982), 522–23.

11. See Ahad Ha-Am, "Shalosh madregot" (Three Steps), in his *Al parashat derakhim,* 2:63–65.

12. Much has been written on this topic. See, e.g., Z. Smilansky [Z.S., pseud.], "Poalim ivrim o arvim" (Sof) (Jewish or Arab Workers [conclusion]), *Ha-Shilo'ah* 19(July–December 1908):462–69. See also Anita Shapira, *Ha-ma'avak ha-nikhzav* (Futile Struggle) (Tel Aviv, 1977), 16–18.

13. Things are repeated. See, e.g., Ahad Ha-Am, "Emet me-Eretz Yisrael," 40; Z. Smilansky, op. cit., 260–68. See also Yaakov Ro'i, "Yahasei Rehovot im shekheneiha ha-Arvim (1890–1914)" (Rehovot's Relations with Its Arab Neighbors [1890–1914]), *Ha-Tziyonut* 1 (Tel Aviv, 1970), 164.

14. The story is detailed in certain documents contained in Druyanow and Laskov, eds., op. cit., vol. 4, docs. 791, 797, 798, 803, and 807. Of especial importance are docs. 791 and 807. In the last item, Elazar Rokeach wrote to Z. D. Levontin (May 20, 1886): "They don't regard the fellahin as human beings; and for every small thing, they beat and punish them with whips."

15. Ahad Ha-Am, "Emet me-Eretz Yisrael," 40.

16. Ro'i, op. cit., 193.

17. Ibid., 165, 175, 195. Other incidents are there reported on, in which Arabs were beaten during a dispute or as a result of provocation on their part.

18. Ibid., 179, 181–83.

19. See A. Y. Ezdin to Rosenhak (official of Jewish Colonization Association), 5 Elul 1913, CZA, J15/6536.

20. See, e.g., Moshe Smilansky, "Hadasa," *Ha-Shilo'ah* 25(July–December 1911): 402.

21. Ahad Ha-Am, "Ha-Yishuv ve-apotropsav" (The Yishuv and its patrons), in his *Al parashat derakhim,* 2:236.

22. Z. Smilansky also wrote in a similar vein on the relationship between colonists and

*For abbreviations of archives, see p. 423.

Arab workers. Those colonists "sometimes permit themselves to pervert the justice due to the Arab worker and arrogantly to trample upon his human rights" (op. cit. 71–79).

23. In Brenner, "Bein mayim le-mayim," 68. It appears in the Babylonian Talmud, Tractate Yevamot, 62a; Tractate Ketuvot, 111a. I am indebted to Aaron Oppenheimer for pointing out these talmudic sources.

24. Moshe Smilansky, "Ma'aseinu yekarvunu, ma'aseinu yarhikunu" (Our Deeds Will Bring Both Fraternization and Alienation), *Ha-Olam,* January 29, 1914.

25. Berl Katznelson to Sarah Shmukler, and Leah Meron, Sukkot 1909, in *Igrot,* vol. 1 (Tel Aviv, 1961), 122.

26. On their presumed laziness, see Druyanow and Laskov, op. cit., doc. 791; Z. Smilansky, op. cit. The assertion that the Arabs were exceptionally diligent was made by the farmers. See, e.g., Brenner, "Bein mayim le-mayim," 68–69.

27. Druyanow and Laskov, op. cit., doc. 791.

28. Ro'i, op. cit., 183, doc. 45.

29. See, e.g., Z. Smilansky, op. cit., 71–79.

30. Ibid., 260–68.

31. Ahad Ha-Am, "Ha-Yishuv ve-apotropsav," 236, n. 2.

32. Z. Smilanksy, op. cit. See also Moshe Smilansky, [Heruti, pseud.] "Me-inyanei ha-Yishuv" (On Matters of the Yishuv), *Ha-Poel ha-Tzair,* Shvat–Adar I, 1908.

33. Elazar Rokeach, in a letter to Z. D. Levontin (May 20, 1886), stated: "Our brethren from Russia, [who] did not know or understand anything about the nature of freedom, suddenly emerged from darkness into the light. Therefore they drank to the dregs the cup of freedom until they were inebriate" (Druyanow and Laskov, op. cit., doc. 807, p. 157). Ahad Ha-Am, five years later, wrote: "They were slaves in the land of their exile and suddenly now find themselves in the midst of freedom without limit, a wild liberty that can only be found in a country like Turkey. That precipitate change led in their hearts to a tendency toward despotism" ("Emet me-Eretz Yisrael," 40).

34. Ahad Ha-Am, "Emet me-Eretz Yisrael," 40.

35. Ahad Ha-Am, "Ha-Yishuv ve-apotropsav," 236, n. 2. On the same topic, see El-R [pseud.], "Le-she'elot ha-yom" (On Questions of the Day), *Ha-Ahdut* (Jerusalem), 14, Nisan 1914).

36. Z. Smilansky, op. cit., pt. 2, 260–68.

37. See, e.g., Ro'i, op. cit., 182–83; Z. Smilansky, op. cit., 260–68; Agnon, op. cit., 49.

38. Eleazar Rokach to Leo Pinsker, April 12, 1886, in Druyanow and Laskov, op. cit., vol. 4, doc. 798, pp. 135–39.

39. Moshe Smilansky, "Ma'aseinu," pt. 1, *Ha-Olam,* January 29, 1914.

40. Ibid., pt. 2, *Ha-Olam,* February 5, 1914.

41. Yosef Klausner [Ish Ivri, pseud.] "Hashash" (Suspicion), *Ha-Shilo'ah* 17(July–December 1907).

42. Ibid.

43. Herzl, *Diaries,* October 29, 1898, 2:742.

44. The exceptional event during this period was the request made by Arab notables in Palestine to the Sublime Porte in Constantinople in 1891 to put a halt to Jewish immigration. This was the only political event with a pronounced nationalist tone in the period before 1908. The most comprehensive book on the attitude of Arabs in Palestine to Zionism prior to 1914 is Neville J. Mandel, *The Arabs and Zionism Before World War I* (Calif., 1976). See also Y. Porath, *The Emergence of the Palestinian–Arab National Movement, 1918–1929* (London, 1974).

45. See n. 19.

46. Druyanow and Laskov, op. cit., vol. 4, docs. 791 and 798.

47. Ibid. on the issue of land disputes; on Metulla, see Ahad Ha-Am, "Ha-Yishuv ve-apotropsav," 241–43. On Rosh Pina and Metulla, see Yitzhak Epstein, "She'ela ne'elama," *Ha-Shilo'ah* 17(July–December 1907). On the general topic of land purchase by Jews in Palestine, see Kenneth W. Stein, *The Land Question in Palestine, 1917–1939* (Chapel Hill, 1984).

48. Epstein, op. cit.; M. Smilanksy, "Ma'aseinu," pts. 1 and 2; idem, "Me-inyanei ha-Yishuv."

49. Ben Gurion, "Bi-Yehuda u-va-Galil."

50. See the discussion on this topic in Anita Shapira, *Ha-ma'avak ha-nikhzav*, 15–32; see also Yosef Gorny, "Ha-ideologia shel kibbush ha-avoda" (The Ideology of Conquest of Labor), *Keshet*, 38(1968). Gorny's *Zionism and the Arabs* (Oxford, 1987) contains the most comprehensive discussion on the Arab question as reflected in the press at the time (pp. 11–77).

51. He did not say this specifically; but it can be deduced from his rhetorical question, "Weren't those people correct who said that it was *precisely that aspiration* on our part that was likely to act as a greater impediment on our path than all other obstacles" (Ahad Ha-Am, "Sakh ha-kol" [All in All], in his *Al parashat derakhim*, 2:172).

52. Nehama Pukhachewsky, "She'elot geluyot" (Open Questions), *Ha-Shilo'ah* 18(January–June 1908). An echo to this approach can be found in Ro'i, op. cit., 152.

53. See, esp., M. Smilansky, "Me-inyanei ha-Yishuv"; Pukhachewsky, op. cit.

54. Pukhachewsky, op. cit.

55. Epstein, op. cit.

56. Pukhachewsky, op. cit.

57. Smilansky stated: "We are even more opposed to that lightheadedness whose result is complete unpreparedness for any clash, so very possible, between us and the Arabs" ("Me-inyanei ha-Yishuv,").

58. See, e.g., remarks by Avshalom Feinberg, quoted in Gorny, *Zionism and the Arabs,* 56.

59. See Porath, op. cit., 20–30; Mandel, op. cit., 63–92.

60. See Dinur et al., *Sefer toldot ha-Hagana*, 1:174–92.

61. See Teveth, op. cit., 16–17; Jonathan Frankel, "The 'Yizkor' Book of 1911—A Note on National Myths in the Second Aliyah," in *Religion, Ideology, and Nationalism in Europe and America,* ed. H. Ben Israel et al. (Jerusalem, 1986), 355–84.

62. An account of the events can be found in Dinur et al., *Sefer toldot ha-Hagana,* 1:207–09. Teveth, op. cit., 12–13; Moshe Smilansky [Ha-Mashkif (The Observer), pseud.] "Hashkafa ivrit" (Jewish outlook), *Ha-Shilo'ah* 18(January–June 1908). Ben Gurion to his father, Sejera, March 25, 1908, *Igrot,* 1:118; Ahad Ha-Am to Mordechai Ben Hillel Ha-Cohen, Odessa, April 14, 1908, in *Igrot,* 4:126–27.

63. A. Reuveni, "Hagana atzmit" (Self-Defense), *Ha-Ahdut,* 3 Ab 1911.

64. El-R [pseud.], "Le-she'elat ha-yom" (On the Question of the Day), *Ha-Ahdut,* 14 Nisan 1914.

65. On the Russian revolutionary roots of the behavior of these young people, see M. Smilansky, "Hashkafa ivrit"; Ahad Ha-Am to Mordechai Ben Hillel Ha-Cohen, Odessa, April 14, 1908, in *Igrot,* 4:126–27.

66. According to Dinur et al., Ha-Shomer was established at Passover 1909 without its founders' knowing that at that same time a watchman and farmer had been killed in Sejera. The bloody events of Passover 1909 are always recalled in the same breath with the establishment of Ha-Shomer, but it is evident that these occurrences did not lead to its foundation.

See *Sefer toldot ha-Hagana,* 1:214. On Ha-Shomer, see pp. 193–314 of the same work and also Y. Ben Zvi et al., eds., *Sefer Ha-Shomer* (Book of Ha-Shomer) (Tel Aviv, 1957); *Kovetz Ha-Shomer* (Ha-Shomer Collection) (Tel Aviv, 1947).

67. See M. Smilansky, "Hashkafa ivrit."

68. Y. Zerubavel, "Zehirut" (Caution), *Ha-Ahdut,* 11 Tammuz 1911; "Shtei ha-shitot" (Two Methods), *Ha-Ahdut,* 18 Tammuz 1911.

69. A series of articles stressed the link between class hatred and national hatred. The ultimate conclusion was that national hatred indeed existed. There is at times an internal contradiction between presenting Arab enmity as a product of their suppression by the farmers and as a consequence of the workers' struggle to advance the cause of "Jewish Labor." In any event, the existence of national hatred was portrayed as self-evident. However, I think there is a ritualistic repetition here of internal persuasion along deterministic Marxist lines— one that does not derive from the actual situation. Characteristic of this is Ben Gurion's "Le-verur matzavenu ha-medini" (Clarifying Our Political Situation), *Ha-Ahdut,* 4 Elul 1910. The entire article is devoted to explaining why it is important for Ben Gurion to travel to Salonika and Constantinople for the purpose of study. Typically Ben Gurion depicts his actions as being the key activity of the period. For that reason, embarking on political activity in the framework of the Ottoman Empire is presented as an essential reaction to national hatred, which should be prevented.

70. Rabbi Binyamin describes how Berele Shveiger wanted to be a bedouin and was envious of the Arabs. Cf. A. Z. Rabinowitz, ed. *Yizko, matzevet zikaron le-halalei ha-poalim ha-ivri'im be-Eretz Yisrael* (In Commemoration of Fallen Jewish Workers in Palestine) (Jaffa, 1911).

71. Note the enthusiasm Ben Gurion expresses on taking a weapon into his hands ("Bi-Yehuda u-va-Galil," p. 109). See also Teveth, op. cit., 13–14; Dinur et al., *Sefer toldot ha-Hagana,* 1:196.

72. On the topic of Ha-Shomer activists' crudeness of manners, consult testimony by Yehuda Almog (in author's possession). On their attitude toward women, see Shulamit Blum, "Ha-isha bit-tnu'at ha-avoda bi-tkufat ha-Aliyah ha-Shniya" (Woman in the Labor Movement in the Period of the Second Aliyah), master's thesis, Tel Aviv University, 1980, p. 72; and note the quotation of Zvi Nadav, taken from *Kovetz Ha-Shomer* (see n. 66), 501.

73. An echo of that criticism can be found in Brenner, "Bein mayim le-mayim," 97.

74. Yosef Aharonovitz, "Klapei pnim" (Internally), *Ha-Poel ha-Tzair,* November 1, 1912.

75. My principal source for this topic has been the instructive essay by Jonathan Frankel (op. cit.). Many of the articles cited in the course of this discussion (such as those by Zerubavel and Aharonovitz) are also cited by Frankel.

76. Bialik, "Be-ir ha-harega," in his *Kol kitvei,* 97.

77. Y. Zerubavel, "Yizkor" (In Memory), *Ha-Ahdut,* January 2, 1912.

78. Idem, "Kavim" (Lines), in *Yizkor,* ed. Rabinowitz, 76.

79. Yehoshua Thon, "Mesirut nefesh" (Self-Sacrifice), in *Yizkor,* ed. Rabinowitz, 20.

80. K. L. Silman, "Me-hirhurei liba" (Personal Reflections, in *Yizkor,* ed. Rabinowitz, 50.

81. Ibid., 50–51; Y. Zerubavel, "Kavim," in *Yizkor,* ed Rabinowitz, 76–77.

82. Y. Zerubavel, "Yizkor," *Ha-Ahdut,* January 2, 1912.

83. Cited in Dinur et al., *Sefer toldot ha-Hagana,* 1:215.

84. Identification of the poem can be found in Frankel, op. cit., 363. I obtained the full version of the poem and information on the poet from Eliyahu Ha-Cohen and am grateful for his help.

85. Y. Zerubavel, "Yizkor," *Ha-Ahdut,* January 9, 1912. The entire article (of which

this is the second part) is full of criticism of the volume *Yizkor* as being too tepid and luke-warm.

86. Ben Gurion, "Bi-Yehuda u-va-Galil." The line from the song was apparently called to his attention while he was editing the Yiddish edition of the book *Yizkor* in New York. See also Shabtai Teveth, *Kin'at David* (The Zeal of David), vol. 1 (Tel Aviv, 1976), 339–58.

87. Ben Gurion to his father, Petah Tikvah, November 8, 1906, *Igrot*, 1:84.

88. H. L. Zuta, "Ba-Aretz u-ve-hutz la-aretz" (In Palestine and Abroad), *Ha-Shilo'ah* 25(July–December 1911).

89. Such complaints are common in the literature of the period. See, e.g., remarks by Shmuel Tolkovski on the matter in Ro'i, op. cit., 165.

90. As an illustration of the stance taken by Poalei Zion, oscillating between universalism and nationalism, see Yitzhak Ben Zvi, "Hagana leumit ve-hashkafa proletarit" (National Defense and Proletarian Outlook), *Ha-Ahdut*, 23 Shvat 1913.

91. Brenner, *Revivim*, 3–4:164. Cited by A. Reuveni [N. Wagman, pseud.] "Ha-she'ela ha-arvit" (The Arab Question), *Ha-Ahdut*, 19 Ab 1913.

92. Ibid.

93. Brenner, "Bein mayim le-mayim," 76.

94. Brenner gave a very strong-worded counterdescription in his critique of an article by Nahum Sokolov, who describes reality in an Arab village in Palestine in idealistic colors "Mi-toch ha-pinkas" (From the Notebook), in his *Kol kitvei*, 6:253.

95. Idem, "Bein mayim le-mayim," 29.

96. Ibid., 32.

97. Ibid., 77; idem, *Mi-kan u-mi-kan*, 153–54, 165, 222.

98. Idem, *Mi-kan u-mi-kan*, 153, 174; idem, "Bein mayim le-mayim," 55, 72.

99. Idem, *Mi-kan u-mi-kan*, 174.

100. Ibid., 154, 174.

101. Idem, "Bein mayim le-mayim," 40.

102. Idem, *Mi-kan u-mi-kan*, 145.

103. Idem, "Gam ele anhot sofer" (Those Are Also the Writer's Sighs), in his *Kol kitvei*, 6:205.

104. According to one view, the reference was to Berele Shveiger, one of the key figures in the volume *Yizkor*. Cf. Frankel, op. cit., 378.

105. Brenner, "Bein mayim le-mayim," 75.

106. Ibid., 75–76.

107. Idem, *Mi-kan u-mi-kan*, 144–45.

108. Moshe Smilansky, "Hadasa," *Ha-Shilo'ah* 25(July–December 1911), 47–48; see also pp. 132–33.

109. See Brenner, "Regashot ve-hirhurim" (Feelings and Reflections), in his *Kol kitvei*, 6:95.

110. Brenner, "Bein mayim le-mayim," 76.

111. Brenner, *Mi-kan u-mi-kan*, 145–46.

112. Ibid., 196. On the "optimists," see remarks by Tomarkin quoted in *Mi-kan u-mi-kan:* "The description is not at all correct . . .—as if our situation were totally precarious. As if tomorrow the natives of Palestine were going to rise up and—God forbid!—kill us!" (p. 212).

113. Ibid., 189.

114. Brenner, "Lama ragzu" (Why Were They Angered?), in his *Kol kitvei*, 6:214; idem, "Ha-ohela" (In the Tent), in his *Kol kitvei*, 6:142.

115. Idem, "Ha-ohela," 142.

116. Ibid., 144.

117. Compare the remarks of those who left Palestine (just mentioned) with the attitude of the "optimists," who actually respond to the implied threat to survival. On Berl Katznelson's attitude toward Brenner, see Katznelson, *Ha-Aliyah ha-Shniya* (The Second Aliyah), ed. Anita Shapira, (Tel Aviv, 1990).

118. A. D. Gordon, "Pitaron lo-ratzionali" (A Non-Rational Solution), in his *Mivhar ketavim* (Selected Writings), ed. Eliezer Shveid (Jerusalem, 1983), 185.

119. Idem, "Ha-kongres" (The Congress), in his *Kitvei* (Collected Works), vol. 1 (Tel Aviv, 1945), 174.

120. Brenner expressed a similar thought when he wrote:

Only fundamental work bestows rights. Only it can give some sort of existence. . . . I do not need to preach about national consciousness and be intent on acting for the glory of nationalism, because all my daily life is *national life in hard cash.*

Very few are those simple Jewish individuals. Very few. But they exist. They're new. A new type among the children of Israel. . . .

Blessed be that sorrowful, sick, rotten nation if such children, even if just a few, were born to her in her old age. There is a great miracle here; and, who knows, it's possible that perhaps indeed [our hope] has not yet been lost ("Hazkarat neshamot" [Memorial Prayer for the Dead], in his *Kol kitvei,* 6:326).

Chapter 3

1. There is a copious literature on the Balfour Declaration and the reasons underlying it. See, e.g., Leonard Stein, *The Balfour Declaration* (London, 1968). M. Verete, "Ha-masa u-matan ha-tziyoni–arvi be-aviv 1919 ve-ha-mediniyut ha-anglit" (Zionist–Arab Negotiations in the Spring of 1919 and the English Policy), *Zion* 32(1967): 76–115. The early period of British rule in Palestine has been described in Christopher Sykes, *Crossroads to Israel* (London, 1965); John Marlowe, *The Seat of Pilate* (London, 1959); Ben-Zion Dinur et al., *Sefer toldot ha-Hagana,* vol. 2 (Tel Aviv, 1959): 53–185; Yehoshua Porath, *The Emergence of the Palestinian–Arab National Movement, 1918–1929* (London, 1974), 31–169.

2. While the sentences in the mandate dealing with the Jews (esp. in paragraphs 2, 4, and 6) are formulated in a positive way and speak about actions to be initiated, the sentences that deal with "other sections of the population" (the Arabs are not mentioned by name) are framed in a language that suggests "safeguarding [of] the civil and religious rights"—and no more.

3. Vladimir Jabotinsky to Chaim Weizmann, August 1, 1920, in his *Mikhtavim* (Letters) (Tel Aviv, n.d.), 146.

4. Porath, op. cit., 70–122.

5. Max Nordau, "Ha-dam u-gmulo" (Blood and Its Recompense) in his *Ketavim tziyoniyim* (Zionist Writings), vol. 4. (Jerusalem, 1962), 20–22.

6. Nili is an acronym-word for the initial letters of the Hebrew verse *Netzah Yisrael lo yeshakker* (The Glory of Israel Will Not Lie, Samuel 15:29).

7. Shaul Tchernichovsky, *Shirei* (Poems) (Tel Aviv, 1968), 52; translation by Chanita Goodblatt.

8. Ibid.

9. Ahad Ha-Am to Joseph Trumpeldor, London, November 9 and 12, 1916, in his *Igrot* (Letters), ed. Arie Simon, vol. 6 (Tel Aviv, 1960), 45–47. My thanks to Shulamit Laskov for calling my attention to those letters.

10. See Aaron Aaronsohn to Julian Mack, October 9, 1916, printed in Eliezer Livne,

Nili: Toldoteha shel he'aza medinit (Nili: The History of a Bold Political Venture) (Tel Aviv, 1980), 421–35.

11. On the conquest of Palestine by the British and the topic of the Jewish Legion, see Yigal Elam, *Ha-Gedudim ha-Ivri'im* (The Jewish Legion) (Tel Aviv, 1984); Dinur et al., *Sefer toldot ha-Hagana,* 1:425–532.

12. Eliyahu Golomb, "Ve'idat ha-mitnadvim," (Volunteers Conference) in *Al ha-Saf* (At the Threshold) (Jerusalem, 1918), 94.

13. Rachel Yanait, "Min he-amal el ha-avoda" (From Toil to Labor), in *Al ha-Saf,* 6.

14. Shmuel Yavne'eli, "Divrei ha-mehaivim" (Views of the Supporters), in *Yalkut Ahdut ha-Avoda* (Ahdut ha-Avoda Anthology), vol. 1 (Tel Aviv, 1929), 157–59.

15. J-Y. [pseud.—Jabotinsky?], in *Al ha-Saf,* 94.

16. Golomb, "Ve'idat ha-mitnadvim," 93.

17. Yavne'eli, "Ve'idat ha-mitnadvim" (Volunteers Conference), in *Al ha-Saf,* 93.

18. Golomb, "Ve'idat ha-mitnadvim," 93–94; Yavne'eli, "Divrei ha-mehaivim," 157.

19. Yavne'eli, "Divrei ha-mehaivim," 157–59.

20. Golomb, "Ve'idat ha-mitnadvim," 94.

21. Yanait, op. cit., 6–9.

22. Anon., "Gilgulei shihrur" (Metamorphoses of Liberation), in *Al ha-Saf,* 103.

23. Berl Katznelson, "Public Statement" in *Yalkut Ahdut ha-Avoda,* 1:173. On this, see also the letter by Katznelson to Mordechai Kushnir, in his *Igrot,* vol. 2 (Tel Aviv, 1974), 529–31, parts of which are reprinted in *Yalkut Ahdut ha-Avoda,* 1:172–73. See also Eliyahu Golomb, "Heshvan–Kislev 1918," in his *Hevyon oz* (Hidden Strength), vol. 1 (Tel Aviv, 1953), 141, 145.

24. Letter by Mordechai Kushnir, in *Yalkut Ahdut ha-Avoda,* 1:170.

25. Ibid., 164.

26. Eliyahu Golomb to Rivka Shertok and Zippora Meirov, in his *Hevyon oz,* 1:146.

27. See *Yalkut Ahdut ha-Avoda,* 1:164.

28. Yavne'eli, "Divrei ha-mehaivim," 158.

29. Mordechai Kushnir, op. cit. 167.

30. See Anita Shapira, *Berl: The Biography of a Socialist Zionist* (Cambridge, 1984), 75–82; Dinur et al., *Sefer toldot ha-Hagana,* 1:25–532; Yigal Elam, op. cit., 259–66.

31. Golomb, *Hevyon oz,* 1:150.

32. Mordechai Kushnir, op. cit., 163; Rachel Katznelson, *Masot u-reshimot* (Essays and Notes) (Tel Aviv, 1946), 28.

33. Yavne'eli, "Divrei ha-mehaivim," 158; see also Brenner, "Nosafot" (Addenda), in his *Ketavim* (Collected Writings), vol. 4 (Tel Aviv, 1985), 1490.

34. Z. Jabotinsky, "Sippur yamay" (Story of My Life), pt. 2 and "Megilat ha-gedud" (Scroll of the Legion)—both in his *Autobiografia* (Autobiography) (Jerusalem, 1947), 304–91.

35. Y. H. Brenner, "Sridei sihot noshanot" (Remnants of Old Conversations), in *Yalkut Ahdut ha-Avoda,* 1:174; see also A. D. Gordon, "Le-zikaron" (In Memoriam), in his *Kitvei* (Collected Writings), vol. 4 (Tel Aviv, 1928), 183–84.

36. A. D. Gordon, "Ketzat iyun be-halakha pesuka" (A Short Review of an Axiom), in his *Kitvei,* 4:149–63; idem, "Mi-shiabud li-geula—mi-shiabud pir'i le-shiabud kulturi" (From Servitude to Redemption—from Wild to Civilized Servitude), in his *Kitvei,* 4:164–79; idem, "Le-zikaron," 4:180–91.

37. Avraham Katznelson, "Li-she'elat ha-tzava ha-ivri" (On the question of the Hebrew army), *Ha-Poel ha-Tzair,* September 24, 1919.

38. Nathan Hofshi, "Tzva'iyut o avoda?" (Militarism or Labor?), in his *Be-lev va-nefesh* (In heart and soul), (Tel Aviv, 1965), 38–40.

39. Ibid.

40. Brenner, "Nosafot" (Addenda), *Ketavim* (Collected Writings), vol. 4, 1985, 1490.

41. Brenner, "Sridei sihot noshanot," in *Yalkut Ahdut ha-Avoda,* 1:174.

42. Izik Ramba, *Ha-magen ve-ha-asir* (The Defender and the Prisoner) (Tel Aviv, 1960), 29.

43. Brenner, "Bibliografia," in his *Ketavim,* 4:1655.

44. Brenner, "Tziyunim" (Remarks), in his *Ketavim,* 4:1724.

45. Ibid., 1687.

46. Ibid., 1639.

47. Ibid., 1640.

48. D. Gogol, in *Yalkut Ahdut ha-Avoda,* 1:181.

49. See Dov Hoz, "Le-kiyum ha-Gedud" (On the Existence of the Legion), in *Yalkut Ahdut ha-Avoda,* 1:187–89; Yitzhak Olshan, "Kitzo shel ha-Gedud" (The End of the Legion), in Yalkut Ahdut ha-Avoda, 192–97.

50. See, e.g., Tmidi, "Le-inyanei ha-sha'a" (On the Present Agenda), *Ha-Poel ha-Tzair,* June 11, 1920.

51. Gogol, op. cit., 180.

52. On Tel Hai, see Dinur et al., *Sefer toldot ha-Hagana,* 1:565–85; an important book on this topic is Nakdimon Rogel, *Hazit beli oref* (Front Without Rear) (Tel Aviv, 1959). See also Shulamit Laskov, *Trumpeldor* (Haifa, 1972).

53. Aharon Sher, "Le-mishmar" (For Keeping), in *Yalkut Ahdut ha-Avoda,* 1:201.

54. Sher's death was reported in *Ha-Poel ha-Tzair,* February 13, 1920.

55. These words by Tabenkin are quoted in Jabotinsky, "Be-asefat ha-va'ad ha-zmani" (At the Meeting of the Provisional Council), in his *Ne'umim,* 1905–1926 (Speeches, 1905–1926) (Jerusalem, 1947), 147, 149. The quote is from Katznelson's "Emda" (Position), in *Yalkut Ahdut ha-Avoda,* 1:208.

56. Y. Soker, "Le-inyanei ha-sha'a" (On Matters of the Hour), *Ha-Poel ha-Tzair,* February 27, 1920 (emphasis mine).

57. Berl Katznelson, "Yizkor" (In Memoriam), in *Yalkut Ahdut ha-Avoda,* 1:211.

58. "Al kevareinu ha-hadashim" (On Our New Graves), *Ha-Poel ha-Tzair,* March 12, 1920.

59. Eliezer Lubrani [E. L., pseud.], "Le-zekher ahai she-naflu ba-Galil" (In Memoriam of My Brothers Who Fell in Galilee), *Ha-Poel ha-Tzair,* March 26, 1920.

60. Y. H. Brenner, "Tel Hai," in *Yalkut Ahdut ha-Avoda,* 1:212–13.

61. Joseph Trumpeldor to Samosha, June 17, 1906, in *Yosef Trumpeldor: Kovetz reshimot ve-kit'ei mikhtavim* (Joseph Trumpeldor: Anthology of Articles and Passages from Letters), ed. Menachem Poznanski (Tel Aviv, 1953), 33.

62. See Brenner, "Tel Hai," 211.

63. Brenner, "Tziyunim," 1685–87.

64. Brenner, "Tel Hai," 213.

65. M. Gluecksohn, "al Kevareinu ha-hadashim" (On Our New Graves), *Ha-Poel ha-Tzair,* March 12, 1920.

66. M. Gluecksohn, "Yom ha-zikaron" (Day of Memorial), *Ha-Poel ha-Tzair,* March 28, 1921.

67. The idiom appears in the poem by Bialik "Im yesh et nafshekha la-da'at" (If You Wish to Learn), in his *Kol kitvei* (Tel Aviv, 1961), 21. My thanks to David Berger, who called my attention to the source of this expression.

68. Gluecksohn, op. cit.

69. See argument to this effect in Yitzhak Laufbahn [Y. L-N., pseud.], "Yom Tel Hai" (Day of Tel Hai), *Ha-Poel ha-Tzair,* March 28, 1921.

70. Nathan Bistritzski, "Yud-alef be-Adar" (11 Adar), *Ha-Poel ha-Tzair,* March 28, 1921.

71. Laufbahn expresses this idea: "We do not want to be 'bridegrooms of blood' [see Exodus 4:25]. We are not a people of heroes and knights. It is 'better to die' for one's homeland than for a foreign country. But even better is to live for one's homeland" (op. cit.).

72. Tchernichovsky, "Mangina li" (I Have a Melody), in his *Shirei,* 52.

73. Laufbahn, op. cit.; A. Axelrod, "Ha-akshanim" (The Stubborn Ones), *Ha-Poel ha-Tzair,* March 28, 1921.

74. D. Shimonovitz, "Tel Hai," *Ba-Wa'ale,* March 5, 1936. It appears that it was also published prior to that.

75. See, e.g., pamphlets for the graduating class of Ha-Noar ha-Oved, first issue, 1931, AKM, Efal, div. 8, cont. 6, ser. 5, sec. A.

76. A good illustrative example of this is an essay written by a young girl named Miryam Mendelblat, from the Ha-Mahanot ha-Olim youth movement, on the topic "11 Adar" (all children were asked to write a composition on the subject). Her essay contained a paraphrasing of Berl Katznelson's "Yizkor," the poem by Jabotinsky, and passages from the poem by Shimonovitz, along with some other flowery phrases. The monument and the grave play a key role in her composition. See AKM, Efal, div. 9, Ha-Mahanot ha-Olim Files, no. 10, pt. 6, cont. 1, file 9.

77. Laufbahn, op. cit.

78. Mordechai Kushnir, "Mi-yemei Tel Hai" (From the Days of Tel Hai), *Niv ha-Kvutza,* Spring 1931.

79. Tabenkin, "11 be-Adar," Mi-Bifnim, March 1928.

80. See Porath, op. cit., 31–69.

81. A description of the historical background from the Zionist perspective can be found in Dinur, et al., *Sefer toldot ha-Hagana,* vol. 1: 554–602. See also Y. Tabenkin, "Me-ha-Galil" (From Galilee), in *Yalkut Ahdut ha-Avoda,* 1:200–201.

82. See, e.g., S. Yavne'eli, "Ikarim le-hityashvut" (Guidelines for Settlement), in *Yalkut Ahdut ha-Avoda,* vol. 2 (Tel Aviv, 1932), 45–50.

83. See the analysis of these events by Porath, op. cit., 97–100.

84. On the policy of Herbert Samuel as high commissioner, see: Elie Kedourie, "Sir Herbert Samuel and the Government of Palestine," in his *Chatham House Version* (London, 1970), 51–82; Moshe Mossek, *Palestine Immigration Policy Under Sir Herbert Samuel* (London, 1978); Bernard Wasserstein, *The British in Palestine: The Mandatory Government and the Arab–Jewish Conflict, 1917–1929* (London, 1979), 73–138.

85. Z. Rubashov [Z., pseud.] in *Yalkut Ahdut ha-Avoda,* 1:223–24.

86. Yavne'eli, *Kuntres* 35.

87. Y. H. Brenner [B., pseud.], "Tziyunim, shalhei Nisan" (Remarks, the End of Nisan), in *Yalkut Ahdut ha-Avoda,* 1:233.

88. S. Yavne'eli [Y-Y., pseud.], "Be-yemei ha-ke'ev" (Days of Pain), in *Yalkut Ahdut ha-Avoda,* 1:238.

89. Anon., "Lifnei ha-ma'ase u-le-aharav" (Before and After the Deed), *Ha-Poel ha-Tzair,* May 13, 1921.

90. M. Kushnir quotes the words of the officer Margulin: "I was born in Russia, and many of the Jews of Tel Aviv stood and looked on. Undoubtedly, what they saw reminded them of the pogrom in Russia perpetrated by Russian officers. And, undoubtedly, they thought that something similar was now happening here, too" (Mordechai Kushnir, "Li-mlot shloshim" (Thirty Days of Mourning), in *Yalkut Ahdut ha-Avoda,* 1:253.

91. Ibid., 250.

92. Yosef Aharonovitz, "Le-ahar ha-pera'ot" (After the Riots), *Ha-Poel ha-Tzair,* May 13, 1921.

93. M. Gluecksohn, "Emet u-politika" (Truth and Politics), *Ha-Poel ha-Tzair,* May 6, 1921.

94. D. Ben Gurion, "Yedei mi shafkhu et ha-dam" (Who Shed the Blood?), in *Yalkut Ahdut ha-Avoda,* 1:260–63.

95. Kushnir, "Li-mlot shloshim," 250.

96. S. Yavne'eli, "Bi-yemei ha-ke'ev," 238. See also Brenner, "Tziduk ha-din" (Justifying the Judgment), in his *Ketavim,* 4:1764–65.

97. See Brenner, "Tziduk ha-din" and "Tziyunim," 1719–1721. See also A. S. Waldstein, [On, pseud.], "La-matzav" (On the Situation), in *Yalkut Ahdut ha-Avoda,* 1:226.

98. Shaul Meirov, "Min ha-Galil" (From Galilee), in *Yalkut Ahdut ha-Avoda,* 1:213. See also S. Yavne'eli, "Bi-yemeni ha-ke'ev," 239; Nahum Benari, "Bein ha-zemanim" (Between the Times), in *Yalkut Ahdut ha-Avoda,* 1:247–48.

99. Berl Katznelson, "Bi-yemei Yerushalayim" (In the Days of Jerusalem), in *Yalkut Ahdut ha-Avoda,* 1:227–31.

100. Yosef Aharonovitz, "Le-ahar ha-pera'ot."

101. See articles in *Ha-Poel ha-Tzair,* May 6, 1921, esp. M. Gluecksohn "Emet u-politika." See also Dinur et al., *Sefer toldot ha-Hagana,* 2:77–118; and Porath, op. cit., 131–37.

102. Cf. Porath, op. cit., 136–37.

103. Elie Kedouri, "Sir Herbert Samuel and the Government of Palestine," in his *Chatham House Version,* 52–81.

104. See, e.g., Berl Katznelson, "Hamesh shnot netzivut" (Five Years of the Commission), *Davar,* June 29, 1925; David Ben Gurion," "La-din ve-heshbon shel Samuel" (On Samuel's Report), in *Yalkut Ahdut ha-Avoda,* 1:305–15.

105. A. D. Gordon, "Mi-Shiabud li-Geula" 164–79.

106. See, e.g., Y. H. Brenner [B., pseud.], "Mi-Tel Hai le-Yerushalayim" (From Tel Hai to Jerusalem) in *Yalkut Ahdut ha-Avoda,* 1:232; Y. Tabenkin, "Gam zehu koah" (This Is Also Power), in *Yalkut Ahdut ha-Avoda* 1:237.

107. See, e.g., Moshe Shertok [Ben-Kedem, pseud.], "Ha-hafgana be-Yafo" (The Demonstration in Jaffa), in *Yalkut Ahdut ha-Avoda,* 1:220.

108. Jabotinsky, "Tokhnit le-shilton zemani be-Eretz Yisrael" (Plan for a Temporary Government in Palestine), in his *Ne'umim, 1905–1926,* 117–88.

109. Brenner, "Tziyunim," 1722–23.

110. Mordechai Kushnir, "Li-mlot shloshim," 254.

111. Brenner, "Mi-hutz u-mi-bayit" (Externally and Internally), in his *Ketavim,* 4:1635.

112. See Jabotinsky, "Tokhnit le-shilton zemani," 117–18; Brenner, "Tziyunim."

113. Y. H. Brenner, "Le-inyanenu" [B., pseud.] (On Our Affair), in his *Ketavim,* 4:1758.

114. Ibid.

115. Rabbi Binyamin, "Misaviv la-kever" (Around the Grave), *Ha-Poel ha-Tzair,* May 6, 1921.

116. D. Shimonovitz, "Al sefod . . ." (Do Not Mourn . . .), *Ha-Poel ha-Tzair,* May 13, 1921.

117. Z. Jabotinsky, "Tokhnit le-shilton zemani," 81–122.

118. On the shortcut, see Anita Shapira, "The Dynamics of Zionist Leftist Trends," in *Jewish History,* ed. Ada Rapoport-Albert and Steven J. Zipperstein (London, 1988), 629–82; on Ahdut ha-Avoda, see Y. Gorny, *Ahdut ha-Avoda, 1919–1930* (Tel Aviv, 1973). On Zionist economic policy in that period, see Yaakov Metzer, *Hon leumi le-vayit leumi, 1919–1921* (National Capital for a National Home) (Jerusalem, 1979).

119. On British foreign policy in the Middle East between the wars, see E. Monroe, *Britain's Moment in the Middle East* (London, 1964).

120. There is a copious literature on the Weizmann–Brandeis controversy. See, e.g., Eviatar Frizel, *Ha-mediniyut ha-tziyonit le-ahar Hatzharat Balfur, 1917–1922* (Zionist Policy after the Balfour Declaration, 1917–1922) (Tel Aviv, 1977), 212–50; G. L. Berlin, "The Brandeis–Weizmann Dispute," *American Jewish Historical Quarterly* 60(1970): 37–68; Y. Shapiro, *Leadership of the American Zionist Organization, 1897–1930* (Urbana, IL, 1971), 135–79. On Brandeis's policies, see Allon Gal, "Hashkafato shel Brandeis al ofen binyan ha-Aretz" (Brandeis's Views on How to Go About Building Palestine), *Ha-Ziyonut* (Tel Aviv) 6(1981):97–145.

121. Chaim Arlosoroff, "Me'ora'ot Mai" (May Riots), in his *Ketavim* (Collected writings), vol. 1 (Tel Aviv, 1934), 5–11.

122. Zalman Aranne, *Autobiografia* (Autobiography) (Tel Aviv, 1971), 177.

123. See Anita Shapira, "Le-shivro shel halom ehad" (On the Breakup of a Dream), in *Ha-halikha al kav ha-ofek* (Visions in Conflict) (Tel Aviv, 1989), 185–86 and 398, n. 81.

124. Brenner, "Mi-toch ha-pinkas" 1833–35.

125. Brenner, "Tziyunim," 1785.

126. Rabbi Binyamin recalls that fact in "Misaviv la-kever," *Ha-Poel ha-Tzair,* May 6, 1921.

127. Even more strange is the explanation he gave for the problem of "Hebrew labor." Brenner dealt with the problem with great candor in his novel *Mi-kan u-mi-kan.* Now he observed, "The Arab worker is a brother for us. Not because of jealousy did we resent his massive presence in the Jewish colonies but because of our grief for him who has to accept being hired for a pittance, and also our sorrow for our brother who employs him . . . that he is not independent, and because exploitation is a basic condition for his existence." See Brenner, "Le-inyanenu," in his *Ketavim,* 4:1758.

128. Y. Tabenkin, *Devarim* (Speeches), vol. 1 (Tel Aviv, 1967), 28.

129. Ibid., 34.

130. Ibid.

Chapter 4

1. See Beilinson to Hugo Bergmann, cited by Anita Shapira, *Ha-halikha al kav ha-ofek,* 296. See also David Horovitz, *Ha-etmol sheli* (My Yesterday) (Jerusalem, 1970), 192.

2. See Y. Porath, *The Emergence of the Palestinian–Arab National Movement, 1918–1929* (London, 1974); cf. also Elie Kedourie, "Sir Herbert Samuel and the Government of Palestine," in his *The Chatham House Version* (London, 1970): 52–81.

3. *Protokol ha-veida ha-revi'it shel Ahdut ha-Avoda,* (Minutes, Fourth Conference of Ahdut ha-Avoda) Ein Harod, 8–16 Iyar, 1924 (Tel Aviv, 1926), 21–22.

4. Ibid., 33–34.

5. Ibid., 35.

6. David Ben Gurion, *Anahnu u-shkheneinu* (We and Our Neighbors) (Tel Aviv, 1931), 61.

7. *Protokol ha-veida ha-revi'it,* 35 (Ben Gurion).

8. Ibid., 172–73.

9. Ibid., 38–39.

10. Ibid., 42.

11. Ibid., 48.

12. Ibid., 47.

13. Ibid., 31–31 (Ben Gurion); ibid., 47–48 (Katznelson).

14. Shlomo Lavi, "Eretz Yisrael o Girgashia" (Palestine or Girgashia), in *Yalkut Ahdut ha-Avoda,* 2:370.

15. Shlonsky refers to the Arab as the person who chopped off the head of John the Baptist and presented it to Salome ("Ohalenu" [Our tent], in his *Ba-galgal* [In the Wheel] [Tel Aviv, 1927], 132). In the poem "Po" (Here), a camel caravan is mentioned, always identified in drawings of the Palestinian landscape with the Arabs, even if there were a few Jewish camel drivers here and there (in his *Ba-galgal,* 149).

16. Yitzhak Lamdan, *Massada* 2d ed. (Tel Aviv, 1929).

17. Idem, *Massada,* 78.

18. S. Zemach, "Massada, Yitzhak Lamdan," *Ha-Poel ha-Tzair,* April 15, 1927; see also the extremely positive critique by Rabbi Binyamin, "Massada," and A. Z. Rabinowitz, "Hirhurim" (Reflections)—both in *Davar,* November 24, 1926.

19. Yitzhak Lamdan, "Ba-Hamsin" (In the Hamsin), in his *Massada,* 48.

20. Ibid., 78; excerpts are translated into English by R. F. Mintz, *Modern Hebrew Poetry: A Bilingual Anthology* (Berkeley, 1966), 134.

21. Rachel [Rachel Blustein] "Rak al atzmi" (Only About Myself), in her *Shirat Rachel* (Poems of Rachel) (Tel Aviv, 1950), 124.

22. Idem, "El artzi" (To My Country), in her *Shirat Rachel,* 54; idem, "Ve-ulai lo hayu ha-devarim me-olam" (Perhaps It Was Never So), in her *Shirat Rachel,* 75.

23. Idem, "El artzi," 54; translation by Chanita Goodblatt.

24. An interesting study that analyzes the special status of Uri Zvi Greenberg as a poet–eschatologist among his admirers, with emphasis on the late 1930s and afterward, is Yaacov Shavit, "'Ad yavo navi ne'eman': Ma'amado shel Uri Zvi Greenberg ke-meshorer eskhatolog" ("Until a Faithful Prophet Comes": The status of Uri Zvi Greenberg as poet–eschatologist), in his *Ha-mitologiyot shel ha-Yamin* (The Mythologies of the Right) (Zofit), 180–206.

25. U. Z. Greenberg, "Me'ein tazkir le-*Davar*" (A Kind of Memo to *Davar*), *Davar,* June 1, 1925.

26. Idem, "Al bsar Yerushalayim" (On the Flesh of Jerusalem), *Kuntres,* 1 Adar II, 1924, for example. The traditional term Sanballat in Hebrew as an epithet for a traitor refers to a satrap of Samaria who figures centrally in the biblical Book of Nehemiah; he opposed Nehemiah and obstructed the rebuilding of Jerusalem.

27. Idem, "Ha-hekhrah" (The Necessity), in his *Be-emtza ha-olam u-ve-emtza ha-zmanim* (In the Middle of the World and the Midst of the Times) (Tel Aviv, 1979), 31.

28. Ibid.

29. Idem, "Alei karka kan" (Here on the Soil), *Kuntres,* 6 Tevet, 1923/24.

30. Idem, "Yerushalayim shel mata" (Jerusalem of Below), *Ha-Poel ha-Tzair,* April 18, 1924.

31. Getzel Kressel, *Leksikon ha-sifrut ha-ivrit* (Dictionary of Hebrew Literature) (Merhavia, Israel 1967), 507; For examples in Greenberg, see his "Ha-tzlav be-Yerushalayim" (The Cross in Jerusalem), *Ha-Poel ha-Tzair,* June 4, 1924; idem "Alei karka kan."

32. Greenberg, "El ever Moskva" (Toward Moscow), *Kuntres,* 19 Shvat 1924.

33. Yosef Molkho, "24 shaot" (24 Hours), *Kuntres,* 17 Adar I, 1924.

34. U. Z. Greenberg, "Histaklut be-tokheinu" (Looking Within Ourselves), *Kuntres,* 15 Elul, 1925.

35. Idem, "Yerushalayim shel mata." A similar version also appears in his *Eima gedola ve-yare'ah* (Great terror and a moon) (Tel Aviv, 1925), 51. My thanks to Chanita Goodblatt for her translation of the poem into English.

36. Idem, "Yerushalayim shel mata."

37. Idem, "Histaklut be-tokheinu."

38. Ibid.

39. Idem, "Mi-sifrei ha-gavrut ha-ola" (From the Books of the Mounting Masculinity), *Ha-Poel ha-Tzair,* January 7, 1926.

40. Idem, "Mi-sifrei Tur Malka" (From the Books of Tur Malka), *Ha-Poel ha-Tzair,* February 20, 1925.

41. Idem, "Li-tfisat ha-matzav etzleinu" (Understanding Our Situation), *Davar,* July 9, 1926.

42. Idem, "Histaklut be-tokheinu."

43. Idem, "Eima gedola ve-yare'ah," pt. B, *Kuntres,* 5 Shvat, 1924.

44. Idem, "Alei karka kan."

45. See, e.g., Greenberg, "Eima gedola ve-yare'ah" loc. cit.; "If an Arab meets him, he will stab him" and "A bedouin will come to slaughter me by the light of the crescent on the wall" ("Yerushalayim shel mata").

46. U. Z. Greenberg [Yosef Molkho, pseud.], "Ha-lahag negdeinu" (Talk Against Us), *Kuntres,* 19 Shvat, 1924. See also Greenberg, "Le-verur svara ahat matmedet" (Clarifying One Steadfast Notion), *Davar,* June 17, 1925.

47. Idem, "Ha-lahag"; idem, "Alei karka kan."

48. Idem, "Ha-lahag."

49. Idem, "Yerushalayim shel mata." There is another reference to the Mosque of Omar as a threatening edifice in Greenberg's "Eima gedola ve-yare'ah" (pt. B).

50. Idem, "Alei karka kan."

51. Idem, "Hazon ahad la-ligyonot" (Vision of One of the Legions), in his *Anakreon al kotev ha-itzavon* (Anacreon on the Pole of Melancholy) (Tel Aviv, 1928), 23.

52. Idem, "Le-verur svara ahat." See also M. Beilinson, "La-vikuah bi-dvar ha-yehasim bein ha-Aravim ve-ha-Yehudim" (On the Debate Regarding Jewish–Arab Relations), *Kuntres,* 25 Tammuz, 1925.

53. U. Z. Greenberg, "Shomer, ma mi-lel?" (Guardsman, What's New?), *Davar,* December 18, 1925 and January 17, 1926; Moshe Beilinson [M. B., pseud.], "Ha-derekh ha-arukha" (The Long Road), *Davar,* January 1, 1926.

54. "It would be right to grab with mournful hands the thread of fire issuing from the great body of Y. H. Brenner, slaughtered by Arabs. It is only proper to listen not to political sophistry, but, rather, to the cry of Louidor's body, stolen by Arabs and not given back to us, even as a *fatality*" (Greenberg, "Shomer, ma mi-lel?").

55. Beilinson, "Ha-derekh ha-aruka."

56. Greenberg, "Shomer, ma mi-lel?"

57. Beilinson, "Ha-derekh ha-aruka"; Greenberg, "Shomer, ma mi-lel?"; idem, "Le-ma'an diktatura ruhanit" (In Favor of a Spiritual Dictatorship), *Kuntres,* 25 Elul, 1925.

58. Greenberg, "Shomer, ma mi-lel?" For a further example of Greenberg's opposition to a joint union, see the exchange of letters between him and David Cohen in *Davar,* October 3, 17, and 26, 1927.

59. Idem, "Le-verur svara ahat."

60. These ideas reappear frequently. See, e.g., Greenberg, "Le-ma'an diktatura ruhanit"; idem, "Me'ein tazkir le-*Davar*"; idem, "Le-verur svara ahat."

61. Idem, "Kefitzat ha-derekh" (Shortcut), *Ha-Poel ha-Tzair,* October 12, 1924.

62. Ibid.

63. Idem, "Shomer, ma mi-lel?"

64. Idem, "Min ha-meshuka u-min ha-oleh" (From the Sunken and the Rising), *Davar,* July 19, 1926.

65. Idem, "Mi-megilat ha-yamim ha-hem" (From the Scroll of Past Days), *Davar,* December 24, 1926.

66. Idem, "Hazon ahad ha-ligyonot," 21.

67. The quote is from his "Mi-megilat ha-yamim ha-hem," *Davar,* April 1, 1927. He refers to his disappointment with the people in "Hazon ahad ha-ligyonot," 9.

68. Idem, "Mi-megilat ha-yamim ha-hem," *Davar*, December 24, 1926.

69. This is a reconstruction by the author of Greenberg's views, based on his entire work in that period, with special emphasis on "Mi-megilat ha-yamim," *Davar*, December 24, 1926.

70. As an example of the shift, see Greenberg, "Mikhtav galuy le-ma'arekhet *Davar*" (Open Letter to the Editorial Board of *Davar*), *Davar*, October 3, 1927.

71. H. Yeivin, "Uri Zvi Greenberg," *Davar* (suppl.), December 4, 1925.

72. N. Benari, "I-havana" (A Misunderstanding), *Kuntres*, 19 Shevat 1924; Y. Yatziv, "Sadna de-ar'a" (The Base of the World), *Kuntres*, 24 Adar, 1925; A. Broides, "Shurot" (Lines), *Kuntres*, 26 Tammuz, 1926.

73. Gershon Hanoch, "Al dorshei he-hazon" (On Those Who Demand a Vision), *Ha-Poel ha-Tzair*, May 20, 1927.

74. See Anita Shapira, "'Black Night–White Snow': Attitudes of the Palestinian Labor Movement to the Russian Revolution, 1917–1929," *Studies in Contemporary Jewry* 4(1988): 144–71. Idem, "Labor Zionism and the October Revolution," *Journal of Contemporary History* 24(1989): 623–56.

75. U. Z. Greenberg, "Mi-megilat ha-yamim ha-hem," *Davar*, December 24, 1926; on the topic of the "revolutionary thrust" or the reluctance by members of the Labor movement to abandon the shortcut, see, e.g., the dispute between Beilinson and Benari: M. Beilinson, "Bein ha-shmashot" (Between the Panes), in *Yalkut Ahdut ha-Avoda*, 2:272–73. For the connection between "pure politics" and "pure revolutionarism," see Beilinson, "S'hufei ha-mediniyut ha-zrufa" (Proponents of Pure Policy), in *Yalkut Ahdut ha-Avoda*, vol. 2:376.

76. Katznelson, "Hamesh shnot netzivut," appeared *Davar*, June 25, 1925; Ben Gurion, "La-din ve-heshbon shel Samuel," *Kuntres*, Tamuz 17, 1925. The Hibbat Zion (Love of Zion) movement, as will be recalled, was the progenitor of the First Aliyah.

77. Hanoch, "Al dorshei he-hazon."

78. MR'I [pseud.], "Pelagot be-Yisrael" (Divisions in Israel), *Davar*, November 1, 1928.

79. Z. Jabotinsky, "Shorshei ha-mashber" (Roots of the Crisis), in his *Ne'umim, 1905–1926*, 322–23.

80. Idem to O. Grusenberg, December 1, 1927, *Mikhtavim* (Letters) (Tel Aviv, n.d.), 85.

81. Idem, "Pitron ha-be'ayot—rak be-shitot mediniyot" (Solution to the Problems—Only by Political Means), in his *Ne'umim, 1905–1926*, 270–91; Idem, "Yesodot rishonim ba-programa ha-revizionistit" (First Principles of the Revisionist Program), in his *Ne'umim, 1905–1926*, 253–57.

82. Idem, "Al kir ha-barzel" (On the Iron Wall), in his *Ba-derekh li-medina* (On the Road to Statehood) (Jerusalem, 1953), 253.

83. Idem, "Aharei hakamat he'il ha-sefar" (After the Establishment of the Border Patrol), in his *Ne'umim, 1905–1926*, 303.

84. Ibid., 296–97.

85. Jabotinsky, "Al kir ha-barzel," in his *Ba-derekh li-medina*, 254–55. The piece is here dated to 1933; but in H. Ben Yeruham, ed., *Sefer Betar: Korot u-mekorot* (Betar's Book: Events and Sources), vol. 1 (Jerusalem, 1969), 154, it is stated that the article was first published in German in 1923 in the periodical *Menorah*.

86. According to Y. Porath, the mid-1920s were years of great weakness in the Palestinian National movement, which recovered only toward the end of the decade under the leadership of Amin al-Husayni (*Emergence of the Palestinian–Arab National Movement*, 241–57).

87. Jabotinsky, "Al kir ha-barzel," 255–60.

88. Z. Jabotinsky, "Yesodot rishonim ba-programa ha-revizionistit," 255–57.

89. Ibid.

90. Jabotinsky, *Shimshon* (Jerusalem, 1950), 305–9.

91. Jabotinsky, "Yesodot risonim ba-programa ha-revizionistit," 254–57.

92. Jabotinsky, "Megilat ha-Gedud" (The Legion Scroll), in his *Autobiografia* (Auto-biography) (Jerusalem, 1947), 204–6.

93. See leaflet by the central command of Betar in Palestine for youth, "Yud-alef be-Adar" (11 Adar), 1928, in *Sefer Betar,* ed. H. Ben-Yeruham, 1:43.

94. On this, see Ben-Yeruham, ed., *Sefer Betar,* 1:136–39.

95. See the article by Yaacov Shavit, "Bein Pilsudski le-Mickiewicz: Meshihiyut u-med-iniyut ba-revizionizm ha-tziyoni" (From Pilsudski to Mickiewicz: Messianism and Politics in Zionist Revisionism), in his *Ha-mitologiyot shel ha-yamin,* 15–62.

96. Jabotinsky, "Shir Betar" (Betar Hymn), in his *Shirim* (Poems), (Jerusalem, 1947), 205–6.

97. Z. Jabotinsky to Yeshayahu Klinov, October 22, 1929, *Mikhtavim* (Letters), 268–69.

98. Quoted in Rachel Katznelson, "Gvulot" (Boundaries), in *Yalkut Ahdut ha-Avoda,* 2:366.

99. Lectures by Jabotinsky to Youth, Eden Theater, Tel Aviv, October 31, 1926, in *Sefer Betar,* ed. H. Ben-Yeruham 1:525–28.

100. M. Beilinson, "Hinuch la-noar" (Education for Youth), in *Yalkut Ahdut ha-Avoda,* 2:233.

101. Arthur Ruppin, *Pirkei hayai* (Chapters of My Life), vol. 3 (Tel Aviv, 1968), 96. An English edition of Ruppin's diaries is Alex Bein, ed., *Arthur Ruppin: Memoirs, Diaries, Letters* (New York, 1971) (hereafter *Ruppin Diaries*). The entry quoted here is not included in the English edition.

102. Nathan Hofshi, *Be-lev va-nefesh* (In Heart and Soul) (Tel Aviv, 1965), 43–44.

103. Arthur Ruppin to Hans Kohn, May 30, 1928, in his *Pirkei hayai,* 3:149. See also *Ruppin Diaries,* 237.

104. *Ruppin Diaries,* April 13, 1923, p. 61.

105. Ibid.; see also April 29, 1923, p. 208.

106. Hugo Bergmann, "Le-verur" (Clarification), *Davar,* August 7, 1925.

107. See S. Schiller, "Ha-medina ha-yehudit ve-ha-bayit ha-leumi ha-ivri" (The Jewish State and the Jewish National Home), *Ha-Poel ha-Tzair,* June 12, 1925; Hans Kohn, "Politika aravit" (Arab Politics), *Ha-Poel ha-Tzair,* June 3, 1926; "Li-dmuta ha-politit shel Eretz Yisrael" (The Political Image of Palestine), *Ha-Poel ha-Tzair,* July 2, 9, and 16, 1926.

108. Gershom Scholem, "Li-ve'ayat ha-parlament" (On the Problem of the Parliament), in *Od davar* (Explications and Implications), vol. 2, ed. Avraham Shapira (Tel Aviv, 1989), 63–67.

109. On his experience in Beirut, see Sprinzak to Robert Weltsch, 17 Tevet, 1930, *Igrot* (Letters) (Tel Aviv, 1969), 2:24.

110. Schiller, "Ha-medina ha-yehudit."

111. *Ruppin Diaries,* April 29, 1923, pp. 207–8; October 30, 1923, p. 211.

112. Hugo Bergmann, "Nedaber gluyot!" (Let's Speak Frankly!), *Davar,* July 2, 1925.

113. Idem, "Ba-derekh le-heskem" (On the Way to an Accord), *Ha-Poel ha-Tzair,* November 11, 1929; idem, "Li-she'elat ha-rov" (On the Question of the Majority), *She'ifoteinu,* Tevet 1929.

114. Idem, "Li-she'elat ha-rov."

115. *Ruppin Diaries,* 207–8, 211. On their misgivings about British imperialism, see also Hugo Bergmann [H.B., pseud.], "Darkei shalom" (Ways of Peace), *Davar,* June 23, 1925.

116. Hans Kohn, "Li-dmuta ha-politit shel Eretz Yisrael," *Ha-Poel ha-Tzair,* July 2 and 16, 1926.

117. Bergmann, "Le-verur"; Scholem, "Li-ve'ayat ha-parlament," 63–64.

118. Scholem, "Li-ve'ayat ha-parlament," 67. See also Hans Kohn, "Martin Buber ve-hat–ziyonut mi-zman ha-milhama va-eilakh" (Martin Buber and Zionism from the War Period Onward), *Ha-Poel ha-Tzair,* April 24, 1929; Bergmann, "Li-she'elat ha-rov."

119. Ibid.

120. *Ruppin Diaries,* May 25, 1928, p. 236.

121. Ibid., Ruppin to Hans Kohn, May 30, 1928, pp. 237–238.

122. Bergmann, "Nedaber gluyot!," *Davar,* July 13, 1925.

123. M. Beilinson, "Mi-pirsumeha ha-rishonim shel Brit Shalom" (From the First Publications by Brit Shalom), in *Yalkut Ahdut ha-Avoda,* 2:400–403.

124. Moshe Beilinson [M.B., pseud.], "Shmira" (Guardship), *Davar,* June 29, 1928.

125. Yitzhak Schweiger, "Al ha-be'erot she-lo yur'alu" (In Order that the Wells Won't Be Poisoned), *Davar,* September 21, 1928.

126. Haim Margolis-Kalvaryski, "Mikhtav galuy le-aheinu ha-muslemim" (Open Letter to Our Muslim Brothers), *Davar,* October 29, 1928.

127. Reply by "Al-Jamiah" to Kalvaryski, *Davar,* October 30, 1928.

128. M. Beilinson, "Al ha-hasbara—drakheha u-gvuloteha" (On Propaganda—its Ways and Limits), *Davar,* November 1, 1928.

Chapter 5

1. Minutes, 23d Histadrut Council, LA, 207 IV, quoted by A. Shapira, *Ha-ma'avak ha-nikhzav* (Futile Struggle) (Tel Aviv, 1977), 55.

2. Y. H. Yeivin, *Al har ga'ash anahnu* (We're Sitting on a Volcano), *Doar ha-Yom,* September 6, 1929.

3. A description of the disturbances is presented in detail in Dinur, et al., *Sefer toldot ha-Hagana,* 2:312–40. The political developments surrounding them in the Arab community are discussed in Y. Porath, *The Palestinian–Arab National Movement: From Riots to Rebellion, 1929–1939* (London, 1977), 1–39. The slogans are cited by Abraham Schwadron, "Yesodei ha-ideologiya shel Brit Shalom" (Foundations of the Ideology of Brit Shalom), in his *Hashkafat ha-tziyonut ha-integralit* (Integral Zionist Outlook) (Jerusalem, 1931), 49.

4. David Ben Gurion, "Al bithon ha-Yishuv u-vitzrono" (On the Security of the Yishuv and Its Strengthening), in his *Anahnu u-shekheneinu* (We and Our Neighbors) (Tel Aviv, 1931), 173.

5. Arthur Ruppin, Jerusalem, December 31, 1933, in his *Pirkei hayai,* 225–26. See also Alex Bein, ed., *Arthur Ruppin: Memoirs, Diaries, Letters* (New York, 1971) (hereafter *Ruppin Diaries), 266.*

6. Public statement of the executive committee of Ahdut ha-Avoda and Ha-Poel ha-Tzair, September 20, 1929.

7. David Ben Gurion, "Darkenu ha-medinit le-ahar ha-me'ora'ot" (Our Political Path after the Riots), in his *Anahanu u-Shekheneinu,* 213.

8. A. Schwadron, op. cit., 50.

9. David Ben Gurion, "Al bithon ha-Yishuv," 173.

10. On this matter, Ruppin already had written on November 3, 1921, "Pogroms smother the enthusiasm and volunteering abroad and undermine the basis of our work

today" (*Pirkei hayai*, 3:26). On December 31, 1930, he wrote, "It should be noted that due to the deterioration in our political situation and as a result of the world economic crisis, world Jewry has no desire to invest money in Palestine or to contribute to Zionist funds" (ibid., 195; see also *Ruppin Diaries*, 255).

11. The poem "Kadru, kadru, pnei ha-shamayim" (The Sky Darkened, Darkened) by Yehoshua Prushansky, an immigrant of the Third Aliyah, was written under the inspiration of Tel Hai. My gratitude to Eliyahu Ha-Cohen for this information.

12. Moshe Beilinson, "Le-heshbonam shel ha-meora'ot" (On the Riots), *Davar*, October 11, 1929, *Bi-yemei masa* (Days of Trial) (Tel Aviv, n.d.), 45.

13. Ibid., 46.

14. On this matter, see David Ben Gurion, "Al bithon ha-Yishuv," 174–76. See also A. Shapira, *Ha-ma'avak ha-nikhzav*, 56.

15. "In the City of Slaughter," *Ha-Aretz*, September 1, 1929; see also *Ha-Aretz*, September 2, 3, and 4, 1929.

16. *Davar*, August 30, 1929.

17. *Doar ha-Yom*, September 2, 3, and 6, 1929.

18. *Ha-Aretz*, September 4, 1929.

19. Moshe Beilinson, "Teshuvatenu ha-amitit" (Our True Response), *Davar*, September 4, 1929.

20. "Bi-zekhut ha-hagana ha-atzmit" (In Favor of Self-Defense), *Doar ha-Yom*, September 6, 1929.

21. U. Z. Greenberg, "Ezor magen u-neum ben ha-dam" (Defense Zone and Speech of the Son of Blood), in his *Be-emtza ha-olam u-ve-emtza ha-zemanim*, 112–13.

22. Chaim Bograshov, "Mishpat ha-hagana" (Trial of the Hagana), *Ha-Aretz*, September 10, 1929.

23. Schwadron, op. cit., 49.

24. Yitzhak Ben Zvi, "Le-zikhron yom Tel Hai" (On the Memory of Tel Hai Day), *Ha-Poel ha-Tzair*, March 14, 1930.

25. Yaakov Eshed, "Li-she'elat ha-hagana ha-atzmit" (On the Question of Self-Defense), *Mi-Bifnim*, October 1929.

26. Details on the disturbances and their supression can be found in Dinur, et al., *Sefer toldot ha-Hagana*, 2, 312–413.

27. Yigal Allon, *My Father's House* (New York, 1976), 164–65; Shosh Spektor, interview with the author.

28. Ahad Ha-Am, letter to the editor of *Ha-Aretz*, September 1, 1922, in *Kol kitvei* (Complete Works) (Tel Aviv, 1961), 462. My thanks to Shulamit Laskov for calling this letter to my attention.

29. *Ruppin Diaries*, October 17, 1929, p. 247.

30. Eshed, "Li-she'elat ha-hagana ha-atzmit."

31. For example, Yaakov Eshed (ibid.) juxtaposed the militarism of Betar to the self-defense of the pioneers.

32. Moshe Beilinson, "Mi hu ha-oyev?" (Who's the Enemy?), in his *Bi-yemei masa*, 27.

33. Ahdut ha-Avoda and Ha-Poel ha-Tzair, public statement, *Ha-Poel ha-Tzair*, September 20, 1929. See also Eliyahu Golomb, *Hevyon oz*, vol. 2 (Tel Aviv, 1953), 29–30.

34. Ahdut ha-Avoda and Ha-Poel ha-Tzair, public statement.

35. David Shimonovitz, "Al sefod" (Do Not Mourn), *Ha-Poel ha-Tzair*, May 13, 1921.

36. David Shimonovitz, "Eretz Yisrael" (Palestine), *Ha-Aretz*, October 4, 1929. My thanks to Eliyahu Ha-Cohen for this reference.

37. Yitzhak Laufbahn, "Mi-tokh ha-mevukha" (In Confusion), *Ha-Poel ha-Tzair*, September 20, 1929.

38. Yitzhak Tabenkin, "Od le-ota she'ela" (On the Same Question), *Mi-Bifnim,* March 1930.

39. Eshed, "Li-she'elat ha-hagana ha-atzmit."

40. Tabenkin, "Od le-ota she'ela."

41. The lullaby "Shekhav beni, shekhav bi-menuha" (Lie My Son, Lie in Slumber), by Emanuel Ha-Russi, was written around the time of the 1929 disturbances, and had its debut in 1931. I am grateful to Eliyahu Ha-Cohen for this information.

42. On caution in expression, see the dispute between Berl Katznelson and David Shimonovitz on the hatred poetry of Aharon Ha-Reuveni—cited in Gorny, *Zionism and the Arabs,* 208.

43. Y. H. Yeivin, "Be-shulei ha-ason" (In the Aftermath of the Disaster), *Doar ha-Yom,* October 18, 1929.

44. See, e.g., *Davar,* August 30 and September 3, 8, and 10, 1929.

45. See comments on these distinctions in Laufbahn, "Be-tokh ha-mevukha"; Beilinson, "Le-heshbonam shel ha-me'ora'ot," 46.

46. Ahdut ha-Avoda and Ha-Poel ha-Tzair, public statement, *Ha-Poel ha-Tzair,* September 20, 1929.

47. On the aspects of mendacity and willingness to accept bribes, see Ben Gurion, Minutes, Meeting on the Topic of the Arab Question, October 10–11, 1929, Joint Secretariat, Ahdut ha-Avoda and ha-Poel ha-Tzair, BB, file 1/1. "Gang of rulers" was used by Berl Katznelson during a debate in the joint meetings of the central committees of Ahdut ha-Avoda and Ha-Poel ha-Tzair, November 24–25, 1929. The matter of corruption and land sales was raised by him in "Li-she'elot ha-mishtar ha-medini ba-aretz" (Questions of the Political Regime in Palestine), *Ahdut ha-Avoda* (Tel Aviv), January–February 1931, p. 213. On the matter of George Nasir, Katznelson, in response to an interpolation, said, "I can bring George Nasir to any framework." On corruption of the effendis in the municipalities, see the meeting of the Mapai secretariat with representatives of the colonies, July 31, 1930, LA, sec. IV Berl Katznelson, file 16. On criticism of Arabs who imitate European culture, see Beilinson, "Le-heshbonam shel ha-me'ora'ot," 52.

48. Minutes of the meeting on the Arab question, October 10–11, 1929, Joint Secretariat, Ahdut ha-Avoda and Ha-Poel ha-Tzair, *Bulletin* no. 1 (October 1929), BB, file 1/1.

49. David Ben Gurion, "Yehasim im shekheneinu" (Relations with Our Neighbors), in his *Anahnu u-shekheneinu,* 61.

50. Berl Katznelson, "Al inyanei ha-sha'a" (On Matters of the Time), in his *Ketavim,* vol. 4 (Tel Aviv, 1946), 288. The source is a meeting of the Mapai secretariat with representatives of the colonies, July 31, 1930, LA, sec. IV Berl Katznelson, file 16.

51. Beilinson, "Le-heshbonam shel ha-me'ora'ot," p. 38; Berl Katznelson, "Bi-ve'idat Poalei Tzion be-Germania" (At the Convention of Poalei Zion in Germany), in his *Ketavim,* 4:105.

52. Debates in the joint session of the central committees of Ha-Poel ha-Tzair and Ahdut ha-Avoda, November 24–25, 1929, BB, file 1/1.

53. Ibid.

54. Berl Katznelson, "Bi-ve'idat Poalei Tzion be-Germania."

55. Ibid., 106.

56. Meeting of Mapai secretariat with representatives of the colonies, July 31, 1930, LA, sec. IV Berl Katznelson, file 16.

57. M. Beilinson, "Le-heshbonam," *Davar,* October 20, 1929, *Bi-yemei masa,* 60.

58. Ibid., 70.

59. About a year after that, Israel Meriminsky, in a meeting of the Mapai Central Committee, noted "In my view, the answer given particularly by Beilinson—'to the entire Jewish

people and to the neighbor [the Arabs] in Palestine'—saved our youth, since that question was on the agenda" Minutes, Mapai Central Committee, December 22, 1930, BB, file 23/30.

60. See, e.g., comments by Hugo Bergmann, quoted in *She'ifoteinu* 4(1930). See also "Tokhnit Brit Shalom" (Program of Brit Shalom) in the same issue.

61. Ernst Simon, "Neum she-lo ne'emar ba-kongres" (Speech Not Given at the Congress), *She'ifoteinu* 2(Summer 1931). See also Beilinson's previous comments on that position, "Le-lo tohelet," (Uselessly), *Davar,* August 13, 1930. See also the interview with Samuel Samborsky, who talks explicitly about a plan in existence then to restrict immigration, in *Iton 77,* January–February 1990, 29–30.

62. Avraham Katznelson, "Li-she'elat he-atid" (On the Question of the Future), *Ha-Poel ha-Tzair,* October 4, 1929.

63. Minutes of a meeting on the Arab question, October 10–11, 1929, Joint Secretariat, Ahdut ha-Avoda and Ha-Poel ha-Tzair, *Bulletin,* no. 1 (October 1929), BB, file 1/1. An analysis of Ben Gurion's position during that period can be found in Shabtai Teveth, *Ben Gurion and the Palestinian Arabs: From Peace to War* (Oxford, 1985), 75–117.

64. See Arlosoroff, "Me'ora'ot Mai" (May Riots), in his *Ketavim* (Collected Writings), vol. 1 (Tel Aviv, 1934), 5–11.

65. On British policy during this era, see Y. Porath, *From Riots to Rebellion;* Dinur et al., *Sefer toldot ha-Hagana,* 2:401–13, 437–72; Gabriel Sheffer, "Intentions and Results of British Policy in Palestine: Passfield White Paper," *Middle Eastern Studies* 9(1973):43–60; idem, "Tadmit ha-Palestinaim ve-ha-Yishuv ke-gorem be-itzuv ha-mediniyut ha-britit bi-shenot ha-sheloshim" (The Image of the Palestinians and the Yishuv as a Factor in Shaping British Policy in the 1930s), *Ha-Tziyonut* 3(1973): 273–94; idem, "Me'atzvei ha-mediniyut ha-mandatorit: Stereotipim o basar va-dam?" (Makers of Mandatory Policy: Stereotypes or Flesh and Blood?), *Keshet* 48(1971): 167–78.

66. Ben Gurion, "Hanahot li-keviat mishtar mamlakhti be-Eretz Yisrael" (Assumptions on the Establishment of a Political Regime in Palestine), in his *Anahnu u-shekheneinu,* 185–96. See the detailed account of this episode in Teveth, *Ben Gurion and the Arabs,* 157–74.

67. Debates in the joint sessions of the Central Committees of Ahdut ha-Avoda and Ha-Poel ha-Tzair, in *Bulletin Mapai,* June 23, 1930; on Katznelson's plan, see his "Li-she'elat ha-mishtar." On the discussion in Mapai about this question, see Shapira, *Berl,* 180–82 (discussed in greater detail in the Hebrew edition of *Berl* [Tel Aviv, 1980], 322–33); Teveth, *Ben Gurion.*

68. Moshe Beilinson, "Ha-zekhuyot al ha-aretz" (Rights to Palestine), in his *Bi-yemei masa,* 111; Ben Gurion, "Darkeinu ha-medinit le-ahar ha-me'ora'ot" (Our Political Path after the Riots), in his *Anahnu u-shekheneinu,* 231.

69. Minutes, Central Committee, Mapai, December 22, 1930, BB, file 23/30.

70. See Shapira, *Berl,* 170–71; Arthur Ruppin, December 31, 1928, in his *Pirke hayai,* 3:165; see *Ruppin Diaries,* 243. See also Y. Laufbahn, "He'ara" (Note), *Ha-Poel ha-Tzair,* October 18, 1929; idem, "Zikhron kedoshei Ab" (In Memory of the Martyrs of Ab), *She'ifoteinu,* Ab–Elul 1932, pp. 146–47.

71. Arthur Ruppin, February 23, 1929, in his *Pirkei hayai,* 3:166; *She'ifoteinu,* Tammuz 1932. See also Ben Gurion, "Ha-mediniyut ha-tziyonit me-aharei ha-me'ora'ot" (Zionist Policy After the Riots), *Ha-Poel ha-Tzair,* December 5, 1930.

72. Shapira, *Berl,* 180–82.

73. Members of Brit Shalom recognized the enormous change in the Mapai position represented by the parity plan; see Gershom Scholem, "Be-mai ka mifalgei?" (What Are We Disagreeing About?), in *Od Davar,* 75.

74. The formula this time stated, "Continuous immigration and settlement and renewal

of full national existence in Palestine, with all features of normal national life" (*Ha-Olam,* July 21, 1931).

75. Gershom Scholem, "Ha-matara ha-sofit" (The Final Goal), in his *Od Davar,* 69.

76. Abba Ahimeir, "Ha-tzorekh be-hinukh medini" (The Need for Political Education), in his *Brit ha-Biryonim* (Covenant of the Biryonim) (Tel Aviv, 1972), 74.

77. Idem, "Betar ki-tefisat olam" (Betar as a World View), in his *Ha-Tziyonut ha-mahapkhanit* (Revolutionary Zionism) (Tel Aviv, 1966), 24.

78. Idem, "Davar el ha-noar ha-tziyoni" (Speech to Zionist Youth), *Ha-Tziyonut ha-mahapkhanit,* 43; idem, "Ha-shalav ha-shelishi" (The Third Stage), *Ha-Tziyonut ha-mahapkhanit,* 13–14.

79. Idem, "Ha-tzorekh be-hinukh medini," in his *Brit ha-Biryonim,* 74; on Ahimeir's repeated attacks on the "vegetarians," see S. Yehuda'i to the editors of *Davar,* November 5, 1928.

80. Abba Ahimeir, "Torat externikim" (Teaching of Externees), in his *Brit ha-Biryonim,* 77.

81. Idem, "Ha-shalav ha-shelishi," in his *Ha-Tziyonut ha-mahapkhanit,* 12–14; idem, "Halutzei ha-Tziyonut ha-mithadeshet" (Pioneers of Renewed Zionism), in his *Brit ha-Biryonim,* 89–90; idem, "Giborim ve-lo kedoshim" (Heroes, Not Martyrs), in his *Ha-Tziyonut ha-mahapkhanit,* 98.

82. Idem, "Itonenu" (Our paper), in his *Ha-Tziyonut ha-mahapkhanit,* 53–57.

83. Ibid.

84. Idem, "Lo ki-venei kushiyim" (Not Like Children of the Ethiopians), in his *Ha-Tziyonut ha-mahapkhanit,* 25.

85. Ibid.

86. Idem, "Ha-teki'ah ha-gedola" (The Great Blast), in his *Ha-Tziyonut ha-mahapkhanit,* 67.

87. Idem, "Zvirko," in his *Ha-Tziyonut ha-mahapkhanit,* 61–63.

88. Idem, "Alcazar ve-havlaga" (Alcazar and Self-Restraint), in his *Ha-Tziyonut ha-mahapkhanit,* 111. Alcazar was the besieged fortress in Toledo that became the symbol of fascist resistance.

89. Idem, "Halutzei ha-Tziyonut ha-mithadeshet" in his *Brit ha-Biryonim,* 90.

90. See, e.g., Abba Ahimeir, "Torat externikim" and "Halutzei ha-Tziyonut ha-mithadeshet"—both in his *Brit ha-Biryonim,* 75–79, 88–90; see also Yosef Nedava, Introduction to Ahimeir's *Brit ha-Biryonim,* xviii.

91. Quoted by Nedava, Introduction, xi.

92. Abba Ahimeir, "Megilat sikarikin" (Scroll of the Sicarii), in his *Brit ha-Biryonim,* 217.

93. Ibid., 218.

94. Ibid., 219.

95. See Nedava, Introduction, liv–lvi.

96. *Hazit ha-Am,* August 9, 1932; quoted by Nedava, Introduction, xxxix.

97. Abba Ahimeir, "Alcazar ve-havlaga," 110.

98. Nedava, Introduction, xl.

99. Abba Ahimeir, "Alcazar ve-havlaga," *Doar ha-Yom,* October 14, 1928, quoted by Nedava, Introduction, x.

100. Abba Ahimeir, "Davar el ha-noar ha-tziyoni," 42; see also his "Alcazar ve-havlaga," 110.

101. Nedava, Introduction, xxxvi.

102. Ibid., xxxv.

103. Abba Ahimeir, "Alcazar ve-havlaga," 110.

104. Idem, "Ha-biryon" (The Hooligan), in his *Brit ha-Biryonim,* 228–29.

105. U. Z. Greenberg, "Ezor Magen" in his *Be-emtza ha-olam,* 114–19.

106. Y. H. Yeivin, *Yerushalayim mehaka* (Jerusalem Is Waiting), 2d ed. (Jerusalem, 1939).

107. U. Z. Greenberg, "Neum ben ha-dam / Kategoriya" (Speech of the Son of Blood / an Accusation), in his *Be-Emtza ha-olam,* 119.

108. The epithets and metaphors are taken from a leaflet, *"Ha-Biryon,"* included in his *Brit ha-Biryonim,* 227–29.

109. See Nedava, Introduction, xxxv and n.

110. For a description of the actions of Brit ha-Biryonim and the ideology of Ahimeir, see Nedava, Introduction *Brit ha-Biryonim.*

111. There is a copious literature on the murder of Arlosoroff. Two recent works are of interest: Shabtai Teveth, *Retzah Arlosoroff* (Arlosoroff's Murder) (Jerusalem, 1982) and H. Ben-Yeruham, *Ha-alila ha-gedola* (The Great Libel) (Tel Aviv, 1982); see also Ahimeir, *Ha-mishpat* (The Trial) (Tel Aviv, 1968).

112. See Nedava, Introduction, xxxvi–xxxvii; on Jabotinsky's position, see pp. xxxvii–xxxviii.

113. There is a voluminous literature on Jabotinsky and his movement. See the biography by Yosef Schechtman, *Zeev Jabotinsky,* 3 vols. (Tel Aviv, 1956–59). Volume 2 deals in detail with this episode. See also Nedava, Introduction, xxxvi–liii. The most important book on Jabotinsky and the Revisionist movement is Yaacov Shavit, *Jabotinsky and the Revisionist Movement, 1925–1948* (London, 1988).

114. See Anita Shapira, "Labor Zionism and the October Revolution," *Journal of Contemporary History* 24 (1989); 623–56.

115. A detailed analysis of this issue can be found in Anita Shapira, "The Debate in Mapai on the Use of Violence, 1932–1935," *Zionism* 3(April 1981):99–124.

116. See Dinur et al., *Sefer toldot ha-Hagana,* 2:251–53; Shlomo Nakdimon and Shaul Meizlish, *De-Haan: Ha-retzah ha-politi ha-rishon be-Eretz Yisrael* (De Haan: The First Political Assassination in Palestine) (Tel Aviv, 1985).

117. See Shapira, *Berl,* 188–94.

118. *Ruppin Diaries,* December 3, 1931, p. 258; on February 21, 1931, Ruppin wrote in his diary, "We are not offered what we need, and what we are offered is of no use to us," *Ruppin Diaries,* 255.

119. *Ruppin Diaries,* February 4, 1932, p. 259.

120. Chaim Arlosoroff to Chaim Weizmann, June 30, 1932, in his *Yoman Yerushalayim* (Jerusalem Diary) (Tel Aviv, 1949), 334.

121. Ibid., 337–342.

122. Ibid., 342.

123. See Ben Gurion, *Pegishot im manhigim arvim* (Meetings with Arab Leaders) (Tel Aviv, 1967), 18–60. For a detailed discussion of this episode, see Teveth, *Ben Gurion and the Palestinian Arabs,* 129–48.

124. Protocol of Mapai Central Committee, April 16, 1936, BB, file 23/36.

125. Arthur Ruppin, May 29, 1931, in his *Pirkei hayai,* 3:199; December 31, 1931, in his *Pirkei hayai,* 3:205 (*Ruppin Diaries,* 259).

126. *Ruppin Diaries,* December 31, 1933, pp. 265–66.

127. *Ruppin Diaries* April 30, 1934, p. 266.

128. Editorial, *She'ifoteinu,* Nisan 1932.

129. On developments in the Hagana in the early 1930s, see Dinur et al., *Sefer toldot ha-Hagana,* 2:510–604.

130. Nathan Alterman's "Shir boker la-moledet" (Morning Song to the Homeland),

written in 1934 for the film *Hayim hadashim* (New life), was set to music by Daniel Sambursky. I wish to thank Eliyahu Ha-Cohen for this information.

131. Nathan Alterman's "Shir ha-emek" (Song of the Valley), written for the film *Hayim hadashim* and set to music by Samburksy, was issued in 1934. My thanks to Eliyahu Ha-Cohen for pointing this out.

132. Rachel, "Ve-ulai lo hayu ha-devarim me-olam" (Perhaps It Was Never So), in her *Shirat Rachel* (Poetry of Rachel) (Tel Aviv, 1950), 75; translated by A. C. Jacobs in *Voices Within the Ark: The Modern Jewish Poets,* ed. Howard Schwartz and Anthony Rudolf (New York, 1980), 148.

133. Shaul Tchernichovsky, "Hazon nevi ha-Ashera" (Vision of the Prophet of Eshtar), in his *Shirei Shaul Tchernichovsky* (Poems of Shaul Tchernichovsky) (Tel Aviv, 1968), 92.

134. Tchernichovsky, "Ahavti ki eta ba-kevish" (I Love to Wander), in his *Shirei,* 100.

135. Tchernichovsky, "Shirat ha-shomer" (Song of the Guardsman), in his *Shirei,* 103.

136. Tchernichovsky, "Ba-mishmeret" (On Guard), in his *Shirei,* 103–4.

137. Eliezer Yaffe, "U-le-Yishmael omar!" (And to Ishmael I'll Say!) in his *Ketavim* (Collected Writings), vol. 2 (Tel Aviv, 1947), 32–40; emphasis mine.

138. Gershon Hanokh, "Klapei penim" (Internally), *Ha-Poel ha-Tzair,* September 20, 1929.

Chapter 6

1. On the Arab Rebellion, see Y. Porath, *The Palestinian–Arab National Movement: From Riots to Rebellion, 1929–1939* (London, 1977), 162ff.; Dinur et al., *Sefer toldot ha-Hagana,* 2:631–63; Yuval Arnon-Ohana, *Falahim ba-mered ha-Arvi be-Eretz Yisrael, 1936–1939* (Fellahin in the Arab Rebellion in Palestine, 1936–1939) (Tel Aviv, 1978); John Marlowe, *Rebellion in Palestine* (London, 1946).

2. Porath, op. cit., 159–61.

3. Y. A. [pseud.], "Tamid" (Always), *Mi-Bifnim,* April 1936.

4. Shmuel Gavish, "Mul pnei ha-ma'arakha" (Facing the Battle), *Niv ha-Kvutza,* Iyar 1936.

5. Chaim Ben Asher, "Bi-tekufat herum u-gzerot" (In the Period of Emergency and Decrees), *Mi-Bifnim,* June 1936.

6. Zerubavel [pseud.—Zerubavel Gilad?], "Bi-tznefat ha-yamim" (In the Web of Days), *Mi-Bifnim,* April 1936.

7. Comments by Zerubavel (Gilad?), minutes (1936?) of a discussion in Ha-Noar ha-Oved, LA, sec. 213 IV, file 15.

8. Y.A. [pseud.], "Tamid."

9. A. Bein, ed., *Arthur Ruppin: Memoirs, Diaries, Letters* (New York, 1971) (hereafter *Ruppin Diaries*), April 24, 1936, p. 277.

10. Moshe Zilbertal, "Ha-emet ha-pshuta" (The Simple Truth), *Hedim,* July 1936.

11. The feeling that the clash was inevitable and the need to accept the "decree of destiny" appears between the lines in numerous essays published at the time. See, e.g., Zerubavel [pseud.], "Bi-tznefat ha-yamim"; Shmuel Gavish ("Mul pnei ha-ma'arakha") states, "We certainly did not wish to accept the Arab affair in this meaning as a historical decree." The quote appears on the last page (unnumbered) of Beracha Habas, ed., *Me'ora'ot 1936* (The 1936 Disturbances) (Tel Aviv, 1937).

12. Zilbertal, op. cit.

13. "Le-ehad be-Mai" (On May Day), *Ha-Poel ha-Tzair,* May 1, 1936.

14. The quotes are from Minutes, Mapai Central Committee, May 21, 1936, BB, file 23/36 and November 26, 1936, BB, file 23/36.

15. Verbal quote of Berl Katznelson mentioned by Berl Locker, Minutes, Mapai Central Committee, June 9, 1936, BB, file 23/36.

16. Fanya Bergstein, "Ani ha-bat" (I'm the Daughter), *Me'ora'ot 1936,* ed. Beracha Habas, 521–22. My thanks to Chanita Goodblatt for her assistance in translating the poem.

17. Habas, *Me'ora'ot 1936,* xiii.

18. Habas, *Me'ora'ot 1936.*

19. Berl Katznelson, "El mul pnei ha-ma'arakha" (Confronting the Battle), in *Me'ora'ot 1936,* ed. Beracha Habas, 349; on the "politics of quotation marks," see Katznelson, "Mekadshei ha-herut u-mehalelei kevarim" (Martyrs of Freedom and Desecrators of Tombstones), in *Me'ora'ot 1936,* ed. Beracha Habas, 391–92.

20. Ernst Simon, "Lifnei shnatayim ve-hayom" (Two Years Ago and Today), *Al Parshat Derakheinu* (At Our Crossroads) (Jerusalem), March 1939, pp. 14–15.

21. Moshe Beilinson, remarks at the Inner Zionist Actions Committee, October 14, 1936, in *Me'ora'ot 1936,* ed. Beracha Habas, 416–17.

22. Yitzhak Tabenkin, "Le-hagbarat atzmautenu" (Augmenting Our Independence), *Mi-Bifnim,* June 1936.

23. See, e.g., the remarks of Ben Gurion, "Some of our comrades have a supposition that the entire Arab uprising (they do not admit its existence and qualify it with quotation marks) is nothing but the product of the failure of the [British] officialdom," Letter from London to the Ihud Council in Geneva, August 18, 1936, in his *Zikhronot* (Memoirs), vol. 3 (Tel Aviv, 1976), 385.

24. Tabenkin, "Le-hagbarat atzmautenu."

25. Minutes, Mapai Central Committee, May 21, 1936, BB, file 23/36.

26. Ibid.

27. Moshe Shertok, speech given before Mapai Central Committee, May 21, 1936, in Moshe Sharett, *Yoman medini* (Political Diary), vol. 1 (Tel Aviv, 1976), 124.

28. M. Shertok, speech given before Mapai Central Committee, June 9, 1936, in Sharett, *Yoman medini,* 1:164.

29. David Ben Gurion to Ihud Council, Geneva, August 18, 1936, in his *Zikhronot,* 3:381.

30. Gavish, op. cit.

31. M. Shertok, speech given before Mapai Central Committee, June 9, 1936, in Sharett, *Yoman medini,* 1:159–60. See also Gavish, op. cit.

32. Ben Gurion to Ihud Council, Geneva, August 18, 1936, in his *Zikhronot,* 3:381; for the tendency to criticize the government, see *Ruppin Diaries,* May 16, 1936, p. 278. For a classic example of accusations against the authorities, see comments by B. Katznelson in a session of the Inner Zionist Actions Committee, Jerusalem, June 22, 1936, in *Me'ora'ot 1936,* ed. Beracha Habas, 354–355.

33. Eliyahu Golomb, "Darkenu ba-Hagana" (Our Path in the Hagana), *Ha-Poel ha-Tzair,* September 16, 1938.

34. Minutes, Mapai Central Committee, November 17, 1937, BB, file 23/37.

35. Berl Katznelson, "Mekadshei ha-herut," 392.

36. Yitzhak Tabenkin, "Le-hagbarat atzmautenu," *Mi-Bifnim,* June 1936.

37. Berl Katznelson, "Mekadshei ha-Herut"; on acts of brutality and terror, see "Al ha-mishmar" (On the Guard), in *Me'ora'ot 1936,* ed. Beracha Habas, 345–418.

38. S. Shalom, "Ayekhem, anshei ha-musar ha-gedolim" (Where Are You, Great Men of Morality?), in *Me'ora'ot 1936,* ed. Beracha Habas, 394–95.

39. Y. Porath, *From Riots to Rebellion,* 188.

40. Robert Weltsch, "Al parshat derakheinu" (At the Crossroads), *Al Parshat Derakheinu* (Jerusalem), March 1939.

41. "Le-ehad be-mai!," *Ha-Poel ha-Tzair,* May 1, 1936.

42. Yitzhak Tabenkin, "Ehad be-Mai, 1936" (May Day 1936), in his *Devarim,* vol. 2 (Tel Aviv, 1972), 264.

43. Meir Ya'ari, "Im ha-me'ora'ot" (With the Disturbances), *Ha-Shomer ha-Tzair,* June 1, 1936.

44. Yitzhak Tabenkin, "Ba-ma'arakha" (In the Battle), in a session of the extended secretariat of Ha-Kibbutz ha-Meuhad, December 1936, in his *Devarim,* 2:280.

45. Ibid.

46. See, e.g., Tabenkin, "Le-heshbona shel tekufa" (Summing Up the Period), in his *Devarim,* 2:338–45.

47. Idem, "Ha-masad le-mediniyutenu" (The Foundation of Our Policy), in his *Devarim,* 2:286; idem, "Le-heshbona shel tekufa," in his *Devarim,* 2:338. See also Eliyahu Golomb, "Darkenu ba-Hagana," *Ha-Poel ha-Tzair,* September 16, 1938.

48. Robert Weltsch, "Al parshat derakheinu."

49. Shapira, *Berl,* 273. See also Golomb's use of the word *appeasement* in the Thirty-ninth Histadrut Council, February 27, 1939, included in his *Hevyon oz,* 2:184.

50. For an example of an analysis of the world situation, see *Ruppin Diaries,* January 1, 1938, p. 289; an updated assessment of British policy in Palestine and the question of appeasement policy can be found in Gabriel Sheffer, "Appeasement and the Problem of Palestine," *International Journal of Middle East Studies* 2(1980):377–99.

51. For remarks by Ben Gurion, see A. Shapira, "Bein teror le-havlaga" (Between Terror and Self-Restraint), *Ha-Tziyonut* 6(1981):418; see also the remark by Ussishkin at the gathering of the Zionist parties in Jerusalem, April 19, 1936, quoted by Ben Gurion, *Zikhronot,* 3:123–27.

52. This is the historiographical line pursued in Dinur et al., *Sefer toldot ha-Hagana,* vol. 2 (Tel Aviv, 1963), 798–850.

53. See, e.g., [M. Beilinson], "Devar ha-yom" in *Me'ora'ot 1936,* ed. Beracha Habas, 340–41.

54. Ben Gurion, remarks at gathering of Zionist parties, Jerusalem, April 19, 1936, in his *Zikhronot,* 3:128–29.

55. Idem, letter to Ihud Council, Geneva, from London, August 18, 1936, in his *Zikhronot,* 3:383; see also A. Shapira, "Bein teror le-havlaga," 418.

56. These matters have been treated in dozens of articles. See, e.g., Y. Cohen, "Be-kav ha-havlaga" (In the Line of Self-Restraint), *Ha-Poel ha-Tzair,* September 1, 1936; Y. Laufbahn, "Ke-tom shana" (In the Wake of a Year), *Ha-Poel ha-Tzair,* April 22, 1937.

57. Eliyahu Golomb, in a meeting of the Histadrut Executive Committee, August 4, 1938, in his *Hevyon oz,* 2:176.

58. For examples of a decline in personal relationships, see Yosef Baratz [Y.B., pseud.], "Me-emek ha-yarden" (From the Jordan Valley), *Niv ha-Kvutza,* April–May 1936; David Zamir, "Mi-tokh ha-alata" (From the Darkness), *Hedim,* June 1938; Efraim Gila'i, "Haver nafal" (A Comrade Fell), *Ha-Shomer ha-Tzair,* October 15, 1938.

59. Tchernichovsky, "Ba-mishmar" (May 13, 1936), in his *Shirei,* 110.

60. Idem, "Shir eres" (A Lullaby), in his *Shirei,* 110.

61. Y. Cohen, "Be-kav ha-havlaga."

62. A. M. Koler, "Le-pe'ulot" (To Actions), in *Me'ora'ot 1936,* ed. Beracha Habas 366.

63. Y. Cohen, "Be-kav ha-Havlaga."

64. A. Z. Rabinowitz, "Be-darkheihem lo nelekh" (We Will Not Take Their Paths), in *Me'ora'ot 1936,* ed. Beracha Habas, 378.

65. [Beilinson], "Devar ha-yom," in Yaacov Shavit, ed. *Havlaga o teguva?* (Self-Restraint or Response?) (Tel Aviv, 1983), 52.

66. Ben Gurion, "Lekah ha-me'ora'ot" (Lesson of the Riots), in *Me'ora'ot 1936,* ed. Beracha Habas, 364.

67. Even in the Hagana, it was stated at the end of a dispute on restraint, "Generally, restraint was easily accepted, since it was basically in keeping with our spirit" (Response to rank-and-file members in Tel Aviv), in Shavit, ed., *Havlaga o teguva,* 85.

68. D. Shimonovitz, "Lo! Et damenu lo nafkir!" (No! We Shall Not Allow Our Blood to Be Shed in Vain!), in *Me'ora'ot 1936,* ed. Baracha Habas, 51.

69. Yaakov Steinberg, "Im onat ha-yisurim" (The Season of Torment), in *Me'ora'ot 1936,* ed. Baracha Habas, 376–77.

70. D. Ben Zvi, "Ve'af al pi khen, havlaga" (Nonetheless, Self-Restraint), in *Me'ora'ot 1936,* ed. Baracha Habas, 377–78.

71. Z. Jabotinsky, "Havlagat ha-Yishuv—ad matai?" (Self-Restraint of the Yishuv—How Much Longer?), Shavit, ed. *Havlaga o teguva,* 73.

72. Moshe Shertok, Mapai Central Committee, June 9, 1936, in M. Sharett, *Yoman medini,* 1:163.

73. Berl Katznelson, comments in a meeting of the Inner Zionist Actions Committee, June 22, 1936, in *Me'ora'ot 1936,* ed. Baracha Habas, 359–60.

74. Binyamin Lubotzky, "Mamlekhet kohanim ve-goy kadosh" (Kingdom of Priests and a Holy People), Shavit, ed. *Havlaga o teguva,* 76.

75. Y. H. Yeivin, "Pesha ha-damim shel ha-sokhnut: hafkarat ha-Yishuv" (The Bloody Crime of the Jewish Agency: Abandonment of the Yishuv), in his *Me-havlaga le-kantoniyut* (From Self-Restraint to Cantonism) (Tel Aviv, 1937); see Shavit, ed., *Havlaga o teguva,* 94.

76. Abba Ahimeir, "Alcazar ve-havlaga" (Alcazar and Self-Restraint), in his *Ha-Tziyonut ha-mahapkhanit,* 106–11.

77. Jabotinsky, "Amen," in his *Ba-sa'ar* (In the Storm) (Jerusalem, 1953), 211–18; Shavit, ed., *Havlaga o teguva,* 137.

78. "Mi-divrei haverim al ha-havlaga" (From Comments of Comrades on Self-Restraint), quoted by Shavit, ed., *Havlaga o teguva,* 82.

79. On pressures among the members of the Hagana, see Dinur et al., *Sefer toldot ha-Hagana,* 2, 837–46; Shapira, *Berl,* 281; Eliyahu Golomb, in a meeting of Mapai Central Committee, November 30, 1937, in his *Hevyon oz,* 2:165; Shavit, ed., *Havlaga o teguva,* 84–86.

80. The description of developments on the radical Right during that period is based on Yosef Heller, *Lehi: Ideologia u-politika* (Lehi: Ideology and Politics) (Jerusalem, 1989), 19–82; Shavit, ed., *Havlaga o teguva;* and my own analysis of the sources.

81. A. Stern, "Ekronot u-maskanot" (Principles and Conclusions), "Omar la-am" (I Will Tell the People) quoted by Heller, op. cit., 77. I am grateful to Eliyahu Ha-Cohen for providing me with the text of "Anonymous Soldiers."

82. U. Z. Greenberg, "Emet ahat ve-lo shtayim" (One Truth and Not Two), in his *Sefer ha-kitrug ve-ha-emuna* (Book of Indictment and Faith) (Jerusalem, 1937), 163. I am grateful to Chanita Goodblatt for her translation of the poem.

83. Yosef Heller, op. cit., 58–59, 64.

84. Y. H. Yeivin, "Pesha ha-damim," 1–6; Shavit, ed., *Havlaga o teguva,* 87–95.

85. David Razi'el, "Nagola herpat ha-havlaga" (The Shame of Self-Restraint Exonerated), in David Niv, *Ma'arakhot ha-Irgun ha-Tzvai ha-Leumi* (Battles of IZL), vol. 2 (Tel Aviv, 1975), 41–42; Shavit, ed., *Havlaga o teguva,* 99–100; IZL, memo to the National Council, July 10, 1938, in Shavit, ed. *Havlaga o teguva,* 107–9.

86. Shavit quotes Yosef Nedava on this, *Havlaga o teguva,* 18.

87. Greenberg, "Ba-hodesh ha-revi'i / Be-fanai el ha-Gola" (In the Fourth Month / Facing the Diaspora), in his *Sefer ha-kitrug ve-ha-emuna,* 154; also in his *Be-emtza ha-olam u-be-emtza ha-zemanim,* 139.

88. Idem, "Rakav le-veit Yisrael" (Rot in the House of Israel), in his *Sefer ha-kitrug ve-ha-emuna,* 14.

89. Ibid., 162, *Be-emtza ha-olam,* 140.

90. Idem, *Sefer ha-kitrug,* 168–69; *Be-emtza ha-olam,* 141–43.

91. Niv, op. cit., 71–72.

92. Shavit, ed. *Havlaga o teguva,* 137–42.

93. See Shavit, ed., *Havlaga o teguva,* 10–14; Heller, op. cit., 53–80; Yehoshua Porath, *Shelah ve-et be-yado* (The Life of Uriel Shelah [Yonathan Ratosh]), (1989), 94–112.

94. Shavit, ed., *Havlaga o teguva,* 137.

95. Ibid.

96. On the spectrum of opinion regarding IZL terror, esp. the views of Ben Gurion, see Anita Shapira, "Bein teror le-havlaga: Ha-kinus ha-yishuvi be-yuli 1938" (Between Terror and Self-Restraint: The Yishuv Conference of July 1938), *Ha-Tziyonut* 6(1981):359–425. See also deliberations during Activists' Day, a meeting of Ha-Kibbutz ha-Meuhad members who were active in security matters, July 29–30, 1938, in U. Brenner, *Ha-Kibbutz ba-Hagana, 1923–1939* (Tel Aviv, 1980), 241–48. On Jewish solidarity, in addition to the two preceding, see Pinhas Lubianiker, "Be-ma'agal ha-teror" (In the Circle of Terror), *Ha-Poel ha-Tzair,* August 12, 1938.

97. On this topic, note Tabenkin's comments: "There is a question about the form of our struggle against the phenomenon of Jewish terror that is actually connected with our struggle against revisionism as a whole. For us, this is a war against fascism, a struggle for the very existence and survival of the Labor movement. The use of acts of terror is common in fascism, and there can be little doubt that it is likely to lead to terror by Jews against other Jews." Cf. the Activists Day deliberations mentioned in 96. This view was heard on countless occasions, e.g., Eliyahu Golomb, session of the Histradrut Executive, August 4, 1938 in his *Hevyon oz,* 2:178; Pinhas Lubianiker, "Be-ma'agal ha-terror"; "Ba-ma'arakha," *Ha-Shomer ha-Tzair,* July 15, 1938; "Milhama lanu ba-teror ha-biryoni!" (We Will Fight the Ruffian Terror!), *Ha-Shomer ha-Tzair,* July 7, 1939. The identification was especially frequent among members of Ha-Kibbutz ha-Meuhad, Ha-Shomer ha-Tzair, and Mapai.

98. On the field squads (Fosh), see Dinur et al., *Sefer toldot ha-Hagana,* 2:939–67.

99. The quote is apparently attributable to Eliyahu Golomb; see "Wingate—yotzer pelugat ha-mahatz" (Wingate–Creator of the Strike Squads), conversation with E. Golomb, *Ba-Ma'avak,* September 1946.

100. On Wingate and his actions, see Christoper Sykes, *Orde Wingate: A Biography* (Cleveland, 1959); Dinur et al., *Sefer toldot ha-Hagana,* 2:911–38; on the responses of men from the field squads, see, e.g., "Mi-yomani" (From My Diary), AHH, Fosh, file 26. Yitzhak Henkin testified to me about Wingate's custom of executing every tenth man. See also the story about the Daburiyya reprisal, AHH, Fosh, file 26.

101. See comments by Yigal Paicovitch (Allon), seminar for emissaries of Ha-Kibbutz ha-Meuhad, May 29, 1945, AKM, sec. 2, box 16, file 105.

102. Moshe Smilanski, in *Neged ha-teror* (Against Terrorism), ed. Rabbi Binyamin and Yaakov Peterzeil (Jerusalem, 1939), 64–66; Shavit, *Havlaga o teguva,* 153.

103. The quote is from Eliyahu Golomb, "Darkenu ba-Hagana," *Ha-Poel ha-Tzair,* September 16, 1938. Moshe Shertok made similar remarks June 27, 1938, see M. Sharett, *Yoman medini,* vol. 3 (Tel Aviv, 1972), 146.

104. Dinur et al, *Sefer toldot ha-Hagana,* 2:877; on the entire Hanita affair, see pp. 872–80.

105. Quotes are from Yaakov Orland, "Hanita"; S. Shalom, "Hanita"; Aharon Ashman, "Kakha kakh ve-lo aheret!" (This Way and No Other!); S. Shalom, "Shir ha-hamisha" (Song of the five); Alexander Penn, "Shir shel Zeid" (Song of Zeid); and Leah Goldberg, "Shir ha-namal" (Song of the Harbor). I am grateful to Eliyahu Ha-Cohen for placing these texts at my disposal.

106. Eliyahu Golomb, "Darkenu ba-Hagana, *Ha-Poel ha-Tzair,* September 16, 1938.

107. Talks on a plan for defense in the event of the establishment of a Jewish state, November 10, 1937, AHH, sec. 116 (Golomb), file 27.

108. Avraham Katznelson, "Bithon ha-Yishuv ve-ha-pitaron ha-medini" (Security of the Yishuv and the Political Solution), *Ha-Poel ha-Tzair,* October 21, 1938.

109. Comments by Ben-Zion Mossinson (principal of Herzliya Hebrew Gymnasia, 1912–1941), quoted by Ahad Ha-Am, "Ha-Gimnasia ha-Ivrit be-Yafo" (The Hebrew Gymnasium in Jaffa), *Al parshat derakhim,* vol. 4 (Berlin, 1930), 152.

110. S. D. Goitein, "Al ha-yesodot ha-ra'ayoniyim shel hora'at ha-tanakh be-veit ha-sefer ha-ivri" (On the Ideological Concepts in Teaching Bible in the Hebrew schools), in *Al ha-hinukh ha-tikhoni ha-ivri be-Eretz Yisrael* (Jewish Secondary Education in Palestine), ed. H. Y. Roth (Jerusalem, 1939), 44–46.

111. Ibid., 48.

112. Ibid., 51.

113. Ernst Simon, "Ha-she'ela ha-arvit be-hinukhenu" (The Arab Question in Our Education) *She'ifoteinu,* October 1932.

114. Z. Lehman, "Kinus ha-noar neged ha-milhama" (Youth Conference Against War), *Ba-Ma'ale,* Augutst 14, 1931.

115. See, e.g. Yuzik Hugim, "Yemei Vina" (Vienna Days), in: *Shnot Ha-Mahanot ha-Olim* (Years of Ha-Mahanot ha-Olim), ed. Yitzhak Kafkafi, vol. 1 (Tel Aviv, 1975), 369.

116. Eliezer Rieger, "Zikat beit ha-sefer ha-ivri el aheinu she-ba-gola" (Relationship of the Hebrew [Jewish] School to Our Brothers in the Diaspora), in his *Ha-hinukh ha-ivri be-Eretz Yisrael,* (The Hebrew [Jewish] Education in Palestine) (Tel Aviv, 1940), 242.

117. Ernst Simon, op. cit.

118. Ibid. The preference for French is mentioned in a meeting of youth to "assess the situation," May 17, 1936, Tel Aviv, AKM, sec. 9, Ha-Mahanot ha-Olim, box 2, file 15.

119. "Pamphlets on the Questions of Educational–Cultural Work in Our Organization," Ha-Noar ha-Oved, "Pamphlet A, for the Senior Class, 1933," AKM, sec. 8, Ha-Noar ha-Oved ve-ha-Lomed, guidance and seminars, organization 1932–1959, ser. 5, box 6, compart. A.

120. Information supplied by Shosh Spektor.

121. See Anita Shapira, "Dor ba-aretz" (A Native Generation), *Alpayim* 2(1990):178–203.

122. Yosef Baratz, "Hesegeinu be-hinukh yeladeinu" (Our Achievements in the Education of Our Children), *Niv ha-Kvutza,* September 1933.

123. See n. 113.

124. Discussion of questions of the movement, conference of the sophomore-level group, Ha-Mahanot ha-Olim, Ha-Hug ha-Ole ve-ha-Hakhsharot (Circle for Graduates and Kibbutz Initiates), Givat Brenner, Hanukkah, December 1936, AKM, sec. 9, Ha-Mahanot ha-Olim, Kinusei ha-Bogrim (Conferences of Seniors), box 1, file 5.

125. Irma Zinger, "Ha-me'ora'ot ve-ha-yeladim" (The Riots and the Children), *Ha-Poel ha-Tzair,* November 12, 1936.

126. Chronicles, in *Me'ora'ot 1936,* ed. Baracha Habas, 525–30.

127. E. Steinmann, "De'aga li-yeladeinu" (Worry About Our Children), in *Me'ora'ot 1936,* ed. Baracha Habas, 530–33; see also Irma Zinger, op. cit.

128. Meeting to "assess the situation," May 17, 1936, Tel Aviv, AKM, sec. 9, Ha-Mahanot ha-Olim, box 2, file 15.

129. "Darkei ha-Hagana" (Paths of the Defense Force), Conference of the senior group, Ha-Mahanot ha-Olim, Givat Chaim, December 2, 1937, AKM, sec. 9. Ha-Mahanot ha-Olim, 10f, box 1, file 20.

130. Discussion (1936?), within the framework of Ha-Noar ha-Oved, LA, sec. 213 IV, file 15.

131. Ibid.

132. Ibid.

133. "Darkei ha-Hagana." See also Minutes, Mapai Central Commitee, November 17, 1937, **BB**, file 23/37.

134. Letter from a child in Jerusalem to his friend, a guest in Moshav Merhavia, early July 1938, BB.

135. Meeting to "assess the situation," May 17, 1936, Tel Aviv, AKM, sec. 9, Ha-Mahanot ha-Olim, box 2, file 15.

136. See n. 124.

137. "Darkei ha-Hagana."

138. Ibid.

139. Ibid.

140. Ibid.

141. Nineteenth Conference of the Permanent Council of Ha-Noar ha-Oved, Tel Aviv, August 19, 1938, LA, sec. 213 IV, file 14; emphasis mine.

142. Ibid.

143. Discussion on questions of the movement, Hanukkah, December 1936, AKM, sec. 9. Ha-Mahanot ha-Olim, Kinusei ha-Bogrim, box 1, file 5.

144. Disucssion (1936?), within the framework of Ha-Noar ha-Oved, LA, sec. 213 IV, file 15.

145. One of those participating in deliberations at the Nineteenth Permanent Council of Ha-Noar ha-Oved, Tel Aviv, August 19, 1938, complained that members were unprepared to accept that action, meaning defense activity. LA, sec. 213 IV, file 14.

146. Yitzhak Tabenkin, "Li-she'elat ha-hagana ve-ha-bitahon" (On the Question of Defense and Security), in his *Devarim,* 2:117.

147. Israel Galili to his father, September 4, 1938, AKM, Galili, box 5, file 3.

148. Israel Galili, comments at Ha-Kibbutz ha-Meuhad seminar (Ein Harod?), May–August 1937, AKM, Galili, box 6, file 1.

149. "Darkei ha-Hagana."

150. Ibid.

151. Nineteenth Conference of the Permanent Council of Ha-Noar ha-Oved, August 19, 1938, LA, sec. 213 IV, file 14.

152. Ibid.

153. Ibid.

154. Arnon Azariahu (Sini) to his parents, fence camp (Sasa), June 24, 1938, Azariahu's private collection.

155. See comments by Shmarya (Gutman) (1936?), Ha-Noar ha-Oved, LA, sec. 213 IV, file 15.

156. Haya Ben Zion, "Mikhtav me-Ein Harod" (Letter from Ein Harod), in Ha-Mahanot ha-Olim, *Bi-vritekh* (In Your Covenant), (Tel Aviv, 1938), 9.

157. Ibid., 45–46.

158. Ibid., 38, 43.

159. Ibid., 37.

160. Ibid., 26–27.

161. Zviya, "Ba-tiyul" (On the Trip), in *Bi-vritekh,* 15–16; emphasis mine.

162. Shabtai, in *Bi-vritekh,* 22.

163. Ibid., 35.

164. Ibid.

165. Ibid., 38–49; quote from p. 49.

166. Ibid., 60.

167. Eliezer Rieger, "Yahas beit ha-sefer el shekheneinu ha-arvim" (Attitude of the Schools to Our Arab Neighbors), in his *Ha-hinukh ha-ivri be-Eretz Yisrael,* 213–23; quote from p. 222.

168. Ibid., 222.

Chapter 7

1. Nathan Alterman, "Ayelet" (Morning Star), in his *Shirim mi-she-kvar* (Poems of Long Ago) (Tel Aviv, 1972), 255.

2. Berl Katznelson to the Mapai Central Commitee, London, June 15, 1937, *Igrot* (Letters), ed. Anita Shapira, vol. 6 (Tel Aviv, 1984), 341.

3. Idem, "Ma be-finu le-yom mahar?" (What Can We Say About Tomorrow?), in his *Ketavim,* vol. 5 (Tel Aviv, 1947) 17.

4. Ibid., 16–26.

5. On the general background of the era, Yehuda Slutzky, ed. *Sefer toldot ha-Hagana,* vol. 3 (Tel Aviv, 1972), 9–37, 91–198; Yosef Heller, *Ba-ma'avak li-medina: Ha-mediniyut ha-tziyonit ba-shanim 1936–1948* (Struggling for a State: Zionist Policy in the Years 1936–1948) (Jerusalem, 1985), 15–113; on the Arab position during the war, see Moshe Shertok, comments in the political committee of Mapai, August 26, 1940, in M. Sharett, *Yoman medini,* vol. 5 (Tel Aviv, 1979), 105–11; Eliyahu Golomb, session of the Histadrut Executive, April 29, 1941, in his *Hevyon oz,* 2:261–64; idem, session of the emergency committee, May 22, 1941 in his *Hevyon oz,* 272–73; idem, session of the Histadrut Executive, May 29, 1941, in his *Hevyon oz,* 279–80.

6. Alexander Prag, "He'arot ve-hatza'ot" (Notes and Proposals), *Ha-Shomer ha-Tzair,* March 7, 1940.

7. Yaakov Amit, "Al ha-perek" (On the Agenda), *Ha-Shomer ha-Tzair,* June 11, 1941.

8. Eliezer Pera'i, "Ba-ma'arakha" (In Battle), *Ha-Shomer ha-Tzair,* February 3, 1943.

9. Letter no. 3 of the secretariat of the Executive Committee, Ha-Kibbutz ha-Artzi, Merhavia, November 24, 1942, GH, 18F.1(16).

10. Protocol of the Inner Zionist Actions Committee, November 10, 1942, CZA, S25/294.

11. Ibid.

12. Ibid.; Ben Gurion, "Ye'udei ha-Tziyonut be-sha'a zo" (Zionism's Current Objectives), in his *Ba-ma'araha,* vol. 4 (Tel Aviv, 1950), 26–27. See also the debate on this issue in *Ha-Shomer ha-Tzair,* February 4, 1942.

13. Eliyahu Golomb, commenting on Zionist plans, stated: "There is even no need for transferring Arabs to other countries, although that is a possibility. In practical terms, the existing number of Arabs in Palestine can remain the same, the number of Jews be increased to five times that number", "Ha-Hagana bi-tkufatenu" (The Hagana in Our Era), lecture in

course for Palmach information officers, July 23, 1943, AKM, Galili archive, box 7(11), file A(C).

14. Moshe Shertok, "Be'ayot mediniyot" (Political Problems), *Ha-Poel ha-Tzair,* April 17, 1944.

15. Moshe Sneh, "Sakanat ha-peshara" (Danger of Compromise), *Alon ha-Palmah,* April–May 1945.

16. Pinhas Lubianiker, "Nokhah pnei ha-metzi'ut" (Facing Reality), *Niv ha-Kvutza,* August 1945.

17. At the end of 1943 and the beginning of 1944, there was a debate in the pages of *Hedim,* organ of Ha-Kibbutz ha-Artzi of Ha-Shomer ha-Tzair, between Aharon Cohen and Simha Flapan. Cohen, although he continued to be a proponent of the joint union as a long-term solution to the Arab problem, also wanted an interim agreement with the Arabs as a means to prevent confrontations in the present. Flapan called him to order, demanding that he repudiate his stand and express his loyalty to the old basic position rejecting any possibility for arriving at an agreement with the current Arab leadership. See Aharon Cohen, "Od le-be'ayat ha-heskem ha-yehudi–arvi" (More on the Problem of the Jewish–Arab Accord), *Hedim,* November 1943; Simha Flapan, "Od le-be'ayat ha-heskem ha-yehudi–arvi" (More on the Problem of the Jewish–Arab Accord), *Hedim,* January 1944. In January 1947, Eliezer Be'eri (Bauer), one of the experts on the Arab question in Ha-Shomer ha-Tzair, wrote that Zionism had to be realized as a historical process. He presented the Biltmore Program as the injection of revisionist ideas into a Zionist program lacking all basis in reality, which thinks the most important thing is to gain certain conditions, that wants to achieve the final goal by a Zionist shortcut with a charter." Cf, Eliezer Bauer, "Ha-Tziyonut be-ma'arakhot yameinu" (Zionism in the Battles of the Day), *Hedim,* January 1947. A detailed discussion of the positions of Ha-Shomer ha-Tzair on the Arab question throughout this period can be found in David Zayit, *Tziyonut be-darkei shalom* (Zionism by Peaceful Methods) (Tel Aviv, 1985); on our topic, see pp. 233–94. See also Yosef Gorny, *Zionism and the Arabs 1882–1948: A Study of Ideology* (Oxford, 1987), 277–320.

18. M. Shertok [Ben Kedem, pseud.] "Ha-ma'arakha she-le-faneinu" (The Battle Facing Us), *Alon ha-Palmah,* November–December 1944.

19. [Moshe Sneh?], lecture (1943?), AHH, 4717, file Moshe Sneh.

20. Moshe Shertok, "Yesodot rishoni'im be-yahas le-emdatenu klapei ha-Britim" (Basic Principles in Our Attitude Toward the British), July 22, 1943, lecture, course for information officers of the Hagana and Palmach, July 21–August 2, 1943, AKM, Galili archive, box 7(11), file (C)A.

21. Eliyahu Golomb, "Ha-Hagana bi-tkufatenu."

22. Moshe Sneh, "Oshiyot ha-irgun" (Foundations of the Organization), August 3, 1943, lecture, course for information officers of the Hagana and Palmach, July 21–August 2, 1943, AKM, Galili archive, box 7(11), file (C)A.

23. Eliyahu Golomb, "Ha-Hagana bi-tkufatenu."

24. [Moshe Sneh?], lecture (1943?) AHH 4717, file Moshe Sneh.

25. On the *Patria* and the *Atlantic,* see Sharett, *Yoman medini,* 5:123–164; the conversation referred to took place with General Nim on December 7, 1940, and is mentioned on p. 139. On illegal immigration during the war and British policy toward it, see Dalia Ofer, *Escaping the Holocaust* (New York, 1990).

26. Slutzky presents a document dated May 18, 1943, written by the Command of the Hagana to field commanders, stating that it is permissible to open fire if British soldiers open fire while searching for weapons. There is no evidence that this order was ever carried out. See Yehuda Slutzky, ed., *Sefer toldot ha-Hagana,* vol. 3 (Tel Aviv, 1972) 1873–74.

27. *Ruppin Diaries,* May 18, 1939, p. 298.

28. Ronald Zweig contends that the policy of the White Paper was never implemented. On this and other matters relating to British policy during the war, see Ronald W. Zweig, *Britain and Palestine During the Second World War* (Hoodridge/Suffolk 1986); Gavriel Cohen, *Churchill u-she'elat Eretz-Yisrael bi-tehilat milhemet ha-olam ha-sheniya 1939–1942* (Churchill and The Question of Palestine at the Beginning of World War II, 1939–1942) (Jerusalem, 1976).

29. On the *Patria* and Mauritius affairs, see Bernard Wasserstein, *Britain and the Jews of Europe 1939–1945* (Oxford, 1979), 62–76. Out of about 1,650 people deported to Mauritius, 130 died. M. Bassok, ed., *Sefer ha-ma'apilim* (Book of the Illegal Immigrants) (Jerusalem, 1947), 299.

30. On this dispute, see Shapira, *Berl,* 285–89.

31. Minutes, Mapai Secretariat (sitting as a political committee), November 12, 1945, BB, file 23/45.

32. Slutzky, ed., *Sefer toldot ha-Hagana,* 3:841.

33. Ben Gurion, "Teshuva le-Bevin" (Answer to Bevin), in his *Ba-ma'arakha,* vol 5 (Tel Aviv, 1951), 32.

34. This speech is quoted, without any date, in *Alon ha-Palmah,* December 1945.

35. Moshe Shertok to members of the Jewish Agency Executive, November 2, 1945, CZA, S25/2308, quoted by Heller, *Ba-ma'avak li-medina,* 424.

36. Weizmann to the Jewish Community of Palestine, London, November 2, 1945, *The Letters and Papers of Chaim Weizmann,* ser. A, vol. 22, ed. Joseph Heller (Jerusalem, 1979), 71–72. There is some doubt as to whether this letter was ever sent; but in any case, Weizmann's views were known. My thanks to Nehama Shalom, archivist of the Weizmann papers, who located the materials relevant to his position on this issue.

37. Minutes, Mapai Secretariat, November 12, 1945, BB, file 23/45.

38. Comments by Zeev Isersohn, Mapai Secretariat, November 6, 1945, BB, file 23/45.

39. "Le-me'ora'ot ha-yamim" (On the Current Events), *Ha-Poel ha-Tzair,* November 7, 1945.

40. Minutes, Mapai Secretariat, November 6, 1945, BB, file 28/45.

41. Weizmann to Moshe Shertok, London, January 20, 1947, *Letters and Papers,* 22:228–32. The original letter was written by Weizmann on June 27, 1946, but was not sent at that time; on January 1, 1947, Weizmann sent Shertok a copy of the letter "for the sake of the record" (p. 232).

42. Sneh to Ben Gurion, September 21, 1946, AHH, Sneh file; the letter appears in *Sefer toldot ha-Hagana,* ed. Slutzky, 3:1933–34.

43. Weizmann, reply to debate at the Twenty-second Zionist Congress in Basel, December 16, 1946, *Letters and Papers* ser. B, vol. 2, ed. Barnet Litvinoff, (New Brunswick, NJ: 1984), 642–51.

44. See the sixth Convention of Mapai, September 6, 1946, in Heller, *Ba-ma'avak li-medina,* 443–46.

45. Galili's transcription of comments by Ben Gurion in the Political Committee of the Twenty-second Congress in Basel, AKM, archive Galili, various notes, November–December 1946. See also the speech by Ben Gurion in the Political Commitee of the Twenty-second Congress, in his *Ba-ma'arakha,* 5:135–38.

46. [Moshe Sneh?], "Arakhim be-mahshevet ha-hagana shelanu" (Values in the Philosophy of Our Defense), *Alon Palmah,* January 1947.

47. On the struggle between Tabenkin and Berl Katznelson for the soul of youth during the 1930s, see Shapira, *Berl,* 208–52.

48. Tabenkin, remarks before the action committee of Ha-Kibbutz ha-Meuhad, Ashdot Yaakov, June 7–8, 1940, AKM, sec. 2, box 5, file 3. A revised version of these remarks appeared in his *Devarim,* vol. 3 (Tel Aviv, 1974), 15–19.

49. Idem, "Beit ha-sefer ve-ha-milhama" (The School and the War), in his *Devarim,* 3:109–12.

50. On the views of Tabenkin and his associates regarding this topic, see Anita Shapira, "Labour Zionism and the October Revolution," *Journal of Contemporary History* 24(1989):623–56.

51. Tabenkin, comments at the council of kibbutz members from Ha-Mahanot ha-Olim, Bet ha-Shita, January 12, 1940, AKM sec. 9, ser. 8, box 1, file 5.

52. Ibid.

53. Idem, comments on conference day, Ha-Tenua le-Ahdut ha-Avoda, January 6, 1945, AKM, Galili archive, Dissenting Organizations cont., file Sezon 1944–1946.

54. Idem, "Beit ha-sefer ve-ha-milhama."

55. Ibid.

56. Ibid

57. For a detailed discussion of this topic, see A. Shapira, "Labour Zionism and the October Revolution"; idem, "The Dynamics of Zionist Leftist Trends," in *Jewish History,* ed. A. Rapoport-Albert and S. J. Zipperstein (London, 1988), 629–82.

58. Tabenkin, comments during a symposium at Ein Harod, November 12–19, 1939, AKM, sec. 1C (Conceptual Clarifications), box 7, file 3.

59. Ibid.

60. Idem, "Likrat he-atid" (Toward the Future), in his *Devarim,* 3:41–45.

61. Idem, "Beit ha-sefer ve-ha-milhama." On discussions about orientation at the Histadrut conference, see Berl Katznelson, *Ketavim,* vol. 5 (Tel Aviv, 1947), 51–94; quote is from p. 72.

62. Tabenkin, "Beit ha-sefer ve-ha-milhama"; idem, "Le-atido shel beit ha-sefer ba-kibbutz" (On the Future of the School in the Kibbutz), in his *Devarim,* 3:381.

63. Tabenkin et al., comments at a gathering, November 10, 1942, AKM, sec. 15— Allon, box 6, file 1. See also Ha-Kibbutz ha-Meuhad Council, Na'an, August 21–23, 1942, AKM, sec. 5, box 6, file 8. On the establishment and formation of the Palmach, see Slutzky, *Sefer toldot ha-Hagana,* 3:374–469.

64. Yitzhak Dubno [Yoav, pseud.], "Be-ikvot nisyon ha-partizanim" (In the Wake of Experience of the Partisans), *Alon ha-Palmah,* March 1945. See also the description of Russian heroism in that periodical: *Alon ha-Palmah,* November–December 1945; "Im hayalim yehudim me-ha-tzava ha-adom" (with Jewish Soldiers from the Red Army), *Alon ha-Palmah,* November–December 1944; see also Tabenkin et al., comments, November 10, 1942, AKM, sec. 15—Allon, box 6, file 1; on experiences in the Palmach, see *Sefer ha-Palmah,* ed. Zerubavel Gil'ad, vol. 1 (Tel Aviv, 1956), 291–434 and *Alon ha-Palmah* in general.

65. Tabenkin, "Keitzad la'azor ba-milhama" (How to Help in the War Effort), in his *Devarim,* 3:457.

66. Council of Kibbutz Members from Ha-Mahanot ha-Olim, Bet ha-Shita, January 12, 1940, AKM, sec. 9. ser. 8, box 1, file 5.

67. Zviya Katznelson et al., comments by members in the Council of Kibbutz Members from Ha-Mahanot ha-Olim, organ no. 4, November 30, 1942, AKM. See, likewise, comments by Asaf Katz, *Gevilei esh* (Scrolls of Fire), ed. Reuven Avinoam [Reuven Grossman], vol. 1 (Tel Aviv, 1954), 636.

68. Zviya Katznelson et al., comments by members in the Council of Kibbutz Members from Ha-Mahanot ha-Olim, organ no. 4, November 30, 1942, AKM.

69. Comments, Council of Kubbutz Members from Ha-Mahanot ha-Olim, Maoz

Hayim, 1943, AKM, sec. 9, box 1, file 4. On the relationship with Berl Katznelson and Ben Gurion, see the meeting with Berl, Seminar of Communes, Gevat, September 10–October 10, 1943, AKM, sec. 9, box 1, file 21.

70. Seminar of Communes, Gevat, September 10–October 10, 1943, AKM, sec. 9, box 1, file 21.

71. Shlomo Drexler (Derekh), Seminar for Instructors, Ha-Mahanot ha-Olim, Yagur, July 31–September 1, 1945, AKM, sec. 9, Ha-Mahanot ha-Olim, ser. 5D, box 6, file 5A.

72. Yitzhak Lamdan, *Massada* (Tel Aviv, 1927), 75.

73. Yosef Braslavsky, "Aharit Metzada ve-ikvoteha" (The End of Massada and Its Traces), *Mi-Bifnim,* January 1942.

74. "Mesibat ha-kibbush ve-ha-ha'apala" (Party on Behalf of the Conquest and Illegal Immigration), final party, camp for intermediate-level youth, Gevat, July 1939, AKM, sec. 9, Ha-Mahanot ha-Olim, (10f), box 1, file 4.

75. Moshe Shertok, Twenty-first Zionist Congress, Geneva, August 21, 1939, cited in Heller, *Ba-ma'avak li-medina,* 270.

76. Exchange of letters between members of Kibbutz Gennosar and the Histadrut Executive, March 12, 1942, LA, 208 IV, file 133/msh.

77. There was a detailed discussion of these matters in the council of Ha-Kibbutz ha-Meuhad, Ein Harod, July 5, 1942, AKM, sec. 5, box 6, file 7.

78. Ibid, comments by Galili.

79. Berl Katznelson, "Im ha-sefer" (With the book), January 1941, in his *Ketavim,* vol. 5 (Tel Aviv, 1947), 334.

80. Galili, notebook, April 18, 1941, AKM, Galili archive, p. 18.

81. Circular letter by members of Kibbutz Na'an et al. 1942, AKM, sec. 8, box 6, file 7; see also Yosef Braslavsky, op. cit.

82. Secretariat, Ha-Noar ha-Oved, to members of the Central Committee, no. 7, February 10, 1942, CZA, S32/1138. See also "Bi-Metzada u-va-Negev" (In Massada and the Negev), Ha-Noar ha-Oved pamphlet, March 1944, LA, 213 IV, file 49.

83. "Hafkidi, Metzada, shomrim al homotayikh!" (Place Massada, Guardsmen, Upon Your Walls!), *Ba-Ma'ale,* March 31, 1942.

84. "Devar Metzada" (Massada's Command), *Ba-Ma'ale,* April 17, 1942.

85. Ha-Mahanot ha-Olim to Department of Youth Affairs, Zionist Organization, December 16, 1942, CZA, S32/435.

86. Circular letter, Secretariat of Ha-Noar ha-Oved, Tel Aviv, April 3, 1945, CZA, S32/1136; see also comments by Azaria (Allon), Fourth Council of Ha-Mahanot ha-Olim, Bet ha-Shita, April 3, 1945, AKM, sec. 9, box 1, file 4.

87. See, e.g., Zviya (Katznelson), "Be-ein nigun" (Without a Melody), *Mi-Bifnim,* January 1946: "All those years that distinguished between us and 'them', what is their inscription on this landscape? . . . All still breathes here with them."

88. Z. Hever, "Elei Metzada" (To Massada), *Ba-Ma'ale,* June 16, 1943.

89. Circular letter to instructors in Ha-Noar ha-Oved, Tel Aviv, February 16, 1943, CZA, S32/1137. See also meeting of the central committee, Ha-Noar ha-Oved, February 13, 1944, LA, 213 IV, file 29.

90. Circular letter, Secretariat of Ha-Noar ha-Oved, Tel Aviv, March 16, 1944, LA, 213 IV, file 245. The line "Happy is the people that goes forth to the wanderings of exile, with Massada in its consciousness and memory" appears there. It is not difficult to discover the source for this literary allusion in the line by Brenner, referring to Tel Hai: "Blessed he who dies in this consciousness, Tel Hai his pillow of earth."

91. Ibid., November 29, 1944, CZA, S32/1136.

92. Ibid., April 3, 1945, CZA, S32/1136; see also "Devar ha-tenua le-olei Metzada be-

Pesah 5705" (The Message of the Movement to the Pilgrims to Massada, Passover 1945), *Ba-Ma'ale,* March 26, 1945.

93. Ha-Mahanot ha-Olim, "Kavim le-tokhnit ha-ta'arukha le-hag ha-tenua" (Outlines for the Program of the Exhibition on the Movement's Celebration), October 19, 1944, CZA, S32/435.

94. Ha-Mahanot ha-Olim, "Na'ar ivri be-milhemet shihrur ha-am" (The Hebrew Boy in the People's Liberation War), program for the young level, July 1945, CZA, S32/435.

95. "Mi-tokh yoman" (From a Diary), *Alon ha-Palmah,* August 1945.

96. Materials for instructors in preparation for Hanukkah, the Histadrut festival, 1945, CZA, S32/1136.

97. On the admiration for Tchernichovsky and its encouragement in Ha-Mahanot ha-Olim, see comments by Yitzhakele (Kafkafi), one of the leaders of the movement seminar for instructors, Ha-Mahanot ha-Olim, Yagur, August 10, 1945, AKM, ser. 5D, box 6, file 5A. See also *Alon ha-Palmah,* December 1946, p. 1. The motto for the article quoted from "Mangina Li," Moshe Halfon, "Le-Harei Efraim Vi-Yehuda" (To the Samaria and Judea Mountains), in *Sefer ha-Palmah* (Book of the Palmach), ed. Zerubavel Gil'ad, vol. 1 (Tel Aviv, 1956), 379; and Yehoshua Porath, *Shelah ve-et be-yado* (The Life of Uriel Shelah [Yonathan Ratosh]) (Tel Aviv, 1989).

98. Omer Hillel, [A. Hillel, pseud.] "Dor ha-Palmah" (Generation of the Palmach), in *Sefer ha-Palmah,* ed. Gil'ad, 1:489.

99. Ibid., 378–97, on the topic of excursions.

100. See A. Shapira, "The Yishuv and the Survivors of the Holocaust," *Studies in Zionism* 7, no. 2 (Autumn 1986): 277–301.

101. See, e.g. Eliyahu Golomb comments, Forty-eighth Council of the Histadrut, December 23, 1942, in his *Hevyon oz,* 2:355–56.

102. See Dina Porat, *The Blue and Yellow Stars of David: The Zionist Leadership in Palestine and the Holocaust, 1939–1945* (Cambridge, MA, 1990) for a detailed discussion of the response by the Zionist Organization to the Holocaust.

103. Lecture, apparently 1943, file Moshe Sneh, AHH, 4717.

104. Tabenkin, "Im ha-edut" (With the Testimony), *Mi-Bifnim,* November 1946.

105. Idem, Seminar of Communes, Gevat, September 10–October 10, 1943, AKM, sec. 9, box 1, file 21.

106. Galili, comments to Ha-Noar ha-Oved, early 1943, work notebook 1943, AKM, Galili archive.

107. Ben Gurion, "El ha-matzpun ha-enoshi" (Appeal to Human Conscience), special meeting of the Assembly of Delegates, November 30, 1943, in his *Ba-ma'arakha,* vol. 3 (Tel Aviv, 1950), 114–19.

108. Lecture, apparently 1943, file Moshe Sneh, AHH, 4717.

109. See, e.g., Nathan Friedel, lecture (1942–1943?), GH, 18F.1(22).

110. Tabenkin, Council of Ha-Kibbutz ha-Meuhad, Ramat ha-Kovesh, January 2, 1943, op. cit., sec. 5, Councils, box 7, file 1.

111. Ibid.

112. Nathan Alterman, "Mi-kol he-amim" (From All the Peoples), in his *Ha-tur ha-shevi'i* (The Seventh Column), vol. 1 (Tel Aviv, 1986), 9–11.

113. Things are repeated over and over again. See, e.g. Moshe Prager, "Ha-mahapekha ha-goralit ba-historia ha-yehudit" (The Fateful Revolution in Jewish History), *Mi-Bifnim,* November 1946; Tabenkin, "Le-atido shel beit ha-sefer"; Idem, "Im ha-edut" (With the Testimony), *Mi-Bifnim,* November 1946.

114. Prager, op. cit.

115. See A. Shapira, "The Yishuv and the Survivors of the Holocaust."

116. Nathan Alterman, "Ha-sertifikat ha-aharon" (The Last Certificate), in his *Ha-tur ha-shevi'i,* 54.

117. Tabenkin, Council, Ramat ha-Kovesh, January 2, 1943, op. cit.

118. Idem, World Convention of the "Dror" (Freedom) Movement, May 1947, Föhrenwald, Germany, in his *Devarim,* vol. 4 (Tel Aviv, 1976), 191.

119. Nathan Alterman, "Aliya Valencia" (Immigration Valencia) in his *Ha-tur ha-shevi'i,* 1:95.

120. Moshe Tabenkin, national convention of graduates of the youth movements of Ha-Tenua le-Ahdut ha-Avoda, Haifa, July 28–29, 1944, LA, sec. 456 IV, file 1.

121. Prager, op. cit.

122. Galili, remarks to Ha-Noar ha-Oved, early 1943, work notebook 1943, AKM, Galili archive.

123. Tabenkin, in *The Fifteenth Convention of Ha-Kibbutz ha-Meuhad, Yagur, June 7– 13, 1946* (Ein Harod, n.d.), 7.

124. Avshalom Tzoref, comments at Twenty-fifth Council, Ha-Noar ha-Oved, Jerusalem, April 23, 1943, LA, sec. 213 IV, file 29.

125. "Berakha le-Antek be-vo'o" (Welcoming Antek), *Alon ha-Palmah,* April–May 1947; see also comments by Ruzka, *Alon ha-Palmah,* February 1945.

126. On futile negotiations to rescue children, see Porat, *The Blue and the Yellow Stars of David,* 149–63; Ofer, *Escaping the Holocaust* (New York, 1990) 218–26; ibid., 147–166 on the *Struma* affair; see Porat, op. cit., pp. 188–211 on the Brand mission.

127. Tabenkin, "Im ha-edut," *Mi-Bifnim,* November 1946.

128. Ibid.

129. Ben Gurion, comments, Zionist Greater Actions Committee, Zurich, August 26, 1947, in his *Ba-ma'arakha,* vol. 5 (Tel Aviv, 1951), 216–19.

130. Council, Ha-Kibbutz ha-Mcuhad, Ein Harod, July 5, 1942, AKM, sec. 4, box 6, file 6.

131. Tabenkin, "Le-afikei hatzala" (On Routes of Rescue), in his *Devarim,* 4:9–10. See also Lova Levite, "Hazkarat neshamot" (Memorial), *Mi-Bifnim,* June 1943.

132. Prager, op. cit.

133. See, e.g., remarks by M. Tabenkin, national convention of graduates of the youth movements of Ha-Tenua le-Ahdut ha-Avoda, Haifa, July 28–29, 1944, LA, scc. 456 IV, file 1; idem, "Ha-gola ha-lohemet" (The Fighting Diaspora), *Alon ha-Palmah,* January 1945; Tabenkin, "Nokhah ha-Shoa" (In the Face of the Holocaust), in his *Devarim,* 4:19.

134. Idem, "Im ha-edut," *Mi-Bifnim,* November 1946.

135. Ibid.

136. See A. Shapira, "Dor ba-aretz" (A Native Generation), *Alpayim,* 2(1990):178–203.

137. M. Tabenkin, national convention of graduates of the youth movements of Ha-Tenua le-Ahdut ha-Avoda, Haifa, July 28–29, 1944, LA, sec. 456 IV, file 1.

138. Galili, comments to Ha-Noar ha-Oved, early 1943, work notebook, 1943.

139. Yigal Allon, "Megamot u-ma'as" (Purposes and Deeds), in *Sefer ha-Palmah,* ed. Gil'ad, 1:596.

140. See, e.g., the remark by Yehuda Ya'ari that there is no reference to the Disapora whatsoever in the booklet *"La-avoda"* (To Work) of Ha-Mahanot ha-Olim. Ya'ari to Ben-Shalom, July 17, 1941, CZA, S32/435. A circular letter from the Secretariat of Ha-Noar ha-Oved also refers to the ghetto revolt, commenting on "our comrades who weren't familiar with the Diaspora and had a cold attitude toward the Jews in the ghettos" (Tel Aviv, June 1, 1943, CZA, S32/1137).

141. Gil'ad, ed., *Sefer ha-Palmah,* 1:352.

142. Benjamin Glücksohn, comments, *Ba-Mivhan,* February 1945.

143. Testimony of Reniya Hershkovitz to the author.

144. Etan Ram, "Yalkut ha-re'im," *Ba-Ma'avak,* September 1946.

145. Yitzhak Sade [Y. Noded, pseud.], "Seviv ha-medura" (Around the Bonfire), *Alon ha-Palmah,* October 1945.

146. Zvika Dror, *Bi-netivei hatzala* (Paths of Rescue) (Tel Aviv, 1988), 124.

147. Testimony of Galili to the author; Zvika Dror, op. cit., 165–67.

148. Berl Katznelson, "Shutfut ha-goral ha-yehudi ki-yesod ba-hinukh" (Jewish Solidarity as a Principle in Education), Mt. Carmel, June 6, 1944, LA, 104 IV, Berl Katznelson, file 16. Published in revised form in his *Ketavim,* vol. 12 (Tel Aviv, 1950), 217–25.

149. Ruzka, a letter on the death of Y. Sade (August 21, 1951), in Ruzka Korchak-Marle, *Lehimata, haguta, demuta* (The Personality and Philosophy-of-Life of a Fighter) (Tel Aviv, 1988), 221.

150. Ben Gurion, "Tzav Tel Hai" (The Imperative of Tel Hai), in his *Ba-ma'arakha,* 3:119–21. See also comments by Yitzhak Gruenbaum before the Council, Ha-Noar ha-Oved, Jerusalem, April 24, 1943, LA, 213 IV, file 29. In this speech, he announced the outbreak of the uprising.

151. Eliyahu Golomb, Secretariat of the Histradrut Executive, May 7, 1943, AHH, Golomb, file 52.

152. Lova Levite, "Hazkarat neshamot," *Mi-Bifnim,* June 1943. Reference to their bond with Palestine and "Tel Hai a pillow of earth" appears in Y. Eshed, "Milhemet ha-Yehudim" (The Jewish War), *Mi-Bifnim,* June 1943.

153. Statement by Palmach Headquarters in *Sefer ha-Palmah,* ed. Gil'ad, 1:525.

154. Eshed, "Milhemet ha-Yehudim."

155. *Ba-Ma'ale,* March 26, 1945; see also circular letter, Secretariat, Ha-Noar ha-Oved, April 12, 1945, LA, 213 IV, file 246.

156. Circular letter, Secretariat, Ha-Noar ha-Oved, June 1, 1943, CZA, S32/1137.

157. *Mi-Bifnim,* January 1946.

158. "La-horim" (To the Parents), *Alon ha-Palmah,* March 1946.

159. *Alon ha-Palmah,* March 1945.

160. Yigal Allon, "Megamot u-Ma'as," in *Sefer ha-Palmah,* ed. Gil'ad, 1:596.

161. See, e.g., "Ha-gola ha-lohemet," *Alon ha-Palmah,* January 1945. See also the testimony by Surika Braverman in Ruzka Korchak-Marle, op. cit., 245, quoting Sade as follows: "These are the Palmachniks who fought in the Diaspora—we fought here, they fought there."

162. Eliezer Shoshani, "Erkhei ha-Palmah" (Palmach Values), *Be-mivhan ha-kravot* (The Test of Battle), *Shenaton Davar 1948/49* (Davar Yearbook, 1948/49), 151.

163. Yigal Allon, "Megamot u-Ma'as."

164. "Partizanim Yehudim" (Jewish Partisans), *Alon ha-Palmah,* October 1945.

165. See, e.g., "Bi-fegishat ha-partizanim ba-aretz" (Meeting of the Partisans in Palestine), *Alon ha-Palmah,* October 1945.

166. See "Ha-pegisha ba-hof" (Meeting on the Beach) (narrated by an illegal immigrant), *Alon ha-Palmah,* September 1946.

167. It is difficult to find a factual basis to this supposed encounter on the shore. The number of ships that made it to the shore was very small, especially in the summer of 1946. On the accusation by Antek, see A. Shapira, "Mifgash ha-Yishuv im she'erit ha-Pleita" (The Encounter of the Yishuv with the Survivors of the Holocaust," in *Ha-Halikha al kav ha-ofek,* 328.

168. Tabenkin, lecture, Ha-Kibbutz ha-Meuhad symposium, January 6, 1945, AKM, Defense Force sec., Dissenters box, file Sezon 1944–1946.

169. "Im tzanhanim" (With Paratroopers), *Alon ha-Palmah,* October 1945.

170. See A. Shapira, "The Yishuv and the Survivors," *Studies in Zionism,* 7 (1986):301.

171. Tabenkin, "Nokhah ha-Shoa."

172. Idem, lecture, Ha-Kibbutz ha-Meuhad symposium, January 6, 1945, AKM, Defense Force sec., Dissenters box, file Sezon 1944–1946. Remarks on the Patria affair were made by Berl Katznelson, in his *Ketavim,* vol. 9 (Tel Aviv, 1948), 374.

173. Berl Katznelson, "Shutfut ha-goral ha-yehudi."

174. Second meeting of Ha-Mahanot ha-Olim Center, January 19–20, 1945, *Ba-Mivhan,* February 1945.

175. See Tabenkin, comments, Ha-Kibbutz ha-Meuhad Council, Yagur, April 27–29, 1944, AKM, sec. V, box 8, file 1; Shmuel Golan, "Al derekh hinukhenu" (On the Path of Our Education), *Hedim,* September 1947.

176. "Im ha-gilayon hazeh" (With This Issue), *Ba-Ma'avak,* September 1946.

177. "Reshut ha-dibur—la-dor ha-Eretz-Yisraeli!" (The Floor—to the Native Generation!), *Ba-Ma'avak,* September 1946.

178. Fourth Council, Ha-Mahanot Ha-Olim, Bet ha-Shita, April 3–6, 1945, AKM, sec. 9, box 1, file 4.

179. N. Alterman, "Prussia shoma'at et kol ha-totahim" (Prussia Hears the Voice of Cannon), in his *Ha-tur ha-shevi'i,* vol. 1 (Tel Aviv, 1986), 46.

180. Dov Stock (Sadan) to Berl Katznelson, December 1940(?), LA, Berl Katznelson, sec. II, 1.

181. Uri (Avneri), "Ha-Hagana be-rosh ha-kol!" (The Hagana in Charge!), *Ba-Ma'avak,* September 1946.

182. Moshe Tabenkin, national gathering of graduates of the youth movements associated with Ha-Tcnua lc-Ahdut ha-Avoda, Haifa, July 29, 1944, LA, 456 IV, file 1.

183. Shmuel Golan, op. cit.

184. Muni Langerman (Allon), "Gormei ha-tkufa be-hinukhenu" (Current Factors in Our Education), *Hedim,* January 1947.

185. Yehuda Bauer et al., Scouts Organization, to Chaim Weizmann, March 8, 1946, WA.

186. Y. Yagur, "Kol ha-samkhuyot—li-meginei ha-Yishuv" (All Authority—to the Defenders of the Yishuv), *Ba-Ma'avak,* September 1946.

187. Heller, *Lehi,* 1:160–61.

188. Ibid., 125–45.

189. Yashke Lebstein, memo, May 5, 1944, AKM, Defense Force sec., Dissenters general file. (1941–1946).

190. On the IZL's attitude toward the British, see the report by Moshe Sneh on his discussion with Menahem Begin, October 9, 1944, in *Sefer toldot ha-Hagana,* ed. Slutzky, 3:1887–93. See, likewise, the minutes of a meeting between representatives of the IZL, the Jewish Agency, and the Hagana, October 31, 1944, quoted by Heller, *Ba-ma'avak li-medina,* 401–10.

191. See lecture by Golomb to the Hagana members, March 16, 1942, AHH, no. 119 (Golomb), file 34.

192. On "Am lohem," see Slutzky, ed., *Sefer toldot ha-Hagana,* vol. 3 (Tel Aviv, 1972), 488–93. See also Uri Ben Eliezer, "Zva'iyut, status, u-politika" (Militarism, Status, and Politics), Ph.D. diss., Tel Aviv University 1988, which sheds a different light on the matter.

193. Moshe Tabenkin, national gathering of graduates of youth movements of Ha-Tenua le-Ahdut ha-Avoda, Haifa, July 28–29, 1944, LA, sec. 456 IV, file 1.

194. Moshe Shertok, "Yesodot rishoni'im be-yahas le-emdatenu."

195. Ben Gurion, response, Twenty-second Zionist Congress, December 16, 1946, in his *Ba-ma'arakha,* vol. 5 (Tel Aviv, 1951), 149.

196. Israel Galili to his friends in prison (ca. November 1945), AKM, Galili archive, box 5, file C. See also "Ma nishtana u-ma lo nishtana" (What Has Changed and What Hasn't?), *Ha-Homa* (The Wall), Adar 17, 1946, AKM, Defense Force sec. Dissenters box, Letters and Articles file.

197. Yitzhak Sade, "Davar la-noar" (A Word to Youth), in *Sefer ha-Palmah,* ed. Gil'ad, 1:803.

198. Eliyahu Golomb [A.G., pseud.] "Al ha-shimush be-koah" (On the Use of Force), *Alon ha-Palmah,* December 1945.

199. Tabenkin, "Mul ha-terorizm ha-aktivisti" (Facing Activist Terrorism), in his *Devarim,* 4:101.

200. Lecture by Hillel (Galili), AKM, Defense Force sec. Dissenters box, Dissenters (1941–1946) general file.

201. Galili asserted that the IZL wanted to stage a "revolt" in Jerusalem along the lines of the revolt under Bor-Komorowski in Warsaw in 1944, which ended with the destruction of the city, (lecture, AKM, Defense Force sec., Dissneters box, Dissenters (1941–1946) general file).

202. Muni Langerman, "Gormei ha-tkufa."

203. This was also Tabenkin's thinking, see Council of Ha-Kibbutz ha-Meuhad, Yagur, April 29, 1944, AKM, sec. V, box 8, file 1.

204. Binyamin Poznansky, national gathering of graduates of the youth movements associated with Ha-Tenua le-Ahdut ha-Avoda, Haifa, July 29, 1944, LA, 456 IV, file 1.

205. "Im ha-yetzi'ah la-hakhshara" (Departing for Kibbutz), *Ba-derekh: Alon Gar'in Erez* (On the Road: Bulletin of the Erez Group), Ha-Noar ha-Oved, Petah Tikvah, 1947, AKM, div. 8, (ser. 3, sec. B), box 11, file C.

206. Shmuel Golan, "Al derkeh hinukhenu," *Hedim,* September 1947.

207. Dov Stock (Sadan) to Berl Katznelson (December 1940), LA, file Berl Katznelson, sec. II/1.

208. Muni Langerman, "Gormei ha-tkufa."

Chapter 8

1. David Ben Gurion, *Yoman ha-milhama* (War Diary), vol. 2 (Tel Aviv, 1982), 427.

2. From an interview by Ehud Ben Ezer with G. Scholem, "Ha-Tziyonut: Dialektika shel retzifut u-mered" (Zionism: Dialectics of Continutity and Revolt), in E. Ben Ezer, *Eyn sha'ananim be-Tziyon* (No Peaceful Souls in Zion) (Tel Aviv, 1986), 292; cited in Scholem, *Od Davar,* 61.

3. S. Yizhar, "Hirbet Hiza'h," in his *Arba'a sippurim* (Four Stories), (Tel Aviv, 1968), 14–112.

4. On the fear of destruction and the readiness to risk a military decision, see David Ben Gurion, "Shalosh hazitot" (Three Fronts), in his *Ba-ma'arakha,* vol. 3 (Tel Aviv, 1950), 239–47.

5. Zvi Guber, "Mekhora" (Motherland), in *Gevilei esh* (Scrolls of Fire), vol. 1, ed. R. Avinoam (Tel Aviv, 1954), 7.

6. Baruch Amon (Rubinstein), in *Gevilei esh,* ed. R. Avinoam, 34.

7. Ben Gurion constantly represented the ratio of attackers of the Jewish state to members of the Yishuv as forty to one, based on a figure that included the general population of the Arab states. Modern researchers tend to focus on the number of conscripts that the Yis-

huv was able to place in the field to confront the Arabs. In that area, the proportion is far more favorable from the Jewish perspective. By the way, David Ben Gurion himself was well aware of his statistical contradiction. In his memo to the Executive of the Jewish Agency in 1929, he spoke specifically about men of conscriptable age that should be included in calculations as potential fighters. One can assume that he did not forget this reasoning in 1948. see "Al bithon ha-Yishuv u-vitzrono" (On the Security of the Yishuv and Its Strengthening), in his *Anahnu u-shekheneinu,* (Tel Aviv, 1931), 174.

8. Chaim Guri, *Ad alot ha-shahar* (Until Dawn) (Tel Aviv, 1950), 124.

9. Minutes of the committe for investigating relations with the Arab worker in the state, Tel Aviv, February 2, 1947, BB, 15/47.

10. Moshe Braslavsky, "Bi-yemei harat am" (A People Is Born), *Mi-Bifnim,* November 1948.

11. Nathan Alterman, "Tzorchei bitahon" (Security Needs), in his *Ha-tur ha-shevi'i,* 1:280.

Glossary

Ahdut ha-Avoda (Unity of Labor) A socialist Zionist association: the dominant party in the Jewish Labor movement in Palestine from 1919 to 1930. Formed in 1919 through the amalgamation of Poalei Zion,* the Non-Affilated Group,* and immigrants from the Third Aliyah.

Aliyah (immigration) Any of five waves of Jewish immigration to Palestine: First (1882–1903) Second (1904–1914) Third (1919–1923) Fourth (1924–1928) Fifth (1933–1939).

Aliyah Bet (Immigration B) Illegal Jewish immigration into Palestine, in violation of British regulations.

Aliyah Hadasha (New Immigration) Liberal moderate party made up largely of Jews who immigrated to Palestine from Central Europe in the 1930s.

Am Oved (Working Nation) The publishing house of the Labor Federation; founded by Berl Katznelson in 1942.

Ha-Aretz **(The Land)** Liberal paper, founded in 1920; first Hebrew daily newspaper in Palestine.

Assefat ha-Nivharim (Assembly of Delegates) Central representative body of the Jewish community in Palestine; established in 1920.

Ba-Ma'avak **(In Struggle)** Influential, activist-oriented periodical of the "new" Palestinian–Jewish generation; founded in 1946.

Bar Giora A secret, quasi-military order set up in Palestine in 1907 as a conspiratorial cell and revolutionary vanguard. Its later legal and open arm was Ha-Shomer*.

Bar Giora, Simon A Zealot leader and central figure in the uprising against the Romans, A.D. 66–70.

Betar Revisionist youth movement. The name is a syllabic acronym of the Hebrew for "Joseph Trumpeldor Alliance" and also the name of the main fortress of Bar Kokhba's rebellion against the Romans, conquered in A.D. 135.

Bilu The first organized group of young Russian Jews who came to Palestine motivated by Zionist ideology; founded in 1882.

Note: Asterisked terms are identified elsewhere in the Glossary.

Bricha (flight) A spontaneous mass movement of Jewish survivors from Europe to Palestine in the wake of World War II; also the name of the underground organization that helped Jews in 1944–1948 to move out of Eastern Europe into Southern and Western Europe as a step toward immigration to Palestine.

Brit ha-Biryonim (Covenant of Hooligans) Radical right-wing organization established by Abba Ahimeir in the 1930s.

Brit Shalom (Covenant of Peace) An association of Jewish intellectuals active from 1925 to 1933; originally chaired by Arthur Ruppin, it aimed to bring about Jewish–Arab accord. Most of its members were of Central European origin.

Bund (Union) Jewish Socialist party, founded in Eastern Europe in 1897, of great influence in Russia until 1917 and in Poland down to the outbreak of World War II. It initially demanded civil rights and political liberty and later on called for Jewish cultural autonomy in Eastern Europe, based on Yiddish language and culture; it was opposed to Zionism.

Churchill White Paper Issued by Colonial Secretary Winston Churchill in June 1922, the first important official statement of British government policy after the Balfour Declaration. It affirmed the rights of both Jews and Arabs in Palestine, and proposed the setting up of a legislative council.

Davar The first Hebrew daily of the Palestinian Labor movement; founded in 1925.

Doar ha-Yom **(Daily Mail)** Right-of-center Palestinian Hebrew daily; founded in 1920.

Elazar ben Yair Leader of the rebel Zealots at Massada in A.D. 70–73.

Eretz Israel The Land of Israel; Palestine.

Fosh (field squads) Small, mobile, attack-oriented squads, operating at night; set up within the framework of the Hagana by Yitzhak Sade in 1937.

Gordonia Pioneering youth movement originating in Eastern Europe, whose members began immigrating to Palestine in the 1930s; served as the manpower reserve of Hever ha-Kvutzot* during the Fifth Aliyah*. Named after Aharon David Gordon, its ideology was socialist but anti-Marxist.

Gush Halav Jewish town in Northern Galilee, fortified by Yohanan ben Levi during the great rebellion against the Romans; conquered by Titus, who murdered all its inhabitants.

Hagana (Defense) Established in 1920 as the Histadrut's* military organization for self-defense in Palestine; later broadened into a people's militia under public control.

He-Halutz (The Pioneer) A nonpolitical association of pioneers preparing for immigration; affiliated to the Labor movement in Palestine through the Histadrut. Founded in Eastern Europe in the early 1920s, it eventually became identified with the left wing of Mapai*.

Haskalah The Hebrew Enlightenment, an intellectual and literary movement from 1750 to 1880 in Central and Eastern Europe.

Hasmoneans   The family of the Maccabees.

Havlaga (restraint)   A policy of self-restraint adopted by the Zionist Executive and the Yishuv* during the Arab Rebellion of 1936–1939; it meant refraining from acts of retaliation against Arab terror.

Hebrew Resistance Movement   United underground movement of the Hagana,* the IZL*, and Lehi*; active from October 1945 to July 1946.

Hever ha-Kvutzot (Kvutzot* Association)   Association of small agricultural communes of non-Marxist inclinations; founded in 1928.

Hibbat Zion (Love of Zion)   A movement founded in Eastern Europe in 1881, advocating the return of Jews to Zion; the progenitor of the First Aliyah*.

Histadrut (General Federation of Jewish Workers in Palestine)   A labor organization founded in 1920 that came to embrace almost all Jewish workers in Palestine.

Ha-Hityashvut ha-Ovedet (Labor Settlement)   The cooperative workers' settlements associated with the Histadrut*; comprised of various forms of cooperative and communal organizations. The most prominent among them were the kibbutizm (communes) and the moshavim (cooperatives). They made their living mostly in agriculture and were the backbone of Zionist colonization of the land.

Hope–Simpson Report   Report issued in October 1930 by Sir John Hope–Simpson, appointed by the British government to report on questions of immigration, land settlement, and development. Its basic conclusion was that there was no margin of land available for settlement by immigrants, given the prevailing methods of Arab cultivation.

Ihud (Union)   Association founded by Judah Magnes in 1942 to promote a binational solution to the question of Palestine. Small in size, it attracted an important group of intellectuals.

IZL (Irgun Zeva'i Leumi [National Military Organization])   Underground Jewish organization founded in 1931; subsequently associated with the right-wing Revisionist party*. It engaged from 1937 in retaliatory acts against Arab attacks and later against the British mandatory authorities.

Keren ha-Yesod (Palestine Foundation Fund, United Jewish Appeal)   Established in 1920 by the Zionist Organization* to raise funds for the development—and particularly the settlement—of Palestine.

Keren Kayemet le-Israel (Jewish National Fund)   Established by the Zionist Organization in 1901 as a financial institution for the purchase of land for Jewish settlement in Palestine.

Ha-Kibbutz ha-Meuhad (United Kibbutz movement)   A kibbutz movement founded in 1927; it became the largest of the kibbutz movements, marked by its revolutionary fervor and devotion.

Kuntres **(Notebook)**   The weekly organ of Ahdut ha-Avoda*.

Kvutza, –ot (group[s])   Communal agricultrual settlement form, based on a small, closely knit group; first established in Degania in 1909 and later organized into a comprehensive, countrywide movement, Hever ha-Kvutzot*.

Labor Palestine *(Eretz Yisrael ha-Ovedet)* The term used to described primarily Ha-Hityashvut ha-Ovedet* and, in a wider sense, all the economic, social, and cultural enterprises associated with the Labor movement.

Labor Settlement See Ha-Hityashvut ha-Ovedet.*

Left Poalei Zion An orthodox Marxist party, created by a splinter from the Poalei Zion* party, the majority of which participated in establishing the Ahdut ha-Avoda party in 1919. Those who opposed the new party became the nucleus of the Left Poalei Zion party.

Lehi (Lohamei Herut Israel [Fighters for the Freedom of Israel]) Radical anti-British armed underground organization in Palestine; founded in 1940 by Avraham Stern (Yair) and other dissidents from the IZL*; also known as the Stern Gang.

MacDonald Letter Letter by Prime Minister Ramsay MacDonald to Chaim Weizmann, February 1931, reinterpreting the Passfield White Paper* so as to nullify its restrictions and make it possible to continue the upbuilding of the Jewish national home.

MacDonald White Paper White Paper of May 1939, published by the Colonial Secretary Malcolm MacDonald. It stipulated restricting Jewish immigration to ten thousand per year for five years, introduced new limitations on the sale of land to Jews, and provided for the establishment of an independent Palestinian state within ten years; regarded by most in the Zionist movement as the final betrayal of Britain's obligations to the Jewish people under the Balfour Declaration and the mandate.

Ha-Mahanot ha-Olim (The Ascending Camps) A pioneering youth movement in Palestine; formed in 1928 by the merger of the first pioneering movement of school youth, Hugim (Circles), and a splinter group from the Jewish scout movement. Labor-oriented, it was later associated primarily with Ha-Kibbutz ha-Meuhad*.

Mapai (Mifleget Poalei Eretz Yisrael [Palestine Workers Party]) Founded in 1930 through the amalgamation of Ha-Poel ha-Tzair* and Ahdut ha-Avoda*; the dominant party in the Yishuv* and, from 1933, in the Zionist Organization*.

Mi-Bifnim **(From Within)** Journal of Ha-Kibbutz ha-Meuhad*; founded in 1927.

Modi'in Home village of the Hasmoneans* (Maccabees).

Moshav Cooperative form of settlement based on individual plots of land and individual households, contrasting with the *kvutza*, which advocated communality.

Moshava (colony) Earliest type of Jewish village in modern Palestine, in which farming was conducted on individual farms mostly on privately owned land. The first such colonies were established during the First Aliyah*.

Mossad le-Aliyah Bet (Organization for Aliyah Bet*) Set up in the late 1930s by the Hagana* under the leadership of Shaul Meirov (Avigur).

Narodnaya Volya (Will of the People) Radical populist–revolutionary movement of Russian youth that emerged in the 1870s.

Nili Espionage group set up by Aaron Aaronson during World War I to gather and supply intelligence to the British Army in Egypt. *Nili* is an acronym for the initial letters of the Hebrew verse *Netzah Yisrael lo yeshakker* ("The glory of Israel will not lie," 1 Samuel 15:29).

Ha-Noar ha-Oved (Working Youth) The youth movement of Jewish working youth in Palestine, established in 1925 by the Histadrut; and eventually associated to a large degree with Ha-Kibbutz ha-Meuhad*.

Non-Affliated Group A trend within the Labor movement that grew out of the Agricultural Workers Union during World War I, led by Berl Katznelson. Along with the Poalei Zion* party, it founded Ahdut ha-Avoda* in 1919.

Notrim (Auxiliary Police) An auxiliary Jewish police force under British command, set up in 1936.

Pale of Settlement Twenty-five provinces in Western Russia under the czar, where Jews were permitted permanent settlement.

Palmach (Pelugot Mahatz [shock Troops]) Striking arm of the Hagana*, set up in 1941. It played a key role in the War of Independence. Was central in molding the military consciousness of Jewish youth.

Passfield White Paper Issued by Colonial Secretary Lord Passfield (Sidney Webb) in the wake of the 1929 riots, simultaneously with the Shaw Report*. The White Paper restricted future immigration on the basis of political criteria, placed limitations on Jewish purchase of land, and concluded that a representative government (majoritarian legislative council) should be set up. The document was severely criticized as a departure from the obligations of the mandate and was eventually abrogated in 1931 by the MacDonald Letter*.

Peel Commission Palestine Royal Commission, appointed in 1936 and headed by Earl Peel. Its report, issued in July 1937, recommended the partition of Palestine into separate Jewish and Arab states, with Jerusalem, Bethlehem, and Nazareth remaining under British Mandate.

Petlyura, Simon Commander of the army of the Ukrainian Democratic Republic, which perpetrated pogroms against Jews in some five hundred towns during the civil war in Russia, following the October Revolution.

Poalei Zion (Workers of Zion) Marxist Zionist party, influenced by the thinking of Ber Borochov; established in Russia in 1906. Those of its members who immigrated to Palestine were active during the Second Aliyah*.

Ha-Poel ha-Tzair (The Young Worker) Populist party established in Palestine in 1905, which merged with Ahdut ha-Avoda* to form Mapai* in 1930. It published a paper by the same name.

Revisionist party A right-of-center, activist-oriented party; founded by Zeev Jabotinsky in 1925.

Shaw Report Report of the Commission on the Palestine Disturbances of 1929 (Shaw Commision), headed by Sir Walter Shaw. It concluded that being disappointed in their political and national aspirations (and consequent feelings of animosity toward Jews) and fearing for their economic future had been the fundamental causes of Arabs' rioting in 1929. The commission accordingly proposed restrictions on Jewish immigration and the purchase of lands from the Arabs.

She'erit ha-Pleta (Surviving Remnant) Appellation (taken from 1 Chronicles 4:43) for survivors of the Holocaust.

Ha-Shilo'ah Major Hebrew literary journal, edited from 1897 to 1903 by Ahad Ha-Am and later by Joseph Klausner. Much of the best Hebrew poetry, fiction, and criticism of the early twentieth century was published in its pages.

Ha-Shomer (The Guardsman) Jewish guard organization founded by a group of Poalei Zion* members in Palestine in 1909 as the legal and open arm of Bar Giora*. Its aim was to defend Jewish settlement and newly purchased land. Absorbed in 1920 into the Hagana.*

Ha-Shomer ha-Tzair (The Young Guardsman) Zionist youth movement established in Central and Eastern Europe toward the end of World War I. Its members immigrated to Palestine from 1919 on, setting up a kibbutz movement (Ha-Kibbutz ha-Artzi ha-Shomer ha-Tzair). From the late 1920s, it was strongly leftist and Marxist in approach.

SNS (special night squads) Small commando units set up by British Army officer Orde Wingate in the 1930s to guard against Arab attacks.

Ha-Tenua le-Ahdut ha-Avoda (Movement for Labor Unity) A militant, activist party founded by Yitzhak Tabenkin in 1944 after he left the ranks of Mapai*; Merged in January 1948 with Ha-Shomer ha-Tzair* to form the Mapam* party, a militantly leftist, pro-Soviet party.

Va'ad Leumi (National Council) Executive body of Assefat ha-Nivharim*. The Jewish community in Palestine was organized in a legal body known as Knesset Israel (Community of Israel), with which every Jew was automatically affiliated unless he elected not to be. The members of the Knesset Israel elected a parlimentary body known as the Assefat ha-Nivharim (Elected Assembly), from which, in turn, the Va'ad Leumi (National Council) was elected.

Völkisch (folk) Of folk-oriented, conservative nationalistic political currents in Germany from the late nineteenth century on; espousing a romantic, organic concept of the nature of the folk and the nation–state deriving from blood ties and common ethnic origin.

Yavneh Site of the school of learning, called Kerem Yavneh (Vineyard of Yavneh); established by Rabbi Yohanan ben Zakkai when he fled Jerusalem in the year 70. Mishnaic literature had its beginnings here.

Yishuv The Jewish community in Palestine before the establishement of the State of Israel. The pre-Zionist community is generally designated the old Yishuv (centered principally in Jerusalem, Safed, Hebron, and Tiberias); the community evolving from 1880 on is known as the new Yishuv.

Yodefat Fortress where Galilean rebels held out against the Romans in the year A.D. 66. Josephus Flavius surrendered there to the Romans.

Yohanan ben Zakkai See Yavneh*.

Zionist Organization Founded in 1897 at the First Zionist Congress as the global structural framework of the organized Zionist movement. The supreme organ of the Zionist Organization is the Zionist Congress, which met, at first, annually and later biannually.

Zionists of Zion Faction in the early Zionist movement headed by Menahem Ussishkin, which demanded that Palestine should be designated as the one and only objective of the Zionist movement and that any alternative settlement schemes, such as the Uganda Plan, ought to be rejected outright. Their opponents were the Territorialists, who were prepared to accept destinations other than Palestine as havens for the Jewish people.

Zippori (Sepphoris) The largest and most important city in Galilee in the first four centuries A.D.; a major Jewish spiritual center, home of many renowned talmudic scholars.

Bibliography

Archives

BB	Labor Party Archive, Bet Berl
LA	Labor Movement Archive, Lavon Institute, Tel Aviv
AKM	Ha-Kibbutz ha-Meuhad Archive, Yad Tabenkin
CZA	Central Zionist Archive, Jerusalem
AHH	Hagana Archive, Tel Aviv
GH	Ha-Shomer ha-Tzair Archive, Givat Haviva
WA	Weizmann Archive, Rehovot

Newspapers and Periodicals

Alon Palmah
Ba-Ma'ale
Ba-Ma'avak
Ba-Mahane
Ba-Mivhan
Davar
Doar ha-Yom
Ha-Ahdut
Ha-Olam
Ha-Poel ha-Tzair
Ha-Shilo'ah

Ha-Shomer ha-Tzair
Ha-Yarden
Ha-Zman
Hedim
Kuntres
Lu'ah Eretz Yisrael
Lu'ah Ahiever
Mi-Bifnim
Niv ha-Kvutza
She'ifoteinu

Works in English

Allon, Yigal. *My Father's House.* New York, 1976.
Bein, Alex. *Theodore Herzl.* Cleveland, 1962.
———. Ed. *Arthur Ruppin: Memoirs, Diaries, Letters.* New York, 1971.
Berlin, G. L. "The Brandeis-Weizmann Dispute." *American Jewish Historical Quarterly* 60(1970):37–68.

Frankel, Jonathan. *Prophecy and Politics: Socialsim, Nationalism, and Russian Jews, 1862–1917.* London, 1981.

———. "'The Yizkor' Book of 1911—a Note on National Myths in the Second Aliyah." In *Religion, Ideology, and Nationalism in Europe and America,* ed. H. Ben Israel et al. Jerusalem, 1986.

Gorny, Yosef. *Zionism and the Arabs, 1882–1948: A Study of Ideology.* Oxford, 1987.

Herzl, Theodor, *The Complete Diaries of Theodor Herzl.* Ed. R. Patai. 5 vols. New York, 1960.

———. *The Jewish State.* New York, 1946.

———. *Old–New Land ("Altneuland").* New York, 1960.

Hess, Moses. *Rome and Jerusalem.* New York, 1956.

Heymann, Michael. *The Uganda Controversy.* Vols. 1–2. Jerusalem, 1970, 1977.

Kedourie, Elie. "Sir Herbert Samuel and the Government of Palestine." In his *Chatham House Version.* London, 1970.

Kohn, Hans. *The Idea of Nationalism.* 1967.

Mandel, Neville J. *The Arabs and Zionism Before World War I.* Berkeley, 1976.

Marlowe, John. *Rebellion in Palestine.* London, 1946.

———. *The Seat of Pilate.* London, 1959.

Monroe, Elizabeth. *Britain's Moment in the Middle East.* London, 1964.

Mosse, George. *Germans and Jews.* New York, 1970.

Mossek, Moshe. *Palestine Immigration Policy Under Sir Herbert Samuel.* London, 1978.

Ofer, Dalia. *Escaping the Holocaust: Illegal Immigration to the Land of Israel, 1939–1944.* New York, 1990.

Pinsker, Leo. "Auto-Emancipation." In his *Road to Freedom: Writings and Addresses.* New York, 1944.

Porat, Dina. *The Blue and the Yellow Stars of David: The Zionist Leadership in Palestine and the Holocaust, 1939–1945.* Cambridge, MA, 1990.

Porath, Yehoshua. *The Emergence of the Palestinian–Arab National Movement, 1918–1929.* London, 1974.

———. *The Palestinian–Arab National Movement: From Riots to Rebellion, 1929–1939.* London, 1977.

Shapira, Anita. *Berl: The Biography of a Socialist Zionist.* Cambridge, Eng., 1984.

———. "'Black Night–White Snow': Attitudes of the Palestinian Labor Movement to the Russian Revolution, 1917–1929." In *Studies in Contemporary Jewry,* vol. 4, ed. Jonathan Frankel. New York, 1988:144–71.

———. "The Debate in Mapai on the Use of Violence, 1932–1935." *Zionism* 3(April 1981):99–124.

———. "The Dynamics of Zionist Leftist Trends." In *Jewish History.* ed. Ada Rapoport-Albert and Steven J. Zipperstein. London, 1988.

———. "Labour Zionism and the October Revolution." *Journal of Contemporary History.* 24(1989):623–56.

———. "The Yishuv and the Survivors of the Holocaust." *Studies in Zionism.* 7, no. 2 (1986):277–301.

Shapiro, Yonathan. *Leadership of the American Zionist Organization, 1897–1930.* Urbana, IL, 1971.

Shavit, Yaacov. *Jabotinsky and the Revisionist Movement, 1925–1948.* London, 1988.

Sheffer, Gabriel. "Appeasement and the Problem of Palestine." *International Journal of Middle East Studies.* 2 (1980):377–99.

———. "Intentions and Results of British Policy in Palestine: Passfields's White Paper." *Middle Eastern Studies,* 9 (1973):43–60.

Stein, Kenneth W. *The Land Question in Palestine, 1917–1939.* Chapel Hill, NC, 1984.

Stein, Leonard. *The Balfour Declaration.* London, 1968.

Sykes, Christopher. *Crossroads to Israel.* London, 1965.

——. *Orde Wingate: A Biography.* Cleveland, 1959.

Teveth, Shabtai. *Ben-Gurion and the Palestinian Arabs: From Peace to War.* Oxford, 1985.

Ussishkin, Menahem. *Our Program.* New York, 1905.

Vital, David. *Zionism: The Formative Years.* Oxford, 1982.

——. *The Origins of Zionism.* Oxford, 1975.

——. *Zionism: The Crucial Phase.* Oxford, 1987.

Wasserstein, Bernard. *Britain and the Jews of Europe, 1939–1945.* Oxford, 1979.

——. *The British in Palestine: The Mandatory Government and the Arab–Jewish Conflict, 1917–1929.* London, 1979.

Weizmann, Chaim. *The Letters and Papers of Chaim Weizmann.* Series A, vol. 22. Ed. Joseph Heller. Jerusalem, 1979.

——. *The Letters and Papers of Chaim Weizmann.* Series B, vol. 2. Ed. Barnet Litvinoff. New Brunswick, NJ, 1984.

Zweig, Ronald W. *Britain and Palestine Druing the Second World War.* Hoodridge/Suffolk, UK, 1986.

Works in Hebrew

Agnon, Shemuel Yosef. *Temol shilshom* (Bygone Days). Tel Aviv, 1947.

Ahad Ha-Am. *Al parashat derakhim* (At the Crossroads), 4 vols. Berlin, 1930.

——. *Igrot* (Letters). Berline, 1924.

——. *Igrot* (Letters). Ed. Arie Simon. Tel Aviv, 1960.

——. *Kol kitvei* (Complete Works), Tel Aviv, 1961.

Ahimeir, Abba. *Brit ha-Biryonim* (The Covenant of the Biryonim). Tel Aviv, 1972.

——. *Ha-mishpat* (The Trial). Tel Aviv, 1968.

——. *Ha-Tziyonut ha-mahapkhanit* (Revolutionary Zionism). Tel Aviv, 1966.

Al ha-Saf. (On the Threshold). Jerusalem, 1918.

Almog, Shemuel. *Tziyonut ve-historia* (Zionism and History), Jerusalem 1982.

Al Parashat Derakheinu (On Our Crossroads). Jerusalem, 1939.

Alterman, Nathan. *Shirim mi-she-kevar* (Poems of Long Ago). Tel Aviv, 1972.

——. *Ha-tur ha-shevi'i* (The Seventh Column). Tel Aviv, 1986.

Aranne, Zalman. *Autobiografia* (Autobiography). Tel Aviv, 1971.

Arlosoroff, Chaim. *Kevatim* (Collected Writings). Vol. 1,. Tel Aviv, 1934.

——. *Yoman Yerushalayim* (Jerusalem Diary). Tel Aviv, 1949.

Arnon-Ohana, Yuval. *Falahim ba-Mered ha-Arvi be-Eretz-Yisrael, 1936–1939* (Fellahin in the Arab Rebellion in Palestine, 1936–1939). Tel Aviv, 1978.

Avinoam, Reuven [Reuven Grossmann], ed. *Gevilei esh* (Scrolls of Fire). Vol. 1,. Tel Aviv, 1954.

Beilinson, Moshe. *Bi-yemei masa* (Days of Trial). Tel Aviv, n.d.

Ben Eliezer, Uri. "Tzva'iyut, status u-politika" (Militarism, Status, and Politics). Ph.D. diss., Tel Aviv University, 1988.

Ben Ezer, Ehud. *Eyn sha'ananim be-Tziyon* (No Peaceful Souls in Zion). Tel Aviv, 1986.

Ben Gurion, David. *Anahnu u-shekheneinu* (We and Our Neighbors). Tel Aviv, 1931.

——. *Ba-ma'arakha* (In the Battle). Vols. 3–5. Tel Aviv, 1950–1951.

——. *Igrot* (Letters). Vol. 1,. Tel Aviv, 1973.

——. *Pegishot im manhigim arvim* (Meetings with Arab Leaders). Tel Aviv, 1967.

——. *Yoman ha-milhama* (War Diary). 3 vols. Ed. Elhanan Oren and Gershon Rivlin. Tel Aviv, 1982.

——. *Zikhronot* (Memoirs). Vols. 1–3. Tel Aviv, 1971–1973.

Ben Yeruham, H. *Ha-alila ha-gedola* (The Great Libel). Tel Aviv, 1982.

——, ed. *Sefer Betar: Korot u-mekorot* (Betar's Book: Events and Sources). Vol. 1,. Jerusalem, 1969.

Ben Zvi, Yitzhak, et al., eds. *Sefer Ha-Shomer* (Book of Ha-Shomer). Tel Aviv, 1957.

Berdichevsky, Micha Yosef. *Al ha-perek* (On the Agenda). Warsaw, 1899.

——. *Ba-derekh* (On the Road). Vols. 2–3. Leipzig, 1922.

——. *Mahshavot ve-torot* (Thoughts and Theories). Leipzig, 1922.

Bialik, Haim Nahman. *Kol kitvei* (Complete Works). Tel Aviv, 1961.

Binyamin, Rabbi, and Ya'akov Peterzeil, eds. *Neged ha-teror* (Against Terrorism). Jerusalem, 1939.

Bi-vritekh (In Your Covenant). Tel Aviv, 1938.

Blum, Shulamit. "Ha-isha bi-tnu'at ha-avoda bi-tkufat ha-Aliyah ha-Shniya" (Women in the Labor Movement in the Period of the Second Aliya). Master's thesis, Tel Aviv University, 1980.

Brenner, Uri. *Ha-Kibbutz ha-Meuhad ba-Hagana, 1923–1939* (The Kibbutz Meuhad in the Hagana, 1923–1939). Tel Aviv, 1980.

Brenner, Yosef Haim. *Ketavim* (Collected Writings). 4 vols. Tel Aviv, 1985.

——. *Kol kitvei* (Complete Works). 9 vols. Tel Aviv, 1927.

Buber, Martin. *Bein am le-artzo* (Between a People and Its Land). Jerusalem, 1984.

Cahan, Yaakov. *Kol kitvei* (Complete Works). Tel Aviv, n.d.

Cohen, Gavriel. *Churchill u-she'elat Eretz-Yisrael bi-tehilat milhemet ha-olam ha-sheniya, 1939–1942* (Churchill and the Palestine Question at the Beginning of World War II 1939–1942. Jerusalem, 1976.

Dinur, Ben-Zion, et al. *Sefer toldot ha-Hagana* (History of the Hagana). Vols. 1–3. Tel Aviv, 1954–1973.

Doron, Yehoyakim. "Ha-Tziyonut ha-merkaz-europe'it mul ideologiyot germaniyot bein ha-shanim 1885–1914" (Central European Zionism Confronting German Ideologies in the Period 1885–1914). Ph.D. diss., Tel Aviv University, 1977.

Dror, Zvika. *Bi-netivei hatzala* (Paths of Rescue). Tel Aviv, 1988.

Druyanow, Alter, ed. *Ketavim le-toldot Hibbat Tziyon* (Documents on the History of Hibbat Zion). 3 vols. Tel Aviv, 1932.

Druyanow, Alter and Shulamit Loskov, eds. *Ketavim le-toldot Hibbat Tzyion vi-yishuv Eretz Yisrael* (Documents on the History of Hibbat Zion and Settlement in Palestine). Rev. ed. 6 vols. Tel Aviv, 1982–1990.

Elam, Yigal. *Ha-Gedudim ha-Ivri'im* (The Jewish Legion). Tel Aviv, 1984.

Frizel, Eviatar. *Ha-mediniuyt ha-tziyonit le-ahar hatzharat Balfour, 1917–1922.* (Zionist Policy After the Balfour Declaration, 1917–1922). Tel Aviv, 1977.

Gal, Allon. "Hashkafato shel Brandeis al ofen binyan ha-Aretz" (Bradeis's Views on How to Go About Building Palestine). *Ha-Tziyonut* 6(1981):97–145.

Gil'ad, Zerubavel, ed. *Sefer ha-Palmah* (The book of the Palmach). 2 Vol. Tel Aviv, 1953.

Golomb, Eliyahu. *Hevyon oz* (Hidden Strength). 2 vols. Tel Aviv, 1953.

Gordon, Aharon David. *Kitvei* (Collected Writings). Tel Aviv, 1928.

——. *Mivhar ketavim* (Selected Writings). Ed. Eliezer Schveid. Jerusalem, 1983.

Gorny, Yosef. *Ahdut ha-Avoda, 1919–1930: Ha-yesodot ha-ra'ayoniyim ve-ha-shita ha-medinit* (Ahdut ha-Avoda, 1919–1930: The Ideological Foundations and the Political Method). Tel Aviv, 1973.

———. "Ha-ideologia shel kibbush ha-avoda" (The Ideology of the Conquest of Labor). *Keshet* 38(1968):49–66.

Greenberg, Uri Zvi. *Anakreon al kotev ha-itzavon* (Anacreon on the Pole of Melancholy). Tel Aviv, 1928.

———. *Be-emtza ha-olam u-ve-emtza ha-zmanim* (In the Middle of the World and the Midst of Times). N.p., 1979.

———. *Eima gedola ve-yare'ah* (Great Terror and a Moon). Tel Aviv, 1925.

———. *Sefer ha-Kitrug ve-ha-Emuna* (Book of Indictment and Faith). Jerusalem, 1937.

Guri, Chaim. *Ad alot ha-shahar* (Until Dawn). Tel Aviv, 1950.

Habas, Bracha, ed. *Me'ora'ot tartzav* (The 1936 Disturbances). Tel Aviv, 1937.

Heller, Joseph. *Ba-ma'avak li-medina: Ha-mediniyut ha-tziyonit ba-shanim 1936–1948* (Struggling for a State: Zionist Policy in the Years 1936–1948). Jerusalem, 1985.

———. *Lehi: Ideologia u-politika, 1940–1949* (Lehi: Ideology and Politics, 1940–1949). Jerusalem, 1989.

Hofshi, Nathan. *Be-lev va-nefesh* (In Heart and Soul). Tel Aviv, 1965.

Horovitz, David. *Ha-etmol sheli* (My Yesterday). Jerusalem, 1970.

Jabotinsky, Zeev. *Autobiografia* (Autobiography). Jerusalem, 1947.

———. *Ba-derekh le-medina* (On the Road to statehood). Jerusalem, 1953.

———. *Ba-sa'ar* (In the Storm). Jerusalem, 1953.

———. *Ketavim tziyoniyim rishonim* (First Writings on Zionism). Jerusalem, 1949.

———. *Mikhtavim* (Letters). Tel Aviv, n.d.

———. *Ne'umim, 1905–1926* (Speeches, 1905–1926). Jerusalem, 1947.

———. *Shimshon* (Samson). Jerusalem, 1950.

———. *Shirim* (Poems). Jerusalem, 1947.

Kafkafi, Yitzhak, ed. *Shenot ha-Mahanot ha-Olim* (Years of Ha-Mahanot ha-Olim). 2 vols. Tel Aviv, 1975–1985.

Katz, Yaakov. "Le-verur ha-musag mevasrei ha-Tziyonut" (On Elucidating the Conception of the Heralds of Zionism). *Shivat Tziyon* (Jerusalem) 1(1950):91–105.

Katznelson, Berl. *Ha-Aliyah ha-Shniya* (The Second Aliya). Ed. Anita Shapira and Naomi Abir. Tel Aviv, 1990.

———. *Igrot* (Letters). 6 vols. Ed. Yehuda Sharett, Yehuda Erez, and Anita Shapira. Tel Aviv, 1961–1984.

———. *Ketavim* (Collected Writings). 12 vols. Tel Aviv, 1948.

Katznelson, Rachel. *Masot u-reshimot* (Essays and Notes). Tel Aviv, 1946.

Korchak-Marle, Ruzka. *Lehimata, haguta, demuta* (The Personality and Philsophy-of-Life of a Fighter). Tel Aviv, 1988.

Kovetz Ha-Shomer (Ha-Shomer collection). Tel Aviv, 1947.

Kressel, Getzel. *Leksikon ha-sifrut ha-ivrit* (Dictionary of Hebrew Literature). Merhavia, Israel, 1967.

Kurzweil, Barukh. "Ha-Yahadut ke-gilui retzon ha-hayim ha-leumi ha-biologi" (Judaism as the Manifestation of the National Biological Urge to Survive). In his *Sifrutenu ha-hadasha: hemshekh o mahapekha?* (Our New Literature: Continuity or Revolution?). Tel Aviv, 1959.

Lamdan, Yitzhak. *Massada.* 2d ed. Tel Aviv, 1929.

Laskov, Shulamit. *Ha-Bilu'im* (The Bilu Group). Tel Aviv, 1980.

———. *Trumpeldor: Sippur hayav* (Trumpeldor: The Story of His Life). Haifa, 1972.

Lilienblum, Moshe Leib. *Derekh teshuva* (The Path of Repentance). Warsaw, 1899.

Livne, Eliezer. *Nili: Toldoteha shel he aza medinit* (Nili: The History of a Bold Political Venture). Tel Aviv, 1980.

Metzer, Yaakov. *Hon leumi le-vayit leumi, 1919–1921* (National Capital for a National Home). Jerusalem, 1979.

Mintz, Matityahu. *Ber Borochov: Ha-ma'agal ha-rishon, 1900–1906* (Ber Borochov: Circle One, 1900–1906). Tel Aviv, 1976.

———. "Ha-Arvim ba-prognozot shel Borochov" (Arabs in Borochov's Prognoses). *Molad*, Adar 1972.

Nakdimon, Shlomo, and Shaul Meizlish. *De-Haan: Ha-retzah ha-politi ha-rishon be-Eretz Yisrael* (De Haan: The First Political Assassination in Palestine). Tel Aviv, 1985.

Niv, David. *Ma'arkhot ha-Irgun ha-Tzeva'i ha-Leumi* (Battles of the IZL). 3 vols. Tel Aviv, 1975.

Nordau, Max. *El amo: Ketavim mediniyim* (To His People: Political Writings). 2 vols. Tel Aviv, ca. 1936–1937.

———. *Ketavim tziyoniyim* (Zionist Writings)). 4 vols. Jerusalem, 1955–1962.

Ofer, Dalia. *Derekh ba-yam: Aliya Bet bi-tekufat ha-Sho'a* (Route by Sea: Illegal Immigration During the Holocaust). Jerusalem, 1988.

Porath, Yehoshua. *Shela ve-et be-yado* (The Life of Uriel Shelah [Yonathan Ratosh]). N.p., 1989.

Poznanski, Menachem, ed. *Yosef Trumpeldor: Kovetz reshimot ve-kit'ei mikhtavim* (Joseph Trumpeldor: Anthology of Articles and Passages from Letters). Tel Aviv, 1953.

Protokol ha-ve'ida ha-Revi'it shel Ahdut ha-Avoda, Ein Harod 8–16 Iyar 1924 (Minutes, Fourth Conference of Ahdut ha-Avoda). Tel Aviv, 1926.

Rabinowitz, Alexander Ziskind, ed. *Yizkor Matzevet zikaron le-halelei ha-po'alim ha-ivri'im be-Eretz Yisrael* (Memorial Service in Remembrance of Fallen Jewish Workers in Palestine). Jaffa, 1911.

Rachel [Rachel Bluwstein]. *Shirat Rachel* (Poetry of Rachel). Tel Aviv, 1950.

Ramba, Izik. *Ha-magen ve-ha-asir* (The Defender and the Prisoner). Tel Aviv, 1960.

Rieger, Eliezer. *Ha-hinukh ha-ivri be-Eretz Yisrael* (The Hebrew Education in Palestine). Tel Aviv, 1940.

Rogel, Nakdimon. *Hazit beli oref* (Front Without Rear). Tel Aviv, 1959.

Ro'i, Yaakov. "Yahasei Rehovot im shekheneiha ha-arvi'im (1890–1914)" (Rehovot's Relations with Its Arab Neighbors [1890–1914]). *Ha-Tziyonut* 1(1970):150–203.

Roth, Hayyim Yudah. *Al ha-hinukh ha-tikhoni ha-ivri be-Eretz Yisrael* (Jewish Secondary Education in Palestine). Jerusalem, 1939.

Ruppin, Arthur. *Pirkei hayai* (Chapters of My Life). 3 vols. Tel Aviv, 1968.

Schechtman, Yosef. *Zeev Jabotinsky*. 3 vols. Tel Aviv, 1956–1959.

Scholem, Gershom. *Devarim be-go* (Explications and Implications). Tel Aviv, 1976.

———. *Od davar* (Explications and Implications. Vol. 2), Ed. Avraham Shapira. Tel Aviv, 1989.

Schwadron, Abraham. *Hashkafat ha-tziyonut ha-integralit* (Integral Zionist Outlook). Jerusalem, 1931.

Shapria, Anita. "Bein teror le-havlaga: Ha-Kinus ha-Yishuvi be-Yuli 1938" (Between Terror and Self-Restraint: The Yishuv Conference in July 1938). *Ha-Tziyonut* 6(1981):359–425.

———. "Dor ba-aretz" (A Native Generation). ed. Ahuvia Malkin. *Alpayim* 2(1990):178–203.

———. *Ha-halikha al kav ha-ofek* (Visions in Conflict). Tel Aviv, 1989.

———. *Ha-ma'avak ha-nikhzav* (Futile Struggle). Tel Aviv, 1977.

Sharett, Moshe. *Yoman medini* (Political Diary). 5 vols. Tel Aviv, 1976–1979.

Shavit, Yaacov. *Ha-mitologiyot shel ha-yamin* (The Mythologies of the Right). Beit Berl and Sharett Institute. Beit Berl, Zofit.

————. ed. *Havlaga o teguva?* (Self-Restraint or Response?). Tel Aviv, 1983.

Sheffer, Gabriel. "Me'atzvei ha-mediniyut ha-mandatorit: Stereotipim o basar va-dam?" (Makers of Mandatory Policy: Stereotypes or Flesh and Blood?). *Keshet* 48(1971):167–78.

————. "Tadmit ha-Falestina'im ve-ha-Yishuv ke-gorem be-itzuv ha-mediniyut ha-Beritit bi-shenot ha-30" (The Image of the Palestinians and the Yishuv as a Factor in Shaping British Policy in the 1930s). *Ha-Tziyonut* 3(1973):273–94.

Shlonsky, Avraham. *Ba-galgal* (In the Wheel). Tel Aviv, 1927.

Shoshani, Eliezer. "Erkhei ha-Palmah" (Palmach Values). In *Be-mivhan ha-keravot: Shen-aton Davar, 1948/49* (The Test of Battles: Davar Yearbook, 1948/49). Tel Aviv, 1949.

Sprinzak, Yosef. *Igrot* (Letters). 2 Vols. Tel Aviv, 1969.

Tabenkin, Yitzhak. *Devarim* (Speeches). 4 vols. 1, Tel Aviv, 1967–1976.

Tchernichovsky, Shaul. *Shirei* (Poems). Tel Aviv, 1968.

Teveth, Shabtai. *Kin'at David* (The Zeal of David). 3 Vols. Tel Aviv, 1976–87.

————. *Retzah Arlosoroff* (Arlosoroff's Murder). Jerusalem, 1982.

Verete, M. "Ha-masa u-matan ha-Tziyoni–Arvi be-aviv 1919 ve-ha-mediniyut ha-anglit" (The Zionist–Arab Negotiations in the Spring of 1919 and the English Policy). *Zion* 32(1967):76–115.

Yaffe, Eliezer. *Kevatim* (Collected Writings). 2 vols. Tel Aviv, 1947.

Yalkut Ahdut ha-Avoda (Ahdut ha-Avoda Anthology). 2 vols. Tel Aviv, 1929–32.

Yeivin, Yehoshua Heschel. *Me-havlaga le-kantoniyut* (From Self-Restraint to Cantonism). Tel Aviv, 1937.

————. *Yerushalayim mehaka* (Jerusalem Is Waiting). 2d ed. Jerusalem, 1939.

Yizhar, S. "Hirbet Hiz'ah." In his *Arba'asippurim* (Four Stories). Tel Aviv, 1968.

Zayit, David. *Tziyonut be-darkei shalom: darko ha-ra'ayonit–Politit shel Ha-Shomer ha-Tza'ir, 1927–1947* (Zionism by Peaceful Methods: The Ideological–Political History of Ha-Shomer ha-Tzair, 1927–1947). Tel Aviv, 1985.

Index

Balance of power
  between Arab states and State of Israel,
    369–70
  Jewish-Arab accord and, 172
  legislative council scheme and, 133, 134
  use of force and, 296
  victim and hero imagery and, 363
Balfour Declaration, 83–84, 89
Ba-Ma'ale (journal), 315
Ba-Ma'avak (journal), 333, 344, 346
Baratz, Yosef, 262–63
Bar Droma, Y., 311
Bar Giora (secret order), 68, 69–70, 74. *See
    also* Ha-Shomer
Bar Kokhba Association (Prague), 8, 14, 74
Bar Kokhba (Berlin athletic association), 13,
    14
Bar Kokhba revolt, 312
Bauer, Eliezer, 406*n*17
Bedouin, 61, 71–72. *See also* Arabs of
    Palestine
Be'eri, Eliezer. *See* Bauer, Eliezer
Begin, Menahem, 347
Beilinson, Moshe, 170
  Arab problem and, 147–48
  August 1929 riots and, 175, 176–77, 179,
    184, 185
  defensive ethos and, 172, 191
  extreme right and, 150, 204
  future of Zionism and, 131
  Jabotinsky and, 163
  policy of self-restraint and, 238
  "politics of quotation marks" and, 225–26
  Zionist propaganda and, 229
Ben Gurion, David, 87, 307
  accord with Arabs and, 209–11
  activism and, 151, 289, 291–96, 348–49
  Arab nationalism and, 187, 228
  Arab Rebellion and, 227–29
  arrival in Palestine, 53, 54, 64
  August 1929 riots and, 174, 175, 182
  Biltmore Program and, 281, 283, 284
  British administration and, 228–247, 292,
    350, 360
  final goal of Zionism and, 193
  future of Zionism and, 131
  ghetto uprisings and, 335
  Holocaust and, 329
  Jaffa riots and, 112
  Jewish fighting force and, 279, 291, 415*n*7
  Jewish state and, 119, 323, 354
  joint union and, 137, 138, 183
  legislative council and, 133, 134–35, 210–11
  national hatred and, 380*n*69
  negotiation with Arab leaders, 209–10
  proposal for constitutional changes, 188–92
  Samuel and, 152
  self-restraint policy and, 235–36, 238
  transfer concept and, 285
  use of poetic passages, 74–75

  Wauchope and, 207
  White Paper and, 279
  World War I and, 278–79
Bentwich, Norman, 201
Ben Yosef, Shlomo, 246
Ben Zvi, Yitzhak, 87, 133
Berdichevsky, Micha Joseph
  Arab problem and, 45–46
  dispute on use of force and, 21–25, 40
  emerging national ethos and, 142
  heroic imagery of, 22–23, 48, 73, 74, 258,
    311, 312
  Jewish life in Diaspora and, 25
  Jewish state and, 17, 18, 21–25
  roots of Betar and, 194
  vitalism and, 17, 18, 21–25
Bergmann, Hugo, 164, 167, 169, 170
Betar youth movement, 161–62, 201. *See also*
    Maximalists
Bevin, Ernest, 292, 293
Bialik, Chaim Nahman, 29, 41, 103, 111, 194,
    352
  emerging national ethos and, 32, 142
  "In the City of Slaughter," 37, 39, 73, 111,
    176, 177, 240, 274, 331
  Jewish self-defense and, 36–37
  "On the Slaughter," 39
Bible
  conflicting elements of national ethos and,
    28–29
  education of young and, 258–59
  heroic myth and, 22–23, 303
  idea of Jewish return and, 41
  land of Israel and, 274
Biltmore Program, 307, 320
  opposition to, 281–84, 308
Bilu (Russian Zionist organization), 55, 56
Binational state proposal, 167–69, 187
Biriya episode of 1946, 318
Birnbaum, Nathan, 11
Biryonim (hooligans), 23–24, 32–33, 74, 197
Bi-Vritekh (Ha-Mahanot ha-Olim booklet),
    311, 316, 318
Black Saturday (Operation Agatha), 294, 295,
    346
Blood motif
  Ahimeir and, 197–98
  Greenberg and, 146
  "In blood and fire" phrase, 33, 75, 93
  Jewish legion and, 90, 92, 96
  Second Aliyah imagery and, 73–74
  Tel Hai myth and, 102, 103, 104
"Bloody Sunday," 219
Bluwstein, Rachel. *See* Rachel
Boger, Haim. *See* Bograshov (Boger), Haim
Bograshov (Boger), Haim, 177
Bols, Louis, 110
Bolshevik revolution. *See* Russian
    revolutionary movement
Borochov, Ber, 48, 67, 321